I0532749

Communes and Conflict

Historical Materialism Book Series

The Historical Materialism Book Series is a major publishing initiative of the radical left. The capitalist crisis of the twenty-first century has been met by a resurgence of interest in critical Marxist theory. At the same time, the publishing institutions committed to Marxism have contracted markedly since the high point of the 1970s. The Historical Materialism Book Series is dedicated to addressing this situation by making available important works of Marxist theory. The aim of the series is to publish important theoretical contributions as the basis for vigorous intellectual debate and exchange on the left.

The peer-reviewed series publishes original monographs, translated texts, and reprints of classics across the bounds of academic disciplinary agendas and across the divisions of the left. The series is particularly concerned to encourage the internationalization of Marxist debate and aims to translate significant studies from beyond the English-speaking world.

For a full list of titles in the Historical Materialism Book Series available in paperback from Haymarket Books, visit: www.haymarketbooks.org/series_collections/1-historical-materialism.

Communes and Conflict

Urban Rebellion in Late Medieval Flanders

Jan Dumolyn
Jelle Haemers

Edited by
Andrew Murray
Joannes van den Maagdenberg

Haymarket Books
Chicago, IL

First published in 2023 by Brill Academic Publishers, The Netherlands
© 2023 Koninklijke Brill NV, Leiden, The Netherlands

Published in paperback in 2024 by
Haymarket Books
P.O. Box 180165
Chicago, IL 60618
773-583-7884
www.haymarketbooks.org

ISBN: 979-8-88890-328-5

Distributed to the trade in the US through Consortium Book Sales and Distribution (www.cbsd.com) and internationally through Ingram Publisher Services International (www.ingramcontent.com).

This book was published with the generous support of Lannan Foundation, Wallace Action Fund, and the Marguerite Casey Foundation.

Special discounts are available for bulk purchases by organizations and institutions. Please call 773-583-7884 or email info@haymarketbooks.org for more information.

Cover art and design by David Mabb. Cover art is a detail from *Construct 50, Morris, Garden Tulip / Malevich, Elongation of the Suprematist Square*, 2006. Paint on paper mounted on canvas (2006).

Printed in the United States.

Library of Congress Cataloging-in-Publication data is available.

Contents

Authors' Preface: Fifteen Years of Systematic Research on Communes and Conflict in the Towns of Late Medieval Flanders

Jan Dumolyn and Jelle Haemers

The research leading to this collection of essays started twenty to twenty-five years ago when – with some years between because of a slight difference in age – we each wrote a *licentiaatsverhandeling* (Master's thesis) at Ghent University with Marc Boone as our supervisor. These dissertations were, respectively, about the revolts of Bruges (1436–1438) and of Ghent (1449–1453) against Philip the Good, Duke of Burgundy.[1] We then subsequently both obtained PhD positions and continued to work on the history of the 'Burgundian state' in Flanders, mostly applying the prosopographical method. Both state formation and pre-industrial collective action had become major fields of interest for medieval historians in the 1990s. The influence of Charles Tilly's historical sociology was especially strong in our department. Wim Blockmans, a Ghent graduate and a leading historian of the medieval Low Countries who, by then, had become a professor in Leiden, cooperated with the well-known American historian and social scientist using, among others, the history of Burgundian state-building as a case study. Furthermore, Blockmans' and Tilly's work also put the collective action of political contenders on the forefront of historical change, which is essential to explain the genesis of local and national power structures (both of the state apparatus, as well as of representational institutions).[2] We owe much to their legacy. In the same line of investigation, of central importance to us has been Jean-Philippe Genet's insights in medieval state-building and his analysis of the sign systems it generated, a method inspired by historical materialism as much as by semiotics.[3]

At the same time, the study of the history of the great cities of medieval Flanders had been a long-established tradition in Ghent. We were fortunate to be trained by scholars with a worldwide reputation like Adriaan Verhulst and Walter Prevenier, who were also the teachers of our own supervisor to whom they passed on this line of research. Verhulst and Prevenier were at the same time classical source-oriented Rankeans and humanist scholars with a great

---

1 Dumolyn 1995, published as Dumolyn 1997; Haemers 2002, published as Haemers 2004b.
2 See Tilly and Blockmans 1994, and many other publications mentioned in the bibliography.
3 For instance Genet 1992 as well as many of his later publications.

deal of imagination and a very open attitude towards young people. Eventually we would both end up as lecturers, one of us staying in Ghent, the other being employed at the University of Leuven. Also, while we developed different interests in other historical fields, and we broadened the geographical and chronological scope of our respective fields of research, we never lost our common interest in popular protest, both perhaps guided by a psychological condition making it difficult to accept authority and abuses of power in general. This includes the injustice we ourselves have done to our friends and colleagues, who have been tormented by our restless minds more than once, just as they have inspired many of our thoughts which you can read in this book. The same goes for the PhD students whom we have started to oppress at both universities for at least a decade. Fortunately, all of them tackled and rejected many of our ideas as they navigated academic life, simultaneously conforming to and challenging it.

We started our systematic study with a first article on the patterns of urban rebellion in medieval Flanders in 2005.[4] Our collaboration eventually resulted in twenty-two joint journal articles and book chapters, of which six are published in this volume (the other ones published here being individually authored by one of us). And more are certainly yet to come.[5] Some of these papers were published in volumes which are difficult to find; others here have been translated into English to make them more easily accessible. We never worked in isolation of course: many, if not most, of the ideas in this volume were discussed during conferences and workshops, or during fellowships, in among other places Oxford, Durham, York, St Andrews, Glasgow, Rome, Paris, London, Boston, New York, Santander, Seville, Gavere, Bruges, and Ghent. Not to forget the lively debates in restaurants, inns and pseudo-medieval alehouses. The discussions with colleagues led to fresh insight in many of our findings, and to new interpretations of previously published thoughts.

The gradual evolution of our ideas on the subject was the main reason why we were initially somewhat reluctant to reprint some of our pieces when it was generously suggested we do so by Andy Murray and Joannes van den Maagdenberg for Brill's Historical Materialism series. Although some of our opinions on various matters evolved over time, we did not rewrite the chapters of this book. Only very minimal changes were made: the correction of some errors, an exceptional bibliographical addition here and there. The result is that this volume is inevitably not a coherent monograph, which would have approached

---

4 Dumolyn and Haemers 2005.
5 See the bibliography. The latest one is Dumolyn and Haemers 2020, in the *Annales. Histoire, Sciences Sociales*, which will also appear in an online English version.

the problem of Flemish medieval urban revolt with a more focused set of viewpoints and methodologies. We do not think that this is a problem, as the book rather shows a quest of more than fifteen years, looking for novel ways to study the phenomenon of medieval urban revolt, in dialogue with other historians and under the influence of the social and political sciences, law, literary theory, cognitive psychology, linguistics and other disciplines.

The focus on Flemish cities, and by extension also on the cities of the other Netherlandish principalities, also including what is now northern France, might seem a limited national point of view. However, we always felt that it was justified to focus on our own homeland, albeit with a constant concern to compare it to other parts of medieval Europe. After all, this region was one that was exceptionally urbanized and economically developed during the medieval period and that made it also into a laboratory of political change. We also brought in comparative perspectives studying the secondary literature on revolts in medieval France, Germany, Italy, Spain and England, but nevertheless decided to continue focussing on one place and its rich source material in depth. In some ways we were also fundamentally challenged by the grand synthesis by Sam Cohn, who had compared Flanders with France and Italy and was working at the same time as us.[6] We agreed with most of what was in his book but certainly also opposed some of his points of view. In fact, it was probably a great deal thanks to Sam that we continued this path so steadfastly, maybe with the unconscious determination to refute what we thought were inaccuracies in his work for, in spite of his vast knowledge, he has not mastered Dutch and did not access a large number of sources and literature in our language. More often his work was inspiring, but we believed could have been explored with greater depth and clarity. Soon, our 'opponent', with his sweeping sense of generalization and brilliancy in seeing the bigger historical picture, also became a good friend with whom we could exchange many sarcastic observations, mostly – and preferably – in less rainy countries than Scotland and Belgium.

Likewise, together with the research of colleagues such as John Watts, Patrick Lantschner and Christian Liddy, our approach challenges the far too often accepted 'national uniqueness' of popular protest. More than ever before, the revolts which we study in this book have been approached from a comparative and international perspective, far away from the focus of 'insularity' that torments the historiography (and even the minds of some inhabitants) of strongly centralised states such as, for instance, England or France. Perhaps the fact that the Low Countries are, since the Middle Ages, a busy crossroad of people,

---

6   Cohn 2006.

languages, and ideas, has inspired us more than we realise in this comparative approach. Furthermore, the multi-lingual environment of Belgian academic life has been very fruitful to our work because interpreting discourse is at the centre of historical work. 'Though they look often similar, the same words mean different things in different languages and different contexts', as Susan Reynolds once gently reminded us on the Piazza Navona in Rome, after a confrontation with the French eloquence of Claude Gauvard during one of the many occasions Jean-Philippe Genet invited us into the 'École Française'. The mobilising power of words is enormous, as Peter Burke also taught us, in particular when raising socialist (considering the location, some would say 'subversive') songs with the late folklorist Roy Palmer at High Table in Hertford College in Oxford. Such hilarious international encounters, too many to mention here, and their stimulating discussions about the interpretation of language, for instance during long evening (or night) dinners at Spanish tables, have been essential to our work. We are sure that this international collaboration will continue to inspire us in the near future and will survive nationalist tendencies such as Brexit or the dire consequences of a pseudo-medieval plague that hit Europe at the moment when we wrote this introduction.

During these fifteen years of working together there have been clear lines of development in our work, although parts of our focus have also remained the same. The emphasis on the craft guilds as the main organisations mobilizing for popular protest in the medieval cities and towns of Flanders and some other parts of the Low Countries and north-western Europe, for instance, or the role played by the 'patrician' merchant class, have been classic features in any narrative on the political history of the later middle ages since the nineteenth century and they obviously also remain present in our work. 'Political guilds' and 'guild politics' were fundamental in the politically, economically and culturally advanced county of Flanders. We were certainly not the first historians to point this out.[7] But perhaps what we were able to show is how politically and socially self-conscious the artisan class was, especially in the great textile towns such as Ghent, the most important centre of the artisanal industry in medieval Europe, or Bruges, the commercial metropolis of northwest Europe. Wageworkers, unskilled proletarians and marginal groups in the medieval town certainly also played a role in revolts, but it was the 'middle classes' of petty commodity producers which were always dominant in the alliances that rebels formed.

In this sense, without using a lot of theoretical jargon, we have always remained inspired by undogmatic readings of historical materialism. Conflicts

---

7   Wyffels 1951; Xhayet 1997; Boone 2010.

between various social groups were essential in the medieval town, though wage relations were not the only or even the most determining factor in these struggles. The principal economic sector of medieval Flanders, the cloth industry, was organized as a complex matrix of power and interdependency between merchant capital, small producers and various groups of wage workers, male and female. Also local producers and retailers, as well as disgruntled parts of the dominant merchant and landowner classes, could participate in rebellious coalitions. At the same time, we have also been fundamentally inspired by Weberian historical sociology, pointing to the importance of types of legitimate authority, for instance, and by a general *Annales* style of structuralism that combines such various influences, including also the importance of demographic movements.

All this, of course, was also not very revolutionary or innovative from our side. The two pioneers of the study of medieval revolt, Michel Mollat and Philippe Wolff, had in fact already combined a *marxisant* view on socio-economic struggles with a Weberian ideal-type approach and an interest in economic movements and cycles.[8] Moreover, the combination of these theoretical influences was always rather easily compatible with older approaches to the study of revolt, including that of our own empiricist 'Ghent school' of medieval urban history. This tradition is still influenced by the fundamental work of Henri Pirenne, a genius historian not because everything he wrote is still valid but because of his sense for grand narratives and synthesis, followed in this regard by Hans van Werveke and Jan Dhondt with their emphasis on technical source analysis and the auxiliary sciences, as well as by traditional insights from legal and 'constitutional' history. Other of his followers and successors, such as François-Louis Ganshof, Egied Strubbe, and Raoul Van Caenegem, made us conscious of the impact of law and custom. And to also appreciate Jelle's now home institution of Leuven: we also owe much to the robust scholarship of twentieth-century historians like Jan Van Houtte and Émile Lousse, on economic history, on 'constitutional' principles, and corporatist thought, not to forget the diversity of topics studied by the late Raymond Van Uytven, particularly about the social, cultural and economic history of towns, a brilliant and authentic scholar who also always supported us.

This more materialist approach, the study of socio-economic causes of revolt, of the role of craft guilds in organizing medieval townsfolk, of states and institutions increasing their power and most of all their capacity for violence – all these are classic features of the debate on contentious politics during the

---

8   Mollat and Wolff 1970.

Middle Ages and they are and will remain present in our work as well. However, we also derived additional perspectives from the social sciences, notably in our work on networks and factions in medieval popular politics. In itself this attention to 'vertical solidarities', as emphasized by conservative historians such as Guy Fourquin, Jacques Heers and, for the Flemish case, David Nicholas, was also not new in itself, but perhaps some of the insights we brought in from social anthropology were, including those of Jeremy Boissevain and Pierre Bourdieu, who allow for a combination of 'class' and 'faction'.

But, perhaps most importantly, there has certainly been a 'cultural' and 'linguistic' turn in our work as well as a 'performative' one, and neither have we escaped the wave of interest in 'memory studies' and even 'emotions' in history. Following the example of the great generation of *Annales* medievalists like Le Goff and Duby, we soon turned our interest 'from the cellar to the attic', from 'base' to 'superstructure' as it were. How else were we to discover what medieval rebels actually thought and said than to focus on their own discursive production? There was much to discover there and apart from historians like Richard Trexler and our friend Peter Arnade, inspired by the interpretative anthropology of Clifford Geertz, who had emphasized the ritual forms of medieval protest, almost no cultural approaches to the phenomenon had been published, be it for Flanders or for other European regions. This new research agenda implied a thorough engagement with historical lexicography and semantics, as well as with more recent perspectives on the dialectical relation between language and society. Notably the classic approaches to hegemonic ideologies by Antonio Gramsci and James C. Scott's more recent elaborations of Gramscian thought, Mikhail Bakhtin's idea of dialogism in the sign, Dell Hymes' sociolinguistics and Norman Fairclough's Critical Discourse Analysis all influenced our approach a great deal. In addition, studies on collective and social memories by Maurice Halbwachs and many other scholars (notably Chris Wickham and James Fentress) have taught us to take care of the selection criteria medieval people used when writing down (or 'forgetting') their memories.

Our interest in subversive language also meant that we looked for new types of sources apart from the traditional charters, account books and chronicles. Thus we started using learned legal arguments, rhetoricians' plays and poems, folk songs, and even names themselves. Could we distinguish 'urban ideologies', 'artisan ideologies', or 'state ideologies' in these discourses? Could we also consider forms of violence, ritual types of mobilization and even customary law as languages, in a general social-semiotic approach? And what about the relations between 'memories' or 'emotions' of rebellion to the dominant ideological framework of the time? These were the main issues we have tried to develop. Most of all we feel that we have been able to show that oppositional discourse was not always concealed muttering in the clandestine sphere with, as a following step, probably an outbreak of uncontrolled, indiscriminate and politically uninformed rebellious violence, but that the talk of popular politics was often uttered out in the open or written down in petitions asking for change. In the same way that Sam Cohn made clear once and for all that popular collective actions were part and parcel of daily medieval politics, especially in the urban environment, we have made a plea to consider subversive speech acts as something equally ubiquitous.[9] The ideology and political control of the leading elites were often less hegemonic than is usually tacitly supposed when it comes to medieval society.

But most of all, we insist that languages of opposition, dissent and revolt should always be studied in conjunction with material realities and social relations: our approach is certainly not a 'postmodern' or constructivist one in the sense that only these cultural and semiotic forms would matter. Once again: a classic empiricist source-based approach as well as a materialist point of departure, grounded in the economy and in power relations, have always remained at the core of our work. And in fact, perhaps now is the time to return to some of these older approaches that have recently been neglected, such as the socio-economic frameworks that determined revolts, including classic analysis of relations of production, wage labour etc. And certainly, other topics need more elaboration as well, notably a gender history of medieval revolt, a field in which especially our PhD students have taken some steps.[10]

And as we have said, our opinions also evolved on some subjects and we would formulate some things differently now than they are printed here. Apart from some errors and details nothing fundamentally has been changed in the chapters that follow and they should all be considered in their original year of publication. On some questions we now have somewhat different opinions. For instance, in 2005 we wrote that medieval Flemish rebels almost never demanded structural changes to society; they just wanted concrete improvements in everyday life (see Chapter 1 in the present volume). Clearly, whatever social tensions Flemish rebellions reflected, rebels almost never attacked an entire social class or fundamentally attempted to overthrow the existing social formation. We stay firm on that, but we disagree now that rebels primarily focused on the defence and restoration of ancient liberties or privileges, striving for an

---

9   See Chapter 12 in the present volume, and Dumolyn and Haemers 2015; Dumolyn and Haemers 2018a and b; Haemers and Demeyer 2019; Vrancken 2017; Haemers and Lecuppre-Desjardin 2020; Eersels and Haemers, eds 2020.

10 Haemers and Delameillieure 2017; Demets 2021.

idealized 'golden age in the past', with an ideology of renovation, not of innovation. This might sometimes have been the case, but on other occasions rebels made truly 'progressive claims' as well, and certainly in late medieval Flanders they fundamentally modified its political culture.

Acknowledgements

First of all, we would like to thank our teachers at the Ghent University Department of Medieval History (now part of the Department of History): Hilde De Ridder-Symoens, Thérèse de Hemptinne, Walter Prevenier, the late Raoul C. Van Caenegem, Erik Thoen, Adriaan Verhulst, Monique Vleeschouwers-van Melkebeek, and of course our former supervisor Marc Boone. We also thank our closest colleagues and friends from the period when we were still young researchers: Jonas Braekevelt, Frederik Buylaert, Jeroen Deploige, the late Laurence Derycke, Bart Lambert, Élodie Lecuppre-Desjardin, Hannes Lowagie, Wouter Ryckbosch, Tim Soens, Peter Stabel, Anne-Laure Van Bruaene and Bram Vannieuwenhuyze. Specifically beneficial to our work on medieval revolts was a loose network of international colleagues and friends working on this and closely related topics, including Peter Arnade, Caroline Barron, Wim Blockmans, Patrick Boucheron, Monique Bourin, Andrew Brown, Peter Burke, Vincent Challet, Sam Cohn, Élisabeth Crouzet-Pavan, Mario Damen, Justine Firnhaber-Baker, Chris Fletcher, Claude Gauvard, Jean-Philippe Genet, Éva Guillorel, Eliza Hartrich, Martha Howell, Alain Hugon, Shennan Hutton, Claire Judde de Larivière, Patrick Lantschner, Christian Liddy, María Ángeles Martín Romera, Pierre Monnet, Nicolas Offenstadt, Hipólito Rafael Oliva Herrer, Mark Ormrod, Alma Poloni, Sarah Rees Jones, Susan Reynolds, Miri Rubin, Louis Sicking, Justine Smithuis, Jesús Ángel Solórzano Telechea, Robert Stein, Susie Sutch, Carol Symes, John Watts, Chris Wickham and Andrea Zorzi. We also want to thank all our former and current PhD students for often offering a fresh perspective on what we thought we had already understood for a long time. Last but not least, Andrew Murray and Joannes van den Maagdenberg were extremely helpful in publishing this volume. Therefore, we are very grateful for the tremendous effort they have put into editing this book, especially in dealing carefully with the nightmare that is called a bibliography.

Thanks are also due to many publishers. Brepols have allowed us to reproduce two articles: 'A Moody Community? Emotion and Ritual in Late Medieval Urban Revolts', which was originally a chapter in *Emotions in the Heart of the City (14th–16th Century)*, published in 2005; and 'Guild Politics and Political Guilds in Fourteenth-Century Flanders', which first appeared in *The Voices of the People in Late Medieval Europe: Communication and Popular Politics* (2014). Brill have allowed us to reproduce 'The Legal Repression of Revolts in Late Medieval Flanders', which originally appeared in *Tijdschrift voor Rechtsgeschiedenis* (2000). Éditions universitaires de Dijon have allowed us to translate and reproduce the article 'Espaces et lieux urbains comme enjeux dans la politique communale en Flandre médiévale', an article originally published in *Territoires, lieux et espaces de la révolte XIVe–XVIIIe siècle* (2017). The Freie Universität Berlin and the *Journal of Dutch Literature* have permitted the reproduction of 'Political Poems and Subversive Songs. The Circulation of "Public Poetry" in the Late Medieval Low Countries', which appeared in the aforementioned journal in 2015. Oxford Academic Journals have allowed the reproduction of two articles: ' "A Bad Chicken was Brooding": Subversive Speech in Late Medieval Flanders', a work that initially appeared in *Past & Present* in 2012; and 'Factionalism and State Power in the Flemish Revolt (1482–92)', which was first published in *Journal of Social History* (2009). Taylor & Francis allowed us to reproduce three articles. These are 'Social Memory and Rebellion in Fifteenth-Century Ghent', a work that initially appeared in the journal *Social History* in 2011; 'Patterns of Urban Rebellion in Medieval Flanders', a work that appeared in *Journal of Medieval History* in 2005; and ' "Let Each Man Carry on with his Trade and Remain Silent": Middle-class Ideology in the Urban Literature of the Late Medieval Low Countries', which was published in *Cultural and Social History* in 2013. The University of Seville gave permission for 'The Vengeance of the Commune: Sign Systems of Popular Politics in Medieval Bruges', a work that originally appeared in 2014 in the collected volume *La comunidad medieval como esfera publica*. Wiley-Blackwell and the editors of *History: The Journal of the Historical Association* have allowed us to republish 'The "Terrible Wednesday" of Pentecost: Confronting Urban and Princely Discourses in the Bruges Rebellion of 1436–8', a work that appeared in their journal in 2007.

CHAPTER 1

Editorial Introduction

Andrew Murray

God and the good city of Ghent, kill all those in government!

∵

Flanders was the site of intensive urbanisation from the eleventh century as it became a nodal point of trade between the Baltic, North Sea and Mediterranean regions. This generated long-lasting antagonisms between a feudal elite (the Count of Flanders, the French monarchy, the dukes of Burgundy from the late fourteenth century and, from the late fifteenth, the Habsburg dynasty); elites composed of urban landowners, wealthy merchants, and aldermen; a 'middle' and 'lower' class of shopkeepers, guilds of artisans; and a 'proletariat' of *le menu peuple*, that is, women and day labourers within and outside the guilds. As well as study the distinctive patterns of conflict between these groups over several centuries from a 'macro' perspective, Dumolyn and Haemers also analyse the more 'micro' behaviours of the rebels: how they would arm themselves, gather into crowds, occupy the main spaces of the town, take over the means of communications (i.e., the town and church bells), sabotage infrastructure and destroy the houses and property of their declared enemies. Rather than disorderly reactions to social, political and economic crises, the authors show that the impact of these rebellions were ever present in medieval Flemish society, latent in shared memory during peaceful times. Their research is therefore not only a history of events, their causes and consequences, but of a broader, ever present culture, one of whispering networks in public houses, commemorations maintained in song, the slogans rebels would rouse themselves with, the legal cases they would use to defend their actions, and the most vulgar insults utterable.

The quotation opening this introduction was a chant used by Ghent rebels in 1467. It condenses three of the recurring cultural aspects of rebellions found in the essays that follow: urban space, linguistic performance and ideas of authority. It is a rallying cry for an urban environment, a means to claim 'the good city' for the rebels (compare with the contemporary ubiquitous chant of British demonstrations, 'Whose street? *Our* streets!'). It is also an oracular perform-ance, its rhythmic structure faintly ringing through its translation into modern English.[1] Finally, it is a claim that the rebels' cause is a just one, backed by God and the good city (as opposed to the 'bad' city, its governmental institu-tions). We have organised the chapters into sections covering these themes. The first provides a general introduction to the subject, with chapters provid-ing a chronological overview of Flemish rebellions and analyses of some of the key institutions involved in them. The second section, 'Assembling the Com-mune', presents material on the visual, material and memorial culture of urban rebellions. The third section, 'Orations and Whispers', looks at oracular and lit-erary performances. The final section, 'Law and Authority', examines how the rebels justified their actions and how they were repressed. The final chapter ends at a crucial moment at the end of the late medieval period, the legal case brought against Maximilian of Habsburg when he was captured in the city of Bruges.

The thematic and methodological range of this volume makes it a devel-opment upon as well as a departure from two previous books by its authors: Dumolyn's *Staatsvorming en vorstelijke ambtenaren in het graafschap Vlaan-deren (1419–1477)*, and Haemers's *For the Common Good? State Power and Urban Revolts in the Reign of Mary of Burgundy, 1477–1482*.[2] These two works were built upon prosopography, an approach to research which, as explained in an art-icle Dumolyn has co-authored on the subject,[3] involves the careful definition of social groups and the critical analysis of the available data required to study the typical characteristics of the individuals within them. While Dumolyn's *Staats-vorming* analysed the ambitions, responsibilities and cliental relationships of civic and courtly functionaries in the developing Burgundian state up to 1477, Haemers's *For the Common Good* studied the relationships between these func-tionaries, the ducal court and regional nobility in the period of crisis after 1477. While both books were well received, during and since their publication their authors have researched Flemish revolts with a more expansive range of meth-ods that address blindspots in their prosopographical work, asking questions about collective memory, urban space, oracular performance, literary and leg-alistic rhetoric.

The methodological pluralism of this volume is therefore the result of its chapters being written across twenty years with the purpose of expanding

---

1   '*God ende die goede stede van Ghent, slaet al doot dat heeft regiment*'. See Chapter 12 in the present volume.
2   Dumolyn 2003; Haemers 2009.
3   Verboven, Carlier and Dumolyn 2007.

the ideas and sources considered in the authors' monographic work. But collectively, these essays provide a cohesive project. By exploring Flemish revolts from multiple viewpoints, they build up a descriptive and analytical depth to the culture they analyse, one which is not fully captured by any single synthesised theory or privileged perspective. This may sound a bit like Fredric Jameson's notion of 'cognitive mapping', that is, research which tries to plot historical reality in its multifacted complexity while, at the same time, acknowledging it cannot fully represent the depth of material reality beyond its theoretical constructions.[4] While there is no direct influence, like Jameson's work, Dumolyn and Haemers's represents an attempt to draw on the strengths of both structuralist and materialist approaches to history and culture. They negotiate, on the one hand, methodologies that examine rebellion as cohesive structures and patterns of behaviour that can be modelled, and on the other, methods that emphasise the complexity of the social composition of medieval rebels and the historical depth of their popular traditions. A brief survey of this broader historiography of revolt shows how the combination of these two methological approaches generates, across this volume, the position that medieval cultures of revolt and contention were a regular component of everyday urban life, rather than exceptional events or symptoms of crisis.

While the historiography of Flemish revolts goes back to the nineteenth century, the attention to the cultures of rebellion in these essays – cultures that are oral, visual, performative and material – are a relatively recent development. This may seem surprising, as the social and cultural histories of the Burgundian Low Countries developed closely alongside one another during the early twentieth century. Each was developed respectively by the two famous historians and contemporaries, Henri Pirenne and Johan Huizinga. Pirenne and his legacy is a notable influence on the essays in this volume, for he applied sociological rigour to the study of Flemish revolts, analysing them not as the expression of the self-interest and solidarity of the guilds (the Romantic view of nineteenth-century historians), but as the result of multiple points of conflict between various agents – peasants, craftsmen, patricians, nobility – and the results of shifting allegiances between these groups. Huizinga, on the other hand, analysed the 'forms of life and thought' of the period, drawing attention not only to art, poetry and theology, but a broader range of behaviour including dress, courting, tournament, prayer, processions, dying and swearing, among others. But despite the familiarity and friendship of these two renowned his-

---

4   Jameson 1988.

torians, Pirenne paid little attention to culture and Huizinga little to economics, urban development and social conflict (his work at times seeming to be more literary than historical).[5]

The analysis of rebellion as a culture required two conceptual developments: firstly, an attention to culture as having its own structure, putting it on a conceptual parity with the economy and society; secondly, and as a consequence of the previous point, an assertion that culture can influence social and economic structures, i.e., it is not simply a function of these other spheres. The earliest analysis of rebellion influenced by these two ideas was Mikhail Bakhtin's *Rabelais and His World*.[6] Combining the Russian formalists' analysis of the estranging effects of literary language with a Marxist attention to class struggle, Bakhtin argued that Rabelais's novels were informed by an older, medieval culture of vulgar speech and the grotesque corporal performances of carnival. Furthermore, the lower classes would draw upon these 'unofficial' modes of speech and behaviour to challenge the 'official' culture of written philosophy, organised religion and state bureaucracy. This was also a well from which Bakhtin drew water, his book being a brave reaction against a Stalinist orthodoxy that demanded a sanitised vision of folkloric traditions as well as crude economic determinism in histories of social and class struggles.

Bakhtin's general approach for studying rebellions as a cultural field with social agency was expanded upon in Western academia during the post-war period. This was not directly due to his influence. Although his book on Rabelais was enthusiastically received when published in 1968, this was because the politics of that moment mirrored his own reaction against economic determinism and his attention to social and sexual alterity. An expansive field of sociological enquiry into language and popular culture, in multiple networks of scholars in Britain, France, and the United States, formed an intellectual habitus known as the 'New Left' or 'post-'68 generation. We can count here the Situationist International and then the structuralists in France, the Centre for Contemporary Cultural Studies in Birmingham and the circle around Herbert Marcuse in the United States. While there are important regional and intellectual differences between these groups (as well as between the individuals within them) they formed part of a reaction not only against Stalinism, but also against capitalist and imperialist oppressions that were not expressly

---

5   On this historiography, see Boone 2008a. The difference in approach between the two historians are evident in their different perspectives on the idea of the 'Burgundian state', with Pirenne studying its emergence in terms of state institutions, and Huizinga an attention to senses of national consciousness and loyalty. See Boone 2019.

6   Bakhtin 1984.

defined on around class, but incorporated other social categories, including youth, race, criminality, gender, sexuality, and nationality. As part of this project, they expanded the attention of Marxists to social conflicts in supposedly 'superstructural' arenas, including the media, law, state, family, the arts, and urban space. Many of these social categories and spheres are analysed in this book through a methodological pluralism that draws on figures as diverse as Maurice Halbwachs, Pierre Bourdieu, Henri Lefebvre, Ernesto Laclau, Chantal Mouffe, Charles Tilly and Max Weber, among others.

Charles Tilly, a regular reference in the following chapters, seems to be an odd one out here. His ideas were generated in the same period as the New Left. However, his politics were also centrist enough for him to contribute his research on the history of European rebellions to the 1968 National Commission on the Causes and Prevention of Violence, which aimed to ascertain the threat posed by social unrest in the wake of the assassinations of Martin Luther King and J.F. Kennedy.[7] It might simply be that his influence on the study of early modern contentious politics is so extensive that it cannot be ignored, especially given his close work with Wim Blockmans, a key figure in the analysis of Burgundian urban and state politics.[8] But as undialectical Tilly's work often is, presenting descriptive schemata and models for state development and rebellions, his research has developed the structural analysis of rebellions as actions with aims, rationalities and strategies that can be compared across places and periods. His work therefore dovetails with the Weberian framework for analysing authority that Dumolyn and Haemers's occasionally draw upon by providing comparative schemata for analysing rebellion as a form of contention, that is, as means of challenging legitimacy. Furthermore, although Tilly's research never fully integrated culture on the same determinative level as economics and politics, from the 1970s it displays a cultural turn with the introduction of the concept of contentious repertoires, a concept used to analyse riots and demonstrations as performative behaviour that draw on collective experiences, customs and tradition.[9]

Alongside social-scientific developments in the analysis of rebellion during the twentieth century, historians were also generating their own specific methods in the study of this subject. While prosopographical methods were developed in German and Anglophone scholarship in the interwar period, particularly for the analysis of socially elite groups, from the late 1960s the Com-

7 Tilly 1969.
8 See Tilly, and Blockmans, eds 1994.
9 See Van der Linden 2009, pp. 270–1 and 274.

munist Party Historians Group applied these methods to the study of rebels and rioters. The most influential have been E.P. Thompson and George Rudé, who demonstrated how crowds, rioters and rebels, in their research of early modern England and France, were not mindlessly violent, but were expressing behaviours embedded in popular traditions and were articulating discontent with the social order.[10] These popular customs and ideals were shown to be either rooted in long-held traditions or emergent from suddenly convergent class interests. While there is no direct influence of Thompson and Rudé in these essays, the prosopography of large social groups was heavily represented at the university of Ghent in the 1990s, and Dumolyn and Haemers were instructed in these methods by their supervisor, Marc Boone.[11]

Dumolyn and Haemers's research draws from both the social scientific and the historical traditions and each of these modes of analysis complements weaknesses in the other. To take the historical methods first, this discipline faces a problem in studying late medieval rebellions, as there is a comparative lack of sources in comparison to later centuries (those studied by Thompson and Rudé). Dumolyn and Haemers expand on the sources for their research into the social and ideological characteristics of late medieval rebels by drawing upon the expanded field of cultural theory, giving particular attention to language, urban space, collective memory, and the construction of legal authority. At the same time, the intensive critical source analysis they developed as historians of medieval culture generates a critical perspective on such theories. The critical perspective afforded by medieval popular culture was first articulated by Carlo Ginzburg in 1976, for whom structuralist and post-structuralist thought would stymie the analysis of oral popular traditions by foreclosing consideration of the historical reality beyond the available sources.[12] For Ginzburg, a history of medieval popular traditions demands a commitment to the reality of what is unrecorded. Similarly, many of the chapters that follow are built on reading sources against their intention to detect how they were combined with or influenced by unrecorded modes of subversive speech and behaviour.

Of course, our conception of this social reality 'from below' requires critical attention. Notable here is Bakhtin, who conceived of a 'grotesque' realism, a universal state of becoming that on a human level was most directly exper-

---

10   Rudé 1981 and Thompson 1993.
11   A survey of prosopographical research at the university of Gent in this period is De Ridder-Symoens 1993. On Marc Boone's prosopographical research from this period, see ibid., pp. 57–8, as well as the bibliography in this book.
12   Ginzburg 1976, p. xxv.

ienced through the destructive and regenerative powers of one's lower bodily organs.[13] More persuasive is Ginzburg's view of the reality underlying his historical analysis: an absent oral culture, now lost, impacting on written documents that have survived, in his case the recorded testimony of a sixteenth-century miller caught up in a heresy trial. Comparable Ginzburgian 'micro-historical' case studies are in this book, notably the legal case brought against Maximilian by Willem Zoete in the final chapter.[14] However, this book's methodological pluralism does not simply represent rebellious culture as an elusive past that is only partially revealed in surviving sources. By mapping the culture and history of rebellion from multi-perspectives, it reveals the depth to which that culture was latent within urban culture, showing it to be an ever-present and everyday part of social life, one integrated with 'official' forms of speech and 'peaceful' modes of organising public space and gatherings.

As Dumolyn and Haemers admit in their introduction, their cognitive map is not a comprehensive one. Gender and sexuality, notably, are analytical categories that are largely absent. Hopefully their work empowers future researchers with heuristic tools to historically analyse these and other constructions. More recently, Haemers has applied his approach to sources to the lives and experiences of women in late medieval Flanders and Brabant, whilst Dumolyn has turned towards the fine arts and Jan van Eyck in particular.[15] Dumolyn's study on van Eyck focuses on the everyday urban and working experiences of artisans to explain the medieval conditions of artists, just as Haemers shows the agency, restrictions, and social transgressions of medieval women through contextualising case-studies. Although some articles in this book were written nearly twenty years ago, they provided a basis for this more expansive research of these historians, and hopefully they will be just as helpful to others.

A notable previous attempt at distributing the history of medieval Flanders to a wider readership was William Morris's *The Revolt of Ghent*, published as a seven-part series in the newspaper *Commonweal* in 1888 and published again posthumously as a book by socialist presses in London, Manchester and Huddersfield.[16] Morris's book could not be more different to the present one in its Romantic hope of a revival of the supposedly medieval spirit of guild solidarity. But then again, one does not need to believe that the struggles of the past

---

13   Bakhtin 1984, pp. 18–19, 52–3.
14   See Chapter 15 in the present volume.
15   Haemers, Bardyn, and Delameillieure 2019; Haemers and Delameillieure 2017; Buylaert and Dumolyn 2020; De Meester, Dumolyn, and Frances Jones 2020.
16   Morris 1910.

are instructive to those of the present to find wonder and pride in this part of history, a heritage that belongs not just to Flanders, but to everyone. Whatever brings us to read about these Flemish revolts, Morris was right in stating, 'it is one of the great tales of the world'.

PART 1

Urban Rebellion

CHAPTER 2

Patterns of Urban Rebellion in Medieval Flanders

Jan Dumolyn and Jelle Haemers

Instead of treating us honourably, you have oppressed us. You have broken your promises and oaths by persecuting us unjustly and perversely. As a lawless and faithless count, you have only one thing to do, and that is to get out and leave your subjects free to elect a successor.[1]

∴

1 Introduction

On 16 February 1128, nobleman Iwein of Aalst declared the reasons that the city of Ghent renounced its allegiance to the Flemish count William Clito. His speech expressed the citizens' latent dissatisfaction with the policy of the count, to whom they felt they owed no further obedience. They rebelled. The frequency of this kind of political conflict in Flanders, especially in an urban context, is a unique phenomenon in medieval Europe. In this contribution, by making use of the concepts for studying 'collective actions' developed by Charles Tilly and other theorists, and in the light of recent historical research,[2] we will systematically reassess revolts and rebellions in medieval Flanders, looking for patterns and repertoires, showing that rebellions formed a fundamental feature of political culture in a county that belonged to one of the most developed regions of Europe. We want both to clarify the origins of these urban revolts in the short term and to shed light on the remarkably rebellious behaviour of the Flemish citizens in the long run, from the twelfth to the sixteenth century.

Romantic historians of the nineteenth century treated revolts of Flemish citizens as chaotic outbursts of mad crowds led by heroic freedom fighters who

---

1 Iwein of Alost, 1128. Written down by Galbert of Bruges and translated from Latin by Van Caenegem 1990, p. 105. Original text: Rider, ed. 1994.
2 TeBrake 1993; Dumolyn 1997 and Haemers 2004b.

resisted cruel oppressors.[3] Nationalist and liberal positivists, however, regarded revolts as a threat to the state they adored and often evaluated them negatively, although they did read the sources more critically. In their positivist search for laws and systematic processes in history, they described regular patterns in medieval revolts. According to Henri Pirenne, several main axes of conflict could split medieval society.[4] Besides class wars between peasants and the nobility in the countryside, Pirenne argued that in the medieval city, citizens were opposed to lords, guilds to patricians, and the poor to the craftsmen. Pirenne's thesis persisted for many years. In the 1960s and 1970s, the study of medieval revolts struck out on a number of different paths. Employing Marxist theories, East German historians, like Karl Czok, saw revolts as expressions of pre-capitalist class struggle.[5] Guy Fourquin held a more conservative interpretation, stressing millenarian movements and the role of family clans and individual leadership.[6] Michel Mollat and Philip Wolff saw conflicts between 'les grands', 'les moyens' and 'les petits' as the root of revolts in the calamitous late Middle Ages.[7] Introducing sociological and political theories, Willem Blockmans detected 'revolutionary mechanisms' in medieval Flanders.[8] In a later article, he elaborated on Pirenne's division of the social battlefield in medieval society. He saw four social antagonisms at work: the count versus the cities, the patricians versus the craftsmen, the peasants versus the nobles and patricians and craftsmen versus other craftsmen.[9] Recently, Wayne Te Brake formulated a triangulated political constellation of medieval society, consisting of top-down claimants to power, local rulers, and ordinary political subjects, in which the three actors fight for political power.[10]

Charles Tilly, identifying repertoires of collective action, divided social upheavals in time. According to Tilly, around 1850 the repertoire of rebels shifted away from local collective actions addressed to local authorities to mediate in conflicts with national elites, to autonomous and national actions in which ordinary people expressed specific claims through representative and formal organisations.[11] In both periods people rebelled with standard routines

---

3   Haemers 2004a, pp. 39–45 and Tollebeek 1998.
4   Pirenne 1933.
5   Czok 1958–9. Pirenne's pupil G. Des Marez already saw class conflicts at work, Des Marez 1900.
6   Fourquin 1972.
7   Mollat and Wolff 1970.
8   Blockmans, Willem 1974b, pp. 138–9.
9   Blockmans, Willem 1997a, pp. 262–3.
10   Te Brake 2003, pp. 127–8.
11   Tilly 1986, p. 395; Deneckere 1993, pp. 345–7.

of action, which for the medieval period were identified by Willem Block-mans, who reconstructed the 'Great Tradition' of revolts of Low Countries cities against their prince.[12] Marc Boone and Maarten Prak further refined this vision by distinguishing a 'Little Tradition' of struggle for power within the city, continuously intermingling with the 'Great Tradition'.[13] Finally, drawing on a great deal of German examples, Peter Blickle detected '*Widerstandstraditionen*', '*Konfliktkontinuitäten*' and spirals of rebellious behaviour in medieval society. In some periods and in some regions, revolts were more likely to appear than in others.[14] This goes especially for medieval Flanders. Since in cities like Ghent and Bruges almost every generation witnessed or joined an urban riot or revolt, it is hardly exaggerated to speak of a 'revolutionary tradition' in collective consciousness.[15] But before retrieving this 'rebellious pattern', we have to define what is understood by medieval rebellions and revolutions.

2 Defining Rebellion

Referring to the framework of Charles Tilly, we consider rebellions or revolts a form of collective action; 'a collective action consists of people's acting together in pursuit of common interests'.[16] People rebel when they are pursuing shared interests, confronting the existing order and trying to gain political power by violence. Dynamics of economic crisis or growth, specific stakes and demands, or socio-political tensions can motivate a significant amount of people to aspire to political power in order to achieve specific aims. Sometimes rebels sought fairer policy. Sometimes they demanded the abolition of repressive measures. At all times they strove for the fulfilment of socio-political or economic wishes.

Medieval rebels almost never demanded structural changes of society; they just wanted concrete improvements in everyday life.[17] Rebellions and revolts are not revolutions, and this distinction remains the most widely used classification in studies of political violence. Rebellions or revolts, in contrast to revolutions, do not result in a basic structural change of society.[18] They are attempts to obtain concessions from the rulers, not to overthrow existing social, political

---

12 Blockmans, Willem 1988a.
13 Boone and Prak 1995.
14 Blickle 1988, p. 46.
15 Lambert and Dumolyn 2002, p. 78; Mollat and Wolff 1970, p. 163; Verbruggen, Raf 2005, pp. 153–69.
16 Tilly 1978, p. 7.
17 Bercé 1980, p. 252.
18 Skocpol 1979, p. 4; Zagorin 1982, vol. 1, p. 22; Johnson 1982, pp. 142–9.

or economic systems.[19] Whatever social tensions Flemish rebellions reflected, rebels almost never attacked an entire social class or institution. Instead, they only wanted to improve institutions or gain the right to participate in them.[20] Moreover, late medieval rebels primarily focused on the defence and restoration of ancient liberties or privileges, striving for an idealised 'golden age in the past', with an ideology of renovation, not of innovation.[21] Fundamentally changing society was never at stake in medieval Flanders.

3   The Communal Movement

Together with Northern and Central Italy, the county of Flanders comprised the most densely urbanised regions in medieval Europe.[22] Since the eleventh century, the process of urbanisation was stimulated by economic developments such as progressive agriculture and a specialisation in export-oriented industrial production.[23] The urban character of the county further determined political and cultural orientation, the organisation of the economy, and the structuring of social relations. Demographic and economic importance determined systems of interaction between commercial gateways and an industrial hinterland, between international and interregional trade centres and regional and local markets, between town and countryside.[24] The dense concentration of wealth enabled the cities to acquire significant autonomy, but the permanent urban aspiration to gain regional power was ultimately stymied by regional princes and their central governing bodies. The first real confrontation between the main cities of the county (Ghent, Bruges and Ypres) and the feudal prince (the count of Flanders, as a vassal to the French king) took place in the years 1127–8, the starting point of the first, 'communal', phase of Flemish urban revolts.

The murder of the Flemish count Charles the Good in March 1127 by the clan of the Erembalds created a vacuum of power in which the Flemish cities emancipated themselves from their feudal lord. The Norman prince William Clito, appointed by the French king Louis VI as the new count in April 1127, showed little sympathy to the ideas of urban liberty, let alone self-government of the

---

19   Brustein and Levi 1987, p. 471; Rotz 1985, pp. 69–70.
20   Rotz 1976, p. 232.
21   Elliott 1969, p. 44.
22   An overview of Flemish history in Nicholas, David 1992.
23   Thoen 2001, pp. 105–11.
24   Stabel 1997; Verhulst 1999, pp. 68–156.

Flemish cities. The latter were ruled by a rich elite who had recently gained fortune through the economic boom of trade in the twelfth century. The conflict between the dynastic logic of the great feudal lords, whom the elite held responsible for the deterioration of commerce and industry (caused by an English embargo of the vital imports of wool) and the fundamental commercial interests of the merchant elite, was out in the open.[25] The count wanted to skim off the profits of trade and, moreover, he seemed to be restoring a classic feudal political system which the Flemish towns had just overcome. In August 1127, the burghers of Lille rose against count William Clito and his officers after they had arrested a citizen during the annual market.[26] His fellow citizens did not want to return to a world ruled by noble arbitrariness that could endanger the basis of citizenry, its privileged juridical status.

After Lille and Saint-Omer, Ghent fought for its juridical and political recognition in February 1128. Even some nobles (among them, Iwein of Aalst) joined the citizens, because an autocratic count also limited their local sphere of regional power on the countryside. Surprisingly, this coalition of forces defeated William Clito, who was killed in battle. The new count, Thierry of Alsace, entered into a political pact with the third estate, making this the first occasion on which it played a determining political role in Flemish history.[27] According to the burghers, political authority ought to rest on a legitimate base, which was none other than a contract between the ruler and his people, including the right of resistance against an unjust ruler, analogous to the feudal *ius resistendi*. This new principle of 'constitutionalism' and the sovereignty of the people became the political basis of Flemish society and was contested throughout the Middle Ages and beyond.[28] During this *Kommunebewegung* (communal development) of the twelfth and thirteenth centuries that took place in other parts of Europe as well,[29] many Flemish cities (and rural districts) would obtain 'constitutional' privileges that organised city government and limited the rights of the count and the lords. The Flemish cities now possessed a large degree of political autonomy from the prince, who was not powerful enough to resist. Making a virtue of necessity, the counts started supporting powerful cities to weaken the third player in the political field, the nobility. The taxes paid by the

25 Boone and Prak 1995, p. 102; Dhondt 1957; Van Caenegem 1994b; Schulz 1992, pp. 101–31.
26 Rider, ed. 1994, p. 141.
27 Dhondt 1950a, pp. 5–52.
28 Van Caenegem 1994b, p. 110; Blockmans, Willem 1997a, p. 259; Boone and Prak 1995, p. 101; Van Uytven and Blockmans 1969.
29 Verhulst 1999, pp. 125–31; Schulz 1992; Petit-Dutaillis 1947. On *Kommunalismus*, see Blickle 2000.

cities were, in a way, protection costs from the grip of this common rival, which never became a powerful player in Flemish politics.[30]

4   Civic Emancipation

After this period of 'communal emancipation', a phase of 'civic emancipation' commenced (1280–1302). Cities had now grown more socially heterogeneous. Flemish sources used a diverse terminology to distinguish the social groups within the urban landscape: 'poor people who work with their hands' versus 'the rich' (Damme 1280 and Ghent 1397),[31] *majores oppidani* and *meliores burgenses* versus *ille de communitate qui opus mechanicum exercerent* (Ghent 1308), or *le commun* versus *les boins de la ville* (Ypres, 1320–32). The leading social group of the patricians – equivalent to the Italian *popolo grosso*[32] – consisted of an oligarchic elite that monopolised political power. Their wealth was based on the possession of urban land and on commercial and financial activities.[33] These merchant-entrepreneurs organised economic life in towns that were predominately engaged in the production of textiles.[34] Under the leadership of these wealthy cloth merchants, the labourers of the textile industry were gradually organised in craft guilds, but the commoners – like the Italian *popolo minuto* – did not participate in political and juridical life.

However, in the second half of the thirteenth century, the first economic disturbances occurred throughout Europe. The vulnerability of large numbers of workers, caused by disruptions in the long-distance trade, made them realise their exploitation.[35] Between 1245 and 1320, the towns in Northern France and Flanders proved to be a real seedbed for social turmoil.[36] This struggle of the *moyens* against the *grands* had similar characteristics all over Western Europe. Petty commodity producers in the craft guilds formed a new kind of middle class, distinct from both the patrician families who monopolised politics, and the lower-class proletarians and marginal groups. Though these groups often participated, they rarely initiated revolts on their own behalf or articulated a

---

30   Blockmans, Willem 1989, p. 750.
31   Prevenier 2002, pp. 180–4.
32   On the divisions in Italian medieval society, see Crouzet-Pavan 2001, pp. 121–62.
33   The classic study remains Blockmans, Frans 1938b.
34   About fifty percent or more of the working population was active in the textile industry: Prevenier 1983, pp. 256–8.
35   Blockmans, Willem 1997a, p. 260.
36   Leguai 1976, p. 281 and Mollat and Wolff 1970, pp. 59–65: in France revolts occurred in Rouen, Laon, Arras and Saint-Quentin.

platform of their own.[37] In 1245, the first strikes (called *takehans*) took place in Douai, and were repeated in 1276.[38] In the years 1252 and 1274, the textile workers of Ghent went on strike. In 1280, a general revolt of labourers spread out all over the county. Disruption of international trade, as in the case of the wool trade with England in the 1270s, could provoke merchants to join in rebellions. Scholars also have described similar revolts in Tournai in 1279–81, Saint-Omer in 1280–3, the Ypres *Cockerulle* in 1281, the Bruges *Moerlemaye* in 1280–1, and Ghent in 1280.

While the rebellions around 1280 all had their specific features, the general recession in commerce and industry explains their simultaneity.[39] However, political questions were foremost in the demands of the rebels, who were led by *nouveaux riches*.[40] During all these revolts, rebels protested against two objectionable practices, namely financial excesses, in the form of heavy taxation, exploitation of the people's goods and work; and corruption and misgovernment of the regime in the form of arbitrary policies, unfair judging, improper use of coercive means, violation of rights and so on.[41] Rising taxes always inflame people with anger during unfavourable economic periods,[42] but being a part of the commune and paying taxes for its government, the working citizen was more concerned that his commune be well-governed. Citizens denounced the unjust division and improper use of taxes by the city oligarchs, not the taxes themselves. The taxes weighed more heavily on those in the population that had the most meagre resources, and this was a source of discontent.[43] In a further stage, the rebels required direct control over the city finances and the urban policy through political representation.[44] In several towns, as in Damme in 1280, dissatisfied citizens, well aware of the fiscal mechanisms that favoured the rich, succeeded in contacting the Flemish count, who saw a chance to diminish the particular power of the city oligarchs.[45]

In 1302, the self-conscious middle-class found allies in rich burghers who had been deprived of a place in the urban government, and also in the count,

---

37 Mollat and Wolff 1970, pp. 53–90.
38 Leguai 1976, p. 281; Espinas 1913, vol. 1, pp. 226–69; Brassart 1883a and 1883b; Prevenier 2002, pp. 184–5; Boone 1998; Bardoel 1994; Dumolyn and Haemers 2016.
39 Wyffels 1966, p. 43.
40 As was studied in Bruges: ibid., p. 57 and Bardoel 1994. On these *homines novi* in Ghent: Märtins 1976.
41 Barth 1974, p. 348.
42 Ardant 1965, vol. 2, p. 728.
43 Hilton 1989, vol. 2, p. 28.
44 Wyffels 1966, pp. 104–7.
45 De Smet, Anton 1950, p. 9.

who faced an aggressive annexation of his county by the French king. The latter, in his turn, was supported by the patrician families of the cities. The outcome of the exceptional synchronism of conflicts is well known. The French army was humiliated at the famous battle of Kortrijk in July 1302 – an event that shook the medieval world – and craft guilds took over power and established themselves as an important part of the body politic within the major Flemish cities.[46] Considering its scale and depth and its repercussions in the surrounding principalities, Blockmans judges the 1302 wave to have been a real social and political revolution, perhaps the first in Europe.[47] According to the terminology we use, speaking of a 'revolution' is perhaps an overstatement, but the crucial importance of the events of 1302 cannot be underestimated. The installation of permanent guild representation in government broadened the base for the exercise of power in Flemish cities for more than two centuries. Craft guilds became a powerful lobby in the urban environment.[48] We argue that the manifest fiscal injustice of the patrician city government was not in fact the fundamental cause of conflict in this second phase of urban rebelliousness. There was a vivid dissatisfaction with the oligarchic character of city policy that only awaited a spark to ignite the fire.[49] But it was the latent socio-political inequality, aggravated by economic evolution, that was the main reason for the conflicts. Gaining access to the polity and control of the financial resources of the city was the foremost objective of the rebels.

5   The Era of the 'City-State'

Financial pressure, caused by the heavy taxation on the county after the disadvantageous peace settlement of Athis-sur-Orges with France in June 1305, and growing economic malaise[50] weighed on the united front of the craft guilds and their allies. In the third phase of Flemish rebellion, from 1305 to 1360, the era of the so-called 'city state', unity disintegrated. Struggles for power deluged the county, on the one hand, between guilds, who fought each other with a

---

46   Boone 2002b.
47   Blockmans, Willem 1997a, p. 261. In the surrounding principalities Holland, Brabant and Liège, the Flemish revolt provoked revolts of artisans demanding the same social and political rights, Blickle 1988, p. 54.
48   Stabel 2004, pp. 187–92 and Black 2003, pp. 66–75.
49   An analysis of fifteenth-century revolts against governmental taxes in France led to the same conclusions, Leguai 1967.
50   Thoen 2001, pp. 111–38.

vital political consciousness fed by their military power that was discovered on the battlefield of Kortrijk in 1302, and, on the other hand, between guilds and patricians who wanted to regain their political power.[51] Revolts took place in Saint-Omer in 1306,[52] in Ghent in 1304, 1311 and 1313,[53] in Ypres in 1303–4,[54] in Bruges in 1309–10 and in Aardenburg in 1309–11.[55]

For the contenders, participation in power and control over city resources, specifically the economic and financial management of the city, was crucial. This included determining tax levies, market regulations, price and wage levels and working conditions.[56] The economic difficulties of the fourteenth century just heightened the latent tensions within guilds containing different social groups. These battles could be vivid because craftsmen who worked for the local market had other interests than those who produced for international trade. The former wanted political stability and stable prices to sell their commodities. The latter were much more dependent on international politics and on the prices of raw materials. They also lived in greater concentrations and were thus more 'proletarianised'. A classic example is the constant fighting between the weavers and the fullers, mostly over wage conflicts.[57] This social conflict was often mixed with the social and political conflicts between the textile guilds and the patricians. In Ghent, patricians and fullers on several occasions actually allied against their common enemy, the weavers. Tension also existed between small commodity producers, who possessed their own means of production, and the wage labourers, journeymen or poor guild-masters who had to sell their labour power to other masters. These contradictions help to explain the frequency and the intensity of the battles for power in major textile centres, as in Ghent thirteen times between 1311 and 1375.[58] At the beginning of the Hundred Years War, between 1337 and 1345, Ghent was ruled by the dean of the weavers, James van Artevelde, who sought international aid to install his autocratic regime throughout the county. He found it especially with the English king who was at that time made king of France. Similarly, Bruges merchants

---

51 A somewhat outdated overview, in Rogghé 1952, p. 103.

52 Hennequin 1955.

53 Fris 1907, p. 428; Boone 2003a, pp. 21–3.

54 Viaene 2004, pp. 13–19.

55 Wyffels 1949–50, pp. 10–11.

56 Mollat and Wolff 1970, p. 282.

57 Verbruggen, Raf 2005, pp. 19–28; Espinas and Pirenne, ed. 1906–66, vol. 2, pp. 402, 533–7, vol. 3, pp. 740–4. A similar rebellion took place in Douai in 1322: Howell 1993, pp. 110–11. More generally, see Sieg'l 1993.

58 In 1311, 1313, 1319, 1325–6, 1328, 1337, 1345, 1347, 1349, 1353, 1359, 1361 and 1373. Nicholas, David 1988; Lucas 1929; Fris 1907; Boone and Brand 1993; Vuylsteke 1895.

might have favoured the revolt of 1323–8 because they feared count Louis would not maintain good commercial relations with England.[59]

We consider the 'peasants' revolt' of maritime Flanders (1323–8) as a partly urban rebellion because it was not purely rural. Facing fiscal pressure and a growing socio-political inequality, a real coalition between powerless citizens and peasants developed. Bruges joined the peasant rebels and so did hundreds of Ghent weavers who were subsequently sent into exile. Not only did major cities like Ypres and Kortrijk at some point join in, but also from at least the beginning of 1324, the commoners of some smaller towns also participated in the rising.[60] The revolt thus spread 'like a plague'. In 1325 the rebels, now clearly uniting peasants and burghers from many cities including Bruges and Ypres, held most of the county and managed to force count Louis, at that time a prisoner in Bruges, to make Robert of Cassel regent of Flanders. Robert was an opportunistic nobleman, uncle to the count, making common cause with the revolt to increase his personal power.[61] This was one of the instances when Flemish rebels managed to form an alternative government, appoint their own functionaries and create a truly 'revolutionary' situation of dual power. It seems, however, that the countrymen had more radical demands and really intended to overthrow the existing social order in the countryside, whereas the burghers did not and were more eager to compromise when the situation seemed lost after a French intervention to support the powerless count.[62]

To an even greater degree than the city of Bruges in 1323–8, James van Artevelde worked out an alternative model to monarchical centralisation, paralleling the Northern Italian cities, but to a lesser degree. His model conceptualised a state organisation based on the autonomous power of the great cities, dominating the surrounding countryside to guarantee the economic interests of the guilds. The firm guild structure, based on corporate solidarity, generated a political culture of 'pre-republicanism' in the powerful cities who wanted to rule the urban space by themselves.[63] Their core position in the European economic system provided the cities such an abundance of resources that

---

59   TeBrake 1993, p. 74.
60   Sabbe, Jacques 1970, pp. 236–47; Sabbe, Jacques 1992, pp. 22, 60–1; and TeBrake 1993.
61   TeBrake 1993, p. 86.
62   TeBrake 1993, p. 87. Contrary to what was claimed in older historiography, Challet has shown that among the Tuchin-movement in the Languedoc (1381–4) there were also urban elements involved, especially artisans. The Tuchin-rebels organised in both rural and urban networks of sociability. Here too, urban rebels were quicker to negotiate with the monarchy than their rural counterparts who were far more radical: Challet 1998, pp. 106–8.
63   Boone 1997b; Schilling 1992.

the princes had no other choice but to leave them an extensive autonomy.[64] However, James van Artevelde was politically finished when the crucial English aid fell away, and he became a victim of rivalries within his own town. The count supported former patricians who expelled the weavers from the city. But in 1359, a year after the Parisian revolt led by Etienne Marcel, a general weavers' revolt spread over the county. In Bruges, Ypres and Ghent, the weavers fought to re-enter the city government.[65] Frightened by this 'national' revolt in his dominion, the count had to confirm the weavers' power in the main cities again. And thus the power of the city-states strengthened.[66]

6 Altering Balances of Power

The time in which the weak counts of Flanders were mere spectators on the sidelines of the political arena came to an end in the fourth period of Flemish urban rebellions (1379–1453). The eve of this phase, the Ghent War (1379–85), exhibited several similarities to revolts and rebellions in preceding years. It coincided chronologically with a wave of socio-political rebellions in Europe that Mollat and Wolff called *les années révolutionnaires*. Though there was no strict synchronism and the events certainly had a different character in different regions. Many parts of Europe witnessed revolts in those years, the most famous of which are the English Peasants Revolt of 1381 and the revolt of the Ciompi in Florence.[67] In the Ghent war, which spread all over the county, a new van Artevelde, Philip, son of James, stood up to the count, once again with the support of English troops. But the alliance of guilds from several towns was not successful this time. In 1380, some Bruges weavers who supported the Ghent rebels were quickly crushed by the Bruges patricians and by craftsmen working for the local markets.[68] After the battle of Beverhoutsveld (1382), a victory for the Ghent rebel troops over the Bruges militia, a revolutionary craft-guild regime took power also in Ypres, but only for a short time.[69]

---

64 Blockmans, Willem 1988a, p. 152; Blockmans, Willem 1989, p. 737.
65 Vuylsteke 1895, pp. 44–6; Fris 1907, pp. 446–50; Mertens 1987, pp. 325–30.
66 Boone and Prevenier 1989b, pp. 85–93.
67 Mollat and Wolff 1970, pp. 139–42; Stella 1993; Hilton and Aston, eds 1984.
68 Demuynck 1951; and Mertens 1973, pp. 6–7.
69 In general, of all the big cities, the guilds in Ypres were in the weakest position *vis-à-vis* the patricians. The only periods they managed to be strongly represented in the urban government was during the revolutionary periods of 1325–8, 1338–48, 1359–61 and 1382: Verbruggen, Raf 2005, pp. 57–8.

The economic landscape had changed. In the face of trade difficulties and foreign competitors, Flemish merchants and entrepreneurs had successfully transformed the structure of the textile industry. After the severe crisis of the fourteenth century, the production of luxury goods and the so-called 'new' and 'light drapery' had replaced the industrial production of the 'heavy drapery'.[70] The fullers became less important in the production of drapery and, as a consequence, their political power fell away.[71] On the contrary, the weavers still remained a politically conscious group, ready to answer attacks on their rights, as happened in 1387 and 1391 in Bruges, and in 1428–9 in Ypres.[72] The fragmentation of the economic landscape into a wider range of medium-sized guilds, and the declining industrial production of textile goods consequently divided economic interests from reasons to rebel.

Moreover, in Ghent and Bruges from about 1360, a balance of power developed between the different guilds, which was reflected in more-or-less fixed systems for the division of economic and socio-political functions within the city.[73] Rebellion was no longer necessary to fulfil political demands, because representatives of the guilds took part in city government. Formerly powerless craftsmen could now demand political changes in legal ways. Especially in the fifteenth century, small elites of the more well-off guild masters monopolised the political functions inside the guilds and the city government.[74] Social divisions had grown deeper, and were still widening under the pressure of the major political evolution of the late Middle Ages, the formation of modern states. As in the Ghent war of 1379–85, in the Bruges revolts of 1411 and 1436–8, and in the Ghent revolts of 1401, 1406, 1411, 1414, 1423, 1432, 1437, 1440 and 1449–53, the Flemish craft guilds opposed their count, who was now the powerful duke of Burgundy. The Burgundian dynasty established a sophisticated and effective, albeit short-lived, state in the medieval Low Countries.[75] The duke's programme for centralisation included the construction and strengthening of central judicial institutions, particularly the Council of Flanders as an appeal court for the local city aldermen, and the undermining of the power of the 'Four Members of Flanders' as a representative institution with the power to approve taxation. The Burgundian state gradually concentrated coercive power by skim-

---

70   Boone 1993; Dambruyne 2001, pp. 356–63; Howell and Boone 1996, pp. 306–11; Stabel 1997, pp. 138–58 and, more generally, Van der Wee 1988.

71   Boone and Brand 1993, pp. 192–3; Haemers 2004b, pp. 44–6.

72   Mertens 1973; Diegerick 1856.

73   Boone 1990b; Mertens 1987, pp. 325–6; Boone and Prak 1995, p. 106.

74   Boone 1990b, pp. 58–93.

75   Blockmans, Willem 1988d; Blockmans and Prevenier 1999; Boone 1990b; Dumolyn 2003.

ming off more and more of the financial means of its subjects and through growing co-option of pro-ducal social and political networks among the urban political elites. In 1385, the Burgundian duke still had to accept a *modus vivendi* with rebellious Ghent as the price for becoming count of Flanders, but Burgundian rule strengthened with the acquisition of new territories in the Netherlands. Once its power was consolidated, the growing ambitions of the ducal state increasingly came into open conflict with parts of the elites and with the urban guilds in the last fortresses of rebellion.[76] This was clearly shown during the bitter but ultimately failed revolts of Bruges in 1436–8 and Ghent in 1449–53.

In the course of these revolts, the craftsmen contested not only the centralising policies of the Burgundian state, but also the decrease in their participation in city politics. Narrower groups of city elites increasingly made the decisions, and the prince and his influential court attracted and recruited these elites to defend the state's ambitions. In most cities this policy worked smoothly, and fifteenth-century political elites became much more docile than their forerunners had been. Unlike the middle class and the common craftsmen, the city oligarchs were less dependent on the urban privileges to ensure their economic wealth and political power. They thus undermined the corporate solidarity of the city which they were supposed to represent.[77] Even the political heads of the guilds took the opportunity to gain personal profit from their position as the privileged suppliers of materials or services for the city. Frustrated members of the urban elites who had not been approached by the duke could forge an alliance with the powerless craftsmen to contest their declining representation in the urban government. But because of intra-urban rivalries, a lack of support by other challengers to the state and the overwhelming strength of such a powerful enemy, rebellious alliances of citizens did not succeed in bringing back the good times when guilds and local potentates independently decided urban policies.[78] Remarkably, during the Burgundian period, his subjects never questioned the authority of the prince. After all, he remained the natural and legitimate lord badly advised by evil councillors. His subjects often had the perception, sometimes rightly, that it was not the duke but his corrupt officials and the bribed city oligarchs who were to blame for the burden of taxation or misled him into revoking urban privileges.

---

76 Boone and Prak 1995, p. 107.
77 Blockmans, Willem 1997a, p. 270.
78 Blockmans, Willem 1978, pp. 588–92; Dumolyn 1997, pp. 335–44; Haemers 2004b, pp. 423–36.

7   The Final Outburst of Crisis

The outcome of the socio-political battle was predictable. Because of their investments in social and political capital, more specifically by marrying into noble families, acquiring feudal land and holding princely offices, an increasing part of the urban political elite was prepared to give up the political autonomy of the city for the consolidation of their personal ambitions.[79] In the long run these 'dangerous liaisons' between city elites and prince were solid enough to handle the resistance of the lower social groups. In this fifth phase, 1467–1540, only in moments of structural weakness in state power could rebel coalitions hold firm. In 1467, during the inauguration of Charles the Bold as the new count, a violent rebellion of the Ghent middle class erupted, and the furious prince responded with a heavy hand.[80] After Duke Charles's death in 1477, a tight collaboration between expelled city elites, middle classes and common craftsmen came to power in the major cities. The repressive measures and the autocratic policy of the duke and his confidants were undone by a sudden and violent attack.[81] However, in spite of rebellions in Bruges and Sluis in September 1477, and in Ghent in February 1479, representatives of the central state could gradually take over power again.[82] However, after the death of his daughter Mary of Burgundy, in 1482, the Burgundian state – which now fell into Habsburg hands with the succession of her husband Maximilian of Austria – faced a serious alternative. Military aid of the French king helped the frustrated elites, middle classes and common craftsmen of all three major Flemish cities plus many nobles to resist openly the autocratic regime of Maximilian, who was portrayed as an unjust and perverse count. Consequently, the representatives of the three Members of Flanders chose regents for his son, Philip the Fair, whom they considered the true count of Flanders. Once again, local authorities were empowered to decide all matters, and enabled decision-making on the higher levels. To summarise: the age-old custom of 'pre-republicanism' was introduced in a monarchical model.[83]

As in the revolts of 1128, 1323–8 and 1339–45, a strong coalition resisted state power. Against this 'popular front' any centralising institution would have to muster an equally formidable coalition of its own. The King of the Romans,

---

79   Blockmans, Willem 1989, p. 753; Tilly 1985; Dumolyn 2002.
80   Arnade 1991; Boone 2001b; Haemers 2004b, pp. 415–16.
81   Blockmans, Willem, ed. 1985a; Hugenholtz 1964; Königsberger 1986 and 2001, pp. 42–72; Boone 2003b.
82   Fris 1909; Janssens 1996.
83   Blockmans, Willem 1974a.

Maximilian himself, had to start a counter-revolt in 1485 to regain political power in the cities. But his claim to power was not broadly based, and after the Ghent revolt in November 1487 and the Bruges revolt in January 1488, rebels imprisoned him in Bruges. To capture the Roman King himself was to do the unthinkable.[84] Nevertheless, internal rivalries, weaker-than-expected foreign aid, an economic blockade of the surrounding countries, and the huge financial and especially military reserves of Maximilian finished the resistance of the coalition. Bruges capitulated first in January, and finally in December 1490; Ghent surrendered in July 1492; and Philip of Cleves, the most rebellious nobleman, held out in Sluis until October 1492.[85]

The repressive measures of the state managed to break open resistance until 1515, when the Ghent guilds contacted Philip of Cleves to disrupt the inauguration of the new count Charles.[86] The repressive reaction of the emperor could not prevent a new revolt against his financial and military policy in 1537–9, put down by extremely harsh repression in 1540.[87] However, the rebellious tradition of the county of Flanders was not exhausted. Partly because of the influence of religious factors, the revolts of the second half of the sixteenth century opened a sixth phase of revolt (1566–84). In itself, however, the religious factor was not new, because during the Great Schism of 1378–1415 it was already an issue in the Ghent war.[88] Moreover, the behaviour and background of the urban rebels of sixteenth-century Ghent who took up arms against Philip II of Spain, did not break new ground.[89] In a vacuum of princely authority in 1576–7, a city coalition made up a programme for the whole county that implemented the formation of a city-state system, bringing the county once again under the control of the three big cities, Ghent, Bruges and Ypres. Iwein of Aalst's words of 1128 echoed more vividly than ever when the Estates-General of the Low Countries enacted an 'Act of Abandonment' in 1581, by which they deposed the 'lawless and faithless prince'.[90]

---

84 Wellens 1965, pp. 29–30; Haemers and Lecuppre-Desjardin 2007.
85 De Fouw 1937; Haemers, Van Hoorebeeck and Wijsman, eds 2007. See Chapter 15 in the present volume.
86 Dambruyne 2002, pp. 614–6.
87 Dambruyne 2003; Decavele and Van Peteghem 1989, pp. 107–13; Blockmans, Willem 2000; Boone 2000; and Te Brake 2003.
88 Boone and Prak 1995, pp. 112–13.
89 Dambruyne 2003, pp. 109–15.
90 Blockmans, Willem 1988a, pp. 145–6; Blockmans and van Peteghem 1976.

8   Coalitions and Leadership

In what follows we try to retrieve structural elements and patterns in medieval rebelliousness in the Flemish cities: i.e., firstly, coalitions and leadership of rebels; secondly, their interests and ideology, and finally, their mobilisation and repertoire. First of all, forging coalitions and alliances was crucial to the rebels. If groups or individuals wanted to gain political power, they could first try to approach the ruling political networks. If these networks did not fulfil the contender's (or contenders') demands, ambitious individuals could form a coalition with other frustrated challengers. Initially, they would try to enter the ruling networks without violence.[91] If the possibilities for a group to attain political involvement were limited, for example in the case of the craft guilds in the 1280s, contenders for power could seek to become members of the polity through collective action.[92] If this collective action used violence to gain power, we speak of a rebellion. The central element in violence is coercion, including an imminent threat,[93] that would force the elites to satisfy rebel demands.

'Coalition' is the key word in a rebellion. People rebel when acting together. The *Moerlemaye* revolt of Bruges (1280–1), for example, shows that the simple opposition between 'commoners' and 'patricians' was not always so clear cut.[94] Revolts cannot be simply reduced to the antagonisms mentioned in the introduction. In every urban rebellion in medieval Flanders, the centre (count and king), patricians, nobles, craftsmen and even peasants formed ever-changing coalitions to gain political power.[95] Facing united groups, power holders easily lost their political support to an alternative body that claimed the city's public space and tried to gain control over coercive powers by replacing the current membership of the city magistracy as the only institution that reflected public authority. Examples of allied forces are numerous in the above survey. The opposition of the period 1280–1302, for example, was a heterogeneous class coalition, a united front of textile workers, middle-class artisans and politically frustrated *homines novi*.[96] Studying a wide range of late medieval urban revolts in Germany, Czok concluded that broader layers of burghers than just the craft guilds participated in united fronts (*Bürgeropposition*) in a struggle

---

91   Tilly 1978, p. 126.
92   Ibid., p. 133.
93   Zagorin 1982, vol. 1, p. 18.
94   Wyffels 1966, p. 38.
95   In many Italian cities as well, popular coalitions managed to break into government by means of revolts before the 1320s and 1330s. See Martines 1972, p. 332 and Jones, Philip 1997, pp. 558–96.
96   Prevenier 2002, p. 176 and Wyffels 1966, pp. 72, 85.

for city government and economic power in general, though with a clearly limited reformist character.[97] Rebellion occurred on a broader scale if the urban elite fragmented into different interest groups. Economic interests, network alliances, or political frustration could unite members of the political and economic elites with dissatisfied craft guilds. Efforts to achieve a more effective central control could weaken older political bonds and sometimes alienated significant elements of the urban ruling classes.[98] Coalitions between guilds could go beyond the city walls, as happened in 1360 (see above). There is even proof that rebels from different cities also formed networks of their own. After the 1323–8 revolt, an anonymous Bruges rebel told the officers charged with the investigation that he had ties with other rebels of the city of Geraardsbergen who had brought him into contact with the Ghent weavers.[99] Noblemen could also divide if a structural crisis threatened the dynasty, as in 1477, when several nobles joined the French king or, as in 1483–5, the Flemish rebels.[100]

Leadership of noblemen like Robert of Cassel during the revolt of maritime Flanders or Philip of Cleves at the end of the fifteenth century gave rebellions additional legitimacy, but these men quickly turned their backs on the rebels when defeat was imminent, since they mostly acted from opportunistic self-interest. Leading rebels always searched for one or more charismatic persons who were to be the compromise figures between several groups and became the leader(s) of the rebellion. As elsewhere in western Europe, rebel leaders mostly originated from the higher classes of society: noblemen, rich merchants, or – in the case of a rural rebellion – wealthy peasants took the lead.[101] Members of the elites had the background, the capital and, sometimes, the political experience to be capable leaders. For the rebellious networks, the leader was an instrument to control the masses. For the guilds, the leader became a symbol of fair resistance to evil; he was supposed to change the course of events.[102] In Ghent, James van Artevelde became the archetype of the rebel leader. In every subsequent revolt rebels referred to his success and his charisma if their leaders did not fulfil their wishes.[103] Van Artevelde, from a wealthy merchant family, can in this respect be compared to Etienne Marcel, *prévôt des*

97   Czok 1960; using a different terminology Maschke 1959 stressed that even dissident patricians sometimes joined rebellions.
98   Forster and Greene 1970, p. 14.
99   Verbruggen, Raf 2005, pp. 83–90; de Pauw 1899a, pp. 670–1.
100 Blockmans, Willem 1985c.
101 Bercé 1980, p. 252; Johnson 1982, p. 15; Leguai 1967, p. 484; Rotz 1985, p. 67; Mollat and Wolff 1970, p. 131.
102 Stone, Clarence 1995, pp. 97–8; Burns, James MacGregor 1978.
103 Boone and Prak 1995, p. 106.

marchands of Paris and leader of the rebels of 1356–8, who sought an alliance with the revolting peasants of the *Jacquerie*.[104] Pieter de Coninck, a great public speaker and leader of the Bruges revolt of 1302, said to be a poor weaver, was a notable exception to this general rule of elite descent. At all events, the position of a rebel leader was risky. If he did not succeed, his fate lay in the hands of the different rebellious networks and factions. If they needed a scapegoat for a lost battle or a lightning rod for dissatisfied guilds, the leader was sacrificed. On one occasion in 1302, Pieter de Coninck was chased out of Bruges. Ghent rebel leader Lieven Boone was decapitated after a lost battle in 1452, and even James van Artevelde was murdered by competing networks in 1345.[105]

The most dramatic expressions of urban political power happened when towns as a whole joined in leagues or alliances, which collectively had far more resources at their disposal than a single prince.[106] And when nobles and even members of the court sympathised, dynastic power was temporarily overcome, as happened, for example, during the periods of the 'regency-council' in 1483–5 and 1488–90.[107] But princely power always had a remarkable resilience. Princes had a far more legitimate position than the rebellious opposition, and they could fall back on a greater experience and tradition of governing. Furthermore, as the state formation process progressed under Burgundian and Habsburg rule, princely reserves of power and finances became too high to resist. Usually, princes tried to tackle coalitions by using divide-and-rule tactics, setting nobles, cities and citizens against each other.[108] The specific urban ideology and the often-diverging interests of the major cities helped the prince to keep the cities divided. Even within the town itself, rebellious coalitions mostly proved to be of short duration. In 1325, for example, a revolt by the Ghent weavers sympathising with their fellow rebels in Western Flanders was defeated inside the city.[109] In the Ghent war of 1379–85, the Bruges weavers were in turn the only group of their town to support the Ghent rebels. They were, however, quickly crushed in 1380.[110] In 1436–8, Ghent left rebellious Bruges on its own, and Bruges did not come to the aid of the Ghent revolt of 1449–53. Both rebellions ended in bitter defeats.

---

104   Mollat and Wolff 1970, pp. 119–25.
105   Lambert, Véronique 2002, pp. 210–16 and Haemers 2004b, pp. 293–6.
106   Rotz 1985, p. 78.
107   Blockmans, Willem 1974a, pp. 278–89 and 293–302.
108   Blockmans, Willem 1989, p. 749.
109   Boone and Prevenier 1989b, p. 84 and Sabbe, Jacques 1992, pp. 47–8.
110   Demuynck 1951; Mertens 1973, pp. 6–7.

Foreign aid also seemed to have been an indispensable requirement for any revolt that questioned the position of the lord, as happened in 1128, 1339–45, 1382, 1451–3 and 1477–92. Economic interests drove the Flemish cities towards the English king, guaranteeing wool trade, and the cities also looked for military and political aid from the French king, the suzerain of the county of Flanders.[111] However, the league between the Flemish cities and supporting kings always failed, because the kings, acting from self-interest, played a double role, and because the Flemish rebels kept their distance, not wanting to replace one centralising lord by another. Alliances with other principalities, as between the county of Flanders and the duchy of Brabant (in 1339, 1488 and 1578), or between two cities, as between Ghent and Liège (in 1381–2 and 1452), never held for long either.[112] And inversely, the prince sometimes had to form his own alliances with 'foreign' powers to defeat his subjects. In 1328 and 1382 the Flemish count needed the intervention of the French army to crush the rebellion.

In this rebellion, a rare alliance between city and countryside occurred. When the peasants of the district of Cassel rose up against ducal reforms of their customary laws (1427–31), the people of Ghent did sympathise,[113] and some urban revolts spread throughout the countryside, as did the Bruges revolt in 1436–7.[114] However, in the latter case, the initiative was clearly urban, and the rural communities seem to have been merely passive followers. Urban and rural interests began to diverge even more because of the urban projects for dictatorship over the rural hinterland since the Van Artevelde period, mainly for economic interests, as discussed below. In addition, during the fourteenth century the Flemish nobility was further weakened and lost much of its grip on the peasants, so the latter had less reason for revolting.[115] Erik Thoen has suggested another reason for the lack of rural rebellions: that during the later Middle Ages, more and more rich peasants became *buitenpoorters* (people with a legal status as burgher of a city but living in the countryside) of one of the cities, thus reducing the social homogeneity of the village communities, a necessary condition for revolt.[116]

---

111 A survey of the relations between Flanders and the English king in Haegeman 1988; for the relations between Flanders and the French king, see Boone 1990a and Blockmans, Willem 1985c.

112 Blockmans, Willem 1988a; De Schrevel 1922. About Liège and Ghent, see Haemers 2004b, pp. 265–70.

113 Vaughan 1970, pp. 75–6; Desplanque 1864–5.

114 Dumolyn 1997, pp. 299–332.

115 Sabbe, Jacques 1992, p. 88.

116 Thoen 1988, pp. 486–7.

9   Interests and Ideology

People acted together in a rebellion because they had shared interests and were conscious of these interests. Urban revolts in medieval Flanders were not the 'irrational' outbursts of the desperate and starving poor. Blind hunger revolts were not typical in Flanders,[117] although rising food prices incited desperate craftsmen and urban poor to join or radicalise a rebellion.[118] Flemish urban rebellions were acts of politicised and self-conscious burghers, whose interests were expressed in very concrete demands. These mostly had to do with the city privileges, the key documents determining relationships within the city and between the city and the count of Flanders. Economically, the privileges provided major sections of the middle class with some sort of protection against the vicissitudes of market fluctuations and other uncertainties besetting the small but independent merchant or craftsman. Socially, they made these people into a community, in which they had status. Politically, it gave the whole of the middle class a claim on the authorities, while at the same time keeping the lower classes at bay.[119] Even if privileges originated from an idea of 'communal rights', privileged groups always reacted to defend their favoured status.[120]

As a consequence, an infraction of the privileges often caused a revolt. When the town hall of Bruges burned in 1280, all the city's privileges were destroyed, and the count deliberately hesitated to issue them again. This was the immediate cause for the mobilisation of the commoners.[121] The count used the repression of the ensuing revolt, however, to impose new and authoritarian privileges on the city. In the years following the 1323–8 rebellion, the count gave new disadvantageous privileges to cities and rural districts that had participated in the revolt, but also to the town of Aalst which had abstained from rebellion.[122] To prevent Bruges from joining the van Artevelde rebellion in 1338, the count cancelled the privileges of 1329 and restored to the city its more advantageous charter of 1304.[123] From this moment forward, the struggle over privileges cut both ways. Rebels demanded new rights, or the confirmation or restoration of established rights. In its turn the comital government used the

---

117   The great famine of 1315–17 did not incite a rebellion, see Van Werveke 1959; Mollat and Wolff 1970, pp. 92–3.
118   Mollat 1978, pp. 192–5.
119   Prak 1991, p. 94.
120   Blockmans, Willem 1997a, pp. 264–7.
121   Wyffels 1966, pp. 60–2.
122   Ibid., p. 75; Van Rompaey 1965, p. 50; Van Rompaey 1978, pp. 117–19.
123   van Houtte 1982, pp. 115–16.

repression of revolts as a tool for political centralisation and undermining the independent position of the towns, or negotiating and bargaining when a new revolt threatened to break out. For the powerful Flemish cities, privileges were a touchy subject. Often, a seemingly minor infraction of the privileges – concerning the juridical prerogatives of burghers, for example – could have important consequences. When, on 5 September 1379, the bailiff of Ghent arrested a burgher, thus violating the Ghent privileges, a revolt broke out that would last for almost six years.[124]

Social groups could have very different motives in joining a rebellion. Specifically, in a commercial city like Bruges, the most important port of Northwest Europe, rebel demands involved economic questions like trade and staple rights. The counts' economic policies and political relations with France and England were often at stake in late medieval Flemish rebellions, because of the importance of guaranteeing wool imports. Artisans, brokers and merchants wanted an attractive and peaceful economic climate, free exchange, judicial autonomy, low tolls and a stable currency.[125] Smaller centres always became the victim of the selfish attitude of the more powerful. Competition between Bruges and its outport Sluis was an issue in the beginning of the civil war of 1323–8 and again in 1436–8.[126] Since the period of James van Artevelde, a recurring demand especially of Ghent and Bruges was the domination over their rural hinterland. They primarily wanted to regulate rural textile industries that posed a threat to urban cloth production because of their lower wages.[127] Furthermore, raising taxes and monetary devaluations without the consent of the subjects endangered the very competitive international market in a city such as Bruges, whose wealth was dependent upon its function as economic gateway with low transaction costs.[128] Fiscal rebellions remained a classic pattern throughout the Middle Ages as well. In 1430, a short-lived revolt of a heterogeneous group of merchants and craftsmen broke out in the small town of Geraardsbergen for fiscal reasons (the taxes on beer were raised) amid charges of the financial mismanagement of the aldermen.[129] When Duke Philip the Good wanted to levy a permanent salt tax in 1447, the whole county stubbornly refused. Members of the urban elite in Ghent quickly allied with the frightened guilds and ambitious members of the middle class who, moreover, saw in this

---

124 Demuynck 1951, p. 308.
125 Blockmans, Willem 1988d, p. 177; Märtins 1976, pp. 179–257.
126 Mertens 1978, p. 98; TeBrake 1993, p. 50; Dumolyn 1997, pp. 89–104.
127 Nicholas, David 1971, pp. 175–200; Boone 1993, pp. 41–4.
128 Stabel 2000, pp. 35–6.
129 Gierts 1996.

coalition the opportunity to regain their participation in the polity lost after pro-ducal political networks took over city politics. A tough battle between competing networks over the resources of the city and the restoration of old rights lasted until 1453, when a Burgundian victory crushed the opposite networks of the princely loyalists.[130]

Flemish social order was an unstable equilibrium, ruled by a lord who guaranteed the unity of the county and a general policy.[131] This balance of tensions found its expression in the ideology of the *bien public, res publica* or *utilitas publica*, the 'common good' that reflected the image of a county as a body politic of several groups with different backgrounds, but living in a common space with common interests like fair justice and economic welfare.[132] Using this ideology in a rebellion united the opposition against the regime and authorised, or legitimised, the use of force.[133] Craftsmen were not primarily driven by ideology, but 'the welfare of the county and all its inhabitants' usually formed the undertone of their protest. The Ghent *communitas* of the end of the thirteenth century and the Bruges guilds of the end the fifteenth century, for example, used the ideology of the *utilitas publica* to justify its claims to the patricians.[134] This common good was expressed in concrete demands: fair wages, a fair use of taxes, 'no new taxation without citizen consultation',[135] no criminal disturbances in the town and accountability of the aldermen. Equality among all citizens was never an issue.[136] The Flemish urban rebels never questioned the fundamentally unequal feudal order. As we have said, apart from millenarian 'communist' movements such as the Bohemian Taborites, some tendencies within the English 'peasants' or 'workers revolt', and perhaps groups of radical peasants in the Flemish revolt of maritime Flanders as well, medieval rebels cannot really be deemed 'revolutionary' in the sense of having a genuine programme to overthrow the existing political order and system of property relations.[137]

When comparing different revolts, it becomes clear that rebels, because of their heterogeneous composition, usually demanded a mix of political and economic measures, mostly based on the restoration or the extension of privileges. Although the heterogeneity of coalitions was always their strength, divergent

---

130   Haemers 2004b, pp. 423–36.
131   Dhondt 1950b, p. 296.
132   On the notion '*bien public*' see Blickle 2000, vol. 2, pp. 195–222 and Eberhard 1985, pp. 203–13.
133   Johnson 1982, p. 26.
134   Prevenier 2002, p. 178 and Haemers and Lecuppre-Desjardin 2007.
135   As in German cities, see Rotz 1985, p. 88.
136   Barth 1974.
137   Mollat and Wolff 1970, p. 283; Blockmans, Willem 1974b, p. 137.

interests of groups within or between cities, stemming from different political and economic interests, could also lead to a lack of cohesion and solidarity. Because of this weak spot, there was often a chance for the beleaguered elite or the count to break the rebellion.[138] Inside the city, the threatened pressure of princely violence could socially divide the community into competing networks, some allying with the count or the former elite, some with those who defended the city privileges. This complicated situation shows that revolts cannot be reduced to battles between craftsmen and patricians, and it also clarifies why 'internal' demands of lower strata to city rulers often intermingled with 'external' demands to the count.[139] Thanks to the 'representative tradition' of the Low Countries, open conflicts could often be avoided. The 'Four Members of Flanders' (Ghent, Bruges, Ypres and the rural 'Liberty of Bruges') regularly negotiated with the prince to arrive at peaceful compromises.[140] But when this proved to be impossible, the 'revolutionary tradition' of the county started a rebellious dynamic of competing and allying networks and alliances, each trying to gain power.

10   Mobilisation and Repertoires

In order to achieve the main goal of every rebellion, gaining power, rebels first had to mobilise. In Flanders, as early as the crisis years 1127–8, a political culture of mass meetings among citizens, *'conjurationes'* or 'assemblies', had started.[141] Sometimes the rebels organised these assemblies under the pretext that they were meetings of religious confraternities, as in Ypres in 1280 and 1348, 1362 and 1370.[142] In fact, these meetings were specific organisational structures originating in old Germanic traditions and developed during the process of political emancipation. Usually, mobilisations took place within the context of the traditional types of solidarity and forms of organisation that structured society.[143] Rebellion was based on former group experience, the backbone of every collective action,[144] on rebellious traditions and on corporate solidarity. These

---

138   Blockmans, Willem 1989, p. 749.
139   Dumolyn 1997, p. 160; Haemers 2004b, p. 429.
140   Blockmans, Willem 1978.
141   Demyttenaere 2003.
142   Doudelez 1974, pp. 232, 246; Verbruggen, Raf 2005, pp. 113–24.
143   Van Uytven 1983, pp. 11–17; Boone 1990b, pp. 57–8; Dumolyn 1997, pp. 344–5; Verbruggen, Raf 2005, pp. 113–24.
144   Tilly 1989, pp. 145–6.

included topographical solidarities (parishes and quarters),[145] professional ties (craft guilds), family ties, political solidarities, factions (like the *Leliaarts* and *Clauwaarts* at the beginning of the fourteenth century)[146] and voluntary associations (confraternities and shooting associations).[147] Rebels always identified with their city, and less frequently with the whole county, in response to outward threats.[148] And as we have noted above, the occasions were rare when craftsmen, usually the weavers, could identify with their 'brothers' from other cities.

'The more closely we look at that same contention, the more we discover order.'[149] According to Charles Tilly, people have standard routines of action, and groups establish a well-known repertoire of contention, the implications of which are understood by everyone.[150] Medieval rebels indeed tended to utilise the same repertoire of violence that they had built up over time. This repertoire included political, financial, social, economic, symbolic, emotional, and ritual violence. When in 1245 the guilds of Douai wanted to gain political influence, they used economic violence by striking, harming the merchants' economic interests. The Bruges rebels of 1436 stood under the banners of their craft guilds on the marketplace, refusing to work (a *ledichganc* or *auwette van der maerct*).[151] The craft guilds also manifested themselves in other collective gatherings. As a reaction to an attack on urban privileges, an impulsive outburst of emotion from the city guilds could quickly evolve from amorphous anger into a cohesive institutionalised protest, namely an armed assembly of the guilds in the city market to defend their corporate identity.[152] The assembled guilds pretended to represent the 'city commune' as a whole and presented this political programme in an emotionally compelling ritual by swearing oaths of unity and mutual aid, gathering armed in the city market, and occupying city space and militarily strategic places. From the existing framework of corporate soci-

---

145   The working classes often populated the suburbs of the cities, see Doudelez 1974, pp. 189, 234.
146   Respectively the pro-French, patrician party and the party of the commoners supporting the count of Flanders.
147   In Italian cities as well, political violence was carried out by well-organised groupings, including associations of noblemen, guilds, family clans or *consorterie* or armed companies of parishes. See Martines 1972, p. 348; Brucker 1972, p. 155.
148   Blockmans, Willem 1997a, p. 265.
149   Tilly 1986, p. 4.
150   Hanagan, Moch and Te Brake, eds 1998, p. xviii.
151   Dumolyn 1997, pp. 158, 185. Similar gatherings happened in 1488, see Wellens 1965.
152   In Ghent this gathering was called a '*wapening*', see [A moody community]. Examples in Bruges: Dumolyn 1997, pp. 152–7 and Verbruggen, Raf 2005, pp. 112–44. To compare with Blickle 1988, pp. 53–4 and Prak 2000.

ety, combinations of signs, such as banners, ringing bells and marching in order were used. The guilds fought and negotiated for political credibility and public prestige on the market square, since it was the economic base of their existence and the theatre of power claimed by the political communities of city and state.[153] The gathering of the united guilds was an institutional vehicle for making demands to those in power. Without this vehicle, opposition activity was doomed to fail.[154] And, in addition to this 'communicative' function, an armed gathering on the central city square was also a mighty coercive tool that frightened the city elite.

If established groups ignored the efforts of the protesting groups to communicate, and if the established groups did not suppress the rebellion because they lacked superior force, either from structural weakness or the overwhelming emotional violence of the mobilised masses,[155] the door was open to the rebels and an alternative political group took power. Sometimes, the new government made institutional reforms, as happened in several cities after 1302, guaranteeing the participation of the rebel coalition in the polity. However, the rebel leaders usually merely filled the gap in authority left by the former regime. Aldermen of the city who had fled out of the town or had been captured and dismissed were replaced by leaders of the revolt. The new power holders had five things to do when they attained power. First, they fulfilled their own demands and those of other coalition members by enacting their political programme. Secondly, after this 'corrective' phase of eliminating the abuse, they retaliated against their opponents.[156] The rebel leaders legitimised their position by punishing those who were responsible for the moral discontent. They removed hostile political networks that could obstruct the new leaders' policy, or, even worse, might take power again. Comital officials were often the first victims in revolts.[157] In 1477 in Ghent, for example, former Burgundian state officials who had carried out Charles the Bold's centralising policy were sent to the scaffold, together with corrupt politicians and abusers of the privileges

---

153 Arnade 1994, p. 497; See [A moody community]; Boone 2002a; Boone and Stabel, eds 2000; Stabel 2001.

154 Forster and Greene 1970, p. 17. See also Hanagan, Moch and Te Brake, eds 1998, p. xvii.

155 By 'emotional violence' we mean frightening insults of contenders, uttering threats to the power holders, caused by the moral discontent of the rebels about political inequalities in town. Violence as a whole is an anti-social action, damaging persons or objects (Tilly 1986, p. 382), used with the intention to disorient the behaviour of others (Zagorin 1982, vol. 1, p. 18).

156 This 'instinct' of retribution in revolts is described in Beik 1997, pp. 49–72.

157 Verbruggen, Raf 2005, pp. 124–7.

charged with misusing their authority.[158] Thirdly, the new power holders had to strengthen their position by the use of violence. Several kinds of violence could be used. Political violence involved the punishment or the execution of princely officers and the revocation of privileges. Exiling members of the elite we consider a form of social violence, and financial violence included fines and confiscations. Forms of violence were usually combined in each punishment. The defenestration of the Ypres burgomaster in 1303,[159] the killing of a former head dean of the guilds who had supported a hated policy of the elite, in Ghent in 1432,[160] or the Bruges murder of the sheriff (*schout*) in 1436, contained political, social, and above all, ritual and emotional violence.[161]

If not used excessively, violence helped to empower the ruling rebels. Banishing the former regime, for instance, symbolically eradicated the evil of people whom the rebels had fought. Sacking and plundering houses of rich burghers, a recurring feature of Flemish urban revolts,[162] would frighten those hostile to the revolt or rebels contemplating desertion, because rebel leaders had to reduce 'free-riding' among participants in the rebellion, the fourth task.[163] Therefore, leaders often admitted the participation of the great mass of craftsmen in policy. While day-to-day decision-making might be left to councillors, major decisions, like going to war or raising taxes, ought to be made by the community as a whole,[164] according to the ideological programme of the *bien public*. During many revolts, the new leaders installed 'great councils' to discuss policy.[165] In 1382, Philip van Artevelde even allowed 'every poor and every rich person' – only men, of course – to participate in political discussions in these councils.[166] Another possibility was to hold referenda on the city market, so the craft guilds, rather than the entire body of citizens, could evaluate the policy of the leaders.[167] And, last but not least, the leaders of the rebellion had to build up a military and financial apparatus, a concentration of funds and forces, to resist attacks from the outside. Often, captains were also appointed, as during

---

158 Boone 2003b, pp. 49–59.
159 Lambin, ed. 1831.
160 Fris 1900a; Boone 2005.
161 Lambin, ed. 1831, p. 11; Rider, ed. 1994, p. 132.
162 For example in Bruges, 1280 (Wyffels 1966, p. 64), 1382 (Verbruggen, Raf 2005), 1436 (Dumolyn 1997, p. 123) and 1488 (Wellens 1965, p. 32).
163 Brustein and Levi 1987, p. 467.
164 Rotz 1985, p. 79.
165 As in Bruges in 1382 (Espinas and Pirenne, ed. 1906–66, vol. 1, p. 602) and in 1436–8 (Dumolyn 1997, p. 164) and in Ghent in 1539 (Dambruyne 2002, p. 627).
166 Nicholas, David 1988, p. 165.
167 As happened in Ghent revolts, Haemers 2004b, pp. 239–65.

the revolutionary leadership of the five *hooftmannen* in Ghent and the military dictatorship of the Bruges *upperhooftmannen* in 1437.[168]

If the count supported the rebels, as in 1302, their participation in politics became permanent. If he did not, and if his interests were damaged, he first negotiated with the rebels, but a stalemate often ended in armed confrontation. An economic blockade could be fatal for the rebels (Bruges, 1437, 1490), just as military battles or exhaustion could bring about their defeat (Ghent, 1385, 1453, 1485, 1492; Cassel, 1328). Conversely a weak count had to give in and confirm rebel participation in the city council, as Louis of Male was forced to do in 1360, or grant privileges or pardon the murders of city councillors, as Philip the Good did for Ghent in 1432, 1436 and 1440.[169] The worst case scenario for the count himself, like William Clito in 1128, was to lose a battle, or, like Maximilian in 1488, to be captured by the rebels. Sometimes ousted urban elites could retake power after internal rivalries enfeebled rebel leaders (as happened to James van Artevelde). After regaining power, the elite deployed its own repertoires to prevent further challenges to their rule. Legal repression of Flemish revolts, discussed in detail elsewhere,[170] usually consisted of fines (*amendes prouffit-ables*) for the cities, revocation of privileges, execution of the principal rebels or leaders, confiscation of their goods and symbolic humiliations (*amendes hon-orables*): removing symbols of corporate identity from public space, organising humiliating processions of burghers and erasing the memory of guilds by committing their archives to the flames. To restore order, the central government in the end pardoned the rebellious cities after the repression. But the aggressive character of the humiliating punishments kept the memory of the revolt vivid, and the repressive measures could, in turn, offer a new reason to rebel. These violent dynamics led to a spiral of rebellion, which once again fed the revolutionary tradition and vice versa.[171]

11 Conclusion

In his survey of the late medieval economic crisis, Guy Bois observed that revolts and rebellions in western Europe almost always appeared in the most developed regions, where ties between cities and the countryside were

---

168 Haemers 2004b, pp. 235–9 and Dumolyn 1997, p. 232.
169 Boone 2005, pp. 25–32.
170 See [The Legal Repression].
171 Verbruggen, Raf 2005, pp. 153–9.

strongest and people, ideas and information circulated continuously.[172] In the county of Flanders, with its highly specialised economy, social interdependence and political tensions within the population had steadily increased since the economic boom of the twelfth century.[173] The cities of the county of Flanders, with their huge concentration of people, power and capital,[174] experienced a quick succession of rebellions and revolts. Capital and power were not divided equally, and long-term economic evolution and the formation of the state in the Low Countries only widened the gap between those who ruled the town and those who did not. If the fluctuating balance of power inclined too sharply, or if the ruling elite did not allow access to power to privileged citizens and did not satisfy their specific demands, those challengers rebelled. This political consciousness, that one should intervene in politics when necessary, created a revolutionary tradition in towns, and also spiralling violence in the county as a whole.

This remarkable pattern of rebellion started in the phase of 'communal emancipation', the period when the counts granted privileges to the Flemish towns, and social and political contradictions began to manifest themselves in the cities. From the 1280s until the end of the fourteenth century, craft guilds constructed alliances with other potential rebels, such as frustrated bourgeois elements, and fought for political representation and control over fiscal and economic policies. During this phase comital power was weak, and the count often could not act independently to regain control over the major cities of Ghent, Bruges and Ypres. As state power became more and more important after the arrival of the centralising Burgundian dynasty in Flanders, the tide began to turn. The urban elites gradually sided with the dukes, and urban rebellions were less successful. This did not mean, however, that the Flemish rebellious tradition was exhausted. The end of the fifteenth century and the sixteenth century would witness new major challenges to princely power.

To start a revolt, rebels needed to forge strong alliances between different social groups and networks that were alienated from the power structure, and leadership was crucial as well for the outcome of a rebellion. Rebels contacted sympathisers in other cities and sought foreign aid. Their demands included a variety of political and economic measures and were inspired by the powerful ideology of the common good (*bien public*). Rebels mobilised in an almost ritualistic fashion and used different types of violence to gain or consolidate

---

172   Bois 2000, p. 156.
173   Elias 1939, vol. 2, pp. 434–54.
174   Tilly 1986, p. 396: 'concentration of capital and political power altered the possibilities and forms of popular collective action'.

rebel power. All these elements were features of what can be considered a true political dialogue between prince and citizen and between powerless and power-holders in the city.[175] Representative organs could solve socio-political and economic problems, but a rebellion usually ended in a struggle between social groups and networks within the towns, and a war between rebel regimes and prince. These two wars continuously intermingled and created a rebellious dynamic, ending in victory or defeat and repression. The outcome of the conflict depended heavily on the amount of resources rebels gathered and on the resilience of the power holders and the state.

---

175 This was also noticed in early-modern France by Beik 1997, p. 1.

CHAPTER 3

Guild Politics and Political Guilds in Fourteenth-Century Flanders

Jan Dumolyn

1 Introduction

A charter in the Municipal Archives of Bruges, issued on 3 September 1361, carries the seals of all fifty-four craft guilds of the city. The document marked the reconciliation between the Flemish commercial metropolis and Louis of Male, Count of Flanders. It was to be preserved in the treasury and read out aloud to all the burghers whenever the city government deemed it necessary.[1] An earlier charter, dated 2 March 1360, referring to this episode of intense political strife in Bruges, was a 'pact of alliance' between all 'good men' of the city.[2] 'In the name of the Father, the Son, and the Holy Spirit, Amen', the document begins, and its *intitulatio* reads, 'We, the mayors, the aldermen, the council, the headmen of the burghers, the deans and sworn men of all the craft guilds, and all the collective commons of the city of Bruges, all hail to Our Lord'. Clearly, this text had been sworn as a collective oath by the city government representatives, the 'headmen' or captains, of the *poorterie* (the class of merchants and urban landowners), and the leaders of the craft guilds. The charter expresses strong regret for the great disorder and the many revolts and conflicts of the last few years. These had been provoked by 'the enemy from Hell', who eternally prevented the well-being of the good people of the city. 'Where there is peace, there is God', the charter continues, and as He Himself had said to His apostles: 'Peace be with You'. Urban peace would prevent the problem that 'good merchants', 'from whom we take our food', stayed away from Flanders. Indeed, discord destroys all cities, so teaches the Holy Scripture.

In this kind of civic ceremony, the Bruges guilds helped to preserve divine peace, political unity and spiritual and economic prosperity in the city. The seals they attached to the first charter testify to their political and judicial

---

1　Gilliodts-Van Severen 1871–85, vol. 2, pp. 117–19; Mertens 1987, pp. 325–30.
2　Gilliodts-Van Severen 1871–85, vol. 2, pp. 107–9.

autonomy and power.[3] In fact, one cannot understand the socio-economic and political history of the fourteenth-century county of Flanders without taking into account the fundamental importance of its urban occupational organisations. In what follows, I will argue that there were few other places in medieval Europe in which craft guilds gained the degree of political power and participation they held in Flanders as well as in some other principalities in the Southern Low Countries. Guilds created spaces for political discussion and patterns of collective action and acted as urban governmental institutions in their own right. Hardly anywhere else did guild organisation weigh as heavily on the relations of production within the urban economy as it did in the large medieval cities of Ghent and Bruges (and also in the cities of Brabant and Liège). And in few other regions – with the possible exception of some towns in Southern Germany – would the ideological and symbolic power of the craft guilds penetrate so thoroughly and endure so long. While craft guilds did play prominent roles in fourteenth-century Florence, Cologne and Strasbourg, in the long run the guilds in those cities did not maintain a position comparable to that held by the guilds in the urban centres of Flanders. For this reason, the structural and institutional features of 'popular politics' in medieval Flanders were to a large degree conditioned by guild organisation. Critical political ideas were often expressed during guild meetings. Craft guilds organised strikes and demonstrations.[4] My central argument is that although Flemish craft guilds have been primarily created as structures for economic efficiency and for defence of the social conditions of the workers, they also functioned as 'political guilds' because of their major political roles. 'Guild politics', with its typical repertoires and ideology, was the primary determinant of late medieval Flemish popular politics.

Since the 1990s, historians have argued that the craft guilds played a more beneficial role in the economy than previous scholars had maintained since the nineteenth century. Stephen Epstein, for instance, wrote that guilds stimulated technological change and diffusion through migrant labour and provided transferable skills through apprenticeship. They also enforced quality standards, lowered informational asymmetries in marketplaces that served more than local needs, and protected their members from exploitation by the urban elites. Scholars such as Jean-Pierre Sosson, Gervase Rosser, Hugo Soly, Catharina Lis, Peter Stabel, Bert de Munck and Maarten Prak have pointed to the economic flexibility and political, social and cultural significance of craft guilds.

---

3 Although there is no systematic study of Flemish guilds' seals, see, for example, De Beer 1931; De Vigne 1857, p. 134; Gailliard, Jean-Jacques 1854.

4 See [Patterns]; and [A Bad Chicken].

Guilds contributed to quality control, human capital formation, innovation and conflict management, as well as reducing costs of searching for products and acquiring information.[5] These researchers have principally focused on the questions of market and production efficiencies, as measured by economic growth and technological innovation. The socio-political and judicial aspects of the guilds have received less scrutiny.[6] Rosser is an exception to this trend, as he has emphasised the diversity and adaptability of different types of guild organisation, and stresses the point that guilds played crucial roles in defending workers' material interests, upholding their public credit, and safeguarding them from the dangers of unemployment and ill health.[7] Likewise, for Flanders, Stabel has underlined the role of craft guilds in defining social structure, cultural experience and political dominance, establishing social networks, and defining festive culture, public ceremonies, and religious practices. Guilds 'defined, often very strictly, the stages of human life from apprenticeship to independent entrepreneurship'.[8] James R. Farr has significantly re-evaluated these 'extra-economic' functions of craft guilds, as well as pre-industrial artisanal production in general. Artisans in sixteenth-century Dijon possessed a solidarity that transcended their specific guilds as they married exogamously. In this 'cohesive culture', Farr saw the 'contours of a nascent class'.[9] However, Farr's primary focus has been on 'honour' and value systems grounded in labour rather than on political value systems and the political role of guilds.[10]

As the field stands, a re-evaluation of the political role of craft guilds is needed in light of the new appreciation of their economic and social importance. If, as I argue, fourteenth-century Flanders was one of the medieval heartlands of politically powerful guilds with judicial and military power, there must be a specific socio-economic explanation. Conversely, the dominant role of the guilds in urban politics must also have heavily influenced the social and economic structure of the region. In one of the few recent articles which attempts to link new insights in economic history with the political role of the guilds, Soly suggests basing the analysis in classical political economy.[11] While my approach builds on his ideas, I will focus on re-evaluating the role of guilds in Flemish urban politics at the apex of their power. First, I need to make a small

---

5   Sosson 1990; Rosser 1997; Epstein 1998; Stabel 2004; Prak, Lis, Lucassen et al., eds 2006; De
     Munck, Kaplan and Soly, eds 2007; Epstein and Prak, eds 2008.
6   An exception is Prak 2006.
7   Rosser 1997, pp. 27–30.
8   Stabel 2004, pp. 188–92.
9   Farr 1988, pp. 10–11, 125.
10 He devotes more space to guild politics and legal and institutional aspects in Farr 2000.
11 Soly 2008.

note on terminology. In medieval Europe, 'religious and social guilds', as Rosser has termed them, certainly played a political role, in addition to that of occupational guilds. In the late medieval County of Flanders, however, the sources demonstrate that craft guilds held a political importance that overwhelmed every other type of corporate association. This fact justifies the limited scope of this article. Moreover, a specialist on medieval Flanders cannot follow the learned Oxford historian when he argues against using the term 'craft guild'.[12] Medieval Flemish documents always distinguished between an *ambochte*, or a craft, and a *ghilde*, or a confraternity organised for religious or secular purpose, such as a *schuttersgilde*, or 'shooting guild'.[13] In other regions of the Netherlands *ghilde* or *gulde* could also mean craft, and in the French speaking regions one mostly finds the term *mestier*. Since historians who study the medieval Netherlands must choose an English equivalent for *ambochte*, the term already most commonly used is 'craft guild', its French equivalent being (*corps de*) *métier*. In contemporary German and Dutch, the word *Gilde* or *gilde* is also more often used to denote merchant guilds, as opposed to *Zunft* or *Handwerk* in German and *ambacht* in Dutch.[14] As the title of this chapter indicates, for the sake of convenience, I use the terms 'craft guild', 'craft' and 'guild' interchangeably, though this inevitably not always does justice to the distinctions the original sources make.

2 Political and Economic Power in the Flemish Cities

Around the year 1300, Flanders was the most urbanised of the principalities of the Southern Low Countries. The region had developed strong, expanding industries and an increasingly diverse social structure since the twelfth century.[15] The county also had the largest number of craft guilds, although it was closely followed by the neighbouring duchy of Brabant and the prince-bishopric of Liège.[16] Fourteenth-century Ghent, Bruges and Ypres, with approximately 65,000, 45,000 and 25,000 inhabitants respectively, had more than fifty crafts each, while the smaller town of Aalst, with 4,000 inhabitants, still

12 Rosser 2006a, 27–42.
13 Crombie 2011.
14 Oexle 1982a, p. 1; Oexle 1985; on the etymology of the Dutch terms see Bruins 1977.
15 Nicholas, David 1992.
16 Sosson 1966; Boone 1994. On the guilds in the Low Countries in general, apart from the references cited in note 5 above, Lis and Soly, eds 1997; Lis and Soly, eds 1994b; Lis and Soly 2006a; De Munck, Lourens and Lucassen 2006; Blockmans, Willem 1999a.

had around twenty craft guilds. In Ghent in 1356–8, there were 14,267 male craftsmen, both masters and journeymen, amounting to 22.3% of the total population.[17] Not all manual labourers were necessarily members of a craft. The industrial cities also had large groups of unskilled workers. In most cases, women's labour was not corporately organised, although women could belong to some craft guilds.[18] In the small town of Eeklo, which had a large cloth industry for its size, only the textile trades were organised into craft guilds.[19] Nevertheless, from the thirteenth century onwards, craft guilds were essential players in urban socio-economic and political relations. The county's political historiography has given guilds a central role, beginning with Henri Pirenne who argued that they were the principal social force pushing for what he termed 'early democracies' in the large cities.[20] While historians today do not accept this anachronistic terminology, they often agree implicitly that corporatist principles provided a universal logic for economic, social and political organisation in Flanders, only rivalled by family and kinship structures. Corporatism became an almost hegemonic ideology which was also reproduced by the elites to some degree. Corporatist discourse had strong and deeply-rooted foundations in religious thought, notably in the principle of *caritas*, as well as in the material relations of production and reproduction characteristic of medieval urban communities. Corporatism consolidated durable social networks and dominated parts of the urban landscape with its sign language and spatial presence. Military mobilisation and political rule were also organised by corporate structures.

By 1300, crafts in many Italian cities, usually called the *compagnie d'arti*, also exercised political influence. However, at the risk of oversimplifying their complex histories as a result of my too limited knowledge, these guilds were usually dominated by small elite groups, and merchant capital remained dominant. In fourteenth-century Flanders and Brabant, at least in the larger urban centres, there were significant differences. In the twelfth and thirteenth centuries, merchants dominated textile production through a system of 'putting-out', or *Verlag*, which gave the international wool merchants control over the labour force of textile workers. Gradually, so the dominant historical narrative goes, the strong position of these 'merchant-capitalists' in the production and marketing of textiles was undermined by the rise of a 'middle class' of 'small

---

17   Prevenier 1975, p. 277.
18   For the organisation of women's labour in Flanders, see Howell 1986; Hutton 2011.
19   Stabel 1995, pp. 144–6, 222–5.
20   Classicly formulated by Pirenne 1910.

commodity producers' and an 'upper middle class' of drapers and other entrepreneurs. The situation may not always have been that straightforward and differed from town to town and from period to period, but this economic contradiction eventually led to a social and political struggle between producers and merchants during a restructuring of the Flemish urban economy. In the prolonged crisis from 1270 to 1350, Flanders faced growing competition from Brabant, Holland and England, as it was also dealing with the general political and military insecurity in Europe. Most of the Flemish textile industry adapted by specialising in high-quality cloth, which made the economy more dependent on imported English wool and consequently more vulnerable to the periods of crisis during the fourteenth century. Caught between England and France during the Hundred Years War, Flanders experienced severe disruptions in supply imports and cloth exports. After the Flemish guild revolution of 1302, which I will discuss below, some of the economic power shifted from the merchants to the 'drapers', small, independent entrepreneurs who belonged to the textile crafts themselves. Soly argues that the rising political power of the guilds produced economic effects, as 'changes occurred in trade and industry that basically benefited the direct producers'. Notwithstanding endemic warfare, during the fourteenth century, the costs of marketing export goods and the risks of transport declined. As a result, master artisans were less dependent on merchant capital and freer to become industrial entrepreneurs, or 'drapers'. Guild masters with an entrepreneurial spirit could hire other artisans as subcontractors and sell their finished products themselves. They now became the key figures in the cloth production. These richer masters had other guildsmen working for them as subcontractors although they could never achieve the same degree of concentration of capital possessed by the thirteenth-century merchant-capitalists. Guilds became more autonomous from city governments and controlled many aspects of the organisation of production. Their more affluent members enjoyed major, enduring influence in urban politics. The socio-economic basis of the guilds' political power was the industrial capital of the drapers along with the power to mobilise a large workforce of small commodity producers and wage workers.[21]

21　The above paragraph is fundamentally based on Soly 2008, pp. 49–53. See also Van Werveke 1946a, pp. 10–11, 24; Duplessis and Howell 1982; Chorley 1987; Sosson 1986, p. 115; Munro 1991; Holbach 1993; Lis and Soly 2006b.

3　　　Strikes and Revolts

The process outlined above only applies to the textile industry. Other sectors of artisanal production were not so focused on international markets, had a less proletarian workforce, such as small shopkeepers who also organised in craft guilds, and did not always play the same political role as the textile workers. Textile guild workers were the 'vanguard' of urban popular politics in Flanders, and during the fourteenth century they remained demographically dominant in most cities and larger towns. Their collective actions most often appear in the chronicles and archival records as signs of the new form of urban mass politics. From the mid-thirteenth century, sources emphasise the difference between *li riches et li povres* in the urban world of the Southern Low Countries. Strike actions became more and more frequent. There was a wave of industrial actions, riots and revolts in the towns of Northern France and Flanders between 1245 and 1320.[22] The first strikes, referred to as *Takehans* in the sources, started around the middle of the thirteenth century. Sources from Douai mention *takehans* in 1245, 1250 and 1266, but the strikes clearly broke out in other textile centres as well. Urban governments quickly reacted with harsh measures and threats. An ordinance promulgated by the Douai alderman in 1245 put a fine of sixty pounds and exile of one year on '*ki face takehans*' ('those who strike').[23] Another ordinance, dated around 1250, prohibited craftsmen from organising an '*assanlée encontre le vile*' ('assembly against the city'), and forced artisans to come before the aldermen to settle conflicts rather than settling disputes among themselves.[24]

Takehan is an intriguing word. It seems to refer to industrial actions as well as to any kind of internal organisation or meeting of workers. Although Georges Espinas and Henri Pirenne have, somewhat speculatively, suggested that this term had a Germanic root in the sense of 'take hands', the expression also appears outside of Flanders and its use was most pronounced in francophone areas. There was a *taquehan ou harelle* of butchers in Saint-Evreux in 1244, and sources used the word *taquehan* for revolts in Rouen. The term was used widely, as other northern French towns also experienced labour conflicts in the second half of the thirteenth century.[25] In a later source, a 1350 city ordinance from the small town of Béthune, the word *taskehem* seems to mean an amount of

---

22　Prevenier 2002; Boone 1995c, pp. 101–5; Leguai 1976, p. 281; Mollat and Wolff 1970, pp. 59–65; Espinas 1913, vol. 1, pp. 226–69; Brassart 1883b; Boone 1998.

23　Espinas and Pirenne, eds 1906–66, vol. 2, p. 22.

24　Ibid., vol. 2, pp. 92–3, 109.

25　Coornaert 1941, pp. 69, 75. More recently Dumolyn and Haemers 2016.

money paid to the guild safety box, as it was ordered *'que nulls ne faiche ban ne taskehem ne autre assise de men mesthier'* ('that no one make a statute, or *taskehem* or other tax on his trade').[26] In the Dutch-speaking region of Flanders, another term for strike was *uutganck* ('going out'), an action in which textile workers collectively left the city to seek better working conditions. In 1252 and 1274, Ghent textile workers organised their first recorded strikes. The cities of Brussels, Mechelen, Leuven, Lier, Antwerp, Tienen and Zoutleeuw pledged not to give asylum to Ghent fullers and weavers who had conspired against that city. The following year, a popular regime temporarily took power in Ghent, but little else is known about this episode.[27] Around 1280, the climate of worker protest reached its zenith as revolts broke out all over Flanders. In 1280, Douai exiled or hung textile workers for organising a strike and trying to prevent other artisans from working. In 1281 Ypres authorities tore out the eyes of ten people and prohibited them from working at their trades (*de prohibitione* operis).[28] As there are few sources surviving from the thirteenth-century Flemish cities, there were probably many other strikes which are now unknown.[29]

After 1250, workers and their collective organisations gained prominence in the urban political scene. During the next fifty years, the craft guilds developed into more autonomous political organisations. The sense of community among guildsmen was reinforced because people of the same trade, especially the textile and leather workers, often still lived close together in the same neighbourhoods and used the same halls, mills, docks and quays.[30] By 1300, as the urban population and the concentration of proletarianised workers in the suburban quarters of the big textile cities grew, their power increased significantly. The earliest Flemish craft guilds – or at least religious confraternities of working men – appear in the sources in the first half of the twelfth century in Arras, which was then the most important city of the county. Although in the early thirteenth century Arras was separated from Flanders as part of the split-off county of Artois, the city and its region shared the economic characteristics of Flanders. Sources attest to these very early craft guilds in the context of their military function, or in the form of religious confraternities. The Arras weavers possessed a war tent in 1232.[31] In 1247, the Arras barbers founded a confraternity, or *carité*, devoted to Saint Dominic and the Virgin, under the spir-

---

26 Espinas and Pirenne, eds 1906–66, vol. 1, p. 313.
27 Ibid., vol. 2, pp. 379–81.
28 Wyffels 1950a; Van Caenegem 1954, p. 22.
29 Wyffels 1951, p. 51; Van Caenegem 1954, p. 22.
30 Van Uytven 1982, p. 210.
31 Espinas and Pirenne, eds 1906–66, vol. 1, pp. 114–17.

itual guidance of the local Dominican convent.[32] By this time, Arras and other French-speaking towns in Walloon Flanders and Artois had been replaced by Ghent, Ypres and Bruges as the most important urban centres in Flanders. After the 1280s, there is more documentary evidence, especially for Bruges and Ypres, which allowed Carlos Wyffels to show that Flemish craft guilds developed for four reasons. Two reasons were fundamentally important: urban governmental supervision of industrial and commercial matters, and artisans' corporate actions taken within the framework created by the authorities. The remaining two, guild military organisation and their function as religious confraternities, seem to have been less crucial factors.[33] At first wardens appointed by the government and called *eswardeurs*, *coriers*, *rewardeurs* or *waerderres* directed the guilds. The Bruges weavers had a *decanus* and *inventores* by 1252. In Middle Dutch, these wardens were titled *dekens* and *vinders*, or sometimes *maners* and *ghezworne*. They were officers appointed by the city magistrates and recruited or elected from the merchant-drapers rather than from the textile occupations. Their primary function was to inspect the markets and the production process. They tried and fined artisans who did not follow craft trade regulations promulgated by the city government.[34]

Although craftsmen were never allowed to elect their own leadership, during the final decades of the thirteenth century, the guilds acquired more power and representation. Gradually artisans themselves were integrated into the guild leadership, undoubtedly because of their technical knowledge. By the 1280s in Bruges, textile workers were already participating in meetings in which wages were discussed, along with other matters.[35] In addition to giving advice on industrial and commercial regulations, they developed their own financial organisations, usually for charity, and served in the city militia.[36] In some cases, craft guilds had the right to draw up petitions. City governments had clearly granted them these concessions to avoid the strikes which were by then frequent. Ironically, it was precisely this integration of the guilds and some artisans into the city government and justice system as advisors that laid the groundwork for their political actions and their quest for autonomy and real representation in politics.[37] After the Flemish victory at Kortrijk in 1302, this

---

32 Espinas 1941–2, vol. 2, pp. 20–4.
33 Wyffels 1951, p. 152.
34 Ibid., p. 61; Espinas and Pirenne, eds 1906–66, vol. 1, pp. 485, 560; Mertens 1981, p. 185.
35 Wyffels 1951, pp. 47–8, 75; Sosson 1984, p. 82; and see for instance Espinas and Pirenne, eds 1906–66, vol. 2, pp. 101–9.
36 Wyffels 1951, p. 103.
37 Ibid., pp. 85–6.

quest resulted in a major victory for the guilds in the Dutch-speaking regions of Flanders. In Artois and French-speaking Flanders, however, real craft guilds, in the sense of economic organisations with a certain degree of autonomy, in most cases did not come into being. They usually remained stuck at the level *confrèries de métiers*, religious associations organised from an occupational base but focused on charitable activities. In contrast craft guilds in Dutch-speaking Flanders usually developed a religious confraternity along their occupational structures proper, a *ghilde* of the *ambochte*, with the same membership but other leadership structures and a separate financial organisation.[38]

While larger political constellations and military and diplomatic developments helped create the strong position of the fourteenth-century Flemish guilds, the single most important cause of the acquisition of autonomy and political power by the craft guilds of Bruges and Ghent was the force of their numbers. Their demographic strength meant that they were militarily powerful. Before 1200, Flemish cities based their military organisation on subdivisions of quarters and neighbourhoods, but during the thirteenth century most cities shifted to forming the city militia by craft guild.[39] In 1280, for example, the pennies paid by new apprentice boys, journeymen and masters to the Bruges textile guilds were used to buy and maintain tents and standards.[40] The *Annales Gandenses*, a chronicle written by an anonymous Franciscan author sympathetic to the urban commons, mentioned that the Bruges and Ghent guilds had well-organised militias by 1300. When Pieter de Coninck, the master weaver who led the Bruges rebellion of 1301–2, first appeared on the popular political scene, he was arrested along with *xxv circiter capitaneis communitatis*, military captains of the guild contingents in the city militia.[41] According to this same very reliable chronicle, Pieter later led '1500 well-armed foot soldiers from the commune of Bruges'.[42] The chronicle notes that the Ghent commoners had war standards (*signis bellicis*), clearly those of the guilds or perhaps of the neighbourhoods inhabited by guild weavers and fullers according to the local pattern of organisation.[43]

38 Espinas 1941–2, vol. 1, pp. 1100–14; on confraternities, including the ones connected to craft guilds, see Trio 1990 and numerous other publications by the same scholar.
39 Wyffels 1951, pp. 56, 105–21; Verbruggen, Jan 1954, pp. 251–2; Verbruggen, Jan 1960.
40 Wyffels 1951, p. 112.
41 Johnstone, ed. 1951, p. 13 gives as a translation 'leaders' of the commune, but the text clearly refers to military captains.
42 Ibid., p. 21; Verbruggen, Jan 1977, pp. 128–32.
43 Johnstone, ed. 1951, p. 14.

4   1280–1302: Towards Political Power for the Guilds

We have already several times referred to the 'commons' or 'commoners', a term used by our sources, but what did this exactly mean? In the thirteenth century, the popular actors in the urban revolts were usually identified as the *communitas* (*meentucht* in Dutch, or *le commun* in French). Sometimes the sources evoked a social struggle of the *majores* against the *minores* or *plebeyos*.[44] The *Annales Gandenses* generally used *communitas* to identify the driving force of the 1301–2 revolts, but the chronicle also employed the terms (*mechanici*) *vulgares* and *minores*. The Franciscan chronicler referred to certain individuals who were wealthy but not patricians as the *divites* or *ditiores de communitate*. This group would probably have included some of the new drapers. At the same time the guilds had now become the most prominent organisations within the opposition.[45] While the organisational structure of earlier strike actions remains unclear, in 1280 documents from Ypres and Damme, craft guilds acquired their full revolutionary agency for the first time. The struggle against merchant rule in the Flemish cities reached its peak that year as coalitions of artisans and small entrepreneurs, 'new men' who had no access to political power, rebelled against the ruling oligarchies in the major cities of Flanders and Northern France.[46] An ordinance dated 28 September 1280, after the first phase of the *Moerlemaye* revolt in Bruges had been repressed, prohibited 'sitting in a guild' (*ghilde te sittene*), organising a guild meeting (*meentucht van ghilde te makene*), or having a guild meal (*in ghilde tetene*) within one mile of the city. Illegal assemblies of workers were called *conspirations, alliances, aconpaignements, assanlees, vergadringhen, meentuchten, sameninghen,* and other Dutch and French terms.[47] Around the same time, in Damme, the port for Bruges, rebels demanded that guild members be governed by a proper administration, led by *deken ende vinders* ('dean and arbiters'), as the commune of Damme specified, elected by 'us, the craftsmen' (*wie, ambochtslieden*).[48] A 1281 source written after the *Cockerulle* revolt in Ypres mentions *li mestier* who took oaths and assembled several times.[49] Count Guy de Dampierre wanted to take political advantage of the situation in Ypres to hurt the local patricians who

---

44   Vuylsteke 1906, p. 181.
45   Johnstone, ed. 1951, pp. 16–18, 21, 30, 95.
46   Wyffels 1966. Similar waves of revolt took place in many French towns as well, see Leguai 1976.
47   Wyffels 1951, pp. 92–3.
48   De Smet, Anton 1950, p. 12.
49   Warnkönig and Gheldolf 1835–64, vol. 5, p. 386.

sided with the king of France against his rule. After the revolt, Guy presented himself as a neutral arbiter between the *eschevins* and *ceaus ki de leur party estoient* on the one hand, and the *drapiers, tisserans, foulons, tondeurs* ('drapers, weavers, fullers, shearers') and *grant plentei dautre gent ki avec eaus se tenoient* ('a large number of other people who were allied with them') on the other hand.[50] Though neither the *Cockerulle* nor other revolts of this period represent pure forms of 'class struggle', they do show that the guilds had taken the lead in organising the popular masses for political goals.

During the two last decades of the thirteenth century, Count Guy de Dampierre increasingly allied himself with the popular classes in the major cities, because the patricians were supporting King Philip the Fair with whom the count had a major conflict. As part of his centralising agenda, the French king was eager to take the rich principality of Flanders for himself and bullied his vassal to the point that Guy of Dampierre renounced his feudal oath to his overlord. In reaction, a French army invaded Flanders in June 1297 and on 18 September Bruges opened its gates to the French, as the merchant class there also favoured direct French rule. Annexation of the county and incorporation into the Crown lands with the support of the Flemish urban oligarchs, known as the *Leliaerts* or the 'Lily' party, in time led to popular revolts in Ghent and especially Bruges, where during the 'Good Friday' revolt of 18 May 1302 (later called *de Brugse Metten* or 'the Bruges Matins') followers of Pieter de Coninck massacred the occupying French soldiers. This uprising was followed by the battle of Kortrijk on 11 July. A Flemish army of urban militia and a few Flemish nobles who had remained loyal to the count defeated and humiliated the French army and their Flemish patrician allies, an event that shocked the ruling elites across Europe. The popular victory drove the French out and brought in a new city government structure which included the craft guilds. The next day, a revolt broke out in Ghent, and the artisan class overthrew the Lily faction in that city as well.[51] All the major Flemish cities installed revolutionary regimes, exiled the Lilies and confiscated their property. A Bruges charter dated 1 July 1302 identified the rulers as 'the council and the whole commune of the city' (*de raed ende al die ghemeentucht van der stede*).[52] Another document, issued one week later, also omitted the aldermen.[53] The bench of aldermen, a princely institution established to rule the city, whose members came exclusively from the wealthy merchants, had been temporarily stripped of its power.

---

50   Ibid., p. 382; Boone 1998.
51   Van Caenegem, ed. 2002; See [Patterns].
52   Municipal Archives of Bruges, political charters, first series, no. 163.
53   Ibid., no. 165.

There was an attempt to return to older communal principles of urban government by a broader representation of the population assembled in a *meentucht* or commune rather than by a limited number of patrician families. Rather than a pure 'guild revolution', the social forces who now took power formed what Karl Czok has called a *Bürgeropposition*, a coalition of different social classes with a programme of fiscal and social justice and political participation.[54] These broader layers of the population reclaimed the older principles of communal government and rejected the logic of oligarchy dominant in the thirteenth century. In Bruges, Ghent and other cities, *nouveaux riches* and some factions of the patrician elite joined forces with the organised middle and working classes. The weakness of the Flemish comital family – the count was still a prisoner in France – *vis-à-vis* King Philip IV had forced these great nobles into accepting the urban 'popular fronts' as allies. In return, the guilds obtained major concessions from the sons of Count Guy and could now for the first time have representatives on the boards of aldermen. The political momentum did not last, however. In 1309, the multi-class alliance of Bruges collapsed under the weight of political opportunism and opposing interests. The butchers, fishmongers and brokers, the three wealthiest craft guilds, joined the Lily party, along with all the *poorters* (*burgesses*, a reference to the merchant class) and wealthy commoners (*ditiores*). Pieter de Coninck and the other leaders of the revolt of 1301–2 were left with the support of the textile workers and other *mechanici vulgares*. They now understood that this was a new political phase, in which the popular party would have to face not only the wealthy and powerful within the cities but also the comital family and the nobles of Flanders.[55]

5 Flemish Guild Power in Comparative Perspective

Farr has rightly observed that 'Flemish incorporated guildsmen may have had greater rights of political participation in their municipal government' than in most other places of Europe.[56] Between the wave of revolts from 1280 to 1309 and the temporary balance of power struck in the 1370s, there was a pattern of constant civic strife in the Flemish cities and towns. In that atmosphere, the craft guilds took shape as institutions within the urban political system.

---

54 Czok 1958–9. A more recent and nuanced view of the importance of alliances of social groups in revolts is formulated by Lantschner 2009.
55 Johnstone, ed. 1951, p. 35.
56 Farr 2000, p. 28.

At different moments and in different ways depending on the size of the city, the guilds became true 'political' guilds, having their own representatives on the boards of aldermen and in the city councils. This pattern was most noticeable in Ghent and Bruges. Guild representatives also served in *smalle wetten* ('small courts of law') to judge infringements of industrial and market regulations. Guilds were also consultative bodies, especially for economic policy and financial and fiscal matters. They sometimes had the power to reject new taxes, for example. After 1302, Flemish guild power was expressed and performed in the city, often within institutionalised political dialogues and sometimes with displays of the force of their numbers and their experience as armed militiamen. To a large degree, principles of corporate organisation shaped the precise forms and discourses used by urban popular politics in future centuries. Even though they also developed elites of themselves, the craft guilds thus acted as a counterbalance to the vested interests of the ruling oligarchic families of merchants and landowners, as the guilds channelled the economic and political opinions of the middle and working classes and framed these ideas with their typical corporatist ideology. Guilds petitioned the aldermen and assembled in armed gatherings. They regulated moral behaviour according to the guild ethos of brotherly love, organised charitable activities, and helped maintain social balance and order. They promoted festive social events and civic ceremonies to strengthen their collective status as a legal and corporate person.

The picture of 'democratic' guilds presented by an older generation of historians is no longer tenable, and the example of fourteenth-century Flanders might seem exceptional within the bigger picture of guild struggle between 1200 and 1800. However, evidence from the fourteenth century suggests that more recent assessments of the elite character of guild leadership have gone too far in the opposite direction to downplay the importance of popular politics.[57] I therefore agree with Prak's argument that the popular uprisings in 1302–6, striking not only Bruges, Ghent and Ypres, but also Brussels, Den Bosch, Mechelen, Antwerp, Utrecht and other small towns in the Low Countries, may still be called 'guild revolutions' even if other social groups participated in them.[58] When the revolution of 1302 failed in a city, that city's institutions developed in a different pattern. In the city of Saint-Omer in Artois and other nearby towns of French-speaking Flanders (Lille and Douai), which were separated from the county between 1305 and 1369, political guilds could not and

---

57 A classic and influential example of this tendency of downplaying the importance of popular agency has been Rotz 1973.

58 Prak 2006, p. 77; Wyffels 1951, pp. 30–1.

did not develop.[59] The revolt in Saint-Omer in 1305–6 failed in the long run.[60] Because the 1302 guild revolutions did not result in guild rule in those cities, or, in the case of Lille and Douai, the cities were annexed to the French crown in the Treaty of Athis-sur-Orge (1305), guilds in the francophone areas of Flanders and Artois never achieved the kind of political power that guilds in Dutch-speaking Flanders did. For that reason, this article will not discuss them further.[61] In the northern Netherlands, as in the County of Holland, guild power was much weaker. Only in Dordrecht were the guilds able to achieve some influence in urban life. In Utrecht, the guilds seized the city government in 1274 and held it for two years before they were crushed by the bishop's troops. In 1302 the Utrecht guilds gained the rights to choose their own leaders, assemble freely, own their own properties and draw up their own rules. In 1304, they again took full power over the city and it thus became the bulwark of guild power in the northern Low Countries.[62] The 1312 guild victory in Liège, in the French-speaking part of the Netherlands, should also be situated in this period of guild struggle. The cities of the Prince Bishopric of Liège had craft guilds by the 1230s.[63] After several struggles which echoed those of 1302 in Flanders, in 1312 the guilds won power in the capital city of Liège itself, and ultimately achieved a joint ruling role comparable to that of Ghent and Bruges.[64] In the fourteenth-century Duchy of Brabant, craft-guild uprisings were less successful – a series of revolts in Brussels between 1303 and 1306 did not succeed in bringing the guilds to power – but the artisans there also remained a constant threat to patrician power and played a vital role within the urban social structure and the political balance of power, and they would again try to gain influence on several occasions during the fourteenth, fifteenth and early sixteenth centuries.[65]

On a wider European scale, thirteenth- and fourteenth-century Florence may present a roughly comparable situation to that in Flanders, Liège and Utrecht.[66] Although a really thorough comparison with the Italian and German towns, however necessary, surpasses the scope of this contribution and cannot be undertaken here, fourteenth-century ideals about the equality of all citizens and joint rule were very similar in some of these cities to Flem-

---

59   Derville 1993; Howell 1993, pp. 127–8.
60   Giry 1877, pp. 154–5.
61   Wyffels 1951, p. 124.
62   Van Bavel 2010a, p. 120.
63   Van Uytven 1982, p. 211.
64   Vercauteren 1943, pp. 66–79; Xhayet 1993, p. 362.
65   Des Marez 1905–6; Favresse 1961; Boffa 2001; Van Uytven 1963; Vandecandelaere 2008; Haemers 2012.
66   Najemy 1982.

ish ideals. Italian craft guilds (often called *compagnie d'arti*) rose in the twelfth century and were firmly established in many cities by the beginning of the thirteenth century. Demographic growth, social diversification and social mobility produced a growing number of occupational guilds which became part of the anti-magnate regimes often referred to as the *popolo*.[67] In these new thirteenth-century city governments, however, the guilds had to share power with other groups, such as armed neighbourhood militias. Internally, the Italian craft guilds were also more elitist than their Flemish counterparts. According to Samuel Cohn, independent political action by guilds was rare in Italian urban insurrections, and labour issues were not a real mobilising factor before the middle of the fourteenth century, and even then they remained limited to Florence and Siena.[68] Although the situation in the peninsula differed from region to region and town to town the political role of the guilds ranged from significant, as in Florence, Siena and Bologna, to powerless in Venice and Verona. Even in those cities where guilds had gained a role in urban politics, that role tended to be restricted during and after the fourteenth century, although this happened by a process of revolts and reactions, as guilds temporarily seized power and were then excluded from it again.[69] Florence experienced the most outspoken 'guild republicanism', since the guild movement sought to make corporate federation the organising principle of communal government in the 1290s, the 1340s, and during the Ciompi Revolt. In the fifteenth century, corporate republicanism finally failed.[70] While there were periods in which the Florentine guilds held some power (1293–6, 1343–8 and 1378–82), this ceased by 1400.[71]

In Germany, strong guild power and participation in city governments were more typical of the Rhineland cities than of the Hanseatic cities, because the latter were usually dominated by merchant oligarchies.[72] Older historians used the term *Zunftkämpfe* ('guild struggles') but after Erich Maschke and Czok published their work, the term *Bürgerkämpfe* ('burgher struggles') became more common in historiography. This refers to alliances of guilds with merchants who had been excluded from power, aimed at fighting for broader political participation, sometimes successfully, sometimes not.[73] There was a wave of

---

67   Racine 1985, p. 128; Hyde 1973, pp. 94–123; Najemy 1979, p. 55.
68   Cohn 2006, pp. 57–62, 122.
69   La Roncière 1991.
70   Najemy 1979, p. 58.
71   Najemy 1982, p. 13.
72   Ehrbrecht 1976.
73   Schmoller 1875; Czok 1958–9; Maschke 1959; Barth 1974; Rotz 1985; Simon-Muscheid 1992; Isenmann 2012, pp. 250–67.

revolts in German episcopal cities, such as Trier, Koblenz, Worms, Speyer and Regensburg, between 1301 and 1304. In some of these revolts, the craft guilds played the same role as they had in Flanders, allying themselves with one patrician faction against another.[74] After the 1332 guild revolt in Strasbourg, the *Zünfte* gained representation in the urban government, in a system quite similar to that of the Flemish political guilds. In practice, however, this was only theoretical, as patricians remained dominant. Several other uprisings followed in the fourteenth and fifteenth centuries.[75] In some other German cities, the guilds managed to maintain their political power until the early modern period.[76] Compared to the fourteenth century, craft guilds throughout Europe generally lost much of their political influence in the early modern period. Nevertheless, artisans and their organisations remained a potent force of political rebellion in many places until the eighteenth century.[77] Although guilds in some regions of Italy and Germany had a roughly comparable status with their counterparts in the Netherlands, French guilds were less of a factor in popular politics. While guilds were certainly present in popular mobilisations, they were never as prominent and central to the struggle as the guilds of Flanders. There were major disturbances in Tournai in 1279, 1302, 1307, and 1365, which featured textile workers as central actors,[78] but Tournai was closer in socio-economic terms to Flanders than to the rest of France. There were a number of revolts in French towns around 1280, 1307–11, 1330–5, 1355–8, and 1378–83. At first the guilds did not play a strong role in organising these, but as the century continued, craft guilds and other corporate organisations did become more important, not only as sources of '*contre-pouvoir*' but also as mediating forces between social groups. In the end, none of these French revolts was as successful as the victory of 1302 had been. The French rebels who showed solidarity with their Flemish brothers and followed their example, shouting slogans like *Vive Gand!* during their own revolts, certainly desired similar power. After 1420, as Chevalier has shown, expanding royal authority imposed social and political peace on the cities, and the guilds never again played a decisive role in urban politics.[79] Finally, in English urban revolts, as Cohn observes in his recent work,

---

74   Haverkamp 1991, pp. 101–7.
75   Dollinger 1977, pp. 230–1.
76   Farr 2000, p. 167.
77   Ibid., pp. 159–90, quote on p. 159.
78   Verriest 1913, pp. 7–14.
79   A recent assessment of the field can be found in Bourin 2008; see also Chevalier 1982; Lalou 1990, pp. 162–3; Challet 2005a.

craft guilds only constituted the organisational base in a few instances. In addition, industrial revolts were much rarer in England than in the Low Countries.[80]

6 The Concept of the Political Guild

The question which logically follows from comparing the degree of power that craft guilds held in late medieval cities is whether guild rule (or at least co-rule) also changed the logic and principles of urban politics, adding more weight to the popular classes and the opinions they voiced. Najemy speaks of a 'corporate approach to political organisation advanced by the Florentine guild community' versus a 'consensus-based approach developed by the oligarchy'. He argued that Florence possessed 'two competing conceptions of communal society and politics, rooted in a fundamental clash of social and political interests'. Florentine guilds operated as 'separate governments exercising extensive legislative, judicial, coercive, and regulatory powers', and were considered 'members' of the body politic.[81] Similarly, in his analysis of political rule in the German cities, Schilling has detected an 'implicit urban republicanism' recognisable in political, social, military and welfare organisations.[82] With his primary focus on towns in the Holy Roman Empire where guilds had gained a role in government, Schulz coined the term *politische Zunft*, which this article also employs. The 'political (craft) guild' was a form of political organisation specific to one developmental stage in European urban history, the *Neuformierung und Neustrukturierung der Stadtgemeinde* (Reformation and Restructuring of City Government): a new theory of communal organisation, decision-making and conflict regulation.[83] Schulz showed that during the late Middle Ages guilds became politically and judicially institutionalised within the governmental structures of many cities and towns, after revolts against German oligarchic lineages who had monopolised power. One of the best examples of this development comes from Cologne, which formed occupational *Gaffeln*, combinations of different craft guilds, to elect members of the city government. Although in Strasbourg guilds gained a strong influence, they never succeeded in gaining a foothold in several other major cities of the Holy Roman Empire, such as Nürnberg, Frankfurt or Lübeck.[84]

---

80   Cohn 2013, pp. 50–4, 104, 185; see also Rosser 1993.
81   Najemy 1982, pp. 3, 8.
82   Schilling 1988, pp. 136–43.
83   Schulz 1994, p. 3.
84   Ibid., p. 4.

Similarly, Marc Boone has argued that Ghent, the largest city of Flanders and the most important industrial centre of medieval Europe, had an urban 'proto-republicanism', *une idéologie pre-républicaine*' or 'corporatism', terms he uses interchangeably to describe a political culture based on corporatist ethics, such as collective honour and virtue, and a system of urban management influenced by the guilds as joint rulers. As after 1302 the Ghent craft guilds continued to have a say in city government, despite ups and downs, they became true 'political guilds', Boone argued, like those described by Schulz. A political equilibrium between the merchant class and the artisans reached institutional maturity around 1360. Since that time the 'Three Members' system, which allocated power among the merchants, the textile sector, and artisans working for the local market, dominated all Ghent institutions. This allocation of power meant that all positions, from the aldermen to the supervisors of charitable institutions to the leaders of the shooting guilds, were equally divided among the Members of the *poorterie* (the successors of the thirteenth-century patricians), the textile guilds, and the 'small guilds' of retailers and service-providers. Conflicts between guilds and guild members were judged and settled by judicial bodies of the superior deans (*overdekens*), who guided the deans of each guild.[85] If we define a political guild as an institution belonging to the new organisational phase of the urban commune during the late Middle Ages, this concept is closely linked to 'corporatist' political practices and discourses. Corporatism has a strong continuity with the earlier dominant communal political system and ideology, but there was clearly a break in the years around 1300. At that time, the guilds tried to become the embodiment of the commune; some succeeded and others failed. They played two roles at the same time, as they were both instruments of popular politics and mobilisation and deputised branches of the urban government which carried out military and legal functions. Being part of the urban government, the deans and sworn men of each craft guild had to swear to uphold the city's privileges when they took office. Furthermore, the military functions of the craft guilds were essential in creating their dual role as 'political guilds', sometimes in opposition to the urban government, but in most cases as loyal members of the body politic. The 1302 privilege of the Bruges butchers, the first privilege granted to an autonomous political guild after Kortrijk, read that all guildsmen were obligated to perform military service for the lord and the land, or 'for the profit of the city and the commune'.[86] While in 1302, the Bruges city militia raised 2,380 men, during

---

85   Boone 1997c.
86   Wyffels 1950b, p. 103.

the van Artevelde period, in 1340, the militia was an even mightier force of 6,044 men. We are well informed on the military organisation of the Bruges and Ghent guilds. They were led by captains or *hooftmannen* recruited from their own ranks. Because these urban foot-soldiers and archers engaged in many campaigns during the fourteenth century, they developed into a formidable force.[87] The Bruges guildsmen even successfully lobbied to receive a salary for the periods when they were campaigning. This was the 'monthly money' (*maendgheld*), first mentioned in the 1349–50 city account.[88]

Since they had gained a large degree of autonomy, the dean, sworn men and 'the whole common craft' of the Bruges glove-makers were free to establish their own regulations in a *keure*, which they completed in 1345. The charter does not mention that the city government had any part in drafting it.[89] And in 1370, for instance, the Bruges purse-makers also autonomously made certain new rules.[90] The craft guilds' legislative or even 'constitutional' powers, as earlier generations of legal and institutional historians termed them, varied in range and scope. In the most widespread model for the craft guilds throughout the medieval and early modern period, the urban government appointed the guild leadership, who only had an advisory voice on economic matters, as they served as experts to inform the policies of the ruling class and to convey some demands from the rank and file in a politically non-subversive manner. At the opposite end of the spectrum, the 'political guild' ideal type was the highly autonomous craft guild, which had the right to elect its own leadership from within (though, in practice, this often required the approval of the urban government), to make its own economic legislation (again with the confirmation of the aldermen), and to serve as a 'lesser court' judging and fining its own members for conflicts or violations of the rules. The actual position of the guilds in each city fluctuated between these two extremes, articulated by the rhythm of social and political struggle within the city and strongly determined by its economic features, and even when craft guilds did not operate autonomously or semi-autonomously from the urban government, they usually had judicial competence anyway. Thus, the massive export industries of the great Flemish cities served as a necessary – but often insufficient – precondition for the devel-

---

87   Vuylsteke 1906, pp. 203–4; De Smet, Jos 1929 and 1933; Verbruggen, Jan 1948; Verbruggen, Jan 1962; Stabel 2011; an example of the military expenses of a specific guild can be found in the account of the Bruges weavers 1372–3, see Espinas and Pirenne, eds 1906–66, vol. 1, p. 589.

88   Gilliodts-Van Severen 1871–85, vol. 4, p. 180.

89   Municipal Archives of Bruges, charters ambachten, no. 546.

90   Ibid., no. 236.

opment of strong political guilds, but their political power was always gained and maintained by means of struggle.

The limited scope of this article does not permit me to address what was arguably the guilds' most important role, regulating production processes and markets in cooperation with the urban government.[91] While this is obviously the primary question for economic historians, from a strictly legal and institutional point of view, guild wardens were responsible for punishing violations of their own privileges (in Dutch: *keuren*). They controlled the quality of raw materials, tools and finished products, inspected weights and measures, oversaw techniques and methods of production, and saw to it that hours and conditions of labour, membership obligations, and monopoly regulations were respected.[92] Their judicial responsibilities and the authority they derived from regulating production and marketing were essential components of the ruling power of the political guilds, and their jurisdiction often dealt with more than just economic matters. As 'small courts of law' (*smalle metten*), the guilds' primary function was to foster reconciliation between their members, judge moral questions related to the trustworthiness of the guild, and maintain peace within the guild and the city. Managing internal conflict and fostering feelings of community, charity and collective honour contributed to social stability. As a result, the judicial power of the guilds was a real advantage for the urban elites.[93] The guilds only took independent political action when they thought their privileges and economic welfare were seriously threatened. In most cases they thus played a stabilising role.

7   The Political Guilds in Popular Politics

Boone's observations for Ghent apply to other major cities in Flanders, although in many small towns the guilds never achieved this degree of power. Even in Ghent, Bruges and Ypres, the merchant class and the counts continued trying to undermine and demolish the political guild phenomenon. After 1302, Flanders experienced a renegotiation of the balance between merchant and guild power within the communal body politic, but the fourteenth century also saw a high incidence of urban strife. In Ghent, there were further revolts in 1311, 1319, 1325, 1332, 1337, 1345, 1353, 1359, 1360, 1373 and 1379–85. In Bruges, political and social struggles took place in 1309, 1318, 1321, 1323–8, 1348, 1351, 1358–61, 1367,

---

91   See the references in notes 5 and 16 above.
92   Mertens 1981, p. 185.
93   Boone 1996a, p. 47; Boone 2005, pp. 20–4.

1369, 1379–80, 1382, 1387, and 1391. In Ypres, riots and revolts broke out in 1303, 1304, 1324, 1325, 1359–61, 1367, 1370, 1377, and 1379–80.[94] Economic and fiscal justice were at the heart of the commoners' demands and would retain their prominence in the core rebel ideology for centuries, along with political participation, financial control and guild autonomy.[95] However, the political system remained fundamentally precarious and the guildsmen jealously guarded their privileges and stood up against oligarchic tendencies. Reports on the revolts of this period, either in chronicles, judicial enquiries, or lists of hostages taken after the revolt had been repressed, almost always classify rebels as belonging to this or that craft guild. They describe the acts and words of guildsmen as protagonists in the struggle.[96] Even immediately after the 1302 victory, the independence of the guilds was limited, as one of the 1303 rules for the Bruges fullers made it illegal for any master or journeyman to organise strikes (*huitghanghe* or *ledichghanghe*), to swear oaths or forge alliances (*bande*), or to send letters or messengers outside the city, without the permission of the city government or the prince.[97]

Craft guild organisations thus became the primary vehicles for popular mobilisation and the main arenas in which popular voices could be uttered. The sources which describe the fourteenth-century Flemish revolts, whether narrative or judicial, unanimously grant guilds or individual artisans the leading political roles in organising insurrections and voicing alternative opinions on how the city should be governed. One Bruges rebel confessed that during the election of new deans and *vinders* in the 1323–8 revolt, he incited others by saying that the deans and *vinders* 'had to belong to the right party'.[98] During his interrogation in Paris in 1328, Willem de Deken, who had been mayor of the commune of Bruges during the revolt, named among the leading rebels two weavers who had been deans of their guild and who *estoient maistre promoteur et faiseur de touz let mauls* ('were the master promoters and makers of all the evil deeds'). The 500 hostages Bruges was required to deliver to the count and the French King after 1328 were also listed according to their crafts.[99] They were mostly fullers and weavers.[100] In fact, in fourteenth-century Flemish collective

---

94 Chronological overview in Verbruggen, Raf 2005, p. 18 (slightly adapted by myself); see also [Patterns] and Boone 2008b.

95 Prevenier 2010, pp. 210–6.

96 Examples are abundant in literature, see Boone 2005; Verbruggen, Raf 2005; and for instance the inquiry on the 1323–8 revolt edited by de Pauw 1899b, pp. 18, 21, 24.

97 Espinas and Pirenne, eds 1906–66, vol. 1, p. 540.

98 De Pauw 1899b, pp. 33–4.

99 Stein 1899, pp. 648–52.

100 Vandermassen 1993.

action, craft guilds were almost the only institutions for popular mobilisation. Parishes or quarters did not take on this role in Flanders, in contrast to their counterparts in other areas of Europe. Some of the larger guilds, such as the Ghent weavers and fullers, lived in distinct neighbourhoods, but these had no autonomous role in social and political mobilisation but instead followed the directives of the guild leadership in which their representatives were elected.[101] While there were also clans and factions in the medieval Flemish towns, these were mainly an elite phenomenon, although from time to time, patrician factions tried to mobilise the guilds for their own purposes, or formed temporary alliances with them.[102] Guilds could also stop a mobilisation. In 1306, for instance, the Ghent weavers' guild decided not to take part in a popular revolt and forbade all members from leaving work, or resisting the count, on pain of exclusion.[103] The practical methods of guild mobilisation are well known. Guildsmen would often assemble first in their guild house, arm themselves and leave, or they would assemble for a so-called *wapening*, a highly ritualised armed gathering on the main square of the town. The 'signs and voices' of guild politics determined the forms and content of Flemish popular mobilisation for centuries to come.[104]

8   Strong but Contested Guild Power in Bruges and Ghent

It was not yet clear in the immediate aftermath of the Battle of Kortrijk that the guilds would become the legal, institutional and ideological successors of the older communal model of popular participation. Rather than explicitly using the term 'guilds', the charters granted to Ghent, Bruges and other cities between 1301 and 1304 identified their forces as the 'commoners'.[105] In Bruges, charters began shortly after this time to name the guilds as the institutions that had the exclusive right to represent the 'commons', the *ghemeentucht, ghemeente*, or *li commun*. These stormy years featured a number of institutional experiments designed to frame the increased political influence of a larger portion of the population. For some time after 1302, the Bruges guilds controlled the institution of the 'Hundred Men' (*hondertmannen*), who were justices of the peace

101 Verbruggen, Raf 2005, pp. 93–102.
102 Braekevelt, Buylaert, Dumolyn et al. 2012.
103 Verbruggen, Raf 2005, p. 97; de Pauw 1890, p. 6.
104 For the *wapeninghe*, see [A Moody Community].
105 For instance the 'constitutional' charter of Senlis granted to Ghent in 1301: Boone 2003a, p. 44, '*ceus du commun*'.

responsible for resolving minor conflicts and maintaining some social order. This institution rivalled the Headmen (*hooftmannen*) of the *Zestendelen* (the six districts of Bruges), which had been responsible for these functions before the Hundred Men took over and resumed their authority after the Hundred Men lost their judicial competence. The Headmen were selected only from the *poorters* (which literally means the 'burghers', but actually included only merchants and property owners), while the Hundred Men were recruited from the guilds as well. After its political compromise with the craft guilds, the merchant class also developed its own institutions for communal representation. After the eclipse of the institutional experiments of the Hundred Men in Bruges and the 'Fifty Men' in Ghent,[106] a similar institution largely composed of guildsmen, the political struggle centred on who would select the individuals who sat on the boards of aldermen, the main political and judicial bodies ruling the Flemish cities and towns.

In 1302 itself, the popular classes occupied approximately seventy-five percent of the governmental offices in Bruges. After 1304 this number began to decrease.[107] In that year, Philip of Chieti, a son of Count Guy of Dampierre, still a prisoner of the French King, gave Bruges a new charter of privileges outlining the city government structure.[108] The final version of the charter drafted by the count's sons omitted a crucial passage giving the craft guilds the right to appoint nine aldermen and councillors. Some versions of the charter preserved by the city contained this passage. In Bruges, as well as other cities, only a fragment of the original volume of documents dealing with the composition of the city government has survived. Most of these 'constitutional' documents regulating city government in Flanders deliberately avoided precise definitions of the guilds' role, which allowed their *de facto* power to be regulated by customary practices. In actual practice, every time the craft guilds suffered a political defeat, their opponents removed the guilds' right, granted in 1304, to appoint the fixed number of nine guildsmen to the board of aldermen and nine to the council. Whenever the guilds revolted, they claimed this right again, even in the 1477 revolt. During each upset, the victors confiscated previous versions of the privileges and issued new ones, which makes the exact chronological reconstruction of this issue a difficult task for the historian.[109] Guild participation

---

106   Dumolyn and Stabel 2002, p. 60.
107   Verbruggen, Jan 1956, p. 43.
108   De Poerck 1931; Gilliodts-Van Severen 1874, vol. 1, pp. 286–307; Berten 1913, pp. 443–4 is the version that states that nine alderman and councillors will be elected by the *ambochten*.
109   Gilliodts-Van Severen 1874, vol. 1, p. 316; Van den Auweele and Oosterbosch 1995, vol. 2, pp. 286–4.

in the urban governments of other Flemish cities similarly varied according to political circumstances and the balance of power at any given time.

For a brief period after 1302, while the alliance between the artisans and the comital family was still solid, the craft guilds managed to obtain favourable political privileges governing their internal organisation and autonomy. They gained the right to elect their own leaders, a demand that the Damme guildsmen had articulated in 1280. The Bruges privileges for the fullers and shearers, probably granted in 1303, laid out a complicated procedure for guild elections which did not entirely eliminate the role of the city government. The 1303 *keure* of the Damme blacksmiths decreed that the *deken* and *vinders* were to be elected by the members. While the Bruges brokers' privilege, dated 8 May 1303, did not mention this autonomy, a later charter, dated 8 June 1306, stated that 'from now on, they shall choose their sworn men themselves'. The butchers gained the right to elect new guild leaders in their privilege of 2 December 1302, which was perhaps the first privilege to be granted to any Flemish guild after the victory at Kortrijk on 11 July of that year. The chosen leaders had to share electoral power with four men appointed by the 'community' (*meentucht*) of the craft guild. Together they were to choose six men, one to be the 'shield bearer' (military leader), and five to be *vinders*, with the offices to be apportioned by lot. Although the text is not entirely clear about the process, it seems that these six men were then to select the dean along with the whole guild, or at least with the approval of all members gathered at a meeting. Though the text does not describe exactly how this was done, the process involved seeking consensus rather than using ballots. However, in this consensus, the voices of the most wealthy and socially prestigious guild members probably dominated. Between 1302 and 1306 the Ghent guilds also received the right to choose their own leadership. The mercers received a privilege giving them this right in 1305. The privilege specified that electors from the guild itself would choose dean and *vinders*. Although another Ghent privilege, granted to the joint craft guild of the joiners, coopers and turners, does not include a passage about election of guild leaders, it does say that the guild would receive half of the revenue collected from fines, which suggests some autonomy. In Ypres, the weavers, fullers, shearers, butchers and fishmongers already possessed their own seals by 4 May 1304, while all the other trades were still directed by two 'headmen'. On that date, all the Ypres guilds gained permission to choose their own captains and deans.[110] The Ghent textile guilds, with their massive memberships, held

---

110 These charters are edited in Espinas and Pirenne, eds 1906–66, vol. 1, pp. 532–41, 542–52; Wyffels 1950b, pp. 94–5, 105–6, 109; Wyffels 1951, p. 223; van der Hallen 1977, p. 107; van Houtte 1950, p. 7.

decentralised elections for guild leaders in every neighbourhood (*ghebuerte*). In 1314 the Ghent weavers were subdivided into twenty-three districts, including two for the shearers, and one each for the finishers, striped-cloth shearers and *uutslagers* (who oversaw the finishing process). Every district had its own banner. Elections for the dean and sworn men of the entire weavers' guild followed an elaborate system of indirect elections.[111] The Ghent fullers were similarly subdivided into nineteen neighbourhoods.[112] By 1309, in Bruges and Ghent, some prosperous commercial guilds, such as the brokers, butchers and fishmongers, began to side with the pro-French Lily faction against the textile guilds.[113] The new Count, Robert de Béthune, lost the support of the guildsmen as a result of his autocratic politics.[114] The initial success of the guilds in gaining positions in city governments clearly encountered patrician reaction between 1310 and 1320. In 1316, twenty-five percent of the Bruges aldermen belonged to the top five percent of taxpayers. In 1315–19, one-third of the Ghent aldermen came from the wealthiest group in the city.[115] A new government was installed in 1302 in Ghent, and it included patricians who did not belong to the Lily party, new men, and members of the craft guilds. In 1312 the Lilies returned from exile. After a series of unsuccessful revolts between 1319 and 1337, the patricians and small guilds dominated Ghent government, while the influence of the weavers greatly diminished. During this phase, Bruges was the city in which the political guilds retained the strongest position.[116] During the 1330s and 1340s, however, the vanguard role in the guild struggle was taken over by Ghent, after the defeat of the revolt of maritime Flanders in 1323–8. During this long, intense revolt, peasants on the coastal plain and the major towns of Ypres, Kortrijk and Geraardsbergen had joined together with a revolutionary regime in Bruges composed of guildsmen and certain patrician factions. At one point the count himself was taken prisoner in Kortrijk and held prisoner in Bruges. A French army ultimately defeated this rebellion in 1328 at the Battle of Cassel.[117] After his victory, the king of France took away the right of Bruges guildsmen to bear arms. The new city government, composed of members of the anti-revolutionary party, asked the king to allow burghers the right to bear arms. The king conceded the right only to those who owned land in the city.[118]

---

111 Boone 1990b, pp. 59–68; De Potter 1882–1933, vol. 15, pp. 163–5.
112 De Pauw 1885, pp. 165–7.
113 Johnstone, ed. 1951, p. 95.
114 Sabbe, Jacques 1970.
115 Van Uytven 1962, pp. 390–2.
116 For Ghent during the same period, see Rogghé 1961, pp. 181–2.
117 Sabbe, Jacques 1992; TeBrake 1993.
118 Gilliodts-Van Severen 1871–85, vol. 1, pp. 402–4.

The reactionary privileges imposed on Bruges in 1329 rescinded the guildsmen's right to elect their own leaders. The city government was to appoint *regardeurs* or *maenres* to govern the guilds instead of deans chosen from the guild ranks. These external supervisors collected fines for infringements of industrial and market regulations, the guilds could no longer tax their own members, and all '*congregations, essamblees de commun ou de mestiers*' were prohibited.[119] This was an attempt to return to the monopoly of power the property-owning class had enjoyed before 1302. However, it was only a temporary setback, and the effort to turn back the clock soon proved futile.

While Bruges was consumed with the revolt, in March 1326, the Ghent reactionary regime of 'the five captains', supporters of the count (1319–29), imposed a tax on the weavers, eager supporters of their comrades in Bruges. The tax was not abolished until 1335. No longer allowed to choose their dean, the weavers were governed by appointed *beleeders*, similar to the *maenres* in Bruges.[120] In 1338, during the opening phase of the Hundred Years War, James van Artevelde, who worked as a broker and may have belonged to the brewers guild, installed a revolutionary government by five captains, each from a different parish. Led by van Artevelde, the captains took charge of military matters and administration in Ghent. The weavers and all the other guilds supported the van Artevelde regime. During James van Artevelde's rule, the five captains from the patricians and the three superior deans (*overdekens*) of the fullers, weavers and small guilds held real power. Three of the captains were rich burghers (*poorters*), but the remaining two were craftsmen. Together with the three superior deans of the weavers, fullers and the small trades, this gave the guilds a numerical advantage.[121] Most other offices were also filled by guildsmen, often the same men who had been exiled by the former regime.[122] Although the government was a coalition of different social groups, the craft guilds, especially the weavers, were heavily involved. While the formal structure of Ghent government by two boards of aldermen was not changed, the captains and the guild deans played important political roles. All the leaders belonged to the anticomital party. Feuds between leading families had a significant impact on the game of allegiances. Soon the other major cities, and finally, the entire county, professed their loyalty to van Artevelde's regime, although sometimes under

---

119   Van Rompaey 1965, pp. 83, 85, '*que jamaiz nulz vindres, dekens, hoofmans, ou autres capitaines de mestiers ne soient en nostre dite ville, ne centhomme pris ne esleu, qu'il soloient prendre par leur volenté*'.

120   Fris 1907, p. 431.

121   Rogghé 1942, vol. 2, p. 10.

122   Rogghé 1952, p. 106.

threat. Van Artevelde installed Ghent captains as leaders in some of the smaller cities. Though less is known about the events in Bruges, the guilds clearly took over there as well. Even before van Artevelde came to power in Ghent, Count Louis of Nevers restored Bruges's privileges of 1304. The van Artevelde regime spread over all of Flanders, leaving the count only a nominal position. During this era the Flemish 'political guilds', reached what was arguably the summit of their power. However, the rebellious coalition in Ghent was internally unstable. The Ghent weavers, who had been readmitted to city government in 1338, murdered van Artevelde in 1345. They suspected him of treason, a common fate of medieval rebel leaders in general.[123] In 1345, the weavers in turn imposed *beleeders* on the fullers. Fullers worked for weavers as wage labourers, and the conflict between the two textile guilds grew sharper during the second half of the fourteenth century.[124] The weavers' regime in Ghent came to an end on the 'Good Tuesday', 13 January 1349, after fullers and patricians slew many weavers in a bloody massacre. The weavers were themselves subjected to the authority of *beleeders* chosen from outside their ranks, and were not allowed to go out on the street in groups of more than three.[125]

9 Towards a New Balance around 1360

In 1348–9, the new Count Louis of Male regained control over Bruges, Ghent and Ypres. As a stronger prince than his predecessor, Louis clearly intended to break the autonomous power of the three big cities, which automatically included eliminating the political force of the guilds. However, urban politics in Flanders remained unstable. A new revolt broke out in May 1359, with severe riots by the textile workers in the Bruges market square. In July of the same year, conflicts erupted between the textile guilds and the other craft guilds. During these years, there were different changes of government, and on 2 March 1360 the guilds sealed the agreement discussed at the beginning of this article to preserve the peace. After renewed rioting in April 1360, a final peace agreement was forged in September 1361. On 1 February 1360, the Ghent weavers triumphed once again over the fullers.[126] In 1362, the Ghent weavers were forced to swear individually never to take arms against the count again.[127] While the Ghent and

---

123 On this period, see Nicholas, David 1988; Carson 1980.
124 Fris 1907, p. 432.
125 Vuylsteke 1895; Demuynck 1951.
126 Vuylsteke 1895, p. 40; Mertens 1987, pp. 325–9.
127 Espinas and Pirenne, eds 1906–66, vol. 2, pp. 503–4.

Ypres guilds were less successful in the end, they had convinced the count and the patricians that the guilds could not be completely excluded from power. As a result, the wave of guild revolts from 1359 to 1361 led to a political balance in Bruges and Ghent, consolidated in the political structure of the 'Members' which organised groups of guilds into the body politic of the city to share power together with the patrician class in a precarious equilibrium. After gradually taking shape during the first half of the fourteenth century, around 1360 the Members were institutionalised in the two major cities of the county: in Bruges there were Nine Members, and power was shared between Three Members in Ghent.[128]

The Nine Members of Bruges were grouped in the following structure: firstly, the *poorterie* or 'burghers' consisted of the merchants and landowners. Every section, or *zestendeel*, of the city had a *hooftman*, or captain. The captain of the Saint John's section, the richest district of the city, was the first of these six captains. Secondly, the four textile guilds (weavers, fullers, shearers and dyers). Thirdly, the butchers and fishmongers. Fourthly, the 'seventeen small guilds', including masons, carpenters, thatchers, plumbers, plaster workers, coopers, potters and others. This member was dominated by the building industry. Fifthly, the guilds of the *Haemere* ('the Hammer'), dominated by the blacksmiths and goldsmiths. Sixthly, the guilds of the *Ledere*, or leatherworkers. Seventhly, the guilds of the *Naelde* ('the Needle') encompassing the garment trades. Eighthly, the bakers, along with the guilds subject to them, including – logically – the millers, but also – less obviously – the barbers and belt makers. Finally, the brokers and other guilds under their leadership, such as the shippers, rosary makers and fruit sellers.[129] In Ghent, the term 'Members of the City' referring at that time to the weavers, fullers and small trades, was first used during the van Artevelde regime (1338–45).[130] The three Members of Ghent gradually grew into separate and institutionalised entities during the first half of the century, although their history remains somewhat confusing. By 1360 through 1369, they took their definitive shape as the member of the *Poorterie*, similar to the one in Bruges, the member of the *Weverie*, dominated by the weavers and excluding the fullers, and the member of the *Cleene Neringhen*, or small guilds, a collective of all the trades working for the local market and in the

---

128   Mertens 1996, pp. 385–9; the logic of the Ghent Member-system is the main topic of the monograph by Boone 1990b.

129   Van den Auweele 1974; Mertens 1961; Dumolyn 1997, pp. 105–15; Vanhaverbeke 1998; Vandewalle 1999.

130   Rogghé 1961, p. 189.

service sector, dominated by the shippers.[131] The distinctions between the different members, however, were sometimes vague. In Bruges, the rich hostellers who controlled the city's international trade sometimes filled positions allotted to the brokers' guild, to which they legally belonged, but were also found among the representatives of the *poorterie*.[132] From the late fourteenth century, some Ghent aldermen took office as representatives of the *poorterie* and later as representatives of guilds. Ghent brokers and hostellers held the same ambivalent position between the members of the small trades and the *poorterie* as did their counterparts in Bruges.[133] Resolution of this problem may come after systematic prosopographical research in the future.[134]

In the two largest cities, during the same period around 1360, new institutions embodying the entire commune seem to have taken shape following a similar logic. In Bruges, the Great Council (*Grote Raad*, or *Ghemeene buke van der stede*) included the six captains of the *poorterie* and the fifty-four deans of the craft guilds. Consulted sporadically on important fiscal and financial issues, it tended to expand its role during later revolts and assume rule of the city as the direct representative of the commune.[135] The Ghent Great Council, or *Collacie*, became a more powerful and continuous institution than its Bruges counterpart. As in Bruges, the *Collacie*'s origin and the precise nature of its operation during the fourteenth century are unclear, because these institutions did not create systematic series of their own records. Nevertheless, the *Collacie* began immediately before or during the time of James van Artevelde and took its definitive shape around 1369.[136] The Ghent *Collacie* usually consisted of ten *poorters*, the *overdeken* of the textile sector, the deans of the five craft guilds under the weavers, the sworn men of the weavers selected by each guild district, the *overdeken* of the small trades and the fifty-three deans of the separate small craft guilds.[137] These more popular institutions were clearly created in the two main cities to channel the discontent of the guilds and include them on a more structural level in the political decision-making process. In theory, this would make bloody confrontations easier to avoid, and the artisans, or at

---

131 First explored by Fris 1907; Boone 1990b has shown how this system continued to function during the whole Burgundian period, and Dambruyne 2002 describes its final days and end.
132 Dumolyn 1997.
133 Rogghé 1949–50.
134 The Burgundian period has been covered by Boone 1990b, but the fourteenth-century situation remains less clear.
135 Blockmans, Willem 1978, pp. 81–7.
136 Boone 1990b, p. 37.
137 Boone 1990b, pp. 28–9; Dambruyne 2002, pp. 23–35.

least their leaders, could legally voice their opinions in an official setting. In the end, a temporary balance of power between the political guilds, the merchant class and the prince was achieved by 1370. Although a new massive revolt directed by Ghent ten years later upset this uneasy equilibrium, the institutional heritage of the fourteenth-century struggle for guild representation lasted well into the sixteenth century.

10   Ypres and the Small Cities of Flanders

The success of the political guilds in Ghent and Bruges should not create the impression that political guilds attained the same degree of power in all the cities and towns of fourteenth-century Flanders. In Ypres, which had approximately 10,000 inhabitants at the end of the fourteenth century (but had counted probably four times that number in the thirteenth century) the textile industry was in sharp decline. Despite the city's large textile workforce, oligarchic rule proved more potent. The craft guilds never acquired the power in city government that their brothers in Ghent and Bruges held. As the Ypres city archives were destroyed during World War I, historians have only the sources that had been edited before that time, and those surviving in other archives. We know that Ypres also had urban councils representing a broader layer of the city's social groups than were represented by the board of aldermen which was always very elitist. Sources attest to a Great Council in 1306. In 1325 – during a revolutionary regime – a document suggests that the deans and *vinders* of the guilds had financial control. The deans belonged to the Great Council in 1344, when van Artevelde dominated the county. In the fifteenth century, a source identifies a 'Council of Twenty-Seven' which included the deans of the craft guilds. It was probably a relic of an older urban communal institution similar to the Bruges *Grote Raed* ('Great Council') and the *Ghent Collacie* ('Ghent Gathering'). In general, the craft guilds were only full partners on the boards of aldermen in popular regimes installed after successful uprisings, as in 1303–4, 1325–8, 1338–48, 1359–61 and 1379–82.[138] Ypres had a political guild system similar to the Members in Ghent and Bruges, but its exact contours are obscure. The 'common trades' (*ghemeene neringhen*) appeared as a group in 1327, and the *poorterie* as another in 1377.[139] The *poortersnering* included in its institution certain Ypres craft guilds, including the butchers, fishmongers, mer-

138   Trio 1997, pp. 335–6.
139   Ibid., p. 337.

cers, silversmiths, shearers, dyers and cloth sellers. The other three 'members' were the common trades, including the blacksmiths, barge operators, tailors and shoemakers, and finally the two main textile guilds, the weavers and the fullers, represented separately.[140]

As the political struggle in fourteenth-century Ypres still awaits systematic study, I can only sketch it superficially. The Ypres regime did not make significant changes immediately after 11 July 1302, which led to an anti-patrician revolt in 1303 in which several aldermen were murdered. On 16 December 1303, Philip of Chieti, son of the count, forgave the Ypres commoners and gave in to all their demands, such as 'que ils fachent echevins et toutes de gouverneurs de loy' ('that they [can] make aldermen and all kinds of legal officials'). This concession granted the Ypres craft guilds the same power to appoint aldermen as the guilds held in Bruges. However, Philip made this concession only to appease the rebellious guildsmen because, supported by the aldermen of Bruges, Ghent, Lille and Douai, he ruled in April 1304 that the surviving aldermen would remain in office and the seven assassinated aldermen would be replaced.[141] There seem to have been few challenges to patrician power in the first few decades of the fourteenth century. During the wide-spread revolt in Western Flanders from 1323 to 1328, a coalition of guilds and 'new men' installed a popular regime in 1325, but this did not last long.[142] The French king tried to craft a peace treaty in 1326. Among other provisions, it stipulated that the inhabitants of the towns in revolt could no longer make alliances, but the men of Ypres were allowed to keep their guild leaders, subject to renewal every seventeen weeks and their oaths of loyalty to the city government.[143] Although events in Ypres before and after the van Artevelde period (1338–45) are less clear, the result must have been disadvantageous because in 1359 the rebellious Ypres guilds again demanded the right to elect their own deans, sworn men and captains.[144] While the count was in the city, on 25 July 1359, the rebellious Ypres weavers and fullers shouted 'in one voice' that they wanted to choose their own deans, vinders and captains, just as the Ghent guilds could, and that they wanted their privileges back that they had held in the time of James van Artevelde. The guilds then organised elections by parish without waiting for authorisation.[145] After guild revolts in 1361 and 1377

140   Ibid., p. 345.
141   Espinas and Pirenne, eds 1906–66, vol. 3, pp. 721–44; Verbruggen, Jan 1991, pp. 69–76; Gilliodts-Van Severen 1908, vol. 2, pp. 53–61.
142   Acke 1986.
143   Gilliodts-Van Severen 1871–85, vol. 1, p. 357.
144   Verbruggen, Raf 2005, p. 42; Espinas and Pirenne, eds 1906–66, vol. 3, p. 782.
145   Ibid., vol. 3, pp. 782–3.

failed, the counts never relinquished their exclusive right to appoint the urban magistrates of Ypres.[146] Ypres also experienced conflicts between fullers and weavers, in 1340 for instance, but these were never as bloody as the violence in Ghent.[147]

Since pre-fifteenth-century guild archives for many medium and small Flemish towns are even sparser than the fragmentary sources for Ypres,[148] there is little preliminary research dealing with their political role. Those official government documents which have survived provide only fragmentary information about guild involvement in urban institutions. However, the struggle for political participation seems to have followed more or less the same general chronology in the smaller towns as in Ghent, Bruges and Ypres. Often the guilds attained limited power in 1303–4, and during the revolt of 1325–8, popular alliances obtained temporary gains. Louis of Nevers abolished these after 1328. In 1330 many small towns received the same 'bad privileges' forced on Bruges in 1329. The privilege issued to Aalst in 1330 required the count's explicit agreement to any attempt by the guilds to proclaim their own ordinances and tax or fine their members, rights they had previously held autonomously.[149] The privileges issued to the Aalst guilds of weavers and fullers by Robert of Béthune were cancelled after the revolt of 1323–8, but restored again by Louis of Male after 1357.[150] In 1328, a new charter for Oudenaarde, a mid-sized textile town in eastern Flanders, prohibited 'starting a new guild without the permission of the aldermen' with the fine of twenty Flemish *groot* pounds.[151] During the next phase, the early van Artevelde period, the weak count restored earlier privileges, including some dealing with the autonomy and rights of craft guilds, to the small towns, but after 1348 these were again abolished. In 1338, the count restored the guild privileges of the Oudenaarde fullers,[152] and in 1359, the Oudenaarde weavers clearly obtained more favourable privileges.[153] Even though these dates match the general chronology discussed above, the town of Oudenaarde seems to have had a more elitist regime, with little political power for the craft guilds.[154]

---

146   Trio 1997, p. 338.
147   Espinas and Pirenne, eds 1906–66, vol. 3, pp. 773–4.
148   For a general demographic and economic assessment of the Flemish small towns, see Stabel 1997 and specifically on the drapery Stabel 1995, pp. 123–37.
149   De Potter and Broeckaert 1873–6, vol. 1, p. 426.
150   Espinas and Pirenne, eds 1906–66, vol. 1, pp. 43.
151   Limburg-Stirum 1882–6, vol. 2, p. 57.
152   Espinas and Pirenne, eds 1906–66, vol. 1, pp. 280–5.
153   Ibid., vol. 1, pp. 285–94.
154   Van Eeckhoudt-De Jaeger 1983.

Although we know little about the political situation in the coastal towns of Flanders, they usually took part in major revolts involving Bruges, which suggest that political regulations there more or less mirrored those of the coastal capital of Flanders. In general, it is safe to assume that in most of the medium and certainly in the small towns of Flanders, guilds were not able to achieve full 'political guild' status. Yet in the town of Geraardsbergen, the guilds made strong attempts to obtain political power. The charter granted to the town by Jean de Namur, son of the count, in April 1303 stipulated that '*k'on fera cescun an wit jurés ens le vile de Grammont des mestiers de le vile, et d'un mestier un juret sans plus*'.[155] This meant that the guilds controlled the communal institution of the eight 'sworn men' alongside the board of aldermen which was still controlled by the count and the patricians. In the reactionary charter of 1331, Louis of Nevers decreed that the sworn men, reduced to seven, would be chosen by the aldermen as they left office without any interference from a meeting of the commoners, or any craft guild. In the same evolution experienced by other Flemish towns, the tide turned in 1338 under the van Artevelde regime, and the craft guilds regained their freedoms.[156] Apparently following the example of its capital, Ghent, the guilds in Geraardsbergen were likely organised in broader units, such as the small trades, who had an *overdeken*.[157] Ghent arbitrated intra-urban conflicts within the smaller towns in the region of the county it dominated. In 1345, Ghent pacified conflicts in Geraardsbergen between the drapers and the journeymen.[158] Little else is known about guild matters there.

Kortrijk, a medium-sized town but a major textile producer, also had combative guilds, but there is not enough evidence to estimate the weight of guild influence in the city government in the first half of the fourteenth century. As in Ypres, communal and corporatist ideas circulated during the revolt of 1323–8, when twenty-four sworn men and councillors represented the commune, and the power of the aldermen seems to have been reduced.[159] Kortrijk imposed taxes on the textile guilds to pay its fine for participating in the revolt. They were clearly blamed for the '*esmeutes*' and the '*mavais gouvernement*', a reference to the short-lived communal guild regime that took power in 1325 in defiance of the count and 'the good people of the city'.[160] In 1338, this tax was abolished.[161]

---

155 Limburg-Stirum 1878, p. 514.
156 Fris 1911b, p. 380.
157 Ibid., p. 380.
158 Espinas and Pirenne, eds 1906–66, vol. 2, p. 652.
159 Limburg-Stirum 1905, p. 153.
160 Espinas and Pirenne, eds 1906–66, vol. 1, pp. 649–51.
161 Ibid., vol. 1, p. 652.

During the van Artevelde years, the Kortrijk aldermen had to share power with a 'college of nine men, but their exact power is unclear'.[162] In 1348, a charter pardoned the Kortrijk fullers and gave back their privileges from the time of Count Robert of Béthune.[163] Significantly, the textile guilds of the large industrial centres showed little solidarity with guildsmen in the smaller textile towns, where wages were often lower, and no sympathy at all for rural producers who worked in the putting-out system. Although weavers formed revolutionary networks on occasion, local chauvinism usually outweighed interurban solidarity. In 1314, the bailiff of Ghent, along with weavers, fullers and shearers, sent punitive expeditions into the surrounding countryside to shut down rural textile industries outlawed by the city privileges.[164] During the revolt of 1323–8, rebels from Ypres who had taken control of their city committed '*homicides, arsins, robberies, brisures de edifices et envaïes par force d'armes et à banières desplijés, par cris et autrement*' ('homicides, arson, robbery, housebreaking and armed invasions with banners flying, by outcry and otherwise') in the neighbouring town of Poperinge and village of Langemark, both regional competitors in the textile industry who paid lower wages.[165] Ghent and Bruges continued to suppress or restrict textile industries in surrounding small towns and villages. In fact, the textile guilds of the big cities made this one of their central demands.

For other towns, there has been no serious study of the few sources that have survived. For example, the bailiff and the aldermen of Deinze issued an ordinance in 1365 on 'reasonable' wages for fullers which was ratified by Count Louis of Male. While this was obviously the result of an earlier petition of the guild, at present almost nothing else is known about the guilds in that small town.[166] Even when normative documents are available, we often lack sources for the prosopographical work needed to evaluate the effectiveness of guild representation in urban institutions. There are fifteenth-century sources that allow extensive prosopographical studies in towns like Hulst, Axel or Eeklo. In these towns, the craft guilds usually had a small degree of representation in the government institutions. Drapers, as the wealthiest members of the textile guilds, along with butchers and brewers, served regularly as aldermen, and members of crafts such as the potters, bakers or millers held this office occasionally. The fourteenth-century Kortrijk evidence suggests that there were usually a few

---

162   De Pauw 1910, p. 221.
163   Espinas and Pirenne, eds 1906–66, vol. 1, pp. 658–9.
164   Vuylsteke 1906, pp. 207–8; in general see Nicholas, David 1971.
165   De Pauw 1899b, p. 191.
166   Espinas and Pirenne, eds 1906–66, vol. 2, pp. 2–3.

guild members, mostly drapers, among the provosts and aldermen, but the majority of the seats were held by men from major patrician families. Therefore, 1302 did produce some guild emancipation in the small towns. Although the political role of the guilds there was much less significant than in Bruges or Ghent, it still contrasted sharply with the purely oligarchic logic of the thirteenth century.[167]

11 Social Divisions between and within the Guilds

Nuances must be added to avoid an overly simple evaluation of the role of guilds in popular politics. Earlier models of 'guild revolutions' and even interpretations that emphasise alliances of diverse social groups have sometimes underestimated the other forces of opposition or solidarity within the medieval city. The simple dichotomy of artisans and merchants was crossed by vertical solidarities, such as client-patron relationships, factional cleavages and lineages, by the social contradictions within the craft guilds themselves and by economic conflicts between different guilds, such as the conflicts between weavers and fullers in Ghent and Ypres. The craft guilds clearly did not always act in political unity. On many occasions, the textile workers found themselves isolated from the rest of the artisans who worked in the food, construction, garment, luxury, and service sectors, who often had a more prudent and conservative outlook. Apart from the dividing line between producers for the international and local markets, the textile guilds themselves were sometimes divided along class lines. While the drapers and other wealthy craftsmen in some places at certain times sided with the common artisans, as in the fourteenth-century revolts in Ghent and Bruges, in smaller towns, the drapers often made common cause with the local merchant class to form the local elite. Craft guilds working for the local and service markets, for instance the blacksmiths or the bakers, sometimes cooperated with the textile workers during urban social struggles, but on other occasions they were 'conservative' forces who allied with the elites to exclude the textile artisans from power. Guilds also could have privileged relations with certain elite families. In these cases, the guild borrowed money or accepted charity from the family.

The Ghent weavers and fullers were in continuous conflict, because the weavers hired the fullers as wage labourers. First documented in 1304, the conflict led to bloody struggles in the mid-fourteenth century. The weavers ulti-

---

167   Stabel 1990, p. 40; Stabel 1992 and 1993; Dupont, Sophie 1999.

mately won and excluded the fullers from any political representation. In practice, the patricians manipulated the fullers against the weavers who were, so to speak, their common enemy. The fifty-three 'small craft guilds', producing for the local market, often joined the anti-weaver alliance. Obviously, the class position of guildsmen could differ and so could their political options. A large draper who acted as an entrepreneur but was a member of the guild of the weavers or a rich butcher who controlled a large part of the meat market must have had a different outlook than a small baker or shoemaker or an impoverished journeyman in the building industry. Certainly, in Ghent such social divisions had clear political consequences. In 1337, the urban government, then under patrician control, distributed money to the fullers to win their allegiance. In 1349, after the overthrow of James van Artevelde and his former weaver allies, the coalition excluded the weavers from power and subjected them to a special tax.[168] However, after the weavers regained the upper hand in 1369, a Ghent city ordinance of 1372–3 prohibited the fullers from refusing work, leaving the city, and bearing arms.[169] Though more research is needed on this issue, in Ypres and in many small towns, the drapers as entrepreneurs in the textile industry may have often sided with the merchant class against the actual producers (weavers, fullers, shearers and dyers), while in the bigger industrial centres drapers and producers joined forces.

In the commercial city of Bruges, the brokers' guild represented the interests of the middlemen who facilitated transactions between foreign merchants. Brokers worked for the rich innkeepers or 'hostellers'. The *keure* obtained by the brokers after 1302 gave them greater power in their relations with hostellers. In the years that followed, as we have seen above, the brokers turned against the textile workers and industrial interests. In 1339 and 1380, the Bruges brokers sided with the patricians. Brokers maintained this allegiance for the rest of the medieval era.[170] Finally, there were also social divisions within guilds between masters and journeymen. Journeymen were almost never represented in the guild leadership. And right after 1302 journeymen in the textile guilds obtained some representation in their own guild leadership. Journeymen could elect a few representatives, although they were only a minor part of the leadership. Journeymen had this right in the Bruges fullers' guild, as stated in their 1303 privilege, in the Saint-Omer weavers' guild in 1306, and in the Oudenaarde and Kortrijk fullers' guilds between 1305 and 1320. There were similar regulations in Ghent for the shearers' guild in 1350 and the weavers' guild in 1359. It is less

---

168 Verbruggen, Raf 2005, p. 20; Boone and Brand 1993.
169 Espinas and Pirenne, eds 1906–66, vol. 2, pp. 526–7.
170 van Houtte 1950, p. 17.

clear whether the journeymen had already formed independent journeymen organisations, such as the religious confraternities often found in the fifteenth century and later.[171]

12 A Guild Oligarchy?

The potential or actual divisions within and between the guilds, and the fact that guilds usually had to ally with members or factions of the ruling classes to obtain political power, pose a significant issue. Was 'guild politics' really a form of 'popular politics', or were the Flemish political guilds merely dominated by another type of elite? David Nicholas claims that '[t]he revolution of 1302 thus merely broadened political participation among the wealthy'.[172] In his view, from their inception Flemish craft guilds never represented working- or middle-class interests, and soon either fell prey to domination by an internal oligarchy, or to manipulation by merchant elites who joined guilds to use them as vehicles for their political careers. The same argument has been made for other regions of medieval Europe and certainly contains a grain of truth.[173] Prosopographical studies, however, show a nuanced picture. Between 1302 and 1312 in Ghent, some patricians were already trying to gain political access by becoming members of guilds.[174] Although there were surely exclusive tendencies within the guilds, the extent of this phenomenon is difficult to discern. In some guilds, such as the butchers and fishmongers, a small number of masters and families monopolised guild institutions. It was logical that political offices, which offered little or no pay, would go to the wealthier guild members, who would also represent their craft in city government as burgomasters, aldermen, or councillors if the guild had rights of election.[175] But there were also less powerful individuals who managed to hold offices, even if only for one term.[176] In the Bruges coopers' guild, a larger and more egalitarian craft guild, between 1375 and 1500, Sosson found that there was no consistent pattern of monopoly by a few individuals over guild leadership, but there were also only a few rich and powerful masters in the guild.[177] Clearly, some craft guilds were

---

171 Van Werveke 1943a, pp. 12–14; Lis and Soly 1994a, pp. 31–4.
172 Nicholas, David 1987, p. 2.
173 For instance, in the classical article of Maschke 1959. For a critique of this 'elite view of urban politics', see Najemy 1991.
174 Rogghé 1944, p. 138.
175 Van Uytven 1962, p. 408.
176 Boone 1994, p. 11.
177 Sosson 1966, pp. 472–4.

far more oligarchic than others.[178] In small, wealthy craft guilds, such as those in the luxury trade, a prosperous class of masters divided power rather equally among themselves, while in the large textile guilds social-economic polarisation between the richer and poorer artisans was far greater. Some worked as subcontractors for others, and drapers monopolised political power in the guild. Some merchants and entrepreneurs opportunistically joined guilds to advance their careers or strengthen their positions in elite factional struggles, but this was probably not widespread in the fourteenth century and became more important during and after the fifteenth century.[179]

The combination of subcontracting and demand for Flemish cloth in foreign markets gave Flemish drapers a greater control over production than their counterparts enjoyed in most other areas of medieval Europe. Flemish drapers had more freedom to achieve economies of scale and introduce innovations precisely because they were organised in strong guilds that also held political power and acted as lobbyists. As a result, city governments could not systematically subordinate industrial interests to those of the merchants.[180] It cannot be denied that drapers usually represented the *weverie* of Ghent on the boards of aldermen.[181] But these guild elites also owed their political position to the support of the more ordinary masters and journeymen, and had to live in symbiosis with a rank and file who could potentially turn against the drapers, even violently, during revolts. While this conflict of interests did not constitute a real class struggle between producers and merchants, the historiographical tendency to emphasise the 'elitist' character of the craft guilds ignores the fact that wealthy drapers and other entrepreneurs, such as the building contractors in the masons guilds, who had more social and political power than their fellow artisans, nevertheless stood up for the interests of those wider layers of their craft guild. Narratives about revolts show that the rank and file put pressure on their wealthy guild leaders time and time again. During guild meetings, especially in times of economic or political crisis, radicals from both inside and outside the guild, poorer masters, and young unruly journeymen aggressively demanded that guild leaders act in the ordinary workers' interest.[182]

---

178   Sosson 1984, pp. 79–81; Mertens 1981, p. 192.
179   In England as well, smaller guilds were more 'democratic' than larger ones, see Farr 2000, p. 160.
180   Lis and Soly 2008, pp. 84–7, 100.
181   Rogghé 1952, p. 112.
182   Dumolyn 2008a.

13 Conclusion: The Legacy of the Fourteenth Century

On 18 December 1380 the Bruges weavers were forced to swear an 'alliance and oath'. Twelve members of the guild had to appear before the aldermen and swear in the name of their craft guild never again to take up arms against the count and city, never to participate in city government, to give up their own work clock, to forego electing their own dean and *vinders*, and to follow the orders of a *maenre* appointed by the lord, among other things. From now on, journeymen would be excluded from the guild militia if the count called up the city to fight in a war, and they were no longer allowed to participate in guild meetings.[183] The contrast between the 1380 oath and the charter sealed by all Bruges guilds on 3 September 1361,[184] described at the beginning of this article, shows the volatility of the political situation in the Flemish cities and the precarious nature of the political guilds' power. In 1380, after the Bruges textile workers and certain other guilds tried to join in the new Ghent revolt led by Philip van Artevelde, son of James, a charter explicitly forbade the weavers from ever sitting as magistrates. In 1384, under Philip the Bold, Duke of Burgundy and the new Count of Flanders, the Bruges system of political representation by the Nine Members was in practice abandoned and would only be restored in 1411. In reality, however, actual guild representation was neglected from the very beginning, and this was one of the causes of new revolts in 1436 and 1477. In Ghent, as well, the power of the guilds was only broken after the city lost rebellious struggles in 1449–53, 1488–92 and 1538–40. Though in fact, all craft guild activity in the sense of self-organising in an interest group was 'political' in itself, the revolutionary events of the year 1302 had accelerated the process of the craft guilds developing into true 'political guilds' who were integral to the urban political system. In the urban world of Flanders, especially in the major cities, the guilds were principal actors in popular politics, but at the same time strove towards acceptance into the established political system. Political power for the guilds was primarily a phenomenon of big cities with export industries, a conclusion which connects directly to Soly's analysis of the power and capital of the drapers.

Robert Duplessis and Martha Howell have pointed out that the urban elites were willing to compromise with the craft guilds 'to uphold order in the city and to perpetuate existing power relationships'.[185] Indeed, the guilds transitioned from their oppositional role and discourse to take part in ruling, managing and

---

183 Espinas and Pirenne, eds 1906–66, vol. 1, pp. 592–601.
184 Ibid., vol. 1, pp. 581–2; Gilliodts-Van Severen 1871–85, vol. 2, 117.
185 Duplessis and Howell 1982, p. 76.

stabilising the city politically and socially. Without any apparent contradiction, corporatism continued to combine these two aspects. Governing the body of the city was a social and moral duty. By taking it up and widening the space for political discussion and negotiation, guild politics opened up the political realm to many more layers of the urban population and involved them in the ideas about the common welfare of urban society and full burgher rights. And sometimes one had to fight for one's interests and convictions. The period of 1302 through 1360 which has been the focus of this article marked the consolidation of the political guilds' power in the major Flemish cities, but the struggle did not come to an end at that time. The 'Ghent revolt' of 1379–85, which actually involved more areas of the county than Ghent alone, highlighted the political contradictions between guild and elite politics again. Clashes, often violent, continued beyond the sixteenth century. What did change during the final two decades of the fourteenth century, however, was the balance of power.

When the Burgundian, and later the Habsburg, dynasties came to power in Flanders, they developed a princely state that had far more resources and soldiers at its disposal than did the generally weak Flemish counts of the fourteenth century. The heyday of the Netherlandish guilds was over by 1500. They lost their military function, and in many cities their direct or indirect participation was taken away or severely limited.[186] Indeed, as Prak stated, 'if guilds did not gain political influence in the Low Countries before 1500, they would never obtain it'.[187] In the city of Liège, guild power in government increased until approximately 1400 and declined after that time, an evolution similar to the Flemish urban world. Geneviève Xhayet has rightly observed that even without considering the precise chronology of institutional guild power in the government, the symbolic value of incarnating the community was central to the guilds' political role.[188] In the fourteenth-century Southern Low Countries, based upon their fundamental role in the production of urban wealth, the ideology and political practice of the political guilds had claimed the entire body politic of the city, or at least claimed its shared ownership with the patrician lineages. This political idea and this way of politically acting would remain as the political guilds' legacy for the next centuries.

---

186   Lis and Soly 2006a, p. 1. This article provides an excellent historiographical overview of the early modern developments.
187   Prak 2006, p. 77, with many references for the other Netherlandish principalities that cannot be treated here.
188   Xhayet 1993, p. 378.

CHAPTER 4

Factionalism and State Power in The Flemish Revolt (1482–92)

Jelle Haemers

It was a damned plague that caused great sadness in Bruges, because the citizens were divided into two factions. Brothers were separated. Even husbands and wives quarrelled about the factions.[1]

∴

1   Introduction

The factional struggle between Monetans and Philippins held Flanders firmly in its grip during the Flemish Revolt. This was the battle for the regency during the minority of the count of Flanders, Philip the Fair, between 1482 and 1492. The faction of the Monetans supported the regency of Philip's father Maximilian, Archduke of Austria, while the faction of the Philippins defended the existence of a regency council that would govern the county in Philip the Fair's name.[2] As the quotation above states, this factional struggle not only separated social entities, such as families and married couples, it also spread a 'plague' of violence in the city of Bruges. Several historians (including Jacques Heers and Willem Blockmans) have already shown that factional struggle made

---

1   '*Twelcke was wel een vermaledyde plaghe, daer dye stede van Brugghe in groot verdriet mede quam, want tvolc was so partyich van dese II benden dat den eenen broedre yeghen dander was. Jae, dat meer es, man ende wijf malcanderen ghetraut hebbende, hadden ompaeys om der partyen wille*', Vorsterman, ed. 1531, fol. 261ᵛ.

2   In 1486 Maximilian of Austria had minted new coins, the '*Moneta archiducum*'. Consequently, the political supporters of Maximilian were called '*Monetanen*'. '*Want het volc binnen der stede gheworden was van twee secten, waerof deene hieten Monetanen, te wetene die metten Roomschen coninc* [Maximilian of Austria] *waren, ende dandere hieten Phelippinnen, dats te verstane die metten hertoghe Phelips* [Philip the Fair] *waren ende metten III Leden slants* [The three Members of Flanders; i.e. the cities Ghent, Bruges and Ypres]', Vorsterman, ed. 1531, fol. 261ᵛ.

medieval and Renaissance politics more violent.[3] They argue that there was no central control mechanism that could stop one faction from using brute force against the other because state power was weak. In a more recent article William Beik states that factional splits were endemic during periods of weakness of the central state because of the nature of the social system. According to Beik, an aristocratic society required effective sharing of resources through taxation, venality, and clientage. When the system of financial and economic redistribution faltered because of the inadequacy of central authority in times of political weakness, 'it produced instead popular unrest, jurisdictional blockage, and factional conflicts'.[4] This article, however, argues that weak state power did not cause factional struggle, because it assesses periods of weakness of central power as an opportunity to grab power that a political alternative to central authority could seize upon. While weakness of the central government does explain why the state could not pacify factional violence in the city, it does not clarify the origins of the conflict. Without the existence of powerful political challengers to the regime factional conflict would not have taken place in periods of weak state power, and therefore, I would argue, we must consider additional social factors in order to understand factional struggle. Challenging factions are powerful when they have at their disposal important economic resources, an alternative political programme, and a cohesive social body. These aspects cannot be ignored when studying factional conflicts.

The goal of the present article is to explore a medieval case in which an urban faction evicted the faction that was supported by central authority: namely, the case of Bruges during the period of the Flemish Revolt. The political position of the state was fundamentally weakened because its sympathizing faction in town did not have a comparable power basis as its opposing faction. The lack of financial and economic means on the state level not only deprived the state elite of the use of force against its adversaries, it also weakened the social networks of its faction in town. By using the opportunity presented by the temporary weakness of central authority, a forceful challenging faction could gain power in town if it felt the need to. In such a case the social support, strong ideas, and sufficient resources enabled the opposing faction to succeed in its mission. In moments power shifted from faction to faction, vengeance reigned over the city, and a spiral of violence held urban society in its grasp. Factional struggle was like a 'damned plague' of which the citizens could not rid themselves.

---

3 For example Heers 1977 and Blockmans, Willem 1990b.
4 Beik 1987, pp. 66–7. See also Beik 1997, pp. 173–98.

In my examination of this case, social theory, especially that of Pierre Bourdieu, will help to formulate my argument, for I define a faction as a 'cluster of social capital'. At the same time, historical research can help to concretise sociological terminology. Firstly, because this article also aims to contribute to the discussion on state building, I will explain what is meant by 'state power' as used above. Secondly, the term 'social capital' and a general analysis of historical samples will give new insights into the social history of factions. Thirdly, a sketch of the Flemish Revolt will consider the political struggle of the factions in Bruges and how they tried (or failed) to grab power in the city. Fourthly, the political, social and economic background of the two fighting factions will be examined, combining prosopographical research and social network analysis (SNA).[5] As John Padgett and Christopher Ansell concluded in their sociological analysis of the Medici faction, a study of the so-called 'social embeddedness' of factions is indispensable to understand their history and the process of statebuilding. We therefore need to penetrate beneath the veneer of formal institutions, down to the relational substratum of people's actual and often contradictory lives. The heterogeneity of localised actions, networks, and identities of these people explains both why aggregation is predictable only in hindsight and how political power is born.[6]

2   The Medieval State and Its Capital

According to Max Weber's famous formula, an 'ideal' state successfully claims the monopoly on the legitimate use of physical and symbolic violence over a definite territory and the totality of the corresponding population.[7] Norbert Elias, Charles Tilly, Richard Bonney, Willem Blockmans, Jean-Philippe Genet, and others have treated the historical state in the same way, namely as a point of concentration of physical and mental coercion.[8] The French sociologist Pierre Bourdieu in his *Rethinking the State* (1994) elaborated on these research results by introducing a new term to social and political science, namely 'state capital' ('*capital étatique*'). In his view, the state is the culmination of a process of concentration of different species of capital (this is the accumulated labour of a person or a group which can be converted into other kinds of labour

---

5 The combination of both methodological tools is an excellent means to discover patterns of social relations. Verbruggen, Christophe 2007, p. 599.

6 Padgett and Ansell 1993, p. 1310.

7 Weber 1968; Bruhns 1988, p. 4; Ertman 2005.

8 Elias 1939, vol. 2, pp. 434–54; Genet 1992; Tilly and Blockmans, eds 1994; Bonney, ed. 1999.

or energy), such as capital of physical force or instruments of coercion (army, police), economic capital (money, economic resources), cultural or (better) informational capital (competencies, the right to determine norms, national culture), and symbolic capital (prestige, honour, authority).[9] All these species of capital correspond to a different field. This is a social arena of struggle over the appropriation of certain species of capital, capital being whatever is taken as significant for social agents. It is the concentration of different species of capital which constitutes the state as the holder of a sort of meta-capital granting power over other species of capital and over their holders. Concentration of the different species of capital leads to the emergence of a specific, properly 'state capital', which enables the state elite to exercise power over the territory and its inhabitants.

Curiously enough, Pierre Bourdieu did not elaborate on 'social capital' when 'rethinking the state', although he did innovative research on the concept. It refers to the sum of the resources, actual or virtual, that accrue to an individual or a group by virtue of possessing a durable network of more or less institutionalised relationships of mutual acquaintance and recognition. Through the application of economic capital, an individual or a group can invest in its social capital.[10] This facilitates cooperative action among individuals and therefore social capital is indispensable for individuals to function in society in general, and for rulers to administer the state in particular. Jan Dumolyn has recently pointed this out for the medieval county of Flanders, which is the case I discuss in this article. According to Dumolyn, following Blockmans, Genet, and others, the most appropriate concept for a definition of the medieval state is 'state feudalism'.[11] State feudalism is a specific set of political relations within a developed and a more or less centralised feudal society. Using the resources from fiscal revenues the prince could distribute money and other goods among his vassals, who, in turn, remained loyal to the prince. Through redistribution of economic capital the prince accumulated social capital. Moreover, all kinds of state capital could be allocated to the local officers and loyal social networks. The symbolic capital of the state, for example, legitimated the appointment

---

9   Bourdieu 1994, p. 4.
10   Bourdieu and Wacquant 1992, p. 119. Following Gaggio, I view social capital not as a publicly owned, unintentionally produced and functionally deployed resource (as James Coleman or Robert Putnam do). It is the property of individuals, and networks, as a resource that is constructed in the arena of political deliberation, and therefore as a relational practice that can be as productive of conflict and inequalities as of order and harmony. See Gaggio 2004, p. 510; and Halpern 2005, pp. 38–9.
11   Dumolyn 2007, pp. 126–8. See also Hicks 1995.

of local officers by members of court. Through this redistribution of state capital, a durable network of more or less institutionalised relationships of mutual trust originated between the sovereign and his officers, and among the court members themselves. As a result, state officers and princely confidants had social networks in town, which facilitated political collaboration between the state and local elites in the cities.[12] This 'urban' social capital was a necessary, but not a sufficient, basis for the political support for the central state, because other kinds of state capital were also needed to govern subordinated cities.[13]

Evidence suggests however that the political influence of the central state in fifteenth-century Flanders was limited. Historians and sociologists have already warned of the 'tyranny of the concept of the modern state'. Contrary to implicit assumptions which could be found in the use of the term state, medieval states were not ideal states in Weber's sense. Historians, of course, have to be aware that the coercion 'monopoly' of medieval states was not as developed as in present-day states.[14] Although the dukes of Burgundy, who were counts of Flanders, had accumulated significant power in the county during the fifteenth century, the urban elites still could rule their cities quite autonomously. Studies of conflict management in late medieval and early modern cities of the Low Countries, for example, demonstrate that the number of vendettas in late medieval cities declined without any interference from the state apparatus. In the course of the fifteenth century the Ghent elite increasingly succeeded in controlling conflicts among members of the elite inside its own milieu. By controlling and solving internal conflicts by themselves, the Ghent elite tried to consolidate their dominant political position in town. The internal pacification of these conflicts hindered subordinated groups in town, but also state officials, from interfering in elite affairs.[15] This article will show that the Burgundian court had accumulated certain means of coercion in fifteenth-century Flanders, but it also argues that elite factions in the Flemish town concentrated sufficient power to act independently from the court.

---

12   Boone 2001a; Dumolyn 2006b.

13   Sociological and political studies confirm Bourdieu's point of view concerning the necessity of social support of a government; see for example: Newton 2006; Jackman and Miller 1998; and Szreter 2002.

14   See for example the discussion between Davies 2003 and Reynolds 2003.

15   Buylaert 2007; Van Dijck 2006.

3   Medieval Factions

The term 'social capital' can also help to identify factions. In his study of medieval factions and their role in the political life of the medieval West, the French historian Jacques Heers defined factions as 'mysterious societies', informal institutions without formal statutes. In Heers' view, they are spontaneous and dynamic formations with a certain coherence, but without a durable organisation, comparable to modern influence and pressure groups.[16] Following Heers, but adding social theory, we can describe the 'mysterious' faction as a 'cluster of social capital'. A cluster is a segment of a (in this case, urban) society with a relatively high (social) density.[17] Members of the faction accumulated a large amount of social capital, which created trust between them.[18] Research on factions in medieval Italy and sixteenth-century England and France, for example, shows a faction consisted of an amalgam of familial relations, pre-existing social networks, economic partnerships, and durable friendships.[19] Jeremy Boissevain and others describe factions as not having clear-cut recruitment rules, nor demarcated boundaries, but that the mutual affection among members was general in factions.[20] Factions by their very nature are dynamic, for they are built up out of personal relations and informal ties, which are highly fluid. In short, an amorphous cluster of social capital united the members of the faction, which created mutual trust among themselves. This social trust facilitated the transaction of economic goods within a faction. Social capital channelled information, it was crucial to keep political secrets in the faction, it excluded non-members, and it generated social connections such as marriages between the members. In short, the social capital a faction assembled through its members was essential for its existence.

The city was the pre-eminent power basis of the medieval faction. Moreover, the political power of medieval factions depended on their power in towns.[21] Factions of different cities could join, however, and form leagues that could compete with factions of neighbouring regions or with state power. But the main political goal of medieval factions remained the growth of their power

16   Heers 1977, pp. 10–11.
17   High density refers to a great number of actual relations or social ties among the set of actors in the cluster, Emirbayer and Goodwin 1994, pp. 1447–9. See also Wasserman and Faust 1994; Carrington, Scott and Wasserman, eds 2005.
18   About this topic: Tilly 2005.
19   Martines 2003; Crouzet-Pavan 2001; Kent 1978; Lansing 1991; Ives 1979; Shephard 1992, pp. 723–8; Potter 2007.
20   Boissevain 1974, pp. 192–205; Nicholas, Ralph 1977, pp. 57–8.
21   Blockmans, Willem 1990b, pp. 32–3.

within a city, and when factions took office in towns, they always tried to monopolise power and to keep it as long as possible. Although they had no fixed political programme, as present-day political parties do, factions were driven by political and economic interests on the one hand, and ideology and religion on the other. For historical research has pointed out that not only money, power, and status, but also ideological and religious ideas were the motivating forces for political involvement by factions.[22] Those interests, ideas, and wishes could inspire factions to prefer a certain political organisation of urban institutions or even of the state apparatus, as would be the case in fifteenth-century Bruges. Because of different interests and diverging ideas on the manner of the government of a city, violent and long-standing political struggles could take place in cities among several factions. Quarrels about honour and prestige were often at the very beginning of factional struggle, and they regularly reignited violence among factions, but factions always had a common goal: the gaining of power to the detriment of (one or more) rival factions. Factional struggle mostly was fed by vengeance between both parties, but it always crystallised a violent confrontation of political and economic interests, and a struggle about valued and scarce resources.[23]

Because a faction is a very dynamic and mobile organisation, its boundaries are vague, and therefore difficult to reconstruct. But this does not mean that factions are a construct of the historian. In the case of the struggle between the so-called *Hoeken* ('Hooks') and the *Kabeljauwen* ('Cods') in fifteenth-century Holland, for example, factions had a definite identity, and contemporaries were very aware of the presence of factions and their struggle for power.[24] Intense factional struggles also appeared in the county of Flanders. In 1297–1304 the supporters of the count, the so-called *Clauwaerts*, were opposed to the *Leliaerts*, supporters of the French king.[25] In fourteenth-century Ghent, allies and rivals of the van Arteveldes struggled for power in the city and the county.[26] In 1446, a quarrel between Duke Philip the Good, on the one side, and the Ghent politician Daneel Sersanders and the allies 'of his party' (*van sijnder partye*), on the other, ended up in a county-wide war.[27] Dividing the citizens of Bruges in

---

22   Block 1993, pp. 2–3. See also Mayer 1985; Duffin 1996; Clay 1997; Luebke, 1997.
23   Crouzet-Pavan 2001, p. 152; Milani 2005, pp. 129–39; Maire-Vigueur 2003.
24   Van Gent 1994; Ter Braake 2007, pp. 258–309.
25   Boone 2002b; Cohn 2006.
26   Nicholas, David 1988.
27   De Potter, ed. 1885, p. 18; Haemers 2004b, p. 140. The mentioned chroniclers used a typical medieval vocabulary to describe political alliance and friendship, see Oschema 2006, pp. 255–69.

'sections' (*secten*) and 'gangs' (*benden*) during the Flemish Revolt, the anonymous chronicler quoted above described the ongoing factional struggle even as a social phenomenon. It is appropriate here to explain what this struggle was about.

4 The Flemish Revolt: The Battle over the Regency of Philip the Fair (1482–92)

On 27 March 1482 the Burgundian duchess Mary of Burgundy died from injuries she had sustained falling off her horse some weeks before.[28] In the turbulent decade that followed her death the regency of Philip the Fair (1478–1506), the minor son of Mary and her husband Maximilian, Archduke of Austria, was at stake. After the death of his wife, Maximilian strove to rule over the Low Countries in the name of his son, because the marriage with Mary had to expand the *Hausmacht* of the Habsburg dynasty. The leading politicians in the county of Flanders, however, determined to exercise power themselves in the name of Philip the Fair through a 'regency council'. The urban elite of Ghent, Bruges, and Ypres (the so-called Members of Flanders) considered the policy of Maximilian to be autocratic. In the years preceding Mary of Burgundy's death, Maximilian had implemented policies that increased the revenues of the ducal treasure-chest. These monetary and fiscal reforms, in collaboration with the belligerent policies of the court, had harmed the economy of the Flemish cities, whose wealth mainly depended on profits from international trade. The urban elite wanted to govern the county according to a federal state model, administered by the regency council, based on the principles of medieval constitutionalism and corporatism. The cities did not dismiss the central state, but reinterpreted it as a federation, a political union comprising a number of partially self-governing cities united by a central ('federal') government, the regency council.

With the inauguration of the 'regency council' in June 1483, the urban elite of Ghent, Bruges, and Ypres ruled as regents over Flanders with the help of several nobles, but without interference from Maximilian. Together with a political faction in Ghent and Ypres, the Bruges faction of Willem Moreel became known as the Philippins, which governed the county for two years. As will be further elaborated later on, Moreel was an important Bruges merchant who had been in Maximilian's service as 'superintendent of finances', together with

---

28   Blockmans and Prevenier 1999, pp. 196–203; Blockmans, Willem 1974a; Janssens 1996.

the Bruges merchant Maarten Lem. But after Moreel had criticised the policies of the archduke, Maximilian had imprisoned his former officer in December 1481. Thereupon, Moreel's political adversaries had taken over power in Bruges, which was the international gateway of the Flemish economy and the most important port and trading centre in northern Europe at this time.[29] Moreel's opponents were also united in a faction, which I will henceforth call the faction of Maximilian because the archduke supported the rule of this faction in Bruges. Maximilian's loss of authority after the death of Mary of Burgundy in March 1482, however, provided an excellent opportunity for Moreel's faction to return to power in Bruges. It successfully expelled Maximilian's faction from the town. In short, the death of Mary launched Moreel's faction on the county level into power. Moreel himself represented the city of Bruges at the county level in the regency council, while other members of the faction assumed political offices in the city itself. Maarten Lem, a close friend of Moreel, became sheriff of Bruges in 1483 and held that post until his death in March 1485. Jan van Nieuwenhove (son of Klaas), a relative of Lem, became burgomaster in 1482, and Moreel himself succeeded him in 1483. Jan de Keyt, Moreel's brother-in-law was responsible for city financing and the finances of the regency council.

But Maximilian and his Bruges confidants did not accept the governance by the regency council and, after negotiations failed, the archduke took up arms against the county in the autumn of 1484. Several military victories of Maximilian and an economic blockade of Bruges forced the city to surrender in June 1485. On the county level, Maximilian suppressed the regency council, and he installed an autocratic rule that deprived the cities of their political autonomy. After his faction (the so-called 'Monetans') had taken power in Bruges in June 1485, Willem Moreel and Jan van Nieuwenhove (son of Klaas) fled to Tournai and Arras. Jan de Keyt was arrested and decapitated in April 1486. Pieter Lanchals, Maximilian's principal financial councillor, became sheriff of Bruges, and another loyalist of the archduke, Joost van Varsenare, was appointed burgomaster. A violent repression by the sheriff and the Bruges city council secured the political position of Maximilian and his loyalists. The city was ruled with an 'authority of violence', a notion elaborated on by Lauro Martines. This special kind of government action spreads fear or even terror in urban society in order to obtain obedience and to silence internal opponents. Archduke Maximilian provided his network in town with the legitimacy and the financial resources for this repression. When they came to power in 1485, Lanchals and his factional partners believed that they had to destroy their internal opponents if they were

---

29   See for example Murray 2005.

to survive and lead. Government was the rule of those who had triumphed, and physical brutality was the carrier of authority. As Martines summarises it, might made right. Through trials and executions, the new urban government of Bruges tried to strengthen its political position, as Marc Boone has shown.[30]

However, in 1488 Maximilian's faction became itself a victim of a violent repression.[31] After the archduke had suffered several defeats in the war against France, the Ghent faction which had supported the regency council in 1483–5 succeeded in seizing power in Ghent. Meanwhile, the Bruges guilds, which had supported the faction of Willem Moreel during the reign of the regency council, rebelled in January 1488. On 31 January, they prevented Maximilian from leaving town at the moment he wanted to join his army to occupy the city. The Habsburg prince lacked the means to counteract the overwhelming political opposition in the town. He remained imprisoned in Bruges for three and a half months. Willem Moreel returned to town as his faction returned to power. Again, Bruges became a city of violence. The victorious rebels beheaded the leaders of Maximilian's faction, namely Pieter Lanchals and his brother-in-law Jan van Nieuwenhove (son of Michiel). Lanchals' head was hung on the city-gate to show the reign of terror was over. Moreel's faction ruled again over town and it took up its position in the regency council that was re-instated in May 1488.

After Maximilian was released from captivity in Bruges in May 1488, however, he gathered troops in Brabant to attack the county of Flanders. In spite of the military support of Philip of Cleves (a nobleman who had joined the opposition),[32] the regency council could not defend its position. After several months of warfare, the council was suppressed in October 1489. Maximilian again took over the regency of his son, and he restored the central authority of the state apparatus. But Ghent and Bruges soon took up arms again. In December 1490 Maximilian's forces managed to conquer Bruges after an economic blockade, and in July 1492 Ghent surrendered definitively. On 12 October 1492, Philip of Cleves, who had made Sluis into a base that could not be captured, accepted a favourable treaty (the 'treaty of Sluis') to lay down his arms. Like the Flemish cities, Philip of Cleves accepted the regency of Philip by Maximilian, who, from then on, fully ruled over the patrimony of Mary of Burgundy. On 12 October, the day that Christopher Columbus first set foot on American soil, the Flemish Revolt came to an end. In contrast to its actions in 1485, however, Maximilian's faction did not organise a severe repression after retaking Bruges

---

30   Martines 2005, p. 33; Boone 2003b.
31   Wellens 1965; Haemers and Lecuppre-Desjardin 2007.
32   Haemers, Van Hoorebeeck and Wijsman, eds 2007.

in December 1490. War continued in the county, and the emperor needed the support of Bruges to attack Sluis, so it focused on pacifying factional conflict in the town. Willem Moreel, who had been appointed sheriff of the city in 1489, was banished again, but no members of his faction were decapitated. Maximilian pardoned Moreel in 1493, when he returned to the city. Willem Moreel was allowed to move freely in the town, but he was not returned to power again. Probably the members of Maximilian's faction had learned from its failure to pacify Bruges in 1485. Because repression would presumably cause a new round of violence, the faction of Willem Moreel was not punished collectively. Nevertheless, any movement against the new regime was severely suppressed, and those who had supported the faction of Willem Moreel were barred from participation in city politics.

Two conclusions can be drawn from the story of the Flemish Revolt concerning state power, factional struggle, and the theoretical framework of this article. Firstly, Bourdieu's work clearly can be put to excellent use in analysing Maximilian of Austria's loss of power in the county of Flanders during the Flemish Revolt, for we are able to say the archduke lacked sufficient state capital to impose his authority firmly in Bruges after the death of Duchess Mary. For example, Maximilian had lost symbolic capital to the regency council in 1483 after the council successfully claimed the regency over his son. Acting as regent, the council possessed the authority to implement a legitimate policy in the county, while Maximilian was seen as a usurper. Nor did the archduke have the coercive means at crucial moments during his reign (for example, at the moment of his capture in Bruges) to suppress a grab for power by political adversaries. In February 1488 he lacked the money to mobilise troops to hinder his imprisonment by the Bruges craft guilds.[33] Because he had needed the political support of one faction in Bruges to rule the city in previous years, Maximilian had not been able to surpass local rivalries in the town. Moreover, he had to join a faction in Bruges to strengthen his political power in the city. But if this faction was chased out of Bruges, he lacked the social capital in town – the social networks and the mutual trust – to execute his policy. In short, to stay in power the state had to assemble a sufficient combination of symbolic, social, and economic capital.

Secondly, it is clear that Bourdieu's terminology is too vague to explain factional struggle. The use of these theoretical tools can help to describe Maximilian's loss of power, but they do not reveal the fundamental causes of the archduke's political defeat. Because state capital is impossible to quantify, a his-

---

33   Stabel and Haemers 2006.

torian cannot indicate how much state capital is needed for a ruler to stay in power. The story of the Flemish Revolt makes clear Maximilian's political position was weakened because a political alternative had succeeded in obtaining a more powerful position in the different fields Bourdieu distinguished, but a historian still has to outline the reasons why this happened. A detailed study on the political legitimacy and the ideological background of the regency council, for example, can explain why it succeeded in claiming the right to appoint officers in the name of the count, and why Maximilian's nominations were not accepted by the inhabitants of the Flemish cities. In what follows, however, I will concentrate on the social capital of Maximilian. Detailed research on the social composition of both factions in Bruges will concretise Bourdieu's terminology, and it can uncover why Maximilian's faction lost power in Bruges, because, as I argue, the social background of a faction is also responsible for its political victory or defeat.

5   The Nucleus of the Faction of Willem Moreel

The structural characteristics of factions differ. According to Jeremy Boissevain, there may be variations in the multiplexity and density of the network of relations within the factions.[34] Generally speaking, a faction consists of a core or nucleus and a periphery; factions display a concentric pattern. The core of the Maltese factions Boissevain studied, and of the faction of the Medici in medieval Florence, for example, consist of a leader who is tied to a number of persons by multiplex ties. The leader and these persons form the core of the faction. But factions in fifteenth-century Flanders differed slightly from this pattern. They did not have a clear central focus consisting of a single person. The term 'faction of Willem Moreel' is actually misleading, because Moreel's faction was not his property. Granted, Willem Moreel was one of the leading figures of the faction, but he could not direct it exclusively, as Lorenzo or Cosimo de' Medici governed his faction in contemporary Italy.[35] The 'godfather' of the Medici faction, the *pater familias*, held all power over the members of the family and their clients. Willem Moreel did not. The core of the faction Moreel consisted rather of several cliques and social networks which had multiple ties among them – there was little centrality in the nucleus of the faction. Willem

---

34   Boissevain 1974, pp. 195–200. Boissevain considers a multiplex network as a social network with two or more types of relations linking actors (see also Emirbayer and Goodwin 1994, p. 1448).

35   Martines 2003. See also Xhayet 1997, p. 397.

Moreel was a member of one clique, while the nucleus of the faction consisted of more equivalent social networks. Willem Moreel was linked to all members of his clique, but not to all members within the nucleus of the faction. This can explain why he was not the leader of the faction, although he held the most political power in the city of Bruges during the reign of the regency council in the Flemish Revolt. A closer look at the Moreel faction concretises these generalisations and demonstrates why one person could not dominate the faction.

The daily economic and social activities of Willem Moreel formed a social network among the Bruges merchants which had the characteristics of a clique. This kind of social network is a collection of actors with direct relations to every other actor in the group and these overlaps are regarded as structural cohesion.[36] Willem Moreel was born around 1425 and he inherited a successful trade business from his father.[37] The wealth Willem accumulated can still be admired because he ordered two portraits by Hans Memling.[38] His fortune was based on trade in spices as part of a family business. Like many tradesmen in fifteenth-century Bruges, he was in business with his relatives. His wife, Barbara van Hertsvelde, alias van Vlaenderenberch, was the daughter of Jan van Hertsvelde, the head of an important company which traded with Venetian merchants and the Holy See.[39] A record from 1488 states that Willem's brother Lieven and Lieven's brother-in-law Jan de Keyt, Willem's son-in-law Boudewijn van Heldinghe, and Willem's brother-in-law Denijs van Hertsvelde were business partners of Jan van Hertsvelde, then recently deceased.[40] The houses, the fiefs, and the immovable goods Willem Moreel and Jan de Keyt had in Bruges and in the countryside are a sign of the wealth of the business partners.[41] The socio-economic network of Willem Moreel was an exponent of the trade endogamy common in the Low Countries, because late medieval Bruges merchants and tradesmen married within their social class, and even within their trade. As Martha Howell has described it for late medieval Douai, this nucleus of relatives generated trust between trade partners, it protected the company from the risks of highly internationalised commerce, and as a consequence it lowered

---

36   Erickson 1997; Scott, John 2000, pp. 114–20.
37   Haemers 2007d; Janssens 2003, pp. 83–4.
38   Borchert, ed. 2005, pp. 168, 172.
39   Schulte 1904, vol. 1, p. 8; Vaes 1919, vol. 1, p. 195.
40   Doehard 1963, vol. 2, p. 102; Mus 1964, p. 96; On the economic activities of compagnies in Bruges: Stabel 1996.
41   Willem Moreel had several houses in Bruges, a fief in Zuienkerke ('*Oostcleyghem*'), Jan de Keyt had fiefs in Moerkerke, Oostkerke, and Dudzele (Janssens 2003, p. 70; Haemers 2007d, pp. 682–3; State Archives of Belgium, Bruges, Burg van Brugge, no. 64, fol. 14ᵛ; Archives départementales du Nord, Lille, B 17732, 'Keyt').

transaction costs in trade.[42] In the Flemish Revolt the nucleus of the faction would also protect Willem Moreel in times of political crisis. In February 1482, for example, Jan de Keyt was one of Willem's sureties when he was released from Maximilian's prison.[43]

A second social network in the nucleus of the Willem Moreel faction was the network of Maarten Lem, the second surety of Willem in February 1482 and his 'political twin brother'. This network was not a clique, but a centralised network with Maarten Lem and Klaas van Nieuwenhove as key actors, connected to the other members without ties between the latter. Like Willem Moreel, Maarten Lem was a wealthy merchant. Both were members of the exclusive crossbow-men's guild of Saint George of Bruges.[44] Maarten Lem imported sugar from the Portuguese island of Madeira and sold it on the international market of Bruges, thereby becoming a sugar baron.[45] Maarten Lem was also a beneficiary of trade endogamy. He was married to Adriana van Nieuwenhove, the daughter of Klaas. This was a lucrative marriage for both parties. Maarten had a considerable fortune, and Adriana came from a wealthy family of Bruges merchants, brokers and politicians. By marrying his children to rich merchants and influential brokers, Klaas van Nieuwenhove had built up a huge socio-economic network. His daughter Margaret married Cornelis Breydel, the dean of the butcher's guild in 1479 and 1483. He originated from a wealthy family which had several fiefs in the countryside of Bruges.[46] In 1484, the Moreel faction made him burgomaster of the Bruges councillors.[47] Another son-in-law of Klaas van Nieuwenhove, Arnoud Adornes, was councillor of Bruges on the 1477 board of magistrates headed by Maarten Lem.[48] Arnoud Adornes originated from a family of foreign merchants who traded in exotic fruit and spices, among other goods. Klaas's sons also belonged to the Moreel faction. His son Jan was kept under house arrest by Maximilian's faction when Willem Moreel was arrested in December 1481, because he also was accused of treason. Maarten Lem was Jan's surety when he was allowed to move freely in town again in February 1482.[49] The faction elected Jan as burgomaster of Bruges after the death

42   Howell 2001, p. 194.
43   Vorsterman, ed. 1531, fols. 222^v–224^v.
44   Janssens 2006, p. 63.
45   Everaert 1993; Paviot 2006, pp. 28–32.
46   State Archives of Belgium, Bruges, chambers of accounts, no. 17404, fol. 4^r; and State Archives of Belgium, Bruges, Burg van Brugge, no. 64, fol. 261^v.
47   Municipal Archives of Bruges, register of the city council, 1468–1501, fol. 141^v.
48   Gailliard, Jean-Jacques 1857–64, vol. 1, p. 139; On the Adornes, see Geirnaert and Vandewalle, eds 1983.
49   Vorsterman, ed. 1531, fols. 222^v–224^v.

of Duchess Mary and he was sheriff of Bruges during the period of the first regency council. Jan was a powerful broker who lived in the house *Casselberg* in the centre of the city – a house that is known as one of the 'seven miracles' of Bruges.[50] A brother of Jan van Nieuwenhove, Antoon, was appointed captain of the castle of Sluis and bailiff for the countryside surrounding Bruges (the *Houtsche*) in 1483.[51] He was dean of the guild of the soap makers in 1480, a craft business which had provided him with the means to afford a fief in Adegem.[52] A cousin of the van Nieuwenhove brothers, Cornelis Metteneye, was burgomaster and military captain of the Liberty of Bruges in 1484, the surrounding countryside around the city. He also originated from a broker's family.[53]

Briefly, two conclusions can be drawn from this short overview of the two networks that made up the core of the faction of Willem Moreel. Firstly, in contrast to generalising statements of modernists about medieval factions, the basic cement of the Moreel faction was not retainership.[54] Because marriage patterns and kinship relations were the most important social structures in late medieval towns, one should not be surprised that relational ties bound the Moreel faction together.[55] As in early modern factions, pre-existing bonds between members of the nucleus seem to have determined which faction an individual would join in the first place. Ties of kinship and comradeship therefore exerted a centripetal pressure. Secondly, the faction also concentrated economic wealth. The political power of the faction reflected a considerable fortune and economic capital. This wealth could be used in times of political need. Several members of the faction had lent money to the financial administration of Maximilian in November 1477 when it urgently needed liquidity to wage the war against France. Jan de Keyt (a member of the Moreel network), Jan de Boot (another surety of Willem Moreel after his release in 1482), his brother Cornelis de Boot, and the already mentioned Klaas van Nieuwenhove (of the Maarten Lem network), for example, lent 750 *livres parisis* on crown jewels to the arch-

50 Municipal Archives of Bruges, Klerk van de Vierschare, no. 828bis, p. 253.

51 He was a captain in the Bruges army that fought against Maximilian and died in battle in 1489. Haemers 2005b, pp. 252–3.

52 Municipal Archives of Bruges, accounts of the city, 1479–80, fol. 167^v. About his fief: State Archives of Belgium, Bruges, Burg van Brugge, no. 64, fol. 263^v; and State Archives of Belgium, Bruges, chambers of accounts, no. 13788, fol. 2^v.

53 Haemers 2005b, pp. 235–6.

54 Reviewing historical research on factions, Shephard 1992, p. 774 stated 'natural ties of local and regional honor' shaped factions in the era of bastard feudalism.

55 See for example Bourdieu 1972 and Lévi-Strauss 1949. For medieval Flemish cities: Dumolyn 2002; Howell 2007, pp. 216–53.

duke. Willem Moreel lent 658 *livres parisis*, Maarten Lem 1200 *livres parisis* on that occasion.[56] The social networks of Maarten Lem and Willem Moreel supported Maximilian's war in 1477 because the invasion of French troops in the Low Countries damaged international trade. But when the archduke's defensive war changed into offensive strikes against France in 1481, he lost his support among the Bruges elite because these costly wars would harm its economic interests again. At that moment dynastic politics served only to knit the social networks of the Bruges merchants even more closely together.

For the members of the nucleus of the Moreel faction, the faction acted as a kind of political and social security. It guaranteed its members protection during risky business ventures, it guarded them from political attacks, and, collectively, it defended their common interests. Because the nucleus of the faction consisted of several dense social networks and cliques, and not of one family alone, as with the Medici in Florence, the faction could not be dominated by a *pater familias*. But its composite character did not prevent a high degree of solidarity among the different networks of the nucleus. As a result of marriages, kinship ties, business contacts, and political activities, the faction seems to have been a cohesive cluster of social capital. Through these means the network consisted of actors connected through many direct, reciprocal relations that enabled them to share information, create solidarity, and act collectively. Numerous direct contacts among all network members dispose a group toward homogeneity of thought, identity, and behaviour.[57] As in the case for example of seventeenth-century La Rochelle, the highly internationalised commerce of Bruges also provided leading urban networks with economic resources, which could be applied in wartime or in a period of political struggle. The socio-economic connections of the leaders of factions consequently were logistically vital for the maintenance of position.[58] The analysis of the social background of the nucleus of the faction of Willem Moreel shows it disposed of considerable economic and social capital that could be used to wield power in the city. But this does not explain the social support the faction had in Bruges during the Flemish Revolt.

---

56   Archives départementales du Nord, Lille, B 3495, nr. 123686.
57   About cohesive groups: Erickson 1997, p. 153; Wasserman and Faust 1994, chapter 7; Knoke and Yang 2008, pp. 72–3.
58   Robbins, Kevin 1995.

6   The Periphery of the Faction of Willem Moreel: From Coalition to Faction

A closer look at the periphery of the faction of Willem Moreel demonstrates that its social capital crossed the boundaries of the nucleus. In 1477 political allies who initially were not linked to the social networks of the faction had entered into a political coalition with its nucleus out of political interests and ideological motives, most of them originating from the urban craft guilds. In a second phase these allies were connected with the core of the faction by social (and maybe economic) ties, forming the periphery of the faction. Or, one can say, the political and ideological factors that were at the basis of the political coalition between the nucleus and the future periphery of the faction in 1477 were replaced by multiple social ties during the following years. These ties connected the nucleus of the faction with its periphery, a connection that was even strengthened during the Flemish Revolt.

The public support and the political authority of the Moreel faction started in 1477. As in 1482, the unexpected death of the head of the Burgundian dynasty in January 1477 had also altered the political history of the county of Flanders. The father of Duchess Mary, Charles the Bold, died in battle before Nancy in an attempt to conquer the Duchy of Lorraine. The Estates-General of the Low Countries required the observance of political privileges at that moment, and in several cities opponents of the dynasty took power from ducal loyalists who had been appointed by Charles the Bold. In early spring 1477, Willem Moreel emerged as the spokesman of a coalition of Bruges merchants and the craft guilds who wanted to obtain privileges from the court.[59] The spice-trader only had a little political experience (he had served as alderman in 1472), and therefore he was not hampered by association with the regime of Charles the Bold. In the new city council that was elected in April 1477 by representatives of the craft guilds and rebelling merchant networks, Moreel was appointed as 'principal committee of the urban treasury'; his brother-in-law Jan de Keyt became burgomaster.[60] With his appointment as burgomaster of the aldermen on 2 September 1478, Moreel reached the top of the political lad-

---

59   In February 1477, for example, Willem travelled to see the widow of Charles, Margaret of York, in Malines to negotiate a resolution to the political crisis (in order to 'vercrighene zekere nieuwe pointen ende artikelen van previlegen'; Municipal Archives of Bruges, accounts of the city, 1467–77, fol. 128ᵛ). On the revolt of 1477 see Blockmans, Willem, ed. 1985a.

60   He was 'principael bouchoudere' of the city, Municipal Archives of Bruges, accounts of the city, 1478–9, fol. 44ᵛ.

der within city government.[61] As a result, Willem Moreel and his social network filled the political vacuum in Bruges after the revolt of 1477. One could say that the revolt made Willem a rising star in Bruges politics. The same can be said of the other members within the nucleus of his faction: Maarten Lem, Jan van Nieuwenhove, Jan van Riebeke, and Jan de Keyt. Except for September 1481, when Maximilian took over power in the city, in every year during the reign of Mary of Burgundy a member of the Moreel faction was appointed burgomaster of the city.[62] After the revolt of 1477, the rebelling social networks of Bruges merchants had become the nucleus of a political faction whose social interdependence and political authority would grow through the years, and would rise to a climax during the Flemish Revolt.

But Willem Moreel and his companions did not rule the city alone during the reign of Mary of Burgundy. For in 1477 representatives and leaders of the urban craft guilds had formed a political coalition with the nucleus of the Moreel faction – a coalition that would govern the city in the following years. Thanks to the coalition with the nucleus of the Moreel faction, the guilds returned to power in 1477 and regained the political position they had lost after the repression of the Bruges revolt of 1438.[63] In April 1477 representatives of the urban craft guilds were elected to the city boards of Bruges. The different parts of the coalition were independent in organisation, but dependent on each other for the fulfilment of their common political goal, namely the gaining of power to the detriment of the supporters of Charles the Bold. Political interests, economic goals, and ideological factors bound the alliance together. Because the common basis of the wealth of the Moreel faction and of the craft guilds was the international economy, it is not surprising the faction had a forceful economic policy in mind. They tried to maintain a stable monetary climate, without the manipulation of the currency. Craft guilds and merchant networks intensely denounced both the warlike policy of Charles (and later on, of Maximilian) and autocratic fiscal policies. In exchange for the maintenance of their economic and social rights, the craft guilds accepted the supremacy in Bruges politics of the social networks around Willem Moreel and Maarten Lem.[64]

---

61   Municipal Archives of Bruges, register of the city council, 1468–1501, fol. 94ᵛ.
62   Maarten Lem was burgomaster in 1477 and 1480, Willem Moreel in 1478, Jan van Riebeke (who was imprisoned together with Willem Moreel in December 1481) exercised this function in 1479.
63   In 1438 Duke Philip the Good had suppressed a revolt of the craft guilds by abolishing the political and economic rights of the guilds. See Dumolyn 1997.
64   About the Bruges craft guilds: Stabel 2004, pp. 187–98; Dumolyn 1999.

Ideological motives, too, united both coalition partners, for the coalition ruled the city in accordance with the principles of corporatism. This was a social system that predicated respect for privileges, the right of self-government of corporations (as the craft guilds), and the political participation of these privileged groups in urban society.[65] During the Flemish Revolt both craft guilds and merchants heavily defended the political autonomy of the city of Bruges and its corporations, and consequently the coalition entered into a conflict when Maximilian tried to impose an autocratic rule in the city. Moreover, the cities in the county of Flanders had a long tradition of defending a political programme of self-governance of corporate bodies in society *vis-à-vis* the centralised mode of government adhered to by the dukes of Burgundy.[66] In Bruges of the 1480s the powerful ideas of corporatism and urban autonomy were defended by a coalition, evolving into a faction, which could mobilise considerable economic resources to resist an unwanted kind of politics.

Through the reign of Mary of Burgundy the initial temporary alliance between merchant networks and the urban craft guilds shifted to a permanent unit of nucleus and periphery of the same faction. Both parts of the coalition, of course, had political reasons for cohesion but slowly, and surely, the political coalition melted together to become a faction because several ties between core and periphery were created. The ties by which the nucleus 'recruited' its followers were diverse: as there were daily contacts, economic partnerships, friendships, etc. These ties increasingly grew in density and in multiplicity between 1477 and 1482, but they are difficult to reconstruct. One can presume economic contacts between the representatives of the craft guilds and the merchant networks of Willem Moreel and Maarten Lem were manifold, but this is impossible to verify because the personal bookkeeping of these persons has not been preserved. The historian unfortunately lacks information about all social ties in the faction, because the sources are very fragmentary. Furthermore, we cannot reconstruct daily contacts between the members of the faction, although they certainly must have taken place.

However, a remarkable marriage pattern does appear in the (scarce) sources. I have already mentioned that some members of the social network of Maarten Lem occupied important political functions in the Bruges craft guilds. His brother-in-law Antoon van Nieuwenhove was dean of the soap makers; another brother-in-law, Cornelis Breydel, was dean of the butchers. But matrimonial bonds also crossed boundaries between the periphery and the nucleus, by

---

65   Prak 2006, pp. 74–82.
66   See [Patterns]; Boone 2007b.

which the faction received a high kinship density. Several members of the social networks of Willem Moreel and Maarten Lem were related to the representatives of the guilds that were appointed to the city council of April 1477, of which Jan de Keyt was burgomaster and Willem Moreel principal treasurer. Councillor Boudin Petyt, for example, the chief of the guild of the cap makers, was married to Katrien Losschaert, the sister of Jan Losschaert, the burgomaster of the board of the councillors (called the *courpse*).[67] Jan Losschaert was married to a niece of Marc van den Velde, the first aldermen in April 1477. He was the brother-in-law of Jan de Keyt, who was married to his sister Catherine.[68] A second brother-in-law of Marc van den Velde was Cornelis de Boot, the brother of Jan who had been a surety of Willem Moreel in February 1482.[69] Two other brothers-in-law of Marc, Steven van den Gheinste and Colard de Labye, who were members of the mercers' guild (Colard was dean of this guild in 1477), were also appointed aldermen on the city board of April 1477. The daughter of Frans Ridsaert (alderman for the butcher's guild in 1477) married the son of Maarten Lem; another daughter of Frans married the already-mentioned Boudin Petyt.[70] Another son of Maarten Lem married the daughter of Jan Dhamere, an influential member of the cooper's guild.[71] All of the above-mentioned relatives exercised political power in the city boards composed by the faction of Willem Moreel during the Flemish Revolt.[72] In short, the single-stranded political tie between rebelling social networks and the political allies of the coalition of 1477 had expanded to many-stranded transactional and social ties between nucleus and periphery of one and the same faction in 1482. Social networks henceforth crossed the boundaries of the periphery and nucleus.

What about the economic position of the members of the craft guilds that were linked to the faction? Unfortunately, their personal wealth cannot be analysed because personal archives are not preserved. Yet if the sale of public annuities by the city of Bruges is taken into account, we can catch a glimpse

---

67   Municipal Archives of Bruges, fonds Adornes, no. 361; State Archives of Belgium, Bruges, chambers of accounts, no. 17412, fol. 1^v.

68   Municipal Archives of Bruges, procuraties, 1485 fol. 132^r, and 1492, fol. 2^r.

69   For what follows, see Gailliard, Jean-Jacques 1857–64, vol. 3, p. 373.

70   Municipal Archives of Bruges, fonds Adornes, nos. 363, 368.

71   Gailliard, Jean-Jacques 1857–64, vol. 1, p. 321.

72   Namely Marc van de Velde and Steven van der Gheinste were made part of the city bench that was appointed after the imprisonment of Maximilian in February 1488; Jan Dhamere was burgomaster. Frans Ridsaert was councillor of Bruges in 1483 and 1488. Boudin Petyt, Jan Losschaert, and Colard de Labye were made part of the city bench of April 1482 that was appointed after the death of Mary of Burgundy (Municipal Archives of Bruges, register of the city council, 1468–1501, fols. 123^v, 172^r). See also Van Leeuwen 2006a.

of their economic and financial background. In cases of acute financial short-age the city of Bruges sold annuities (*renten*) on the urban domain to raise the urban income. Citizens therefore could invest in the public debt of the city by buying annuities, which were paid off with an annual interest of six to seven percent. An in-depth analysis of the social and economic background of the annuity purchases of the period this article deals with has shown that not only wealthy members of the urban elite but also broad middle classes could afford these *renten*.[73] The concern of supporting urban politics certainly was a motivation for an annuity buyer to invest in the public debt of the city. But a purchaser needed financial reserves in the first place to buy an annuity. The purchase of an annuity therefore can provide information about the financial background of the annuity buyer. As expected, Willem Moreel held many annu-ities from Bruges. Fourteen annuities bought during the reign of Mary of Bur-gundy provided him with an annual income of 1302 *livres* 10 *sous parisis*.[74] The above-mentioned members of the craft guilds however could not afford such a high number of annuities. Nevertheless, they also invested personal finances in the public debt of the city. During the reign of Mary of Burgundy Steven van der Gheinste, Boudin Petyt, Jan Dhamere, Frans Ridsaert, and Colard de Labye bought a total of nine annuities, providing them with a total annual income of 348 *livres parisis*.[75] The purchase of these annuities demonstrates that these five persons did not belong to the financial nor to the economic elite of town. But nevertheless, their economic activities as craftsmen provided them with a certain wealth that allowed them to invest in the public debt of the city. The relatives of the nucleus of the faction therefore did not belong to the 'popular crowd' of Bruges, but probably to what can be called the middle class of the town. As in medieval Ghent, the Bruges middle class therefore appeared to be a fierce advocate of urban autonomy and the corporate model of urban govern-ment.[76]

In times of need the faction members invested their financial reserves in politics. One of these public investments can even help us to say more about the extent of the political support of the Moreel faction in town. After Max-imilian of Austria was released from the city, the urban government organised

---

73 Derycke 2003.

74 Municipal Archives of Bruges, accounts of the city, 1476–7, fols. 99^v, 110^v; 1477–8, fol. 118^v, 126^v–128^r; 1478–9, fols. 151^{r-v}.

75 Steven van der Gheinste and Boudin Petyt had bought one annuity each, Frans Ridsaert and Colard de Labye two each, and Jan Dhamere three. Municipal Archives of Bruges, accounts of the city, 1477–8, fols. 115^{r-v}, 118^v, 122^{r-v}; 1478–9, 150^r; 1481–2, 143^r.

76 Prak 2006, pp. 74–6; Dambruyne 2003.

two voluntary loans by citizens to pay the wages of soldiers who fought German troops in Brabant under the leadership of Philip of Cleves.[77] We can presume that the creditors who subscribed to the loan, supported the Philippin regime because the loans were voluntary and the city did not pay off its debt with an interest (in contrast to public annuities). In May and July 1488, 494 citizens and forty-seven craft guilds lent a total sum of 58,937 *livres 4 sous parisis*.[78] With this sum 1,000 unskilled labourers could be paid for twenty-five days' work.[79] The citizens lent 49,021 *livres 4 sous parisis* (83.2% of the total amount of the two loans). One-hundred and eighty-nine of the 494 citizens lent twice. We were able to find a social tie between fifty-four persons of those who lent twice and the nucleus of the faction of Willem Moreel. The fifty-four faction members (11% of the total number of creditors) lent for a total sum of 10,075 *livres 12 sous parisis* (20.6% of the total loan of the 494 citizens).

Three other observations can be made regarding these figures. Firstly, the archival sources of the city of Bruges are inadequate to reconstruct the political support of the Moreel faction. Possibly all creditors were linked socially with the nucleus of the faction, but information about the social ties of most creditors is absent. Secondly, what does this voluntary loan tell us about the number of supporters of the faction? About 1% of the population of Bruges supported the regime financially.[80] Of course, only wealthy political supporters with a lot of cash available could lend to the city. The figures mentioned above therefore only reflect the political support of the economic elite and the (upper) middle class of the town and not the popular support of the faction. Logically, several members of the nucleus of the faction lent giant sums of money, such as the mother of Jan van Nieuwenhove (son of Klaas), who lent a total sum of 240 *livres parisis* to the city in both loans – Jan van Nieuwenhove himself and Willem Moreel had not yet returned to the city in May 1488. Also the members of the craft guilds who had married relatives of the members of the nucleus of the faction, such as Steven van der Gheinste, Colard de Labye, Boudin Petyt, Frans Ridsaert, and Jan Dhamere, contributed to the loan (for a total sum of 1488 *livre parisis*).[81]

---

77   Haemers 2007c, pp. 55–8.
78   The list of taxpayers is edited by Blockmans, Willem 1973. A short analysis of the political circumstances of these loans: Blockmans, Willem 1971, p. 138. The original account in Municipal Archives of Bruges, accounts of the war, no. 5 (1488–9), fols 4ʳ–19ᵛ.
79   An unskilled labourer daily earned about 48 *denarius parisis* in 1488 (Scholliers 1965, vol. 2, pp. 87–160).
80   In 1477 Bruges had about 40,000–45,000 inhabitants. Janssens 1983; Dumolyn 1999, p. 63.
81   Respectively 204 *livre parisis*, 300 *livre parisis*, 600 *livre parisis*, 96 *livre parisis*, and 288 *livre parisis*. Blockmans, Willem 1973, pp. 234, 240, 244, 267, 278.

Thirdly, faction members, who formed one tenth of the creditors, therefore provided one fifth of the total loan. This observation can confirm the presumption that at least this group of creditors were political supporters of the Philippin regime. The political sympathies of all moneylenders are difficult to reconstruct, but we can presume the financial efforts of the above-mentioned members are a sign of their political loyalty to the nucleus of the faction. The social capital of the faction therefore was a handy tool for the mobilisation of logistically vital resources for the political and military actions of the leaders of the faction. It made economic resources available for the leaders of the faction, which defended intensively common interests and ideas. The voluntary loan of 1488 and the presence of the social networks described above demonstrate that the political programme promulgated by Moreel's faction enjoyed the support of a powerful segment of Bruges society. Although it is difficult to prove due to the lack of sources allowing us to uncover the social ties of the members of the faction with lower classes in urban society, connections with other networks and political allies probably made the faction a deep-rooted political organisation. During the Revolt, the faction nevertheless became a reservoir of social relations through which it was able to recruit support to counter its rivals and mobilise support to attain its goals. Its social capital was a powerful mobilising force, a treasure chest in times of need, and a strong conductor of political ideas on corporatism. At this point we can ask if the rival faction had a similar weapon.

7   The Social Composition of the Faction of Maximilian

The faction of Maximilian the – the Monetans – which supported the regency of the Habsburg prince during the Flemish Revolt, had branches in every town in Flanders. They had a similar composition to the Bruges faction of Willem Moreel, and the factions of Maximilian in the different cities were bound together politically and socially on a county-wide level.[82] As was true for the Moreel faction, the nucleus of Maximilian's faction in Bruges consisted of a core and a periphery. The core of the Maximilian faction in Bruges was the social network of Pieter Lanchals, Maximilian's financial advisor. A native of Bruges, Pieter Lanchals originated from a lower social stratum, but because he was very talented in financial affairs, he rose high in ducal service. Charles the Bold had a

---

82   The two daughters of Mathijs Peyaert, the leader of the Ghent faction of Maximilian, were married to members of the Bruges faction of Maximilian: Yeronimus Lauwerein and Filips van den Berghe. Fris 1901e; Haemers and Soens 2007.

use for commoners with political insight, talent, and familiarity with financial techniques, because, like Maximilian, he needed politically independent servants who could devise clever policies to support his political ambitions with financial means. In these circumstances, Lanchals progressed rapidly through the bureaucratic ranks.[83] Maximilian appointed Lanchals to the 'financial commission' he erected in the Autumn of 1477 and from then on the Bruges native made financial policy for his lord – he did this for a short time together with Willem Moreel and Maarten Lem in 1479–80. After the departure of Maarten Lem and the imprisonment of Willem Moreel in 1481, Lanchals would become a personal rival of his former colleagues. During the reign of the regency council he was banished from the county, and his goods were confiscated. However, after Maximilian had conquered the county in June 1485, Lanchals was appointed sheriff of Bruges, a position he used to carry out Maximilian's policies. In short, Pieter Lanchals obeyed his master, and probably even influenced Maximilian on financial policy issues. In return, Lanchals was rewarded with gifts, money, and luxurious goods with which he could live a lavish 'noble' lifestyle.[84] For his task as Maximilian's financial commissioner, for example, he received a daily wage of 48 *sous parisis* in 1480 from the general treasurer of Burgundian finances.[85] As a part of bastard feudalism, this kind of patronage was a typical tool of centralisation used by princes in the construction of their state apparatus.[86] Due to his loyalty to Maximilian, the *'parvenu'* Lanchals was able to climb the social ladder. Thanks to the loyalty of talented officers, the court could increase its social capital in town.

When governing Bruges, Pieter Lanchals was surrounded by a network of relatives. Maybe it was a clique, but there is a lack of source material to reconstruct all the social ties between the members in order to confirm this hypothesis. Pieter Lanchals was married to Catherine van Nieuwenhove. Her father, Michiel van Nieuwenhove, was the brother of Klaas, whose children were part of the Moreel faction. But the children of Michiel chose the opposite side of the political spectrum. This fact demonstrates that kinship does not always determine political choices. All kinds of ties and contacts between people are responsible for their political behaviour. As the already mentioned Bruges chronicler stated: political lines sometimes crossed families during the Flemish Revolt. Jan van Nieuwenhove (son of Michiel), for example, one of Lanchals' brothers-

---

83   Boone 1990d.
84   A similar case, of Pieter Bladelin, is dealt with in De Clercq, Dumolyn and Haemers 2007.
85   This is about twelve times the daily wage of an unskilled labourer in Bruges (Archives départementales du Nord, Lille, B 2121, fol. 93ᵛ).
86   A case-study about patronage in fifteenth-century Flanders in Blockmans, Willem 1988c.

in-law, became burgomaster of Bruges in September 1487, when Lanchals was sheriff of the town. Jan's son Maarten, whose portrait was painted by Hans Memling, also made a career in ducal service. He was the receiver of extraordinary revenues for the count of Flanders after 1490.[87] While Maximilian held power as regent for his son (June 1485–January 1488), other members of Lanchals' social network also held political office in Bruges or at court. Michiel van Theimseke, another of Lanchals' brothers-in-law, was treasurer in the city in 1487.[88] Jacob Dheere, a cousin of Jan van Nieuwenhove (son of Michiel), was appointed alderman in June 1487, the same year that his brother Michiel Dheere became treasurer of Bruges in June 1485. Pieter Lanchals' son-in-law, Wouter Merghaert, was a process-server in the Council of Flanders.[89] Another son-in-law, Nicolas van Delft, was clerk of the city council from June 1485 until its demise in February 1488. He would be appointed burgomaster of Bruges after the surrender of the city in December 1490.[90] These examples show that Pieter Lanchals utilised a social network that joined him in political service to Maximilian during his regency. Lanchals therefore acted as a broker for the distribution of rewards, honours, and offices controlled by the Burgundian court. This patronage and brokerage was the vital glue of the core of Maximilian's faction in town, which created strong resemblances with early modern court factions.[91]

The periphery of the faction comprised two components, which entered into a coalition with the social network of Pieter Lanchals after the death of Mary of Burgundy in 1482. But in contrast to the Moreel faction, the Lanchals faction hardly had left the stage of political coalition, because the two components were hardly linked between themselves. The first component consisted of a group of frustrated wealthy citizens who had been sidelined during the reign of Mary of Burgundy by the faction of Willem Moreel. For example, several aldermen appointed by Maximilian in June 1485 after his conquest of the country had previously held office during the reign of Charles the Bold, but had been removed from office by the revolt of 1477.[92] Personal rivals of Willem Moreel were also put into office during Maximilian's regency. The brothers Houtmaerct

87   Archives départementales du Nord, Lille, B 2140, fol. 92^r. In 1487 he was already in civil service as receiver of tolls in Bruges (Municipal Archives of Bruges, accounts of the city, 1487–8, fol. 31^r). His portrait is reproduced in Borchert, ed. 2005, p. 173.

88   Municipal Archives of Bruges, register of the city council, 1468–1501, fol. 165^v.

89   Municipal Archives of Bruges, accounts of the city, 1477–8, fol. 154^v.

90   Municipal Archives of Bruges. register of the city council, 1468–1501, fol. 185^r.

91   Shephard 1992, pp. 723–4; Ives 1979, pp. 3–7.

92   For example, Geraard de Groote, Jan van Wulfsberghe, and Jan Dhondt (Municipal Archives of Bruges, register of the city council, 1468–1501, fols. 148^v, 157^r).

who had a personal quarrel with Willem Moreel in 1478, henceforth joined the Maximilian faction.[93] Some of the members of this component of Maximilian's faction also had made a fortune in international trade, such as Donaas de Moor. But because they had implemented a severe fiscal policy during the reign of Charles the Bold, they were condemned for corruption in the revolt of 1477 or banished from town. After the faction of Willem Moreel had taken over power, Donaas de Moor, for example, had to pay back the wages he had earned as city councillor in the years preceding the revolt – he was banished in 1483.[94] During the period 1485–8 the personal and political rivals of the Moreel faction finally found the opportunity to return to the political scene. But the social support for this coalition partner of the network of Pieter Lanchals was low. Most of the wealthy patricians married internally and none of them had social connections with representatives of the guilds.

Some of them, however, had social ties with the second component of the periphery of the faction, which consisted of noblemen from the Liberty of Bruges. Those noblemen were also ousted politically from the city of Bruges during the reign of Mary of Burgundy, because the Bruges craft guilds had fought in 1477 against the political power of the Liberty of Bruges, the surrounding countryside of Bruges that was ruled by a council (termed the fourth 'Member of Flanders'). The main source of animosity between the Bruges craft guilds and the council of the Liberty of Bruges council was economic competition, because the Liberty was home to economic rivals of the craft guilds. By abolishing the political power of the council of the Liberty of Bruges in 1477,[95] the city of Bruges again became the political centre of its surrounding countryside. When the guilds gained power in the city council of 1477, they again had the means to dominate the surrounding countryside – to the detriment of the rural nobility that had previously governed the Liberty. As a consequence the nobles joined Maximilian in his opposition to the growing power of the coalition between the networks around Willem Moreel and the urban guilds in 1477. The nobles of the Liberty of Bruges were wealthy men who had lost

---

93 In August 1478 Renier Houtmaerct (alderman in 1486) was forced to go on a pilgrimage by the Bruges city council, led by Maarten Lem, because he had called Willem Moreel a 'son of a whore' ('hoerezuene'; Municipal Archives of Bruges, Memoriael van de Camere, 1478, fol. 19^r). In June 1485, Maximilian appointed his brother Willem Houtmaerct, who also had quarrelled with Moreel in 1478, as one of the new treasurers of the city (Municipal Archives of Bruges, register of the city council, 1468–1501, fol. 148^v).

94 Municipal Archives of Bruges, accounts of the city, 1467–77, fol. 34^v and 1482–3, fols. 40^v–41^r.

95 In spring 1477, the Bruges craft guilds successfully had strived for the loss of the political rights of the Liberty (Prevenier 1961).

power in 1477, but in the Flemish Revolt they finally got the chance to return to the highest political levels. In June 1485, Joost van Varsenare, a nobleman who had a number of fiefs in the Liberty of Bruges, became burgomaster of the aldermen of Bruges.[96] Several nobles, like the brothers van Halewyn, joined the burgomaster in his attempt to dominate Bruges politics in the following years. The burgomaster of the councillors in 1485 was Joost van Halewyn. His half-brother Karel van Halewyn became bailiff of the city and the Liberty of Bruges. Joost's father-in-law, Guy de Baenst, was appointed burgomaster of the Liberty of Bruges, restored in its political rights by Maximilian in October 1485.[97] Pieter Lanchals married the daughter of one of them, Roeland van Halewyn, in October 1486.[98] In short, the nobles of the Liberty of Bruges regained power in 1485 by joining the social network around Pieter Lanchals. They were socially connected by family ties, and some of their daughters were married to Bruges aldermen during the reign of Charles the Bold. Jacob Dheere was married to Kateline van Stavele, daughter of Jan, a noble alderman of the Liberty of bruges. Jacob was the burgomaster of the Liberty in 1486 and decapitated by the faction of Willem Moreel in March 1488.[99] But the nobles had neither political nor social connections with the craft guilds of Bruges, which had become their political rivals in 1477.

The basis of the wealth of the Maximilian faction depended on courtly patronage, feudal revenues, and income derived from land. As in the case of Pieter Lanchals, several members of the faction held important positions at court which gave them annual or daily revenues. Jan van Nieuwenhove (son of Michiel), Lanchals' brother-in-law, was *waterbaljuw* of Flanders (i.e., heads of the water authorities that maintained dykes). He had an annual income of eighty *livres parisis* from this office, and with the profits of the office his personal loans to Maximilian were paid back.[100] An in-depth analysis of the feudal income of Joost van Varsenare and Guy de Baenst (respectively, burgomaster of Bruges and of the Liberty of Bruges in 1485) shows both noblemen not only had accumulated wealth from their offices, but also from feudal revenues and land holdings. Because he was an heir of the former general receiver of the dukes of Burgundy Pieter Bladelin, Joost van Varsenare had inherited the castle and city of Middelburg in Flanders. In 1476 he sold his rights on this seigneurie

---

96   Haemers 2005b, pp. 223–5.
97   Buylaert 2005.
98   Boone 1990d, p. 472.
99   Gailliard, Jean-Jacques 1857–64, vol. 5, p. 149.
100 Archives départementales du Nord, Lille, B 5346, fol. 1^r; and B 2121, fol. 62^r.

to Guillaume Hugonet, the chancellor of Burgundy, for 16,800 *livres parisis*.[101] He had fiefs and land in Sint-Kruis, Moerkerke, Varsenare, Woumen, Cadzand, Aardenburg, Oostkerke, Maldegem, and Oostburg. Guy de Baenst had comparable possessions in Aardenburg, Oostkerke, Lapscheure, Boekhoute, Sint-Kruis, Sluis, and in the county of Zeeland.[102] These fiefs provided Maximilian's allies with revenues, prestige, and status.

The wealth of the faction could likewise be invested in political power. As was true for the faction of Willem Moreel, the faction of Maximilian financed its politics with the sale of annuities. Laurence Derycke's research on annuity buyers points out that a select company of leading figures dominated the public annuity market during the faction's reign. Their participation in public debt probably was inspired by economic gain, but it also has to be understood within a broader context of consolidating political power structures in the city. Since large investments in the public debt could lead to an increased grip on the urban government and public finances, considerations about the strengthening of the faction's power position were of decisive importance in the strategies of investment of these leading figures.[103] Pieter Lanchals, for example, bought twelve annuities in the period between 1485 and 1487. This purchase provided the city with a total sum of 13,944 *livres parisis*, and Lanchals henceforth had an annual interest of 1,104 *livres parisis*.[104] Also members of the components of the periphery of the faction bought annuities, albeit less intensively. Willem Houtmaerct bought four annuities in 1486 for a total sum of 2,002 *livres parisis*, Joost de Baenst (the brother of the above-mentioned Guy de Baenst) bought one annuity in April 1486 for a sum of 1,043 *livres parisis*.[105] Most of these finances were spent on 'aides' (these are voluntary subsidies for the state), which the city had granted to finance Maximilian's war against France. The investment of the Maximilian faction therefore directly supported archducal policy, while the costs of the annuities were paid with urban taxes.

The only voluntary loan to the city granted by the faction of Maximilian merits further attention because of a remarkable fact. In January 1488, ten citizens lent voluntarily to the city (for a total sum of 3,560 *livres parisis*).[106] This loan was a panic measure of the faction in order to fight the Ghent army which

---

101   Haemers 2005b, pp. 222–5 (for what follows).
102   Buylaert 2005, pp. 212–4.
103   Derycke 2003, p. 181. For comparable evidence in Ghent: Boone 1991.
104   Municipal Archives of Bruges, accounts of the city, 1485–6, fols. 114^v, 117^v, and 1488–9, fol. 108^v.
105   Municipal Archives of Bruges, accounts of the city, 1485–6, fols. 115^v, 116^v, and 1488–9, fols. 104^v, 109^r.
106   Municipal Archives of Bruges, accounts of the city, 1487–8, fol. 30^v.

had invaded the surrounding cities of Bruges – but their efforts would be in vain. Because of the urgency and the political aim of the loan, most creditors belonged to the wealthy part of the Maximilian faction. Lanchals' brother-in-law Jan van Nieuwenhove (son of Michiel), for example, lent 300 *livres parisis*. One creditor, however, did not belong to Maximilian's faction. Jan de Boot, a member of the core of the Moreel faction in 1483–5 voluntary lent 300 *livres parisis* to prevent challengers to archducal power from taking power in the county. How to explain Jan de Boot's strange act? At first sight it can indicate the regime had exerted a certain political pressure on its adversaries to lend money to the urban administration. But there can also be another explanation. Maybe Jan de Boot's tie with the Moreel faction was based on mutual usefulness, and therefore he switched to the other faction when he could no longer exploit the Moreel faction for some reason. I categorised Jan de Boot as a faction member of the Moreel faction because he exercised power during the reign of the faction in town and he was surety for Willem Moreel in February 1482. However, Jan de Boot was married to Lysbette Dhondt, the sister of Jan Dhondt. Jan Dhondt was a wealthy citizen of Bruges who was appointed receiver of Bruges by Maximilian in June 1485.[107] Jan de Boot therefore had a relational tie with a member of the periphery of the Maximilian faction. Maybe Jan Dhondt convinced Jan de Boot to contribute to the loan of January 1488. Or did Jan de Boot opportunistically lend to the new regime because he thought the Moreel faction would never return to power again? This complicated case shows an historian cannot always reconstruct boundaries of factions because he lacks adequate sources, but also because of their own vagueness. The case of Jan de Boot serves as a warning to the historian who wants to rationalise political history. Some faction members could have been quite opportunistic in their political choice. As was noticed for sixteenth-century factions, followers could move from one faction to another especially in times of political turmoil.[108] This opportunism can be explained by the nature of political conflicts themselves. Because their outcome never was clear for the contemporary, he had to make the best of the opportunities that presented themselves. On such occasions, economic interests, social ties, ideological factors, but also opportunistic choices could determine an individual's political position.

---

107   Archives départementales du Nord, Lille, B 4121, fol. 79^v; Municipal Archives of Bruges, procuraties, 1485, fol. 131^r.

108   Shephard 1992, p. 733.

8   The Two Factions Compared

As did the faction of Willem Moreel, the faction of Maximilian clustered social capital. Their nuclei consisted of dense and cohesive networks, bound together by relational ties and patronage. But their resources differed widely. While Willem Moreel and his companions gained economic goods and financial means from international trade, the members of Lanchals' network gained their economic capital from fief holding, court patronage, and political services when governing the city. The economic state capital Maximilian invested in Lanchals through patronage therefore seeped through to the members of the sheriff's network. But the strong relationship that the faction of Pieter Lanchals and his companions had with the archduke was also its downfall. Once Maximilian of Austria was imprisoned in Bruges in February 1488, the network lost its political protector. It no longer received the economic capital of the state, and it was evident that if the legitimacy of the archduke was attacked, the network would lose its authority to govern Bruges. Factions are difficult to maintain if their resources become exhausted.[109] The lack of filtered state capital seriously weakened the social network of Pieter Lanchals in spring 1488. When imprisoned in the city of Bruges, the archduke and his local faction were deprived of state finances and military forces to prevent the rival faction from striking back. The execution of Pieter Lanchals and Jan van Nieuwenhove (son of Michiel) was not only a vengeful act, it was a resolute strategy of Moreel's faction to erase the social capital of Maximilian's state apparatus in the city. Once Lanchals's social network was gone, its rivals could take power. Only political allies who had joined the Lanchals faction in the preceding years in its periphery remained loyal to the archduke, but they too became the victim of repression.[110] Once Maximilian lost his faction in town, he no longer had access to the necessary social capital to govern the city. Patronage therefore is a weak tie between the ruler and local factions. When patronage disappears, the court no longer has the people in town to rule it. From this point of view, Heers, Blockmans, Beik, and others are right when they claim the weakness of the central state apparatus stimulated factional struggle.

But factional conflict would not have taken place without the presence of a cohesive alternative political body in town. The Moreel faction was a dense kinship group, and its social base was more deeply rooted in urban society than the social base of Maximilian's faction. In contrast to the latter, the components of

---

109   Boissevain 1974, pp. 196–7.
110   Wellens 1965, pp. 45–8.

the Moreel faction did have the support of a wide range of merchant networks and the craft guilds in town. Neither the noblemen of the Liberty of Bruges, nor the social network of Pieter Lanchals, nor the wealthy Brugeois who joined them had social connections with representatives of the guilds. The 'authority of violence' Maximilian's faction professed during the regency of the Habsburg prince was designed to mask the inadequate social support of the regime and its lack of political legitimacy and social trust. However, by using violence, the regime could not destroy the structural social and political ties between the members of the Moreel faction. Because Pieter Lanchals and his companions did not have powerful social networks to rely on when Maximilian was imprisoned, neither their relatives nor other faction members could stop their execution. The challenging faction now could fill the political vacuum because the social capital of the faction enabled it to disperse persuasive ideas and to mobilise sufficient resources in times of need.

But the faction of Willem Moreel also had its weaknesses. Twice during the Flemish Revolt, in spring 1485 and autumn 1490, Archduke Maximilian succeeded in conquering the city. In each case a blockade of the city was efficient at eroding the economic power basis of the faction. Without the revenues from international trade, the faction lost its vital resources. But other aspects also weakened the faction. Although I did not study the aspect of the legitimacy of the faction in detail, it is possible the faction never succeeded in accumulating sufficient authority to contest the legitimacy of the regency of Maximilian. The suggestive evidence of shifting faction members can prove that some members only adhered to the faction out of opportunistic motives, not because they were convinced of the legitimacy of its rule. Although social ties between people seem to have been one of the most important guidelines in factional struggle, it was not the only one. The faction had assembled sufficient social capital in town to overtake the rule of rivals in times of their weakness, but it did not succeed in gaining political support outside town. Maximilian of Austria could mobilise financial and military means from regions other than the county of Flanders after he was released in Bruges. The Flemish Philippins had very few allies outside Flanders in their revolt against Maximilian of Austria. The lack of social capital and political support for the Flemish 'rebels' in other regions was difficult, if not impossible, to overcome.[111]

---

111   Haemers and Sicking 2006. More generally, see Blockmans, Willem 1989, pp. 733–55.

9   Conclusion

This article demonstrates that social theory (especially Bourdieu's thinking, social network analysis, and social capital theory) is a valuable tool for describing factional struggle, but historical research is needed to concretise sociological terminology. Although social capital helps to define the structure of factions, it does not explain why and when a faction succeeded in seizing political power. Detailed historical research has pointed out that differences in social structure, political ideas, and the economic resources of factions can explain why one faction was more powerful than another in moments that state power was weak. Both factions in Bruges – the faction of Willem Moreel, and the faction of Maximilian – had a dense and cohesive core. Both were clusters of social capital, which created trust among the members, channelled information, dispersed ideas and goods, and protected members of the faction from political attacks. In contrast to the faction of Maximilian, however, the resources of the faction of Willem Moreel originated from international trade. The Maximilian faction in contrast only received profits from fief holding and courtly patronage. When the economic and symbolic capital of the state was insufficient to govern the county – for example when tax revenues collapsed and the legitimacy of power was undermined – the local court faction could lose power in the city for its resources were insufficient to avert the political attack of its rivals. Because its social capital was provided with sufficient resources, the Moreel faction could easily regain power when the Maximilian faction lost control over coercive means.

As elsewhere, factional struggle in Flanders was about economic interests, political motives, and strong ideas. In Bruges, the faction of Willem Moreel tried to protect its economic wealth by introducing a corporate model of urban government, and in collaboration with the Ghent elite, a federal model of territorial government. In contrast, the Burgundian-Habsburg dynasty tried to increase its fiscal revenues by governing the cities and the county of Flanders in an autocratic way. But in its attempts to accumulate financial means, the dynasty was a giant with feet of clay. At moments when its authority was contested, violence could keep the local networks of the court in power only for a temporary period. Loyal networks of the prince could not survive politically (or even physically) the combination of contested legitimacy to wield power, insufficient economic resources, and weak social support in Bruges. State structure was fragile in Flanders, and it would remain politically weak when powerful alternatives to the dynasty were present in the main cities of the county. The patronage relation of the state could hardly break the economic and marriage networks of urban rivals. Revolt could spread out like a plague when challengers felt the need to gain power to the detriment of the state elite and if they got the opportunity. It was a 'damned plague', not only for the inhabitants of the cities who became the victim of violence, inherent in factional struggle, but also for the central state and its local allies.

CHAPTER 5

A Moody Community? Emotion and Ritual in Late Medieval Urban Revolts

Jelle Haemers

1 Introduction

'A quick overview of the Ghent Annals of the fifteenth century is enough to be fully aware of the instability of the mood of the "community": from 1432 to 1492 and after, large and small revolts of urban craftsmen happened in quick succession. One is inclined to think 'that they rebelled ceaselessly, just because they cannot be peaceful', to quote Chateaubriand'.[1] To Victor Fris (1877–1925), a follower of Henri Pirenne, the restless mind of the Ghent craftsman accounted for the rebellious tradition of his beloved city. In this quotation and in the rest of his works, Fris valued the role of emotions in history negatively. As a positivist, he was above appreciating emotions. Normally positivists did not inject emotions into rational models. Their paradigm explained historical evolution using processes and structures that were regulated by mechanical laws, not by emotions. And if emotions occurred, they had a destructive effect on the history of mankind, as Victor Fris noted. The positivists' romantic predecessors wrote bloody histories shaped by cruel leaders and docile masses who were driven by instincts. Positivists abandoned these irrational emotions. History was reconstructed in universities by means of serious scrutiny.

Moreover, the intellectual positivist based his history on sources written by the medieval political elite. In these sources the medieval rebels were often portrayed as an unstable element, ready to attack the rights of the lord and the upper class violently at any moment. Positivists took over that image uncritically and added a common attitude of disgust arising from their devotion to the nation-state. Henri Pirenne, for example, had no mercy for urban guilds rebelling against the Burgundian state. The anger of craftsmen was not based on rational arguments, and their revolts threatened the genesis of the Belgian

---

1 Fris 1913, p. 115, '*Il suffit de parcourir les annales gantoises du XVe siècle pour se rendre compte de l'humeur inconstante du "commun": de 1432 a 1492, c'est une liste interminable de grandes et de petites révoltes des gens de métier. Et l'on est tenté de leur appliquer ce mot de Chateaubriand "qu'ils tendaient sans cesse a s'insurger, sans autre raison qu'une impossibilité d'être paisibles"*'.

state that Pirenne adored.[2] As a result, the emotions of medieval craftsmen were seen as useless and not worth studying.

Following social scientists, I want to re-evaluate medieval emotions. Victor Fris, Henri Pirenne and other positivists made an artificial distinction between the rational mind and so-called irrational emotion. In contemporary psychological, anthropological and sociological literature emotions are no longer seen as irrational behaviour caused by uncontrollable feelings or by untamed reactions to stimuli. Researchers now posit that emotion itself is a basis for moral and social behaviour. Emotion no longer needs to be opposed to rationality, but rather interacts with it.[3] Some scholars consider emotions even as social constructions and as a product of social interactions. In these studies, emotions emerge as both social shapers and socially shaped.[4] As a consequence many scholars have concluded that different social organisations promoted or inhibited different emotions. It falls to anthropologists to investigate the cross-cultural expression of emotions and to historians to enhance the social and cognitive aspects of emotions by diachronic research.[5] In this short contribution to the history of emotions, I will concentrate on periods during which fever ran hot in the blood. But in contrast to Elodie Lecuppre-Desjardin and Jan Dumolyn, who discuss the *expression of emotions in language*, I will examine, as do Lauro Martines and Vincent Challet, *emotional behaviour* in late medieval cities.

What is new in my approach is the use of urban sources, such as bills, civic acts and chronicles written by urban administrators. These civic narratives offer us a portrait of urban experience from a very different social perspective. In these sources we hear a civic voice.[6] Most of these sources are written by the administrative staff of the city or by citizens who were not threatened by the emotional violence of the rebels. We will discuss this further on. But as a result of this broadened spectrum of sources, a more comprehensive approach to urban revolts and the demands of the rebels takes the place of the previous undisguised contempt for the 'moody community' and its emotions.

---

2 On this topic see Haemers 2004a, pp. 45–50.
3 Larrington 2001, p. 252; See also Rosenwein 1998b, p. 247; For an excellent *status quaestionis*, see Rosenwein 2002.
4 Lutz and White 1986, p. 417; Abundant literature concerning the social construction of emotion is cited in Rosenwein 2002, pp. 824–6; We specially refer to the work of the Stearnes, among others: Stearns and Stearns, eds 1988.
5 Sommers 1988, p. 35; On the strategies of studying emotions: Abu-Lughod and Lutz 1990, pp. 3–10.
6 Arnade 1996b, pp. 103–4.

2   Emotional Behaviour in Flemish Revolts

Firstly, we will concentrate on how medieval emotions arose. In the opinion of the Dutch psychologist Nico Frijda a person becomes emotional when he has an interest in something. A group always reacts emotionally to a new situation when its members have shared advantages (or disadvantages) in regard to it.[7] Emotions emerge when changes in the relationship between a group and the world around it threaten the group's interests. The 'proto-typical scenario' of the genesis of social and emotional processes worked out by anthropologist Catherine Lutz bears out this conclusion. Her schema, outlining a generalised scenario of action, represents emotions as arising in social situations and compelling certain types of responses.[8] This theory fits in wonderfully with the facts described below. In revolts of the Flemish urban population feelings started running high if interests were harmed, as the following three examples show.

After the death of the Burgundian duke Charles the Bold in January 1477, a particularist wave washed away the autocratic regime of the duke and his staff in the county of Flanders. After a period of 'legal struggle' in which the so-called 'Members of Flanders' (Ghent, Bruges and Ypres – the major cities of the county) regained their lost privileges, which lasted from January to February 1477, the revolt against the Burgundian regime became more violent. In March, the new regime in Ghent decapitated several members of the former city council, and in Bruges, the city guilds went out on strike. At the end of the month even the peaceful city of Ypres was agitated – for the first time in the fifteenth century. On 29 March the magistracy of Ypres imprisoned Pieter Cockuyt, a member of the lower class, after he had insulted the city aldermen.[9] The Ypres fullers were fully aware of the fact that not only Pieter Cockuyt and the members of his family, but also other craftsmen who had supported the unfortunate fuller, were threatened by the city magistracy. Moreover, this imprisonment could endanger the position of the whole guild of the fullers. These were very uncertain times! As a consequence, the offence against the autonomy of the common craftsman rapidly stoked the anger of the fullers, and they felt a corrective action was needed. The expression of their anger, as the behavioural implication of their collective emotion, was a furious occupation of the city market.

---

7   Frijda 1998, pp. 11–17.
8   Lutz 1987, pp. 293–4; White, Geoffrey 1990, pp. 47–8.
9   Diegerick 1848, p. 433; the general context of 1477 is studied by Arnould 1985, pp. 23–36; Hugenholtz 1964 and Boone 2003b, pp. 43–59.

Bruges in 1488 offers a similar example. On 27 March 1482, the sudden death of Duchess Mary of Burgundy, the daughter of Charles the Bold, made her minor son, Philip the Fair, duke of Burgundy and count of Flanders. In spite of the strong opposition of his father, Archduke Maximilian of Austria, the Members of Flanders governed the county in Philip's name. But the Members of Flanders could not stand up to Maximilian's military pressure, and in June 1485, he took over the regency for Philip the Fair.[10] His autocratic policy, however, forced the Ghent guilds into renewed rebellion. In November 1487 they took over the control of the city, and in January 1488 the Bruges guilds were urged to do the same. In Bruges, tension built up, and the nervous Maximilian, who was staying in his palace in the city, tried to avert a crisis by bringing in his German troops. A psychosis of fear arose. The frightening thought of a military invasion drove the Bruges guilds to the city gates, which they quickly occupied. The personal intervention of the archduke himself acted like a red rag to a bull; the 'agitated and coarse' guild of the carpenters in cooperation with the other guilds closed the gates.[11]

The last example brings us back to Ghent, the most rebellious city in the county of Flanders. On 3 November 1451, the city government of Ghent made known its intention to judge corrupt politicians. This administration was held responsible for the policy that had neglected the demands of the town's smaller guilds for many years. Finally, an end of the continuing humiliation came. The news of the approaching trials spread through the town like wildfire.[12] Some craftsmen, reacting very angrily, felt that the time for justice (or vengeance) had come. They took wooden sticks and ran to their guild house where they waited for a sign from their superiors to act. As the guild leaders called an unofficial general strike, the violent period of the Ghent revolt (1449–53) commenced.[13] Just as they had in 1432, 1437, and 1440, the urban craftsmen rebelled with arms against the city aldermen and the lord. These revolts were not premeditated; as Duke Philip the Good said of the riots of April 1437, 'fever was running in the blood' (*in hitten van bloede*).[14]

---

10   Blockmans, Willem 1974a; Königsberger 2001, pp. 42–72; Cauchies 2003, pp. 3–40; See [Patterns].

11   The '*upgheroerden onbeclokerden ghemeente*' did not want to give in, see Despars 1837–40, vol. 4, p. 322 (to a lost medieval chronicle of Rombout de Doppere). The events were also noted down by a civil clerk in Carton, ed. 1859, p. 177. The context in Wellens 1965, pp. 21–5 and Haemers and Lecuppre-Desjardin 2007.

12   Leguay 1984, p. 198, '*Les révoltes urbaines naissent, se propagent, s'exacerbent dans la rue*'.

13   Haemers 2004b, pp. 208–13; Fris, ed. 1901–4, vol. 1, pp. 135–7.

14   Philip the Good pardoned the rebels because '*de voorschrevene faiten niet bi vorraden, nemaer in hitten bloed ghesciet zyn bi ghemeenten*', Fris, ed. 1901–4, vol. 1, pp. 204–5.

As in Bruges and in Ypres, the guilds of Ghent responded very emotionally and violently to a concrete incident. In these cases, a 'collective emotion' arose, that is an emotion that was shared by a group of people. Of course, people did not react in the same manner, but they felt a similar emotion of anger and fear at the same moment. In such situations, 'pioneers' of the emotional wave rise up, while other participants play meeker or more docile roles. The emotional reaction of a single person, however, could never give birth to an urban revolt. In our opinion, an orchestrated collective emotion conducted only by one or two persons is impossible.[15] Leaders of revolts always channel existing collective emotions, in particular collective anger, grief or fear. These emotions only arise when common interests are harmed, as they are with the threat of a military invasion, the violation of a social right, or the symbolic judgement of a scapegoat. Irrational impulses are not the cause of rebellious deeds; instead collective anger is caused by the simple threat of harm to the common interest of a significant amount of people.

The outcome of this collective anger was the so-called *wapening*. '*Een wapenynghe scheen rijsende*' (a *wapening* is rising), wrote an anxious civil clerk of Ghent in 1452 after the guilds took up arms.[16] What is meant by this medieval term? A *wapening* is a unique urban phenomenon and it is the ultimate manifestation of Flemish revolts. I argue that the *wapening is* the revolt.[17] When we look at the etymology of this word, we see the term *wapen*, meaning 'weapon' or 'arms'. In a *wapening*, the Flemish guilds took up their weapons, which were sticks in the case of Ghent, to defend their corporate selves. A *wapening* is an armed assembly of the urban guilds in the city market.

A *wapening* is a collective action. Medieval guilds always responded collectively to a disadvantageous situation and the strong guild structure formed the basis of this concerted action.[18] The *wapening* was the temperate outcome of an impulsive outburst of the collective emotions of the urban guilds, whose interests were threatened. Every single violation of a right of one craftsman did not end in a *wapening*, however. Only when the higher authorities glaringly attacked the rights or privileges of all the urban guilds did this emotional

---

15 We refer to the similar remark of Dumolyn 1997, p. 346. Collective anger is not studied as such. The arousing of individual anger is discussed in White, Geoffrey 1990, pp. 48–52, and Larrington 2001, p. 253; based on Rozin, Lowery, Imada et al. 1999.

16 Fris, ed. 1901–4, vol. 1, p. 137, the craftsmen '*voorsaghen hem alle haestelic van stocken, zo dat een wapenynghe scheen rijsende, maer bleven in huus ligghene*'. A similar situation occurred on 13 November 1451, Ibid., vol. 1, p. 155.

17 For a detailed analysis of the Flemish *wapening* see Haemers 2004b, pp. 195–205 and Verbruggen, Raf 2002, pp. 124–55.

18 Our analysis of guild collective action is based on Tilly 1978.

collective action arise. More than an emotional response to a past political act, this display of armed but not violent anger also demonstrates a quasi-juridical appraisal of the act and of the person or persons deemed responsible for it. To display anger about an action publicly is to construe the action as an injury, as a wrongful act causing harm, as an offence against the guild's honour.[19] As a reaction, the guilds armed against further provocation. Each guildsman took up his weapon and, as is said in the sources, the guilds 'laid' (*liggen*) armed in their guild houses, waiting for the sign to march to a central place in the city. As we study the background of the rebels, one of the most striking features of the *wapening* is the prominent role of craftsmen who practised a job that requires heavy physical labour. In 1477, the Ypres fullers lead the revolt and in 1452–3 the bricklayers took the lead in Ghent. And after they had initiated the closing of the gates on 1 February 1488, the Bruges carpenters rebelled again several times 'with a furious wild head' in March.[20]

The guilds tried to get the duke's attention to show their dissatisfaction with his policies by making a lot of noise in the heart of the town. After the occupation of the city gates in 1488, for example, the Bruges guilds marched straight on to the city market, where Maximilian was staying.[21] The guilds complained about both the military threat to the city and Maximilian's autocratic policy of the past years. But the lord was not the only target; the *wapening* was in several cases also directed towards the city government. In the case of Bruges, Maximilian's network of supporters, which had taken over civic authority in the years 1485 through 1487, had pursued a tough policy towards the guilds. This resulted in an economic decline and in the political elimination of the guilds.[22] The emotional reaction of these guilds was aimed at reversing this policy through the execution of Pieter Lanchals, the most detested appointee of Maximilian.[23] In Ghent's *wapening* of 1452, the guilds protested against the weak response of the city government to the duke's hostile policy, but they also had an internal demand. They wanted corrupt politicians to be condemned. The revolt of the guilds of Ypres in 1477 had also a double goal. First the rebels tried to force the city government to release the imprisoned Pieter Cockuyt, but

---

19   White, Stephen 1998, p. 140.

20   Despars 1837–40, vol. 4, p. 375, '*met eenen verwoeden dulle hoofde*'. For the role of the brick-layers in 1449–53, Haemers 2004b. More generally, Tilly 1978, pp. 65–7.

21   Wellens 1965, p. 23. For a detailed account of the events, Vorsterman, ed. 1531, fol. 229ᵛ; Despars 1837–40, vol. 4, pp. 323–4 and Carton, ed. 1859, p. 178, the guilds came '*up de grote Merct, ter plaetse ghecostumeerd, in voorme van wapinghe*'. On the Bruges *wapeninghe*, Dumolyn 1997.

22   About the economic decline of late medieval Bruges: Van Uytven 2001.

23   Boone 2003b, pp. 59–62.

in addition, they demanded lower taxes, the restoration of old rights and a say in policy-making. In the case of Ypres the imprisonment of Pieter Cockuyt was a little spark that ignited a fire, the fire of collective anger. In tumultuous and uncertain situations when the city government or ducal authority threatened the position of the guilds, a simple event such as the capture of Cockuyt could give rise to an impulsive eruption of anger, an emotional answer to continuing danger.

Chroniclers who were clearly linked to the Burgundian or Habsburg court labelled this anger as a mad rampage of the furious masses, who took up their arms against the dynasty and its appointees and loyal supporters, sometimes against the chroniclers themselves. Jean Molinet expressed his disapproval of the assault in the Bruges Grote Mark in his *Chroniques*:

> *au commencement du mois de febvrier, tres horrible et fière commotion du peuple de Bruges s'esleva contre le roy des Romains estant illec et contre ceulx de son hostel*

> at the beginning of the month of February, a horrendous and savage commotion of the people of Bruges rose against the King of the Romans and those of his household).[24]

Jacques du Clercq saw the Ghent revolt of 1451 as a plot of some malicious villains (*gens de moindre estat d'icelle ville et povres gens*) against his lord, Duke Philip the Good. They swayed the masses (*avoient emeu et esmouvoient le peuple*) with a view to fighting the lord.[25] These chroniclers often were not familiar with the political discourse used in the revolts, because most of them were foreign and misunderstood Flemish political gestures and expressions. They interpreted the *wapening* incorrectly and saw the violence of the lower class as a threat to public order. Moreover, chroniclers had to persuade their audience that rebelling against the lord was reprehensible, because chronicles told the people how to behave.[26] Chronicles had a kind of moral function, especially when they were written by clerics. Positivists, who based their view of history on those chronicles, fell into the trap of accepting these accounts uncritically and condemned, as Victor Fris said, the violent outbursts and the rebellious nature of the moody community.

---

24   Molinet 1935–7, vol. 1, p. 587.
25   Reiffenberg, ed. 1835–6, vol. 2, p. 12.
26   Similar remarks by Chevalier 1982, pp. 35–6.

3   Emotional Regulation

How should we interpret the *wapening* correctly? According to the emotional model of the Dutch psychologist Frijda, emotional behaviour is always followed by an emotional regulation. Not only do humans react emotionally, they also *use* their emotions. Humans have to regulate their emotions to stop themselves from hurting others. This regulation normalises human relations again. This calm after the storm is the logical result of the universal concern for living together and the fear of revenge or retribution.[27] In the case of the medieval *wapening*, the urban craftsman knew what to do when there was a violent attack on the rights of his guild. He reacted very emotionally (he angrily took up his stick), but custom and collective memory forced him to run to his guild house. The leaders of the urban guilds tried to channel seditious emotions and became the leaders of the revolt. They originated for the most part from the middle class or from the lower elite of the town, as studies of the fifteenth and sixteenth centuries point out.[28]

Then, the actors followed an accustomed script. Francois Olivier Touati, Claude Gauvard, and Rodney Hilton have already noticed a number of '*traits de rationalité*' at work in urban revolts. More than once revolts followed a stereotypical scenario, known by all the participants. Serge Moscovici called this the 'choreography of the masses', a term which approaches the notion of the repertoire of collective action of Charles Tilly.[29] Every population had a specific choreographed way of rebelling, and in late medieval Flanders this choreographed response was the *wapening*. The collective emotions of the craftsmen provided the driver, but these emotions only became a powerful political instrument if they were expressed collectively in a central public space of a city. More than once the marketplace was chosen as background, like the Vrijdagmarkt in Ghent or the Grote Markt in Bruges and Ypres, as in other cities in Western Europe. The market was a playing field upon which the political communities of city and state claimed, fought and negotiated for political credibility and public prestige.[30] It was the theatre of power.

To occupy the city market the leaders of the revolt called together the dissatisfied craftsmen by the use of the city-bells. If the leaders of the revolt could

---

27   Frijda 1998, pp. 17–20. About the repression of revolts, See [The Legal Repression].
28   As in the Ghent revolt, Haemers 2004b, pp. 423–36; and in the sixteenth century, Dambruyne 2002, pp. 613–77 and Dambruyne 2003.
29   Touati 1990, pp. 12–14; Hilton 1989; Gauvard 1989; Moscovici 1981 and Tilly 1978, pp. 151–65.
30   Arnade 1994, p. 497; Boone 2002a; See contributions in Boone and Stabel, eds 2000, especially Crouzet-Pavan 2000; Stabel 2001.

not reach the bells of the belfry, they assembled the rebellious crowd by ringing the guild house bells.[31] The ringing of the bells in medieval urban revolts was a European-wide phenomenon.[32]

The bells became the voice of power, a vital medium to mobilise the masses. When the bells rang, the city rebelled. The inscription on bell Roeland, the main bell of Ghent, is revealing: when it is rung, the county is on fire.[33] The bells gave voice to collective anger, as its loud and dominant ringing filled the air with emotional tension.

The bells were to be rung only in the case of a city-wide public event. On 18 June 1488, a month after Maximilian was released, an anonymous Bruges craftsman caused an enormous commotion in town when he managed to ring the bell of the belfry without the permission of the city council, a council that had been installed in February of that same year by the leaders of the city guilds after they had taken control of the city.[34] Several armed members of the city guilds had run to the city market, and they became very angry when they discovered the wrongful use of the bells. The city aldermen arrested the man and after a public trial he was executed on the city market (!) because he had acted 'with his bad will in his *own* head'.[35] The ringing of the bell was a common right and nobody had the right to threaten this privilege. While it is hard to know why the anonymous craftsman rang the bell, it is clear that he did not succeed in setting the city on fire. This anecdote supports our argument that a collective emotion cannot originate with a single individual's emotion. A collective emotion only arises when common interests are harmed.

The most important tool used to express medieval collective emotions was ritual. 'Ritual is a kind of social action', Peter Arnade stated in his *Realms of Ritual*.[36] But ritual has also several emotional functions. First, ritual regulates emotions, as it channels anger into a more acceptable, more social form. In the cities of medieval Flanders mutinous emotions were channelled by ritualised parades. These spectacles displayed the emotions visually, but the ritual char-

---

31   As the Ghent revolt of February 1479 points out. After the inauguration of a new tax some members of the weavers' guild ran to their guild house and '*luutden tclocxen te storm om huerlieder adherente te vergaderen*', as noted down by the bailiff of the town, John of Dadizeele, see Kervyn de Lettenhove, ed. 1850, p. 14. On this revolt, see Fris 1909.

32   Garrioch 2003; Van Uytven 1998, pp. 129–43; Verbruggen, Raf 2002, pp. 125–31. Compare with Challet 2005b. Sometimes the guilds used light to express their presence, Lecuppre-Desjardin 1999.

33   '*Als men se luut, es storme in 't landt*', Van Uytven 1998, p. 134.

34   '*Ende [hij] stelde daer mede die gheheele stede in roere*', Vorsterman, ed. 1531, fol. 255ᵛ.

35   Ibid., he acted '*huyt eenen quaden wille huyt sijnen eyghenen hoofde*'.

36   Arnade 1996a, p. 212. See also Arnade 1997 and Arnade 2003, pp. 105–24.

acter of city parades made the released emotions of the carnavalesque crowd less dangerous, just as, for example, carnival did.[37] In periods of revolts, as in 1451, in 1477 and in 1488, after assembling in the guild house, the craftsmen marched under their banners to the marketplace. The sight of the civic symbols and the presence of his workmates at the market put the heart and the mind of the craftsman at rest. Thus the ritual parade was built on emotions and kept emotions vivid. The ritual use of space and the dramatic quality of symbols provoked an emotional response by the participants.[38] Every time the craftsman beheld his banner, he was reminded of the reason why he was not at work. He stood on the market to defend his rights, and he would not temper his emotions until these rights were restored. The ritual also unified a possible diversity of meanings and it created a vital bond among all participants. The *wapening* presented a picture of a world, ruled by the guilds, that was so emotionally compelling that the message of the *wapening* and the leading role of the middle class were beyond debate.[39]

The purpose of the *wapening* was to convey this uncontested message to the authorities. Ritual became a form of rhetoric, the propagation of the message through a complex symbolic performance.[40] Through the emotional *wapening* the guilds sought to enter negotiations with the city government or with the duke. Traditional literature often neglects a fundamental aspect of emotions, namely, that humans use them to gain a certain interaction. Following recent research that focuses on the communicative aspect of collective action,[41] I advance the thesis that this communicative aspect was performed by ritualised emotions. Communication in medieval public life was decisively determined by demonstrative acts and emotional behaviours.[42] Emotions telegraphed information. The use of emotions – their performance – indicated the possibility of peace to the authorities.[43] For Gerd Althoff, emotions have social functions and follow social rules.[44] Our research on the Flemish *wapening* confirms

---

37 Verbruggen, Raf 2002, pp. 163–9, and De Roos 1994.

38 Kertzer 1988, p. 11. Kertzer also proposes that rulers designed and employed 'rituals to arouse popular emotions in support of their legitimacy and to drum up popular enthusiasm for their policies', p. 14. We already discussed that this proposition does not hold for the medieval *wapening*; the emotions of the craftsmen did not have to be created by the leaders of the revolt. More generally about the use of symbols, Althoff 2002a.

39 Haemers and Lecuppre-Desjardin 2007. See also Kertzer 1988, pp. 99–101 and Blockmans and Donckers 1999, pp. 81–3.

40 Kertzer 1988, p. 101.

41 Haemers 2004b; Verbruggen, Raf 2002 and Lecuppre-Desjardin 2004a.

42 Althoff 1998, p. 74.

43 Rosenwein 2002, p. 841.

44 Althoff 1996; Rosenwein 2002, pp. 841–42.

this conclusion, because policy was discussed by using emotions. The *wapening* was a well-understood socio-political code, in which anger appeared as a 'social signal' which, paradoxically enough, helped to keep the peace.[45] Through the *wapening* guilds became a participant in policy, a 'polity member', according to Tilly.[46] The *wapening* was a symbolic sign to start negotiations about the rights of the guilds. If the authorities did not react in a comprehensive way, the diplomatic bridge between both parties would be destroyed. In these negotiations, collective emotions were a useful political tool. With the real danger of a furious and armed crowd on the city market, the city government or the central authority was forced to find a fair solution. Thus, the *wapening* not only had a defensive character, but it was also an offensive reaction to the policy of the central authorities.

4   The History of the Wapening

Whether or not the *wapening* was successful depended on the strength of the authorities and the intensity of the rebellion. Sometimes a count was forced to surrender by a sudden display of furious emotions, as Duke Charles the Bold had to do in 1467. After their military defeat on the battlefield of Gavere in July 1453, the Ghent guilds were oppressed by ducal networks that had assumed power. Under constant ducal monitoring, Ghent remained quiescent during the reign of Duke Philip the Good, but after his death the urban craftsmen gave their frustration free reign. During the provocative inaugural oath of Charles the Bold in 1467, in which the duke made the tactical mistake of not following city customs, the toll houses collecting the taxes and which had been installed in 1453 were stormed. The leaders of the guilds channelled the anger of the craftsmen by gathering on the Vrijdagmarkt. The first *wapening* in fourteen years forced important political concessions from the powerless duke. The crowd responded with an exuberant jubilation.[47]

In less vulnerable moments the count, in cooperation with the civil government, had enough means to oppress overt resistance to his policies. One example is the *wapening* of February 1488 in Bruges. After occupying the city gates, Maximilian of Austria, King of the Romans, through his loyal confidant Pieter Lanchals, invited a delegation from the urban guilds to the negotiating table. The guilds wanted Maximilian and his supporters in the city banks to

---

45   Rosenwein 1998a, p. 5; Barton 1998 and White, Stephen 1998, p. 139.
46   The political strategy to become a member of policy is discussed by Tilly 2003, p. 29.
47   Arnade 1991; Boone 2001b and Fris 1923.

adjust their policy concerning the deplorable economic situation of the city and the general treatment of the guilds. The haughty king and his loyalists did not want to give in to the rebellious crowd and offended the guild delegation more than once. This released the emotions of the craftsmen who rushed to the market and demolished the house of Pieter Lanchals. The guilds were sensible enough to leave Maximilian untouched, but they kept him imprisoned in town for more than three months.[48] So even if the emotions of the craftsmen got the better of them and the emotional outburst became violent, they still acted very purposefully and in an organised fashion.[49]

This contrasts sharply with the outcome of the *wapeningen* of the fourteenth century. The script of the *wapening* remained unchanged in the period between 1300 and 1500, but in the age of the van Arteveldes, the *wapeningen* in Ghent more than once ended in inner conflicts and brutal fights on the city market, as one guild drove out its competitor. For example, the fullers' guild removed the weavers guild from the political scene several times. Executions (in 1328, 1328 and 1337), massive exiles (in 1326, 1328, 1337, 1349 and 1353) and financial punishments (in 1326–33, 1349–53 and in 1356–9) of weavers stirred up hatred against the fullers in the city. When the weavers got the opportunity, they struck back.[50] In those bloody combats for power emotions were running high and the city was uncontrollable. By contrast, in the fifteenth century *wapeningen* never ended in violence, except for the focused destruction of symbolic buildings. Brute force was gradually transformed into symbolic violence.

I can conclude that the more time passed and the more power the state got, the less violent the *wapening* became. Is this a significant example of the civilising process of Norbert Elias? A telling argument in favour of this theory is the leading role of the middle class in the late medieval *wapening*. In Elias's theory of the civilising process, the middle class adopts the more dis-

---

48   Despars 1837–40, vol. 4, p. 324, the reaction of the guilds was extremely furious ('zo *lieper terstondt een deel van den ghemeente zeer furieuselick van de marct naer thuys van den schouteetene Lanchals'*). See also Vorsterman, ed. 1531, fols. 229^v–230^r and Wellens 1965, pp. 23–5.

49   Boone 2003b, pp. 60–64, describing the execution of Pieter Lanchals two months after Maximilian's capture, noted that blind violence remained absent. 'Pas de violence aveugle, mais une maîtrise de la violence, ciblée et raisonnée', p. 63. Patterns of revolts in late medieval Flanders are described in [Patterns] above.

50   Nicholas, David 1988. To our opinion Nicholas, by adopting the sources too uncritically – that more than once followed the discourse of the Flemish count – exaggerates the cruelty of the *wapeningen*. That, however, the *wapeningen* in the fourteenth century were more violent than in the following century is confirmed by Boone 1990b, pp. 199–235; Boone and Brand 1993; Verbruggen, Raf 2002, pp. 59–115 and Boone and Prak 1995, pp. 104–7.

ciplined way of life and the less emotional or less violent political methods of the ruling classes. In regions with a highly specialised economy, such as in the county of Flanders, social interdependence between townspeople grew quickly in the fifteenth century. If people wanted to live together, they had to temper the expression of their emotions. To be civilised meant to repress anger.[51] The middle class observed that an emotionally-informed policy was no longer tolerated by the ducal court. At the end of the fifteenth century, an indignant lord would not negotiate with emotional craftsmen. In the above-mentioned example of Maximilian in 1488, as long as the guilds remained armed on the market, the king would be unwilling to give in to their objections. To achieve its political goals, the middle class tried to temper the emotions of the common craftsman through a more intensive use of ritual. This can clarify the central position of ritual in late medieval urban society. Ritual served to temper – and thus 'to civilise' – the emotions of the common man. By taking part in the ritual, the craftsman adopted this more tempered model of outing emotions, and in a later stage he internalised social constraint to an increasing degree, to become – as a far later stage – increasingly self-disciplined.

As several historians have pointed out, the lord also had interests to defend in achieving or maintaining control of behaviour and conflict management. Just as Elias did, we link the mounting chains of social interdependency with the process of state formation. During the fifteenth century, the state intensified its use of ritual and symbolic mass communication to increase its control of the masses. To the lord, it was in every respect more efficient, and considerably cheaper, to use symbolic measures to involve the populace emotionally in the state than to force them with an iron hand.[52] Sizeable groups driven by unstable emotions (such as the fourteenth-century fullers of Ghent) threatened the position of a lord and his local representatives. The princes considered an uncontrollable fever running hot in the citizens' blood to be dangerous, as we read in the courtly chronicles. Collective anger or grief had to be suppressed. Permanent control over the emotions of the subjects, although often forgotten in the traditional scholarly literature, is a crucial pillar of the state's legitimacy. According to William Reddy, politics is 'just a process of determining who must repress as illegitimate, who must foreground as valuable, the feelings and desires that come up for them in given contexts and relationships'.[53] This 'emotional control' is just one of the sites of state power, but at the end of the Middle

---

51   Rosenwein 1998a, p. 3, and the conclusion of Elias 1939, vol. 2, pp. 434–54. *Status quaestionis*: Schwerhoff 1998; very useful in this context was: Van Krieken 1989.
52   Blockmans and Donckers 1999, p. 82; Blockmans, Willem 1997b, pp. 267–301.
53   Reddy 1997, p. 335. See also Rosenwein 2001, p. 230.

Ages influencing the emotions of the common man began to be one of the main concerns of an ambitious lord. In the Habsburg Netherlands ceremonial entries, pompous plays, drama contests and regional festivals were organised 'pour esmouvoir les ceurs et coraiges des homes a joye et a recreacion' ('to move the hearts and minds of men to joy and recreation'). The principal motive of the princes was to pacify citizens with semi-religious rituals and the symbolic violence of the theatre.[54] Maximilian of Austria and Philip the Fair (1482–1506) were particularly interested in dramatic media as part of their political 'project' to rule their subjects. More than once chambers of rhetoricians were called in to influence the emotional behaviour of the common citizen. As a consequence, the rhetorician confraternities affirmed a new urban cultural elite: literate, skilled exemplars of the emerging early modern aspiration to refined manners and restrained emotions.[55]

When the common man questioned the policy of the lord, the middle class tried to regain control over the citizens through an overwhelming use of ritual. The emotions of the craftsmen had to be channelled by ritual, in this case the *wapening*, and reduced to a more acceptable form. When a revolt ended, the ritual power of the rebels had to be washed away by an overwhelming *Joyeuse Entrée*, like those of 1440 in Bruges or of 1458 in Ghent. In contrast to the more emotional political style of the rebels, the prince entered solemnly into the city as an exemplary icon ('*un prince iconique*') perfectly in control of his passions and emotions both in his behaviour and in his policy, a pattern of conduct evolving into an ideal of '*virtus*'.[56] Thus both parties, the urban guilds and the central authorities, had a vested interest in redefining common manners and medieval emotions. They both wanted a peaceful and civilized urban society that was easier to control, and gradually the *wapening* became the victim of this 'civilising process'.

The *wapening* did not disappear, but in a later stage of the process of state formation, the emotionally tempered *wapening* lost its ability to overawe the lord. Emperor Charles v, for example, had enough financial and political means not to be frightened by a *wapening* on a city market. In the sixteenth century the state had grown too powerful to admit to the demands of rebellious subjects. The Ghent rebellion of 1540, for example, was suppressed very easily by the emperor. He destroyed the privileges of the urban guilds and removed their cultural symbols (banners, guild houses, city-bells ...), and thus banned guild ritual

---

54 Van Bruaene 2002, pp. 233–4 and Van Bruaene 2008. About ceremonial entries of Burgundian dukes: Lecuppre-Desjardin 2004a and 2004b.

55 Arnade 1996a, p. 187.

56 Dumolyn and Lecuppre-Desjardin 2005.

from politics.[57] After this last appearance of guild power, late medieval emotional behaviour faded out of political discourse. Other scholars have observed a similar trend towards less emotion in politics, particularly in late medieval England and, among others, Charles Phythian-Adams even argued that it was this ceremonial decline that truly marked the end of the medieval era in towns and cities.[58]

How can this extraordinary transformation in the use of emotions and ritual in politics be explained? Recently Barbara Rosenwein proposed that distinct emotional communities existed in different historical periods. Every society evokes, shapes, constrains and expresses emotions differently, and even within the same society, contradictory values and models have their place.[59] In sixteenth-century Flanders, the emotional community of late medieval urban society had been exchanged for another, more 'suitable' one. The new public order created by the absolute monarchy defined and assessed emotional behaviour in terms of its value or harm to the regime. A new mode of emotional expression and behaviour replaced the old-fashioned one.[60] The causes of this abrupt change are very complex, but a key component is the socio-economic transformation that undermined the economic and political position of the late medieval guilds. At the end of the fifteenth century, the economic decline in traditional trade sectors eroded the guilds' political capacity to counter the lord's drive towards centralisation.[61] Moreover, the economic transformation strengthened the social position of the urban middle class, which facilitated their dominance over a reduced urban proletariat and its modes of expression.[62] And perhaps the religious disturbances in the turbulent sixteenth century were a decisive factor. As it is up to modernists to clarify this remarkable evolution, I only can conclude that the prince as icon won the ritual battle of the market-place.

---

57   Arnade 1996a, pp. 189–209; Dambruyne 2003 and Boone 2000. In a more general context: Blockmans, Willem 1989.
58   This is discussed by McRee 1994, pp. 202–3.
59   Rosenwein 2002, pp. 842–5.
60   Arnade 2005.
61   About the economic decline of the traditional guilds, Stabel 1997, pp. 138–58, 262–9; Boone 1994, pp. 15–21; and Howell and Boone 1996, pp. 323–4.
62   About the rise of the urban middle class: Dambruyne 2001, pp. 345–68; Dambruyne 2002, pp. 723–7. About the transformation of the economy of late medieval Flanders: Van der Wee 1988, pp. 321–47.

5   Conclusion

In contrast to the opinion of Victor Fris our overview of the history of urban revolts in the county of Flanders in the fourteenth and fifteenth century has taught us to re-evaluate and appreciate medieval emotions. But writing the history of emotions is a difficult task. On the one hand, political, social, economic, cultural and religious aspects have to be studied in order to contextualise the emotions of the time people felt. On the other hand, the historian cannot do this job alone; he must consult the scientific results of sociological, psychological and anthropological research in order to reconstruct an emotional community of medieval society.

Was late medieval urban society a world reigned by moody craftsmen? Again, in contrast to Victor Fris, I have discovered a stable emotional community that did not rebel because it had a rebellious nature. In the fourteenth and fifteenth century, medieval Flemish guilds rebelled only if their rights were attacked. Medieval craftsmen reacted very emotionally in these precarious situations; but late medieval urban revolts were never a calamitous outburst of a mad crowd, as we read in the chronicles that were written at the court. On the contrary, the urban guilds used emotions as a political instrument to achieve political goals, for emotions are among the tools with which humans manage social life as a whole.[63] Moreover, as some anthropologists have concluded, emotion can be seen as a strategy for defending a group's preferred type of social organisation.[64] Through the use of their emotions the medieval guilds demanded the preservation of their rights. The collective emotions were channelled by a theatrical ritual of communication, the *wapening*, which warned the local and central authorities not to continue their policy. But the state gradually became stronger, too strong to be influenced by the emotions of urban guilds, and increasingly the lords succeeded in controlling the emotions of the common citizen. So, despite the remarkable disciplining – or 'civilising' – effect of the *wapening*, the urban middle class and the craftsmen finally tasted defeat. Their emotional community could no longer adapt to the changed social context in general and sixteenth-century politics in particular. Emotions never disappeared from politics, but they were never again used so politically as in late medieval urban society.

---

63   Rosenwein 2002, p. 842.
64   Lutz and White 1986, p. 420; Douglas and Wildavsky 1982.

PART 2

Assembling the Commune

CHAPTER 6

The Vengeance of the Commune: Sign Systems of Popular Politics in Medieval Bruges

Jan Dumolyn

1 Introduction

'Overt conspiracies', wrote the late fifteenth-century Flemish jurist Filips Wielant in his 'Brief Instruction into Criminal Matters', 'happen in three ways: the people against the governors, the governors against the people, or the governors and people together against the prince'. What Wielant called 'overt' conspiracies, as opposed to 'covert' plots, in fact refers to typical patterns of popular politics in the medieval Low Countries. According to his legal point of view, when the people rebelled against their governors because the latter had provided no justice and had taxed them too much, they should not be considered to have committed the crime of *lèse-majesté*. In such cases, only the principal instigators of the revolt ought to be punished. Those seditious persons, Wielant writes, who organise illicit meetings ('*ongheoorlooftde vergaderynghe*') and stir up the people ('*tvolck beroeren*') should indeed be hung, decapitated or exiled. Illicit meetings were always forbidden but, the jurist insisted, if a 'mutiny of the people' against its local rulers was caused by the injustice of the latter the punishment should only be a moderate one. When a revolt had started because of envy or party strife, however, this certainly represented an act of *lèse-majesté* and the punishment should accordingly be more severe. And if the governors of a local community had also joined in the rebellion against the prince, 'killing his officers, closing the gate before his nose, demolishing his houses [*werpende zyn huusen*] and committing other enormities and rebellions', this was clearly also considered *lèse-majesté*. In such cases, the lives and properties of all inhabitants of the city should be at the mercy of the prince, their privileges and liberties should be abolished, and the town's belfry, gates and walls should be demolished. However, Wielant remarks, in such cases the prince is usually gracious and only punishes the ringleaders by executing them, confiscating their goods or sending them on faraway pilgrimages. The 'body of the city' (*tlichame van der stede*), he writes, would thus be reduced to poverty with a large fine.[1]

2   Medieval Contentious Politics and the 'Cultural Turn'

During the last decades, the types of medieval Flemish popular revolts this learned jurist was reflecting on have been analysed with more or less traditional socio-economic and political perspectives, emphasising economic structures and conjunctures, social struggle, resistance against oligarchy and state formation, social networks, factions and political alliances and programmes.[2] Since the 1980s, the influence of Charles Tilly's historical-sociological model for the study of 'collective action' – he later preferred the more general term 'contentious politics' – has been very influential within this line of research.[3] Tilly considered the 'repertoires' of political protest as a limited set of tactics deployed by those challenging official authority. In given societies, these repertoires – for instance strikes, marches or armed revolts – tended to change slowly over time, and though groups of protesters might have sometimes experimented with new forms, usually few exceptions can be observed. However, Samuel Cohn, one of the foremost specialists of medieval revolts, has criticised Tilly's distinction between the pre-modern 'communal' and the modern 'associational' types of revolt, the former being local and uncoordinated and the latter type, starting in the middle of the nineteenth century, being larger in scale, more disciplined, and deliberately organised in advance, such as the modern demonstration or coordinated strike action.[4] Cohn emphasises the ability of the medieval popular classes to organise themselves in a fundamentally political manner with clear programmes and objectives, and not just under the influence of leaders from the upper classes or of millenarian ideologies.[5]

Such critique notwithstanding, Tilly's point that 'in general participants in uprisings and local struggles followed available scripts, adapted those scripts, but only changed them bit by bit' remains a valid and useful one. Rebels 'drew their claim-making performances from standardised, limited repertoires'.[6] Accordingly, in medieval Flanders, contentious repertoires often remained quite similar for centuries but were at the same time adapted to new social and political contexts, testifying to the organisational creativity of rebels from the

---

1   Wielant 1995, pp. 80, 188; on repression of Flemish revolts see [The Legal Repression]; Boone 1997a; and Van Caenegem 1954.

2   Mollat and Wolff 1970; Fourquin 1972; Cohn 2006; for Flemish revolts in particular: Pirenne 1910; Van Werveke 1946b; Nicholas, David 1992; Blockmans and Prevenier 1999; Boone and Prak 1995; See [Patterns].

3   Tilly 1978; McAdam, Tarrow and Tilly 2003; Tilly 2008.

4   Cohn 2012b.

5   Cohn 2006.

6   Tilly 2008, p. xiii.

popular classes. Tilly himself observed similar patterns of adaptability, and his later work moves from a more structuralist analysis of 'repertoires' to an emphasis on their 'performances', that is, from a kind of *histoire immobile* of pre-modern politics to a history of variation and adaptability in methods of collective actions. Here Tilly is in line with a general 'cultural' approach to the repertoires of medieval revolt, in Flanders and elsewhere, that became fashionable since the 1980s among scholars of the Middle Ages. For instance, in 1989, the French specialist of heraldry Christian de Mérindol listed a number of 'symbols' medieval cities used during revolts: colours, emblems, bellringing, closing the gates, pillaging and burning the houses of enemies, and lynching.[7] Especially during the last two decades, as in other fields of historical writing, the so-called 'linguistic', 'cultural' and 'performative turns' left their mark, notably dealing with revolts in Flanders, one of the heartlands of medieval collective action. Peter Arnade applied a Geertzian approach to the 'reading' of collective action in Ghent.[8] Thomas Boogaart similarly applied a semiotics grounded in a post-structuralist 'cultural geography' to the events in Bruges in the period between 1280–1302 while Marc Boone, Raf Verbruggen and Jelle Haemers reflected on ritualised patterns of violence in Flemish rebellions.[9] Not exclusively focusing on contentious politics, Élodie Lecuppre-Desjardin widened the scope to all 'ceremonial' aspects of political communication between rulers and subjects in the Burgundian lands.[10] And in his recent overview of medieval revolts, Cohn has also devoted a chapter to the 'flags and words' used during collective actions. For revolts in France and Flanders, he stresses the importance of guild banners and of hoods and, most of all, of the culture of assemblies and fierce rebel leader speeches. In Italy, he writes, flags, pennons and other icons and pictorial symbols specific to the rebellions themselves would have been more important.[11] Most recently, with Haemers, I have studied the fundamental role of speech acts and ideologies in Flemish popular politics, changing the focus from the 'ritual' forms of political communication to those of the plain spoken and written word.[12]

Even if such a 'cultural reading of popular politics' is a fruitful product of the developments in historiography over the past couple of decades it should in my

---

7   Mérindol 1990, pp. 289–93.
8   Arnade 1996a; Trexler 1980.
9   Boogaart 2004; Boone 2005; Verbruggen, Raf 2005; See [A Moody Community]; Haemers 2007f.
10 Lecuppre-Desjardin 2004a; Haemers and Lecuppre-Desjardin 2007.
11 Cohn 2006, pp. 177–205.
12 See [A Bad Chicken]; See [Let Each Man Carry]; Dumolyn and Haemers 2015a.

opinion not be taken too far. The study of the 'forms' of collective actions ought not to make us forget about the importance of their 'contents' and 'functions': the structural, socio-economic contradictions in society that they stemmed from and the political visions that their active participants formulated. Politics is not just about political culture, 'rituals' or 'symbolic communication' but mainly about power relations. Medieval politics is also not merely about the agency of the dominant classes who are the usual actors in the narratives inspired by the performative turn. In a study of the discourses and practices proper to what I refer to here as 'popular politics', from mostly British historians in using the term,[13] what is always primarily at stake is rather straightforward issues of disparity in wealth and power: resistance against oligarchic and corrupt forms of class rule, fiscal and monetary injustices, power abuses, inflation, pressures on wages and other direct threats to the living standards of the middle and lower classes, and, last but not least, the demand for popular participation in urban government.[14] The notion of 'popular politics', in contrast to the 'oligarchic politics' of the ruling classes, includes 'collective actions' or 'contentious politics' but is in itself a more encompassing term. Rumours and muttering, anger and discontent formulated in daily interactions, the threats of revolt or strike and negotiations between social groups were all part of the same system of popular politics as violent collective actions. In medieval Flemish urban political practice the middle and lower classes were often able to challenge elite authority in institutionally acknowledged forms such as councils drawing up petitions, in which the expression of popular voices could serve as a safety valve for the political system and reflected a certain balance of forces at a given moment. When necessary, however, popular politics made use of concealed or semi-clandestine forms of discourses and practices and also of open mobilisations, reclaiming central public places in a city or village community.[15]

The type of overt popular politics that was typical for medieval Flanders, so typical that a jurist in the service of the Burgundian-Habsburg dynasty like Filips Wielant thought it should be treated with some lenience, consisted of political performances that were, as I will argue below, fundamentally 'communal' in nature. These communal sign systems remained more or less inert, very visible and even ideologically dominant within the Flemish towns as power means of mobilisation, political ethics and moral justice even as they competed against symbols rooted in the oligarchic logic of patrician rule based

---

13   For instance, Whittle and Rigby 2003, pp. 69–70.
14   Dumolyn 2010b.
15   See [A Bad Chicken]; Liddy and Haemers 2013.

on lineages, factions, and economic monopolies. The sign systems of the Flemish commune had a relative autonomy of which the origins are not primarily liturgical or religious in nature but should rather be sought in the discourses and practices of justice of the earliest urban communities between the eleventh and the thirteenth centuries. Using the rich political history of Bruges, one of the foremost commercial and industrial centres of medieval Europe, I want to consider the Tillyan concepts of 'rebellious repertoire' or 'contentious performance' from a semiotic point of view, without losing sight of concrete socio-economic and political processes. Such sign systems cannot be limited to linguistic systems in the strictest sense of 'political languages' or 'ideological discourses'[16] as they were formulated in slogans or in the demands in a petition. They also include visual, spatial, auditive and performative codes: the wearing of insignias and deploying of banners, collective assemblies and marching to occupy crucial sites within urban space, bodily gestures, looting, demolishing or burning down specific buildings, drinking, armed gatherings and other acts of symbolic and physical violence, and the sounds of bells and drums.[17]

3   Communal Politics in the High Middle Ages

The first part of the title of this article is based on an old work by the legal historian André Delcourt called *La vengeance de la commune*.[18] Delcourt was referring to typical elements of communal criminal law. The inhabitants of communes in Flanders and Hainaut took violent revenge on their enemies by burning or demolishing their houses. I use the phrase 'vengeance of the commune' as a metaphor for the sign systems of urban popular politics because it cannot be emphasised enough that if repertoires of collective action had a 'ritualised' character, these rituals were in the first place those of the administration of customary justice. Medieval urban communities were groups of persons inhabiting a common space bound by secular justice and by networks of kinship and friendship.[19] This justice was delivered according to the laws and customs of what medievalists have generally called 'the commune'.[20] The Lombard communes were the oldest ones to develop in Italy, having appeared

---

16   Dumolyn 2012b.
17   See similar observations in Cohn 2012a; and Oliva Herrer 2012.
18   Delcourt 1930.
19   Blockmans, Willem 2010.
20   The literature is too vast to extensively quote here, see for instance Petit-Dutaillis 1947 and, recently, Blickle 2000.

in the middle of the eleventh century, and in the centre of the peninsula this happened around the middle of the twelfth century.[21] Typically in the communal movement, a *conjuratio*, the sworn oath of the city-dwellers, was at the basis of what German historians have called the *Eidgenossische Bewegung* forming *Schwurgemeinschaften* since the eleventh century in the Holy Roman Empire.[22] Oath-takers were mostly merchants and artisans, though they often included knights, ministerials and clerics. Closer to Flanders, in France, well-known examples are the commune of Le Mans (1070), the commune of Noyon (1108–9), the commune of Amiens (about 1113) and that of Laon (1112), which was recognised as an *institutio pacis* in 1128.[23] For the North of France, Petit-Dutaillis defined the commune as essentially this *conjuratio* of the burghers, their oath of mutual aid.[24] Vermeesch, on the other hand, emphasised the aspect of *pax*, as an extension of the *Pax et Treuga Dei*. This urban peace aimed to protect its members against knightly violence, pillages and extortions. It was not revolutionary, however, because the fundamental ties of dependence between lords and their subjects were not broken by the commune, and oath-takers continued to pay their land rents.[25]

Obviously, the lack of clear sources for this early period of the Middle Ages is the main cause of the still ongoing debate about the precise nature of the commune. Keller already pointed out the different problems for the Italian communes,[26] and for the German, French and certainly the cities of the Dutch-speaking region of Flanders the lack of clear sources is even more manifest.[27] But the factor which complicates the issue most, as for instance in German and Italian historiography, is that of whether the commune was primarily a legal and institutional phenomenon or, rather, a fundamentally socio-political one.[28] The nineteenth-century Belgian historian Léon Vanderkindere saw the legal form of the commune appearing everywhere in the Southern Low Countries because later sources mention *jurés, jurati, coremannen, keurheren* or other similar titles, seeming to designate offices which would have been the successors of the early communal institutions. He claimed that all Flem-

---

21   For instance, Volpe 1970; Dilcher 1967.
22   Classically formulated by Planitz 1954, pp. 102–25.
23   Vermeesch 1966, pp. 105, 113.
24   Petit-Dutaillis, 1947, pp. 80–4.
25   Vermeesch 1966, pp. 177–9; Platelle 1971, pp. 145–56; Ross, ed. 1991 (see especially the introduction); Hoffmann 1964; Oexle 1996a.
26   Keller 1988; Gilli 2011.
27   For the French speaking part of Flanders, the commune has been studied by older scholars such as Espinas 1941–2; Bertin 1947; Rolland 1931; and Derville 1995.
28   Dilcher 1988.

ish towns had originally been communes in the legal sense, governing themselves and autonomously administering justice within the community.[29] Henri
Pirenne used a more flexible concept of commune that Vanderkindere and also
emphasised elements like the *droit d'arsin*, the cry '*commune!*' or '*ghemeente!*',
the possession of communal bells or a belfry, mutual aid in times of hardship
and the right to be judged by one's own sworn men.[30] But at the same time,
Pirenne and, especially, his successor François Ganshof denied that there had
been legal communes in the Dutch-speaking part of Flanders, including the
capital cities of Ghent, Bruges and Ypres. Instead, they emphasised institution
of the aldermen (*schepenen, scabini, échevins*) as having been present at a very
early stage in Flemish cities,[31] instituted by the beginning of the twelfth century, sometimes in continuity with Carolingian institutions, a view which is in
my opinion a questionable one.[32] For now, I shall not focus on this institutional
and legal question as to whether the early Flemish commune had autonomous
institutions or was ruled by comital aldermen from its very beginning; rather, I
will examine the 'political logic' of the commune as a fundamental source for
popular politics for the centuries after the first phase of urban history in the
eleventh and twelfth centuries.

From a social-anthropological perspective, the commune was a community
of labour and solidarity, almost comparable to a large kin group and replacing
the latter's functions in the context of the medieval city, as towns were always
full of newcomers from the countryside whose social ties with their places of
origin would often have been totally severed. However, communes were in fact
not necessarily urban. Susan Reynolds considers them as a continuation of a
long tradition of communities such as the Carolingian guilds, and a similar view
was elaborated by Otto Gerhard Oexle.[33] Flanders also certainly had rural 'communes' in the form of politically privileged communities, such as the Liberty of
Bruges, i.e. the rural district or *kasselrij* or *châtellenie* around the city of Bruges.
Though Flemish communal struggle was more intense and frequent in the cities than in the countryside, the role of the rural commune should certainly not
be underestimated, notably that of the coastal regions of the county, where
strong communities of free peasants had existed since the high Middle Ages

---

29   Vanderkindere 1909a and 1909b. His views were contested, but without really sound arguments, by Pirenne 1939, vol. 1, pp. 201–18; and by Pirenne's successor Ganshof 1951.

30   Pirenne 1939, vol. 1, pp. 183–91.

31   According to Frans Blockmans 1938a they would have existed even earlier, but his reasoning is largely speculative.

32   This point is prudently questioned by Van Caenegem 1978; by Wyffels 1968; and more explicitly by Verhulst 1999, p. 130.

33   Reynolds 1984, p. 156; Oexle 1996b.

often on land won from the sea.[34] In all such cases, a sworn *communio* (in medieval Flanders also referred to as an *amicitial, pax, communaulté, ghemeente* or *meentucht*) had the function of preserving peace and security and of safeguarding, most notably in the urban context, a climate beneficial to trade and industry. The commune could not tolerate feuds and violent conflict among its inhabitants. Through systems of reconciliatory justice, it forced its members to conflict settlement, known in Flemish as the *zoenrecht*, a fundamental feature of urban private and criminal law. Already in the eleventh century, there are proofs of measures reinforcing 'friendship' and 'peace' on the scale of entire urban communities.[35]

Thus, the foundations of communal urban legal and political organisation were basic principles of social order, reinforced by mutual oaths, held by men who needed peace and security so as to live, produce, own property and trade together in a densely built environment. These principles, though clearly combined with older elements from Germanic law, formed the basis for the customary laws of the commune. Of course, even with regard to the beginnings of the communes we should refrain from any illusions about egalitarianism or romantic ideas of *Genossenschaftsrecht*.[36] However, we can safely assume that around 1100 the social polarisation was less sharp than it would become after the thirteenth century.[37] As populations grew, the oaths and meetings of free men soon had to give way to a delegation of power to those who were the richest and most powerful, the *boni homines* and *nobiles*, and surely also to those who reasoned and spoke best, sometimes called the *prudentes viri* or similar terms. It was in their judgment, whether about legal or economic policies, that the common burghers could trust, and they provided the elementary political action necessary to direct these precocious urban communities. Often, early communes included or merely reshuffled earlier local elite social groups. Most Italian and Flemish communal regimes merely rearranged institutional power structures while leaving members of the same ruling classes (local merchants, landowners, clerics and often also the knights, ministerials and officers of the local comital castle or important abbey) in their dominant position.[38] So, was the communal movement a 'popular' or 'revolutionary' one? The answer must be more nuanced. Violence as an aspect of communal revolu-

---

34   TeBrake 1993; Van Bavel 2010b.
35   Van Caenegem 1956, p. 5.
36   Von Gierke 1868–81.
37   Dumolyn 2012a.
38   Hyde 1973, p. 48.

tion, as famously described for the case of Laon in 1112 by Guibert de Nogent,[39] was in fact rather exceptional and more typical for cities ruled by ecclesiastical lords. Such forms of conflict happened, for instance, not far from Flanders in 1077 in Cambrai. Though Galbert of Bruges's description of the aftermath of the 1127 murder of count Charles the Good placed the Flemish burghers on the stage of history as emancipatory and conscious groups,[40] fully prepared to take up arms for their rights, the communal movement in this region was in general not characterised by violent upheavals and confrontations with the authority of local lords or bishops (in Flanders, there were in fact no episcopal towns as the county mostly fell under the clerical authority of Tournai and Cambrai).

Though the sources usually remain vague, the communal movement looks rather like a more gradual and smooth process of urban emancipation that was ultimately sanctioned by the strong Flemish counts. At the end of the eleventh century, they already clearly seem to have realised that granting the privileges of jurisdiction and partial self-rule to these productive urban communities and that liberating merchants from excessive toll tariffs and arbitrary seigneurial violence was also in their own economic interest.[41] The term 'commune' is explicitly mentioned for Saint-Omer and for Ghent, but in other towns other names are used for what is essentially the same phenomenon. Some other terms used for the Flemish communes and for those of neighbouring regions like Hainaut, Brabant and Liège point to their fundamental socio-economic, political, legal and ideological features, for instance *pax* (for Valenciennes) for the peaceful and secure situation they sought to preserve, or *amicitial* (for Aire-sur-la-Lys) for the mutual aid and free consent of the sworn men of the *conjuratio*. Another keyword in this sense is the common term used for an urban privilege or liberty charter: the *cora* or *keure*, that is, the 'chosen law' of the community.[42] The general picture the scattered sources offer us is that in all probability, somewhere between the rules of count Robert the Frisian (1071–93) and William Clito (1127–8), the Flemish towns became factually and perhaps sometimes also judicially autonomous bodies, separated from the countryside.[43] During the eleventh and twelfth centuries, after an initial impetus by the Peace and Truce of God movement which had been influential in Flanders since about 1030, the counts of Flanders increasingly assumed the

---

39 Saint-Denis 1994; Deploige 2008.
40 Rider, ed. 1994.
41 Schulz 1992, pp. 101–31.
42 Vanderkindere 1909a, p. 254; and see Ganshof 1951, Derville 1995 and Verhulst 1999 for more details and references about the chronology and geography.
43 Dhondt 1948; Oexle 1995.

role of warrantors of the peace, especially Baldwin VII (1111–19) and Charles the Good (1119–27).[44] At the same time, local 'communities of peace' came into existence in towns and rural areas, assuming a *de facto* legal and semi-autonomous status.[45] The idea of *pax* provided an ideological framework in which burghers could express their desires to be free of knightly and irrational justice such as ordeals and duels and in favour of market peace and toll freedom in order to develop trade and industry. At the beginnings of the movement, the counts and the young urban populations had the same interests in communal development, and subsequent counts, notably Philip of Alsace at the end of the twelfth century, would take many measures to stimulate growth which were advantageous to both the urban economics and to his own revenues.[46]

4 Communal Justice

As the majority of the few sources at our disposal are of a legal nature, the legal-historical approach is still the key to understanding the economy, society and politics of the early Flemish urban communities. From the point of view of social and economic history, however, one might say that the Italian communes were eventually accepted as permanent political and legal institutions precisely because they were the most efficient levels of power to provide for the basic needs of the city-dwellers: the administration of justice within a group of people living closely together, the management of common property such as markets and sea and river ports, and the liberation of the burghers from imperial tolls and taxes.[47] The Flemish communes had to fulfil exactly the same tasks in order to reduce transaction costs and insecurities that hampered economic growth. It is my main argument here that without a clear understanding of the origins and nature of the commune in the shape that it took between the eleventh and thirteenth centuries it is also impossible to fully grasp the political and socio-economic stakes and the repertoires or sign systems of urban politics in the later Middle Ages and the early modern period. The sign systems of popular politics in medieval Flanders were fundamentally shaped in this early urban context and were fundamentally repertoires of customary law. The oldest documented Flemish communal law, as classically

---

44 Hoffmann 1964, pp. 143–58.
45 On the principles of communal law in Flanders see Van Caenegem 1954, pp. 3–25. Of specific importance are the notions of market peace ad urban peace, ibid., pp. 67–9.
46 Verhulst 1967.
47 Hyde 1973, p. 97.

studied by Van Caenegem, was a collective response to the established system of criminal law from private origin in the sense of *weregeld* ('compensation'), feuding and conflict settlement. In the new, more developed and socially diversified urban community conflict had to be settled not with the kin group of the victim but with the entire community. Its 'peace' had to be preserved. Though customary law is often conservative, it was not at all immutable. Contrary to a general misconception, medieval customs were very much open to change, adapting themselves to new social and political circumstances. Indeed, communal law was considered 'old law' but could also be changed, a right that was for instance explicitly recognised for Bruges in 1127.[48] In the context of the growth of comital authority in Flanders, princely law was often an ally of communal law but gradually became an ever stronger rival. Thus, the principles of Germanic law that were fundamental in Flemish communal law until the twelfth century and beyond, were altered and replaced by a much more direct and intensive intervention of the count, certainly since the end of the twelfth century, the time of the strong count Philip of Alsace who introduced authoritarian and centralising principles favouring the power of 'the state'.[49]

There were a number of violations of the law considered to be specific 'offences against the commune' as a peace community with a collective responsibility. Going back to old Germanic custom, members of the commune were supposed to carry out police tasks themselves to arrest criminals. If they failed to do so they could risk a fine or face exile themselves. They should act 'like brothers' and answer and come to the aid (*ad auxilium advenire*) of fellow citizens crying out (*faire cri*) *bourgesie, poorters* or *communie*, which indicates that strangers had attacked.[50] Communal law was also not as sanguinary as one might expect. Exile as a specific urban punishment clearly derives from the character of the town as a free community of labour and solidarity within a defined space. Someone who did not collaborate or who sabotaged the common welfare of the town was useless and dangerous. Exile made one *vredeloos* or 'outside the peace' of the commune.[51] Another typical communal punishment as the destruction of the house of an enemy of the city: the *droit d'arsin*, literally burning down the house, or the *abattis de maison*, as in demolishing it (common to the urban context in which setting fire to a house meant an obvious risk for other buildings), was another old Germanic legal principle.[52] In

---

48   Van Caenegem 1994a.
49   Van Caenegem 1956, p. 317; Van Caenegem 2000.
50   Van Caenegem 1956, pp. 133–6.
51   Ibid., pp. 137–55; Brunner, Heinrich 1890.
52   Van Caenegem 1956, pp. 175–90.

the context of popular politics, the main point here is that even after the institutional and legal stripping of its powers by the comital benches of aldermen in the cities, the notion of the commune still provided a discourse of ideological legitimacy and mobilisation. The commune implied a powerful and long-lasting set of ideas with an accompanying sign language of buildings, walls, gates, towers, of bells, clocks and intimidating but uniting rally cries and solemn oaths of brotherhood and mutual aid, a common space of local saints and collective devotion, an arena for ritualised expressions of both violence and peace. Thus, as an urban authority and territory of markets and collective properties, which had to control infrastructure, streets, roads, rivers and canals, even though it was internally ridden with potential and explicit conflict and sharp inequalities, the commune was a metaphor for revenge against outside enemies and an inclusive form of exclusion. The political language of the commune was principally a judicial language, performed through speech acts such as swearing oaths and formulating complaints according to the practice and procedures of customary law.

5 From Communal to Corporatist Popular Politics

By the year 1300, already more than 400 years after the development of an early urban community there, Bruges, at the edge of the maritime plain of the county of Flanders, was a thriving commercial metropolis with a population between 40,000 and 50,000 people, famous throughout Europe for the range of commodities which were sold on its markets. Probably since the ninth and certainly by the eleventh century, Bruges had already had a modest *portus* (or *wik*) function. Gradually, around a comital castle (*castrum*) that had been constructed as a stronghold against Norman invasion at the crossroads of a land and maritime trade route, an urban agglomeration (*suburbium*) of artisans and merchants developed. By the mid-twelfth century, after the port of Bruges had become more easily accessible because of the opening up of the Zwin estuary as a result of a flood in 1134, the city witnessed a demographic and economic take-off that lasted until well into the fourteenth century. In the suburbs around the twelfth-century inner city the textile industry expanded enormously, though it would never acquire the absolute economic and demographic dominance that it had in other large Flemish cities like Ghent, Ypres and Saint-Omer. But even more that these other towns, Bruges gradually also became a centre for the luxury and fashion industries, economic activities which reached their high point during the 'Burgundian' fifteenth century, when painters like Jan van Eyck and Hans Memling were active there. Most of all, however, the Zwin city was a commercial gateway town, a central node in the European commercial network. Beginning in the final decades of the thirteenth century, as is generally known, merchants from all over Europe settled semi-permanently in Bruges, and the Zwin city became the most important hub between the Mediterranean and the North Sea commercial zones. By the later Middle Ages, the social structure of Bruges thus consisted of a large unskilled and skilled workforce active in the textile, leather and metal industries; a prosperous middle class of shopkeepers and highly trained artisans in the luxury industries; and a commercial elite of merchants, hostellers and brokers (the two latter professions controlling the trade between foreigners).[53]

In 1127, when economic diversification and social polarisation were not as visible yet as they would be in later epochs, the burghers of Bruges entered the scene of politics for the first time, at least as clearly recorded in the sources, demanding more privileges from the new candidates for the office of count after the murder of Count Charles the Good. The sources on political development in Bruges between 1227 and 1280 are very scarce, but after the complete takeover of power by the merchant class in the thirteenth century and the erosion of communal institutions, which were now both on the judicial and administrative levels replaced by the authority of aldermen appointed by the count, the communal idea seems to have become mostly one of popular opposition to oligarchic politics. On the political level, the much more diversified socio-economic structure of Bruges since the rapid economic and demographic growth of the later twelfth and thirteenth centuries would result in a perennial political struggle. On the one hand, there the popular classes, usually directed by the independent artisans engaged in petty commodity production but also encompassing wage labourers and the poor, and, on the other hand, there were the commercial elites, represented since the mid-fourteenth century by the drapers, the butchers, fishmongers and the guild masters of the luxury trades. This social cleavage was not as clear cut, however, as disgruntled members of the elite or 'new men' deprived of political power often formed temporary alliances with the middle classes to contest oligarchic power, and, at the same time, members of the guild elites would often become part of the establishment. After the revolutionary period, which began in 1280 and culminated in the Flemish popular victory at Kortrijk in 1302, power in the city

---

53 The most important dates, facts and general developments of the history of medieval Bruges, including the principal scholarly articles and the older references, can be found in Brown 2011; Haemers 2009; Murray 2005; Lambert, Bart 2006; Dupont, Guy 1996; Dumolyn 1997; Paviot 2002; Geirnaert and Vandamme 1996; Nicholas, David 1992; Ryckaert 1991; van Houtte 1982; De Roover 1999 and Häpke 1908.

government had to be shared with the guild elites in a corporatist form of government. The commune was at this time confronted with the logic of the political guilds and their internal processes of oligarchy and social mobility, with the rising power of the princely state, with changing structures in the elites, with patrician faction struggle, and with conjunctural economic and demographic crises and structural transformations.

By this time, the meaning of the term *communitas* had gradually altered. The *Annales Gandenses*, a chronicle written by an anonymous Ghent Greyfriar, which is the best narrative source on the events in Flanders that led to the battle of Kortrijk in 1302, recounts the struggle between the *communitas* and the *majores* in Bruges and Ghent.[54] This *communitas* was still reminiscent of the older communes and their institutions about which we are almost totally uninformed,[55] but it had transformed since the early twelfth century. In a 1241 privilege for Bruges, it was explicitly stated that all aldermen had to be members of the merchant guild and could not perform manual labour.[56] However, even if all power was in the hands of these patrician aldermen, thirteenth-century charters still speak of the 'aldermen and the commune' (*communitas* or *communaulté*) in their *intitulatio*. The precise institutional nature of this 'community' involved in the decision-making process leading to a certain charter must have changed considerably over time and in different contexts, but before the end of the thirteenth century the sources for this question are almost non-existent. In this diplomatic formula, rather than being a precisely defined institution, the term commune seems to stand for 'those who are ruled' in a representative manner, not just one guild or one group in the town but a unity or *universitas*, representing the commonweal or common body of the city. In practice, this could have been a group of notable burghers (*ghoede lieden* or *bonnes gens*) acting as advisers, sometimes along with artisans assisting in technical questions. Then in 1280, as the social gap between *li riches* and *li povres* had become even larger, a wave of revolts struck Flanders, and the popular classes formulated their demands in meetings called *meentucht* or *ghemeente*, terms closely related with that of the commune, or *li kemuns* in French, as was the case in Bruges during the *Moerlemaye* revolt and in the Bruges outport of Damme.[57] In claiming to speak for the entire urban community, rebel alliances, including craftsmen and factions of the elite, were reclaiming the political power of the

---

54   Johnstone, ed. 1951, p. 20.
55   With the exception of some towns in French speaking Flanders such as the *amicitial* of Aire-sur-la-Lys, see Bertin 1947.
56   Gilliodts-Van Severen 1874, vol. 1, p. 194.
57   Prevenier 1978; Wyffels 1966, p. 43; Bardoel 1994.

commune against the oligarchy and misrule of those lineages that controlled the benches of aldermen. 'The commons' or 'the commoners' were now also more and more used to denote a social group in the city. In the fourteenth and fifteenth centuries, *het ghemeen, li commun, les communes*, or similar variants primarily carried the more restricted meaning of the 'commoners' as in 'the popular classes' (as in *den beroerte van den commune ieghen die heeren* or 'the revolt of the commoners against the lords').[58] At the same time, the term always retained the connation of the commune as a political community, as in *la communauté* or *de ghemeente*, those who were ruled and not the *poorters* or the *heren* (lords) who usually dominated the city government.[59]

6   After the Revolution of 1302

By the later Middle Ages, the character of political rule over the major Flemish cities had decisively changed. The manual workers, who had been systematically excluded from the city government but who had massively entered the stage of politics around 1280, now successfully obtained political participation at least in the bigger cities such as Bruges and Ghent. After the Bruges revolt of 1302, followed by the general Flemish popular victory at a battlefield near Kortrijk, the cities received new constitutions in which urban government was shared between the old patrician class and the now fully emancipated craft guilds.[60] Thus, after 1302, we can speak of the age of 'corporatism'. This development, which had itself been a result of economic processes of growth and the division of labour, strongly changed communal popular politics. For centuries to come, the guilds would remain the dominant mobilizing forces, and their languages of signs – banners, slogans, armed gatherings and strikes – would fundamentally colour popular contentious politics.[61] The Flemish political revolution of 1302 had been a clear victory for the middle and working classes, but the merchant elites also retained a lot of their power, especially because the count of Flanders soon sided with them again and abandoned his temporary coalition with the commoners against the king of France. The uneasy political equilibrium thus having become unbalanced, new smaller-scale revolts, disturbances and riots took place in Bruges in 1309, 1310, 1318 and

---

58   Lambin, ed. 1839, p. 213.
59   Compare with Watts 2007; and Gleba 1989.
60   The latest synthesis, including the many references to older works, is Van Caenegem, ed. 2002.
61   Boone 1997b.

1321, followed by the massive revolt of 1323–8.[62] This major popular uprising was in fact not merely a peasant revolt but a movement of the city and the Liberty of Bruges together, and of other cities and rural districts in mostly Western Flanders.[63] This Liberty of Bruges (*Brugse Vrije, Franc de Bruges*) was the *kasselrij* (in French *châtellenie*) or rural district around Bruges, a prosperous area of free and independent peasants. Indeed, the rural communes of the coastal plain of Flanders, where new land had been massively won from the sea, had the same traditions of popular meetings and assemblies that had developed in the cities, though these have been much less studied and also left fewer sources, so their internal dynamics remain unclear. During mobilisations in each rural district, captains were elected by local meetings. These captains also played a role in popular politics in normal years, among other things, authorising the local levy of taxes. It seems that the rural communes were led not by the most downtrodden and exploited peasants but by the more important farmers and those of middling wealth of each community. They were persons who resisted rising rents and taxes imposed on them by the local nobility.[64] So in the countryside as well as the city, 'the commune' as a privileged community of free men with a certain degree of popular representations, came to the foreground as the institutional form of popular mobilisation.

This alliance between the urban popular classes and the free peasants of the Flemish coastal area against the nobles and the elites in general was not a new one, and it would also persist during later revolts such as those of 1379–82, 1436–8 and 1477. Since the days when it was first documented in 1127, the Bruges commune had had a continuous tradition of resisting and fighting neighbouring noblemen threatening the communal space and market function, including the Zwin estuary connecting the city to the sea and the other canals and landed routes vital for commerce. In 1127, the burghers of Bruges had temporarily supported the Erembald clan who had murdered the count of Flanders because both had a common enemy in the lords of Straten who from their castle (in what is today the Bruges suburb of Sint-Andries) controlled the route to Ypres. With the Erembalds, who had a feud with this same family, they burned the castle of Thancmar of Straten.[65] During the thirteenth century the merchant class that now dominated the city found a certain *moyen de vivre* with important noble families such as the lords of Assebroek, the lords of Gistel and of Praet. The city gradually bought up their toll rights and landed property just

62   Verbruggen, Raf 2005, pp. 32–40.
63   Sabbe, Jacques 1992, pp. 24–5.
64   TeBrake 1993, pp. 57–8, 135.
65   Ross 1959.

outside the first city walls, and this was annexed to the urban territory. The lord of Gistel, however, tried to make Bruges pay as much as possible to sell his lands in 1275, and the countess had to intervene. But the strongest local bully was the lord of the neighbouring seignory of Sijsele who, so the *Annales Gandenses* state 'had always been an enemy of the city'. After the victory of the Flemish army – largely made up by the Bruges and Ypres militias – at the battle of Kortrijk, Bruges seized all his territories in the immediate vicinity of the city.[66] Even more intensive was the conflict over the Bruges outport of Sluis in 1323 with Count John of Namur, an arrogant nobleman who was great uncle to Count Louis of Nevers. Since 1305 John had become lord of the newly established outport of Lamminsvliet or Sluis. This was the small port along the Zwin estuary closest to the sea (the other Bruges outports were Muide, Hoeke, Monnikerede and Damme) and with the gradual silting of the stream it became even more important as ships could no longer enter the Zwin and their freights had to be shipped on smaller boats there. For Bruges, it was vital that the city controlled full access to the sea itself without noble interference and with comital authority the sole check on communal power. The presence of John of Namur at their 'gateway' to the sea was a thorn in the city's side that eventually had to lead to serious problems. When, in July 1323, John also obtained the judicial office of 'water bailiff' in the Zwin, including full policing of all traffic on the stream, the commune reacted immediately. On the 31st of the same month, a Bruges urban militia marched towards Sluis and completely burned it.[67] When the count of Namur obtained the office of water bailiff in 1323, those of Bruges and Damme *turbati sunt vehementer*; they said they wanted to keep their law without infraction.[68] Thus the rural and urban participants of the revolt of 1323–8 had different motives, but their forms of mobilisation and popular politics and their demands were all fundamentally communal in nature.

7   Instability in the Fourteenth Century

Though the revolt of maritime Flanders was ultimately crushed by a French army at Cassel and the liberties of Bruges were severely diminished with the 'bad privilege' of 1329,[69] guild power in the city was soon re-established during the period of 1338–48 as Bruges joined in the rebellion of Ghent against

---

66   Johnstone, ed. 1951, pp. 8, 14.
67   Sabbe, Jacques 1992, pp. 19–20.
68   De Smet, Joseph Jean, ed. 1837a, p. 184.
69   Van Rompaey 1965.

the count under the famous rebel captain James van Artevelde.[70] The period that followed the middle of the fourteenth century, also witness to the Black Death and the popular religious movement of the 'Brothers of the Cross' or 'flagellants', was a very tumultuous time marked by economic crises within the textile industry and subsequent attempts of the weavers, fullers, shearers and dyers to maintain their political power. The textile guilds were the most radical group in the city as they defended the communal programme of a more popular rule against the oligarchic tendencies represented by the merchants, brokers and richer craft guilds. In 1344, a strike of the shearers took place followed by outbursts of small riots and larger revolts in which textile workers played the main role in 1348, 1359, 1361, 1367, and 1369.[71] The years 1358–61 were particularly tumultuous. Several riots and popular assemblies followed each other, and the guilds were divided among themselves, notably the fullers and weavers against most of the others.[72] This political constellation should be interpreted in the context of the crises affecting the Flemish textile industry. Though the number and power of textile workers were diminishing, a new compromise between commoners and patricians such as the one after 1302 had to be established. Around 1360, the representative institutions of the city that were the successors of the commune took a more stable form and were referred to as 'the common body' (*ghemeenen buucke*) of the city.[73]

At the same time, the principle of guild representation on the bench of aldermen, one that had been installed in 1304 but was in practice often neglected, now became institutionalised in the system of the 'Nine Members' in which every 'member' of the city comprised a certain group of craft guilds.[74] The 'community' more and more took the form of an institutionalised 'great council' including the captains of the burghers and the deans of all the guilds, and there were even more restricted consultative meetings with the *bonnes gens* or *goede lieden* of the elites. Nonetheless, taxes and troops could only be granted to the prince by meetings of *den ghemeenen van den stede* ('the common of the city'), or *al tghemeente* ('the whole commune'). In 1464 at the latest, the nine deans were called the 'heavy deans' or *zwaerdekens*. By the fifteenth century, the Great Council, also called *de ghemeene buke van der stede* ('the common body of the city'), took shape as the institutional form of the old communal idea and

---

70   See Nicholas, David 1988 and the older works he quotes. Until now, these revolts and this
     period in the history of Bruges have not been sufficiently studied.
71   For this period, see mostly Verbruggen, Raf 2005; Mertens 1987, pp. 326–7; Boone 2008b.
72   Gilliodts-Van Severen 1874, vol. 2, pp. 416–34.
73   Dauwe 1987, vol. 2b, p. 317.
74   Vandewalle 1999.

obtained competence over all important financial and fiscal matters, including the sale of annuities. The Great Council was an institution which assembled regularly during peacetime, although there were also more restricted meetings with only six headmen and the nine or eighteen most important deans present along with former aldermen and burgomasters, usually from the commercial class of merchants, hostellers and brokers.[75] Guild representation in the city government, however, was in practice often prevented by the latter political elite. Except for periods of real revolt, usually only some representatives from the richer guilds such as the butchers, fishmongers, and luxury trades, or those weavers or stone masons who were actually big entrepreneurs, managed to become aldermen, and the guild majority in the city government remained a fiction. In 1477 it was demanded that the aldermen would be elected from each member of the city, showing that this practice had already long been abandoned.[76] Later traditions to be found in the Bruges chronicles claimed that the system of the Nine Members electing the aldermen went back to Count Baldwin IV's alleged privilege of 1036.[77] This was of course a myth, but it shows that during the fifteenth century the idea was common that this was an 'old law' that ought to be re-established and that it was part and parcel of the collective memory and programme of the commune.

8   The Burgundian Epoch

The politically unstable fourteenth century culminated in the participation of parts of the Bruges popular classes in a revolt led by Ghent in 1379–82. During some months in 1382, the Ghent rebels occupied Bruges with the collaboration of the most radical parts of the Bruges commoners (*alianche aveukes le people et comun de Bruges*), the textile guilds and blacksmiths, and installed a communal regime.[78] Ghent would only capitulate on very advantageous terms in 1385, but in Bruges repression was extremely harsh, and the commercial class came out victorious and assumed full power in the city with the strong support of the new Valois Burgundian dynasty that now ruled Flanders. The most anti-communal measure in the restrictive charter imposed on Bruges by Duke Philip the Bold

---

75   Blockmans, Willem 1978, pp. 81–7. A thorough study of the great council is still lacking.
76   Haemers 2009.
77   Warnkönig 1835, vol. 2, p. 131; Dauwe 1987, vol. 2c, p. 645.
78   Gilliodts-Van Severen 1871–85, vol. 4, p. 8. See an interesting 'manifesto' of this communal government, emphasising the freedoms and equality of all burghers in ibid. vol. 3, pp. 467–71.

in 1384 was the clause *que toute la communaulté d'icelle ville de Bruges soit gouvernee par six connestables et gouverneurs des six parties d'icelle.*[79] Granting the policing of the entire commune to the captains or *hoofdmannen* of the patricians alone and completely eradicating the role of the guilds from the body politic meant returning to the regime of the 1270s when the six sections of the city or *zestendelen* had been first erected to control the recently added suburbs. This repressive measure against guild power was soon followed by a 'revolt, alliance and conspiracy' (*upset, verband ende vergaderinghe*), a failed plot by the weaver Jan Groeninc in 1387 to kill the *goede lieden* of the city.[80] Like another minor textile workers riot in 1391, it was crushed before it had even started, and these events were symbolic of the loss of demographic and political power of the textile guild. In addition, in the period between 1392 and 1394, some riots concerning the Western Schism took place – the city remained Urbanite while the new Duke of Burgundy and Count of Flanders supported Avignon – but the final decades of the fourteenth and the first years of the fifteenth century were mostly a period of intensified factional strife among the elites. Guild power had suffered a very strong blow, and the crafts had been demilitarised and robbed of their political power, their banners and other symbols, but now the elites turned against one another. In 1407, Duke John the Fearless supported a factional coup in the city, but in 1411, this new regime was overthrown by the guilds, which reinstalled the previously dominant patrician faction and regained many of their privileges as a form of recompense.[81]

After twenty-five years of general political stability, a decisive showdown was the major Bruges revolt of 1436–8 which, as in 1323–8, also resonated in the countryside and in the smaller towns of Western Flanders.[82] Once again, during the 1436 revolt, it was 'the commune', or at least the communal idea in its form of the united community of all burghers and guilds, confirmed by a sworn oath of all the guildsmen and captains of the six sections, which took direct power and ruled the city through the Great Council while the power of the aldermen was severely restricted in practice. This 'direct rule' implied that the rank and file of all the guilds had to be informed on and consulted about all political decisions. For instance, at one point in 1436, the men of Bruges blamed the deans of the blacksmiths and dyers '*qui sans le scue de la commune*' allowed their representatives to negotiate with Ghent.[83] Traditional communal

---

79   Ibid., vol. 3, p. 2.
80   Ibid., vol. 3, p. 233; Mertens 1973.
81   Dumolyn 2010a.
82   Dumolyn 1997, pp. 120–1.
83   De Smet, Joseph Jean, ed. 1865, p. 322.

demands once again came to the foreground. Still in 1436, the lady of Gistel was arrested by the Bruges rebels because as the possessor of the toll which she held in fief from the count it was her duty to protect all access to the sea from pirates, and she had clearly failed to do so. If she did not want to organise this herself, they said, the city would do it at her expense.[84] After the defeat of the great revolt of 1436–8 and a subsequent outbreak of famine and plague, more than two decades of economic prosperity followed. Although some representatives of the guilds retained symbolic seats in the city government, political rule would remain predominantly oligarchic until a new uprising broke out in 1477, after the death of Duke Charles the Bold, and the guilds once again gained political participation.[85] The situation in Bruges would remain highly unstable until a final revolt in 1488 against Maximilian of Austria, who had claimed effective power as guardian of his son after his wife Mary of Burgundy had died in 1482 but was strongly contested by most of his Flemish subjects.[86] At the same time, this period would also mark the steady economic downfall of the city and its gradual transformation into a merely provincial town after the middle of the sixteenth century.[87]

9 Oaths and Privileges: The Signs and Speech Acts of the Political Contract

Urban political language might have come to maturity in Flanders earlier than anywhere else in Northern Europe,[88] and though the conditions of urban life changed considerably over the centuries, this language seems to have remained rather constant until the end of the Middle Ages. Throughout this period of four centuries and longer, communal politics was associated with a semantic field consisting of ideological keywords such as *pax, amicitia, communio, communitas, corpus, universitas, bonum commune, utilitas totius urbis* or *consuetudo*. These concepts are obviously not specific for the Flemish cities, where notions like *meentucht, ghemeente, meente, ghemeene, buke, leden, keure, costume, hulpe, eeninghe, bistandichede, broederlike minne* or *ghemenen orbor* appear frequently in the sources.[89] In what follows, I will approach the recon-

84   Dumolyn 1997, p. 193.
85   Haemers 2009.
86   Wellens 1965.
87   Van Uytven 1995.
88   Stein, Boele and Blockmans 2010.
89   Dumolyn 2012b.

struction of a general typology of the sign systems of communal popular politics by placing a lexicological analysis in the context of the changing socio-
economic and political conditions of medieval Bruges. A first important point
is that town politics and communal ideological discourses were fundamentally defined within a dialogue of power between the urban community and
the prince, in other words, between 'the commoners' in the later sense of 'the
commune' as 'those who are ruled' or 'the entire community of the city' and
the count of Flanders.

The first Bruges privilege defining the relations between the urban community and the count that we know of is mentioned in Galbert's chronicle. In
1127 *chartula conventionis inter comitem et cives nostros factae de telonio con-
donato et censu mansionum eorundem* was read out before the population. It
contained typical economic concessions to an urban commune dealing with
toll freedom and land rents. But this could not have been the first privilege granted to the city as Galbert goes on to mention that after the count of Flanders
and the king of France, who had been present at the proclamation, had sworn
on these privileges, so did the burghers of Bruges, the text says, just as they had
done to the count's predecessors: '*quoque cives juraverunt fidelitatem comiti,
sicut moris erat, et hominia fecerunt ei et securitates sicut prius praedecessoribus
suis naturalibus, principibus terrae et dominis*' ('The citizens also swore allegiance to the count, as was custom, and they paid homage to him and securities
just as [they had] to their natural predecessors, the princes of the land and
lords').[90] We know that, for instance, the small Flemish town of Geraardsbergen received an oral privilege around 1070, and the same probably goes for the
amicitia of Aire-sur-la-Lys.[91] Hence, we can safely assume that, as Galbert suggests, before 1127 an important city like Bruges would have been granted such
recognition by the count, most likely also only in oral form.[92] Thus, from its
earliest stage, oral expressions of the political relations between the commune
and the prince, through speech acts of mutual oaths, took on the character of a
'political contract'.[93] In the centuries to come, chronicles dealing with urban
matters would continue to use the terms *juramentum, fidelitas* or *securitas*
frequently in similar contexts of the contractual relation between the prince
and the city community.[94]

---

90   Rider, ed. 1994, p. 112.
91   Blockmans, Frans 1938a.
92   *Cfr.* Van Caenegem 1994a, p. 104. The earliest privilege conserved in the original is the one
      for Saint-Omer. See Espinas 1947; Van Caenegem 1991, pp. 61–70.
93   A concept coined in this sense by François Foronda, see Foronda, ed. 2011.
94   De Smet, Joseph Jean, ed. 1837a, pp. 196–7 and *passim.*

As was the case in other Flemish towns, on the first occasion when a new count made his solemn entry into Bruges, he had to swear to respect the city's privileges. The judicial officers who represented the prince in Bruges (the *baljuw* or 'bailiff' and the *schout* or 'sheriff') also had to swear oaths in front of the urban community.[95] This oral performance was crucial in establishing 'contractual' power relations in front of the burghers present, but privileges were no less symbolically important in their material and written form. They even had a fetish-like character. The charters containing the 'privileges, rights and freedoms' of Bruges were kept in coffers in two barred alcoves in the Belfry. Each leader of one of the City's nine 'Members', eight groups of guilds plus the patricians, held one of nine keys to the alcoves. Leaders representing the guilds were the 'heavy deans' (*zwaerdeken*), such as the dean of the weavers who headed up the Member of the drapery, which also included fullers, shearers and dyers. The captain or 'headman' (*hoeftman*) of the *Sint-Jans zestendeel*, the most important of the city's six sections represented the patricians, the ninth Member of the *poorterie*.[96] Typically, in times of revolt, the armed guildsmen would demand that the privileges and other documents be read out to them, as they were always suspicious that either the urban elite or the prince had not been respecting them, or that the aldermen had 'sold out' to the count, which was indeed often a justified suspicion.[97] In many ways, the city privileges were the written crystallisation of the political balance of power both between the prince and the city and between the oligarchs and the popular classes. Thus, in most cases their contents also formed the main stake of contentious popular politics and strongly inspired popular political ideology. After a succession revolt, city privileges would become more advantageous from the point of view of the commoners. This was the case with the charters granted to Bruges after 1302. When the revolts failed, however, the counts imposed centralising measures on the city and restricted the power of the guilds and of popular representation in general. The new privileges imposed on Bruges in 1329 and 1384, for instance, were reactionary attempts by the count and the patricians to completely destroy the communal-corporatist principles of government and return to pre-1302 conditions.[98]

In 1407, the men of Bruges said that they did not want a comital arbiter to judge on the differences between themselves and the Liberty of Bruges with respect to the rural textile industry, another classic conflict of interest between,

---

95   Lecuppre-Desjardin 2004a, pp. 96–7.
96   Gilliodts-Van Severen 1871–85, vol. 9, p. 48.
97   Dumolyn 1997; Dauwe 1987, vol. 2b, p. 313; Van Leeuwen 2008, pp. 306–11.
98   Van Rompaey 1965.

on the one hand, the urban working and middle classes, who wanted to suppress it, and, on the other, the merchant elites who could profit from the lower wages in the villages. The commoners said 'that they had beautiful and well-sealed privileges of count Louis of the drapery and the lord had confirmed them, and they were willing to show them to the whole world if necessary'. Duke John the Fearless decided to make a compromise and to grant the Liberty of Bruges and the outport of Sluis, a perennial rival of its capital city, some minor rights for the sale and production of cloth. Fearing for their lives, the aldermen of Bruges present at the negotiations begged their lord to send a councillor with them to announce this decision to the crowd, 'because in no way would they dare take up this burden'.[99] The assembled mob of guildsmen on the marketplace could indeed have an intimidating effect. In 1411, the Bruges artisans rose up against the Calf Skin (*calfvel*), the ducal charter of 1407 that had installed the *cueillote*, a new tax of grain or, as the *Chronicon Comitum Flandriensum* puts it, an exaction '*communitati super modium bladorum*' ('on the community over bushels of grain'). The wooden cabin on the Bruges grain market where this tax was collected was subsequently destroyed and the Calf Skin itself was torn into pieces ('*Nam domus queliote desposita est et charta illa, quae Kalfsvel vocabatur, fracta et lacerate est*').[100] Also during the revolt of 1477, on the demand of the rebels and with the permission of Countess Mary of Burgundy, the Bruges nobleman Louis of Gruuthuse symbolically destroyed the Peace of Arras in front of the revolting popular classes, a charter that had been imposed on Bruges after the failure of the earlier revolt in 1438.[101] An entirely new generation of rebels had collectively remembered that this 'bad privilege' had to be cancelled as it was the result of a previous popular defeat. On 9 April of the same year, the armed craftsmen also demanded, with the support of the rural commoners, that the Liberty of Bruges be abolished as the 'Fourth Member of Flanders', thus losing its place in the representative institution of the count next to Ghent, Bruges and Ypres. This too was part of the 'historic programme' of the Bruges commoners. Mary of Burgundy, powerless after the death of father Duke Charles the Bold of Burgundy, had to submit to their demands and confirmed in a charter the same day that the Bruges rural district would lose its autonomy from the city. This was not enough for the rebels, though; they demanded that any mention of the Fourth Member of Flanders as such be removed from every copy of the General Privilege for Flanders which

---

99   Lambin, ed. 1835, pp. 33–5.
100   De Smet, Joseph Jean, ed. 1837a, p. 252.
101   Van Leeuwen 2008, p. 313.

had been issued on 11 February of the same year. The peasants of the Liberty of Bruges now joined the communal army of the city.[102]

10   Meetings, Bells, Banners and Calls for Action

At times when the popular classes felt that their privileges and their communal peace had been harmed, voices were usually raised to collectively mobilise and restore justice in the city. 'The song of the Flemish insurrection', an English popular song probably written directly after the Flemish victory at Kortrijk on 11 July 1302, testifying to the strong symbolic impact of this event on other regions, mentions an oath sworn by 'the commune of Bruges': '*Gedere we us togedere hardilyche at ene*'. Especially the weavers and fullers stood out as the most vigorous rebels: '*The webbes and the fullaris assembleden hem alle,/Ant makeden huere consail in huere commune halle*'. They chose Peter the King (the weaver and people's tribune Pieter de Coninck) as their captain.[103] But before such assemblies were convoked, they were usually preceded by a period or more concealed 'muttering', spreading 'rumours' and defying the enemies of the city in popular songs or in leaflets distributed in the streets. On Christmas Eve 1407, for instance, 'many leaflets were sown on the streets and on the Burg square', threatening Jan Biese, Lubrecht de Scutelare, Clais de Soutere, and others of the city government who had forced on the guilds the Calf Skin, a charter of Duke John the Fearless very unfavourable to the popular classes.[104] With Jelle Haemers, in a later chapter in this volume, I study in detail such political languages of mobilisation, deliberation and complaint, the *murmuratio, clamor, derision, calomnia, collation* and *petitiones* that came before every collective action.[105] The commoners might first secretly convene ('*convene secreto vulgares*'),[106] or they might openly meet in their guild houses to draw up a *clachte* or petition to be handed over to the urban authorities or to the count during one of his visits to the city.

   A 'call' or 'shout' (*roupe* or *roupinghe* in Middle Dutch) was the typical term for a call for action.[107] Such calls were a ubiquitous practice in medieval Europe.

---

102   For the context, see Haemers 2009.
103   Fieuws 1977; Robbins, Rossell, ed. 1959, pp. 20–1.
104   Lambin, ed. 1839, p. 40.
105   See [A Bad Chicken].
106   De Smet, Joseph Jean, ed. 1837b, p. 307.
107   Dumolyn 2008a.

They could be something like *'As Armes'* (mentioned in a French language chronicle, which in Dutch would have been *Te Waepen*),[108] 'Bruges and friend' (*Brugghe ende vriend*),[109] alluding to the commune as a sworn society of friendship, 'All those who love the city of Bruges, follow us!',[110] or just 'Bruges!'. In the history of medieval Flanders, the most famous of all cries is 'shield and friend' (*scilt ende vrient, scultetus et amicus*) the slogan of the Bruges rebels of May 1302, the revolt of the Bruges Matins during which French occupying soldiers were massacred. As one later version of the story has it, Pieter de Coninck entered the city at night 'fiercely shouting "shield and friend and kill them all!"' (*'Roupende met verstoremden sinnen /Scilt ende vrient ende slach al doot'*).[111] The traditional explanation of the phrase *scultetus et amicus*, as provided by the Annales Gandenses and other chronicles is that the Flemish sounds of the phrase *scilt ende vrient* were impossible for the French to pronounce. Whoever failed to correctly repeat this phrase would then have been slaughtered. However, this story is too much inspired by the biblical motif of the *shibboleth* to be taken at face value. The origin of this line should rather be sought for in the fact that the popular party in Bruges and elsewhere was at that time usually called the *amici comitis* or the *parti le conte* so the 'shield' stands for supporting the arms of the count against his enemy the king of France, while 'friend' simply refers to the terms 'friends' used in an alliance or faction.[112] Clearly, such calls for popular action had their origin in the idea and practice of the 'vengeance of the commune', the collective mobilisation typical for urban customary justice when one of the inhabitants was attacked by outsiders. Once a communal cry was uttered, it was everyone's duty to come to the rescue of a fellow burgher or, as in this case, of the *universitas* itself. By the later Middle Ages, such procedures of criminal law enforced by the people themselves had largely been banned and put in the background by the development of the princely administration of justice, but their subversive and mobilising potential was still feared by the rulers. In 1384, after a revolt which had also led to tensions between the city and the surrounding countryside, the new count Philip the Bold banned the people of Bruges and of the Liberty of Bruges from shouting out 'Bruges! Bruges!' (*'Brugghe! Brugghe!'*), or, referring to the Liberty of Bruges, *'Vrije! Vrije!'*. So severe was this law that if a row would start as a result of such a cry, the instigator would be decapitated. It was also forbidden to ring bells in the Liberty to mobilise against Bruges.[113]

---

108 Pirenne, ed. 1902, p. 19.
109 Dauwe 1987, vol. 2c, p. 766.
110 Dumolyn 1997, p. 192.
111 Brinkman and Schenkel, eds 1997, vol. 2, p. 1404.
112 Braekevelt, Buylaert, Dumolyn et al. 2012.
113 Dauwe 1987, vol. 2a, pp. 183–4.

The practice of using bells for popular mobilisation to which I have referred above has been remarked upon by medieval historians for a long time, and is obviously also not specific to the Flemish situation.[114] After the suppression of the original communal authority by the growth of comital power in the twelfth century, ringing the official bells was always considered a usurpation of public authority. According to later medieval notions, sounding the urban bells in fact belonged to the count's right to command or *bannum*, but during popular uprisings rebels seized this right to demonstrate their communal authority. On 21 February 1324, for instance, the bells of the parish churches of the villages and small towns in the sphere of influence of Bruges were rung to mobilise all men in support of the revolt. The peasant rebels '*fisrent capitaines et grandes assemblées et coururent avant le pays et abatirent les maisons des nobles*' (made captains and large assemblies and ran through the country and destroyed the houses of nobles). The count granted them a peace treaty on the condition that they could not assemble any more '*par son de cloche ou autrement*' ('through the sound of the bell or otherwise').[115] In this rural context, it must have been the bells of the village parish churches that were rung, but in Bruges itself, the main bells were the ones on the belfry or 'hall tower'. The origins of the city bells are obscured by the lack of sources before the end of the thirteenth century, but it seems plausible that the Flemish and Northern French bell towers replaced the secular functions of the bells of the parish churches at the time when belfries came into existence as the typical symbol for the communes, even as they maintained a strong link with symbols of comital power. In smaller towns and villages that did not have a belfry, the main communal bells remained those of the parish churches.[116] In Bruges, the belfry (*belford, belafroid, beffredum, halla* or *torre van der halle*) was a tower directly connected to the merchant hall. We know that this hall was there at least from the beginning of the thirteenth century and probably already existed in the twelfth century. By the middle of the thirteenth century it had a wooden tower which subsequently burnt down in 1280 and was rebuilt in brick.[117] The communal bell of the belfry was the *magna campana*, the *campana in halla* or *de clocke*. There was also a *scepenen scelle* (a *scelle* was a smaller type of bell), a *bruudclocke* or *campana nuntiarum* to announce weddings, and a *clocke van der maeltyt* and a *werc clocke* to organise the rhythm of labour and leisure in the city. Bells were rung to announce the

---

114   For instance, in Mollat and Wolff 1970, pp. 293–4 and Cohn 2012a.
115   Verbruggen, Raf 2005, pp. 104–7; De Smet, Joseph Jean, ed. 1865, pp. 292–3.
116   Van Uytven 1998, p. 127.
117   Gilliodts-Van Severen 1871–85, vol. 9, p. 38.

annual market or *Brucghemaerct*, the procession of the Holy Blood of Christ,[118] visits of the count, and every morning, noon and evening to announce the start and the end of the working day.[119] Even more than in peacetime, during periods of popular revolt, bells functioned as the principal way of mobilising the commune. On 19 October 1436, at two o'clock in the afternoon, the bell of the hall tower was rung and a mass of people gathered before it on the market square (*'na der noenen ten 11 hueren men slouch de clocke up den Halle, ende up de maerct van Brugghe vergaerderde een onghetallic volc'*). The rebel government proclaimed its ordinances before the urban community, liberating from banishment those who had been exiled for petty crimes by the former sheriff, allowing all men of the Liberty to become burghers of Bruges and enacting other measures. As was typical, after these public utterances, a letter of pardon by the duke for acts of rebellion was read out along with a charter proving that the Calf Skin of 1407 had been destroyed.[120]

Richard Trexler was the first to draw systematic attention to the role of flags in the Ciompi revolt of Florence and Arnade emphasised the importance of guild banners in Ghent revolts.[121] In Bruges, there was an official banner with the arms of the city, including signs for each section or *zestendeel*; the shooting guilds as well as craft guilds had their own banners. We know, for instance, that one city banner made in 1425 as a military standard measured 3.85 by 1.75 metres,[122] but we need more in-depth studies of Flemish guild symbolism, including their guild houses, patron saints, confraternities and processions. The Calf Skin episode of 1407–11 in particular is heavily laden with symbols of the commune and the guilds. In 1384 the guilds had been stripped of any political and military power. Moreover, their banners and candles for the procession of the Holy Blood were seized and it was proclaimed that a burgher would no longer be free from confiscation if he was found guilty of mutiny.[123] The guild banners had been confiscated officially to prevent the guilds from fighting each other, most notably the weavers against the butchers (*'om dat de ambochten niet risen en souden ieghen de heeren, ende om dat sy onderlinghe niet vechten en souden, een ambocht ieghen dandere, ghelyc dat de wevers, de welke bi wilen plaghen te vechtene ieghen de vleeschouders'*). But the fact that Philip the Bold

---

118   For the multiple links between the communal and corporate structures and popular devotion and processions, see Brown 2011.
119   Gilliodts-Van Severen 1871–85, vol. 9, pp. 48–9.
120   De Smet, Joseph Jean, ed. 1856c, p. 66.
121   Trexler 1984b.
122   Gilliodts-Van Severen 1871–85, vol. 9, p. 38.
123   Ibid., vol. 4, p. 4.

had also taken away their candles for the procession of the Holy Blood was an equally important blow for the corporate identity of the guilds.[124] These issues were closely connected to other special privileges the Bruges commune possessed. Most notably, the burghers of Bruges had been liberated from confiscation through a privilege granted by Louis of Nevers in 1338.[125] The issue of whether the material goods of the burghers could be confiscated by the prince was highly sensitive as it touched on the original communal emancipation from servility, but in 1384 Philip the Bold made an exception to original exemptions from confiscation for those who rebelled against his princely authority.[126] After the coup that he arranged in Bruges in 1407, John the Fearless once again explicitly stated in the Calf Skin that those who brought their guild banner to the marketplace before the count's banner had been there would have their goods confiscated. By this time, the guilds had gotten their banners back after their confiscation in 1384 as a concession to make them accept the financial measures in the Calf Skin, but the duke was keen on preventing that they be used in an armed gathering.[127] In 1411, however, the restrictive measures of 1407 were abolished and in 1414, while negotiating a substantial sum of money with Bruges for his wars against the Armagnacs, John again abolished the confiscation of rebel goods completely.[128] Entirely within the logic of changing the urban privileges after a popular defeat, in the charter of Arras of 1438, Philip the Good once again reversed this decision.[129]

11 Demonstrations, Strikes, and Armed Gatherings

Apart from the specific use of the term *roupe* or 'shout' for the mobilisation for a revolt, there are a number of other interesting Middle Dutch words dealing with popular politics. They all have very precise legal and political meanings, the understanding of which is essential to grasping Flemish popular politics. The first mention we have of a communal revolt in Bruges takes place during the events in 1127 and is described by Galbert: *'gravis tumultus obortus est inter Gervasium et suos et cives nostros* [...]'. A man was captured on the market square (the *forum*) by a knight of Gervase of Praet, the Bruges viscount who

---

124 Lambin, ed. 1839, p. 293.
125 Gilliodts-Van Severen 1871–85, vol. 1, p. 483.
126 Ibid., vol. 3, pp. 1–2.
127 Ibid., vol. 4, pp. 14–15.
128 Ibid., vol. 4, p. 323.
129 Ibid., vol. 5, p. 151.

was in fact siding with the citizens and had laid a siege against the assassins of Count Charles the Good. The men of Bruges now turned against Gervase and his knights (*'Continuo tumultus infinitus factus est inter cives et prosilientes ad arma'*) and they attacked his residence (*'Conclamaverunt enim se nunquam velle pati dominium cujusquam, imo in sua potestate staret hoc malefactum corrigere'*).[130] The *tumultus* mentioned here is the running to arms by the members of the commune of Bruges because their *potestas*, in other words their legal competence, had been infringed upon. The later equivalent in Middle Dutch of the *tumultus* is clearly the *loop, gheloop, lopinghe* or *uploop*. This literally means a 'run', in other words: a 'mobilisation'. The term is also used in the meaning of 'attack' or 'conflict', even a simple conflict with words, but here it denotes a performance of spontaneous popular justice by a community defending its rights. In French sources, the term generally used is *course*, which also refers to popular crowds 'running' towards a rebellion. We also sometimes encounter the words *uprisinghe* ('uprising'), *destourbanchen, roeringhen, beroerte* ('troubles'), *meute* or *muyt* ('mutiny'), *rebellicheit* ('rebellion'), and derived from these: *oproerighe, rebel* ('rebel'), *muytmemaker* ('rebel', 'mutineer').[131] An *upset*, however, usually seems to be a more deliberately planned revolt, conspiracy or factional struggle, 'set up' by *upsetters*.[132]

As a repertoire for mobilisation an *oploop* or popular demonstration had to intimidate the enemies of the commune and reinforce its own strength. It was often accompanied by a lot of shouting and kettle music and the display of signs and banners.[133] During the Bruges Matins of 1302, for instance, the rebels were making *'sonoribus et vocibus ac clamoribus terribilis'* ('with sounds and voices or terrifying cries').[134] When rebels marched in a fashion similar to a procession through specific parts of the city, as Haemers and Lecuppre-Desjardin have shown, this popular 'movement' also intended to symbolically occupy important public spaces such as the main squares or the commercial areas, thereby demonstrating its authority over the body of the city.[135] More specifically in the context of labour relations and conditions, another form of

---

130 Rider, ed. 1994, p. 100. See also Van Caenegem 1994b.
131 Dauwe 1987, vol. 2a, p. 35.
132 For instance, Gilliodts-Van Severen 1871–85, vol. 3, p. 233. See also our observations on the vocabulary of Flemish factional struggle in Braekevelt, Buylaert, Dumolyn et al. 2012. Earlier assessments of these and other terms in Verbruggen, Raf 2005, pp. 164–5; and Boone 2005. Additional evidence comes from searches in Verwijs and Verdam, ed. *Middelnederlandsch Woordenboek* (http://gtb.inl.nl/).
133 See [A Moody Community].
134 De Smet, Joseph Jean, ed. 1837a, pp. 166–7.
135 Haemers and Lecuppre-Desjardin 2007.

demonstration, the *ledichganck*, literally 'going idle', refers to a strike action by the guildsmen. Sometimes a strike is also called an *uutganck* ('going out'), in the case when the craftsmen left the city to make an even stronger point. Only reliably documented since 1245 in Douai, such early industrial action, notably in the export-oriented textile industry, seems to have been a major problem since the middle of the thirteenth century. These medieval strikes, as a feature of the more developed urban economy, the accumulation of capital and the concentration of labour in the suburbs, remained present as a form of action for centuries to come.[136] As later chronicles remark about a strike in Bruges in 1302 against the French occupation 'nobody wanted to work in Bruges, it was mass day every day' (*Te Brugghe en wilde niement weerken, het was allen dach mesdach*)[137] even though, as another chronicle mentions, governor Jacques de Châtillon planned to hang all the *mechanicos nolentes operari* ('manual workers who did not want to work').[138] The city accounts also suggest that in 1344–5 there was a *ledichganc* as a result of a conflict between the weavers and the shearers as the latter worked as wage labourers for the former.[139] The major revolt of 1436 also started with what a Burgundian charter called a strike *appelé en Flameng ledichganc*, but at that point a specific circumstance was that the craftsmen had just come back from the failed siege of Calais with the city militia in the service of Duke Philip the Good, and they used this occasion for refusing to start to work once back in Bruges.[140] Still, during the revolt of 1477 and 1488 the *ledichganc* remained a permanent feature of Bruges popular politics.[141]

As in other cases, looking for the origins of these repertoires of popular politics remains a speculative endeavour because of the scarcity of twelfth- and thirteenth-century sources, but the general picture seems to be one of both continuity and adaptation to economic and social developments. Many of the above performances of contentious politics may have found their origin in older systems of communal mobilisations of customary justice, but clearly by the fourteenth century their formal aspects were dominated by the military organisation and ideology of the craft guilds, who organised popular politics in a rather planned and disciplined manner.

The urban militia and rituals of watch and guard have been central to the politics of the commune since its origin, but we are poorly informed on the

---

136 Verbruggen, Raf 2005, pp. 145–51.
137 Lambin, ed. 1839, p. 159.
138 De Smet, Joseph Jean, ed. 1837a, p. 166.
139 Gilliodts-Van Severen 1871–85, vol. 8, p. 393.
140 Ibid., vol. 5, p. 154.
141 Wellens 1965.

earliest phase of communal military organisation. We know that the Ghent urban militia of 1127 is referred to as a *communio* by Galbert, and there are some examples of urban troops fighting in twelfth- and thirteenth-century conflicts, but only for the later Middle Ages are we somewhat informed on aspects like uniforms, banners, weaponry etc. In connection with the rights to possess their own banners,[142] after 1302, the guilds also obtained a large degree of military autonomy. The Flemish urban soldiers were especially renowned as crossbow-men, pikemen and foot-soldiers in general, but they also realised that military mobilisations in the service of their prince gave them an important power they could make use of to obtain political goals.[143] Thus in 1411, the militia of Bruges, which had just returned from a Burgundian expedition against the Armagnac enemies of John the Fearless in Picardy, remained in arms on a field just out-side Bruges. They refused to take off their arms and enter the city unless the Calf Skin would be given to the army to tear up and the tax house demol-ished with hammers and thrown into the canal. The faction that had come to power in 1407 had promulgated the Calf Skin without the knowledge of the commune when they had ordained the deans of every guild and had returned to them their privileges and their banners, but the deans had to seal the let-ter without knowing what was inside it and *under threat*.[144] So it was in the context of an armed gathering of the guild militias, referred to in the sources as an *auweet* or *wapening* (literally 'watch' or 'muster') that on 19 October, as mentioned above, the Calf Skin was handed over to the deans of the guilds on their banners. Every dean tore off the seal of his craft and the whole parch-ment was then torn to pieces by the artisans using their teeth for this symbolic act.[145]

Boone, Arnade, Haemers and others have already amply described that per-haps the most archetypal pattern of popular mobilisation in Ghent was the *wapening*, a ritualised armed gathering of the guilds, banners fully deployed, on a central square in the city, displaying the collective anger of the crafts-men through an intimidating but at the same time disciplined choreography.[146] Combining this bodily and spatial performance with auditory signals of mobil-isation, the bells of guild houses, if they had any, would be rung to mobilise the rank and file, thus imitating the 'storm bell' of city government when the

---

142   Already attested in the *Annales Gandenses*, see Johnstone, ed. 1951, pp. 12–13.
143   See a synthesis in Verbruggen, Jan 1977.
144   Dauwe 1987, vol. 2a, p. 243; De Smet, Joseph Jean, ed. 1837a, p. 252; Lambin, ed. 1839, p. 294; Fris 1911a, pp. 242–3. Fris is right in judging that this was a typical myth.
145   Ibid., p. 82.
146   See [A Moody Community]; Boone 2005; Arnade 1994.

rebels could not get access to the latter. Guild flags would hang from above the windows and further visualise the power of the commoners. However, it has perhaps not been emphasised enough that in itself the Middle Dutch *wapening* in most occurrences simply meant 'battle' or 'military campaign' in general. In fact, the *wapening* for a military campaign ordered by the prince, as the guilds would assemble for a muster on a central square of the city, mostly took place along the same lines as a 'rebellious one' would have.[147] Yet again, a popular *wapening* implied the usurpation, or, in fact, the reappropriation of forms of public power and authority by the commune. The purpose of such a *wapening*, which in Bruges is usually called the *auweet* or *auwette* (derived from the French *guêt*), though the term *wapening* is also sometimes used there,[148] was to deploy the symbolic and physical strength of the guildsmen in order to enter into negotiations with the authorities, either the city government or sometimes the prince if he was present. This was in some ways a play with staged emotions, channelling the collective *ira* of the people. In the previous chapter, Haemers has argued that the *wapening* was 'a well-understood socio-political code, in which anger appeared as a social "signal" which, paradoxically, helped to keep the peace'. The *wapening* or *auweet* made the middle and lower classes participants in the polity again for some time and temporarily created new balances of forces within the commune.[149] Thus, in 1477, it was the Bruges craft guilds who once again mobilised according to customary communal patterns, breaking into the belfry to examine the city's privileges, assembling and arming themselves in their guild houses with the guild banners raised from there, drawing up a petition in the Great Council, and assembling in a *wapening* through a *roupinghe* or call for action. They were soon followed by 'the commune of the Liberty of Bruges', the smaller and middle peasants who, in revolt against the noble aldermen who dominated the Liberty rural district of the Liberty of Bruges, demanded to be directly ruled by the city. This seems remarkable given the fact that the Bruges rebels repeated their traditional demands of economically dominating the countryside and the outports. Clearly, however, the commoners of the Liberty of Bruges, most likely smaller and middle peasants, preferred this to being ruled by their own aldermen, most of whom were nobles. Apart from the problems with the urban hinterland, the Bruges popular programme was a traditional communal one: removing obstacles to trade and industry such as tolls and market restrictions, restoring the political and

---

147 Dauwe 1987, vol. 2b, p. 291.
148 For instance, Gilliodts-Van Severen 1871–85, vol. 4, p. 136; Dauwe 1987, vol. 2b, p. 328.
149 See [A Moody Community], pp. 63–81.

military rights of the guilds, ratifying urban privileges and fighting corruption among the political elites.[150]

12   Conclusion: The Sign System of Popular Justice

In many ways, Flemish medieval rebels formulated a moral lesson for the rulers or to the wealthy and powerful in general when the latter had failed to safeguard the commonweal of their community. In the final analysis, all of the sign systems of contentious politics that the rebels deployed were languages of justice, codes of the collective vengeance of the community on its internal and external enemies who were deemed useless or harmful to the city. Corrupt burgomasters, aldermen, treasurers, speculating grain merchants or princely officials, city rulers failing to defend the customs and privileges of the town or those persons or groups accused of sowing factional strife and discord (including even the most radical rebels who were supressed by middle-class revolt leaders themselves) – all would meet with the vengeance of the commune. Thus, the Bruges commoners who gathered on the market square in 1436 sought to impose justice on the captain of Sluis Roeland van Uutkerke who had called them 'mutineers'. They refused to lay down their arms even when the burgomasters, aldermen, bailiff, sheriffs and army captains went from banner to banner to ask every guild to do so.[151] This was a moment of communal justice, of the commune in its totality represented by the constituents of the corporate body politic, demanding that customs be carried out and overruling the judicial power of the bench of aldermen. We have noted how essential the city privileges were both as perlocutory speech acts and in their materiality, but the repressive signs of communal justice against those who did not uphold and defend these privileges included the burning and demolishing of the houses of enemies, lynching or imprisoning town rulers, subjecting them to mock executions or real ones, exiling them and confiscating their property. During a smaller Bruges revolt in 1310, for instance, Michiel de Loo, an alderman, was killed.[152] Though the circumstances of this event are not very clear, it would probably be mistaken to consider this as merely an act of spontaneous violence by a mob out of control. During outbursts of violent popular politics, the rebels once again carried out the communal criminal justice that had been forbidden for the centuries during which the rendering of justice had been monopolised

---

150   Haemers 2009, pp. 156–73.
151   Dauwe 1987, vol. 2b, p. 312.
152   Verbruggen, Raf 2005, p. 124.

by the aldermen instituted by the count, but which was still practised in times of revolt. They did so most arrogantly during the great revolt of 1323–8 when, after Count Louis of Nevers himself had been captured by rebels in Kortrijk and had been imprisoned in Bruges, his six principal noble councillors were cut into pieces, despite the fact, so one chronicle tells us, that the count was begging 'with tears in his eyes' that they be saved.[153] From the point of view of the commune, this was not murder but a political execution. During the revolt of 1488 against Maximilian of Austria, King of the Romans, who would also be imprisoned in Bruges, the rebels arrested the previous aldermen and 'plusieurs autres gens de bien et d'auctorité' and nine or ten of them were publicly tortured and beheaded.[154]

But the overall picture of the centuries of popular revolt is not such a bloody one, and executions were not all that frequent. As is already attested in the earliest sources of Flemish urban criminal law, exile was a more accustomed way of dealing with the internal enemies of the commune.[155] After the popular victory at Kortrijk, for instance, about 250 Lilies were exiled from Bruges as 'enemies of the city', and their goods were confiscated.[156] Another typical form of punishment of the enemies of the commune was the ritual destruction or burning of their houses. The droit d'arsin was the right to burn down a house or castle of an enemy, usually outside the city because within the city burning houses obviously endangered whole neighbourhoods. Also practised was the woesten of a person, meaning banishing him so all his properties could be confiscated and his house would be destroyed. In Bruges, the urban practice of demolishing houses, the droit d'abattis or huus asselieren was already banned by the anti-communal Keure of 1281, as it had been practised by the rebels of the meentucht of the Moerlemaye revolt of 1280 against the properties of patrician oligarchs.[157] Clearly, the count felt the need to explicitly forbid this practice because it was still considered an acceptable form of collective justice by the Bruges commoners, and during the fourteenth and fifteenth century it remained one of the most frequently utilised methods of resistance in the repertoire of popular politics. We already saw how in 1323–38, 'chil de Bruges, du Franc et d'entour cachèrent les chevaliers et nobles homes hors du païs et en ochirent pluiseurs, et abatirent leur forteresse' (those of Bruges, of the Liberty of Bruges and of the district chased the knights and noble men from

153 Dauwe 1987, vol. 2a, p. 19.
154 De Smet, Joseph Jean, ed. 1856a, p. 719.
155 Van Caenegem 1954, pp. 22–3.
156 Verbruggen, Jan 1991, pp. 19–21.
157 Warnkönig 1835, vol. 2, p. 103.

the country, slayed many of them and demolished their fortress).[158] The most radical rebels burned them completely (*'audaciores effecti apposuerunt ignem in domibus nobelium'*),[159] and it was even reported that the leaders of the revolt made an ideological point of preventively destroying all noble castles in the area *'considerantes non esse bonum nobiles habere fortes domos et mansions'*, as these were their strongholds from which the rural population was terrorised.[160]

During the revolt of 1436, all those who had been magistrates of the city within the last thirty years were ordered to come to the market square. Gheer-art Ruebs, 'of whom it was known he was no friend of the commune and that he and his retainers wanted to force the commune into submission', and Dolin van Thielt did not show up, so they were sought for in their houses and these houses were stormed (*'geselgiert'*) and partly demolished as all their windows were broken. The wine barrels in the cellars were also destroyed.[161] Subsequently, the Bruges rebels also attacked the country house of Guy de Baenst, a local nobleman who had been exiled during the revolt, in the parish of Heile outside the city.[162] Typically, in this practice, it was usually enough to break windows and roofs and the rest of the house would soon fall into ruin. So they smashed the glass windows 'and some other things and inflicted great damage to the house'.[163] We have already seen how tax houses would be destroyed, and breaking into prisons was yet another typical feature of communal revolts, and another re-appropriation of criminal justice.[164] However, the chronicle of Adrian de Budt, a later writer, tells us that when Pieter de Coninck had been captured by the bailiff of Bruges with twenty-five 'criers' (*'cum fere xxv clamatoribus'*) he was freed by the common people (*'communitas rupto carcere cum omnibus violenter'*).[165] By analogy, in 1436, when the people of Bruges had been insulted by those of Sluis who had refused to let them in, they even wanted that *'les portes et murs de l'Escluse fussent abbatuz'*.[166] Unable to carry out such a plan directly, the commoners stormed the house that Roeland of Uutkerke, the captain of Sluis, possessed in Bruges and destroyed it.[167] Thus the sign system of

---

158   De Smet, Joseph Jean, ed. 1856b, p. 143.
159   De Smet, Joseph Jean, ed. 1837a, pp. 187–8.
160   De Smet, Joseph Jean, ed. 1837b, pp. p. 318; TeBrake 1993, pp. 24–6, 67–9.
161   Dauwe 1987, vol. 2b, pp. 318–19; Lambin, ed. 1839, pp. 327–8.
162   Dumolyn 1997, p. 192.
163   Dauwe 1987, vol. 2b, p. 342.
164   *'Quem communitas rupto carcere cum omnibus, violenter aliquibus Liliardis occisis et in fugam conversis, eduxit.'* De Smet, Joseph Jean, ed. 1837b, p. 307.
165   Ibid., pp. 307–8.
166   De Smet, Joseph Jean, ed. 1865, p. 317.
167   Dauwe 1987, vol. 2b, pp. 309–10; compare with Boone 1997a.

popular politics was and remained in the first place one of popular justice and customary moral discourse on the duties of rulers.

Other historians have made similar observations, though have not made them central to their arguments, and I believe that they can indeed be generalised into wider parts of medieval Europe. Though medieval revolts have been a rather popular topic of research since the 1970s, their pristine history during the very early days of the communal movement between the eleventh and the thirteenth centuries has been neglected. It was in fact then that urban popular politics took its first shape, and though a lot changed as urban Europe demographically and economically exploded during this period, a lot also stayed the same. Even the 1566 Calvinist iconoclasts of the Low Countries were still very much using the same traditional codes of collective action, connecting their religious protest with what Peter Arnade calls 'the language of (masculine) labor'.[168] By then, politically and socially a lot had changed since the earliest revolts in Ghent, Bruges, Lille and other cities in the years 1127–8, or even since the classic epoch of textile guild uprisings in the middle of the fourteenth century. Customary communal forms of popular mobilisation to protect the sworn peace of the city and the security of every inhabitant had first been appropriated or banned by the count and his aldermen in an effort to monopolise justice and legitimate violence. After 1302, this communal idea of justice was subsequently framed according to the logic, military organisation and symbolism of the corporate rule of the town by the political guilds. Communal justice as corporate rule became part of the middle-class ideology on labour and brotherly love. The communal sign systems became hegemonic in the urban context, but they remained contested between the popular classes and the elites. In the meantime, social and political conflicts between the lower, middle and upper classes in the town itself had been complicated by the growing external pressure of the centralising Burgundian state. In the age of the Reformation, where the sequel of this story could be written, Flanders proved to be a particularly fertile ground for radical Protestantism resulting in the blending of new religious motives with older social and political rebellious ideologies. Communal sign systems interacted in form and function with these structural changes but always retained a strong relative autonomy because their fundamentally moral and customary character moved more slowly than social and political reality.

---

168   Arnade 2005, pp. 95, 103; Arnade 2008.

CHAPTER 7

Social Memory and Rebellion in Fifteenth-Century Ghent

Jelle Haemers

Retrouver le passé dans le présent; c'est bien ainsi qu'on peut définir la mémoire.[1]

∵

1 Introduction

Since the 1950 posthumous publication of an unfinished book by Maurice Halbwachs (1877–1945), and its rediscovery in the last decades of the twentieth century, scholars have agreed with his view that collective memory is a constructive force in society. Expanding on Emile Durkheim's writings and reacting to Henri Bergson, Halbwachs looked at memory in terms of minds working together in society, with operations structured by social arrangements. The French sociologist and philosopher wrote that memory is not a purely individual affair, but rather shaped by social frameworks and identities. Halbwachs argues that although individuals remember within their own minds, what they remember is determined by the larger social group and the setting surrounding the event. Consequently, Halbwachs and many current scholars of memory believe that the collective memory of groups shapes identities and marks social differentiation.[2] Moreover, current scholarly work posits memory as a sociocultural mode of action.[3] Memory is defined as a disparate range of practices

---

1 Halbwachs 1950, p. 104 (English translation Halbwachs 1992). For a survey of this work see Olick 1999, pp. 334–6.

2 Olick and Robbins 1998, pp. 105–40; Kansteiner 2002; Climo and Cattel 2002.

3 Confino 1997, p. 1390. The notion of 'cultural memory' elaborates on this, for it is 'a form of collective memory, in the sense that it is shared by a number of people and that it conveys to this people a collective, that is, cultural identity'. Assmann 2008, p. 110. See also Assmann 1992; and Erll 2005.

and processes which are involved in producing consciousness of the past. It is the means by which a conscious sense of the past, as something meaningfully connected to the present, is sustained and developed within society.[4] The image created by each society of its history gives us a sense of the past through its present use. Memories stir emotions, motivate people to act, give meaning to objects and places, and legitimise social hierarchy and political power. Through its collective remembering, a group constitutes its social relationships, its culture and identity, and even its future. As Maurice Halbwachs postulates in the above quotation, we can define memory by recovering the past in the present.

Although this article reflects many of the ideas of Halbwachs (and his followers), it will not employ the term 'collective memory' as a conceptual category, because of the problems scholars have identified with this term. James Fentress and Chris Wickham, for example, noted that those who follow Halbwachs end up with a conception of memory which, in the attempt to do full justice to the collective side of one's consciousness, renders the individual into an automaton passively obeying the interiorised collective will.[5] These scholars do not deny that social groups construct their own images of the world by establishing a common version of the past; they still emphasise that these pasts are created by communication, not by private remembrance. However, Fentress and Wickham argue that individual memories, and even the cognitive processes of memory, contain much that is social in origin. Therefore, they prefer the notion of 'social memory', which accentuates the important role of social structures in creating and maintaining collective memory practices. Adding his adherence to the term 'social memory', Geoffrey Cubitt elaborates on the concept. He sees it as a process through which knowledge or awareness of past events is developed and sustained within human societies, while also giving individuals in those societies a sense of a past that extends beyond what they themselves personally remember.[6] Cubitt's point is that the notion of a 'collective memory' transmitted from generation to generation as a fundamental part of social identity masks what are often radical discontinuities in social consciousness. To him, social memory is the continuously modified result of a set of processes that within any community are likely to generate a diversity of understandings. Setting aside the theoretical debates on these nuances, which are well beyond the scope of this article, I find Cubitt's concept of social memory constructive because he sees the process of memory as primarily a dynamic social phenomenon. In addition, as Olick says, social memory is a useful concept

---

4 Cubitt 2007, pp. 5, 9.
5 Fentress and Wickham 1992, p. ix.
6 Cubitt 2007, pp. 14–15.

for a wide variety of mnemonic processes, practices and outcomes (neurological, cognitive, personal, aggregated and collective). Unlike collective memory studies, social memory studies do not raise confusion about their objects of reference.[7]

I also prefer the concept of 'social memory' because 'collective memory', as it is defined in Halbwachs's writings, appears to assume that there is just one collective memory working in a society. Although Halbwachs was himself aware of the distinct uses of memory by various groups in the same community,[8] research on collective memories often concludes that a social memory in a community is 'monolithic'. Of course, different individuals can share the same memories about a certain event in the past, even when they belong to totally different social groups, but people can also react very differently to the same event. After all, because social memories originate in a community in which different social groups live together, different social memories can be produced and maintained – as long as the social 'barriers' of the memories endure. Consequently, two or more social memories can co-exist in the same society. Both memories are still collective (in the sense that they are shared by a group), but they are not shared in common by all social groups, nor does one memory have hegemony. Building on an interpretation of Michel Foucault's work, some scholars even employ the term 'counter-memories' to assess different 'competing' social memories. Some use the term 'counter-memories' for memories that differ from and often challenge dominant discourses, but Foucault himself did not develop this notion.[9] By offering a divergent commemorative narrative representing the views of subordinate groups within the society, a counter-memory challenges the hegemony of the elite's construction of the past, a construction which serves the elite's special interests and promotes its political agenda. Through the development of an alternative vision of the past which opposes the hegemonic one, remembrance of the past becomes a contested territory in which groups engaging in a political conflict promote competing narratives in order to gain control over the political centre or legitimise a political position, as Yael Zerubavel has convincingly shown for a contemporary case.[10]

---

7   Olick 1999, p. 346.
8   He studied, for example, the social memory of medieval nobility, for which he definitely acknowledged that this was just one 'social framework' in which a certain memory came into existence; see Halbwachs 1923.
9   Foucault 1971, p. 167; reprinted in Foucault 1994, vol. 2, p. 143; translated in Foucault 1977, p. 160; and in Foucault 1991, p. 83.
10   Zerubavel, Yael 1995, p. 11. See also Lipsitz 1989, p. 123.

This article presents a case study of an alternative social memory of less prominent citizens which challenged the social memory of powerful elites, but set this time in a medieval context. It concerns the social memory of the urban craftsmen of fifteenth-century Ghent, and it reconstructs a 'sociomental topography' of the Ghent craft guilds,[11] highlighting the marked social dimension of human memory by recovering how this specific social group, rather than just the individual craftsman, remembered the past. In a similar manner to other examples, the social memory of the Ghent craft guilds framed guild identity, legitimised their quest for power, provided justification for their frequent rebellions and made their mobilisation more efficient. But this specific 'artisan memory' did not hold a monopoly in the city, because it had to compete with the social memories constructed by other groups, such as the urban elite, the nobility who resided in the city and the court. The different social memories of the elite and craftsmen were not diametrically opposed to one another, but each propagated a distinct vision of history in order to legitimise its own political views. As will be shown, the history of fifteenth-century Ghent was dominated by a struggle between the Ghent craft guilds and a growing state power which contested the corporate autonomy of the guilds. This article illustrates that the craft guilds not only had to defend their privileges but also their social memory against the aggressive court elite. The political and sometimes military contest between the state and the craft guilds was accompanied by a battle between memories. In the end, the state elite won the struggle, because almost all traces of the alternative memory of the craft guilds were erased. However, by a careful reading of the sources and recovery of exceptional archival material, it is now possible to retrieve traces of the lost social memory of the craft guilds – although it has not survived the clash with its powerful enemy unscathed.

There are many reasons why scholars have not studied the social memory of lower echelons of society, a subject which poses many difficulties. A political battle in which one social group succeeds in dominating its challenger and destroys the media of its memory and thus the potential sources of the historian is just one of them. Others include the extinction of a social group (and thus its memory) and the small chance that its objects and writings will survive. In contrast, the social memories of elites, monastic communities or court nobles have been exhaustively studied, because these groups left behind essential sources for historians to mine. A monastic community, for instance, had an institutional continuity and traditional methods for efficiently maintaining archives, which other groups in medieval society lacked. Of course, communit-

---

11   Zerubavel, Eviatar 2003, p. 2.

ies of monks could manipulate history and ignore certain memories, cultivating in this way a culture of 'social forgetting' if such moves were necessary for political or other purposes.[12] Political tensions within the monastic community may also have influenced its construction of a certain vision of the past, but usually the most influential group succeeded in wiping out the view of its competitors. In that event, the memories maintained by the community might not have been as monolithic as its historiographical production leads us to believe. However, the weaker group did not have the traditions, means or structures to pass on alternative views of history equivalent to that of the more powerful group. After those who experienced the events died, future generations began to manipulate the commemoration of those events in a way that was useful for themselves.[13] Consequently, the social memory faded away as a group disappeared from the social spectrum, or when their media of communication were targeted by political repression (as my case will show). As a result, historians do not dispose of the sources to study alternative social memories. In contrast, sources of the powerful groups in society are abundantly preserved. Epic stories of early medieval noble families, for instance, were copied all over Europe because these families had the funds to preserve their parchment documents.[14] Wealthy families in Renaissance Italian or German-speaking cities left abundant chronicles (the *ricordanze* or *Stadtbücher*) in which the history of the family was exhaustively detailed and often contextualised into the city's history.[15] However, the oral traditions of artisans and craftsmen in the same cities were rarely written down, and if they were, these mnemonic narratives did not survive repression, or less than optimal storage conditions.[16] The scanty remains of such memories must therefore be studied in 'an archaeological way', by carefully retrieving the context, the social background, and the intellectual and cultural tradition in which the memory was embedded. Moreover, since this trace evidence comes to us second hand, we must carefully assess its authenticity. Finally, the historian has to consider why these small fragments have survived, because the reasons for that survival contribute to an understanding of the conditions which assist the maintenance or hasten the disappearance of a social memory. This article searches out such traces, in order to demonstrate

---

12   Vanderputten 2004. See also Haverkamp and Lachmann, eds 1993.
13   Assmann 1992, p. 40. Or, as Geary argued, a social memory is about how the present should be, because of how the past had been, Geary 1994, p. 8. See also Geary 2005.
14   Wandhoff 2004.
15   Zotz 2000. For other case studies, see Ciapelli and Rubin, eds 2000; Brand, Monnet and Staub, eds 2003; Studt, ed. 2007.
16   Haines 2000.

that the lower orders in medieval urban society actively opposed repression of their social memory. Evidence of oral and written mnemonic practices will reveal that those groups had an alternative social memory that contradicted the stories of the city's rulers. The Ghent craftsmen developed their own self-conscious narrative (in oral and written form) and used it politically when it was needed. But I will also examine why, in spite of its remarkable resilience, the social memory of the late medieval Ghent craft guilds in the end disappeared.

2   The Media of Memory in the Medieval City

Medieval culture was fundamentally memorial.[17] In creating, maintaining, and propagating social memories, medieval citizens used a wide range of communicative practices and media. Several *Objekten mit Appellfunktion*, as Peter Johanek has called them, such as places, buildings, flags, images, relics, texts, songs and rituals, evoked historical remembrance in the medieval city.[18] Memories resided in many mnemonic sites and practices, which can be labelled 'sites of memories'.[19] In Halbwachs's eyes, the spatial environment is one of the most important areas in which social groups frame their representations of the past.[20] Sculptures, buildings and monuments, as symbols of remembrance, act as boundaries around a social group's identity. Social historians rightly consider how (rural and urban) landscapes contain a vital collection of mnemonic devices which structure local memories, customs and practices – a repository of knowledge which can be passed on to successive generations.[21] Consequently, static symbols in stone were not only clearly visible landmarks, but also sites of remembrance, appropriated by social groups to display their views of history. A focus on political conflicts makes it important to stress that the symbolic meaning attributed to buildings and places can be contested by other groups. Consequently, the appropriation of a certain place or building can provide the focus for conflict. As historians have amply proven, urban public space was a forum for contests between political opponents in the cities of the medieval

---

17   Carruthers 2008, p. 8.
18   Johanek 2002, p. 343. Compare Geary 2000; and Innes 2000.
19   Climo and Cattel 2002, p. 17.
20   Halbwachs 1950, pp. 86–8. See also the numerous studies on the so-called *lieux de mémoire* – in France: Nora 1984–92; in Germany: François and Schulze, eds 2003; in Belgium: Tollebeek, Buelens, Deneckere et al., eds 2008.
21   Rollison 1992; Whyte 2007.

Low Countries, cities which were spatial realms of locations inflected with economic, political and cultural importance. When they took over and claimed public space, urban social groups vied with one another and with regional and state authorities. The original geographical core of the commune was constantly refashioned as patricians, guildsmen and representatives of the state crafted their ritual statements of power. Newly empowered elites did not so much redraw the spatial map as they appropriated established sites, symbols of authority and loci of mnemonic significance.[22] Through just a few striking examples, I intend not only to clarify the importance of this 'spatial medium of remembrance' in late medieval society, but also to outline the objectives of political struggle between the Ghent craft guilds and the ruling dynasty of the Burgundian dukes in fifteenth-century Flanders.

In 1453, Philip the Good, Duke of Burgundy and Count of Flanders, gave the order to lock one city gate of Ghent, the *Spitaalpoort*, permanently, and lock two more gates, the *Heuvelpoort* and the *Percellepoort*, each Thursday, as part of the punishment he allotted to the city after his conquest ended four years of open revolt.[23] During this revolt, the craft guilds had taken over rule of the city by removing ducal loyalists from their seats on the city's benches of aldermen. Those aldermen who had been the duke's supporters had not stopped Philip the Good from violating the city's custom that the craft guilds had the sole right to choose their own deans. Ghent recognised fifty-three so-called 'small craft guilds', each governed by its own dean and a 'chief dean' (*overdeken*) over all.[24] By personally manipulating the election of the chief dean in 1447, Philip the Good and his loyalists had clearly violated the right of self-government of the Ghent craft guilds. Since this custom was the main guarantee of the craft guilds' political autonomy, they had forcefully rebelled to counter violation of their privileges. Such revolts were continual in the history of late medieval cities all over the Low Countries, as urban craft guilds tried to hold on to acquired rights and corporate benefits which protected their privileged position in city politics.[25] The duke's flamboyant provocation actually concealed his true goal, abolition of the political autonomy of the craft guilds, who had opposed his centralizing policies for decades. Seeking redress for this aggravation, the craftsmen chose one of the duke's fervent political opponents, Daneel Sersanders, as new chief dean in 1449, and he led the city of Ghent dur-

---

22   Boone 2002a, p. 640; Lecuppre-Desjardin 2004a.
23   Haemers 2004b, p. 387; Arnade 1996a, pp. 120–1.
24   About the institutional structures of Ghent, see Boone 1990b; on its craft guilds, see Stabel 2004; and on the 1477 conflict, see Haemers 2004b, pp. 138–46.
25   Prak 2006.

ing the first years of the revolt against the ducal regime. The uprising ended in a military conflict between the two parties, which the duke won at the battle of Gavere in July 1453. As a consequence, the duke abolished certain privileges of the Ghent craft guilds, such as the right to elect their deans. He also imposed a fine on the city and marked the city landscape with signs of remembrance. As part of the symbolic punishment, Philip the Good ordered the closure 'for perpetual memory' of the *Spitaalpoort* through which the craft guild militias had marched in 1452 on their way to attack the duke's troops at Rupelmonde, a battle in which Ghent forces killed a bastard son of the duke.[26] The other two gates were only forced to close on Thursdays, because the craft guilds had marched out of these gates on White Thursday 1452 to attack the ducal army at Oudenaarde. By blocking the gates, the duke intended that the city's inhabitants would eternally remember that fighting against his armies was an illegal act rendered impossible for the future.

In June 1467, however, the craft guilds unlocked the three city gates.[27] The reopening of the gates marked the beginning of a new revolt against the Burgundian dynasty and an effort to regain the privileges that the town had lost in 1453. The immediate cause of the revolt was the Joyous Entry of Duke Charles the Bold, who had succeeded his father Philip the Good some months before. The political vacuum at the state level had empowered the craft guilds to rid themselves of the punitive measures Charles's father had enacted in 1453. The rebels also removed another ducal symbol by demolishing the duke's tax houses in the Cornmarket Square. These tax houses had been constructed after the treaty of 1453 for the express purpose of collecting taxes to pay the fine imposed on Ghent by the victorious duke. Clearly, the craft guilds wanted to rid the urban landscape of the painful scars from the military defeat of 1453 constructed by the Burgundian dynasty. Retaking symbols of political resistance lost in 1453, the rebels returned to the city the craft guild's banners, which the guilds had frequently deployed during the 1449–53 revolt in the streets and the Friday Market (*Vrijdagmarkt*), Ghent's central public square, as symbolic markers of occupation.[28] The purpose of this ceremonial activity in the centre of the city was to overwhelm viewers emotionally so that they would never forget, a primary function of the ceremonial use of rituals.[29] In the following months, the craft guilds managed to replace the city aldermen who had been loyal to

---

26   Duke Philip the Good stipulated that the '*Ospitaeleporte, en perpetuelle memoire, soit fermee et muree*' (Gachard 1833–4, vol. 2, pp. 152–3).

27   Arnade 1991.

28   Arnade 1994; See [Moody community].

29   As, for instance, has been shown by Althoff 2002b, p. 72.

the duke with their own representatives, a logical outcome of their new victory in the struggle against the Burgundian dynasty.

In 1467, all the markers which might remind the city of its military defeat of 1453 had been eliminated from urban space and replaced by the craft guild banners, symbols of their political power. In Ghent, as in other late medieval towns, these large flags bearing the insignias of each guild symbolised the right to self-government of these corporate entities and, as such, they functioned as an important mnemonic medium. Their colourful appearance in the streets and the central market square reminded citizens of the newly gained political power of the craft guilds. The events of 1467 therefore demonstrate that the Ghent craft guilds readily took advantage of opportunities to conquer urban space with their symbols – as was the case in other revolts of craftsmen in Flanders and throughout late medieval Europe.[30] By waving the banners and tearing down the visible reminder of ducal punishment (the tax houses), the craft guilds made the spectators think of the glorious days when the guilds had been in power. The ceremonial opening of the city gates erased the humiliation of 1453, and afterwards the unblocked gates reminded each passer-by that the craft guilds had recovered their political autonomy. The social memory of the craft guilds was again overtly visible in the city, after they had succeeded in effacing the symbols which had inscribed the memory of repression.

The events of 1467 reveal that the struggle between the Ghent craft guilds and the ruler of the Low Countries, the dynasty of the dukes of Burgundy, was a profound political battle. Revolts in Flanders were fought with violence, political tactics and military clashes in which the financial resources of each side often predicted the outcome. In this continuous conflict between supporters and opponents of the Burgundian dynasty, mnemonic practices were just one of several weapons. Both sides tried to manipulate people by using symbolic objects and intervening in urban space. However mighty mnemonic practices may have been, they could not counteract the power of the sword. After a few months of rebel ascendancy, Charles the Bold struck back. In 1468 he imposed a severe punishment on Ghent, levying heavy fines and establishing a new institutional structure which deprived the craft guilds of power.[31] As the duke had just sacked the city of Liège, the rebels knew they could not overcome his military and political power. The symbols of the rebel's victory of 1467 had to disappear. The city gates were closed again, and the tax houses were rebuilt. But in spite of the severe repression which followed the duke's punitive measures,

30   Trexler 1984b; McRee 1994, pp. 202–3; Haemers and Lecuppre-Desjardin 2007.
31   Boone 2001b.

the social memory of the rebels did not fade away. The craft guilds maintained their social memory of rebellion, making it available to be used again to legitimate their bid for power after the sudden death of Duke Charles in 1477. But before moving to the remarkable events of 1477, we must examine the ways in which the guilds maintained the social memory of their rebellious tradition, in spite of the incessant repression of which the guilds were the victim. Rare traces of songs and poems about rebel leaders show that the rebellious tradition of the Ghent craftsmen was maintained through oral media of remembrance in the first place.

3 Oral Practices of Remembrance

By restructuring the past and telling distorted stories about it, the Ghent craftsmen cultivated a social memory based on heroic episodes from successful or repressed revolts. Craftsmen defined themselves through these narratives, and urban rebels used them to legitimise both past and future uprisings. In contrast to the official historiography, written at court by chroniclers who condemned violent actions against princes or urban elites, rebels maintained a kind of 'counter-memory' about the same events, transmitting them from one generation to the next. Studies of urban revolts in medieval and early modern England and France have demonstrated the probable endurance of a widespread social memory of popular rebellion which conditioned protest and legitimated its ideology.[32] As these examples show, memories of rebellions gave labouring people a historical context within which to make sense of contemporary power relations and resistance. In medieval Ghent, the existence of several fragments of poems and songs suggests that a similar kind of oral rebellious tradition thrived among the city's inhabitants. Through the popular and accessible formats of songs and poems, political opinions circulated in the late medieval town and, as Fox argues, such informed criticism helped to provide a political education for the wider populace.[33]

Only glimpses of the tradition of popular oral narratives have come down to us, always in written form, and in most cases indirectly and in a distorted way. The nature of these written texts, in rhyme, verse or song form, suggest that they belong to an oral culture, which has totally disappeared. Subaltern groups

---

32 Wood 2007, p. 10; Kesselring 2007, pp. 175–8; Harvey 1991; Davies 1995; Joutard 1977; Jouhaud 2009.

33 Fox 1997, p. 617.

in the society used subversive words to criticise the dominant ideology, sometimes by copying, subverting and manipulating it. Michel de Certeau calls this practice the 'prise de parole' of less powerful groups, who borrowed words from the authorities in order to proclaim an alternative 'truth' with them.[34] These thoughts allow us to contextualise speech acts of rebels within the broader repertoire of 'popular orality' and to see them in relation, rather than in opposition, to other forms of conflictual negotiation with the authorities. Subjects never completely interiorise the hegemonic discourse of the ruling classes, though they pretend to do so on the 'public stage'. 'Off-stage', outside the control of the ruling elites, they are free to speak, by singing subversive songs in alehouses, for instance. From the urban rulers' point of view, there were several reasons why songs and poems were dangerous media which had to be suppressed. Rebellious speech acts were a public event, a performance, a circulating oral jingle, easily memorised and freely altered, as historical examples show.[35] As a result of censorship but primarily because of their orality, only a few of these openly political literary works in Middle Dutch have survived.

Nevertheless, for reasons which are not entirely clear, sixteenth-century rhetoricians wrote down a few rebellious songs about medieval Ghent. Although some of these songs as oral media have inevitably changed over time, they still contain elements of the rebellious songs. A very careful and critical reading is necessary, but there is a pattern of repeated references to certain rebel leaders, for instance, which shows that their cult was remembered through oral narratives. Although this cult was not purely religious in nature, some Flemish authors deployed it through the literary genre of 'pseudo-prophecies', which purported to be from an earlier time commenting on past events as if they were still in the future. Different versions of these pseudo-prophecies, such as the Prophecy of Amisins or The Prophecy of the Huise Blacksmith, refer to medieval political events. Probably written around 1360, the Amisins prophecy predicted the coming of a human saviour for Flemish citizens, a likely reference to the Ghent weaver James van Artevelde who had led the city in a long revolt against the count of Flanders.[36] Using the bestial allegory which is typical for this genre, the author predicts that the 'boar', clearly meant to be James van Artevelde, would help 'the small animals' against the 'big animals' in 'the land of the lion' (the lion was the emblem of the counts of Flanders). The boar would bring an end to unjust rule and chase out those who had governed the county

---

34   Certeau 1994, pp. 59–69.
35   Martines 2000, p. 51; Kuhn 2007; Lentz 2002; Walter 2009.
36   Nicholas, David 1988.

so badly.[37] Writing approximately two decades after the revolt, the anonymous author of the prophecy clearly wanted to keep van Artevelde's message alive in a genre of writing which mixed religion and politics and could potentially play an inciting role.

The appearance of James van Artevelde in several songs and poems written after the revolt of 1338–45 demonstrates that the remembrance of his rebellious deeds appealed to the sentiments of like-minded individuals who similarly wished to fight for their rights. The revolt James van Artevelde led defended Ghent privileges, especially those of the craft guilds, against the growing influence of the count in city politics. Surviving remnants of medieval songs, some still popular in the sixteenth century, remind us of the deep impact these songs had on their audience. *Van Kort Rozijn* ('Of Short Raisin'), for example, is a song about a companion of James van Artevelde, Zeger van Kortrijk, who was imprisoned in 1337 by the count of Flanders. In the song, van Artevelde avenged this unjust provocation by asking the king of England (Edward III) to attack the count of Flanders (Louis of Nevers).[38] The song distorted historical reality and simplified the social, economic and political complexities of the opening manoeuvres of the Hundred Years War. As Fentress and Wickham argue, this is typical of events which, once integrated into social memory, undergo a process of simplification, resulting in an easily memorisable and usable version of that event.[39] This simplification, interpretation and distortion of reality is socially conditioned, as Burke explains.[40] Although the stories about rebel heroes are based on actual elements from past events, the commemoration of that event becomes a fictive construction, rather than a long-acknowledged and collectively remembered 'truth'.[41] Van Artevelde had sought English aid in his struggle against the count, and the English king had sent troops to aid Ghent in the struggle. However, this aid was in the mutual interests of both parties, because in exchange for Ghent's support of Edward's claim to the French throne, Edward promised to guarantee the export of English wool to Flanders. England was the main supplier of wool for the Ghent cloth industry, the mainstay of the city's economy. The fact that James van Artevelde was the chief dean of the weavers' guild exposes his own interests in supporting the English king and indicates that the political reality of the revolt was much more complicated than the song *Van Kort Rozijn* narrates. However, the

---

37 De Keyser and Verrycken 1983, pp. 446–7.
38 Van de Graft, ed. 1968, pp. 67–8.
39 Fentress and Wickham 1992, pp. 39–40.
40 Burke 1989, p. 98; see also Schudson 1995, pp. 346–9.
41 Foot 1999, p. 188.

most important function of the Artevelde songs was not their exact representation of the facts, but their meaning within popular political consciousness. As
James Scott noticed, autonomous myths about heroes play a vital role in the
thoughts about everyday resistance.[42] This song filtered the unjust rule of the
count from historic reality and highlighted the valiant deeds of van Artevelde
against injustice. The key function of these stories was spreading the message
that Ghent had the tradition and, because tradition and customs had legal force
in medieval society,[43] therefore the right to fight violations of its privileges by
higher authorities.

The mythical proportions James van Artevelde assumed among Ghent
craftsmen in later years is even clearer in an anonymous pamphlet from 1451.
During the year of rebellion by the Ghent craft guilds against the Burgundian
Duke Philip the Good, this document was hung on the doors of the city hall.
In this seditious tract, the anonymous author cried out for van Artevelde to
come back if the city's aldermen failed to oppose the duke's violations of Ghent
privileges. 'We will ask for a new Artevelde', the pamphlet predicted, trying to
force the urban government to appoint decisive leaders for an impending revolt
against the duke.[44] During the following turbulent events, the craftsmen did
choose new leaders, some of whose names resounded from Ghent's rebellious
tradition. On 25 April 1452, Pieter van den Bossche and Willem van Vaernewijck
were elected as military captains of Ghent parishes.[45] Since neither had any
military experience at all, it seems that their famous surnames, the same surnames as those of rebel heroes, accounted for the public offices they were given.
In 1338–42 a Willem van Vaernewijck had been a key supporter of James van
Artevelde in the city's administration.[46] A Pieter van den Bossche had taken up
arms with James's son, Philip van Artevelde, in a revolt against Philip the Good's
grandfather, Philip the Bold.[47] When in 1423 one of the duke's councillors insulted the burgomaster of Ghent for his political opposition to Duke Philip the
Good, the councillor not only called the burgomaster an 'Artevelde', but also a
'Pieter van den Bossche'.[48] The names of rebellious heroes seem to have been

---

42   Scott, James 1990, p. 135.
43   In a review of Halbwachs's work, Marc Bloch considers customs as a mnemonic practice,
      Bloch 1925, p. 81.
44   'Ghy slapscheten van Ghendt, die nu hebt 't regiment, wy en zullen 't hu nyet meet ghewa-
      ghen, maer zullen 't eenen nyuewen Artevelt daghen' (Fris, ed. 1901–4, vol. 1, p. 129). See also
      Van Leeuwen 2004.
45   Haemers 2004b, pp. 291–2.
46   Nicholas, David 1988, p. 23.
47   Ibid., pp. 144–6.
48   Prevenier 1985, p. 298.

synonyms for rebellious behaviour and defence of the city's privileges, because names assumed special meaning and performed the function of a code in late medieval society.[49] Since uprisings were remembered by their leaders rather than by their date, as Harvey has shown for late medieval England, rebel names were an important point of reference which encouraged and fortified potential insurgents.[50] In our case, the names of rebel heroes related to an idealised version of the past, in which rebel leaders had successfully fought against political adversaries. The popular cry for charismatic leaders in the revolt of 1452 was coupled with a search for namesakes of deceased heroes from the past. When there was no actual van Artevelde to protect the craft guilds' interests, the craftsmen sought leaders with the same names as van Artevelde's companions. These remarkable facts show that the rebellious tradition in Ghent was maintained by the common practice of remembering rebel idols from former revolts. The presence of these names in the sources implies the endurance of a shared body of local knowledge concerning tumultuous times. Traces of archival evidence strongly suggests that, despite the best efforts of late medieval rulers to repress forms of everyday resistance, alternative memories of past revolts endured.[51]

A political ballad written down at the beginning of the sixteenth century features another Ghent rebel leader who had taken up arms against Duke Philip the Good in 1452, Lieven Boone. The composer expressed his hope that Boone would rule the city of Ghent again, because otherwise the city would no longer be 'worth a crown'.[52] Another song compared the Ghent military captain Jacob Meeuwsone with Saint George fighting his powerful draconic enemy. It warned that all those who served the lord 'must be beaten to death', as Saint George had done with the evil dragon. This ballad was composed on the rhyme scheme of a contemporary Latin drinking song, which supports the theory that these political ditties were sung during drinking sessions in alehouses.[53] Another Ghent song of 1467 described the demolition of the duke's tax houses.[54] Poems and songs about popular leaders and rebellious events in the city kept the memory of revolts alive for many decades while, at the same time, they must have

---

49   Postless 2006, p. 36.

50   Harvey 1995, pp. 167–8.

51   As in the English 1549 risings, see Wood 2007, p. 245. See also Jones, Amanda 2009.

52   'O Ghent, Ghent scone, den zijst niet weert een croone, want di zults die laten hoonen, tenzij datti regiert Lieven Boone', de Pauw 1893–1914, vol. 2, p. 388. About Lieven Boone, see Haemers 2005a.

53   'Sent Joris ende vrient, slaet al doot dat den heere dient, zonder den prince ende kint, haut die op, waer ghij se vint', de Pauw 1893–1914, p. 390.

54   'God ende die goede stede van Ghent, slaet al doot dat heeft regiment', ibid., p. 395.

been used to criticise the policies of the current regime in a veiled manner. While van Artevelde was a real historical character, the fictional folktale hero Tijl Ulenspiegel in some ways played a similar role. The Middle Dutch story of *Ulenspiegel*, about an innocent boy labourer who subverts the social order, mocking clerics, nobles and guild masters alike, is comparable with the stories told about Robin Hood in England.[55] According to Rodney Hilton, the wide dissemination of such tales from the late Middle Ages onwards reveals the political functions of this textual tradition. In one of the versions of the story, the 'Gest of Robyn Hode', a ballad from before 1500, the peasants saw the king as the fount of justice, which for them meant protection against wicked landlords and officials. Such discourse was not critical of society as a whole but only a 'protest against immediately felt hardship'.[56] That could have been one of the functions of the later evocations of the Flemish rebel leaders in popular literature as well.

Through a fluid oral tradition within a family or a guild, such discourses transmitted certain political opinions which inspired a new generation of rebels and even contributed to the practical organisation of rebellions. As Wood has revealed for early modern England, stories about rebellious traditions caused popular upheavals to follow a similar organisational pattern, ideological cohesion and course of events.[57] The same process seems to have been active in Flanders. Old veterans of Flemish rebellious movements clearly shared their experiences with the younger generation, because the major revolts in Bruges in 1411, 1436, 1477 and 1488, and in Ghent in 1432, 1436, 1453, 1467, 1477 and 1485, showed striking similarities in patterns of mobilisation and political programmes.[58] The participants were well aware of what their fathers and grandfathers had said and done before them. Children probably learned revolt stories as artisans told each other subversive anecdotes about earlier uprisings on the shop floor. It is through such 'mnemonic socialisation', as Eviatar Zerubavel has called it, that memories passed on from generation to generation.[59] But remarkable evidence from the Austrian archives shows that Ghent craftsmen not only had oral media of remembrance, but also a tradition of written accounts of rebellious customs.

---

55   Geeraedts 1986.
56   Hilton 1999, p. 209.
57   Wood 2007, p. 246.
58   See [Patterns].
59   Zerubavel, Eviatar 1997, p. 87.

4   Lettered Resistance: The Book of Jan De Rouc

In the archives of the Habsburg emperors in Vienna, a small piece of paper survives among thousands of copies of sixteenth-century charters and imperial correspondence. It is a copy of a document entitled *An extract taken from a certain project of Jan De Rouc, found in the house of his late father Jan De Rouc, written by his father to hold in his memory*.[60] The fragment, which is only three pages long, describes the Ghent revolt of February 1477. This was the previously discussed revolt of the craft guilds to reverse the repressive policies of Duke Charles the Bold. After the revolt of 1467 the Burgundian duke had abolished several privileges of the Ghent craft guilds and installed local governors loyal to himself. In February 1477, however, after the sudden death of the duke on the battlefield in Lorraine, the craft guilds got their revenge.[61] They took back their privileges, punished the duke's sympathisers and resumed appointing the aldermen of the city, just as they had done in 1467. Although the son's copy only gives us a short excerpt, the 'book' of Jan De Rouc senior describes the beginning of this revolt in detail. He records how the tick weavers' guild (the '*tijkweversambacht*' made mattresses) started the revolt by mobilizing its members and occupying the Friday Market, displaying its banners and enacting the characteristic rituals. Accentuating the attempts of the former city power holders to influence the court, Jan says that some aldermen intended to submit 'false letters' to Mary of Burgundy, the daughter and heiress of the late duke. Jan describes how these letters, designed to mislead the duchess about the reasons for the craftsmen's resistance, were not sufficient to influence events in the former aldermen's favour. On the contrary, when Mary of Burgundy swore her oath as duchess on 16 February 1477, she restored all the old city privileges (and thus also those of the craft guilds). The fragment ends with a list of the names of the new city aldermen, who were elected by the craft guilds on 18 February 1477. The chronicle fragment is therefore a silent witness to the craft guilds' takeover of power in Ghent, which lasted until 1485.[62]

Although the fragment of Jan De Rouc's book is unique in that no other comparable document describing revolts by rebels has been found in the Low

---

60   Haus-, Hof-, und Staatsarchiv, Vienna, Belgica PC, Liasse 1, Konvolut 2 (Ghent, 1476–92), 'Gand 1476', 127ʳ–128ᵛ: *Extract getrocken uuyt zekere proiecte toebehoorende Jan De Rouc, twelcke hij gevonden heeft int selfs huys wijlen Jan De Rouc zijnen vader ende bij der handt van zijn voirnoemde vader gescreven ende genoteerd tzijnder memorie.* It is edited in Haemers 2010a, appendix 2.

61   Blockmans, Willem, ed. 1985a; Vaughan 1973, pp. 399–432.

62   Haemers 2009, pp. 228–42.

Countries, there are typical elements in it which indicate that Jan's book was not exceptional in its own time. Several aspects of this extraordinary source, its contents, the author's social background and its polemical style, clarify why the book was written. Moreover, it gives us exclusive insight into the nature, genesis and maintenance of the social memory of the Ghent craft guilds. Comparison of its content with other stories about the revolt of 1477 shows that Jan De Rouc's book was not neutral. Jan disapproved of the aldermen's attempt to misrepresent the revolt's causes to the duchess and deplored their efforts to suppress the revolt with force. As a fervent advocate of maintaining guild privileges, such as their representation in the civic institutions, Jan De Rouc defended their occupation of the market square and punishment of the deposed officials. He applauded the duchess's decision to ignore the 'false' attempts of the aldermen to repress the revolt, writing that the aldermen should have pacified the conflict instead of aggravating it by using force. As a craftsman, Jan senior defended guild privileges and justified their uprising. By carefully describing the events from a biased perspective, the text disseminated the guild's position on the revolt. It gave readers arguments to use against the policies of the former authorities and advised other guildsmen to take the same measures. In its simplified form, the exciting story could be easily memorised and copied, in order to convince others that the guild's revolt was justified. Since the document summarised the rebellious arguments and ideological ammunition of the craft guilds, it seems to have been a touchstone of their social memory.

The polemical narrative of Jan De Rouc is not the only version of the events. At the other end of the political spectrum, court chroniclers wrote in pejorative terms about the revolt of 1477. Jean Molinet, the *indiciaire* of the Burgundian dukes (the official court chronicler), labelled the actions of the Ghent craft guilds '*conspirations*', '*mutineries*' and '*machinations*' of '*les petis contre les grans*'.[63] He said that the inhabitants of Ghent, 'taken by a great fury', had started the 'bad dance' of 1477.[64] Molinet's discourse displayed remarkably little insight into the political vigour and socio-economic desires of the aggrieved craftsmen. Because the chronicle, like others composed at court or in noble milieus, had no pity for the Ghent craftsmen, it reproduced narratives that legitimised the power and repression of the prince and the ruling classes. Georges Chastellain, Molinet's predecessor, condemned the city of Ghent as '*une ville de grand dangier*', whose citizens were incapable of formulating their own polit-

---

63   Molinet 1935–7, vol. 1, p. 213.
64   '*Gantois, espris de grant fureur* [...] *commencèrent ceste maleureuse danse*', ibid., p. 214.

ical desires.[65] Court chroniclers described craftsmen as social inferiors with no right to contradict the decisions of the lord and his officials, who were supposed to act for the common good of all subjects. This infantilising view of the lower layer of society was a characteristic expression of the court and the urban elite, who constructed their social memory based on these premises.[66] The story of Jan De Rouc shows the rebels' distinct view, presenting rebellions as legal acts of subjects who are victimised by arbitrary power. In the same manner as court narratives, the counter-vision of the Ghent craftsmen was written to legitimise political action, making the book of Jan De Rouc as biased as the chronicle of Molinet. They are different perceptions of the same events, created in totally different social settings.

Though sparse, details about the social background of Jan De Rouc and his son give us a rare insight into the specific social conditions behind the rebellious memory of the craft guilds. Father and son might have been members of the tick weavers' guild, as it is the only guild mentioned in the document. This craft guild belonged to the larger weavers' guild, which had the right to select aldermen (when this right was not suppressed by the dukes). Jan De Rouc junior was chosen as an alderman by the weavers' guild in 1503 and 1523.[67] Jan's appointment to public office indicates that he had power in his craft guild, but he did not belong to the city's elite. As research on Ghent has shown, only the burgomaster and a few other aldermen held real authority in the city.[68] Although Jan's office did not give him the opportunity to influence city politics, it does show that he had a considerable reputation in his guild, because only powerful persons of the guild would be selected for this office. Evidence of his economic circumstances supports this assessment. He owned a house in the *Leeuwstraat* in a weaver neighbourhood, and in 1511 he left money to two illegitimate sons.[69] Jan De Rouc was not a rich man, but this archival evidence demonstrates that he belonged neither to the city's poor nor to the urban elite. Jan therefore seems to have been a member of what has been called 'the Ghent middle class' in the historiography of the Low Countries, a social group with a certain amount of wealth and power who were the driving force behind guild revolts in the city.[70]

---

65 Quoted by Jan Dumolyn, who studied the vision of court chronicles on urban rebels in detail, in Dumolyn 2009, p. 179.

66 To be discussed widely in Haemers 2010b.

67 Van der Meersch 1852–61, vol. 2, pp. 5, 59.

68 Boone 1990b, pp. 55–6.

69 City archives of Ghent, series 330, no. 44, fols. 119^v, 251^v; no. 45, fol. 8^v.

70 Haemers 2004b, pp. 110–11; Dambruyne 2003; Boone 2005.

Several studies on the social reality behind the urban craft guilds in Flemish towns have demonstrated that the craft guilds united, firstly, rich elite merchants, secondly, a relatively wealthy group of middle-class artisans, and thirdly, the urban poor (daily wage-workers).[71] Whereas what could be called the urban 'mob' in the medieval Flemish urban social structure often included poorer guildsmen, and wageworkers, the 'middle class' in town consisted of better-off guild masters, skilled artisans, secondary merchants and shopkeepers. While the first group often served as storm troopers in the collective actions of the craft guilds, the middle class, on the contrary, led these political movements in order to force the elite to recognise them as an important political player in town. In some periods of the political history of late medieval Flanders, the urban middle class had the right to appoint aldermen and to make part of the political decision-making process in town through the participation in several governing councils, but in other periods it had to fight literally for its political and social recognition. The middle class, therefore, did not belong either to the group of powerless citizens or to the rulers of the town, as they had the means and the finances to support, for instance, the performances of processions and plays in order to deliver instructive messages to other citizens. In short, as elsewhere in Europe, the 'middling sort of people' in the Flemish cities were united in craft guilds, which had political rights and economic privileges to defend.[72] Although I did not find evidence of Jan senior in the archives, the limited information about his son indicates that Jan De Rouc junior (and probably also his father) were 'typical' agents of the self-conscious urban middle class of Ghent, which continuously defended its rights with a remarkable tradition of revolts. In that case, the literary legacy of Jan senior reveals that the Ghent middle class maintained this tradition in part by preserving a powerful social memory in the city.

Jan De Rouc's 'book of memory' was a common written medium of remembrance well known to the urban society of the late Middle Ages. Though it might seem astonishing that someone from Jan De Rouc's social milieu possessed this kind of book, urban elites all over western Europe kept written accounts which included personal and family mementos, sometimes intermingled with individual book-keeping records.[73] Wealthy urban families also commissioned masses and liturgical memory-foundations in their testaments in order to be publicly remembered by future generations.[74] But similar com-

---

71   Prak 2006, pp. 74–80; Dambruyne 1998.
72   Compare with Barry 1994.
73   See note 16 above and the case studies of Klapisch-Zuber 1991, pp. 253–7; and Monnet 2001.
74   Petti Balbi 2008; Oexle 1982b; Richard 2009.

memorative texts written by persons from the urban middle class are rare archival finds, and therefore hardly studied. Nevertheless, the book of Jan De Rouc had much in common with the elite 'memory books', as it included a list of aldermen (elected during the revolt) and reports about civic history (albeit focused on rebellious events). Both were also preserved by and transmitted within a family.[75] Jan De Rouc might have made entries in the book each year, as the elite did in their accounts. The difference is that Jan De Rouc wrote the reigning 'counter-memory' book in Ghent history. Since only a fragment of it survives, a definitive analysis of its form and content is impossible. But the manner and the context in which it was transmitted, and the nature of the surviving excerpt, suggest that it was mixture of several genres: a personal diary, a subversive chronicle of city events and a middle-class 'memory book'. While it is possible that Jan's book is a survivor of a wider literary practice in late medieval Ghent, it is the only one known to this date.

Jan De Rouc senior composed his book from a clear ideological background, in a specific social and political setting, and following a certain historiographical tradition, but also because he felt the need to write down an account of an important event in the social memory of the craft guilds. In the same fashion noted by other historians of social memory, the record of events that Jan De Rouc wanted to preserve in memory was not only his own personal view, but also the view of those in his social milieu. Since Jan De Rouc was probably one of the craftsmen who occupied the market square in February 1477, he may have added some personal memories to his story. He may have stressed the role of the tick weavers' guild in the revolt because he was a tick weaver. However, despite the likelihood that it contained personal elements, the memory book depended on common ideas and a wider practice of social remembering. Through the process of remembering a functional vision giving an idealised civic history, the Ghent craftsmen preserved their collective identity in order to maintain a privileged position in the city. By restructuring the past in a selective, distorted and commonly accepted manner, by carefully telescoping the view to certain facts and events, and then by interpreting those within a given political framework, the craftsmen defined themselves through a common narrative commemorated from generation to generation. As scholars have noted for medieval England, Spain and France, the Ghent rebels clearly cultivated a literature of clamour that was used for justifying revolts and supporting political positions when needed.[76] In addition, it is likely that the use of

---

75   An excellent study of 'memory books' in Ghent is Van Bruaene 1998.
76   Kesselring 2007; Justice, Steven 1994; Challet 2008; Oliva Herrer 2007, pp. 188–92.

written media of remembrance continuously overlapped and interacted with the use of oral mnemonic practices in reciprocal and mutually reinforcing ways. In textual communities – the term Stock uses to denote micro-societies which were organised around the common understanding of a script – texts were read in public, and their contents were memorised and orally dispersed.[77] The oral culture of less educated groups, which refers to the common illiterate culture of late medieval society, was a mighty 'weapon of the weak' for the spread of ideas and memories.[78] The written account of Jan De Rouc was copied by his son, probably read within the family and in wider circles, narrated to friends and colleagues, and so on. The mnemonic socialisation through reading aloud and speaking was used to educate children, convince opponents and guide future rebels. In short, it was a key tool for the maintenance of social memory.

The most significant evidence that Jan De Rouc's book served as an instruction manual for revolts appears in a notation in the surviving fragment of his chronicle. The passage says that the copy of the book (which now survives in Vienna) was made on 10 September 1539,[79] in the middle of a revolt of Ghent against Emperor Charles V, the great-grandson of Charles the Bold. In September 1539 the craft guilds refused to pay for the emperor's costly wars any longer, and protested, as usual, the violation of their privileges by the emperor's trusted officials. Some of these loyalists were arrested by the rebellious craftsmen, who went on strike and occupied central city sites. They presented their grievances to the emperor's regent, who was forced to give in due to the emperor's absence and the resulting weakness of the Habsburg dynasty.[80] Even this brief summary of events points to a remarkable resemblance between the revolt of 1539 and its predecessors. As in June 1467, and in February 1477, the Ghent craft guilds used a vacuum of power at court to criticise the alleged misbehaviour of local officials and punish those held responsible for the violation of treasured privileges. It is not a coincidence that the book of Jan De Rouc senior was 'discovered' by his son during this turbulent September of 1539. The events of 1477 may not have directly motivated the craftsmen to act in 1539 in the same ways as they did in 1477, but the remarkable similarity between the rebellious events in both episodes (and in others) strongly suggests that narrated stories and written memories inspired rebels who were attacking the authorities.

---

77   Stock 1990; Innes 1998; Fox 1999; Finnegan 1988.
78   Coleman, Joyce 1996. See also Clanchy 1979, pp. 214–20; and Watts 2004, pp. 166–7.
79   'Als dit gescreven was int jaer duust vijfhondert XXXIX, den X^{en} van september', Haus-, Hof-, und Staatsarchiv, Vienna, Belgica PC, Liasse 1, Konvolut 2 (Ghent, 1476–92), fol. 126^{r}.
80   A full summary of the events in Dambruyne 1990; Blockmans, Willem 2002.

While the causes of the 1539 uprising are found in contemporary complaints about government policies, the mobilisation, rituals and methods of the revolt were clearly taken from memories of past events.

Considering the content and purpose of Jan De Rouc's book, it is not surprising that it was locked away in the Habsburg archives in Vienna after Charles v severely repressed the Ghent revolt of 1539. With the so-called 'Carolingian concession' of 1540 the emperor not only changed the institutional structure of his native city, but also tried to erase the rebellious tradition of the city of the van Arteveldes. The '*Concessio*' peace treaty imposed heavy fines on the city, and ordered the execution of the revolt's leaders and the construction of a castle on the site of Ghent's oldest monastery, Saint Bavo's abbey.[81] Building a symbol of repression upon the emblematic location of the abbey served to remind citizens that the balance of power in the city had shifted. The emperor went further in manipulating the commemoration of revolts within the city by confiscating the houses, revenues, goods and archives of the Ghent craft guilds, who also lost their right to elect aldermen. With these unprecedented measures, Charles v intended to break the Ghent craftsmen's political power and tradition of resistance decisively. Obviously, the emperor could only destroy written commemorative media and not oral counter-narratives, but his confiscation of the craft guilds' archives deprived them of important documents which might have been used to reconstruct their history. The confiscators may also have taken the original book of Jan De Rouc senior, or his son might have destroyed it himself, but the copy made during the revolt was deposited in the Habsburg state archives in Lille. After the French conquest of that city in the seventeenth century, parts of the archive were moved to Brussels, and then to Vienna in the following century, where they remain today.[82]

With his characteristically pompous Joyous Entry ceremonies and dissemination of imperial propaganda after the Ghent repression, Charles v (and his successors) tried to impose their historical vision of the Ghent revolt on to the city. This vision condemned uprisings as dangerous for the dynasty and against the common good of all subjects.[83] These ideas had already circulated at court before the repression of the Ghent revolt, but in 1540 the growing state power of the Habsburg dynasty (which had added Spain and the Americas to its crown) provided them with the political and financial means to overshadow alternative political powers and ideas in their territory. In the end, the political views of

---

81   Decavele and Van Peteghem 1989.
82   Laenen 1924, p. 292.
83   About the practice of Charles v to influence people's minds by Joyous Entry ceremonies, see Arnade 2000.

the victorious central state succeeded in dominating people's minds, creating a cultural hegemony in its own territory, as Gramsci would say.[84] This means that the authorities achieved ideological supremacy in subjugated towns (like Ghent), a situation which still left room for alternative political thoughts, but not for their public utterance. The remnants of the social memory of the opposition (like the Ghent craft guilds) were repressed and, over time, disappeared. In addition to the burgeoning power of their mighty state adversary, the changing economic situation in Flanders weakened the Ghent craft guilds. Over the sixteenth and seventeenth centuries, the waning of the Flemish economy in favour of Antwerp, and later Amsterdam, undermined the economic and social position of the Ghent craftsmen.[85] Their economic decline cost the craft guilds their social significance in the city, with the consequence that their social memory slowly but surely evaporated over the following centuries. Put another way, the social memory of the rebels was not maintained by future generations, which instead manipulated rebel narratives, distorting them to tell a completely different story. Jan De Rouc's narrative was, however, removed from its context, and no longer adapted to suit changing political circumstances. As a little booklet in the immense imperial archives in Vienna, comparable to a fossil concealed in unexcavated ground, his book is now one of the only witnesses to the effaced counter-memory of the defunct Ghent craft guilds.

5 Conclusion: A Battle of Memories

In late medieval Ghent the tradition of revolts by craftsmen lasted for more than two centuries. From the first revolt of the craft guilds in 1280 until the imperial repression after the revolt of 1540, a remarkable pattern of urban rebellion existed.[86] This article makes clear that the social memory which the craft guilds developed through time was responsible for the striking similarity between the numerous uprisings which fill Ghent's history during those centuries. The commemoration of times of commotion, stories about rebel heroes, written accounts of rituals, victory ballads, poems about defeats and other reminders maintained this extraordinary rebellious tradition within the Ghent craft guilds. Due to multiple mnemonic practices, spatial arrangements, oral customs and written accounts, rebels knew how to act during a revolt, how to mobilise effectively, how to deploy rituals and banners, and the like. The

---

84 Hoare and Nowell Smith, transl. and eds 1971, pp. 244–5.
85 Prak 2006, pp. 83–6; Dambruyne 2002, pp. 721–44.
86 See [Patterns]; Boone 2007b.

ideological consistency and ritual coherence of revolts spanning almost three centuries was preserved through many media of remembrance. Even though the existence of an inherited memory within the craft guilds explains why the revolts were so similar, it was still the balance of the guilds' political, economic, social and financial power against that of their opponents which determined the outcome of the revolt. Nevertheless, widespread powerful memories of an idealised past heavily influenced maintenance of a collective identity among the craftsmen, the efficiency of their mobilisation and their justifications for seizing power. In short, the social memory of the Ghent craftsmen explains their characteristic rebellious tradition.

This social memory was a kind of counter-memory, as identified by Foucault, because it collected alternative ideas about power which challenged the cultural hegemony of the elites' construction of the past, by offering a divergent commemorative narrative of subaltern social groups. Public expression of the craftsmen's alternative memory was suppressed, and written accounts were destroyed when they surfaced. However, the social memory of the craftsmen was autonomous, and maintained a continuous dialectical relationship with the memory of the urban rulers. But it did not survive the double-edged sword presented by the increasing power of the central state of a dynasty which would not tolerate alternative nuclei of power within its territory. In their quest for political domination, the state elite and local officials continuously tried to erase the social memory of their opponents. The remarkable resilience of the social memory of the Ghent craft guilds was not eternal, when presented also with the harmful consequences of early modern economic evolution. The craftsmen's social memory lost its social significance during the sixteenth century and lost all chance for a continued existence. Ironically, the confiscation of written accounts containing the Ghent craftsmen's social memory by powerful enemies shaped conditions necessary for some evidence of its influential presence in late medieval society to survive. Rulers possessed better archival conditions, more powerful repressive methods and a stronger economic position, which enabled them to dominate society, but in spite of their efforts to suppress alternative memories, the social memory of the Ghent craftsmen has not been totally forgotten.

CHAPTER 8

Urban Spaces and Places as a Concern of Communal Politics in Medieval Flanders

Jan Dumolyn (translated by Andrew Murray)

1   Introduction

Since the work of Henri Pirenne, the towns of medieval Flanders and, by extension, those of northern France and the rest of the southern Low Countries, being regions where the urban landscape had very similar traits, have been the object of a rich historiographical tradition.[1] They have attracted attention for their early and strong industrialisation, their commercial character as well as their social and political struggles between different social groups. Recently, a new aspect to the research on the socio-economic, political and cultural history of the Flemish town has been systematically introduced: space. The 'spatial turn' in historiography – a term that applies to a varied group of theoretical debates in geography – implies that historians reorient their research in terms of the following premise: the totality of events and practices are not situated in an abstract and homogenous place, but in specific environments within a space characterised by material, socio-economic, political and symbolic standpoints.[2]

In this context, certain medievalists have been influenced by the approach advocated by Henri Lefebvre in his *La Production de l'espace*. With regards to the Flemish and Italian cities of the Middle Ages, they have formulated the following observation: from the second half of the thirteenth century, urban authorities actively sought to transform communal space and a similar scenario emerges during the following centuries in other European regions. The spaces, buildings or central and symbolic monuments in the urban landscape progressively became major issues that different social groups and central authorities disputed. In Flanders, the conflict between the prince's political

---

1   For a recent synthesis, see Boone 2010.
2   On the 'spatial turn' see Scott, James 2009, p. 1; and Guldi 2011. For an excellent bibliography and major conceptual discussions relevant to medieval and early modern Europe, see Arnade, Howell and Simons 2002; Deligne and Billen 2007; Classen 2009; and Boone and Howell 2013.

power and the towns known for their tradition of rebellion forced these two parties to assert their claims in terms of urban space.[3]

This claim and appropriation of parcels of urban space was done by means of violence, physical or symbolic, either through direct confrontation between antagonists or, in the context of 'ritual' or 'ceremony', political dialogue between the prince and town. These sites are presented as the principal stakes of the spatial struggle: the squares and the markets, the official building such as the belfries, the houses of aldermen, the prisons or the princely residences, or even certain monumental symbols typical of urbanity such as the walls and gates. The research on the 'spatial politics' in medieval Flemish towns is therefore concentrated on the 'places' specific to the urban 'space' as a whole,[4] even if the authors always stress that the specific appropriations must be situated in a larger spatial logic and ideology.

In this brief contribution, we propose to deepen the approach of our predecessors in order to define the traits of this specific communal, politico-spatial logic. The situation of the urban, Flemish network, understood in a broad sense and also accommodating neighbouring urban zones such as the county of Artois or the duchy of Brabant,[5] can without doubt be generalised and projected, *mutatis mutandis*, to the other European regions marked by a strong urbanisation and by the presence of industrial and commercial metropolises. From this perspective, we regret that the comparison – a necessary one – with the medieval towns in Italy has to be reduced here due to a lack of space.[6]

Class struggle occupies a central place in the theoretical model of Lefebvre and it is often the conflictual situations, rooted in a specific social construction, which best instruct us on the politico-spatial logic of the medieval town. Thus, the revolt of Saint-Omer of 1468 led against the local elite and Duke Charles the Bold had urban space itself as its fundamental issue. Ostensibly, this collective action broke out for fiscal reasons, but in reality it touched on a much vaster problematic subject: who did urban space belong to and who controlled its

---

3 Crouzet-Pavan 1992 and 2000; Boone 2002a; Deligne 2013. For Venice, similar findings have been observed by Crouzet-Pavan 2000; Boone and Porfyriou 2007; Lecuppre-Desjardin 2004a; Verbruggen, Raf 2005. Among the other work relevant to the study of urban space in Italy, one could cite Najemy 2006; Maire-Vigueur 1995; Herlihy 1976, pp. 174–94.
4 It is important to remark that the principal paradigms of geographic theory in the Anglo-Saxon world use the term of 'place' and 'space' often completely differently than does Lefebvre. See, notably, Tuan 1977. The town would here be considered often as a 'place', that is, a place invested with a social sense. Among those who write in this tradition, see Lilley 2014.
5 Blockmans, Willem 1999b; Stabel 1997 and 2008a.
6 A recent primer for such comparisons between Flanders and Italy is Crouzet-Pavan and Lecuppre-Desjardin, eds 2008.

material, financial and symbolic management? Such are the questions which underlined this revolt, as many others. The rebels had come primarily from the industrial outskirts of the town and claimed political rights equivalent to those which benefitted the inhabitants of the town's centre. They also demanded participation in the management of water across the length of the Aa river to guarantee the maintenance of this infrastructure, as well as the restoration of their right to use the town's public grounds. In their struggle to obtain complete citizenship, the rebels took actions and formulated demands in which the symbolic value of space was very evident. They obtained, for example, the keys to the gates of the town adjoining their *suburbium*, they gathered at the town hall, being the centre of urban power, and they opened the gates of the prison.[7]

2   The Construction of Communal Space

In 1468, the inhabitants of the suburbs of Saint-Omer still acted according to a logic of 'popular politics' which originated with the economic and juridical construction of the commune as it had existed four centuries earlier. For Lefebvre, the medieval town was above all a 'space of accumulation', being a place reserved for markets and production. Here is an impactful image which is certainly valuable for this region of north-west Europe, where the renewal of urban life can be observed clearly from the eleventh century, with a spectacular growth from a commercial and artisanal perspective from the twelfth century and above all from the thirteenth.[8] In the world of the Christian west of the epoque, only Paris and the large merchant towns of Italy surpassed in power the towns of Flanders. Due to increased agricultural productivity, a commercial revolution and improvements in public security, the Flemish town was able to transform itself to become a specific social construction. In what follows, we will concentrate on and prioritise these most important industrial and commercial centres.

Blockmans showed that from a spatial point of view the construction of the Flemish towns reflects above all the needs of merchants and tradespeople.[9] It is known that proto-urban agglomerations initially developed in the shadow of seigneurial and ecclesiastical centres of power. But in the course of the high and central Middle Ages, during the social, institutional and topograph-

---

7 Dumolyn and Papin 2012.
8 Lefebvre 1974. The first great specialists of the medieval town such as Henri Pirenne similarly conceived of the town as being a marketplace before anything else.
9 Blockmans, Willem 1994a.

ical emergence of urban centres in the region, the principal role fell back on the producers and traders of the towns. Situated at neural nodes in networks composed of routes over water and land, the military fortifications, abbeys and episcopal residences attracted merchants and artisans. These populations constituted settlements, called *burgus, suburbium, portus* or *vicus* in the sources, which were stimulated in their development by the demand of goods and services emanating from the elites. Numerous other zones in Europe testify to the same scenario, some with and some without continuity with previous Roman urbanisation.[10]

In Lefebvre's approach, urban space constitutes a productive force maintained with other social forces in a dialectical relationship. Through the interaction between, on the one hand, the material and economic structures in place and, on the other hand, the actions, interests and ideological concepts of the different social groups, there emerge very specific urban spaces in Flanders. In the context of the strong economic and demographic growth in the period between 1050 and 1280, a confluence of factors such as immigration, the growth of markets, industrial specialisation, social diversification and the extension of political, religious and caritative functions of the town as a 'central place', led to a new form of communal life which was subsequently consolidated during the period of crisis and transformation that was the fourteenth and fifteenth centuries. This emergence of the medieval town as a specific social construction was accomplished in a direct, permanent interaction with urban space, both as a material reality and as a perceived entity, lived and represented.[11]

3   Communal Space and Communal Politics

In parallel to the economic and demographic expansion observed during the second half of the eleventh and throughout the twelfth century, the first urban settlements of the north of France and then also of the county of Flanders (to which still belonged the zone which would become the county of Artois) were transformed into 'communal spaces'. They were delimited territories benefitting from a certain juridical autonomy and arranged according to a specific politico-economic organisation. This *communio* (also called *amicitia, pax, communauté, ghemeente* or *meentucht* in medieval Flanders) was a community

---

10   Verhulst 1999; Keene 2004.
11   Ennen 1972; Stabel 2002.

founded on individual liberty, work and solidarity.[12] The communal movement thus led to a distinctly spatial conception of the urban political economy. The town was a space offering a quantity of assets: collective and juridical security, individual property rights substantial enough for commerce and production, the collective management of communal property – the 'commons' – necessitating the maintenance of battlements, paved roads and bridges, common pastures, ponds and waterways, and often also urban spaces specifically reserved for fullers, shearers, brewers and dyers.[13] In the privilege of Saint-Omer of 1127, a certain number of aspirations emanating from the first urban population already illustrate these spatial-communal elements: the limitation of arbitrary feudal taxes on the inhabitants of the territory of the city, the maintenance of waterways and infrastructure, boat transport around the town, the management of common pastures and the public participation in the political and financial management of the town.[14]

In the domain of criminal justice, the commune could exclude whoever transgressed its laws and customs and breached the urban *pax, communio* or *amicitia*, or whoever neglected in any other manner their duties to the community.[15] A whole series of offences were susceptible to be punished by exile: the refusal to appear before a court of justice, homicide, theft, rape, the corruption of minors, prostitution, etc. Banishment as well as legal practice consisting of destroying the houses of exiles and other 'enemies of the commune', what one calls the *droit d'arsin* or the *droit d'abattis*, thus became typical traits of urban custom. These penalties therefore aimed to remove criminals from urban space and often also to destroy the places that they had occupied in the town. In as much as it was an inclusive social construction, the town equally had to be a space of potential exclusion.[16]

The oldest sources related to the towns in the region often testify to oppositions in terms of the statutes and juridical law between, on one side, the *clerici* and the *milites* of the local garrison, and the *burgenses* on the other. However, during the period of economic growth of the central Middle Ages, these oppositions, which were often of a socio-topographical nature and meant that towns often developed from multiple centres, progressively faded away. More and

---

12 Reynolds 1984, p. 156; Oexle 1996b; Van Caenegem 1956, p. 5. The best study on the communal movement in this region is Saint-Denis 1994. See also Schulz 1992.
13 For these socio-economic aspects of communal space, see Schofield and Vince 1994; and Lilley 2002.
14 Van Caenegem 1982, pp. 260–1 and Van Caenegem 2009.
15 On the oldest charters of Flemish liberty, see Van Caenegem 1968.
16 Delcourt 1930; Van Caenegem 1956.

more, the town was experienced and perceived as a juridically privileged space in its unity. This does not exclude the upkeep, within themselves, of seigneurial and ecclesiastical enclaves susceptible to stimulate juridical and fiscal conflicts. In the settlements of the Flemish urban zone in its wider sense, with the exception of certain episcopal towns such as Arras and Tournai, the ecclesiastical presence was always relatively restrained compared to those of the Italian town, for example. However, if the towers of the church continued to dominate the Flemish urban landscape, it was the commercial component which became preponderant. During the thirteenth century, the merchant elites governing the town always sought more systematic means to unify the urban territory according to juridical and political plans and to extend their jurisdiction outside of the town. At the same time, the town looked to acquire from noble proprietors the seigneurial rights which acted as a brake on both the spatial and economic development of the town: rights over custom duties, weighing houses and other economic rights.[17]

4 Socio-spatial Oppositions in the Town of the Thirteenth Century

The concept and the forms of initial political organisation of the town rested on the *Schwurvereinigung* of free men and the practices of merchant guilds. But these elements disappear in the thirteenth century and urban society began increasingly to diversify socially. The development of urban production and commercial exchange provoked a growing polarisation between rich and poor. The symbols of seigneurial and ecclesiastical power were no longer the only ones to dominate the urban landscape, even if the thirteenth century was the grand epoque of the emergence of Gothic cathedrals. But on the political plan, it was the merchant class, who possessed the majority of urban lands, which dominated the town. These lands – following demographic and economic growth – experienced a strong increase in value and became an object for financial speculation. Their merchant-entrepreneur owners set themselves up in stone houses situated in areas inside of the town and invested in cheaper, smaller dwellings (*cameren*, litterally, 'rooms': small houses with one room and an attic) rented to their workers.[18] At first these were constructed in woods and then in stone. Then one sees belfries erected, typical monuments of this region that were the pride of the towns.[19] Thus the big merchants and proprietors

---

17   Strubbe 1963.
18   Raveschot and Laleman 1986.
19   Battard and Lestocquoy 1948; Van Uytven 1998; Billen 2010.

of land increasingly concurred that urban space was theirs exclusively, from a social and political point of view. In Flanders, it was equally the urban elite who obtained the control of hospitals, leper-houses and other charitable institutions which developed rapidly from the second half of the twelfth century, with only the indirect involvement of ecclesiastical institutions.[20]

After the control of the means of production and of communal lands, another political stake with spatial dimensions took a growing importance: the control of labour. The massive movement of labour to the towns from the thirteenth century expanded the suburban industrial zones. They sheltered above all textile workers, and to a lesser extent tanners. The elite who lived in the centre of the town saw these 'labouring classes' as the 'dangerous classes': not only did crime and prostitution flourish in their quarters but a direct line can equally be established between these 'marginal' suburbs and social protests. This is illustrated by a first wave of strikes touching the Flemish towns in the years 1240–50, as well as a wave of revolts which affected the textiles town around 1280. The merchant class put in place a strategy combining policing and charity in order to reinforce their control over the industrial suburbs but, in the majority of cases, they could only avoid extending complete civil laws to the inhabitants of these zones. From the thirteenth and fourteenth centuries, many towns enlarged their battlements in order to include these suburban zones. But in certain industrial towns such as Ypres and Saint-Omer, the spatial opposition between the richer centre and the industrial suburbs was strongly maintained even towards the end of the later Middle Ages.[21]

5   From Urban Communal Space to Urban Corporative Space

The wave of revolts that marked the Flemish towns around 1280 ended, admittedly, with failure. However, it is clear that the complete integration of artisans into the political system and therefore also in all aspects of urban space had become inevitable, at least in the large towns. After the rebellion of 1302, which constituted a defeat for the patricians allied with the French occupier, tradespeople obtained political participation in towns such as Ghent and Bruges. The late Middle Ages was subsequently marked by recurring confrontations between changing coalitions. These generally saw the elite merchants in opposition to the productive classes of the artisans, including their elites and large

---

20   De Coninck and Blockmans 1967; Maréchal 1978.
21   Prevenier 1978; Keene 1990; Boone 1998; Dewilde and Van Bellingen 1998; Dumolyn 2012a and 2015; Dumolyn and Haemers 2015b.

businessmen. The incontestable stranglehold of the merchant class over urban space had to partially cede place to a new spatial logic, that of 'corporatism'. This new model of communal organisation characterises the more complex and diversified urban space of the late Middle Ages. The artisans aspired to an ideological transformation of the town in order to make a 'corporative space', an urban political and religious space that would metaphorically represent the *Corpus Christi* venerated by the townspeople during processions.[22]

The social topography of the Flemish towns of the late Middle Ages certainly necessitates much more empirical research, but the global image which emerges shows the partial effacement of spatial oppositions between the poor suburbs and the more comfortable centre. There is certainly not the capacity to speak of social segregation. It is true that the rich lived predominantly in the centre or in the roads leading to the gates of the town, and that the homes of the poor were most often situated in the roads adjacent and at the periphery, but the most well-off groups equally constructed residences in the open spaces situated in proximity to the battlements.[23] The fourteenth and fifteenth centuries are also characterised by the specialisation and the diversification of economic activities, by a more variated spatial distribution of businesses and social groups, and also by markets whose topography changed over time. This spatial development was articulated by the struggle for power between the corporations and the commercial elites. The collectivist principles of corporatism often conflicted with the more individualist principles of the free entrepreneuriat and of private property. Furthermore, the symbolic dimensions tied to prestige and to domination were also present.

The study of 'microscopic' conflicts emanating from different corporative groups and from individual businessmen remains to be done: in effect, the concern of these rivalries was urban, commercial and industrial space, here understood in their symbolic dimensions. These conflicts were less spectacular than the great revolts and civil wars in late medieval Flanders – which have until now motivated the analyse of urban spatial politics – and have left fewer traces in the sources. But incontestably they were more frequent and probably also much more present in everyday life. Therefore, little is known about conflict between the proprietors of houses and their tenants, with the exception of the notorious case of the merchant-entrepreneur Jehan Boinebroke from thirteenth-century Douai, who used his status as a landlord to extort rent and work from destitute widows.[24]

---

22 See Chapter 3 in the present volume.
23 Boogaart 2004; and Leguay 1984, pp. 115–23.
24 Espinas 1933.

The spatial aspects tied to the corporate control of workshops and markets constitute another crucial issue susceptible to creating conflict.[25] The small businessmen, artisans and merchants disputed the control of industrial and commercial zones and the right to inspect the workshops. By controlling the spaces of work as well as markets, the halls and the local shops, the corporations also tried to impose their demand on other corporations, to distributors and formally organised workers and to the street-sellers.[26] As in many other European towns of the Middle Ages, the socio-economic struggle for the control of space was also often ecological in nature. In effect, certain trades occupied specific zones in the town. Thus, the space reserved for tanners, fullers, dyers, shearers or brewers was tied to the indispensable proximity to water or to open spaces, or even to the stench or the fire hazards they generated.[27] Finally, the urban tissue also comprised other actors making their own demands on the various economic sectors in order to defend their interests. The count of Flanders and the local lords counted on the sums collected from taxes and tolls. The ecclesiastical institutions managed the urban zones where indirect taxes were lower and they would therefore enrich themselves by selling alcohol. The commercial elite, notably the hoteliers, the regional merchants, the entrepreneurs and the proprietors of land looked to generate profit from commerce, entrepreneurial active, rent and political and symbolic domination.

In the course of the fourteenth century, a new dimension to the socio-economic and political struggle for urban space emerged: the control of the countryside and of roads and waterways.[28] During the period of crisis of the fourteenth century, demands on urban space expressed themselves at first in continuity with the traditional practice of the *droit d'abattis* and the *droit d'arsin* led against the 'enemies of the commune'. However, a new dimension came into the mix: the tension between urban and rural industries. The opposition between the town and the countryside, as that between the large and the small subordinate towns, was accentuated by the economic crisis and reconversion affecting the cloth industry in Flanders, as well as by the growth of violence which disrupted commercial exchange. This was above all the impulsion of the textile trades as well as the militias of Ghent and Ypres, and to a lesser extent those of Bruges, performing raids led against competing rural industries, destroying their looms and fulling tanks. The access routes, by land or by water, and certain aspects tied to them – staple rights, the position within the commercial

---

25 Stabel 2008b, pp. 80–1.
26 Stabel 2008c.
27 Nicholas, David 1987, pp. 169–70; Dumolyn 2012a; Lecuppre-Desjardin 2002.
28 Nicholas, David 1971.

networks – were considered as being an integral part of communal space. The Ghent navigators ferociously protected their privileges and in 1379 attacked the Brugeois workers hired to dig a new canal that risked their position. This was the direct cause of a revolt that lasted until 1385. As for the Brugeois artisans, just as for the commercial elites, they distrusted the outer harbours of their mercantile metropolis, because they could short-circuit the port of Bruges. Notably, the threat came from Sluis, which was much more accessible from the sea than Bruges. Thus, in 1323 as in 1437 the Brugeois rebels attacked Sluis because they saw the privileges of their town threatened.[29]

6 An Urban Landscape of Political Action and Communication

The urban Flemish network developed particularly quickly between the twelfth and the thirteenth century with numerous routes and canals connecting the large urban centres and the small towns, so that one would never find oneself further than twenty kilometres from a medium-sized settlement. This infrastructure permitted not only the emergence of a hierarchical network with intense economic and demographic interconnections between different urban functions,[30] but also a veritable political landscape. The towns remained in part autonomous public spaces, but they also had an interdependency that meant that socio-political troubles could easily pass from one to the other, notably by the mobility of the literate workforce and by the flow of information. Thus, in the course of the eventful year of 1302, the popular classes reacted constantly to the revolts led against the occupying French and their patrician allies by expressing their solidarity or by trying to seize power themselves.[31] Furthermore, the revolts often led to wide waves of unrest that affected the whole or a large part of the county, as during the years 1323–8, 1359, 1379–82, 1436–7 or 1477.[32]

Consequently, in the great industrial centres of Flanders and of the north of France, urban medieval space constituted a system of intense communication with a vast expanse. A very coherent political and communicative space formed in the crucible of the great towns in which space and the population were relatively easy to control, even for the largest among them which

---

29 Boone 2008b, pp. 33–4; Nicholas, David 1971; Ryckaert, Vandermaesen and Coornaert 1979; Dumolyn 1997, p. 240.

30 Stabel 1997; Thoen and Verhulst 1986; Blockmans, Willem 1994a.

31 Verbruggen, Raf 2005.

32 See [Patterns]; Verbruggen, Raf 2005, pp. 79–90.

accommodated between ten and sixty-five thousand inhabitants. In the Flemish region (in the expanded sense), these towns were: Oudenaarde, Kortrijk, Dendermonde, Douai, Arras, Saint-Omer, Lille, Tournai and Ypres and above all Bruges and Ghent.[33] This space accommodated the speech, commercial transactions, information exchange (both news and gossip), laws and regulations promulgated by the gatehouse of the belfry, but equally subversive conspiracies, secretive meetings and rebel slogans.[34] The town also attracted the theatre, and popular songs resounded there, sometimes bearing a political message.[35] This was a place where inscriptions and placards adorned the walls and where the sounds of clocks and of trumpets created, so to speak, a sonic landscape.[36] Thus there emerged a system of urban signs, in dialogue with the material aspects characterising space, with religious and secular architecture and notably with the architectural elements such as belfries, the houses of aldermen, the houses of artisans, the gates and the walls of the town.[37] This system constantly mediated the politico-ideological values discussed above that different urban groups use to express their aspirations and their identities in the urban landscape.[38]

The Ypres urban chronicle attributed to Olivier van Dixmude and his successors is a very interesting source to understand the spatial dimensions of the 'popular politics' of the late Middle Ages, including those which extended beyond the frontiers of the town.[39] This work provides a clear image of the confusing situation of the years 1379–90 when the Ghent rebels 'headed out' (*trocken ute*, a phrase that appears multiple times) to roam through the whole Flemish urban network in order to obtain the solidarity of other townspeople or to attack a place controlled by the adversaries supporting the count. These mobile rebel troops were designated by the term 'travellers' (*reisers*). In a context of civil war, the dense urbanisation of this zone permitted rapid and unexpected movement and was suited to rumours and news.[40]

The text describes energetically and simultaneously, on the one hand, the spatial oppositions on the socio-economic plane, and on the other, the forms of rebellions, civil war and repression. The first of these gave shape to the struggles

---

33 Stabel 2002.
34 Lett and Offenstadt, eds 2003; See [A Bad Chicken].
35 See [Political Poems]. See recently, for example, multiple contributions in Dumolyn, Haemers, Oliva Herrer et al., eds 2014.
36 Lecuppre-Desjardin 2010; Billen 2010; Strohm, Reinhard 1985; Haverkamp 1996.
37 Lecuppre-Desjardin 2003.
38 Lecuppre-Desjardin 2007.
39 Lambin, ed. 1835. On this text see Trio 2008.
40 Lambin, ed. 1835, pp. 3–10.

of different groups, the second had material and symbolic space as its concern. Thus, central public spaces were often the theatre of conflict between partisans and opponents of a revolt. In 1379, the main square of Ypres saw a confrontation between the radical urban militia of Ghent, the *Witte Kaproenen* (White Hoods) and the local partisans of the county. And in 1380, at the Friday Market square in Bruges, the Ghent rebels and the comital party of Bruges clashed yet again. The resounding bells summoned the people, sometimes from outside the town, to throw themselves into the melee, crying slogans of war like 'Flanders and Lion! Our freedom will be maintained!' (*Vlaendre en Leeuw ons vryhede behoudende*).[41] The central markets of the town also accommodated revolutionary meetings. On these occasions, there would be public consultations with the people who would have their cries forcefully state 'aye' and 'nay'.[42] It sometimes happened that the count would personally involve himself in these tense situations specific to these assemblies, either as a form of premeditated provocation or with the intention of calming the situation or re-establishing his symbolic domination in the town. He appeared either on horseback surrounded by an armed guard or on the balcony of one of the houses of the aldermen.[43]

7   The Static and Dynamic Struggle for Communal Space

As we have recalled, Marc Boone was the first to stress the importance of politically symbolic spaces in the medieval town as a factor in the numerous sociopolitical conflicts that marked Flanders. The Friday Market at Ghent and the main square at Lille (presently La Place Charles de Gaulle) were then partially created by the administrative councils of the towns to serve as *décor* for political rituals. Later, it was precisely these central places that rebel artisans tried to symbolically occupy.[44] During the revolts, the Flemish tradespeople also had the habit of opening the prisons, pillaging and destroying the house of seigneurial functionaries and urban tax collectors. The control of bells belonging to central, communal buildings such as the belfries and the houses of aldermen provided further facilities for mobilisation.[45] Armed and partly choreo-

---

41   Ibid., pp. 2–3; and Ryckaert, Vandermaesen and Coornaert 1979.
42   Lambin, ed. 1835, p. 4.
43   For example, ibid., p. 11.
44   Boone 2002a; Deligne 2013. Similar findings were formulated for Venice by Crouzet-Pavan 2000.
45   Boone 2002a, p. 634; Verbruggen, Raf 2005, pp. 103–13.

graphed assemblies of artisans, regulated by the ringing of bells, the rhymes and rhythms of slogans and the deployment of banners, in combination with popular gatherings in open air, even political murders, pseudo-executions or the throwing of corrupt office holders from windows from symbolic buildings such as the house of aldermen, all characterised the revolts that were often present at Ghent and Bruges, but also in the smaller towns. This type of mobilisation was called *wapeningen* or *auweeten*, a word derived from the French word *guet*, and which referred to inspections of military troops organised by the urban militia. Through this type of action, the holders of power expressed their demands in an intimidating manner in very specific places in order to stress that they were an integral part of the commune and therefore had political rights within public space.[46]

Another collective action undertaken by the tradespeople of the Low Countries to intimidate the authorities was what was called the 'course' (*loop, ghel-oop, lopinghe, uploop* or *oploepe*).[47] 'To run around the town' or 'organise a course', meant to run through the street in order to reclaim urban space and its central symbolic spaces.[48] One such *oploop* or popular demonstration was that which took place during the Matins of Bruges in 1302, during which the rebels demonstrated '*sonoribus et vocibus ac clamoribus terribilibus*' ('with noises, voices and terrifying clamours').[49] The formal and symbolic analogy with popular processions is here striking, an aspect of them that has been remarked on numerous times by Élodie Lecuppre-Desjardin.[50] When the rebels marched in the manner of a procession around specific parts of the town, this popular movement with a 'para-religious' character also aimed to symbolically occupy important public spaces such as the main squares or the commercial zones in order to demonstrate their stranglehold on the body of the town.[51]

Another way to politicise the urban landscape consisted in collectively destroying certain symbolic places. This form of popular mobilisation was also directly derived from *droit d'abattis* or *huus asselieren*. At Bruges the anti-communal charter of 1281 had suppressed this form of popular communal

---

46 See [A Moody Community]; Boone 2005; Arnade 1994; See [The Vengeance].
47 Boone 2005.
48 See [The Vengeance]; Boone 2005. Courses also appear in French sources and in Italy, *correre la città* was equally a metaphor for urban troubles. On this see Trexler 1984a.
49 De Smet, Joseph Jean, ed. 1837a, pp. 166–7.
50 Lecuppre-Desjardin and Van Bruaene 2013; Lecuppre-Desjardin 2004.
51 Haemers and Lecuppre-Desjardin 2007; Boogaart 2001a, pp. 82–5; Brown 2011, pp. 42–4; Arnade 1991.

justice, seeing that it had been applied by the rebels of the *meentucht* on the occasion of the revolt of the *Moerlemaye* in 1280, a revolt led against the possession of patrician oligarchs.[52] However, this practice remained one of the favourite methods of resistance in the popular repetoire. Whether it be the destruction of the houses of tax collectors, the assault on prisons during revolts or even, in an indirect manner, the iconoclastic crisis of the sixteenth century, these were in each case variations of this practice. These acts added a symbolic and spatial dimension to communal ideas on law and justice, here including the levying of taxes which was resented as an injustice.

At other times, the princes also used destructive interventions in the urban landscape. They thus condemned the rebellious towns to demolish their battlements or to block up their gates, which happened regularly in Flanders.[53] Such seigneurial interventions intensified with the Burgundian and Habsburg dynasty. The entourage of Philip the Good, after having considered razing the rebel towns for some time, gave up on the idea for economic reasons. It was Philip's son, Charles the Bold, who put the idea into practice with the pillage of Liège in 1468. Finally, Charles v, the Holy Roman Emperor, raised the stakes by having built a strong castle at Ghent called the 'Spanish Castle'.[54]

The *ledichganc*, the collective refusal to work among the artisans of the town or certain trades, notably the textile workers, which sometimes transformed into an early type of 'general strike', was a later form of action relevant to the repertoire of communal actions and to the context of employment conditions for the workforce.[55] Seeing that artisanal production was spread across diverse workshops, it was impossible to envisage similar strike action that we know today: there were simply not places that lent themselves to action similar to an industrial occupation or a picket line. The static and dynamic actions described above therefore permitted the tradespeople to stress their demands. They served not only to reclaim the spaces tied to the production process, but also the political and symbolic space of the town. To underline their refusal to work, there finally remained the possibility of collectively walking out of the town. In this case, a strike was also called '*uutganck*' (exit).[56] This type of early industrial action, notably in the textile sector oriented to exportation, became a major problem from the middle of the thirteenth century. From that point, medieval strikes, tied to a developed urban economy, capital accumulation and

---

52   Warnkönig 1835, vol. 2, p. 103.
53   Verbruggen, Raf 2005, pp. 116–20.
54   Boone and de Hemptinne 1997; Boone 2013.
55   See [The Vengeance].
56   Boone and Brand 1993.

the concentration of the workforce in the suburbs, were forms of action present throughout the following centuries.[57]

On the occasion, the militias of the town, composed in the majority of artisans, purposefully camped in a field situated just outside of the town before re-entering to resume work. This occurred in Bruge in 1411 and in 1436, in each case triggering a revolt.[58] In 1379, the Ghent rebels assembled in a field situated outside the gate of Bruges before leaving to 'assail and break' (*saelgieren ende breiken*) the castle of the count at Wondelgem. Afterwards they returned to Ghent.[59] This way of playing with the symbolic frontier with the town and also of defending their interests outside of the walls occurs from the twelfth century in the traditions and the directories of penal law – with the *droit d'abattis* – and in the exploits of urban militia.

The creation of a corporative political space within the town was not only a demand in times of conflict. The tradespeople also worked to attain this objective in a peaceful manner and during periods of political stability. During the late Middle Ages, they dedicated for this guild houses situated on the principal roads and squares, or even more in the chapels and almshouses.[60] The Bruges guild of weavers, for example, had their almshouse next to their chapel with a cemetery dedicated to Saint John and Saint Severin. It must have existed from the middle of the fourteenth century. The smiths had one from 1352. These two buildings marked the urban space at the entry of the principal roads, next to the gates of the town.[61] But despite the demands emanating from corporative groups, it was the commercial sector that continued to dominate communal space in the late Middle Ages, just as it was the merchant elite, along with the ecclesiastical institutions, who imposed themselves in the urban landscape. Like the urban nobility, they displayed their riches and their power through private residences, church endowments and communal construction projects.[62]

---

57 Verbruggen, Raf 2005, pp. 145–61.
58 Dumolyn 1997.
59 Lambin, ed. 1835, p. 1.
60 Dambruyne 2006.
61 Maertens 1940, pp. 71–3.
62 Buylaert, De Rock, Dumolyn et al. 2015.

8 Conclusion

Since the beginning of the communal movement, urban space in Flanders and in the surrounding regions, for reasons of its specific socio-economic and juridical-political character, was at stake in struggles between different social groups and centres of power. The crucial element in this context was the communal management of symbolic places, buildings and frontiers as well as semi-rural, artisanal and commercial zones, markets and infrastructures. The town was a well-defined space, materially situated at the centre of a network of routes and rural hinterlands and ideologically in a context of economic and political privileges, industrial monopolies and staple rights fearlessly defended by the townspeople. With socio-economic growth and diversification as well as growing political polarisation, it was completely logical that this communal space witnessed the emergence of a struggle between different artisanal and commercial groups, a struggle which inevitably took on a spatial character. It was articulated around property rights, conflicts in the location's domain, control of common urban elements, the workforce and markets. These conflicts were forms of action that took place either in a static manner, through occupation, the destruction or construction of symbolic places or buildings, or in a dynamic manner, by the spatial appropriation of communal space as a whole. In all cases, the parties concerned always operated in a politico-spatial logic where the commune was understood as a whole.

PART 3

Oration and Whispers

Political Poems and Subversive Songs: The Circulation of 'Public Poetry' in the Late Medieval Low Countries

Jan Dumolyn and Jelle Haemers

1   Introduction

A chronicle on the 'wondrous wars' of Maximilian of Austria composed at the end of the fifteenth century recounts the story of Jan de Gheest, leader of the Ghent militia of the *Groententers*, those who sleep in 'green tents', in other words, out in the open field. In 1477, this commoner and his 4,000 strong army of simple folk, also known as the *Ghelapte Schoen* or 'mended shoes', had inflicted great losses on the French invaders who had taken advantage of the general instability in the Burgundian lands after the death of Duke Charles the Bold. 'Thus, the Mended Shoes were very strong', the text relates, 'and they displayed feats of arms about which songs were sung in the streets'.[1] Likewise, after the 1481 victory of the city of Utrecht in the county of Holland, the mob dragged artillery through the streets singing refrains 'about the lords', songs the chronicler dared not name because, he wrote, 'I am too small a man to mention them'. The songs were mocking the mayor who had illegitimately appropriated a valuable tabard from the war booty.[2]

Although only a few of these songs composed before the middle of the sixteenth century have survived, this genre of popular songs about both contemporary and past political events must have been omnipresent in the late medieval Low Countries.[3] Like the nearly indistinguishable streams of gossip and political information running from town to town, from inn to inn, and from one artisan's workshop to another, songs were an important way to communicate military and political news and also to incite action. This was true long before the age of the printing press, although the practice perhaps became more frequent afterwards, as printing facilitated production of this ephemeral

---

1 Alberts, ed. 1957, p. 36. All translations are ours unless indicated otherwise.
2 Van 't Hooft 1948, pp. 22–3.
3 Van de Graft, ed. 1904 identified forty-nine 'historical songs' dated before the sixteenth century but her list is problematic and certainly non-exhaustive. See also Grijp 2000.

genre. Especially during times of war, dynastic crises, or civic conflicts – as also happened in England, France and elsewhere[4] – songs, as well as poems, with political messages circulated in and between the towns and cities of the Netherlands.[5]

A primary purpose of this article is to fill a historiographical gap by drawing systematic attention to the ubiquitous circulation of political songs and poems in the urban world of the Low Countries between the fourteenth century and approximately 1540. During the last two decades, historians and literary scholars have paid far more attention to the intersection between politics and literary production in medieval English and German urban societies than have current specialists in Middle Dutch literature.[6] In the scholarly work of Dutch and Flemish specialists of the period – with the notable exceptions cited below – only those works that predate the middle of the twentieth century generally examine the political context of a literary text. More recent studies merely note political context in passing or analyse it sporadically in scattered case studies.[7]

As yet, there has been no systematic attempt to establish links between the flourishing study of Middle Dutch literature as a broad cultural history on the one hand and the increasing attention of political historians to questions of 'communication' and 'political culture' on the other.[8] The genre of 'historical songs' (as they have traditionally been called) or 'political songs' (a better term) offers the opportunity to reflect on the intense relationship between literature, society and politics in the medieval Low Countries. These songs could be descriptive, propagandistic or polemic.[9] We argue that these intriguing texts should be classified as what medievalists now generally call 'public poetry', a 'genre' defined by the ideological contents, functions and audiences of literary texts, to transcend the research that mainly targets generic distinctions made by scholars in the past between different types of poems, songs and tales.[10]

---

4   Martines 2001, pp. 232–48; Cheesman 1994; Darnton 2010; Salzberg and Rospocher 2012, pp. 9–26.
5   Van der Bom 1985; Pleij 2007, pp. 604–6.
6   For instance, Scattergood 1971; Honemann 1997; Mairey 2007b; Scase 2007.
7   Kalff 1884; Te Winkel 1884. See also more general and recent work on medieval Dutch songs: Reynaert 1999; and most of all the many publications by Frank Willaert on Middle Dutch songs, including: Willaert, ed. 1992, Willaert, ed. 1997 and Willaert 2008.
8   Although the publication of the repertory of Dutch songs before 1600, including classification of genre for each song, now strongly facilitates such studies: de Bruin, Oosterman and Strijboch, eds 2001.
9   Van Bork, Delabastita, Van Gorp et al., eds 2012b.
10   Middleton 1978, p. 94; Arens 1989, p. 168.

2 Official Political Literature

From the fourteenth century onwards, travelling acrobats, musicians, street and market singers, magicians and illusionists regularly appear in the sources of the medieval Netherlands, but it is likely that political literature, whether recited or sung, began first at court. Heralds would sing the praise of their lords and their feats of arms in panegyric songs.[11] Many 'political' Middle Dutch literary works were clearly composed for a princely or noble audience.

These political works represent the dominant ideologies and princely politics of the time. The oldest known Dutch text lauding a prince is the *Wapenlied van hertog Jan III van Brabant* ('The Epic of Duke Jan III of Brabant') of 1369 which compares the Duke of Brabant to a boar.[12] *Die Claghe van den Grave van Vlaendren* ('The Complaint of the Count of Flanders') and *Die Claghe van den hertoghe Wenselijn van Brabant* ('The Complaint of Duke Wencelin of Brabant'), each by Jan Knibbe (about 1383–4), are other examples of allegorical poems with similar mentions of heraldry, presumably written for a noble audience.[13]

Among other political texts written from the viewpoint of the political elites is the poem *Een exempel van partyen* ('An Example of Parties'), by the late fourteenth-century Holland storyteller Willem van Hildegaersberch. While it did not directly discuss a specific historical event, the poem clearly referred to the partisan strife in Holland between the Hooks and the Cods in its moralising message promoting unity.[14] From the fifteenth century onwards, panegyrical texts were also produced in urban environments. In 1477, the Bruges rhetorician Anthonis de Roovere wrote one for the deceased Charles the Bold, *Den droom van Roovere op die doot van Kaerle van Borgonnyen saleger gedachten* ('Roovere's Dream of the Death of Charles of Burgundy of Blessed Memory').[15] After her untimely death in 1482, a text praised Charles's daughter Mary. It was written from the perspective of the city of Bruges but recorded in the 1544

---

11   Te Winkel 1884, pp. 4–5; Van Anrooij 1985.

12   Fredericq 1894, pp. 15–16.

13   Serrure 1855, pp. 303–8; Hogenelst 1997, vol. 2, pp. 79–80.

14   Hogenelst 1997, vol. 2, p. 140; Bisschop and Verwijs, eds 1870, pp. 102–3. About Van Hildesgaersberch, see Meder 1991. Other examples are *Hoe die yerste partie in Hollant quam* ('How the factional party came to Holland') by the same author. It carries a message against hate and slander but situated within the history of the Holland dynasty. In the allegorical text, *Van den sloetel* ('Of the Key'), Hildegaersberch defends the Leiden city council after a failed workers revolt in 1393 (ibid., pp. 122–3 and 164–9). See also Van Oostrom 2013, pp. 412–9.

15   Mak, ed. 1955, pp. 351–9; Oosterman 1999.

Antwerp Songbook (a variant is preserved in a Brussels manuscript as well). In addition to this song, obviously performed in music, Anthonis de Roovere paid written tribute to her in an acrostic inserted into his 'Excellent Chronicle of Flanders' (*De Excellente cronike van Vlaenderen*).[16]

3   Subversive Songs

Besides these rather 'official' works of politically motivated literature, many of the people singing songs and observed by contemporary writers actually belonged to the lower classes. Their songs probably had more 'folk characteristics' than did the lyrical songs with complex forms composed by courtly singers. Common singers were often women, or sometimes groups of children, and a number of them also seem to have been blind or disabled. Some sung occasionally or joined in with crowds; others were professional street singers. After the fifteenth-century shearer François van den Broucke, for instance, was mutilated and could no longer practice his trade, he started 'to roam about the country singing songs and selling them'.[17]

Although the vast majority of these songs dealt with the deeds of epic heroes, or love and life in general, many also contained ideological elements from the 'popular politics' typical of the cities in the late medieval Netherlands. With a moralistic critique on the failings of their political adversaries, these elements condemned urban elites who were guided by elite or factional interests.[18]

For instance, a song chanted during factional conflicts in Leiden and Haarlem in 1478 was called *Brederoede hout dy veste* ('Brederode, hold the keep'). This song sympathised with Frans van Brederode, a nobleman who supported the faction that had rebelled against the count of Holland. Details aside, the song shows that using common idioms, such as the colourful term 'liver eaters' to denote greedy princely officials and looting soldiers, and well-known rhyme and rhythm schemes helped speed oral transmission of political messages.[19] According to sources, the *Brederode* song was sung as a refrain to the Latin hymn *Dies est laetitae*. Apparently, both the rebels who sang *Brederoede hout dy veste* and the informers among the count's supporters who reported the singing to his officials recognised the song and its rhythm scheme (as the

---

16   Fredericq 1894, pp. 43–4; Van de Graft, ed. 1904, pp. 96–100; Van der Poel and Grijp, eds 2004, vol. 1, pp. 288–9 and vol. 2, pp. 300–2; Oosterman 2005, pp. 98–105.

17   Stalpaert 1959, pp. 12–4 (and other examples).

18   See [Patterns]; Liddy and Haemers 2013.

19   Van Gent 1990, p. 132.

sources noted the title of the song to which *Brederoede* referred). Urban dissidents thus adopted older and well-known melodies which made taunting songs easy to repeat in order to spread the message rapidly.[20]

These examples can be considered 'rebellious' or 'subversive' songs because they contain critical views of rulers, city governments, and political and moral behaviour of public officials. However, those studying these ephemeral subversive texts of the late medieval period often find it difficult to distinguish among rhyming slogans, leaflets in verse, party songs meant either to forge a common identity or simply to serve as a way to distinguish friend from foe, defamation chants meant to intimidate opponents, poems written years after the events, and actual songs put to music. On 4 October 1451, a broadside posted on the door of the Ghent city hall read *'Gy slapscheten van Ghendt, / die nu hebt 't regiment, / wy en zullen 't hu nyet ghewagen, / maer zullen 't eenen nyeuwen Artevelt claghen'* ('Thou feeble farts of Ghent, who art in power now, we won't tell you / but we'll complain to a new Artevelde'). The leaflet called for a 'new Artevelde', referring to the fourteenth-century rebel leader of the city, to take up arms against the Burgundian Duke Philip the Good. In the authors' view, the aldermen had not taken sufficient action against the duke whom the rebels believed had violated their privileges. Although the chronicler who copied these few lines into his general narrative added that the citizens were clearly agitated after having read the subversive phrases, it is hard to judge whether such slogans in rhyme were later read out loud to groups of bystanders, rhythmically chanted or sung to a melody.[21] At any rate, once the authorities tore down the broadside, the words would only have been further diffused in oral form.

Few of these subversive, or even openly rebellious, texts, whether intended for oral or musical performance or no performance at all, have come down to us in full, although frequent references to them in chronicles, ordinances issued by the urban authorities and judicial records demonstrate that they were common and feared by the social and political elites. For instance, a singer from the town of Kampen was arrested in Guelders in 1335 for singing songs mocking the county.[22] In the respectable wine tavern *De Munt* ('The Mint') on the main commercial street of medieval Bruges, Thuene de Budt of the nearby small town of Oudenburg sung two 'regretful songs' in 1491, reproaching people with the events of the recently concluded revolt against Maximilian of Austria. To

---

20   Brinkman 1997, p. 57.
21   *'Int dwelcke de wet ende 't volck eensdeels beroert waren'*, Fris, ed. 1901–4, vol. 1, p. 129. See also Van Leeuwen 2004; Lecuppre-Desjardin 2010.
22   Van 't Hooft 1948, pp. 2, 22.

make matters worse, this happened 'in the presence and before the audience of many good and honourable men'.[23] The public character of this speech crime and, in this case, its intended audience of respectable people, were aggravating circumstances. The large majority of such cases of drunken political ranting must have gone unnoticed because they took place in much lowlier environments. Yet, sometimes, these songs were performed within the public space. In 1429, Lamin Fabriel from Ypres was exiled for fifty years because he had participated in an uprising during the previous year. Along with other crimes, he had disseminated a song entitled *Ypre, ghi waert een zoet prayel* ('Ypres, you were a sweet garden of delight') referring to the city's glorious economic past. Undoubtedly, the now lost song accused the Ypres authorities of failing to prevent the city's decline. Mary, Charles van Kooigem's wife, was banished as well because she had sung 'songs blaming and confusing' the city's aldermen. Significantly, the commission charged with investigating the revolt after it had been repressed, argued that Lamin had composed the song in Tournai, and Mary 'had brought it to Ypres'. Presumably, this referred to leaflets with the text of the song, which Mary had taken with her. According to her verdict, this action and the singing had incited the weavers to take up arms against the city council for encroaching on the weavers' privileges in previous years.[24] Defamatory songs were also used in private conflicts between families, in feuds, partisan strife, and even during a 'walkout' (*uutganc*) in Gouda in 1478–9. In 1544 Leiden, angry textile workers sang songs insulting the merchants because they had not bought wool in Calais. Although most of these songs are only mentioned in other sources, some songs from the Hook-Cod civil war in Holland have also survived.[25]

Of course, performing a rebellious song and disseminating subversive rhymes only led to an uprising if the citizens had political or economic reasons to take action. Yet, these texts did have a mobilizing or accelerating effect, recognised as such by late medieval authorities. Almost everywhere in Europe, repressive measures against 'protest singers' were in place, although these singers must have often been difficult to apprehend, and their performances and

---

23   For this example and others see [A Bad Chicken]; and see also Maes 1947, pp. 249–50, 680.

24   '*Ommedat zoe ghezonghen hadde liedekinne ter blame ende confuse van den heere van der wet*', Diegerick 1855–6, p. 310. The report of the commission states: '*Aussi lui a dit le dit Lammin Fabriel en ceste ville de Tournay qu'il avoit fait le canchon vituperable contre ceulx de la loy d'Ippre qui commence Ypre, ghi waert een zoet prayel etc, et lequelle canchon le femme du dit Karle porta de Tournay à Ypre*', Ibid., p. 305.

25   Interesting examples from Leiden in Brinkman 1997, pp. 48–62; Van Gent 1994, pp. 421–4; and similar songs in a German city in Roth 1996 and Honemann 2008, pp. 232–3.

flimsy pamphlets clearly a challenge to regulate.[26] A 1514 bylaw in Bruges prohibited the singing of ballads about princes and kings accompanied by the display of 'tekenen', which were presumably painted placards adding visual information to the lyrics.[27] However, if a public performance by a singer was too risky, dissidents were able to spread written copies in more covert and anonymous ways. Some years later the city of Antwerp banished rhetoricians who had posted 'famous broadsides, poems and ballads' on church doors and city gates.[28]

In 1539, a man from Hasselt and his wife were publicly humiliated in Mechelen because they had printed and spread 'controversial libels' (fameuse libellen) in Mechelen and Dendermonde. It is likely that the authorities took immediate action against the agitators as there had recently been a violent revolt in the city of Ghent. The libels were hung around the man's neck and then publicly burnt. His wife was sent on a forced pilgrimage.[29]

4   Political Songs

Political songs are an important component of public poetry. The first political song about which we are reasonably well informed is Van Cort Rozijn.[30] Cort Rozijn cannot be anyone else than Zeger van Kortrijk, known in French as Sohier le Courtraisin, whose name was literally changed into Flemish to literally mean 'Short Raisin'. The historical facts upon which the song is based must date to 1337, when Zeger, an influential knight and trusted counsellor of count Louis of Nevers who also had close ties to the city of Ghent, was executed by the count due to his alliance with the king of England at the onset of the Hundred Years War. All this is left out of the story, however, and the reason why Cort Rozijn is beheaded is because he angers the count by refusing his offer to become ruwaerd ('governor') of Flanders. Another famous song is the Kerelslied ('Song of the Villains') preserved in the Bruges Gruuthuse manuscript composed around the beginning of the fifteenth century. Along with other codicological features, analysis has identified the social and political circle that surrounded the manuscript as an elite circle in Bruges that

---

26   See examples mentioned in Scattergood 2000, pp. 200–25; Kuhn 2007; Martines 2000; Salzberg 2010.
27   Stalpaert 1959, p. 11.
28   'Famose billetten, dichten, rondeelkens ende balladen', de Bock 1969–70, p. 249.
29   Foncke 1928, p. 82.
30   Van de Graft, ed. 1904, pp. 49–53; Van der Poel and Grijp, eds 2004, vol. 2.

opposed radical popular groups in the Flemish towns. The *Kerelslied*, probably written at the end of the fourteenth century to deal with the revolt of 1379–85, portrays Flemish rebels as primitive and dangerous villains. Brinkman thinks that this song belongs to the 'protohistory' of the historical song genre.[31] Fortunately, a systematic study of the manuscript context, transmission and oral features of most political songs will be published soon by Brinkman.

The limited scope of this article allows only a brief discussion of the ways in which versions of political songs have been passed down to the present day, despite the methodological importance of this analysis.[32] There is, however, one outstanding source that reliably and directly transmitted late medieval and early sixteenth-century political songs in Dutch: the *Schoon Liedekensboeck* ('Fine Songbook') printed by Jan Roulans in 1544 in the metropolis of Antwerp.[33] It contains the lyrics of 221 songs, alphabetically ordered but without musical notations or illustrations apart from a woodcut on the title page. In the time of its publication, it was one of the most important collections of secular songs in Europe. The editor, Jan Roulans, probably compiled the *Songbook* from written sources: printed broadsheets, pamphlets, handwritten booklets and bits of paper.[34] Only one complete copy has survived, not only because the songbook was a cheaply printed item of everyday use, not meant to last, but also because the authorities prohibited its circulation, undoubtedly due to its contents (it was put on the *Index Librorum Prohibitorum* in 1546). Some of the songs were sexually explicit, and approximately thirty were political songs. Many of the lyrics dealt with the recent armed conflict between Charles V and the Duke of Guelders, known as the third Guelders Succession War of 1538–43. The *Antwerp Songbook* divided most of the lyrics into *oudt liedekens* ('old songs'), dating back to the fourteenth century, and more recent ones. Vellekoop's musicological research led him to conclude that Jan Roulans placed songs that had existed before approximately 1510 in the 'old songs' category. The general dividing line between old and new songs was roughly 1510–25.[35]

---

31   Brinkman 2002, p. 113.
32   We deal with this extensively in Dumolyn and Haemers 2018a.
33   This *Antwerp Songbook* was first edited by Hoffmann von Fallersleben, ed. 1830–62, vol. 2, but has recently been re-published in a modern edition of high quality: Van der Poel and Grijp, eds 2004, vol. 2.
34   Van der Poel and Grijp, eds 2004, vol. 2, p. 23.
35   Vellekoop 1985.

The *Antwerp Songbook*, or at least the surviving version, probably from the fourth print run, was hastily updated with twelve *nyue liedekens* ('new songs') about the struggle with Guelders in order to have more currency.[36] Some of the chivalric ballads, such as a Dutch version of the Song of Hildebrand (*Van den ouden Hillebrant*), must be older than the middle of the fifteenth century. The same is true for many historical songs of Flemish origin.[37] There was a marked increase in the number of historical songs, written by both sides in the conflict, from the second half of the sixteenth century during the revolt of the Netherlands against Spain (1568–1648).[38]

Many attestations to political songs supporting this pattern as well have been lost.

5 Questions of Genre

Songs were a popular object of study for Romantic historians because they were sources that seemed to represent the so-called 'folk' element, obviously a problematic and essentialist notion, and reflect what the Romantics thought of as the inner soul and spirit of a people. In their collections, German scholars, such as August Heinrich Hoffmann von Fallersleben and Rochus von Liliencron, sometimes included songs in Middle Dutch, a crucial stimulus for Dutch and Flemish scholars to study them by.[39] At the same time, the Romantic Movement in the historical and philological sciences became influential in Belgium and the Netherlands. However, the collections made by nineteenth-century and early twentieth-century folklorists and erudite scholars, such as Louis de Baecker, Jan Willems and Johannes van Vloten, and the later, more scholarly and systematic collections of Paul Fredericq and Cornelia van de Graft, did not have coherent criteria to delineate the corpus and therefore, understandably for their time, they did not sufficiently analyse the problems of social origin, intended audience and textual tradition.[40] Despite the recent public-

---

36 Van Wissing 1993, pp. 235–6.
37 Van der Poel and Grijp, eds 2004, vol. 2, pp. 9–14.
38 Blommaert, ed. 1847 contains mainly pro-Catholic and pro-Spanish songs, while the *Geusen Lietboek* contains songs about the 'Beggars'; see Leendertz 1924–5 and Buitendijk 1977.
39 Von Liliencron, ed. 1865–9. On the notion of the 'folk song' in Dutch and Belgian literary history, see Grijp 2000.
40 Fredericq 1894 was the first critical approach, along with Te Winkel 1887, pp. 425–7, 451–4. De Baecker 1855; van Vloten 1864.

ation of several important case studies,[41] these late medieval songs have generally received scant attention, in contrast to the significant work on historical and political songs from the sixteenth and seventeenth centuries, particularly the so-called *Geuzenliederen* ('Beggar's Songs'), which include the *Wilhelmus*, the national anthem of the kingdom of the Netherlands since 1932. In other European countries, there have been advances in the study of historical songs from the same time period. Recent scholarship on popular political discourses and practices in the later medieval Low Countries also provides useful context for this project.[42]

There are a number of problems associated with establishing a corpus of Middle Dutch political songs and poems. Along with other genres, such as 'battle songs', 'social satires', and 'Beggar's Songs' (named after the rebels in the sixteenth-century revolt of the Low Countries against Spain), the lyrical genre of the 'historical song' is hard to define. An extensive tradition of scholarship uses the terms *Geuzenliederen* and battle songs (*strijdliederen*) to categorise historical songs about the Eighty Years' War.[43] Scholars studying the sixteenth-century Netherlands revolts have given ample scrutiny to the *Geuzenliedboek* and the Protestant martyr songs.[44] However, the 'genres' of the *Geuzenliederen*, martyr or battle songs, contain distinctly different types of messages, registers and influences. The *Gentsch Vader Onze*, for instance, a text defending the Calvinist Republic of 1578–84, was influenced by prayer (The Lord's Prayer or *Onze Vader*).[45] However, 'A Song on the Tenth Penny' (*Een lied op den tienden penning*), composed in 1569 to protest against the taxes levied by the Duke of Alva, was written in the same pre-Reformation tradition of complaints against heavy taxation.[46] The genre also includes 'faction songs' (*factieliederen*), short ditties sung at the end of allegorical plays known as the *factiespelen* ('faction plays'), which were performed on the street. Some scholars also hold that 'street songs', often about current events, which market singers sold in leaflet form, were a separate genre.[47]

Other genres, such as the heroic epic, the romance or *chanson de geste*, story-telling ballads, prophetic texts, and even Christian hymns recounting the lives

---

41   For instance, Brinkman 2002; Pleij 1973; Van Anrooij 2002a; Mareel 2010b, pp. 72, 132–40.
42   See the survey in Dumolyn, Haemers, Oliva Herrer et al., eds 2014.
43   Van Bork, Delabastita, Van Gorp et al., eds 2012a; de Bruin 2001.
44   For instance, 'The History of a Martyr Burned' (1525) in Buitendijk 1977, pp. 29–30; and for singing martyrs in general see Grijp 1977. On the *Geuzenliedboek*, see Bruch 1971, pp. 14–18.
45   Fredericq 1894, pp. 52–3.
46   Loman 1872.
47   Martin 1984, pp. 422–6; Grijp and de Bruin, eds 2006; Dekker and van der Pol 1982, pp. 486–94; Grijp 2004; van den Berg 2004.

of saints and martyrs, often have some 'historical value' because they are partly based on historical fact. In addition, all these medieval 'genres' are intertextually related.[48] Distinguishing between a Middle Dutch *sproke* (similar to a French *fabliau*), a lyrical text to be recited (*Sprechspruchdichtung*) and a song that was actually chanted to a melody (*Sangspruchdichtung*) is often a difficult methodological issue.[49]

Leaving aside the problems of subgenre and performance to focus on the content of the texts, the general consensus among scholars is that historical or political songs and poems provide accounts of actual events. According to folklorists, cultural anthropologists and oral history specialists, these songs or poems may have been intended as propaganda or panegyrics, but since they were 'popular', they are comparable to other folk songs.[50] For instance, direct speech, which features in most of the 'historical' or 'political' songs we examine below, added vivacity. Typically, the plot was vague and underdeveloped, perhaps because the composer assumed the intended audience would already be familiar with the political context. This strategy also stimulated fantasy formation and self-engagement in the minds of the listeners.[51]

Vladimir Propp argues that historical songs, even if they were factually incorrect or incoherent, were usually composed by participants in or witnesses to the actual events that form the subject of the songs. Thus, a song about a military operation may have originated among the soldiers, composed by a talented and poetically gifted individual, been taken up by the rest of the group, and then diffused and gradually altered.[52] Historical songs aim to transmit the significance of an event rather than to recount it exactly. As Propp put it, the historical value of political songs lies in 'the people's expression of its historical self-awareness and in its attitude towards past events, persons and circumstances' rather than in their correct depiction of events and persons.[53] Composers used insults, metaphors, black-and-white oppositions, and polemical street language to present a colourful image of the past aimed at releasing emotions and distorting the memory of a certain event. The vivid lyrics of many Middle Dutch historical songs, such as those in the *Antwerp Songbook* about the war against Guelders, perfectly illustrate this observation.

---

48 Van Puffelen 1966.
49 Hogenelst 1997, vol. 1, pp. 59–70.
50 Vansina 1973, pp. 148–50. For other examples, see several good studies of French folkloric songs: Joutard 1983; Guilcher 1989; Guillorel 2010.
51 Van 't Hooft 1948, pp. 15–16.
52 Propp 1984, pp. 35–6.
53 Ibid., p. 51.

The positivist question about the historical 'truth' in these texts is not a consideration; rather these songs are significant in terms of the evidence they contain concerning beliefs and ideas about governance and their change over time. This type of analysis is complex. Political songs deal with the people's past and present political lives; they not only describe the events but also evaluate them. Songs about revolts, for instance, may reflect class struggle, but their later transformations are determined by subsequent social developments. The significance of the text lies in its relationship to the moment of performance, rather than to a putative but improved tradition.[54] Songs and chants about past events were composed for present needs. From this perspective, every version of a song is an 'original' version with a special function for the community in which it circulated, as it served to maintain the 'social memories' that a group needed to define itself.[55] For instance, songs about rebel heroes gave members of craft guilds exemplary stories about the mobilisation of rebels, along with historical arguments to justify an uprising.

6   Authorship, Intended Audience and Circulation

The terms 'historical song' and 'political song' are actually hybridised, and perhaps should be abandoned altogether, because the texts packed together under these labels belong to diverse types, were produced for many objectives in different environments, and were preserved and transmitted in many forms through multiple methods. The songs under scrutiny here circulated in the towns and countryside, but this did not necessarily make them 'popular'.[56] For some time historians have been aware of the danger of making a hard and fast distinction between 'popular' and 'elite' literature. Songs could easily cross social boundaries, especially in medieval towns. The urban landscape was an arena of cultural dissemination in which literate culture came into contact with 'illiterate' culture.[57]

---

54   Hopkin 2012, p. 256.
55   Burke 1989, p. 98; Fentress and Wickham 1992, p. ix; Cubitt 2007, p. 7. For individual case studies of the functionality of literature and 'social memories' in a political context, see Wood 2013; Haemers 2011; Kuijpers and Pollmann 2013.
56   Reynaert 1999, pp. 90–100. About the urban embedding of literary activities, see amongst others Brinkman 2011; Doudet 2008–9; Mareel 2010b.
57   Bouza 1999; Bellingradt 2012.

As a consequence, precise information about the social context is a crucial part of understanding a song's contents. The context not only affected the creation and adaptation of a song, but also its function. However, information about the authors and the audiences of political songs is scarce. When a source mentions the author and singers, we usually do not have the lyrics; conversely, for most surviving complete song texts, there is no indication of the author's name. This even holds true for songs from the late sixteenth century, although there are generally more authorial details. One example is the Amsterdam merchant Laurens Jacobsz Reael, who wrote 'Beggar Songs'.[58] Songs that praised the revolt against Spain were often composed by rhetoricians, such as Laurens Reael, G.H. van Breughel, D.V. Coornhert and Lucas d'Heere.[59] Earlier in the century, the rhetorician Mathijs de Castelein wrote six political songs.[60] And the famous sixteenth-century poet Anna Bijns from Antwerp also referred to contemporary problems in some refrains.[61]

All these well-known rhetorician authors belonged to the urban middle and upper classes and had much to lose if their city was punished for a rebellion. Although rhetoricians did write about the political and social problems of their times, they usually did not call for social or political revolt, but encouraged passive resistance instead.[62] Their relative wealth depended on the advantageous privileges held by the craft guilds in prosperous cities, such as Bruges and Ghent. However, other songs arose in urban public space, the streets and the inns, places for hearing and chanting songs, as recorded in the judicial and historiographical sources. Rhetorician authors, members of official literary guilds, explicitly condemned unorganised street and pub singers from the lower classes. A sixteenth-century ballad, for instance, described them pejoratively as *cluijtenaers*, those 'who make songs for small pieces of money'.[63]

The 'popular' or 'public' character of some political songs is also indicated by their widespread diffusion throughout the military forces around 1500, when the new professional armies recruited and hired soldiers from the lower social groups in the town and countryside. In the songs of the *Antwerp Songbook*, soldiers often drink cool wine and admire the beauty of fair girls with white arms and brown eyes. In one song, a soldier addresses a frivolous girl named

---

58   Leendertz 1924–5, vol. 1, pp. xviii–xix.
59   Van Bork, Delabastita, Van Gorp et al., eds 2012a.
60   Van de Graft, ed. 1904, p. 31.
61   Pleij 2011.
62   See [Let Each Man Carry].
63   '*Om liedekens te maken om sgelts vertieren*', Lyna and van Eeghem, eds 1929–30, vol. 2, p. 135; See Mareel 2011, pp. 40–3.

Margret, asking her to come with him to Thérouanne, the site of a battle. This city and its hinterland were the site of hostilities involving the Habsburgs, the French and the English during the early sixteenth-century wars, particularly in 1513.[64] The song *Van Keyser Maximiliaen*, about the failed marriage project between Maximilian and the daughter of the Duke of Brittany in 1490, claimed to have been first sung, according to the final stanza, by three penniless soldiers in Cologne.[65]

Philologists of earlier generations distinguished a specific genre for songs performed in a military context, usually dealing with exploits of war, the so-called '*landsknechtliederen*' or '*ruiterliederen*' (literally, songs of 'routiers' or professional soldiers). Most date from the period after 1450, and their number increases after Maximilian's reign. These songs were written by or for soldiers, or at least they present themselves as belonging to the military environment in order to claim authenticity. This pattern applies throughout fifteenth- and sixteenth-century Europe. One of many contemporary examples from the same region is a French poem about the capture of Saint-Omer by the Lord of Esquerdes in 1487.[66] By 1544 this genre was well represented in the *Antwerp Songbook*.[67] After the sixteenth-century war against Guelders, the number of surviving songs increased sharply (which does not necessarily mean that more were produced during that time, but rather that more songs from that period survived). According to Pleij, the events of 1542–3 provoked the 'first media-hype in the Low Countries', about Martin Luther and Maarten van Rossum. While the widespread increase in printing, often in the form of leaflets, must have enhanced the impact and circulation of these songs, Pleij emphasises the continued importance of orality and aurality.[68]

Sometimes in these texts a kind of proto-nationalist feeling comes to the surface as well. The common identity of the soldiers is 'Burgundian', but there is also a sense of pride in the Flemish language. *Een Liedeken van den Slach van Blangijs* ('A Song of the Battle of *Blangijs*') commemorates the Battle of Guinegatte on 7 August 1479, as it describes the Flemings united behind their prince Maximilian defeating the French army. The battle cry '*Vlander de*

---

64   Van der Poel and Grijp, eds 2004, vol. 1, pp. 276–9, and vol. 2, pp. 285–7.
65   Ibid., vol. 1, pp. 262–3, and vol. 2, pp. 276–9. This song clearly had a German origin.
66   Paris, ed. 1935, pp. 96–7. Many war poems have been attested as well for fifteenth-century England: Arens 1989, p. 176; also an extensive Franco-Burgundian tradition exists in Middle French, see most recently Marchandisse and Schnerb 2016, with references to older literature. For German war songs: Moser 2006, pp. 17–18.
67   Brinkman 2002, pp. 111–12.
68   Pleij 2000.

leeu!' ('Flanders, the Lion!'), expressed *'Met Vlaemscher tonghen'* ('in the Flemish language') is repeated at the end of each stanza.[69] Anthonis Ghyseleers, or perhaps an anonymous editor who collected Ghyseleers' works into the manuscript now attributed to him, may have been a *ruter* in the service of Maximilian, who 'from a young age had learnt nothing except rhyming and singing'.[70]

The author described himself as 'a horseman from Brabant born in Landen', although this might also be a topos.[71]

It is also likely that at least some of these soldiers – or literary pseudo-soldiers – either belonged or were connected to the urban militias that fought together with the armies of regional lords or in conflicts between different towns. For instance, the *Kloekmoedigheid der Mechelenaeren* ('Song of the Hardiness of the Men of Mechelen') seems to be linked to the city militia fighting against Brussels, as it reflects the frequently vicious economic and military conflicts between towns in the Netherlands.[72] Many literary historians think that the authors and performers of these songs were not themselves soldiers, but rather that the authors adopted a stereotyped soldier's voice to make frequent references to military matters. Others suggest that the songs about the military events were first composed for the armies themselves and later diffused among the general population.[73] Another theory is that popular poets actually joined the armies, even though there were certainly soldiers who could read and write and would have been capable of composing songs.[74] Even if the anonymous authors only styled themselves as 'men of the people' with military or artisan professions as a literary trope to convey a moral and political message to the community, there is sufficient evidence to prove the circulation and reception of songs about military events and political struggles, past and present, among the 'popular layers' of society, urban and rural, small merchants, artisans and professional soldiers.[75]

---

69   Van de Graft, ed. 1904, pp. 91–5; Verbruggen, Jan 1993, pp. 137–8.
70   Te Winkel 1922–7, vol. 2, pp. 240–1. Van de Graft, ed. 1904, pp. 74–5.
71   Fredericq 1894, p. 56; Van de Graft, ed. 1904, p. 137 (who presents a strong argument that Ghyseleers was not the poet himself). Further codicological research would be necessary to prove this. *Ruters* were hired soldiers who could serve on horse or on foot, rather than 'horsemen' in the strict sense, like *routiers* in French (*cfr.* Brinkman 2004, pp. 5–9).
72   Willems, Serrure and Snellaert 1848, pp. 52–5.
73   Van 't Hooft 1948, p. 9.
74   Van de Graft, ed. 1904, p. 36; Sabbe, Maurits 1928, pp. 80–5.
75   Similar remarks by Honemann 1997, pp. 412–14. See also Strassner 1970, pp. 230–1.

7   A Part of a General European Tradition of Public Poetry

We have seen that several scholars have argued that 'historical songs' should be classified as 'political songs'.[76] Katarina Kellerman proposes 'historisch-politische Ereignisdichtung' (literally: a historico-political event literature) as a genre with specific functions, aesthetic principles and significant public impact.[77] As mentioned previously, a more accepted term is Anne Middleton's concept of 'public poetry', literature meant to be a 'common voice' to serve the 'common good', which addressed its audience directly as an ideal community on issues of politics, justice and morality. In addition, Wendy Scase has identified a wider 'literature of clamour' in late medieval England. She shows that social and political complaints were expressed in a variety of modes and genres, which were vehicles of expression relevant to different layers of society.[78] The circulation and impact of this 'genre' of public poetry were considerable. Scholars are beginning to consider such texts among the more widely circulated genres rather than as occasional pieces to be analysed as curiosities or mined for historical information. This contribution emphasises that public poetry in the late medieval Low Countries also transmitted critical ideas about the social and political order and thus deserves more systematic study. This was fundamentally a literature of public performance, sometimes bringing about important effects, such as protests, riots or even rebellion. These 'voices of the people' used spoken language to call for action and, in doing so, created something new.[79] They had the capacity to underwrite or undermine, to inspire or disable political initiatives and social relations.

---

76   Sauermann 1975.
77   Kellermann 2000.
78   Scase 2007, p. 135.
79   See the theoretical reflexions of Strohm, Paul 2005, p. 8; Pocock 1987, pp. 19–38; and more generally Bourdieu 1991.

CHAPTER 10

'Let Each Man Carry on with His Trade and Remain Silent': Middle-Class Ideology in the Urban Literature of the Late Medieval Low Countries

Jan Dumolyn and Jelle Haemers

1 Introduction

According to Anthonis de Roovere, a master stonemason and rhetorician poet from Bruges (c. 1430–82), the Devil was responsible for both tyranny and rebellion. In his poem *Sondighen is menschelijck* ('Sinning Is Human') he wrote: 'He [Satan] makes one mutter, he makes the other dominate'. Both the grumbling of the discontented commoners and the arrogance of the elites, 'those lords who ride high horses' as he called them in another text, were signs of the sin of pride.[1] De Roovere preached obedience to God and to the prince. 'Do not mutter', he warned in a poem entitled *Vander obedientie* ('On Obedience'), but 'live according to reason; do more with love than through violence. For he who obeys shall be esteemed'.[2] At the same time, he sternly chastised corrupt lawyers and government officials, because he thought 'that the rich destroyed the poor'.[3] In a bitterly sarcastic poem, 'Hoordt nae my ghy spitters ghy deluers', which could also be called 'Porridge and Bread for Future Days', Anthonis described the fate of the common workers of Bruges. If they slave their entire lives, he wrote, in old age they shall be rewarded with porridge and bread.[4] In these and other texts Anthonis de Roovere, arguably the most important fifteenth-century writer in the Dutch language, expressed harsh social and political criticism via a moralist discourse. He could not, however, have the simple folk doing the same thing in their plain manner, since people who 'ride on their tongues' commit devilish sins as well.[5]

---

1   Mak, ed. 1955, pp. 241, 335; See Oosterman 2001; Oosterman 1995–6. Many of the Middle Dutch texts quoted in this article can be consulted online at the Digitale Bibliotheek voor de Nederlandse Letteren (DBNL), www.dbnl.org.
2   Mak, ed. 1955, p. 250.
3   Ibid., p. 322.
4   Ibid., pp. 342–3.
5   In *Van Quade tonghen* (ibid., pp. 326–7).

Engaged in the activities of the *rederijkers* (rhetoricians), whose work is the most common expression of urban literary culture in fifteenth-century Netherlandish towns, De Roovere in many ways functioned as the ideological mouthpiece of the middling sort of people in the commercial metropolis of Bruges: master artisans and petty shopkeepers, organised in craft guilds, with a specific social and political consciousness.[6] These urban 'middle classes' or 'artisanal classes', prosperous guild masters, skilled artisans, petty merchants and shopkeepers, belonged neither to the patrician elites, who based their power and status on commercial activities and landed property inside and outside the city, nor to the lower groups of humble wage labourers, nor to marginal groups, such as beggars, thieves and prostitutes.[7] In all probability, De Roovere was one of the richer masters of the Bruges stonemasons' guild, and an independent building contractor who employed other artisans to carry out the actual work. In the towns and cities of the Low Countries, literate middle-class laymen produced texts which systematically criticised their own social class along with other groups.[8] Much of De Roovere's work is deeply religious, but in his texts on more worldly matters he articulated the ideology of the independent artisan, a petty commodity producer who clung to his privileges as a guildsman and a burgher. Confronted with urban political conflict or revolt – a frequent occurrence in cities such as Ghent, Bruges or Ypres – a typical middle-class man like De Roovere would condemn the violation of guild privileges by the urban elite or the count of Flanders, but also distance himself from lower-class rebels, such as journeymen and unskilled labourers, when the situation got out of hand. Poets and playwrights in the densely urbanised Netherlandish principalities of Flanders, Brabant and Holland generally shared De Roovere's opinions about the political failings of their rulers and the unreliable loyalty of the proletarian mob. In the Low Countries there were many popular revolts against what was perceived as unjust rule, and thus such political creeds were frequently put into practice.[9]

There are a number of studies of the physical violence, collective actions and ritual performances deployed by urban rebels in the Low Countries.[10] The literary productions of the organised artisans who were the driving force in these revolts have received less scrutiny, even though their writing offers

---

6   Small 2005.
7   Compare with Barry 1994.
8   Coleman, Janet 1981, pp. 62–5; Sosson 1977; Stabel 2004.
9   See [Patterns]; Boone 2007b.
10   Arnade 1994; Boone 2005; Liddy and Haemers 2013.

insight into their sophisticated political consciousness and into the ideological discourses which both inspired and reflected popular political views and actions. Social and political motives drove middle-class authors to compose texts about the moral standards of their rulers and fellow citizens. The standard academic interpretation is that the rhetoricians supported prevailing morality. Thus Herman Pleij influentially claimed that rhetoricians had a clear and 'elitist' policy to transform less 'civilised' citizens into inoffensive and conformist burghers who followed the new bourgeois morals of the elite.[11] He suggests that urban literature in Netherlandish towns played an active role in forming, defending and propagating 'burgher virtues', revolving around the key concepts of practicality and utilitarianism. Pleij's concept of *burgermoraal* ('burgher' or 'civic' morality) is characterised by values – pragmatism, individual independence, reason and practical skill – adapted from other ideas and discourses, such as Christian and Stoic morality.[12] The art historian Paul Vandenbroeck, formulating more or less the same thesis, emphasises the fundamentally 'middle-class' origins of these ideological values found in many later medieval Dutch literary texts.[13] We do not find the term 'burgher morality' very useful, because it fails to do justice to the social diversity of the late medieval urban world. Nonetheless Pleij's insights have been helpful for placing urban literature in its social context, and the discourse produced by citizens of the thriving industrial and commercial cities and towns does contain elements of pragmatic utilitarian rationality. However, for Pleij, almost all urban literature seems to belong to a 'civilizing offensive' by the urban elites (whom he confusingly calls 'middle classes', in contrast to the nobility and clergy).

In this narrative the urban middle and lower social groups seem to exercise little cultural agency themselves. Van Bruaene points out that the chambers of rhetoric recruited most of their membership from the middling sort of people, which contradicts Pleij's hypothesis about the elite 'civilizing intentions' of the rhetoricians' texts. Instead, she argued, the fifteenth century saw the development of a distinctive urban culture dominated by an educated artisanal class who shared the values of lay devotion, collective honour and social harmony.[14] Building on Van Bruaene's argument, we assert that the moralistic judgements on elite behaviour in Middle Dutch poems, though inspired by existing literary models, contained a clear political message, expressed from a moderate

---

11   Pleij 1983 and Pleij 1990, pp. 629–47.
12   Pleij 1994, p. 63; Pleij 2007, pp. 100–2.
13   Vandenbroeck 1990, pp. 21–3.
14   Van Bruaene 2010, p. 139.

reformist viewpoint and typical of the upper layers of the craft guilds. The frequent expression of disapproval of the moral failings of city rulers indicates a degree of political subversion inherent in many of these texts.

2   Rhetoricians' Literature as a Cultural Expression of Guild Values

In the fifteenth century, beginning in the economically and culturally dominant county of Flanders, poets and playwrights started to organise themselves in literary corporations, the *rederijkerskamers*, 'chambers of rhetoric' or 'rhetoricians' guilds'. Urban culture in the Netherlands was strongly influenced by corporate forms of organisation and thought. A plethora of guilds and confraternities regulated and organised the religious and ideological lives of laymen.[15] As most craft guilds had their own confraternities, these corporate organisations were often linked together. In the period that literary scholars consider the starting point of 'urban literature' in the Low Countries, the second half of the fourteenth century, the guild structure had come to dominate the organisation of cultural activities. While urban theatre was often officially staged during religious festivals, princely entries and other civic events, guilds and religious confraternities performed plays in guildhalls, in churches and on wagons in the street.[16]

Of course, the craft guilds were in the first place economic interest groups. In most cities and towns in the Netherlands, guilds united local retailers, a relatively wealthy group of middle-class artisans, but also large segments of the working poor.[17] While, schematically speaking, the urban 'mob', including poorer guildsmen and unskilled wage labourers, served as shock troops when the guilds took collective action, the artisanal classes usually kept firm control over these political movements so that they would be able to negotiate with the patrician elite or the ruler. In the major cities of Flanders and Brabant, such as Ghent, Bruges and Brussels, as well as in other towns of the Low Countries, the guilds often had the right to appoint a specified number of aldermen and so participate in the political decision-making process, although they had to struggle with the merchant class to gain political and social recognition at times. In other words, as expressed in De Roovere's social-issue poems, the middle-class guildsmen had legal rights and economic privileges to defend.

---

15   Trio 2009, pp. 99–110.
16   Strietman 1998; Mareel 2010b.
17   Prak 2006; Boone 2010, pp. 29–56.

These guild masters were the driving force behind the establishment of the rhetoricians' chambers and so maintained a remarkable cultural and literary tradition, producing many poems and plays. Although some chambers were more elitist than others, the social composition of their membership usually corresponded with the upper levels of the craft guilds. The *rederijkers* chambers were organised in the same form as the latter, led by deans or governors and ruled by statutes that granted equal rights and duties to all members. The rhetoricians wrote poems and plays for competitions and, upon request, staged *tableaux vivants* for princely entries and played significant roles in the performance of civic ritual.[18] Thus, the rhetoricians' chambers of the Low Countries not only contributed to the forging of urban identity through their associational practices but also helped to shape urban public space through theatrical representations. Both urban political elites and subordinate groups used the plays to influence public opinion in the city.[19] From the more than six hundred known dramas, mostly on religious subjects, the Dutch literary historian Jacobus Mak found approximately thirty what he called 'social plays'. Although some social plays were performed at a celebration of a victory or peace treaty, or during an entry ceremony of a prince, others seem to have offered the playwright the chance to give voice to subversive thoughts.[20]

3   Performance and Political Dialogue

Though their social positions, daily lives and surroundings clearly differed, urban elites and the lesser townsfolk understood each other's arguments, because they used similar media to express political beliefs. The public guild ceremonies during an urban uprising, and the symbolic rituals of submission employed by urban elites and princes to suppress revolts, used comparable procedures, gestures and speech acts, such as parading through the streets, waving banners, ringing bells, and chanting slogans and rhymed verses. The civic rituals of artisans and urban authorities took place in the same spaces, in and around the central marketplace, public buildings (the city hall, the bell tower, the city gates) and parish churches. Guildsmen and patricians used the same literary media of plays, songs and verses to communicate political opin-

---

18   Van Bruaene 2006, pp. 374–405.
19   Bonicel and Lavéant 2010, pp. 95–105.
20   Mak 1944, p. 75; for an overview of Dutch rhetorican drama, see Hummelen 1968.

ions in identical spaces during a conflict.[21] As is generally known, written texts overlapped with the diffusion of oral and visual culture to a large degree in the medieval period. The circulation of medieval popular ideas about politics and society has to be situated in a communicative framework of 'aurality'.[22] Written texts were not only copied and dispersed in a textual form, but also read out loud in public, memorised and circulated further. Although subversive political discourse did circulate on paper pamphlets, public speech was its natural medium. In the same way that libels and slogans in verse spread widely, the brevity and form of popular political songs facilitated their circulation across social boundaries, among both literate and illiterate people, and through a variety of social settings.[23]

While only a limited number of popular songs dealing with current political issues have survived, we still have a fair amount of Middle Dutch rhetorical drama, the genre *par excellence* for combining words and images.[24] The plays that have come down to us are scripted remnants of performances that drew on a shared language of visual display, aural stimuli and spatial orientation. Document and performance, text and presentation were interdependent.[25] Written, iconographic and oral codes served as complementary means of communication, employed interchangeably, according to the needs of the moment, in no preconceived hierarchy, and in an arena of cultural dissemination in which the culture of the literate met that of the illiterate.[26] Gervase Rosser has drawn attention to the 'socially creative and disruptive qualities' of medieval guild drama and its potential to subvert order. Plays could 'objectify and revise social relationships'.[27] Indeed, during times of hardship or political uncertainty, rhetoricians' plays sometimes enacted in drama a symbolic accusation and indictment, prompting governmental distrust of their performance.[28] Rhetoricians' drama was at the heart of urban politics.

---

21   Arnade 1996a; Lecuppre-Desjardin 2004a.
22   Zumthor 1983; Coleman, Joyce 1996.
23   See below [A Bad Chicken], pp. 60–4; Lecuppre-Desjardin 2010; Liddy 2011; Maddicot 1986, pp. 130–44.
24   Strietman 1991; Ramakers 2006.
25   Symes 2007, p. 2; Postlewate and Hüsken, eds 2007, p. 7.
26   Bouza 1999, p. 15; Bellingradt 2011, pp. 305–6.
27   Rosser 2006b, pp. 142–3.
28   Dekker 1987.

4   Social and Political Drama

The early sixteenth-century Bruges master fuller, dyer and rhetorician Cornelis Everaert wrote the most overtly 'political' drama surviving today.[29] Like his predecessor Anthonis de Roovere, Everaert criticised rich merchants, but he excoriated poor workers (for laziness, thievery, incompetence and excessive drinking) just as severely. He often attacked merchants who wore fur coats and rings yet did not pay their debts and bills, and, as in other medieval texts, he denounced grain speculators.[30] His discourse remained framed by Christian ideas such as the sin of pride; yet Everaert's plays are not mere moralist rhetoric, as they provide sharp analysis of periods of economic crisis and its social effects. The dialogues uttered by his allegorical characters reflect a profound understanding of economic and financial mechanisms among the urban common people. In his remarkable play *dOnghelycke Munte* ('On Unequal Coinage'), Everaert explains how floating exchange rates destabilise the economy, bankrupting the middle and labouring classes, while speculators reap huge profits. One character, *Ghemeene Neerynghe* ('Common Trade'), who represents a textile guild master, has to fire his wage labourer *Sulc Scaemel* ('So Poor'). So Poor then tries to convince his employer not to let him go, offering to work for Common Trade for a penny less per day, and even to accept payment in kind.[31] Gossip and muttering are also central elements in Everaert's drama in general. *Den Daghelicxschen Snaetere* ('The Daily Cackling Hen'), for instance, is a woman selling hazelnuts on the street, a gendered voice of popular discourse. At one point, she tells the audience that another character, *Den Scaemele Aerbeyder* ('The Shabby Worker'), was fired by his employer *Menichte van Volke* ('Multitude of People'), and comments that wage labourers suffer worst in a crisis because the guild masters pass down the effects to them. But the main cause of the crisis seems to be *Den Tyt van Nu* ('The Present Time'), a figure dressed as a war-mongering soldier.[32] In Everaert's political plays, war is always a major cause of social evil, along with human sinfulness in general, as he emphasises in his *tSpel vanden Crych* ('Play of the *Crych*', a *jeu de mots*, because in this specific context the Middle Dutch word *crych* can mean both 'war' and 'greed').[33]

---

29   Hüsken, ed. 2005; Mareel 2008.
30   Van Gelder 1911, pp. 209, 230.
31   De Vries 1942, p. 190.
32   Müller 1907.
33   Hüsken 1999, pp. 242–6.

The literature produced by the rhetoricians presents all the usual medieval satirical topoi of greedy officers, sinful priests and unworthy noblemen. But in the end authors like De Roovere and Everaert did not call for social or political revolt, but rather encouraged passive endurance. The same is true of the anonymous writer whose poem survived in the sixteenth-century collection compiled by Jan van Stijevoort, to which the title of this article refers. In this anonymous poem, called *Elc doe sijn neringhe ende swijch al stille* ('Let Each Man Carry on with His Trade and Remain Silent'), the writer complains that some are singing in the streets about the deeds of great lords and the wars lords wage, as if the singers 'knew the lords' secrets!' The poet calls them *clappaerts* ('babblers' or 'blabbermouths'), evil fools who sow seeds of discontent. 'A lot of babbling is not right', he wrote, as people ought to trust the wisdom of their prince. They should work and simply be silent. In another poem from the same collection, the poet holds such 'evil tongues' responsible not only for the usual sins of envy, slander and discord, but also for the more political crime of mutiny. The word *clappaerts* usually denotes gossipers in general and may specifically refer to jealous talk about lovers, but in this usage their gossip is an illegitimate political speech act. 'I say that each man must control his tongue', the anonymous rhetorician warns against the danger of subversive talk.[34] This interesting interpretation of the word *clappaert* also occurs in the work of the sixteenth-century Bruges poet Eduard de Dene, who wrote: 'Even if it was pierced with a pike from Liège, the blabbermouth cannot easily control his tongue'.[35] Other writers condemn autonomous actions of the lower townsmen even more harshly, calling them *lodders* ('scoundrels'), as in a poem by Anthonius Stalin. This fifteenth-century parish priest wrote that 'if scoundrels want to be lords, and get the upper hand, then the country will be destroyed' (*als lodders willen heeren wesen, als lodders hebben die overhant, so wert ghedestrueert dat lant*). But Stalin concluded, with some relief, that the mob 'can babble, insult and act, but the lords will stay lords for ever'.[36]

In the plays of Cornelis Everaert, characters such as 'Shabby Worker' and 'Multitude of People' overtly condemn the ruinous monetary policies of the prince and bemoan their effect on the trade and industry of Bruges. These were strong and dangerous statements. Even though at first glance Everaert seemed to distance himself from this 'popular speech' because it was uttered by farcical

---

34   Lyna and van Eeghem, eds 1929–30, vol. 2, pp. 134–6; van Elslander 1953, pp. 166–7.
35   Waterschoot and Coigneau, eds 1979, vol. 2, pp. 86–8.
36   '*Moghen clappen, scelden ende driven, maer heeren sullen altoes heeren bliven*', de Pauw 1893–1914, vol. 2, p. 393.

and rather stupid figures, use of the comical genre and the dialogue format, in which allegorical characters present their opposing views, allowed the rhetorician to speak out in a manner otherwise considered politically subversive. The critique does ultimately appear half-hearted, as at the end of Everaert's plays another allegorical character comes in to restore moral order by blaming the babbling fools of the populace for their pride and stupidity. However, the political subversion had been uttered; the audience heard it and could perhaps even have cheered in approval.[37] Everaert was likely a sincere poet who did not aim to incite any kind of popular protest, although this did not stop the authorities from banning his *On Unequal Coinage* on at least one occasion.[38] One of the most elaborate political dramas to criticise city government was *Een Spul van Sinnen van den siecke Stadt* ('Play about the Sick City'), a bitter satire, written around 1536, denouncing corruption, injustice and persecution of heretics in the city of Amsterdam, which was governed by an oligarchy. In a style similar to that of Everaert's contemporary drama, allegorical characters, such as 'Hypocrisy', 'The Commune', 'Finance', 'Pre-emption', 'So Much' (a rich man) and 'More than One' (an artisan), represented social groups and embodied economic forces discussing political issues. This later play was clearly anti-Catholic and was engaging in Reformation debates, but the literary form had been established in the medieval period.[39] Its critical undertone continues to reveal the social and political ideology of the guildsmen. In addition, an earlier example of political theatre performed in Bruges also shows that spectators understood the contents of such plays very well and could also react if they disagreed with the ideological message. In February 1478 the burgomaster of Bruges organised a play performed in the Great Market square before an audience of guildsmen. The play was designed to convince the citizens that it was necessary to levy a new city tax, in order to pay troops for the war against France. Anthonis de Roovere wrote in a contemporary chronicle that 'some of the commoners' got angry and threw objects at the actors.[40] This play was not subversive theatre: the city government had ordered its production to convey an official ideology that was then rejected by some in the popular audience. It is a remarkable reminder and example of the audience's agency.

Beyond the devotional uses of urban literary performances, and their association with sixteenth-century religious reform movements,[41] the performance

---

37   Van Gelder 1911, p. 216; Hüsken 1996.

38   Mareel 2010b, p. 199.

39   Bloemendaal, ed. 2009; Te Winkel 1922–7, vol. 2, pp. 455–8.

40   Vorsterman, ed. 1531, fol. 198ʳ. The passage has been translated by Hüsken 1997, p. 186.

41   Waite 2006; Strietman 1997.

of urban literary texts aimed to reinforce social identity and brotherly love among members of a guild, sometimes in a serious way and sometimes in a playful and ironic manner. *Van den boeghe* ('Of the Bow') and *Van ghilden* ('Of Guilds'), two *sproken* (short tales, a Middle Dutch genre comparable to the French *fabliaux*) by Willem Van Hildegaersberch, were probably written and performed for a shooting guild and a religious confraternity.[42] *Of the Bow* is a poem about the qualities of bows, which can win both love and royal office for the archer. Emphasizing the need for mutual accord, the poet wrote that the strongest wall protecting the town is unity.[43] Everaert's *Een tafelspeilken op een Hoedeken van Marye* ('Play about Mary's Hat') was performed before the guild of the Bruges hatters, during their 1531 Epiphany banquet, at which they elected their 'King', a custom typical of the Low Countries. Playing with the meanings of the word 'hat' and Mary's 'rose hat', or rosary, the text reinforces the unity of the guild through the association of their products with the virtues of religion and devotion.[44] This typical ideological discourse served to strengthen the symbolic identity and internal unity of a guild, or of the city as a whole, to mask or prevent internal dissension, and to accentuate its collective honour, faith and social status.[45] But in the disrespect for hierarchy and status, encouragement of reversal, and erasure of the line between spectators and participants, the performance of these texts and the imagery and associations of revelry also offered a vehicle by which a heterogeneous group of craftsmen were briefly able to set aside customary deference.[46]

As in late medieval England and France, the central focus of 'political' or 'public' poetry in the Low Countries was on the moral failings of those held responsible for contemporary problems.[47] The guild ethos needed negative images, mostly provided by Christian thought, to demarcate moral, social and political group identities. A song, or recited poem, called 'Van den plaesteraers' ('About the Plaster Workers'), which may have been performed before a Shrove Tuesday plasterers' guild banquet in an unidentified town (perhaps Brussels), is a sarcastic text praising the good qualities of the real plasterers, 'who work for two or three pennies a day'. At the same time, the text employs word-play with the metaphorical Middle Dutch meaning of 'plasterer' in the sense of 'flatterer', 'fawner' or 'crook' to lavish ironic praise on others who 'plaster' their

---

42   Hogenelst 1997, vol. 1, p. 185.
43   Ibid., vol. 2, p. 179.
44   Hüsken, ed. 2005, vol. 2, pp. 785–802.
45   Clark, Robert 1999, p. 36.
46   Strohm, Paul 1992, p. 56.
47   Fletcher 2008; Mairey 2007a, pp. 40–3.

way through life, such as lawyers, corrupt shopkeepers and dishonest millers.[48] Even more clearly linked to a particular guild is a piece called *De hel vant brouwersgilde* ('The Hell of the Brewers' Guild'), written for the brewers in the town of Haarlem in Holland. Although it has been dated to the early 1560s, this text represents a much older tradition of satirical 'devilish plays' performed by or for guilds during their Easter banquets. In plays of this tradition, Lucifer hears reports from his devils working on earth about their efforts to promote sin and then dictates to his secretary a new list of candidates for eternal hellfire. All social groups are then chastised for their greed, corruption, cupidity and other sins.[49] As the Haarlem brewers' play exemplifies, the task of the guild was to prevent fraud and abuse of power in a brotherly form of organisation upholding Christian values, and to oppose sinners who committed mainly 'economic sins' such as greed and gluttony.

5 Religion, Morality and Politics in the Middle Dutch Literary Tradition

Though this article focuses on the social and political content in the rhetoricians' literary production, religious themes and discourses unsurprisingly predominated. However, in analysing these texts, we cannot treat religion and politics as separate spheres; some elements of popular religiosity could have had a political character as well.[50] While some rhetoricians were clerics, the large majority were laymen who also constantly referred to Christian thought in their writings.[51] Integral to their mental world, religion was a deeply rooted source of inspiration for political criticism and for guild and urban ideology in general. Late medieval Flemish writers followed the widespread medieval tradition of social criticism, and sometimes utopianism (eschatological and prelapsarian in tone), rooted in Christian moral discourse. This radical potential within reformist religious discourse is nonetheless often foreclosed by a more conservative, static model of social role and hierarchy, also drawn from Christianity. There are many examples of this stereotypical social criticism in Middle Dutch texts. The moralist critique of the ruling estates, expressed via a discourse of sins and virtues, was another common theme in the Middle Dutch 'didactic genre', as in other types of European medieval literature. Many Flem-

---

48   Brinkman and Schenkel, eds 1999, pp. 354–7.
49   Erné 1934, pp. 1–16; Hüsken, Ramakers and Schaars, eds 1992, pp. 16–43.
50   Arnold 2009, pp. 151–2; Fletcher and Oates 2009, p. 299.
51   A situation similar to that in England: Clopper 1989, p. 113.

ish and Brabantine writers of the thirteenth and fourteenth centuries launched severe attacks on the elites in their didactic works. Therefore, we can say that the literary production of the most important among them, namely Jacob van Maerlant, Jan De Weert, Jan van Boendale and Jan van Leeuwen (whose work will be discussed here), preceded the social criticism of the fifteenth- and sixteenth-century rhetoricians. The latter could thus fall back on a strong tradition of subversive texts on morality in the vernacular.

Jacob van Maerlant, the thirteenth-century 'founding father' of Dutch didactic literature who came from the region of Bruges, set the literary standard for the social critique genre in the medieval Netherlands. In his *Martijn* cycle, a series of moralist dialogues written in the 1260s, Maerlant depicted the deplorable moral condition of the world.[52] However, his 'Christian communism', praising the original state of nature before there were nobles or serfs, is relatively conventional and stems principally from Vincent of Beauvais (c. 1190–c. 1264), one of the most widely read medieval authors.[53] Maerlant also deplored the state of lordly power, no longer based on virtues, and the lack of loyalty and trust, in a world now dominated by greed and the pursuit of profit. He addressed 'the great lords', asking them to 'spare the small people'.[54] He posed the question common to this type of moralist social criticism: why were there nobles, freemen and serfs, if all men had descended from Adam? Influenced by Eike von Repgow's *Sachsenspiegel*, a text also circulating in the Netherlands, Maerlant wrote that 'there are only two words in the world, "mine" and "thine". If one could chase away those words, there would be peace, all would be free and none a serf, neither men nor women, and the wheat and wine would all be held in common'.[55] Maerlant was also strongly influenced by Franciscan ideology, the appropriate Christian answer to increasing social polarisation in a major thirteenth-century industrial and commercial city such as Bruges. Although this subject needs further systematic study, the newly prominent mendicant orders were clearly important in shaping middle-class ideology in the Netherlandish cities. Maerlant himself translated Bonaventure's *Life of Saint Francis* into Middle Dutch, along with the life of Saint Claire (for the Bruges Clarissans), although this latter text is now lost.[56] Writing for an elite audience of lords, local nobles and merchants, who donated money to the mendicant orders and other charities, Maerlant

---

52   Van Oostrom 1996; Gruijs and Mertens 1975.
53   Te Winkel 1877, pp. 265, 276. See Serrarens 1928, pp. 1–32, 77–127.
54   Te Winkel 1877, pp. 248–9.
55   Verwijs, ed. 1879, p. 26; Schott and Schmidt-Wiegand, eds 1984.
56   Maximilianus (van Dun, Petrus), ed. 1954; Van Mierlo 1946, p. 91.

preached love of one's fellow man. However, in many ways he was also a political radical, who adapted classic religious and literary ideas in order to address the increasing inequality in the Netherlandish cities during the second half of the thirteenth century, with their growing 'proletariats' who had come from the countryside and lived in the suburbs. In the area of critical social thought, the influence of this 'father of all Dutch poets', as he was called by his successors, was widespread.

Maerlant's chief successor, Jan van Boendale, a city clerk in Antwerp (c. 1290–c. 1365), set a similar 'progressive' tone when dealing with social issues. He lauded peasants, fullers, tailors and working people in general.[57] People earning their money by manual labour or a trade are the most virtuous, Boendale wrote in *Jans teestye* ('Jan's Testimony'):

> You fuller, weaver, merchant, tailor or shipper, and all of you who labour, you who are the least esteemed and who win your bread with pain. There you shall be among the best, and much more – this I know for sure – than the deacon or prelate who despises and oppresses you.[58]

Jan van Boendale also praised those who were shrewd in commercial and juridical matters – his own social milieu of merchants and administrators. Like Maerlant, he condemned the rich if they did not give alms to the poor, but he also typically attacked those poor men who were too lazy to work and beggars who were healthy enough for manual labour. On occasion, he exhibited a more radical outlook. In his *Boec van der wraken* ('Book of Wrath'), a peculiar work dealing with the Wrath of God and showing apocalyptic tendencies, he wrote that 'common property is divine and good', and more important than individual forms of property. Common property should be spent for the common good, to the benefit of poor and rich alike. At the same time, human sin is the collective responsibility of all orders in society. If the common people do not correct their misbehaving lord, they are accomplices in his transgressions and will be punished along with him.[59]

Reflecting the urban ideological discourse typical of many official and legal documents produced in towns, Jan van Boendale's political ideas centred on peace, justice, the *bonum commune* and the duty of city governments to uphold these values.[60] In his chronicle *Brabantse yeesten* ('Brabantine Histories'),

---

57　Van Gerven 1976; Kinable 1998.
58　Van Moerkerken 1904, p. 35.
59　Snellaert, ed. 1869, pp. 287–488; Faems 2009, pp. 33–4; Wuttke 2010.
60　Van Anrooij 1994; Van Uytven 2002, pp. 22, 27.

Boendale applauded the leading cities of Brabant for taking over effective political power in the duchy between 1314 and 1320, while the duke (who was still in his minority) was practically a captive of his noble entourage. The financial mismanagement of these nobles had caused the arrests of Brabantine merchants abroad and the confiscation of their goods. As a result, the cities had taken over the government and had settled the duchy's debts to foreign creditors 'so that the merchants could travel for their trade, wherever they wanted, without being arrested and their goods confiscated'.[61] Boendale considered this political action justified in the interest of commerce and industry and in view of the lords' short-sighted and abusive behaviour, but in the same chronicle he also wrote that 'if the commoners are in uproar' (als die ghemeente wert in rueren), 'the land would be lost'.[62] Exactly as in the case of the rhetoricians a century later, despite voicing this political criticism of elites, the Antwerp clerk attacked the mob and the common guildsmen for their arrogant behaviour, especially when they revolted. If Maerlant had remained rather abstract in his political comments, Jan van Boendale – who stood with both feet in the world of administration, commerce and industry, even though he also wrote for the nobility – was directly involved in his city's political life and urban ideological discourse.

Another follower of Maerlant was Jan de Weert. Probably a master surgeon from Ypres, a major textile industry centre in the county of Flanders, he lived in the early or mid-fourteenth century and often displayed rather radical ethical and political ideas. He addressed an urban audience and evoked the norms and values of city life, similarly to his contemporary Boendale and more clearly than Maerlant. De Weert strongly condemned city taxes which unjustly targeted working people and raged mercilessly against the corruption of the patrician rulers. At the same time, he also warned the labouring classes to work hard so that they would not fall into poverty, their daughters would not end up as prostitutes, and the whole family would not be dishonoured.[63] Sparing not a single urban social group, De Weert chastised craftsmen and shopkeepers who rigged weights and measures to cheat their customers.[64]

Perhaps the most intriguing Middle Dutch moralist writer was Jan van Leeuwen, a layman who was also the most radically religious writer in this group. He differs somewhat from the others mentioned above because of his mystical tone, another strong tradition in Middle Dutch literature. Jan van Leeuwen was

---

61   Quoted by Avonds 1994, p. 176.
62   'Dat lant verloren es', ibid., p. 171.
63   Brinkman 1991, pp. 107, 111.
64   Hermersdorf 1980, p. 382.

a cook for the convent of the famous mystic Jan van Ruusbroec near Brussels. He came from a middling or lower-class family in Brussels. He used direct language and was often extremely severe in his moral judgements. In his *Dboec van den tien gheboden* ('Book of the Ten Commandments'), Van Leeuwen followed the convention of blaming lords for not observing justice, and, like Boendale and De Weert, he chastised all social classes. Under the sixth commandment, he condemned a long list of thieves, from wealthy misers who refused to share their wealth with the poor to simoniacal clergy, counterfeit dealers, fraudulent merchants and retailers, and poor servants who stole from their masters.[65] Thus even though Maerlant and his followers could viciously condemn the rich and powerful, they did not excuse the moral failings of the middle, working or poor classes.

Although these texts share many of the general characteristics of didactic writing, they also show that by the fourteenth century a specifically 'urban' kind of ideological discourse, or at least a discourse shaped by the urban experience, had emerged. This literature was read, or heard, by patricians and probably by the more educated guildsmen as well. Moreover, the texts contained many of the ideological ingredients later found in the rhetoricians' works. However, the moralist writers' primary struggle was against sinfulness, and their political and social judgements derived from an ethical system of sins and virtues, and moral schemes of honour and dishonour, reason and foolishness. Joris Reynaert identified these characteristics as the core ingredients of what he has called a 'lay ethics' of the late medieval Netherlands.[66] This system of lay ethics did have 'political' features. The writers formulated an ethico-political ideology, drawing intertextually from the institutionalised oral culture of negotiation, written vernacular texts by mystical and other Christian writers, didactic dialogues between master and student, and, by the fifteenth century, public performance of rhetoricians' dramas. The novelty of the rhetoricians' works in the fifteenth century is found, therefore, less in the content of their writing than in the guild milieu from which they emerged. While the rhetoricians' social and political discourses fundamentally followed the tradition begun by Maerlant, these playwrights expressed the ideas in other genres, particularly public performances which directly involved audience and organisers. Moreover, with corporatism now fully established as a political and social system in most major cities of the Netherlands, their discourses echoed urban and guild ideologies even more clearly than the discourses of earlier Middle Dutch writers.

---

65   Axters 1943, p. xxxix; Stoop 2001, pp. 207–8, 214–15.
66   See articles in Reynaert, ed. 1994.

6 Petitioning the Rulers

Thirteenth- and fourteenth-century writers may also have had a direct link to ruling authorities and opposition groups. Although the available sources permit only hypotheses about their actual roles, we have seen that abuse of power was a dominant theme in Jacob van Maerlant's social morality. In several didactic poems, including 'Der nature bloeme' (a significantly adapted Middle Dutch translation of Thomas of Cantimpré's 'De natura rerum'), Maerlant clearly chose the side of the people against the aristocracy. Frits van Oostrom, the authoritative specialist on Maerlant's work, rightly emphasises an apparent paradox: Maerlant wrote this text while he was under the patronage of the same princely and noble authorities he was criticizing. One patron was Lord Nicolas van Cats, one of the most powerful noblemen from the county of Holland and a member of the comital court. The storyteller Willem van Hildegaersberch was likewise active in the Holland court and urban elite circles. Even though these authors wrote and performed for the amusement of the upper classes, they sometimes deployed a genre in which they criticized their primary audience, indirectly through allegory and dream visions or directly by holding up a moralistic mirror to the elite's vices and emphasizing their earthly duties as good lords and governors, rather than pleading for radical reforms of society. In this way, literature offered a certain 'safety zone' for social critique.[67]

Several Middle Dutch didactic writers worked as clerks, copyists, schoolmasters or officials for the city government or the guilds. City clerks were immersed in the discourse, technical knowledge and procedures of law, politics and administration. Often they were closely tied to the political elites, even though many had artisanal origins.[68] Van Oostrom suggests that Jacob van Maerlant might have been the clerk who in 1280 recorded the demands of the people of Damme, a port for Bruges, when they petitioned the count of Flanders, protesting against the ruling patricians' abuses of power and asking for a participatory role in local government. This is speculation (the recorder could have been any other local clerk, notary or secretary) but attractive: this petition and others composed by Flemish towns and cities between 1275 and 1280 show a strong affinity with Maerlant's ideas about the struggle between 'the rich' and 'the poor', and the evils of lordly greed and abuses of power.[69] In other words, it is certainly plausible that somebody *like* Jacob van Maerlant

---

67 Van Oostrom 2006, pp. 512–16.
68 Van Gerven 1978, p. 49.
69 Van Oostrom 2006. See also Prevenier 2002.

was the author of that petition, which had been dictated to him at a meeting of angry citizens in order to be read out before the aldermen or the count when he entered the city.

There are also formal and substantive arguments for the similarities between the political discourses formulated by petitioning subjects and the moralist literary genre.[70] Middle Dutch ethical theory as expressed in the *sproken* genre (mentioned above) was often organised in *poenten* ('points'), as in 'These are all the points a lord who will rule his land should possess' or 'On ten points of love'.[71] There is a strong similarity between a text organised by enumerating different 'points' or 'items' and the financial and administrative documents of the urban world, particularly petitions, which listed demands to rulers in the same fashion. The normative ideological discourse of rebel petitions has exactly the same moralist undertone, notably on the duties of good rulers, found in the didactic literature. A city clerk, such as Jan van Boendale, who confronted city elites with their obligations and their vices, was an intellectual well versed in urban administration and capable of recording the decisions and demands made at a guild or city assembly and rephrasing them in the normative judicial language suitable for the petition genre. In his 'Der leken spieghel' ('Layman's Mirror') Boendale urged the urban 'rich man', who with the nobility formed his intended audience, not to hold on to the workers' daily wages. He advised the ruling families to seek peace with each other rather than engaging in factional struggles.[72]

Towards the end of the fifteenth century, direct allusions to political issues increased in texts not easily categorised in a 'genre', but which used a similar ideological vocabulary to that of petitions. In his 'Complaincte up t'Land van Vlaendre' ('Complaint about the Land of Flanders') (1490), an allegorical political *lamentatio*, the Bruges cleric, notary and rhetorician Rombout De Doppere attributes the faltering economy of his city to the disputes that had divided Flanders for the past ten years.[73] Between 1482 and 1490 there was a serious conflict between the city of Bruges and Maximilian of Austria, regent and guardian of the minor count of Flanders. De Doppere writes that the time had now come to find an agreement. Just as with Cornelis Everaert's work several decades later, some of De Doppere's allegorical characters represent social groups while others portray ethical categories. 'Necessity must make friends who understand each other, in order to settle the disputes before Flanders is totally wasted', De

---

70   See also Giancarlo 2007.

71   Hogenelst 1997, vol. 1, p. 117; Van Anrooij 2002b, pp. 65–80.

72   Kinable 1998, pp. 51–2, 58, 140.

73   Ricour 1857–9, pp. 183–5. For the context, see Haemers 2007c.

Doppere writes. 'Conscience' must be made 'clean', and crimes had to be for-
given. 'Compassion' and 'charity' had to rule the land, or it was 'doomed'.[74] On
a more realistic level, De Doppere urged the Flemish ruling elites to listen to
each other's complaints and find mutual agreement instead of fighting each
other, referring to the classic medieval political discourse on the duty of city
government officials to uphold the common good of all citizens instead of their
private interests.[75]

City aldermen, councillors and mayors had to swear public oaths when they
took office, and the prince had to swear an oath when he first entered the
city after his succession. These solemn promises obliged rulers and officials
to be mindful of the common good of every citizen or subject during their
term of office.[76] In his 'Complaint', De Doppere reminded the authorities of
these promises as he criticized both the members of Maximilian's administration and their urban opponents. During the same political crisis, in the performance (in 1490) of an allegory by an Ypres poet known as Gleyscoof, four
characters tried to reach an agreement on county monetary policies; they were
'Labour', 'Money', 'Reason' and 'Everyone'.[77] In 1490, different county factions
sought to influence currency policy for the Flemish pound. While the followers of Archduke Maximilian wanted to devalue the pound by a third, the two
main cities, Bruges and Ghent, stubbornly refused to accept this autocratic currency manipulation. The craft guilds and most of the wealthy merchant families strongly opposed the manipulation because the archduke's officials had
not negotiated it with the representative political institutions of the county.
Gleyscoof's poem sought a middle course, because he wrote it in Ypres, a city
that tried to negotiate between Ghent and Bruges on the one side and the archducal court on the other. Whereas 'Reason' tells 'Everyone' that 'Money' ought
to reduce its value by thirty percent, 'Reason' does condemn the practice of
manipulating coinage without the consent of all concerned parties. 'Labour'
then adds that he would not accept a different currency in different parts of
the county, as the people would start muttering. After hearing the arguments of
all parties, the poet chooses sides, putting the monetary initiative in the hands
of the prince but reiterating the need for political dialogue to decide this sort
of issue. In the end, therefore, Gleyscoof concludes that 'often discord leads to
mischief', which harms the county as a whole.[78]

---

74   Ricour, 1857–9, p. 185.
75   Prevenier 2010.
76   Van Leeuwen 2005.
77   *Labuer, Ghelt, Redene* and *Elckerlyk*, Ricour, 1857–9, p. 188.
78   Ibid., p. 190.

While this text supported the prince and stayed within prudent and conservative bounds, the modern reader finds that it also brilliantly presents complicated economic problems in a comprehensible manner. The economic ideas expressed in this allegory and other similar texts, such as Cornelis Everaert's *On Unequal Coinage*, are reminiscent of the economic demands in contemporary petitions of the craft guilds. Using ideological concepts and frames of reference identical to those of the literary texts, the 1488 demands made by Bruges craft guilds suggested that the Flemish counts owed their power and authority to the urban craft guilds. They requested the count to uphold the privileges of the county and ensure 'justice' and 'peace', including fair prices, taxes and interest rates, in order to create a favourable climate for investment, 'so that trade and industry might flourish as they had before'.[79] The ideologies of both the rhetoricians and craft guilds held that maintenance of corporate privileges determined the common welfare of the prince and his lands. Princely interests and urban prosperity were mutually enhancing forces. As an anonymous Brussels poet of the end of the fifteenth century put it: 'Poor people, poor land; poor land, poor lord.'[80] The emphasis in these texts on the maintenance of guild privileges, monetary stability and the political virtue of carefully managing the land as one would manage a household fundamentally reflected the economic interests of the urban artisanal classes.

7   Conclusion

The Dutch literary historian Bart Ramakers has called the rhetoricians both 'conformists and rebels'.[81] The *rederijkers* of the Low Countries put forward Christian and corporate ideals, such as the maintenance of social order, privileges and political stability in the cities and throughout the realm, as a moral and political guide for those who governed them. The middle-class rhetoricians did not propagate a general 'burgher morality'; nor did they engage in a so-called 'civilizing offensive' to discipline the marginalised classes. In their political discourse at least, they held up an ethico-political mirror to the authorities, in the same way that guildsmen would present a petition. The more explicit political plays, such as those of Cornelis Everaert, were grounded in keen observations of social and economic structures and changes. Appropriating the liter-

---

79   Dumolyn 2010b. For similar conclusions on the importance of 'peace' for De Roovere, see Oosterman 2003.
80   *Erm volc, erm lant; erm lant, erm heere*, edited by Mareel 2010a, p. 226.
81   Ramakers 2003, p. 20. See also Sutch 2003.

ary tradition of criticizing behaviour that was perceived as 'immoral' by earlier writers such as Maerlant (who primarily wrote for the princes, nobles and urban elites), the rhetoricians introduced their middle-class ideology, advocating a moral economy and emphasizing corporately organised labour, brotherhood and Christian charity, into the older literary form.

When they expressed ideological discourses, the authors we have examined were fundamentally spokesmen of the corporate middling sort of people in Netherlandish urban society, even though they shared much of their language and culture with both the patrician rulers and the 'mob' of poor journeymen, unskilled workers and marginal groups. Their 'guild discourse', drawing inevitably upon Christian moral thought, particularly the idea of *caritas*, normally called for harmony and brotherly love between different groups in the city. When the middling sort perceived that their interests were threatened, however, the more prosperous guild master had to juxtapose his anger at the elite and his fear of the mob. Having a lot to lose, he had to defend his privileges from onslaught by the count and the urban elite, but he was always reluctant to empower unskilled workers in periods of political turmoil. More than once in the rebellious history of the county of Flanders, guild leaders silenced the 'criers' and 'shouters', as the radical rebels are called in the chronicles (often written by rhetoricians). The leaders prevented strikes and riots that were too radical and urged the common worker to go back to work.[82] When the guilds did use violence against the upper class, leaders limited the violence so that they would not risk losing privileges after the tumult. Radicals had better remain silent and carry on with their trade instead of taking their political views to the streets.

The rhetoricians lamented the moral failings of their rulers, charging them with alleged political misbehaviour, but failed to seek any fundamental change in society. Evidence from the Low Countries demonstrates a strong link between the ideological discourses of the rhetoricians and the thirteenth- and fourteenth-century didactic writers, such as Maerlant and Boendale, who were widely read by urban audiences. There is a remarkable similarity in wording and tone between these literary works and the politically critical discourses in juridical documents, chronicles, petitions and pamphlets, which emanated from the urban middle classes. The guild masters shared a conformist, but self-conscious, corporatist ideology that advocated urban prosperity, maintenance of political prerogatives and economic privileges, and a stable monetary climate and defence of trade – a view that coloured their poems and plays as

---

82   See [A Bad Chicken].

well. Though they often took up the banner of revolt themselves, the urban middling sort of people in Flanders usually did not agree with the violent and radical political actions taken by the lower classes. The wide dissemination of rhetoricians' literature spread these views on political power and so helped to forge in the Flemish cities a typical political discourse that warned the artisanal class about the unstable character of 'scoundrels' (*lodders*) and dangerous 'blabbermouths' (*clappaerts*), but also inspired these craftsmen to take up arms against the 'lords riding their high horses'.

Because of lack of space we have only cited sources in Middle Dutch, but one of the most remarkable dramas in thirteenth-century French, Adam de la Halle's *Jeu de la feuillée*, expresses a similar political and social critique, firmly anti-patrician but also morally critical of the lower social orders. This 'Northern-French' early drama tradition of Arras, in the county of Artois, the south-western part of Flanders that was split off from the county around 1200, is quite distinct from the drama traditions of the rest of the francophone area and belongs in fact to the common literary and political culture of the Low Countries.[83] Later, during the Reformation and the beginning of the Dutch Revolt, perhaps the harshest literary critic of urban politics in the Low Countries was the late sixteenth-century rhetorician Lauris Jansz, from the city of Haarlem in Holland, a county which was by then economically dominant. He blamed not only rich speculators but also the sins of the people – thus still expressing the same fundamentally medieval middle-class economic and political values.[84] According to Mak, Cornelis Everaert 'starts as a revolutionary, a social rebel, and ends as penitence preacher' in all his plays.[85]

Rhetoricians' literature of the later medieval Netherlands thus provides a fascinating source for reconstructing the social and political ideas of the middling sort of people in this vibrant urban society. It is true that the rhetoricians were not revolutionary demagogues, but they seem to have sympathised primarily with the common people, provided that these commoners worked and did not sit idle. Opinions on current political events could be heard all over these prosperous cities, but, unless forced to react and defend guild privileges, it was usually better to remain silent and carry on with one's trade.

---

83   Langley 1999, pp. 57–77; Koopmans 2001; Lavéant 2007, pp. 93–6.
84   Strietman 1999, pp. 135–45; Hummelen and Dibbets, eds 1985.
85   Mak 1944, p. 109.

CHAPTER 11

'A Bad Chicken Was Brooding': Subversive Speech in Late Medieval Flanders

Jan Dumolyn and Jelle Haemers

1 Introduction

In March and April 1477, the guilds of Ypres were in open revolt. They took advantage of the defeat and death at Nancy of Charles the Bold, count of Flanders and duke of Burgundy, to start a rebellion against the ruling patrician class and demand the restitution of privileges that had been abolished in earlier decades. Burgundian power was weak as the French king attacked its territory, and the new countess of Flanders, Charles's daughter Mary of Burgundy, did not have the means to suppress revolts in Ghent, Bruges, Ypres and other cities and towns in the Low Countries. In Ypres, guild leaders took control of the urban government and several of the privileges favourable to the craft guilds were restored. Once the Burgundian court had recovered and Mary of Burgundy had married Maximilian, the Habsburg archduke of Austria, the central power retaliated. In a joint action with the urban elite of Ypres in the autumn of 1477, the ruling dynasty started an in-depth investigation into the circumstances of the revolt's outbreak in order to punish its leaders. The prosecutor wanted to know not only what exactly had happened, but also what the rebels had said to each other before the rebellion had started. At some point, one Jan Wouterman, a draper, confessed that he had overheard two other men, Ghislain and Maylin Everaert, in conversation at the Ypres Corn Market. They had said they knew where 'a bad chicken was brooding' (*een quaet kiekin broedde*). Wouterman was referring to some apprentice weavers who had secretly assembled in an inn at the market square around three tables, declaring that they would not take up work again until they had regained the old privileges.[1]

---

1 Jan Wouterman said '*dat hij hoorde zegghen Ghilein Everaerde ende Maylin Everaerd, up de maerct staende thender coorenmarct, datter in weet waer een quaet Kiekin broedde, ende dat de cnaepwevers up enen zekeren dach vergadert waren te Clemmekins in den Beere, an de maerct, ende dat zij daer waren in drien tafelen, ende ooc dat zij spraken ende sloten dat*

'A bad chicken was brooding', as linked to the expression 'Bad egg, bad chick' (*Quaet ey, quaet kuke* or *malum ovum, mala gallina*), was a common proverb in the Middle Ages. The phrase is attested in the oldest Middle Dutch proverb collection with Latin translation, the *Proverbia communia* of 1487.[2] In this context it meant that wicked people were hatching a malicious plan. Jan Wouterman used it to describe the rebellious speech acts uttered by the apprentice boys during their illicit meeting. They 'were brooding on' subversive plans that had to remain hidden from the city government (especially the spies of the bailiff who hung around inns), until they could take action and openly call for a strike in the textile industry. The testimonies of Jan Wouterman and other inhabitants of the city show not only that rebels planned their political actions in clandestine meetings, but also that even groups completely excluded from political power, as the young apprentices of the Flemish textile guilds were, commonly exchanged dangerous political ideas amongst themselves without the initial knowledge of the urban rulers or the deans and masters of their guilds. When these bad eggs were hatched, subversive speech could pose a serious threat to the authorities. During the last two decades, medieval Flemish revolts have been systematically studied in terms of their chronology, economic background, social composition, patterns of mobilisation, ritual repertoires and symbolic choreography.[3] The stereotypical discourses of princely, noble and patrician power elites about rebels and revolts have also been considered.[4] But what about the discursive production and oral utterances of the popular opposition itself? How do we study rumours and mutterings, the slogans and battle cries, the party names, the songs and poems that could be heard before and during revolts?

2   **Language as the Scene of Struggle**

It has long been commonly accepted that political history cannot restrict itself to formal organisations of power. The political historian must also be con-

---

zij niet weerken en zouden voor anderstond dat zij hadden huere oude kueren also zij van ouds gheordonneert waren, ende anders niet', see Justice, Jean 1891, p. 39. The context of the Ypres revolt of 1477 and its repression, are studied at length by Haemers 2009, pp. 256–61.

2 Jente, ed. 1947, p. 257.
3 See [Patterns]; See [Factionalism]; Boone 2007b; Arnade 1996a.
4 Dumolyn 2008a; Haemers 2008.

cerned with languages, ideas and their structures.[5] In the medieval world, there were large bodies of interconnected discourses that made up the frameworks of political thinking.[6] According to James C. Scott, subaltern groups, operating in opposition to 'hegemonic ideology', develop their own political languages which remain concealed or only temporarily come to the surface.[7] In this view, people never completely interiorise the dominant ideology of the ruling class. What Scott calls the 'hidden transcripts', in contrast to the 'public transcripts' of the authorities, are expressions of 'infrapolitics', the type of discussions and complaints that fall 'somewhere between wholehearted consent and open rebellion'.[8] However, the distinction between a 'hidden' and a 'public' transcript is not an easy one to make.[9] The overlaps are manifold. The lower social strata criticise and mock the dominant ideology, sometimes by parodying, subverting and manipulating it. In the same way, the political elite can depart from convention by using verbal forms and expressions which originated from 'popular slang'. But most importantly, the question of how the social consciousness of a subaltern group manifests itself and how it interacts with official communication should always be studied in specific historical contexts. The theoretical insights discussed above can only be of help when we take into account the specific features of medieval Flemish urban politics. As is generally known, Flanders was one of the most urbanised and economically developed regions of medieval Europe. Since the fourteenth century, its cities and towns had a strong tradition of communal politics and of guild participation in their governments and riots. So, we must ask ourselves, within this specific social and political balance of power, could Flemish rebels construct and voice their own political discourses or could they only partly subvert the official ideologies?

We argue that they did both things at the same time. The available sources show that the production, circulation and political outcomes of subversive speech largely depended on two elements: the specific circumstances in which the rebels uttered political speech and their social and political background. According to the sociolinguistic framework of Dell Hymes, the setting, moment, place and physical circumstances of the utterances determine the degree of 'seriousness' and legitimacy of those utterances.[10] The scene of speaking, the

---

5   A point particularly emphasised for medieval political history, which has generally been
     less receptive to this approach than is the case for other periods, in the recent work of
     Watts 2009, pp. 35–6.
6   Ibid., pp. 131–2; Burke 1987, p. 3; Black 2002, pp. 2–10.
7   Scott, James 1990.
8   Walker 2000, p. 33.
9   See the critique of Bourdieu 1991, p. 93.
10   Hymes 1977, pp. 55–6.

institutionalised space of the gathering, and the physical setting conditioned the linguistic register that was used by the speakers. But it is not only the concrete speech situation in the late medieval town that explains why rebels used certain words; their social background and political importance also has to be taken into account in order to understand what has been said. We therefore argue that the expressions of the popular classes in medieval Flanders varied according to the speakers' social position and their ability to take advantage of the possibilities offered to them to express grievances. In what follows, we broadly distinguish between two main types of political speech used in the context of Flemish popular politics in the late Middle Ages. The first type of language is the typical ideological discourse used in the official meetings of the guildsmen and rebel leaders from the urban middling sort, a discourse which had a direct dialogic relationship with the dominant political languages of the time. Urban elites used a number of learned juridical arguments to legitimise their opposition to the count of Flanders when his politics were or were judged to be harmful to the county. The ideological chains of signifiers in these texts, among which the concept of the *bonum commune* was the most important, were strongly influenced by juridical, biblical, Aristotelian, and other normative vocabularies, and do not greatly differ from those encountered in clerical or princely political discourses.[11] For instance, such language can be found in the exemplary genre reflecting political discourses used by medieval subjects: the petition. In this sense, petitions, as Mark Ormrod has argued, formed a specific textual framework of political language that structured and limited the way in which the rebels' clamour was voiced.[12]

Apart from the 'official' rebellious discourse of the petition, we must also consider types of direct, less theoretically informed popular speech, such as the threats and insults of the rioting mob. The social background of speakers located within the urban mob usually differed from those who handed over petitions to the lord or the urban magistrate. Whereas the 'mob' often included poorer guildsmen and unskilled wage-workers, what we might refer to as the 'middle classes' consisted of better-off guild masters, skilled artisans, petty merchants and shopkeepers. While, schematically speaking, the first group often served as storm troops in the collective actions of the craft guilds, the middling sort of people, on the contrary, usually kept firm control over urban political revolts in order to negotiate with the urban elite or the prince.[13] Though the language used by both groups differed, it is important to recognise from the start

---

11   Dumolyn and Haemers 2011 [see les bonnes causes]; Dumolyn 2006a.
12   Ormrod 2009. See also the case studies in Millet, ed. 2003.
13   See [Patterns].

that this distinction between the more 'middlebrow' rebellious discourse found in official documents and the popular utterances on the street is not clear-cut at all. There were numerous overlaps and borrowings between the political languages of different social strata, as demonstrated by the way middle-class leaders, such as the deans of the craft guilds, used words and expressions belonging to the official political discourse of the city in order to confront the ruling patrician elites with the inconsistencies between their deeds and promises. Mikhail Bakhtin's notion of 'heteroglossia' is helpful in this context. The Russian literary theorist coined the term to express the 'polyphony' of social and discursive forces in a text or, in other words, another's speech in another's language.[14] By appropriating and altering elements of the dominant ideology, subaltern discourse can parody or express a kind of irony towards it. At other moments, however, radical rebels used more autonomous popular expressions to convey political grievances. To summarise, our case shows that a neat distinction between 'popular' and 'elitist' speech cannot be recognised in late medieval Flanders. The linguistic reality of politics in the Flemish urban space was a polyphonic world in which language was a scene of struggle, and in which the choice of words was conditioned by circumstantial and social factors.

3   The Voice of the Common People

Although the vocal utterances of a rebelling mob were more aggressive than the discourse that can be found in surviving petitions to urban governments and the counts of Flanders, the former should certainly not be considered naive or coarse. Instead, such popular 'speech acts' often had a significant political impact. In addition to the systems of thought which are usually the primary objects of study for historians dealing with political ideas, this article considers the performance of speech in the Flemish cities as a socio-political action vital to urban political systems. Medieval and early modern speech events constituted and even defined political relations between rulers and subjects.[15] As is the case in modern society, the expression of subversive thoughts in public can be considered a 'perlocutionary speech act', an utterance that brings about important effects, in our case a seditious mobilisation or an urban revolt.[16] Of course, more was needed to incite a rebellion than the shouting of a slogan, but a subversive speech act could function as a spark that lit the fire. Or in

14   Bakhtin 1981. See also Holquist 2002.
15   Wood 2007, chapter 3; see also Wood 2001.
16   Terminology derived from Austin 1971.

the words of the fifteenth-century chronicle of Saint-Denis, it was the transition from the *scintilla* to the *incendium*.[17] The Middle Dutch dialect spoken in Flanders even had a specific word for such incitements to revolt: a *roepinghe* (a 'shouting'), indicating the prominence of speech acts in the social and political struggle that was so characteristic of the prosperous urban centres in the county of Flanders.

Finding traces of these popular subversive utterances is at first sight not an easy task. Rebellious speech usually evaporated quickly because of its oral and clandestine nature. Although the sources appear to be scarce, fragmented and usually socially and politically distorted from the viewpoint of the elite, we try to evaluate the character, the sociolinguistic setting, the dissemination and the ideological contents of the Flemish rebels' words. Most of the subversive speech under scrutiny in this article can only be studied in an 'archaeological' manner because, as is usually the case in this field of study, it has come down to us in the form of fragments and indirect quotations in hostile chronicles, fictional texts, as well as political, legal and repressive documents. Moreover, forms of communication like mockery and insults are usually intentionally transitory, as are oral traditions such as gossip.[18] Because of the consequences for the authors, social criticism and other subversive ideas were rarely written down. If they were, the number of copies was usually very limited in the period before, or at the dawn of, the age of the printing press. Contrary to the widespread assumption held by historians of the Reformation, political pamphlets were in fact common in the medieval Low Countries. But most of the libels, complaints, petitions and other written documents that were produced by rebels were quickly destroyed by the ducal or urban government. Nevertheless, our systematic search in a variety of Flemish medieval sources has yielded a large number of results, of which this article only cites a small part. Inevitably, of course, some methodological doubts surround these sources. Chroniclers, judges and clerks of the courts filtered and rephrased the words of the rebels through their own socially and legally determined discursive frames. Therefore it is hard to retrieve the precise formulations used by political criminals.[19] Repression had to be legally justified by the courts, however, and even chroniclers who dealt with political protest mainly in stereotypes had to quote rebels more or less exactly in some cases to persuade their intended audience of the rebels' maliciousness and potential danger. Hence, we argue that histori-

---

17   Guenée 2002, p. 49.
18   Vansina 1985, pp. 17–18; Wickham 1998, pp. 11–12.
19   See Le Roy Ladurie 1975; and the interesting discussion about this study's sources: Benad 1990; Arnold 2001.

ans should not be excessively negative about the sources' lack of 'authenticity' and their stereotypical character, because in combination with other data, they have the potential to reveal a good deal of the discursive reality surrounding medieval revolts.

The circulation of medieval popular ideas about politics and society should be situated in a communicative situation of 'aurality'.[20] Written texts were not only copied and dispersed in a textual form, they were also read in public, memorised and dispersed orally. Libels were posted at church doors and read aloud by bystanders. Manually copied leaflets circulated, probably read out loud by those who were able to, and were discussed in groups. Although subversive political discourse did indeed circulate on paper, speech was its natural medium. The problem we are dealing with is essentially one of retrieving the politics of the spoken word, an issue central to medieval society. Situations of speech and silence were important matters for normative theories on law and religion. The 'sins of the tongue' were manifold: gossip, boasting, slander but also blasphemy and political subversion. Ideas of who was supposed to speak and who was supposed to remain silent, under which conditions and in whose presence, were crystallised in moralistic works like the *Ars loquendi et tacendi* of Albertanus of Brescia (1245) on the *vitium linguae*.[21] John Gower's dream vision *Vox clamantis*, which is usually directly linked to the Peasant Revolt of 1381, also offers us a metaphoric description of the repertoire of late medieval rebels. It focuses on the noises they produced, comparing them to different kinds of animals. They were rebellious asses whose 'braying terrified all the burghers, as they loudly redoubled their usual "hee haw" again and again' and 'they refused to carry sacks to the city anymore'. They were oxen who would not let themselves be led by their ploughmen. They were dogs barking 'as if there were tens of thousands, and the fields shook with their voices', so that when this noise descended to Satan's ears there was great rejoicing in hell. Their looting and plundering was done by 'foxes and innumerable cats', and 'a Jackdaw, well instructed in the art of speaking, which no cage could keep at home', was the demagogue rebel leader of service.[22] Gower's poem perhaps echoes the words of Isaiah (17.12): 'Woe to the multitude of many people, which make a noise like the noise of the seas; and to the rushing of nations, that make a rushing like the rushing of mighty waters!' The metaphors of noise, as in 'the buzzing crowd', reveal the impact of late medieval subversive speech acts. The beastly crying, or the muttering resembling the sound of bees and birds for which the elite

---

20   See Coleman, Janet, ed. 1996; and, for the Low Countries: Lecuppre-Desjardin 2010.
21   Casagrande and Vecchio 1991, p. 14.
22   Stockton, ed. 1962 pp. 54–69.

writers reproached lower-class rebels, reflects their judgement of the common person's linguistic competence. In the opinion of elite writers, the masses were incapable of using the appropriate words to express their anger in a strategic manner and were unable to persuade the crowd except with furious cries and acts of violence.[23]

From a sociolinguistic point of view, these negative opinions are very informative, but most of all, they reveal an awareness of the potential danger of popular speech. *Vox populi, vox Dei* was a well-known expression, first recorded in a letter by Alcuin of York, though he reports that it was already in use.[24] This proverb did not mean that the voice of the common man was wise or good, but simply that it was overwhelming and could not be ignored.[25] Nevertheless, although the popular classes were always reckoned to be a potential political force, it was usually dangerous for them to articulate their political thoughts. In the later medieval Low Countries, ecclesiastical and lay authors legitimised the sometimes harsh repression of subversive words and slogans by urban and princely authorities. The *Duytschen Catoen*, a Middle Dutch moralistic poem based on the *Disticha Catonis*, one of the classic ethical texts of the Middle Ages, stressed the importance of shutting one's mouth in social life.[26] Examples of this moralist genre were very popular in late medieval Flemish cities and towns and similar views appear in legal discourse. The Flemish jurist Filips Wielant (1441/2–1520), evoking the notion of *diffamatio* in Roman Law, stipulated that not only writings such as songs, books or stories, but also oral utterances that were harmful, false or undeserved had to be prosecuted.[27] This rule was enforced by municipal and state authorities through violent, public physical punishments that were intended to discourage any political challengers of their regime from voicing political grievances. In addition, the fact that the authorities punished oral protest in a similar way to written protest should prevent the historian from making too great a distinction between the oral and written expression of the same subversive ideas.

In recent years, several specialists of the early modern period have studied the 'public voice' of subordinate groups in order to understand the political beliefs and behaviour of these 'historically inarticulate'.[28] They have shown that

---

23 Steiner 2003, pp. 200–1; Barr 2001.
24 Boas 1969, p. 8, who quotes Dümmler, ed. 1895, p. 199.
25 Gallacher 1945; Brewer 1898, p. 1279. See also Walther, ed. 1967, vol. 5, p. 919, no. 34182.
26 Van Buuren, ed. 1998, pp. 47–9. The original Latin included the lines '*Virtutem primam esse puto compescere linguam: / Proximus ille deo qui scit ratione tacere*' (ibid., p. 47).
27 Wielant 1995, pp. 267, 273.
28 In addition to Wood (see note 15 above), see Walter 2006; Beik 2007.

crowds combined verbal violence with other forms of violent action in the pursuit of their political agenda.[29] Some medievalists have also recognised similar characteristics in the political culture of crowds,[30] but the importance of political speech acts in the later medieval city has never been the subject of a study in itself. In his recent survey of revolts in late medieval Europe, Samuel Cohn evokes a communicative world in which rebels maintained and exchanged a particular political ideology, providing many interesting examples of clandestine meetings and demagogic speeches, but he does not discuss the mechanisms of this communication process or its ideological content in detail.[31] Even if in recent years medieval historians have paid somewhat more attention to these linguistic phenomena in addition to the significance of ritual practices, emotions and symbolic violence,[32] standard accounts of revolts and 'popular politics' remain dominated by the image of the violent crowd fighting in the streets. In general, the importance of the spoken word still remains far too underexposed in the study of medieval popular politics. We argue that subversive speech was one of the omnipresent features of political life in Flemish cities because it formed a continuous threat to the position of the rulers, a threat more dangerous than the regular outbursts of violence that specialists of Flemish urban politics have usually focused upon. Using a variety of sources, we try to reconstruct systematically those speech situations that allowed for political expression, together with the effects of political speech acts and their ideological content.

4   Murmuratio: The Imminent Threat of Revolt

'Muttering' is the collective speech act that invariably precedes every preindustrial uprising and a discussion of this phenomenon is the best way to start our empirical analysis. The Book of Wisdom (1.11) is clear on the dangerous character of *murmur* or *murmuratio*: 'Keep yourselves therefore from murmuring, which profiteth nothing, and refrain your tongue from detraction, for an obscure speech shall not go for nought: and the mouth that belieth, killeth the soul'. The word was also explicitly used in the *Regula Benedicti* warning

29   Bercé 1976; Dupuy 2002; Randall 2006; Kesselring 2007; Arnade 2008.
30   Barron 2004, p. 130; Schubert 1975; Scase 2007.
31   Cohn 2006, pp. 193–201.
32   See the essays in Van Leeuwen, ed. 2006b; and in Lecuppre-Desjardin and Van Bruaene, eds 2005.

the monastic community of the danger of mumbling monks.[33] The onomato-poeic character of the word *murmuratio*, which is first mentioned in Roman sources (to indicate the sound of a flock of birds), typically points to the ruling elites' inability to understand the speech of the lower classes, who were put on the level of animals. At the same time, the condemnation of muttering was part of the systematic normative discourse on illicit speech acts, or sins of the tongue, established by the religious and legal theorists of the later Middle Ages. The thirteenth-century Dominican Guglielmus Peraldus, for instance, wrote a *Summa de vitiis et virtutibus* in which he mentions the murmur or complaint among other *peccati linguae*, next to *blasphemia, periurum* and *derisio*.[34] And the two leading medieval jurists, Baldus and Bartolus, whose legal treatises usually reflect the political conditions of their days very well, made a distinction between the *vana vox populi* consisting of perverted rumours, and the *notorium facti* based on clear evidence.[35]

Muttering was also closely associated with uncontrollable rumour and, in that context, it usually had a more explicitly political meaning. In lay writings from France and the Netherlands, concepts that were used for public knowledge such as *nouvelle, renommée*, or *(nieu)mare* had a more positive connotation, while *murmur* often had a subversive twist to it. Numerous Latin and vernacular treatises demonstrate that rumours and murmurs frightened moralist writers, since *murmuratio* could lead to an outburst of anger. Medieval authorities were very familiar with grumbling as a form of veiled complaint and shared anxieties about the obscure and undecipherable nature of this subversive circulation of discourse. Usually the intention behind the grumbling was to communicate a general sense of dissatisfaction without taking responsibility for an open, specific complaint. The subject of the complaint may have been clear to listeners but, by muttering, the complainer avoided an open incident and could always disavow any intention to complain should the authorities hear about it.[36] On many occasions, the Flemish sources refer to murmur as a sign of growing discontent. In 1301, for instance, when the French king wanted to reintroduce taxes that he had abolished some months before, the people in the streets of Ghent 'began to rage fiercely, complain, and grumble shrilly'.[37] And also much later, on 9 April 1477, the inhabitants of Bruges began

---

33 Vogüé and Neufville, eds 1972–3, vol. 2, p. 542.

34 Lindorfer 2003, pp. 27–8.

35 Gauvard 1994, pp. 168–9.

36 Scott, James 1990, p. 154.

37 '*Quod communitas audiens, ferociter cepit fremere et acute conqueri et murmurare*', Funck-Brentano, ed. 1896, p. 18.

'to clear their throat and to murmur' when the city council refused to take their wishes into account (*'te rochellene ende te murmureren'*).[38] This meant imminent danger to the public order. Flemish chroniclers often warned their audience against muttering, which was described as a form of the sin of *ira* ('anger'); for example, when the commons of Ypres murmured, they were 'disturbed and angry' (*'verstorbeirt ende gram'*).[39] Most of all, the fact that the government took the dangers of popular grumbling very seriously is shown in various ordinances of the dukes of Burgundy for Flanders. In the *narratio* at the beginning of the charter, where the law ordained by the duke had to be justified, there are often suggestions that certain legislative measures were made precisely to prevent popular anger. An ordinance on the night watch in the town of Veurne in 1465, for instance, was issued because *'a ceste cause pluseurs grans murmures, debatz et inconveniens sourdent et aviengnent souvent entre le menu people'* ('because many great murmurs, debates and improprieties arise and happen among the lesser people').[40] A 1452 charter for the port town of Nieuwpoort dealing with aldermen being accused of corruption also mentions *'les oblocucions du peuple'* ('the disputes of the people').[41]

The phenomenon of concealed or semi-public complaining should be understood in the context of the networks of oral communication which circulated political information and opinions in the form of rumours. *Murmuratio* was thus closely connected to another form of rebellious speech act, spreading the rumour. Studies of medieval and early modern rumours in England show that the urban commons could be surprisingly well informed about politics.[42] Regardless of people's individual beliefs, rumours were a medium through which communities monitored their own vital signs, canvassing attitudes and reactions and testing the boundaries of the 'sayable'.[43] They also had a strong mobilising power during revolts and civil wars. Muttering and rumours were considered dangerous phenomena by the authorities precisely because they referred to the circulation of political views that the authorities were unable to control. In Venice, the *mormoratione* was harshly repressed by the doge and his army of spies. Often, these rumours were unfounded, but what was especially alarming was the possibility that real information would be dissem-

---

38   Vorsterman, ed. 1531, fol. 182^v.
39   Lambin, ed. 1835, p. 2; see also Lett and Offenstadt, eds 2003, p. 14.
40   Veurne Municipal Archives, charter 206.
41   State Archives of Belgium, Bruges, Oud archief stad Nieuwpoort, charter 124.
42   Harvey 1995; Watts 2004.
43   Shagan 2001, pp. 30–1; Highley 1998, pp. 63–4; Fox 1997, p. 598.

inated through the urban social networks.[44] Many chroniclers took notice of the muttering with the potential political consequences in mind, didactically cautioning rulers not to neglect such warnings 'from below'. By quoting the dissatisfaction of the 'small people', the medieval chroniclers acknowledged the influence of popular grumbling, and 'semi-legitimised' it. As mentioned above, rebellions and groups of rebels were often designated with onomato-poeic words that pejoratively labelled them as mutterers. The accusation of unintelligibility was certainly belittling but it may also reflect the authorities' anxiety in the face of covertly circulating information. The murmuring with which the Bruges revolt of the 1280s started gave its name to the entire revolt: the so-called *Moerlemaye*, derived from the Middle Dutch words *morren* ('to mutter') and *maaien* ('fiercely waving one's arms').[45] In late medieval Flanders, similar derogatory onomatopoeic words were also often used to denote people who engaged in illegitimate speech acts. For example, the term *reutelaer* (as in the 1534 'guild of the *reutelaers*' in Bruges) is mentioned, which refers to unruly young men who gathered in the convent of the Clarissans and mocked the religious women with a combination of rough music and early reformat-ory activities, shouting and hurling objects during mass. The city government could only warn that in the future such conduct would be punished with flog-ging.[46] *Reutelen* means to make a rasping sound with one's voice. A *reutelaer* is a chattering fool, a rattler, windbag or blabbermouth.[47] The sixteenth-century Flemish poet Anna Bijns further associated the *rueteleers* with the *preuteleers*. *Preutelen* means to grouse or to gripe, the speech of someone who mumbles in the back of his mouth, as it were in an act of semi-concealed protest.[48] Another similar onomatopoeia is *lollen*, eating one's words while praying or mumbling or quietly singing prayers, and this Middle Dutch word is the generally accepted etymology of 'Lollard', the term applied to the subversive heretics of late medi-eval England. The fact that Middle Dutch, spoken in one of the most rebellious regions of medieval Europe, also had so many words for these uncontrollable speech acts and for those who spoke idly or dangerously, such as *clappaert* ('babbler'), is clearly more than a mere coincidence.

---

44 Crouzet-Pavan 1994, pp. 210–12.
45 Boogaart 2001b. The simultaneous revolt in Ypres was called the '*Cockerulle*', probably also referring to cries and noises produced by the rebels, although its exact meaning remains unclear: see Boone 1998, p. 147.
46 Dewitte 1982, p. 37.
47 Verwijs and Verdam 1907, vol. 6, pp. 1644–5.
48 Soens 1900–2, p. 214.

5   Songs and Pamphlets

The onomatopoeic origins of 'murmur' and these similar words demonstrate that the authors of repressive documents or chronicles in many cases did not know exactly what was being muttered, since this speech act was mostly performed in the private or semi-private sphere. Many insults, *lèse-majesté*, mockeries and subversive songs, however, were also uttered or 'performed' in speech situations like inns and alehouses. These public places often attracted large numbers of unruly young people, including servants and apprentice boys. They were spaces where boys could meet without the supervision of their families or guild masters, and form their own peer groups, a situation that always had the potential for subversion and class struggle.[49] Inns were also news centres in which travellers and messengers met, and gathering places for the marginal elements of society, including people who had been exiled from other cities, and criminals in general.[50] In combination with the ability of alcohol to loosen tongues, these factors made pubs principal sites for subversive talking, or often singing. The large majority of such cases of drunken political ranting must have gone unnoticed because they took place in lowly environments.

Moreover, subversive thoughts were often also expressed playfully, though not harmlessly, in subversive songs, popular theatre, and public poetry and storytelling – all widespread phenomena in late medieval Flemish cities. From the urban rulers' point of view, songs and poems were dangerous media for several reasons. They were public events and they were contagious; a circulating jingle was easily memorised and freely altered.[51] As a result of censorship, self-censorship, and of course the oral character of their transmission, the full text of only a few of such openly political literary works in Middle Dutch have come down to contemporary historians. Sometimes, historical accounts refer to them indirectly. This was the case with the decree of 5 January 1518 issued by the Bruges city government strictly forbidding any public mockery of those in office in the form of songs, poems or plays.[52] The play *dOnghelycke Munte* ('On Unequal Coinage') by the sixteenth-century Bruges rhetorician and master fuller Cornelis Everaert could not be staged because of its criticism of princely monetary manipulation but, fortunately, the text survives

---

49   Clark, Peter 1983, p. 183.
50   Fox 1997, pp. 607–8; Soly 1983, p. 569.
51   Martines 2000; Maddicot 1986; Kuhn 2007.
52   Hüsken 1992, pp. 223–4.

in a manuscript.[53] Everaert's plays feature allegorical characters with names like 'Poor person' or 'Common tradesman' debating the economic situation in early sixteenth-century Bruges – never in a very radical manner, though often sharp and to the point. Plays like these, composed by rhetoricians, were usually written for guilds and confraternities to be performed during Church holidays, and it seems that there was space for mild social critique on these occasions.

We also have evidence of political singing on the streets, as in the case reported to the Bruges aldermen by blacksmith Jan van de Kerchove. He had heard a blind man playing an instrument and singing songs, the words of which were allegedly directed 'against the prince and the prosperity of the land, and there was nothing virtuous or good in them'.[54] Unfortunately, the exact words of the blind singer have not come down to us. Sometimes we do know what people were singing about, as in the case of *'une jone fille'* in the city of Saint-Omer in the neighbouring principality of Artois, who was exiled for three years and three days *sur le langhe* in 1431 because she had sung a song about the Cassel peasants' revolt, criticising the duke of Burgundy. She was later pardoned, however, because of her age and 'because she had not thought that it would anger anyone'.[55] Chroniclers also quote possibly reformulated fragments of political songs and ballads, as do later printed collections of popular songs. Quite a few of the Middle Dutch 'historical ballads' that survive deal with rebellions against the prince. A political song transcribed at the beginning of the sixteenth century features a Ghent rebel leader, Lieven Boone, who had taken up arms against Duke Philip the Good in 1452. The author expressed his hope that Boone would rule the city of Ghent again, because otherwise the city would no longer be 'worth a crown'.[56] Another song compared the Ghent military captain Jacob Meeuwsone to Saint George fighting his powerful dragon-like enemy. It warned that all those who served the lord 'must be beaten to death', as Saint George had done to the evil dragon. This ballad was composed using the rhyme scheme of a contemporary Latin drinking song, supporting the theory that these political ditties were sung during drinking sessions in alehouses.[57]

---

53 Mareel 2008.

54 Municipal Archives of Bruges, register van de Vierschaar, fols. 45ᵛ–46ᵛ.

55 Pas 1930, p. 138. 'Sur le langhe' meant that she was on pain of having her tongue cut out if she returned to the city within the period of exile.

56 'O Ghent, Ghent scone, den zijst niet weert een croone, want di zults die laten hoonen, tenzij datti regiert Lieven Boone', de Pauw, 1893–1914, vol. 2, p. 388. On the revolt, see Haemers 2004b.

57 'Sent Joris ende vrient, slaet al doot dat den heere dient, zonder den prince ende zijn kint, haut die op, waer ghij se vint', de Pauw, 1893–1914, vol. 2, p. 390.

Poems and songs about popular leaders and rebellious events in the city kept the memory of revolts alive for many decades, while at the same time they must have been used to criticise in a veiled manner the policies of the current regime.[58]

Indeed, rebels were sometimes courageous enough to leave the semi-clandestine world of disreputable alehouses and utter their subversive words in public. If the political climate was unstable, an anonymous pamphlet might be spread throughout the city or be attached to a central or symbolically important building, such as the belfry or an important church. Even if these forms of political graffiti were quickly removed by the authorities, someone would undoubtedly remember their contents since the pamphlets were often written in verse, and he or she would orally transmit them to friends, kinsmen, neighbours or guild brothers. In most cases, pamphlets demanded that rulers correct a certain political situation. Sometimes there were also threats involved.[59] In November 1487, an anonymous Bruges rhyme that was posted on the Belfry, the central building in which the urban privileges were stored, warned the aldermen that the following night they would be deprived of 'life and property' if they continued to ignore protest.[60] In 1407, leaflets with similar contents were found across the city.[61] In Ghent in 1460, several 'horrible' letters were dispersed, insulting the duke of Burgundy.[62] In 1481 in the same city, six sheets of paper with political messages surfaced after the faction that supported the duke of Burgundy tried to influence the election of the aldermen by violating the city's privileges.[63] Even before printing, or in its very early days, it was an established practice in Flemish cities and towns to spread rebellious discourse by means of pamphlets, the limited edition of which was compensated for by the speed of the consequent oral transmission of their contents in narrow urban streets, crowded inns and small workshops.

---

58   In another chapter, we show that widespread, powerful memories of an idealised past heavily influenced the maintenance of a collective identity among the urban craftsmen in Flanders, the efficiency of their mobilisation, and their justifications for seizing power: See [Social Memory].

59   See Darnton 1996, p. 198; Scase 1998; Walter 2009.

60   'Ghy, heeren van Brugghe, zijt ghy niet wel up u hoeden, ghy zult by nachte berooft zijn van lijve ende van goede', Despars 1837–40, vol. 4, p. 298. See also Lecuppre-Desjardin 2010, pp. 155–60; Van Leeuwen 2004.

61   Lambin, ed. 1835, p. 40.

62   'Horrybele quade ende veynselicke brieven', Fris, ed. 1901–4, vol. 2, p. 188.

63   Van der Meersch, ed. 1852–61, vol. 1, p. 321.

6 The Oral Politics of Popular Assemblies

From muttering in the inn to libelling, from speaking one's mind in the guild assembly to shouting slogans in the marketplace, each further step of coming into the open was successively riskier. Most of the muttering, cries, shouts, songs and poems we have quoted in the preceding paragraphs were considered as *ongheoorloofdelic zegghende* ('illicit' or 'improper speech'), uttered in what were stereotypically called *assemblees illicites* ('illicit meetings').[64] Within the context of specific political situations and institutional settings, however, the expression of political opinions was tolerated to a certain degree. This often seems to have been the case during meetings of the guilds or of urban popular councils. In these meetings, the specific physical setting of the 'licit gathering' legitimised the speech act. However, social and political rules determined which kind of utterances remained unpunished. The oppositional discourse was allowed as long as it remained within clear boundaries: the closed and usually completely masculine space of the meeting place, mostly the guild house in the case of a guild gathering. Of course, certain rules had to be followed, but dissident ideas about the city's politics regularly seem to have been voiced freely, without punishment by the urban authorities. Although the debate in these meetings must often have been heated, the 'culture of deliberation' lent legitimacy to the political decisions which were taken, but also imposed clear limits on who was allowed to speak and who was not, when, and on which matters. We can be sure that, apart from really 'revolutionary' situations, even the most 'democratic' guild or burgher meetings were dominated by the better-off, older men. The sources of the Flemish towns do not reveal any woman's voice in this context. And apart from the girl singing the rebellious song mentioned above, literary texts stereotyping women as gossips or the occasional chronicle depicting them in emotional scenes, fearing for the fate of their rebel husbands, they remain conspicuous by their absence in the context of revolt.[65] Although women do seem to have been present on the streets, in most cases the opinions of women may simply have been overlooked by the sources. Clearly, as was the case among rebels, it was the established adult male who had the most right and power to speak: he was seen as a legitimate agent of political discourse, an *émetteur légitime* in the words of Pierre Bourdieu.[66] A dean of a guild in a

---

64 Justice, Jean 1891, p. 19. Froissart speaks of the people of Ghent who *'parloient villainement'*, Kervyn de Lettenhove, ed. 1867–77, vol. 2, p. 410. On the use of the word 'illicit' concerning speech acts, see Casagrande and Vecchio 1991, p. 37.

65 Dumolyn and Lecuppre-Desjardin 2005.

66 Bourdieu 1991, chapter 1.

meeting of artisans, for instance, was also allowed to articulate his opinions more freely than a person of lower rank and status.[67]

Although in many cases we do not have a precise understanding of how assemblies of 'all the burghers' or 'all the commoners' (later usually the meetings of the different guild leaders) functioned due to the scarcity of sources, we do know that they convened at irregular moments. Flemish urban institutions such as the Bruges 'Great Council', the Ypres 'Council of Twenty-Seven' and the Ghent 'Collacie', clearly had their origin in the original assemblies of the communal movement of the twelfth century. The earliest known Flemish popular political meeting is the one in Bruges in 1127 described by the cleric Galbert of Bruges in his report of the events after the murder of Count Charles the Good in the same year.[68] This assembly of the burghers of the early commune of Bruges took place in Zand square, *apud Harenas* as this sandy ridge just outside the first city walls was called – apparently the field where those who had sworn the communal oath debated important issues. During the later twelfth and thirteenth centuries, however, the power of these communal institutions in the cities and towns was weakened and replaced by the authority of the aldermen appointed by the counts of Flanders among the international merchants and rich landowners who had taken firm control over the urban space. Soon, social polarisation between these elite groups and the growing numbers of poor textile workers who lived in the suburbs of cities like Saint-Omer, Douai, Ghent, Ypres and Bruges led to new forms of popular conspiracies and riots. In Old and Middle French, these kinds of revolutionary meetings, strikes and riots, ever more frequent since the 1250s, were usually called *conspirations, alliances, aconpaignements, assanlees, takehans* or *routes*; in Middle Dutch *vergaderinghen, gaderinghen, meentuchten* and *sameninghen*. Obviously these meetings were a privileged setting for subversive talk, with potential revolutionary effects, but they could not be entirely suppressed. In 1280, for instance, a political meeting took place in Bruges which called itself the *meentucht* (literally meaning 'the authority of the commoners' or 'the meeting of the commune'). They claimed to speak for the city as a whole and formulated fiscal and political demands. This event started the aforementioned revolt that became known as the *Moerlemaye*. On the eve of that uprising, the city government had issued an ordinance forbidding artisans to organise meetings consisting of more than seven persons and in the absence of their dean.[69]

---

67   Research for Lyon confirms this, see Fargeix 2007.
68   Demyttenaere 2003.
69   Wyffels 1951, pp. 92–5.

From the second half of the thirteenth century, with the mass of industrial workers in the towns and cities and their suburbs growing ever greater, the ruling merchant elites of the Flemish cities had to choose between the strategy of forbidding independent guild meetings and other popular assemblies altogether, or trying to integrate them into their political structures in order to neutralise the threat they could pose if muttering led to forms of self-organisation and mass political meetings. Of course, regulating the social and institutional space as a locus for legitimate political discussion was a matter of concern in many medieval cities. In the small Italian commune of Macerata, for instance, there was even a ban on any kind of political talk outside the official councils. Measures were also taken against forms of derogatory painting with *pittura infamante* ('political messages'). People who did not agree with the leading party had to live 'quiet as a mouse in the flour' (*quatti como topo in farina*).[70] Such popular gatherings (and guild assemblies in particular) existed in many European towns, but the Flemish cases can most easily be compared with their better-studied Italian counterparts. After the revolt in Bruges in 1302 and the victory of the urban militias against the French army at Kortrijk, the bigger cities such as Ghent and Bruges were co-ruled by the guilds, and the degree of political participation among the middle class was considerably augmented.[71] During the fourteenth and fifteenth centuries, the ruling city magistrates, usually called the *scepenen* ('aldermen'), had to present important decisions to larger councils, often including the deans of the craft guilds. In Bruges, the metaphor of the urban body politic was used; the 'Great Council', made up of the fifty-four deans of the guilds and the six headmen of the burghers, was referred to as 'the common belly of the city' (*de ghemeene buke van de stad*). The representatives of the guilds and the burghers were thereby compared to an essential part of the human body, which stood for the entirety of urban society.[72] Separate meetings of the craft guilds were also common, each in their own guild house (*elc int sine* or *elc in zyn ledt*, meaning 'each in his own', or literally 'each in his limbs' – which again refers to the 'body politic' of the city).[73] In these houses the governors of the guild and representatives of the craftsmen were allowed to gather and speak their minds freely, to a certain degree at

---

70   Jones, Philip 1997, pp. 512, 574, 608. See also Cherubini 2008.

71   Stabel 2004; Prak 2006.

72   Head, belly and feet each symbolised a certain social or political organisation, which taken together formed a closed society. All limbs had a specific function, and they all acted for the 'common good' of the body. This 'organology' goes back to Aristotle and was continued by John of Salisbury, see Struve 1984, pp. 309–10.

73   For example in Ghent in 1450, Fris, ed. 1901–4, vol. 1, p. 112; in Bruges in 1436, Loncke 2007, p. 131; and in Ypres in 1477, Diegerick 1848, p. 428.

least. In 1449 in Ghent, for instance, representatives of the craft guilds delivered a document to the city council, the content of which was 'deliberated, advised upon in concord, concluded and handed over' in a meeting of the members of each guild.[74]

At particular moments during a revolt, when the urban craft guilds were assembled in arms in the market square and in control of the urban public space, these gatherings of guildsmen were no longer held inside but out in the open. The act of making complaints public had to be handled in a more collective manner, in keeping with the gravity of the economic and political climate. Such disciplined and orderly armed gatherings were called a *wapeninghe* or an *auweet*, and they were occasions for the presentation of petitions to the urban government.[75] Once again, the scene of the speech act and its particular circumstances influenced the way in which grievances were formulated. Mostly, craftsmen voiced their dissent as slogans or catchy phrases which were shouted collectively. In February 1478, for example, the guilds gathered in the market square of Bruges when it became clear that the city wanted to mobilise foreign troops in order to support Maximilian of Austria in his war against France. The guildsmen 'said publicly and in a very loud voice that they did not want to give money for something they could do themselves'.[76] They would not tolerate the violation of the custom that they had the right to mobilise urban militias if the city had to defend itself. Because it was an established tradition that Flemish guilds gathered in the main market squares to voice their political demands, collective shouting was not often subject to prosecution by the urban government and, in any case, each craftsman could hide behind corporate collectivity. In Bruges in 1477, a wooden *parc* ('stage') was set up in the market square with seats for the deans of the guilds so that they could 'speak together, have council daily and advise each other'.[77] In 1488 a cleric (probably a mendicant, but the sources are not clear on his identity) preached on a similar stage, after which guild leaders addressed the assembled crowd of craftsmen.[78] Chroniclers report that on such occasions, the guilds made their decisions 'by

---

74   *'Ghemeenlic vergadert zynde, te wetene elc in zyn let* [...] *met deliberatie ende advys daerup ghehadt hebbende, hebben eendrachtelic gheadvyseert, ghedelibereert, overeenghedreghen ende gheconclueert'*, Fris, ed. 1901–4, vol. 1, p. 72.

75   See [A moody community]; Boone 2005.

76   *'Zegghende openbaerlick ende overluydt, dat hemlieden gheenen noodt was ghelt te ghevene voor tghuene dat zy zelve doen consten'*, Despars 1837–40, vol. 4, p. 161.

77   *'Om dagelicx tsamen te sprekene, raet ende advijs met malcanderen te nemene'*, Vorsterman, ed. 1531, fol. 182ᵛ.

78   Carton, ed. 1859, pp. 221–2.

knowledge of the market square' or 'with public consent'.[79] The highly symbolic setting of this wooden stage, standing in the economic and political centre of the city, and the way in which these concerted decisions were reached, gave more legitimacy to the discourses of the rebel leaders. Conversely, when guild leaders made important political decisions during revolts without the consent of the assembled craftsmen, the rank and file started muttering against their own leadership.[80] In 1452, the military captains of the Ghent rebels, who, after three years of open revolt, were heading towards a final military showdown with Duke Philip the Good of Burgundy, decided that the Ghent Collacie was no longer competent to take political decisions. It was now up to all ordinary artisans assembled at the Friday Market to rule the city directly.[81] The Collacie had apparently lost its legitimacy in the eyes of the common guildsmen, and perhaps the military captains hoped to lead the revolt as demagogues with the blessing of the mob. Froissart paints a vivid picture of Jan Yoens, the demagogue leader of the violent militia of the so-called *Witte Kaproenen* ('White Hoods') in 1380s Ghent, who spoke *'de si belle rétorique et par si grant art'* ('with such fine rhetoric and great skill'), so that all the bystanders hearing him shouted: *'Il dist voir!'* ('he speaks truly') and *'Il dist bien!'* ('he speaks well').[82] Sometimes the multiplicity of rebel voices also reveals the chaotic situation during revolts. The sources on the Ypres revolt of 1477 provide a picture of total confusion about who was in power. They describe different sorts of meetings (both official ones and others, including meals and drinks): of guilds in their guild houses or little groups of patricians; of the urban institutions with a new role and function in these revolutionary times; and of clandestine groups of conspirators in inns, trying to fill the power vacuum, swearing oaths of mutual aid 'to be joined with lives and goods', and plotting actions and formulating arguments. Rumours were everywhere, and it was the talk of the town which leader was to be trusted, who could speak with legitimate authority, and who might be a traitor or a spy.[83]

---

79   'Ter kenesse van der merct', in Bruges in 1488, ibid., p. 202; 'openbaren den volcke tzelve consent', in Ghent in 1452, Fris, ed. 1901–4, vol. 2, 71.

80   'Tsdycendaechs was tvolc murmurerende ende grootelicx beroert', Fris, ed. 1901–4, vol. 1, p. 171.

81   Haemers 2004b, p. 222.

82   Kervyn de Lettenhove, ed. 1867–77, vol. 9, pp. 174, 176; also mentioned in Cohn 2006, p. 194.

83   Justice, Jean 1891, p. 44.

7   Ideological Discourses of Urban Elites and Craftsmen

Using the slogans that were shouted during guild assemblies, the written accounts of these meetings, and the petitions which resulted from them, we
can reconstruct a good deal of the ideological content of the guildsmen's
discourse. Although petitions are obviously conserved in written form, other
sources testify that complaints were primarily delivered orally to those who
were thought to possess the power to remedy them. In 1280 in Damme, a small
port town near Bruges, the commons 'clamoured' for justice, handing over a
written petition to the count.[84] During the 1323–8 revolt, a delegation of the
city of Ypres had delivered a $clachte$ ('complaint') about their government to
the French king, quite radically 'saying that we protest against all things'.[85]
Such oppositional discourse was only tolerated by the authorities because it
was presented to them in a 'legitimate' manner, composed by clerks or lawyers
who provided the necessary skills and expertise to write such documents.[86]
Whereas the demands in the petitions were undoubtedly formulated in quite
a different manner by the artisans present at a rebel meeting, they were subsequently written out in a judicial register, so that they could be directly incorporated into a law or ordinance. Their tone was usually humble; the subjects
were pleading to their governors or prince to 'remedy' what, in their eyes, was
a distorted situation. In comparing rebels' political claims with this elitist discourse, one is struck by the very similar choice of words. The notion of $utilitas$
$communis$, for instance, had become a routine political cliché in the late medieval city. Under different circumstances, it was a mobilising concept employed
by the political elite of Flemish towns, as well as by various oppositional movements and groups.[87] The same is true for the ideological discourse on privileges.
Expressions like $nobles\ francisses$ or 'beautiful and well-established privileges'
($scoone\ ende\ wel\ beseigelde\ previlegen$) were central to the guildsmen's and the
urban elite's ideology.[88] The typical language of this kind of document presents
the political ideas of artisans at their most moderate, wholly expressed in a dialogue with more dominant political languages. However, even if the subjects
voiced their demands and anxieties in a politically 'appropriate' manner and
in a language understandable to the elites, they did in fact subvert its meaning.

84   De Smet, Anton 1950.
85   'Dat wi zegghen zullen, wie maken vor alle dinghen protestacie', de Pauw 1899a, p. 702.
86   Van Nierop 1997, pp. 280–90; Scase 2007.
87   Prevenier 2010, p. 216.
88   See, respectively, Kervyn de Lettenhove, ed. 1867–77, vol. 9, p. 173, and Lambin, ed. 1835,
      p. 30. In general, see Dumolyn 2008b, pp. 20–3.

It was because these political utterances often sounded 'reasonable' (framed as they were in hegemonic terms) that they were so dangerous. As Antony Black and others have shown, notions of the common good, of peace, privileges, law, rights, customs, freedom, unity and concord were central in the dominant medieval ideologies.[89] Also for the Flemish rebels, the notions of 'custom' and 'privilege' were the most important elements of this semantic field. When the craft guilds took power, they read the urban privileges out loud in front of a crowd as large as the ones the prince would face during his ceremonial entries.[90] In several cases, privileges were the subject of rumours; they were alleged to have been falsified, lost or sold to the prince. Rebels had them copied and translated after taking power. They called them *quaede* or *scone* privileges ('bad' or 'beautiful'). The symbolic force of these freedoms, not least in their material form as parchment charters with seals, was even more important than the precise juridical interpretation of their contents. The least popular charters issued by the Flemish counts, for example in both Bruges and Ghent, were called the *calfvel* ('calf skin'). During revolts they would be ritually torn into pieces and even eaten by artisans,[91] just as the prince could 'cancel' a privilege by cutting it with a knife. Such was the power of these words, whether spoken aloud or in written form.

A common slogan of the Flemish craft guilds in the middle of the fourteenth century was *gemeente ende vrient* ('community and friend').[92] *Eendrachticheyt* ('unity') and variations on *broeders al eens* ('brothers all together') were also popular.[93] Such cries not only served to unite the political opposition against the urban rulers or the count; 'unity' with all its related concepts of 'brotherhood' and 'concord' were weighty elements in the 'corporate' ideology of the Flemish burghers. Flemish craftsmen always maintained at least the fiction of unity amongst themselves. With rallying cries such as 'Everybody who loves the city of Bruges, follow us',[94] 'Ghent! Ghent!',[95] and 'Bruges and friend',[96] craftsmen displayed their chauvinistic urban identity, but also insisted on defending an urban community protected by specific privileges. The urban political elites conventionally used the same arguments to defend their own point of view

---

89   Reynolds 1982; Black 2003, p. 70; Blickle 2000; Watts 2009, pp. 131–53.
90   Bibliothèque municipale, Douai, ms. 1110, fol. 180ᵛ.
91   Arnade 2003, p. 117.
92   De Smet, Joseph Jean, ed. 1841, vol. 2, p. 287.
93   Vorsterman, ed. 1531, fol. 183ᵛ; Lambin, ed. 1835, p. 157.
94   *Alle diegone die de stede van Brugghe liefhebben, die volghen ons!*, Bibliothèque municipale Douai, ms. 1110, fol. 188ᵛ.
95   Kervyn de Lettenhove, ed. 1867–77, vol. 10, p. 33.
96   Bibliothèque municipale, Douai, ms. 1110, fol. 238ᵛ.

while negotiating with the central government about taxes.[97] Local pride and identity were feelings which the urban elites shared with the popular classes. In Ghent, the most unruly city of Flanders, the almost mythical cult of James (or, in Dutch, Jacob) van Artevelde, which was maintained by defenders of the urban privileges, inspired craftsmen to shout his name during revolts, making it a slogan in itself. Van Artevelde had ruled the city between 1338 and 1345, choosing the side of the English king at the beginning of the Hundred Years War in order to protect the city's privileges against the attempts of the counts of Flanders (who were supported by the French king) to undermine them.[98] Later Ghent rebel leaders are reported to have told crowds, at least in Froissart's colourful language, that 'if James van Artevelde were still alive, the city would be in good shape'.[99] *Artevelde* became a homonym for rebel leaders defending privileges in late medieval Ghent. Even courtly officials used this association; in 1423 one of the councillors of Duke Philip the Good called the burgomaster of Ghent an *Artevelde* for his political opposition to the duke.[100] In addition, we should note that even though the slogans of Flemish craftsmen show some unique traits, they generally correspond to what is recorded in the publications on revolts in other European regions. Artisans and townsmen throughout the French kingdom shouted 'Paix!', 'Commune!' and 'Bourgeoisie!' during revolts in the late Middle Ages.[101] These had been the political keywords in urban life since the communal movement of the eleventh and twelfth centuries.[102]

'We want justice first', the 1477 Ypres rebels shouted during a meeting, intimidating the aldermen present.[103] The central ideological concept of *justitia* ubiquitously appeared in legal and theological medieval texts in relation to concepts such as *res publica, pax, bonum commune* or *utilitas publica*, but it also included an understanding of economic justice. Here we see the social and political struggle reflected in a discursive struggle over what this notion exactly meant in different contexts. The Flemish rebels phrased their demands of an

---

97   Dumolyn 2008b, pp. 22–3.
98   Nicholas, David 1988.
99   'Se Jaques d'Artevelle vivoit, nos coses seroient en boin estat; nous arions pais à nostre vollenté, et seroit nos sires li contes tous lies, quant il nous poroit tout pardonne', Kervyn de Lettenhove, ed. 1867–77, vol. 9, p. 373.
100   Prevenier 1985, p. 298.
101   Lett and Offenstadt, eds 2003, p. 14.
102   Slogans in Italian cities are well recorded. In 1318, for instance, the inhabitants of the city of Siena who suffered hardships under the patrician regime of the Nine shouted 'Viva il popolo!' and 'Long live the people and the guilds!', see Bowsky 1981, p. 133. For a similar case in Florence in 1370, see Cohn 1999, p. 117.
103   Justice, Jean 1891, p. 16.

economic, monetary or fiscal nature in terms of the discourse of responsible city governance that the urban governments usually propagated themselves. The guilds' position on taxation is a case in point. Tax increases frequently inflamed the populace of Flemish cities during unfavourable eco-nomic climates. As in many medieval cities and towns, the slogan 'Down with the taxes' often resounded through the guild gatherings in Ghent, Bruges and Ypres, but in fact this was not the central issue for the Flemish craftsmen. Being a part of the commune and paying taxes for its government, the common townsfolk were primarily concerned that their city be well governed. Burghers usually denounced the unjust division and improper use of tax money by the city oligarchs, but, apart from the most radical groups of rebels, they did not necessarily denounce the taxes themselves. A very early example of this type of protest was the so-called 'complaint of the commoners of Damme' in 1280. This petition shows a clear understanding of the difference between what we would today call progressive and regressive taxes.[104] In Ypres in 1477, the craft guilds gathered in the market square shouting 'Abolish the *cueillote*' (*tafdoen van den cueillote*), which was an indirect tax imposed by Charles the Bold's hated officers.[105] The economic programme of the Flemish urban rebels, however, went much further than mere fiscal protest. 'Stop collecting the tax, before we start asking for more', other craftsmen threatened during the same Ypres revolt.[106] Fiscal demands were inextricably connected to a more general opposition to urban economic policies and were expressed in the classic terms of peace, justice and the common weal. On different occasions, such as in Bruges in 1436, 1477 and 1488, rebels formulated elaborate petitions listing very concrete measures concerning economic and monetary policies designed to create a stable climate of investment, so that, according to the keywords of their ideology, 'trade and industry could flourish'; these were 'the foundations of the land of Flanders'.[107]

There was often a thin line between insults and threats to the mob's political opponents and the display of a social and political consciousness such as the one encountered in the rebel petitions. Rebel insults often derived from genuine political reflections similar to the central ideas expressed in more official examples of guild ideology. A typical term of abuse, present in both judicial and literary sources of the medieval Low Countries, for instance, was the expression *leevereeter* or *mangeur de foie* ('liver eater'). This offensive term was generally

---

104   Prevenier 2002.
105   Justice, Jean 1891, p. 18.
106   'Cortet en doetter al af, eer wy meer heerschen', Diegerick 1848, p. 429.
107   Examples are quoted in Dumolyn 2010b.

aimed at corrupt officers or aldermen, or the city or princely government in general. In an early sixteenth-century rhetorician poem, which expresses an ideology typical of these middle-class literary guilds, the liver eaters are presented as the main enemies of peace, as greedy pigs filling their gluttonous bellies, and as burning and looting wolves and scorpions.[108] Over the course of the fifteenth century, the insult was used during several different Flemish rebellions. In Bruges, for example, wage-workers shouted 'the big liver eater is imprisoned' at the sheriff of the town when he was arrested for corruption in March 1488.[109] The armed Ghent rebels of 1432 marched to the city hall, crying 'by the wounds and bowels, we will find the liver eaters'.[110] This formulation probably referred to the wounds of the Lord, but the term 'liver eaters' was also linked to the aforementioned 'organologic' views which compared the city to a body that could be harmed by the corrupt acts of individuals. In this case, according to rebel ideology, people who ate the 'liver' of the city damaged the most important part of its 'body politic'. Medieval medicine saw the liver as the source of all necessary body fluids, but, medical models aside, the basic idea of eating one's liver is expressive enough. Shouting slogans and uttering threats as they marched, the rebels inflicted symbolic violence on the internal enemies of the city. Shouted slogans, such as 'Bad government!', also charged the urban governors with comparable misdeeds.[111] The next step could be looting and burning their houses, acts that were not carried out in a random fashion, but rather in a very selective and almost disciplined way. By accusing someone of this severe crime, rebels legitimised the punishment of those who were accused of corruption, since they claimed that it was a necessary action to cure 'a wounded town'.

In 1467, a group of rebels used the rallying cry 'God and the good city of Ghent, kill all those in government! And all those who have collected taxes, kill them all, let no one escape'.[112] The rhythmic structure of the Middle Dutch text, and of several other similar examples, shows that it was meant to be chanted or sung. If a mob of thousands was shouting such phrases in unison, this would obviously have an extremely intimidating effect on the aldermen hiding in the

---

108 Lyna and van Eeghem, eds 1929–30, vol. 1, pp. 135–7. The fifteenth-century Bruges poet Anthonis De Roovere also puts the word *leevereeter* into the mouth of the babbling people, see Mak, ed. 1955, pp. 326–7.

109 *'Die grooten leveretere es ghevanghen'*, Despars 1837–40, vol. 4, p. 382. He was called a 'merciless rascal' ('*onghenadighe bouve*').

110 Fris 1900a, p. 169. See also the *mangeurs de foie* mentioned by Kervyn de Lettenhove, ed. 1863–6, vol. 5, p. 270.

111 '*Quaet regiment*', Fris 1900a, p. 175; '*quaet beleet*', Lambin, ed. 1835, p. 5.

112 '*God ende die goede stede van Ghent, slaet al doot dat heeft regiment ende die de kaliote hebben ontfaen, slaet al doot, laet nyemans ontgaen*', de Pauw, 1893–1914, vol. 2, p. 395.

city hall. Using a rhetoric of violence targeted at the moral failings of rulers, these shouted slogans did not attack the urban government as a whole, but just those who had failed to fulfil their proper role as good governors. Here again, having 'dialogically appropriated' (in the sense given to this expression by Bakhtin) learned political discourses about 'good lordship' or 'good government', rebels sought to hold up the mirror to magistrates, asking them to correct their faults and remedy the particular grievance that lay at the heart of the protest.[113] Cries like *justicie* ('justice'), as in Ghent in 1451, were utilised by rebels to legitimise the elimination of their political opponents and to persuade fellow inhabitants of their own 'just' intentions.[114] But the primary reason rebels employed cries for justice, which was also a common practice in Mediterranean cities, was to show the rulers that the inhabitants of the city had had enough of corruption and arbitrary justice.[115] Other typical terms of abuse, like *les traitteurs* ('the traitors', 1378, in Ghent) or *mal fauls echevins* ('evil, false aldermen', 1320, in Ypres), had the same intention. Considering the rulers of the city to be traitors or bad rulers who did not pursue the *bonum commune*, the rebels voiced a set of expectations about the proper exercise of civic power, turning the official political discourses of the elites against them and accusing them of 'bad government' (typically referred to in the sources as *maulvais gouvernement* or *quaede regheringe*).[116]

8 Radicals' Speech

But apart from the ideals of the politically emancipated groups about just government and moral economy, there also existed another type of mental and social world in the major Flemish cities. The political speech circulating among unskilled workers newly arrived from the countryside and of the poorer and younger artisans who did not hold political power in their craft guild seems to have been rather more unpolished and direct, expressed through coarse laughter and scatological language, insults and violent menace. This rude language was also uttered among the urban elites. In 1478, for instance, Renier Houtmaerct, a respectable man in Bruges, publicly offended the future burgo-

---

113 A similar analysis was made by Walter, who studied discourse about 'good kingship' in early modern England, Walter 2007, p. 99. See also Offenstadt 2007, pp. 137–8.
114 Fris, ed. 1901–4, vol. 1, p. 173.
115 Brucker 1983, p. 152; Challet 2005b, p. 90.
116 See, for instance, Kervyn de Lettenhove, ed. 1867–77, vol. 9, p. 179; De Pelsmaeker 1914, p. 255.

master Willem Moreel with the common insult *hoerezeune* ('son of a whore').[117] Such vulgar language was therefore not used only in the lower ranks of the craft guilds, as it seems to have been quite common in all social strata in the town.[118] However, circumstantial factors and the social position of those who uttered the subversive speech determined which type of language was considered illicit, or an infraction against the rules of speaking. There are numerous examples of rude protest that occurred during guild meetings in a guild house, in which rules, customs and hierarchies had to be respected. Those who broke the rules with bad-mannered language and behaviour were severely punished. In 1532, the shipper Willem Van Cuul was exiled from the city of Bruges because he had 'loudly insulted' the governors of his guild, who were gathered in the chapel of their guild house. He had called them 'thieves, drinkers, eaters and lickers who were not worthy to be in the council'.[119] In 1527, the fishmonger Thomas Haghebaert had shouted to the dean and the sworn men of his guild: 'I will have nothing to do with you or with the magistrate. I shit on you and on the aldermen and on all those who think they can harm me!' He was exiled as well, a heavy punishment for a serious crime.[120] In the same year, Peter Mansepreuve was exiled from Bruges because, 'rebelliously and foolhardily', he had publicly sworn that guild rules would not hinder him from taking revenge in a quarrel with another artisan.[121] In this case Mansepreuve was banished, not so much because he had promised revenge, but because he had publicly questioned the authority of the leading members of the craft guild.

Yet, during several rebellions in late medieval Flanders, ordinary craftsmen succeeded in disrupting the dominant discourse of their middle-class leaders by shouting loudly during meetings in the guild houses or in the market square. These radicals clearly belonged to a more adversarial and largely oral political culture and were often inexperienced in politics. They were not sufficiently integrated within the institutional structures of the craft guilds and had not mastered the official discourses used in presenting demands or requests to superiors. When radical proletarians went too far in brutally confronting the elites during guild assemblies in the market square, they would usually be

---

117 Haemers 2009, p. 222.
118 Hendrik Callewier has shown that similar insults were also commonly used among the Bruges clergy, see Callewier 2011, pp. 379–82.
119 'Zegghende ende roupende overluudt, dat zy alle bouven, scudden, zuupers, eters ende leckers waren ende niet weerdich te zyne in den eedt', Schouteet 1962, p. 425.
120 'Ic en hebbe met u, noch met de wet niet te doene, ic schyte in ulieden ende in scepenen, ende in al deghonne die my deeren moghen', ibid., p. 420.
121 Ibid., p. 416.

silenced by their own middle-class leaders, since the latter wanted their petitions to be heard in accordance with institutionalised practices. In April 1477, after five days of assembly in the market square of Bruges, the first signs of protest appeared against the craft guild leadership who had led the revolt. A chronicler informs us that while they were remonstrating against the high taxes the Burgundian dukes had imposed on the city, 'a curious shout' arose in the market square, a claim that the leaders of the guilds had been bribed by the city government.[122] This was not a wild rumour, but rather a political message from the craftsmen who were asking their guild leaders to take decisive action. The term 'shout' not only meant that they used a high tone of voice, a *roup* or *roepinghe* also meant a slogan or a rallying cry for seditious mobilisation. The radical craftsmen came from a different political and social background from that of the craft guild leaders who had demanded political participation at the urban council a month earlier. Cries of 'Kill them! Kill them!' (*slaet doot, slaet doot*) resounded through the square. The extremists shouted that they wanted other, more radical leaders who would force the urban government to make concessions, with violence if necessary. But a significant number of craftsmen shuddered at the thought of chaos and feared a takeover by radicals. Recognising the danger to their authority, guild leaders scrambled to regain control over the assembled craftsmen. The dean of the blacksmiths took the lead and called the craftsmen to order, yelling: 'Everyone under his banner!' After shouting a renowned formula in guild ideology, that of 'Unity!', the craftsmen obeyed.[123]

It is because of the threat posed by the 'perlocutionary' act of the *roepinghe*, not only to the patrician elites but also to middle-class revolt leaders themselves, that the Flemish chronicles generally referred to these most radical urban rebels as 'shouters and criers' (*roupers ende creesers*).[124] Documents of repression often called them the 'shepherds and instigators' of a revolt.[125] During the Ypres revolt of 1477, at a certain point a man named Arnoud Scoop came towards the gardeners of the city who were weeding the field outside a city gate, 'and he made a cry' (*ende gaf enen roup*) that all prisoners would be released. 'With that cry', so testified the dean of the small trades of Ypres afterwards, 'the people came inside the city', and upon reaching the market they

---

122 'Eenen wonderlicken roup', Vorsterman, ed. 1531, fol. 183ʳ.
123 The 'alleman onder sijnen standaert' was followed by 'eendrachticheyt', ibid. For a more detailed discussion of this protest, see Haemers 2009, pp. 170–1.
124 Dumolyn 2008a, p. 120.
125 'Meeste sceperaers ende upstellers', see Justice, Jean 1891, p. 22.

set up a mock execution for a local nobleman called Jan Van Lichtervelde.[126] A certain Maes Raffin was one of the most dangerous criers in Ypres. He was accused, among other things, of being the principal leader and demagogue who incited the commoners to close the gates to prevent John of Luxembourg, a noble from an important family connected to the Burgundian court, from entering the city. Raffin was reported to have been in the marketplace shouting to the common people: *Filz de putain, fermez les portes*' ('Sons of a whore, shut the gates').[127] Leaders of the craft guilds were aware of the revolutionary potential of the crowd, and therefore often tried to prevent such slogans from being uttered. In 1451 the rebellious government of Ghent (made up of representatives of the craft guilds) decided that any kind of *roupynghe* would be punished with hanging, and the same went for making a *loope*, literally a 'run', in the sense of 'riot' or 'tumult', the bodily movement that went hand in hand with the seditious 'shout'.[128] Craftsmen who wanted to say something in public during the guild meetings in the market square first had to ask their guild dean for permission.[129] The deans therefore remained in control of the 'verbal space' during the collective action of the rank and file.

As was the case with the threats against the liver eaters, radical slogans were often accompanied by calls for retribution for the injuries that the 'bad rulers' had inflicted upon the 'body politic' of the city. The most typical and direct slogan of this kind was obviously *slaet doot* ('kill them'), as at Bruges in 1488. This 'culture of retribution', as William Beik has termed it, publicly demonstrated which acts would not be tolerated by rebels.[130] Accordingly, variations on the slogan 'kill the traitors', used in many European regions, demonstrated a clear political vision.[131] In the revolt of 1477, the Ypres criers were extremely unhappy with the moderate approach to tax reform which was proposed in the meeting of the Ypres burghers. Certain well-off burghers had expressed 'different opinions' (*diversche opinioenen*) about abolishing the grain taxes, but this was not enough for the radical party. Men from the 'small guilds' (the retail trades) entered the meeting and 'illegitimately' said: 'We want them all abolished: all means all!' One burgher tried to propose the abolition of the taxes on food, *mercerie* and salt, but a radical rebel who was there with his compan-

---

126   Ibid., p. 15.
127   Ibid., p. 49 (the original phrase was probably spoken in Dutch, but written down in French).
128   Fris, ed. 1901–4, vol. 1, p. 216.
129   Ibid., p. 184.
130   Beik 1997, chapter 3.
131   For instance in Ferrara, in 1385, Dean, ed. 2000, p. 175.

ions, 'without having been asked', simply kept repeating: 'we don't want some of them to remain', and 'all means all!'[132] The same man is also reported to have said: 'if they want us to sleep, we shall wake, because everything the lords think is false'.[133] At one point during the same revolt, the apprentice weavers of Ypres thought that their own leaders were too weak. 'We want the stick in our hands, like those of Ghent and Bruges have!', they shouted to the headman of the textile industry, who was one of the main figures in the rebel leadership.[134] When the four captains of Ypres, who at that time were the military leaders of the revolt, proposed that the prisoners should be brought before the aldermen, the criers found this too moderate. 'We don't want them before the magistrate, we want a new magistrate!', *tghemeente* ('the commoners') said.[135] There was widespread impatience at that moment, and radical ideas circulated through the city streets and alleyways. A certain Foriaen Denis had supposedly said *'que le temps estoit venu que les riches n'auroient rien à leur, ne les povres à leur vie'* ('the time had come that the rich would have nothing for themselves, nor the poor their lives for long').[136] A comparable radical shout arose against the count of Flanders, Louis of Nevers, during the revolt of coastal Flanders in 1323–8. Hendrik de Meyere was punished after the revolt because he had said in public that he hoped that the castle of the count in Wijnendale near Bruges would be burnt down. De Meyere allegedly wished that a spark of the fire, which had been started by troops of the count in order to destroy the village of Deinze, 'should fly to the castle of Wijnendale', he said, 'so that he [the count] would suffer enough'.[137]

These fragments present some of the political discourse uttered by popular classes without having been restyled and rephrased in the more acceptable language which was spoken in the guild house and which can be encountered in medieval petitions. It was a rather brutal language but also an intelligent one. The 'criers and shouters' understood that they had to demand immediate change when they had the advantage, when it was too difficult to punish them for their illegitimate utterances in official meetings – the sort of outbursts which would normally be paid for with their heads. The artisans could often claim discursive space in the political scene, but the impunity with which

---

132   Justice, Jean 1891, pp. 18–19, 26, 34. In this context *mercerie* referred not to cloth but to fancy goods such as jewellery, glassware and pottery.

133   *'Car tout est faulx que les seigneurs pensent'*, ibid., p. 63.

134   Ibid., p. 28.

135   Ibid., p. 25.

136   Ibid., p. 52.

137   *'Datter wel ene spaerke vlieghen mochte van Duensen te Wynendale omme Wynedale te verbarne, ende dat hi dicken ghenoech daerbi lede'*, de Pauw 1899a, p. 687.

their incursions could be carried out was dependent on status, laws and social rules as well as the balance of political forces at a given time. There were many moments when even the most powerful of princes were forced to listen to their unruly Flemish subjects. At such points, individuals were perhaps not allowed to speak for themselves, but the *populus* or *communitas* could speak as a whole. When the French king Philip the Fair entered the city of Ghent in 1301, the inhabitants 'loudly clamoured and at the same moment petitioned' (*fortiter clamavit et instanter ab ipso petiit*).[138] This fragment of the Ghent Annals written by an anonymous Greyfriar demonstrates that political clamour often went hand in hand with the formulation and the presentation of a petition. The shouting of the mob that accompanied the presentation of grievances to the lord was one form of disobedience, but remaining silent could be another form, the so-called *malum taciturnitatis*, which showed great *superbia*.[139] When King Philip the Fair entered Bruges for a second time in 1301, to his great surprise the people did not cheer him but '*stetit quasi muta*', in order to demonstrate their protest against the taxes.[140] Indeed, at that point the act of collective silence must have been the most powerful way for the commoners to show their defiance.

9   A Culture of Subversive Speech

There are a number of Flemish examples of 'pseudo-prophecies' or 'political prophecies', a genre that allows for a kind of indirect discourse on contemporary reality. These so-called prophecies, full of religious and symbolic references, were falsely backdated and commented on past or contemporary political events as if they would take place in the future.[141] One of these texts, the 'Prophecy of the Blacksmith of Huise', which contains some curious references to the social and political struggle in Flanders, predicts that a human saviour will come to help the Flemish citizens. Probably written at the end of the fourteenth century, it is loaded with indirect references to the so-called Ghent War of 1379–85, led by rebel leader Philip van Artevelde, son of James. Employing a bestial allegory quite typical for the genre, the text says that the 'boar' (a reference to van Artevelde) would help 'the small animals' against the 'big animals' in 'the land of the lion'. The text describes a variety of rebellious utterances,

---

138   Funck-Brentano, ed. 1896, p. 14.
139   Casagrande and Vecchio 1991, pp. 313–14.
140   Funck-Brentano, ed. 1896, p. 14.
141   De Keyser and Verrycken 1983.

such as the *roupe* of the 'small worms' in their struggle against the 'middle' and 'big worms', and the frequent meetings of the worms 'in their houses' (in other words, their guild houses). The 'middle' worms, the middle-class rebel leaders such as van Artevelde, are set in this text against the 'smaller' ones, the more radical craftsmen who used uncouth speech to utter their claims. The worms object to new taxation ordained 'without consent of the small animals'. More specifically, the prophecy speaks of a *roupe* ('call') uttered by a mysterious old man who suddenly appeared in Kouter square, a site where the Ghent weavers used to gather. The old man says to the artisans: 'Dear beloved brothers, why are you still standing here while your friends in the market square are in need of you?' In the narrative that follows, this prophet-like figure's rebellious call to action is associated with the prophecy of events to come. Another version of this text states that the call was made by a shoemaker, who threw his boot tree so hard at the French soldiers invading Ghent that they ran back to the gates in fear, and many of them were slain by the citizens.[142]

These fascinating allegorical political texts confirm the vital importance of rebellious speech acts in the urban landscape of medieval Flanders. Subversive or critical talk of the political and economic state of affairs was indeed a daily and fundamental force in places like Ghent, Bruges and Ypres. In the final analysis, the political power of the urban popular classes in medieval Flanders may have resided in their numbers and demographic concentration, and in the potential outbursts of violence they could deploy, whether the organised mobilisation of the craft guilds led by the middle-class masters or the more spontaneous and uncontrolled rage of the lowest townsfolk. Endemic urban riots and large-scale revolts were indeed an integral part of Flemish popular politics. But the power of the word – of the critical, subversive or openly defiant speech of ordinary burghers – was an even more consistent factor. Everywhere, even when no real violence broke out afterwards, there could be grumbling, complaining, discussing, shouting and chanting about politics. The belief that the 'authentic' muttering, rumours, jokes, cries and slogans of the medieval common men and women can be fully grasped might be a romantic or idealist illusion, but the relics of such utterances can be found in numerous types of sources originating from medieval Flanders, each imposing specific interpretative obstacles. The general picture, however, is clear: the speech acts through which political discourses were expressed (swearing, speaking out, arguing persuasively in official meetings, or intimidating enemies with brutal threats) did not only exist as 'hidden transcripts', but were instead vital elements within

---

142   De Pauw, 1893–1914, vol. 2, pp. 486, 490.

the political system of the Flemish cities and towns. Middle-class guild masters were not the only ones to envisage distinct political goals by delivering petitions and shouting slogans during assemblies. The political speech of the crowds, which might at first sight seem irrational and uncultivated, was in fact also highly politically effective, and formed an essential part of a rebellious repertoire of symbolic violence. But like the reactionary, moralising Hieronymus Bosch, who painted an evil chicken brooding its egg in the foreground of his Saint Anthony Triptych,[143] contemporary elite writers could not always understand the grievances of the muttering rebels, even if they knew that they posed a potential threat. A man who had been held prisoner by the Ypres rebels in 1477 (and who was therefore clearly a partisan of the urban elite and of Mary of Burgundy) later testified that he had asked a rebel: 'What is it that you are trying to say? In fact, do you even know what you are saying, and what you really want?' The latter answered 'We want the calf skin, and we want it!'[144] Perhaps this rebel did not fully understand in precise legal terms the 'bad privilege' to which he referred when he mentioned the calf skin, but he definitely knew what was at stake, and why he said it.

During the course of the frequent social and political struggles in late medieval Flanders, no single successful ideologically hegemonic discourse can be seen at work, whether it be one associated with the prince and nobles, the rulers in the towns and cities, or the middle class in their guild houses. True enough, the urban middle classes certainly had a rival political culture and self-consciousness, but they never really developed a fully 'alternative' or 'autonomous' political discourse that clearly stood apart from the dominant political languages used by the courtly, noble, clerical and patrician elites. In their utterances in the vernacular, they used the same keywords as those which can be found in almost all learned medieval political discourses (the body politic, the common weal, peace, justice and good government), dialogically rephrasing this dominant ideological register by emphasising political values pertaining to what could be called a guild ideology, in the process reflecting the direct needs of the common townspeople. Their speech acts remained within a dominant ideological framework, but they also demonstrate a struggle over the exact meaning of these keywords within this discourse. Ranging from the rallying cries of lynch mobs to an elaborately constructed juridical justification of a revolt, elements of legitimate political discourses were strategically appropriated by the rebels, who entered the field of negotiation in order to be heard

---

143   Vink 2001.
144   Justice, Jean 1891, p. 18.

and to accomplish their aims. Common workers who did not have the political power to influence daily politics used a more violent and brutal language, vulgar slang and 'popular' expressions to make their wishes clear, but these expressions could be understood by all social strata in the town. The forms and outcomes of these rebel speech acts were determined by the space in which they were performed, and on the specific political balance of forces of the given moment. Only when they failed to influence political decisions with words did the popular classes resort to physical violence to make their point. Violence remained the exception. By contrast, subversive utterances, though always risky, must have been the rule of daily politics in the urban centres of late medieval Flanders and, clearly, in many other European towns and cities as well.

PART 4

Law and Authority

∴

CHAPTER 12

The Legal Repression of Revolts in Late Medieval Flanders

Jan Dumolyn

1 Introduction

Charles Tilly introduced the concept of collective action for studying revolts.[1] Subsequent scholars have fruitfully utilised this framework to analyse a variety of collective acts. Increasingly the concept has also attracted the attention of medieval historians 'from below', especially those interested in analysing organised and spontaneous resistance against authority, the processes of state formation, and the development of capitalism.[2] In medieval Flanders, the concept of collective action can be applied to quite a variety of different movements: revolts of entire communities, spontaneous riots, strikes motivated by hunger, illicit assemblies of workers ('conspiracies'), resistance to princely officers, aldermen, or guild authorities. When consulting many of the general studies of popular revolts during the medieval period, it is striking that not even one of them (Zagorin, Mollat and Wolff, Fourquin, Bercé),[3] devotes even a paragraph to the legal methods authorities used to repress rebellions. Apparently, most authors judged this unnecessary, because they considered themselves to be dealing strictly with social and political phenomena.[4] A similar sentiment can be found among legal historians. The leading scholar of Flemish criminal law never gave the major revolts serious treatment, because he judged that this constituted political rather than legal history.[5] This point of view can be defendable, but it does not diminish the importance of under-

---

1 Tilly 1978 and 1989.
2 Tilly 1990.
3 The most important studies on medieval and early modern revolts include: Mollat and Wolff 1970, for the English translation by Lytton-Sells, see Mollat and Wolff 1973; Czok 1958–9; Barth 1974; Schulz 1992; Blickle 1988; Chevalier 1982; Hilton 1989 (and some other contributions in Gambrelle and Trebitsch, eds 1989); Zagorin 1982; Bercé 1980; Fögen, ed. 1995. For contemporary Belgium in the modern period, see Van Honacker 1994.
4 A notable exception: Romano 1995.
5 Van Caenegem 1954, p. 83, n. 6.

standing the legal forms the repression of revolts took, or the legal discourse authorities used to justify and legitimise the application of these mechanisms.

Tilly considers repression as any act by one group which raises the stakes of collective action for its opponents. The modern state's development culminated in the invention of new and powerful repressive tools. Like contemporary authoritarian regimes, medieval and early modern states and town authorities discouraged popular politics almost by definition. It is not the intention of this article however, to apply a concept developed by sociologists to analyse medieval revolts, revolutions, social struggle, or their repression. Neither will I undertake a detailed analysis of Flemish revolts during the medieval period, either of their causes or organisational forms.[6] Such issues will be discussed only tangentially when they arise in connection with our main topic of concern: the legal discourse used to repress revolts inside medieval Flanders, and how central and local governments organised such repression. The medieval county of Flanders was certainly no stranger to social struggle or different forms of collective action. Quite to the contrary, it is fair to say that within Europe Flanders' experience with such struggles was unrivalled excepting perhaps Northern and Central Italy, which on the whole shared Flanders' high degree of urban development. The medieval Flemish city – and in some cases the countryside as well – proved to be a veritable seedbed for unrest. This was due certainly to an extensive division of labour, the presence of prominent export industries and an educated and politically conscious upper and middle class (including master artisans and relatively independent 'peasants'). These conditions obviously generated a sharp polarisation within medieval society. My study will leave aside private feuds and family vendettas, or any other form of violence that did not have a clear political or social character, although, obviously such phenomena often intermingled with concrete collective acts.[7] I also leave out the crime of treason, despite the fact that many collective actions were often considered treacherous and their leaders deemed traitors. I also exclude phenomena of popular culture such as *charivari* ('rough music') or carnival, which could also be considered collective acts. Most cases of 'collective action' described here could be called 'revolts', 'riots' or 'tumult', dependent on scale and success.

---

6 See Chapter 1 in the present volume.

7 The importance of which – as far as later medieval Flanders is concerned – is blown out of proportion by Nicholas, David 1988; for a balanced view, see Blockmans, Willem 1990b, pp. 21–30.

In a number of cases the documents authorities used for repression are the only sources we have to evaluate past collective action.[8] Consequently, a study of the legal forms repression took is important not only from the point of view of legal history (our primary concern here), but also for sharpening our understanding of the concrete events themselves. More specifically, it is useful in helping to identify connections between the social profile of rebels and their political aims.

In his *Recueil des Antiquités de Flandre*, an institutional and political history of the county of Flanders written in the early sixteenth century (about 1512), the Flemish jurist Filips Wielant devotes over sixty-three pages (over one fifth of the nineteenth-century edition) to rebellions of Flemish people against their prince.[9] Wielant was not some ivory tower philosopher, but one of the most important politicians and practical legal thinkers of his time. He had ample experience with rebellions and revolts himself. At one point he had stood up against the first Habsburg prince of the Netherlands, Maximilian of Austria, although he later submitted together with the rest of the Flemish political elite. On other occasions, he took shelter from urban riots caused by the furious middle and working classes. The social struggles inside Flanders were generally considered by contemporaries to constitute an inescapable feature of their social and political lives, or, to put it more provocatively, one of the oldest and most venerable 'institutions' of their county.[10] Although many of Wielant's comments concern an already relatively distant past, they are particularly significant in relation to Burgundian ideas about collective action and repression. Nevertheless, Wielant's description of more than three hundred years of social struggle and princely reaction to it, in combination with legal sources, indicates that the Burgundians relied upon an already existing and elaborate repressive system for coping with collective action. In addition to Wielant's views on revolts, I have used edited material, primarily comital and urban charters. I also supplemented often outdated monographs on repression with my own research into Flemish revolts during 1436–8.[11] This research included archival sources, accounts of ducal officers, and chronicles. Primary emphasis is placed on the fourteenth and fifteenth centuries, not only because

---

8   Boone and Brand 1993, p. 169.

9   De Smet, Joseph Jean, ed. 1865, pp. 278–342; also see Buntinx 1972 and the introduction in Wielant 1995; on this chronicle: Fris 1901b, pp. 393–407.

10   No medieval man, and not even the chroniclers who were usually more interested in personal than social relations, reduced the main cause of social struggle in Flanders to 'clan politics', as some contemporary authors claim on the basis of one-sided evidence.

11   As in other periods (1323–8, 1379–85, 1449–53) a revolt in a major city triggered or strengthened social struggle in smaller towns and the countryside, see Dumolyn 1997.

more documents survived, but also because collective action became more frequent and intense due to the higher concentration of people, capital, and coercive measures. In an attempt to abstain from further sociological generalisation, let me just observe that a textile workers' quarter in late medieval Flemish cities proved a more fertile place for the genesis of what we might call 'class consciousness', by which I mean insight into mechanisms of exploitation and the common interests of social groups, than a small scale eleventh-century rural manor. According to Wielant, however, the Flemish had already started rebelling in the eleventh century, when several cities defended the claims of count Robert the Frisian. This assumed independent political role of the cities – even before their determined action after the murder of count Charles the Good in 1127 – is however an exaggerated back projection by Wielant of their later positions.[12] The bitter feud between the Ingherkins and the Blavotins in Western Flanders during the twelfth and early thirteenth centuries also merited his attention in the context of revolts. Though this had been a real 'clan war', Wielant saw in it yet another manifestation of rebellion.[13] Anyway, he was right in stressing the precocious political consciousness in the Flemish political space, foremostly in the cities. Since the wave of 'communal revolutions' – urban and rural – in Flanders proved victorious (given the concessions of the succeeding counts), there was no repression at all after revolts like that of Ghent in 1128 against count William Clito, who had broken his oath in disrespecting the urban privileges he had confirmed himself.[14]

2 Legal and Intellectual Background

In general studies of medieval political thought, little attention is given to revolts, rebellions, or any other collective action. This is somewhat surprising in the light of the ample attention given to loyalty and treason.[15] But possibly we can attribute this to the fact that all major theologians and political

---

12 The count had in fact concluded an alliance with the major cities, so as not to be fully dependent on the nobles and knights who had elected him: see the account of these events in Verlinden 1935 and Schulz 1992, p. 118; on 1127, see Ross, ed. 1991; Van Caenegem 1994b; and especially Schulz 1992, pp. 112–18 and *passim*.

13 Warlop 1975–6, vol. 1, pp. 261–4; Fris 1906a; though this struggle involved a refusal of one of the parties to pay taxes to the countess who supported the other side, this was primarily an archaic war between clans led by local ruling families.

14 The most recent reference study is Schulz 1992, pp. 18, 112.

15 Canning 1996; Black 2002; Krynen 1993: some of these do not even devote a single paragraph to revolts.

thinkers were in agreement concerning the atrocity of this crime, typically committed by low life villains, that it was not deemed worthy of discussion. In contrast, treason was a crime usually reserved for more 'notable' people. The early fifteenth-century political theorist Jean de Terrevermeille, who equated all disobedience and rebellion to the crime of *lèse-majesté*, focused on *rebellio* in connection with the feudal concept of *diffiduciatio* (renouncing one's homage to one's lord, in this case principally by the duke of Burgundy) and similar problems of the *ius resistendi* (i.e., the right to resist). Some authors speak of the *rebellio* of the sons of Louis the Pious in 833 (although in this case they believed it justifiable).[16] These were people worth mentioning in learned treatises. Perhaps another reason for the lack of scholarly comment on the subject was Thomas Aquinas's influential opinion. With philosophical rather than theological arguments, quoting both Cicero and Saint Augustine, he concluded that revolt constituted a mortal sin, since the common good was greater than the private good. Only revolts against tyrants were deemed justifiable, because a tyrant was, by definition, not working for the common interest. Unless, he added, interestingly enough, a revolt was so disorderly as to cause more harm to the people than the tyrant's rule.[17]

Apart from the legal tradition already mentioned in connection with feudal law, there also existed other legal concepts for dealing with collective action. In conceptualising this very 'public' criminal act, the influence of Roman law proved influential, primarily in terms of terminology. The political character of collective action tended to generate variation, and even a certain inconsistency, in the terms used to describe it. For instance, specific political circumstances or the prevailing balance of power might dictate quite different responses from the authorities, ranging from full pardons to harsh and bloody repression.

The Romans were certainly no strangers to civil wars, political treason, or revolts of all kinds. In the later Roman period, the concept of *perduellio* (treason) was gradually replaced by the broader term *crimen laesae maiestatis*. In the *Lex Julia Maiestatis*, all crimes against the state fell under this rubric. The *Lex Quisquis*, issued by Arcadius and Honorius in 397 AD, and later recorded in the *Codex Jusitinianus*, further expanded this concept to include the

---

16 Burns, James Henderson, ed. 1988, pp. 220, 224, 489, 492, 506; the new edition of 2008 does not add anything on this subject; on *difficuciatio*, see Ganshof 1957, pp. 157–8; in the later middle ages, this concept was replaced by the more general loss of fief, see Heirbaut 1997, pp. 272–6.

17 Carlyle and Carlyle 1903–36, vol. 6, pp. 81 and 87, quoting Thomas Aquinas, *Summa Theologica*, 2.2, 42.2: '*manifestum est ergo, quod seditio opponitur et justitiae et communi bono; et iseo ex suo genere est peccatum mortale*'.

murder of councillors of the emperor *'nam et ipsi pars corporis nostri sunt'* ('for they are too a part of our body').[18] Under the Roman Republic, violent transitions of power were the rule rather than the exception. This condition ensured that the definition of treason remained quite fluid depending on the context of such acts. In addition, it must be remembered that treason was a concept applied only to collective acts which failed. Gradually this notion of treason evolved from an offence against the *familia* to a political crime against the state.[19] This evolutionary development would repeat itself during the Middle Ages.

In the Merovingian and Carolingian periods, and even later, legitimate political resistance without any result often does not survive in the evidence.[20] Similarly, political crimes are often confused with other capital crimes. According to Carolingian capitularies, lawless people and participants in a *conjuratio* should be tried under the king's law. During the reign of Charles the Bald robbery, rape and conspiracy are treated in the same chapter.[21] The notion of treason, however, was considered a violation of the peace, punishable by the death penalty.[22] Except for military violations, the early Germanic kingdoms knew only one felony against the state: high treason (or treason of state if this is not a somewhat anachronistic formulation for this period): *traditio*. This included revolts and conspiracies. Originally, the notion of treason escaped definition under feudal law. Only later would the concepts of *felonie* and *proditio* emerge. There existed no essential difference between treason against the king and treason against one's political community, which often was defined as treason against the 'peace'. During the 614 council of Paris, an edict of king Clotharius II had already stated: *'Ut pax et disciplina in regno nostro sit, Christo propiciante, perpetua, et ut revellus vel insulentia malorum hominum severissime reprimatur'* ('So that peace and discipline be in our realm, favourable to Christ, and so that the rebel and insolence of evil people by severely punished').[23] In this sense, the Frankish notion was clearly influenced by the *cri-*

---

18   Cuttler 1982, pp. 6–7; *Lex Julia Maiestatis*, Digest 48.4; *Lex Quisquis*, Codex 9.8.5; the *Lex Julia* was presumably issued not by Caesar, but by Augustus, *cfr.* Lear 1965, p. 22; see also Allison and Cloud 1962; Bauman 1967 and 1974. I want to thank Dr. Frederik Vervaet, who studies revolts under Roman rule, for suggesting some of this literature.

19   Lear 1965, pp. 5, 17, 43; we have unfortunately not been able to consult the work of Sbriccoli 1974.

20   Brunner, Karl 1979, p. 14; see also the (often mechanical) 'Marxist-Leninist' views of GDR historians like Epperlein 1975, pp. 211–27.

21   Brunner, Karl 1979, p. 16.

22   Lear 1965, p. 65.

23   Boretius and Krause, eds 1883–97, vol. 1, no. 22, cap. 11, p. 22.

men laesae majestatis of Roman Law, and consequently Frankish sources make frequent use of the expression.[24] Rebellious Lotharingian nobles were at one point referred to as disturbers of the peace and as a *multitudo predonum* ('a multitude of thieves'). In Roman Law *hostes* ('enemies') and *latrunculi vel praedones* ('brigands or thieves') were distinguished. The first referred to external enemies of the state with certain rights of the law of nations, while the later denoted plain robbers, who should be judged under criminal law.[25] The confusion between revolt and other capital crimes persisted throughout the Middle Ages.

The justice of the king and his counts was competent to repress *causae inclitae, coniurationes vel ceterae nefandae res* ('renowned causes, conspiracies or other nefarious things'), such as social and religious guilds: *collectae, quas geldonias vel confratrias vulgo vocant* ('collections [of people] which are commonly called guilds or confraternities'), *convivia* or *conventicula* which brought together people of different social classes, maybe in connection with an ancient pagan rite. These phenomena were far from exceptional during the ninth century, or so it seems.[26] The chief perceived danger with such sworn oaths was that they competed with the oath of fidelity owed to the king.[27] After all, Carolingian laws were written for a tiny elite layer of society. For that reason we might expect that these statutes condemning rebellion were primarily meant for them. Instructions to *missi dominici* ('officials of the lord'), for example, enumerated different criminal cases that endangered the peace: '*De clamatoribus vel causidicis qui nec iuditium scabinorum adquiescere nec blasfemare volunt antiqua consuetudo servetur. De conspirationibus vero, quicumque facere praesumserit et sacramento quamcumque conspirationem firmaverint ut triplici ratione iudicentur*' ('Ancient laws are to be protected for plaintiffs and lawyers who neither want to assent to the judgment of aldermen nor to blaspheme, the ancient custom is to be preserved. However, whoever presumes to produce and secretly strengthen whatever conspiracy, conspiracies are to be condemned for three reasons').[28] However, this sketchy attempt to study some legal concepts

---

24   His 1964, vol. 1, pp. 30–9, 41; a clear summary of the development of the juridical notion of treason can be found in Maes 1947, pp. 318–19; Brunner, Heinrich 1892, vol. 3, pp. 685–7.

25   Brunner, Karl 1979, pp. 17–19; see also Kern 1954, p. 170.

26   Brunner, Karl 1979, pp. 17–19; see also Coornaert 1948, p. 31; Oexle 1995 and 1985; for Carolingian *conjurationes*, see Epperlein 1969; Staab 1975, pp. 371–9.

27   His 1964, vol. 1, p. 20, '*Genossenschaftliches und monarchisches Prinzip standen einander unversöhnlich gegenüber*'.

28   Boretius and Krause, eds 1883–97, vol. 1, no. 44, cap. 8 and 10, pp. 123–4: '*Capitulare missorum in Theodonis villa datum secundum, generale. Ad omnes generaliter. De pace, ut omnes qui per aliqua scelera ei rebelles sunt constringantur*' which according to de Clercq

of these confusing and nebulous periods is perhaps not very relevant here. In fact, there seems to be little continuity between Merovingian and Carolingian terminology and the actual topic of this article. Nevertheless, it can serve as an indication for the continuity of the phenomenon of collective action – including some of its organisational forms – and its repression throughout Western European history.

3 Manorial Rebellions

In eleventh- and twelfth-century documents from the Southern Low Countries it is interesting to note the context in which words like *rebellio, insurgere* or *seditio* ('rebellion', 'to rise', 'sedition') were used.[29] A charter given by Emperor Henri VI to the abbey of Saint-Ghislain notes that *'si quis de familia monasterii abbati suo rebellis inventus fuerit ex iudicio et districtione parium suorum ad satisfactionem abbatis cogatur'* ('If anyone of the household of the monastery is found to be rebellious to his abbot, he should be constrained by the judgement and discretion of his peers to the satisfaction of the abbot.').[30] In another charter for the Flemish abbey of Ninove, issued by count Philip in 1167, *rebellis* is again used in the general sense of resisting or offering opposition to authority.[31] The verb *insurgere* (apart from its use in the sense of 'to occur') holds the same meaning in many other charters.[32] For example, a 1116 charter of the chapter of Saint Lambert in Liège mentions *'in popularibus sturmis et burinis'* (roughly, 'in risings and riots by the people'). Jan Niermeyer's *Mediae latinitatis lexicon minus* gives even earlier examples of these terms meaning 'riot' and 'violent fight': *'numquam [advocatus] se intromittet de aliqua justitia ibi facienda vel de sturma sive burina'* ('so that no lawyer intervenes in whatever judicial mat-

---

1936, vol. 1, p. 208, should be dated in 805–6; see also Ganshof 1955. I thank Dr. S. Vanderputten for suggesting literature on the Carolingian epoch.

29   *Thesaurus Diplomaticus*, now available at www.diplomata-belgica.be/colophon_fr.html. On this database for 'Belgian' charters before 1200, edited by Brepols, Turnhout 1997, see Demonty 2000.

30   Thesaurus Diplomaticus, D4246, *familia* relating to serfs of the abbey in this case; Niermeyer 1976, p. 885, translates *rebellio* as 'contradiction' or 'protest'.

31   Thesaurus Diplomaticus, D5152, *'siquis vero rebellis nos ausire noluerit sed dominium nostrum subterfugerit'*; Ibid., D4840 (a° 1088), *'et si forte ipsa persona episcopo inobediens a judicio sinodali se substraxerit vel sibi vel abbati rebellis extiterit ...'*; Ibid., D3625 (a° 1082), *'monachus qui abbati fuerit rebellis'*.

32   Thesaurus Diplomaticus, D3983, D4442; this meaning is also given by Niermeyer 1976, p. 547.

ters are there be done or in *troubles* or *disturbances*', Liège 1034). In my view the word *sturmus* or *sturma*, derived from the Germanic 'Sturm' – this refers specifically in the Walloon area to *burina* – could perhaps be a typical word for a collective action inside the manorial context.[33] Maybe, these phenomena could be considered in the context of the introduction of seigniorial power or new levies,[34] a process that was undoubtedly often resisted by peasants. Many of these charters evoke the respective judicial rights of ecclesiastical institutions and their *advocati*. We are probably dealing here with very small-scale local 'rebellions' or 'revolts'. These actions perhaps involved a dozen farmers refusing to pay certain seigniorial dues to their lord or to appear before his court, or even smaller and more isolated forms of protest. The sources for these kinds of collective actions are of course extremely few in numbers for continental Europe. Nevertheless, the fact that these crimes got specific names proves that they reflected a certain social reality. The case of a potential *'rebellione aliqua rusticorum'* ('some rebellion of the peasants'), mentioned in the 1103 charter for the abbey of Saint-Jacques in Liège, is difficult to put inside this context, since the document is considered a forgery by diplomatists.[35] As a comparison: the Norman cleric Wace who wrote the *Roman de Rou* around 1170 offers an interesting description of a peasant revolt that took place in Normandy around 1000. The peasants assembled in groups of twenty to a hundred (*'parlemenz'*), swore oaths, and labelled their lords enemies because among other things they had usurped common fields and woods.[36] In any case his narrative reflects twelfth-century realities.[37] Similar small-scale phenomena might have been much more prevalent during the high Middle Ages than the scarcity of sources suggests. They were usually violently smashed rather than tried before a court.[38]

During the eleventh and twelfth centuries, the church condemned rebels as *corruptores*, *violatores pacis*, *perfidies* and *infidels* ('corruptors', 'violators of the peace', 'betrayers', 'infidels') because they joined a *conjuratio* or *pactio communis* not based on the church itself. Apart from this classic condemnation of any type of grouping, the key word here is *pax*. It represents an ideology

---

33   Thesaurus Diplomaticus, D1389.
34   For a recent assessment of these problems see: Köhn 1991; Hilton 1973, pp. 63–95; Eggert 1975 and 1971; Epperlein 1989; Hilton 1974.
35   Thesaurus Diplomaticus, D5306; Niermeyer 1935, pp. 38–41; Stiennon 1951, pp. 38–42, 98–9; however, this does not mean that the document was entirely fake or that the expressions used are necessarily completely alien to the period.
36   Oexle 1995, pp. 122–3; Holden, ed. 1970, vol. 1, pp. 191–6.
37   Köhn 1991, p. 373.
38   Ibid., p. 375; Hilton 1973, p. 65.

used by princes and cities to extend their powers under the device (or pretext) of 'preserving the peace'. Robert Fossier cynically defined this peace as the 'expression of legalised violence'. Rebels refused to submit to peace because they were crushed by it.[39] According to the theories of Marx, Weber, Elias, Tilly and others, the monopoly on legitimate (or *legitimised*) force constitutes one of the principal criteria for the development of state power. In Flanders, this phenomenon took shape for the first time with the introduction of the *pax comitis*.[40]

4   A New Public Law

To construct a new public law, that left behind purely feudal and religious principles – which of course had still included the *ius resistendi*, an unthinkable concept in the developing modern state – not only Roman laws were invoked, but also the influential concept of *utilitas publica*.[41] The interests of the prince were identified with that of the 'public'. This can be seen quite explicitly in places that witnessed an early and thorough influence of Roman law, like twelfth-century Sicily.[42] In Flanders, in the course of the twelfth century, all major crimes were considered offences against the count and his *pax comitis*. As such, they were subject to his jurisdiction and punishable by a fine of sixty pounds paid directly to him.[43]

In medieval Flemish sources (documents of the repression, chroniclers, and hagiographers like Galbert of Bruges, Walter of Thérouanne and the jurist Wielant) we meet the words *traditor, tradere, perfidus, conspirare, rebellare, insurgere, trahison, trahir, conspiration, desloyauté, sedition, verrader*. The knights who conspired against Robert the Frisian were called *traditores* ('traitors'). The 1127 murderers of count Charles the Good were labelled *perfidi* ('disloyal'), guilty of *conspirare* ('to conspire') and *rebellionem parare* ('to prepare rebellion'). The feudal concept of disloyalty, the breaking of personal ties and treason remain interwoven in their terminological usage.[44] The early thirteenth-century large scale clan war in coastal Flanders inspired the count to secure his jurisdiction over the construction of illegal fortifications and viol-

---

39   Fossier 1973, pp. 46–9; see for the *pax dei* Strubbe 1984, pp. 489–501.
40   Van Caenegem 1954, pp. 17–24; Lévy and Rousseaux 1992, pp. 251, 262–3.
41   Cuttler 1982, p. 15.
42   Romano 1995, p. 141.
43   Van Caenegem 1954; De Gryse 1969, pp. 7–13; Platelle 1971, pp. 115–16, 119–23.
44   Van Caenegem 1954, p. 81.

ence inside churches, which originally belonged to the aldermen of the rural castellanies. These rural courts never judged cases of rebellion. They were comital from the very beginning.[45] In the cities, on the other hand, the main comital officers, the *burchgraven* ('castellans'), seem to have lost jurisdiction to urban aldermen – who were appointed by the count as well – already by 1127. Although the new comital office of bailiff received most of the rights of the earlier castellan, city aldermen acquired more and more autonomy during the twelfth and thirteenth centuries. Especially during the twelfth century, urban benches were created everywhere.[46]

5   Lèse-majesté

In his classic study on the *'cas royaux'* Ernest Perrot did not clearly state whether the medieval notion of *lèse-majesté* was derived from the German concept of *infidelitas*, or whether it was a Roman idea which had survived from antiquity. In its full development in later medieval French jurisprudence, *lèse-majesté* already encompassed various crimes. First, it included every assault on the person of the king or his sovereign power. Secondly, there was a tendency to include assaults on his patrimony, that of officers and servants, or any failure to obey his explicit commands. In most cases, however, *lèse-majesté* only included clear attacks on the *res publica*. Related offences were labelled *conspiraciones, monopolia illicita* or *congregationes*.[47] The wider, more 'state-orientated' notion of *lèse-majesté* seems to have remained theoretical until the fifteenth century. This is revealed in Jean Boutillier's distinction between *lèse-majesté* and crimes against the public order (sedition, monopoly and conspiracy).[48] On some occasions, princes proved more outspoken about whose interests were at stake. In 1324, the count of Flanders ordered his uncle Robert of Cassel to punish the rebels of the Liberty of Bruges. He regarded this revolt not only as contrary to his own interest, but to that of proprietors in general, *'de nous, de vous et de tous*

---

45   Ganshof 1932, p. 44.

46   Blommaert 1915, pp. 29–30; Ganshof 1938, pp. 164, 175; on the *schepenen* ('aldermen') see Boone 1995a.

47   Perrot 1910, pp. 27–8: in 1335 Philip VI mentions *'pluribus conspiracionibus, monopoliis, congregacionibus illicitis, et super pluribus aliis casibus et excessibus enormibus per ipsos in nostrum jurisque nostri regni ac majestatis regie subditorumque nostrorum prejudicium atque dampnum'* perpetrated by revolting merchants of Carcassonne, Toulouse and Montpellier.

48   Ibid.; Boutillier 1603, pp. 170–2.

signeurs terriens.[49] Mentioning the ideological fiction of the public weal in this private letter was not necessary. This was a clear appeal to the class consciousness of large landowners.

The medieval concept of *lèse-majesté* developed further as the state expanded by slowly appropriating principles of Roman law.[50] According to Germanic custom, *lèse-majesté* was only possible against the king himself. From the twelfth century onwards, however, it came to be applied to any revolt or conspiracy against the lower territorial princes, especially in those principalities where the central authority was most fully developed. An 1142 comital charter given to the abbey of Ninove stated that whoever caused damage to the abbey was guilty of offending against the *'Flandrensis maiestatis reus'*.[51] In the later Middle Ages, the dukes of Brittany judged themselves competent in cases of *lèse-majesté* against themselves.[52] In the case of Normandy, Perrot even uses the expression *'cas ducaux'* to stress how from the twelfth century onwards the duke of Normandy deemed himself competent to enforce the 'peace' around his person.[53] At the end of the twelfth century, the theory of 'reserved cases' arose not from a reworking of Roman legal precepts, but from feudal principles. Although there never was a full enumeration of such cases composed (not to hinder further extension of royal competence), *lèse-majesté* or any infringement on the public order and public peace were definitively labelled 'royal cases'. In Flanders, however, this theory was still not fully developed during the fourteenth century. The ordinance of 1409 for the Council of Flanders, the superior comital court in Flanders under Burgundian rule, remained vague on reserved cases and its terminology was not very explicit.[54] It was only in 1540 that the term *cas de souveraineté* was used for the first time in the so-called *Concessio Carolina*, by which emperor Charles V punished the rebellious city of Ghent. In the comital *Audiëntie*, predecessor of the Council of Flanders during the fourteenth century, these cases were referred to as *'mesdaet jeghen min heere'*, *'meffait devers monseigneur'* (meaning the same thing, 'misdeeds against my Lord') and cases belonging to the rights and seigniory of our lord (*'also minen heeren rechte ende herlicheit toe-*

---

49   Limburg-Stirum 1879–89, vol. 2, p. 369.
50   Van Caenegem 1954, p. 83.
51   His 1964, pp. 40–1; see the edition of this charter in de Hemptinne, Verhulst and De Mey 1988–2009, vol. 1, pp. 112–13; a similar example is the charter the same count issued for the abbey of Marchiennes in 1155, *'Quisquis igitur privilegio nostro obviare temptaverit iram dei et nostram incurret et reus maiestatis'*.
52   Jones, Michael 1984, p. 91.
53   Perrot 1910, p. 304.
54   Ibid.; Buntinx 1949, pp. 180–1, 188–9, 195–205; Leyte 1996, p. 169.

behoort'). These expressions cannot be equated with the crime of *lèse-majesté* because they only indicated the reason why a particular criminal offence was judged by the court. The legal theories jurists later invoked to explain the handling of such cases by the count's council, were nothing but justifications of a factual situation. In other words, there was an extension of comital power at the expense of the lords and the lower courts of justice. In a 1350 conflict concerning the textile industry between two cities, Louis of Male stated that the case belonged to him because it arose from mutiny and civil war.[55]

In the writings of the early fifteenth century French jurist Jean de Terrevermeille there was a fusion of feudal and Roman concepts: *crimen laesae maiestatis* was used in connection with *infidelitas* ('disloyalty'). Indeed, a fifteenth-century sentence in France (though concerning treason *stricto sensu* in this case and not rebellion) described the crime as '*crimen laesae maiestatis*', '*proditio*' and '*conspiratio*', conceived '*contra fidelitatem ad quam domino Regi tenetur*' ('against the loyalty that is held for the lord King').[56] As a foremost anti-Burgundian intellectual, De Terrevermeille accused duke John the Fearless of *lèse-majesté* because he caused damage to the *status regis*, the *status regni*, and the *res publica* ('the condition of the king', 'the condition of the kingdom', and of the 'commonweal'). According to his political philosophy, the duke was a 'mystical member' who was not obedient enough to the *voluntas capitis* ('the will of the head') of the political body and this implied *lèse-majesté*.[57] It does not seem, however, that theories of this kind had any real influence on the categories judges used for repressing *lèse-majesté*. However, these concepts indicate that the medieval concept of *lèse-majesté* was a mixture of Roman law, feudal law, and theology. Philip of Leyden, a fourteenth-century political theorist writing for the count of nearby Holland and famous for his *De Cura Rei Publicae et Sorte Principantis* ('On the care of the state and the role of the ruler'), looked for casuistic arguments in Roman Law to support the count's authority. He concluded that, strictly speaking, the crime of *lèse-majesté* was only possible against the emperor, not against a duke, count, or baron. He acknowledged, however, that others believed it also applied to lower princes recognised as wielding imperial authority. Some also argued that lower princes acting inside their own jurisdiction should be considered a *princeps* in his own territory, since the empire

---

55 Buntinx 1949, p. 187; de Pauw 1899b, p. 248; it was the abbot of Saint-Bertin, lord of Poperinge, who had claimed competence, see below note 94.

56 Cuttler 1982, p. 24.

57 Barbey 1983, pp. 246–7.

was divided. In this sense any attack on a count's councillor constituted *lèse-majesté*. Others steadfastly denied this.[58]

The fourteenth century jurist Philippe de Beaumanoir did not pronounce himself on the problem explicitly, but he speaks of *mefés* committed against the count of Clermont. This essentially refers to the same idea. In the early fourteenth century, Petrus Jacobi in his *Practica* argued that *lèse-majesté* was impossible against the king because he was not the emperor. Degrassalius, however, in his *Regalium Francie Jura Omnia* (lib. II, jus XX) stated that it was '*quia rex Franciae est imperator in suo regno*' ('because the king of France is the emperor in his kingdom').[59] In contemporary ideological writings (favourable to him), the duke of Burgundy was portrayed as the defender of the *chose publicque* and as a representative of God. A rebellion against him and the public order constituted a revolt against the Creator himself.[60] The *Anciennes Coutumes* of the duchy of Burgundy state that the duke of Burgundy was competent '*à cause de sa pairie*' (i.e., due to his seigneurial dignity) on *lèse-majesté* committed in Burgundy against his person.[61] He was not competent to judge those committed against the king. However, in a 1390 requisitory the royal prosecutor before the Parliament of Paris noted that '*il y a crime de leze majesté, de quoy monseigneur de Bourgogne ne peut cognoistre*' ('there is a crime of *lèse-majesté*, of which My Lord of Burgundy has no jusridiction').[62] The juridical reasoning behind the conviction referred to the *crimen laesae majestatis*. Wielant mentions conspiracies and rebellions in several of his works. In his *Corte instructie in materie criminele* ('Short instruction on criminal matters') he lists conspiracy and sedition as crimes against temporal majesty. In so doing, he makes explicit reference to the *Lex Quisquis* and the *Lex Julia Majestatis*. According to Wielant, a conspiracy can be directed against the person of the prince, against his honour and prosperity, but also against his councillors or 'senators'. Seditions were aimed against 'the common profit' (*'t gemeen proffijte*). A mutiny or conspiracy against the officers or government of a city was also a *crisme de lese-majesté temporelle*. Accomplices, or anybody who failed to report a plan for a rebellion, were also considered guilty.[63] Explicit use of the term *lèse-majesté*, however, remained unusual during the Burgundian epoch.

---

58   Leupen 1981, p. 142; Feenstra 1970, pp. 71–5.
59   Perrot 1910, pp. 29–31.
60   Vanderjagt 1981; Boone 1997a, p. 14.
61   Bouhier 1742, vol. 1, p. 116, art. 53.
62   Perrot 1910, p. 34, n. 1; Cuttler 1982, p. 68.
63   Wielant 1995, pp. 186–8. The fact that Wielant used the term 'senators' should once again warn us of the fact that his study was neither a treatise on theoretical Roman law, nor on practical law, but a mixture of both, which has misled a number of historians.

On 10 July 1440, Philip the Good pardoned Ghent for an illicit assembly held six days earlier about his fiscal policies. He considered this act as offending his *'haulteur et seignourie en commetans criesme de lese majesté'* ('Pre-eminence and lordship by committing the crime of *lèse-majesté'*).[64] The explicit mention of this term in a verdict remains a (notable) exception. The earlier Blankenberge remission of 1330 said that the rebels had acted: *'en vituperant nostre seignorie et noblece, et en desobeissant du tout et a nos commandemens'* ('by outraging our lordship and nobility, and by disobeying all of our commands').[65] The remission for Dunkirk given by Duke Philip the Bold in 1385 described how the rebels had *'encourru son indignacion et offendu sa personne et singnourie'* ('incurred his indignation and offended his person and lordship').[66]

These were the usual motivations invoked. One year before the first explicit use of the *lèse-majesté* idea in 1440, the duke had given Ostend a letter of remission for supporting the Bruges revolt of 1436–8. In this he only mentioned that they had offended his *'haulteur et seigneurie'* ('pre-eminence and lordship'),[67] the common expression used. Failure to make explicit use of the term *lèse-majesté* in legal documents can possibly be explained by the fact that this would have endangered diplomatic relations with the king of France, who might have interpreted it as a usurpation of his own rights. Nevertheless, Duke Charles the Bold (1467–77), a stubborn, arrogant and power-hungry prince, used a rather broad concept of *lèse-majesté*. This is particularly evident in his political speech given to the Estates of Flanders on 12 July 1475, where he berates delegates for refusing to mobilise the soldiers he called for. Although it was far from the first time the Flemings refused taxes or soldiers to their prince, Charles took it personally. He accused the Flemish delegates of holding secret meetings against him and shouted:

> *sont toutes ces choses de faire machinacions occultes et secretes en la mort de son prince* [...] *N'est pas crisme de leze magesté? Certes oy, et non pas le moindre, car c'est en la personne de son prince. Quelle punicion il y sciet? Chascun le scet, car ce n'est pas privacion et confiscacion des biens d'eulx tant seulement, mais ausii de leurs heritiers, et non la punicion capitale, mais quarteleure de corps.*

---

64   Boone 2005; Boone 1990b, pp. 224–5 for the facts; the charter is in the Ghent City Archives, charter 582.

65   Gilliodts-Van Severen 1890–3, vol. 1, p. 595.

66   Espinas, Verlinden and Buntinx 1959–61, vol. 1, p. 335.

67   Vlietinck 1910, pp. 68–70.

all these things are for making occult and secret plans for the death of their prince [...] Is this not a crime of *lèse-majesté*? Certainly yes, and not the least because this concerns the person of the prince. What punishment lies there? Everyone knows it, because it is not only the privation and confiscation of their possessions and estates, and not only capital punishment, but the quartering of the body.

It proved politically and practically impossible to draw and quarter all the delegates of the estates, but the threat served its purpose of intimidation. At war with France, and having designs of his own for a crown, Charles did not censor himself in using the expression '*leze magesté*'. Indeed, he presented himself as a *personne publicque*, guarantor of the *chose publicque*. Though it must be pointed out that in conveying such 'modern' terms, he also invoked knightly concepts of honour and glory concomitantly.[68] The punishment of Ghent after one of its last great revolts in 1540, was drafted by Lodewijk van Schore. He served as president of the Council of State and the Privy Council, the top institutions of the emperor in the Netherlands. Ghent was deemed guilty of '*crymes de desloyauté, desobeyssance, infraction de traictez, sedition, rebellion et de leze majesté*'.[69] Maybe this usage reflects the disappearance of French sovereignty over the county of Flanders after 1526–9. Then again, it might have been due to the influence of specific jurists. Whatever the case, it is clear that from the fifteenth century onwards, the repression of collective action invoked the Roman concept of *crimen laesae majestatis*.

6   Later Medieval Terminology

The terminology in Middle Dutch and Middle French to describe collective acts proved diverse. One can find *beroerte, commocien, conspiratie, meute, tumult, upset,* or *wapeninghe* in Ghent sources.[70] In his chronicle, Wielant referred to the revolt of maritime Flanders of 1323–8 as '*la grande mutinerie*'.[71] Other words and expressions used for types of collective action include: '*rebellion,*

---

68 Blockmans, Willem 1996a. The confiscation of the heirs of rebels had been out of use for a very long time in the Middle Ages, indicating to us the direct and explicit influence of Roman Law on Charles's ideas; there is a further parallel in that after Charles's 1462 ordonnances for the Council of Holland, insulting the court also was seen as explicit *lèse-majesté*, see Bailly 1998.

69 Boone 1997a, p. 16, n. 42.

70 Lenaerts 1972, p. 5.

71 De Smet, Joseph Jean, ed. 1865, p. 254.

assemblee et armee desordonnee' (Ghent 1432); *'deliz, crimes, exces, rebellions, desobeissances, mefassances'* (Gent 1385, Peace of Tournai); *'rebellions, violenses et outrages'* (Bruges 1324); *'uploop ghedaen met menichten'* (Ypres 1361); *'conspiracions, commotions, maleficions, rebellions, desobeissances, oultrages et mesusances'* (Cassel 1385); *'ces derraines muetes et guerres de Flandre [...] pluseurs offenses, mesusances, deobeissances et griefs contre nous, noz gens et officiers, tant en empeschant noz lois, justices et signeuries comme autrement, dont nous avons eu pluseurs grans perdes et damages'* (Dunkirk 1384); *'overhoricheden, beroerten, rebelheden ende vergaderinghen ongheoorloofde ende verboden'* (Bruges 1436); *'guerres et divisions'* (Ghent 1492, Treaty of Cadzand).

The *Bouc van tale ende wedertale*, a presumably early fourteenth century guide for jurisprudence written by an Aardenburg city lawyer, describes a case of attempted mutiny which he terms a *'burghstorme'*. A certain Jacob filius Heinric had protested violently against a sentence of the aldermen of Aardenburg inside the courthouse. He had drawn his knife and boasted that he had mobilised the burghers against them. The anonymous writer of the *Bouc van tale ende wedertale* used this example to argue that anybody who started a fight or a violent scene in the *scepencamere* ('courthouse of the aldermen') was guilty of *burghstorm*.[72] In later sources, this expression disappeared. Possibly, the idea survived from the older seigniorial crime of *sturma* (only now in the context of a *burgus*). The crime of openly rebelling against the decisions of the courts and benches continued to be considered a form of mutiny.

Jean Boutillier distinguished between *lèse-majesté*, treason, sedition, conspiracy and *monopole*. On *lèse-majesté* he remained rather vague, and his concept of treason was entirely traditional. But the differences between sedition, conspiration and *monopole* are subtle. Sedition threatens the life and body of the prince, which is different from conspiracy in Boutillier's eyes. A *monopole* (derived from the Roman legal terminology) refers to an illegal assembly, but not directed against the prince. It proved especially popular to describe meetings for dealing with labour conditions and taxes.[73] It must not surprise us

---

72   Gilliodts-Van Severen 1890–3, vol. 1, pp. 288–90; also edited by Vorsterman van Oyen 1892. Though L. Gilliodts-Van Severen, editor of the *Coutumes* dated it a late thirteenth century document, Strubbe 1950, pp. 1–2 preferred dating it in the fourteenth century. Compare with the phenomenon of *valsschelden* (*faussement de jugement*): Ganshof 1935, pp. 115–40.

73   Boutillier 1603, pp. 170–2: a *monopole* happens when assemblies are organised *'disant nous devons estre ainsi traictez et menez et devons de tel mestier avoir telle franchise et gagnage'*; compare the *Codex Justinianus* 4.59 (we thank Prof. Dr. Em. Robert Feenstra for attracting our attention to this); on Boutillier, see van Dievoet 1951.

that this creative jurist from fourteenth-century France tried to re-establish a distinct legal category for a 'new' social phenomenon: labour conflicts (be it under the direct and clear influence of Roman law). In medieval France, confraternities of workers were often held responsible for revolts *'pour oster toute matiere de faire assemblees, harelles et conspirations'* ('to avoid all ways of making assemblies, riots and conspiracies'); mutinies were held *'sub ficto velamine confratriae quasi monopola'* ('under the false cover of confraternity resembling *monopole'*). Beaumanoir is sometimes cited by authorities because he harshly condemned the alliances of workers against the public weal and of commoners of some city united in force against their lord, alliances referred to as *monopoles* or (in the North of France) *taquehans*.[74] From the latter half of the fourteenth century onwards, the primary cause of social upheaval is no longer sought in confraternities or alliances, but rather in the similar organisational forms of craft guilds and their militias with banners. For example, Parisian crafts were put under custody of visitors ordained by the authorities in 1383.[75]

During the Moerlemaye revolt of Bruges (1280–1),[76] guilds were formally abolished (rather than in practice) after a collective action in 1280. The eyes of violators of this ordinance would be put out.[77] A Bruges ordinance on the eve of the Moerlemaye specified that artisans could no longer assemble in groups of more than seven without special authorisation, associations of any type were forbidden.[78] In punishing the smaller contemporary *Cockerulle* revolt in Ypres, the count strictly forbade all *'conspirations, alliances, accompagnements, serments, quel que soit le nom qu'on leur donne, faites sans le congé du seigneur'* ('conspiracies, alliances, companies, sermons, whatever the name they are given, done without the authorisation of the Lord.'). In practice, this meant that any kind of alliance or association, or practically any grouping of more than ten persons at a time was illegal. This was still applied especially to organisations formed under the cover of religious fraternities.[79] In a personal memoir to the duke, Bruges's former alderman Nicolas Barbezaen talks about an *'allianche,*

---

74   Chevalier 1982; Leguai 1976, 281–303: the first strike mentioned in historical sources was the 1245 *takehan* in Douai.

75   Chevalier 1982, pp. 37–8; comparative measures were taken in Flemish cities on different occasions, see Fris 1911a.

76   Wyffels 1966 and 1973. There were also complaints of commoners in neighbouring Damme, *cfr.* De Smet, Anton 1950, p. 89.

77   Gilliodts-Van Severen 1874, vol. 1, p. 235; the same happened in Ypres in July 1281, see Van Caenegem 1954, p. 23.

78   Warnkönig and Gheldolf 1835–64, vol. 4, p. 251.

79   Doudelez 1974, pp. 188–292; Boone 1998; Saint Genois 1843–6, pp. 86–7.

congregacion et asanblee' with the objective to '*destrure toute bonne gens*' ('destroy all good people'). The latter, of course, included him. He was referring to only a minor attempt at revolt by the Bruges weavers in 1386. Another conspiracy of textile workers in 1391 is no less subtly described as a '*cruele alianche pour toutes boines gens mordryr*' ('a cruel alliance to kill all good people').[80] In 1451, inhabitants of the minor drapery centre Wervik had organised '*certaines assemblees secretes et machinations illicites*'.[81] It was never questioned by the authorities that illicit convocations or assemblies were treasonable.[82] Wielant said that assemblies called by ringing bells or through other means were strictly forbidden if not explicitly ordered by the prince or one of his lieutenants.[83] An assembly at night by the inhabitants of the village of Bellem in 1441, for unclear reasons, but not demonstrating any hostile intent, was crushed by a bailiff of Ghent, who called it an '*assamblee illicite par maniere de commocion*' ('an illicit assembly by way of riot') and ordered those responsible arrested.[84] Perhaps a possible protest was in the making there, or alternatively, any kind of public gathering not officially invoked was considered dangerous. Labour actions such as strikes or collective exodus from the city were also considered dangerous forms of collective action. In 1374 there was a general strike and an *uutgang* (a 'walk out') of the fullers of Ghent.[85] In 1436 all the craft guilds of Bruges called a general strike (*ledichganck*) and assembled under their banners on the marketplace.[86] In 1423, Philip the Good issued an ordinance, trying to quell the recurring conflicts between weavers and fullers in Ghent. The fullers had convoked illicit assemblies, participated in an *uutgang*, and had even organised a strike fund.[87] Comparing these strikes to labour actions under modern capitalism is hazardous.[88] Usually medieval strikes in Flanders were part of larger revolts. They were not organised in a daily workers' struggle because simply holding a meeting was considered to posit a direct challenge to authority which could not be tolerated by the count or the urban ruling classes who saw concepts like *pax* or *utilitas publica* from the perspective of their own interests.

---

80   Mertens 1973, pp. 8, 11; edited in Gilliodts-Van Severen 1871–85, vol. 4, p. 10.
81   De Sagher 1922, p. 110.
82   Cuttler 1982, p. 44.
83   De Smet, Joseph Jean, ed. 1865, p. 292.
84   Van Rompaey 1967, p. 50.
85   Nicholas, David 1987, p. 8.
86   Dumolyn 1997, pp. 158–9.
87   Boone and Brand 1993, pp. 178–9.
88   For a recent study see Sieg'l 1993.

7   Competence

In the 'modern' legal system of Flanders, the two main executors of criminal law were the count and the urban *schepenen* ('aldermen').[89] The general rule was that only the prince and his council were competent to judge crimes against the temporal majesty.[90] In France, Jean Boutillier was categorical on this: nobody but the king, not even a *'haut justicier'* had competence to judge a case of *lèse-majesté*.[91] Unlike the French *cas royaux* which could be judged by a bailiff (who served not only as prosecutors in most cases, but as judges as well), the Flemish 'comital cases' were tried before the count's council.[92] When possible, the count would intervene personally in repressing a revolt. When a revolt erupted in the Waasland-district in 1310, count Robert of Bethune set out with mounted knights to suppress it. He promptly organised an inquiry, had its five principal leaders executed, while 25 co-conspirators were exiled.[93] During the period of the Flemish captain James van Artevelde (1338–45), a certain Jacob de Bets had served as a rebel captain of the small town of Poperinge. The abbot of Saint-Bertin of Saint-Omer possessed extensive rights as lord of Poperinge, including high justice. After Jacob died, some of his goods were confiscated by the abbot. The count ruled, however, that because this was a case arising from mutiny and war, the property belonged to him.[94] Another clear illustration that a 'comital case' could not be judged even by a powerful lord with extensive jurisdictional rights.

In spite of this principle, there are a number of examples in which town aldermen judged such cases, albeit often minor ones which did not directly challenge the count. The following examples indicate how difficult it is to evaluate in what cases the prince or the major cities were legally competent to repress collective action. In 1435, the accounts of the bailiff of Ghent mention a case where the prince was insulted. This was clearly a case of *lèse-majesté*, yet it was tried before Ghent's *schepenen van de keure* ('aldermen') invoking *'l'ordonnance du dit bailli'* ('the ordonnance of the said bailiff').[95] In cases of powerful

---

89   Van Caenegem 1956, pp. 3, 5; of course, there were rural castellany courts and comital feudal courts with criminal jurisdiction as well.
90   Wielant 1872, p. 87 to be replaced by the new edition of Wielant 1995, pp. 186–8.
91   Boutillier 1603, p. 170.
92   Buntinx 1949.
93   Fris 1913, p. 60; Funck-Brentano, ed. 1896, p. 99.
94   Gilliodts-Van Severen 1897–1902, vol. 6, pp. 326–7, *'om dat de zake sprutende es ute meeu-terien ende den orloghen touchiert, ende zoe bi dien redenen ons toebehoort te berechtene'*, see above note 55.
95   Lenaerts 1972, p. 9. For the ordinance referred to, see Van Caenegem 1971; and the edition of Prevenier 1964–71, vol. 2, pp. 437–47.

cities like Ghent, execution of comital justice against a rebel who was a burger, needed to take place within the city itself.[96] However, as we have seen, there existed a communal peace in juxtaposition with that of the count. In the duke's collective 1440 pardon for Ghent on account of illegal assemblies against fiscal policies, everyone was exiled by city aldermen *'d'esmeute ou de conspiration ou d'avoir fait et commis aucune chose qui geust alencontre de nous [...] ou contre le bien de la paix et transquillité de notre dit pays de Flandre et de notre ville de Gand'* ('for riot or conspiracy or for having done and committed anything found contrary to ourselves, or against the good of the peace and tranquillity of our said lands of Flanders and our town of Ghent').[97] Within the city of Ghent, rebellion was in some cases considered an infringement on the 'peace and rest in the city'. In other words, the communal concept of peace had developed independently from the *pax comitis*. In this way, a rebel became an 'enemy' of the city.[98] On 15 February 1477, riots broke out in Ghent with an appeal made for *wapeninghe* ('armed assembly') on the Friday Market, the traditional point of assembly for the craft guilds. This was prevented by city aldermen, who beheaded nine of the riot's leaders and put their bodies on display outside the *Muidepoort*.[99] The fourteenth century proved particularly bloody with frequent changes in the Ghent government in a three way power struggle between patricians, weavers, and fullers allied with small craftsmen working for the internal market. Each new regime used exile as a weapon against their adversaries.[100] Occasionally the count intervened by means of a 'selective' repression, which favoured one of the parties. In some cases, he favoured the weavers, directing his repression towards the fullers and their allies. In other cases, it was the other way around.[101] We do not consider these cases systematically because they were untypical in the light of an exceptional situation motivated more by political than legal principles. In fact, they were purely political settlements of accounts. In any case, the city of Ghent had the biggest pretensions on autonomy and self-rule. This expressed itself in the city's policy towards collective action, sometimes favouring it, while at other times brutally repressing it (when it endangered the interests of the city). During the period when James van Artevelde held power and ruled Ghent as a vir-

---

96   Ibid., vol. 2, p. 10.
97   Boone 2005.
98   Lenaerts 1972, p. 5.
99   Hancké 1995b, p. 22.
100   See e.g. the literature on captain Jacob van Artevelde: Van Werveke 1943b; de Pauw 1920; Nicholas, David 1988 and 1987; Vuylsteke 1895.
101   Espinas and Pirenne, ed. 1906–66, vol. 2, pp. 533–7.

tual city state dominating all of Flanders, he on several occasions repressed revolts against his dictatorship in smaller cities.[102] Ghent assumed the role of sovereign, taking over comital strategies of repression. In repressing the revolt of the Cassel-district (1427–31), the Four Members of Flanders (the three big cities and the rural district of the Liberty of Bruges) mobilised troops but the legal mechanisms were organised by the duke's commissioners.[103] The city of Ghent, dominated by a reactionary patrician faction, also remained loyal to the count during the revolt of maritime Flanders (1323–8). In august 1324, peasants outside Ghent became agitated. The patricians retaliated by organising armed expeditions to the small towns of Aardenburg, Assenede and Deinze, which destroyed the property of the *populares* and brought back the ringleaders to Ghent for public execution. What is striking here, is that they went as far as Aardenburg, a city in the administrative and jurisdictional orbit of Bruges and not in the sphere of influence of Ghent. During the summer of 1325, Ghent's aldermen feared a revolt of the weavers, who did not hide their open sympathy with the rebels in Western Flanders. They promptly banished the leaders of the weavers as a pre-emptive measure. Count Louis of Nevers, who had been kept prisoner in Bruges for months before being liberated in February 1325, affirmed all the exiles, confiscations and executions in Ghent, since that was the one large city which had remained loyal to him.[104] These independent actions of Ghent were even more justified since the count was in no position to rule. In 1329, Philip VI, king of France, ordered the count of Flanders to enforce the payment of a fine of 100,000 pounds by Bruges and Ypres to Ghent and Oudenaarde, who had remained loyal during the revolt of 1323–8.[105] Indeed Ghent – famously feared or admired throughout all of medieval Europe for its incurable tendency to revolt – had on this occasion arranged itself completely on the side of the repression. In 1330, the city, together with count Louis of Nevers, wrote a letter to the count of neighbouring Hainaut asking him to arrest 625 rebels sentenced by Ghent's magistrate. They had temporarily taken shelter inside this principality. The joint letter called them prime movers of murder, treason, robberies, alliances and conspiracies against the count and the city.[106]

Since the twelfth century, the foremost guardians of the comital peace were the removable comital bailiffs. They were the first to intervene during a revolt

---

102 De Pauw 1878; de Pauw 1910; Fris 1913, p. 79: revolts in Oudenaarde (1340), Ypres and Dendermonde (1341) against the Ghent regime.
103 Desplanque 1864–5; see also Petit-Dutaillis 1908, pp. 112–26; Coppens 1969.
104 Fris 1913, p. 65.
105 Van Duyse and de Busscher 1867, pp. 115–6.
106 Ibid., pp. 118–21.

or mutiny – when this proved possible. They prevented rebels from seizing the bells (a typical way to convoke rebels and start a commotion). They arrested rebels and organised the prosecution of armed gangs of mutineers in the countryside. Often they were also the first victims of a revolt, being beaten to death by an angry mob, or symbolically – though painfully – thrown to their death from the belfry.[107] In the *castellany* around Bruges (the 'Liberty of Bruges'), like in other districts, there was a *'duerghaende waerhede'* (literally a 'passing inquiry') organised three times per year. This was a common procedure for handling cases that had not yet been prosecuted because they apparently escaped the bailiff's attention. They served to ensure full compliance with the *pax comitis*.[108] One of the crimes that could be prosecuted on such occasions was 'leading people in an assembly to fight'. This carried a fine of 60 *livre parisis*.[109] For the city of Kortrijk, a list has been preserved mentioning all the questions that were customarily asked during the local *duerghaende waerhede*: among other things they inquired into who had committed sodomy, who had thieved, who was notorious for gambling or cheating people, who was a regular visitor of prostitutes or a known fornicator, who was always sitting in bars or shouting at people, who used to throw urine on the streets. Grouped among such offences was an inquiry into who had served as an organiser of 'alliances in the craft guilds, contrary to the count and the city'.[110]

A specific comital officer who dealt with all forms of rebellion and mutiny was the sovereign bailiff of Flanders, an office created in 1372. His primary task was to secure public order throughout the county of Flanders, or as Wielant stated it: *'Purger le pays de maulvaises gens'* ('purge the land of bad people'). He was only nominally superior to the regular bailiffs. For the most part his role proved complementary. Instead of having a fixed residence, he travelled through the county. He was informed by his sergeants, spies and informers, sometimes through the Council of Flanders (the highest court in the county created by the duke of Burgundy in 1386 as a continuation of the comital *Audience*), which dispatched him to specific pockets of unrest. In 1420, the Council sent him to Kortrijk to repress a minor abortive revolt there. The case was clear and no time was wasted with a formal trial. The rebels were arrested and beheaded. These methods of terror were naturally meant to intimidate other

---

107   Nowé 1928, pp. 229, 233–4. Van Rompaey 1967.
108   Van Caenegem 1956, pp. 35–50.
109   Gilliodts-Van Severen 1879–80, vol. 1, p. 790.
110   Limburg-Stirum 1905, p. 305.

potential rebels.[111] Being public prosecutor and judge at the same time, the sovereign bailiff held extraordinary powers – he could, and often did, abuse them – and was from the point of view of the prince, the ideal officer for repressing collective action. His power was contested however, not only by the big cities, whose privileges he systematically tried to violate, but also by the more rational and learned jurists of the Council of Flanders.[112] Such an officer however, was necessary for the prince to ensure the administration of princely criminal justice everywhere in the county against collective actions and other dangerous phenomena such as wandering bands of exiles. 'Composition' (buying off the prosecution) was the only alternative considered for the death penalty by the sovereign bailiff.[113] This was practised even with whole cities. During the wave of repression (and at the same time illegal exactions) organised by the sovereign bailiff after 1438, this officer and his men went to the small town of Oostburg, in the vicinity of Bruges, and forced the magistrate there to pay 700 pounds as compensation for having assisted Bruges's rebels.[114]

The sovereign bailiff not only intervened in minor riots or failed conspiracies led by minority opposition groups, he also led the military expedition against the revolt of the Cassel-district.[115] But for the repression of major revolts of complete cities or territories, which sometimes lasted for years and even assumed the form of full scale civil wars, such normal mechanisms of repression proved insufficient. In France, the legal suppression of local or urban revolts was usually handled by special commissions appointed by the king for the occasion.[116] The counts of Flanders and dukes of Burgundy used the same system. This implied that any collective action larger than the average was handled by ducal commissioners, who usually judged the case on the spot, just like the sovereign bailiff. There is no proof that the central comital courts (in chronological order, the *Audience*, and the Council of Flanders) administered justice to rebels, although the registers of the latter institution have never been systematically studied as far as the medieval period is concerned. As a rule, the count, or later the duke of Burgundy would appoint a commission *ad hoc*, consisting of high nobles from the prince's immediate surroundings, often members of his council, jurists within the higher courts (*Audience*,

---

111   Van Rompaey 1967, p. 49.
112   Boone 1989a.
113   Ibid., p. 58; Van Rompaey 1961.
114   Dumolyn 1997, p. 51; Van Rompaey 1967, pp. 76–8.
115   Van Rompaey 1967, p. 51.
116   Cuttler 1982, p. 239.

Raad van Vlaanderen or *Grote Raad* or Great Council of the dukes, the judicial section of their council) and officers knowledgeable in local politics and customs.[117] After the revolt of maritime Flanders between 1323 and 1328, which included Bruges and Ypres,[118] count Robert ordered an inquiry commission consisting of some knights, valets and comital bailiffs, to investigate what had happened in Gravelines, Nieuwpoort, Dunkirk and Mardike, all of them small towns of coastal Flanders involved for five years in the revolt which had just ended. He explained that *'nous nous volsissiemes enfourmer de la verité pour savoir comment nouz les porriemes, ou cas que nous les volriemes punir, ou quelle grace nouz leur feriemes ou cas la grace appartenroit et nous leur volriemes fere'* ('we would have wished to inform ourselves of the truth as much as we would be able to, in the case that we would want to punish, or which pardon we should grant them').[119] The commissioners examined all the 'the horrible things that were done in Bruges against the peace' (*'horrible faite, die ghedaen sijn in Brucghe jeghen der vorme van den paise'*). All the aldermen were examined to see if they had deliberately supported the revolt. Some were completely acquitted. Several craftsmen (including members of their political elites) were considered separately because they were *'moverre in sijn ambocht van allen horiblen faite binnen der stede'* ('promoters within their craft of all the horrible events within the town') or *'moverre van den moyten die gheweest hebben'* ('promotor of the troubles that have taken place'). Another man was *'sustineerre met sinen rade'* ('had given support and advice'). There was a list of names composed. After taking testimony and checking stories a mark was appended to the name of the guilty. They were deemed the principal leaders of all the *'roeringhen'* and *'moiten'* ('uproars'), which had occurred since the Peace of Arques. Others solemnly swore that they had not been *'hulpers of moverres of promoveres'* ('helpers or promotors or starters') in the rebellion. These individuals could, however, identify others who had acted *'contraryen den payse'* ('against the peace'). Another specific crime perpetrated during the revolt was the installation of new aldermen by the rebellious city government itself. Or similarly, the fuller Pieter de Backere was accused of making himself *'here ende justichierre, ende leide lieden up raden'* ('lord and justice, and imposed counsel on people').[120] After the repression of the 1436–8 revolt, the duke had ordered his nephew John of Cleves to lead a commission to find the forty principal guilty

117   Buntinx 1949; Van Rompaey 1973.
118   TeBrake 1993; Sabbe, Jacques 1992; Pirenne 1900; Hugenholtz 1949; Blockmans, Frans 1940.
119   Espinas, Verlinden and Buntinx 1959–61, vol. 1, p. 12.
120   De Pauw 1899a.

persons, *'par voyes ordinaires et extraordinaires'* ('by ordinary or extraordinary means'), implying the use of torture was normal.[121]

Sometimes people were excluded from a collective ducal pardon (see below) given to a city because an inquiry was still in the process of identifying the guilty. Philip the Good pardoned the city of Ostend in 1439 for having supported the rebels of Bruges, but he specifically mentioned that any inhabitant of Ostend who was later found as having been involved with the killing of certain officers (notably his admiral Jean de Hornes who had been assassinated in the dunes in 1436, but also officers who had been killed by the Bruges rebels themselves) or with the armed resistance of Bruges against the duke on May 1437, would forfeit their right to the collective pardon.[122] The pardon was given here for political reasons, before there had been time to organise a proper inquiry.

The 1428 conspiracy of textile workers in Ypres fully illustrates the complexity of the issue of competence. This was only a minor attempt to start a revolt of textile workers in December 1428, probably led by drapers. The Ypres textile industry would never recover from the heavy blows it had received in the fourteenth century, and now it had to cope with competition from the surrounding countryside where labour was cheaper. Just like Bruges in the 1380s and 1390s desperate conspiracies among textile workers hoped to turn the tide. The repressive documents accused them of wanting to take power in the city and start a kind of city-state regime. It was a miserable failure and the city authorities immediately arrested the ringleaders *'comme conspirateurs'*. As burghers of Ypres they demanded to be tried before the aldermen according to the privileges. The aldermen, however, delivered the conspirators to ducal officers *'pour estre puniz et corrigiez selon leur demerite'* ('to be punished and corrected according to their crimes'). In the presence of the sovereign bailiff of Flanders two of them were executed on the scaffold on 12 January 1429. A third conspirator was executed one week later. The brother of the latter was exiled for ten years on pain of death because he had known of the projects but had not informed the magistrates. Although we might have expected that ducal officers and certainly the sovereign bailiff would have had jurisdiction in a case such as this, which could be considered as the *crimen laesae majestatis*, the duke, nevertheless, gave a *lettre de non préjudice* to Ypres (that is, a letter stating that what has occurred has no legal precedent). The aldermen had first maintained *'que la congnoissance leur en doye appertenir'* ('that the jurisdiction should have been theirs') because the conspirators were their burghers.

---

121   Dumolyn 1997, p. 280.
122   Vlietinck 1910, pp. 68–70.

The duke, however, argued *'tout le contraire'*. In the end, the aldermen gave in, but obtained this letter from the duke to ensure that this did not infringe upon their privileges in any way, which was, according to the logic of princely justice, the truth. The dukes of Burgundy must have considered that it was the big cities who had appropriated elements of what should definitely be princely justice. As we have said, the fifteenth-century city of Ypres was not what it used to be. It was weak, and its ruling circles were normally servile partisans of the duke. But still they only reluctantly gave in to the prince. Nevertheless, in the month of July, a dozen more alleged conspirators were banished, and this time by the aldermen. This had clearly been a new attempt to seize power in the city. Four of them were exiled for fifty years on pain of death because they had planned to kill the aldermen and others. This clearly was *'contrarie Gode van hemelrike, onzen natuerliken heere ende prinche ende alle goeden lieden'* ('against God, our natural lord and prince and all good people': *Crimen laesae majestatis* here extended to the urban ruling classes!). One of these principal rebels had fled to the jurisdiction of nearby Tournai. But a few weeks later he was beheaded by the authorities there. This *'criesme de monopolle, conspiracion, commocion et sedicion'*, the *prevotz et jurez* of Tournai judged (quoting Jean Boutillier?), was too serious to be left unpunished in a law-abiding city. Others were executed in Bruges and elsewhere. Three other men from Ypres were exiled by the aldermen for ten years because they had failed to report the intentions of rebels to the authorities, although a fourth man and his wife received only two years exile on account that it was *'van onproffitelic in de stede tsine'* ('being useless to the town'). Another, Charles van Kooigem, was exiled for six years *'van onoorborlyc in de steide van Ypre tsine'* ('being disruptive in the city of Ypres') and his wife banished one year *'up den pit'* (which meant she was to be buried alive if she came back!) because she had recited a song attacking the prince and the city government. Symoen van den Dyke was exiled for one year for cursing some members of the city council (*'ruwe woorden angaende eeneghe van der wet'*). Finally, a priest, sire Olivier van Kooigem, father of Charles above, was held as an accomplice because he hid armed men in his house. The bailiff of Ypres handed him over to the rural dean of Christianity of Ypres for judgement.[123] But this handing over to an ecclesiastical court would surely not have happened if he had committed a major offence.

The period from 1407 to 1411 in Bruges comprises a confusing segment of history which included riots, various uprisings, and a putsch of the city govern-

---

123   Diegerick 1856. *Onprofitelic* en *onorborlic*, meaning literally 'without any profit for the city', or 'disadvantageous to the city' which could have a very wide interpretation. This kind of accusations was clearly used as a political weapon.

ment supported by duke John the Fearless. It sheds another interesting light on the problem of competence. In the end, the craft guilds earned a moral victory because some of the aldermen who had belonged to the ducal faction installed in power in 1407 were banished for three or six years 'van tansemente' ('for extortion') and 'being disadvantageous to be in the city' ('van onproffitelic in de stede te zine'). They themselves had orchestrated the banishment of the opposing faction four years earlier 'for rebellion and extortion' ('van muten ende tassemente'). It is clear, however, that all these claims were entirely arbitrary and political. Bruges's patrician factions were manoeuvring between the revolting middle and working classes on the one hand, and the duke on the other. One can also mention a few other movements which occurred during the same period: in 1409 and in early 1412 individual rebels were arrested by the schout of Bruges. In 1409 a Bruges mutineer was banished for fifty years and all his property was confiscated, because he had forged alliances with different persons 'pour en faire esmouvement de peuple dont grant effusion de sanc estoit taillié' ('for making a disturbance of people from which great gushing of blood flowed'). Being an orphaned minor (a category of the personae miserabiles), he was not sentenced to death. In 1412 another conspiracy was revealed, started by three men who wanted to organise an armed insurrection 'contrarie onsen prinche ende der welvaert van der stede' ('against our prince and the welfare of the town'). They were brought to the castle of Male, a princely residence near Bruges. There they were apparently questioned by ducal officers. When the rebels started to accuse members of the Bruges political elite of being accomplices, city aldermen asked for their extradition so that they could be questioned.[124] During the pro-ducal regime of 1407–11, anybody who expressed the slightest criticism about the prince or the city government was immediately banished from the city by the town's schout ('bailiff') 'as contrary to our lord'.[125] Just as in Ypres, both city government and ducal officers seemed to have jurisdiction over political crimes and collective action. Obviously, this was a question of politics and power, rather than hard and fast legal principles. In periods of prolonged insecurity, as during 1477 and 1492 when the big cities of Flanders temporarily reclaimed their position in the county and for many years refused to recognise their new prince Maximilian of Habsburg, the question of who had competence for repressing revolts became even more political than before. After the Ghent riots of 1479[126] a wapeninghe supported only by a minority of some craft guilds, city aldermen organised repression on their own. The

---

124   Fris 1911a; Dumolyn 1997, pp. 129–43.
125   Fris 1911a, p. 246.
126   Fris 1903; Fris 1909.

leaders were beheaded '*pour avoir faicte commocion*' and some dozen others banned from Flanders for fifty years.[127] In July 1486, however, the military and political position of Maximilian was far stronger and he handled such affairs himself.[128] The *Dagboek van Gent* ('Diary of Ghent') describes this riot as '*eene dangereuse wapenynghe die noeynt man en ghebeet*' ('a dangerous armed uprising that was ever witnessed'), but this didn't keep the archduke from repressing the revolt in the manner he had wanted to do for years: seven leaders were beheaded, hundreds were exiled, the city had to pay a fine of 127,000 *riders*, and all city privileges which had been abolished before, but which the city had gained back in 1477, were now again banned. The sentence of Maximilian was also called the *calfvel* ('calfskin').[129] Another riot, started by some fullers in September 1486, was even more easily crushed by the pro-princely party that now firmly held the city government: two were executed, fifteen exiled.[130]

The pretentions of the big cities concerning the jurisdiction over revolts went even further, at least for Ghent, the biggest and most stubborn of them all. During a minor revolt of the craftsmen at Geraardsbergen in 1430,[131] rebels occupied the marketplace and destroyed the city seal to protest against the financial and fiscal policies of city government. The riots were easily pacified by the magistrates. Later it was said that the rebels had planned to kill some aldermen. Pretending to cave in, the aldermen offered wine to the rebels, but immediately notified the Ghent aldermen of the *Keure* and the Council of Flanders: This was a clear case of illicit '*assamblees de peuple*', '*rebellion, conspiration ou meute*', '*rudesses et rebellions ... par aucuns de la communauté d'icelle ville*'. An inquiry commission was organised consisting not only of ducal officers but of both representatives from Ghent and the central government: some Ghent aldermen and a city clerk, the bailiff of Ghent, the prosecutor general of Flanders, the receiver of fines and some councillors of the Council of Flanders, supported by the local bailiff (of the Land van Aalst) and some aldermen of Geraardsbergen itself.[132] Though this was a clear case of *crimen laesae majestatis*, and theoretically only the prince's officers should be have jurisdiction over the matter, we can see once more that the political and judicial reality of the county was different. The major

---

127   Fris 1903, pp. 107, 111.
128   Blockmans, Willem 1974a; Fris 1906b; Hancké 1995b, pp. 41–7.
129   Ibid., p. 44.
130   Ibid., p. 47; confiscations of these and former riots are to be found in the accounts of the bailiff of Ghent, e.g. State Archives of Belgium, Chamber of Accounts, 14118, fol. 68.
131   Gierts 1996; Fris 1912; Boone 1990b, p. 195; Blockmans, Willem 1978, p. 345.
132   Fris 1912, p. 4.

cities, and most of all Ghent, wanted to exercise as much power as possible over their rural hinterland. They had always made use of the legal principle of *hoofdvaart* (*chef de sens*) to extend legal domination over smaller cities and rural districts.[133] In this situation a mixed commission that guarded the fundamental jurisdiction of the count (the rebels were sentenced '*bi heerlike justicien*', 'by lordly justice'), but allowed the aldermen of Ghent to participate, was undoubtedly the most elegant solution. The duke congratulated both the aldermen of Ghent and his councillors for their quick and efficient action.

Perhaps the most interesting document for studying the repression of collective action inside a city, and issued by the city aldermen themselves, is a register of sentences issued by the aldermen of Ypres.[134] We have seen that the aldermen's competence on rebellions was questioned by the duke in 1429, but in this register, dating from the end of the fourteenth century, he does not indicate that this was already the case at that time. The aldermen banned rebels forever from the county because of alliances and conspiracies against the count and the city government.[135] Minor offenders who had spoken vile words on the '*gens de boin estat*', and had started a commotion in the neighbourhood, were exiled for three years, or seven in those more dangerous cases when agitation had taken place on the '*place des tisserans*', which could have provoked riots throughout the whole city, according to the argument of aldermen.[136] Another case of 'terrible words' spoken about the aldermen resulted in an exile of one year.[137] In some cases the use of propaganda (spreading bad news) was used to start the riots. This seems to have been a three-year offence as well.[138] All this was different from a real attempted '*muete et conspiration*' in 1370 when craftsmen made sworn oaths and alliances against their lord and aldermen. Although nothing had actually happened, they were broken on the wheel. A year later another failed conspiracy resulted in the hanging of three rebels.[139] In all these cases, the sources do not mention intervention by comital officers (apart from the normal actions of the bailiff who indicted *ex officio*). The prince seemed to have tolerated the jurisdiction of the aldermen of big cities as long as they were effective and defended his interests. It was always easier to install

---

133 Monier 1928.
134 De Pelsmaeker 1914.
135 Ibid., pp. 256, 267: two women were exiled for life in 1329.
136 Ibid., pp. 267, 278–9.
137 Ibid., p. 300.
138 Ibid., p. 287.
139 Ibid., pp. 300, 304, *cfr.* Vandenpeereboom, ed. 1878–83, vol. 7, pp. 214–15.

princely partisans in the benches of aldermen than to change privileges or even the judicial practice of the big cities. When he had the opportunity, however, the count reinforced his position inside the cities. A Bruges rebel of 1323–8, whose name is not conserved in the records but who apparently belonged to the upper classes and was a member of the political elite, has left us an interesting written confession. He humbly acknowledges to have for the most part passively supported the revolt: *'Item, je confese que je sui coupables en che ke je ne repriis mie chieus ki gouvernoient le vile, ensi ke je deuse, et bien croi ke il eusent aucunes choses mauvaises laisiet, se je les euse repriis, ensi que je deuse'* ('Item, I confess that I am culpable in that I did not contest those who govern the town, as I should have, and I well believe that they would have been allowed no bad things, if I confronted them, as I should have done.') He even had some good advice for the count to prevent future rebellions: *'Item, il me sambleroit boin ke mesires de Flandres eust deus secrees amiis en chacune paroiche de Flandres, qui li raportasent loiaument chou k'il oroient kaleer poorroit contre lui et contre le boen estaet dou paiis'* ('Item, it would appear to me that my lords of Flanders should have secret friends in each parish of Flanders who would report loyally what they will hear that might happen against him and against the good state of the land').[140] After the involvement of the Bruges textile workers in the revolt led by Ghent (1379–82 for Bruges), the duke of Burgundy slightly reorganised the administration of criminal justice in the city in order to improve repression of collective action. All the city's privileges were confirmed, except for two points. There would be six *hoeftmannen* ('captains') installed, each one responsible for policing one of the six sections of Bruges in order to buttress the authority of the aldermen. Secondly, confiscated property of rebels sentenced by the Bruges aldermen would belong to the count of Flanders.[141] The reason why the captains were introduced was explained by Nicolas Barbezaen, who as a *hooftman* himself, had helped prevent a revolt of radical textile workers in 1386. But he found himself banished for alleged *'moyte'* ('uproar') and conspiracy in 1407, in a plea to the duke to prove he was not a rebel himself.[142]

Since medieval Flanders was juridically part of the kingdom of France, on several occasions the French king intervened to crush Flemish rebellions. In 1328 and 1384, the defeat of Flemish rebels came at the hands of French troops assisting the count of Flanders because he proved too weak to handle them on his own. After the battle of Cassel in 1328, the French king also intervened in

---

140   De Pauw 1899a.
141   Gilliodts-Van Severen 1874, vol. 1, p. 433.
142   Gilliodts-Van Severen 1871–85, vol. 4, pp. 7–13.

the repression of the revolt of maritime Flanders. Willem de Deken, one of the leaders of this revolt, was accused by the Parliament of Paris of having 'esmeu tout le commun de Flandres' to forge alliances, to act rebelliously, and to disobey their lords. He denied this, saying that the people did it without needing him. Apart from this, William de Deken was accused of inciting the Flemish people to refuse French coins and to wage war against the king even after his victory at Cassel. In addition, he was accused of going to England on several occasions to conclude alliances. Denials could not save him from a horrible death.[143] The king also confiscated the property of Flemish rebels by invoking the law of lèse-majesté without consulting the count. This obviously had as its goal to demonstrate French sovereignty over Flanders. Once this was clear for everybody concerned, the king generously accorded one third of the proceeds to his vassal, Count Louis and to Robert of Cassel, who held a part of the county in apanage.[144]

At one point even the pope intervened, albeit on the request of his patron, the king of France. On 4 November Charles IV sent a letter to all bishops holding title over Flemish territory inciting them to impose the ecclesiastical interdict upon the county. This missive was drafted to buttress his earlier promulgations against opponents of the treaties between King Philip IV and former count Robert of Bethune. He sought to excommunicate those who disobeyed the interdict.[145] Pope John XXII feared so much that the Flemish rebellion of 1323–8 would spread throughout Europe, that he energetically supported the French king by issuing an interdict against the rebels in April 1327.[146]

8   Pardon and Mercy

In her seminal study of French letters of pardon, Claude Gauvard concluded that explicit use of lèse-majesté occurred only infrequently in letters of remission for the Tuchins, rebels from Southern France. Despite this region being a country of written law, few rebels were found explicitly guilty of lèse-majesté, conspiracy and sedition. In most cases, the political crimes of rebels are put

---

143   Stein 1899, p. 655; see also the corrections made by Van Caenegem 1953, pp. 140–1.
144   Pirenne 1900, p. xxxvi.
145   TeBrake 1993, pp. 95, 107. A priest was brought before the Inquisition because of breaking the interdict, cfr. Fayen 1912, vol. 2, part 1, pp. 349–50; Limburg-Stirum 1879–89, vol. 2, p. 374; Pirenne 1900, p. xxiv.
146   Stein 1899, pp. 660–2.

in categories of common criminal law: they are *crimineulx* and *malfaiteurs*, guilty of pillage or brigandage within the pretext of revolt. *Lèse-majesté* was not clearly distinguished from other capital crimes, and it was clearly not 'irremissible' at all.[147] Neither was the expression often found in letters of pardon or *arrêts* of the Parliament of Paris, despite being used during legal proceedings.[148] In the collected series of *lettres de grace* and *lettres de remission* issued by the dukes of Burgundy, there are surprisingly few which concern political crimes. This seems to indicate that the dukes gave only few individual pardons for this kind of offence.[149] The counts of Flanders had done so earlier. Jan de Hase had violently struck out at the count's banner during a guild's mobilisation on the Friday Market in 1359, culminating in his exile. As late as 1365 he received a comital pardon.[150] The documents do not allow us to judge whether this was a regular practice.

But as shown by some of the examples already mentioned, collective action in which a whole political community – or large sections of it – participated, was almost invariably sentenced in the terms of a collective pardon. This often included some punitive measures and did not exonerate the rebellion's principal leaders. Marc Boone already pointed out the fact that the collective remissions for rebellions often took a form which closely resembled formulas used in individual letters of pardon.[151] This is striking indeed, when we compare form and terminology of the letter of pardon given to the city of Bruges on 18 December 1348 (in which all its privileges were confirmed though Bruges had more or less supported the famous Ghent leader James van Artevelde) with individual letters of remission written just fifteen days earlier for Willem van Vaernewijck, a knight who had also supported the rebel party.[152] Filips Wielant justified the pardon Louis of Nevers had tried to give to the rebels of maritime Flanders in 1326 in a failed attempt to stop the revolt, by saying that the people who got killed during the revolt had in some ways caused it themselves and it all happened in the context of a popular commotion *'que ne se doibt si rigoureusement punir comme s'il estoit fait par particulier'* ('which should not be so rigorously punished as if was done individually').[153] To motivate these pardons, emphasis was put primarily on the spontaneous or irrational aspects of a

---

147   Gauvard 1991, pp. 564–71, 832, 835.
148   Ibid., p. 124.
149   Petit-Dutaillis 1908, p. 1; Boone 1989b.
150   Nicholas, David 1987, p. 8.
151   Boone 2005.
152   Limburg-Stirum 1898–1901, vol. 1, pp. 13–16.
153   De Smet, Joseph Jean, ed. 1865, p. 291; TeBrake 1993, pp. 98–9; Sabbe, Jacques 1992, pp. 52–3; this treaty was published in Limburg-Stirum 1879–89, vol. 2, pp. 385–403.

particular collective action, when in fact, urban revolts in particular were often more highly structured, deliberate, and premeditated than they appear at first sight.[154]

The ultimate punishment for a rebellious city was its complete destruction. A method evidently inspired by classical examples such as the levelling of Carthage by Rome. Although Wielant also mentioned fines as a way of punishing a city (reducing it to poverty), legally speaking these were simply payments for the pardon bestowed upon it. Consequently, destruction might be considered as the only penalty for a rebel city perfectly consistent with medieval legal principles. However, it was of course seldom put into practice. On several occasions the Burgundian dukes destroyed rebel cities, but always reserved this punishment for cities lying outside their own territory (like Liège and Dinant) not desiring to suffer any economic penalty themselves. Usually full destruction was not required, simply confiscating or destroying a municipality's 'symbolic capital' sufficed: its gates, walls, seals, or bells were particularly popular targets.[155] In 1479 the French king Louis XI punished the city of Arras for remaining faithful to Duchess Mary of Burgundy, by stripping it of its name, exiling its inhabitants, and attempting to establish a 'new' city called 'Franchise'. This proved a miserable failure and the king abandoned his plan in 1482.[156] Since such absurd ideas were in fact the only penalty a prince could levy upon cities as a point of law, he usually granted a pardon.

The prince was always moved with pity and compassion by humble supplications offered by his kneeling subjects. This ritual demonstrated their true repentance and earnest desire to return to proper obedience to their natural lord. This classical formula was applied through letters of remission. A good example of the discourse used in such letters can be found in the 1330 remission charter which Blankenberge received after its participation in the revolt of 1323–8:

> Et nous meu par pitié et misericorde en sievant les oeuvres de Dieu, qui est plus pieteus et misericors que pecheor nose requerir et qui mie ne veut la mort de pecheor, mais que il se convertise et vive, et aussi les vois de nos devanchiers, combien de droit il euissent desiervi a perdre corps, biens et toutes autres choses, les rechuemes en nostre volente.

---

154   Boone 2005.
155   Boone 1997a.
156   Boone 1997a, p. 25; Higounet and Billot 1984.

And we, moved by pity and mercy in following the works of God, who is more piteous and merciful than our sinner requires and who does not want the death of the sinner, but that he changes and lives, and also the ways of our predecessors, even if by right they had deserved to lose their body, possessions and all over things, they receive in our will.

The men of Blankenberge (presumably their aldermen) had to swear an oath before the local comital bailiff formally submitting themselves to the count and pledging never to rise against his authority again. Suppliants participated in this by a public instrument made by a notary describing the whole scene and including the count's letter. Despite the generosity of the count, penalties needed to be given to discourage others from committing the same or worse. Alternatively, some of the 'guilty' were executed and the city was made to pay a perpetual fine to the count and his successors.[157] In 1384 a similar series of letters of remission were issued, in this instance for all cities who had supported rebellious Ghent. In this case, however, no privileges were altered and no fines were imposed: conditions of pardon were a mere political function. In 1384, Philip the Bold was still involved in a civil war with Ghent, so he was more lenient towards Bruges, Ypres and the smaller cities who had already surrendered or switched sides (in many cases because of internal changes of power).[158]

Constant emphasis on the prince's clemency thus often functioned to disguise his weak political position. Sometimes pardons concealed the precarious political or military situation he found himself in. In other instances they were meant as a show of force. Pardons were always a very sensible political tool for defusing explosive situations. The political balance of power at a certain moment, between the social classes, between cities and the central authority or on a European level, could force the count not to repress social upheavals at all. He or his councillors often judged it wiser to yield to some demands of the rebels, even if only as a tactic for temporarily allaying tension or to prevent its further diffusion. A typical example is the pardon given by Mary of Burgundy

---

157 Gilliodts-Van Severen 1890–3, vol. 1, pp. 593–603: most smaller cities in Flanders who had participated in the revolt got exactly the same charter, only with different fines, probably according to their demographic size.

158 See e.g. the pardon and confirmation of privileges given to Veurne in May 1384, *cfr.* ibid., vol. 4, pp. 135–6 (the lack of a more precise date indicates that all these charters were written down at one time in the comital chancery and order was probably formally restored in a ceremony of submission by the local aldermen in the presence of a comital officer such as the bailiff).

on 12 April 1477 to rebels who had executed several of her functionaries.[159] The duchess could not prevent the explosion of malcontent after ten years of constant war and fiscal exploitation by her late father Charles the Bold. A similar scenario developed in Bruges during 1361 after serious troubles. The count did not intervene as a condemning judge but presented himself as a gentle arbitrator who desired to 'establish peace' and put an end to the discords plaguing the city. These efforts proved fruitless. In later years riots flared up several times before the count finally managed to settle the matter through an act of pacification in which all the craft guilds were compelled to serve as guarantors.[160] A revolt of Bruges's city militia occurred when they returned from a military campaign in 1411 to support John the Fearless in his war with the Armagnacs. They refused to enter the city until the *calfvel*, a hated charter degrading their privileges, be cancelled, a grain tax abolished and the city government replaced. The young Philip the Good, count of Charolais and governing Flanders in his father's absence, conceded most of their demands, after deliberating with his chancellor and council. He realised that his military position was too weak to enable him to react forcefully against Bruges. In this way the rebels managed to take advantage of the international aspirations of the duke of Burgundy.[161] In 1432 a monetary reform announced by duke Philip the Good caused dangerous friction and rioting among the commoners in Ghent. Some members of the pro-Burgundian faction of the political elite (called the 'liver eaters' by the crowd) were threatened, others beaten to death. However, a few days later, the aldermen and deans of the guilds went to the duke and duchess in Kortrijk to plea for mercy for the killings claiming that all that transpired was for the benefit of the city and the lord. Again, external circumstances enabled them to get away with it. When the mutiny recommenced a few months later, Philip gave in a second time and extended the privileges of the weavers and other craft guilds, while one would have expected exactly the opposite. In these cases the prince had to present himself as the 'bringer of the peace' in order to save his face.[162] In September 1436, during the revolt of Bruges, while the duke was staying in Ghent, some of this city's craftsmen organised a *wapeninghe* (armed assembly of the craft guilds) occupying the Friday Market for five days. The duke, who already had enough on his mind with a war going on against Eng-

---

159   Van Duyse and de Busscher 1867, p. 247; the same pardon was given to rebellions in other
        cities, see for Ypres Diegerick 1853–68, vol. 2, pp. 34–5.
160   Mertens 1987; Gilliodts-Van Severen 1871–85, vol. 2, pp. 107–9, 117–19.
161   Fris 1911a, pp. 260–5.
162   Fris 1900a; Boone 2005.

land and the revolt of Bruges, pretended to give in to their demands, written down on no less than sixty-six rolls of paper. He handily forgot about all this later.[163]

In an early and famous case, the pardon – and certainly the repentance of the subjects – was merely a fiction. The Peace of Tournai of 1385, which finally ended the conflict between the count – and later the first duke of Burgundy who ruled Flanders, Philip the Bold – and Ghent, can be considered a 'draw'. The city did not really submit and retained all its privileges. Still, the treaty was composed in the form of a pardon, suggesting that there was a need for genuflection on the part of the notables of Ghent. They, however, stubbornly refused even this symbolic indulgence to their prince. The duke was furious and felt humiliated. Somebody had to bow before him to restore the juridical, moral and political order. The problem was resolved when the duke of Bavaria, count of Holland, intervened and had the duchess of Brabant and the countess of Nevers bow to the duke in place of Ghent. The duchess of Burgundy and countess of Flanders, Margaret of Male, joined them in this submission.[164] Another revealing case: the new duke of Burgundy Charles the Bold immediately faced the mutinous Ghent population when he made his solemn entry in the city as count of Flanders in 1467. He was forced to concede their demands during his next entry ceremony. Temporarily, because as soon as he got out of the city, the old regime was gradually restored, and revenge was taken when he decreed a charter in 1468, later known as the 'circumcision of Ghent', already indicating that it cut off some further pieces of the city privileges. Another humiliating *amende honorable* (see below) took place in January 1469.[165] It is revealing that the Ghent rebels of 1467 immediately had Charles sign a document in which he had to promise to forgive them all offences. The rebels thus used the same legal fiction of grace in their political tactics, reversing the system of the prince. They had offensive demands but agreed to restore the moral order immediately.[166]

We can see that whenever the prince was not strong enough to harshly repress collective actions (or did not perceive this to be a good tactic during negotiations, since he presented himself as the reconciliating arbiter, eager to prevent and resolve *'guerre et division'*), a neutral terminology was more appropriate on such occasions than long lamentations about how the natural order was disturbed. He also used this terminology after the repression of a revolt – even after a particularly harsh repression – not insisting any more on the ques-

---

163   Fris 1913, p. 119; Dumolyn 1997, p. 172.
164   De Smet, Joseph Jean, ed. 1865, pp. 311–12.
165   Fris 1923, pp. 57–142.
166   De Smet, Joseph Jean, ed. 1865, p. 326.

tion of guilt but in a manner of giving everybody an opportunity to make a fresh start and return in his grace, as it were.[167] Persons who had been banished, suffered or fined by a rebellious city government, naturally received the automatic grace of the duke, after the suppression of the revolt.[168] And also in normal periods the sovereign bailiff had a right to reprieve exiles, even those who had been banished for commotion or conspiracy, his motivation allegedly being they had been exiled *par envie et rapport d'aucuns ses hayneux'* ('by desire and testimony of some of their enemies'). This resulted in political clashes with the cities.[169] And sometimes the count issued an intra-urban 'reconciliation' on top of the comital 'pardon'. The Cockerulle-revolt of Ypres, 1280, a minor clash between patricians on the one hand and drapers and textile workers on the other, was never actually aimed at the count. The form of the charter issued by Guy de Dampierre afterwards reminds us of a *zoendinc* ('reconciliation process'), because the count wanted a so-called reconciliation of the *'parties et lignages'*, while in fact favouring the patricians. There were no executions or confiscations, the two confronting parties each had to pay a fine; the ruling political elite, however, was acquitted of its part later; the textile workers, of course, were not.[170]

9   **Penalty and Repentance**

The great terminological variety in the conceptualisation of medieval collective action matched a broad spectre of punishments. The *Lex Quisquis* had established the punishment for the *crimen laesae maiestatis* as execution and confiscation.[171] In the Frankish epoch the typical punishment for this crime (though as we have said the meaning had changed), including conspiracy and revolt, was hanging or decapitation.[172] Sometimes, pillory, or cutting off toes and fingers were alternative corporal punishments. Rebels who had already fled, were exiled.[173] Already in the twelfth century the punishments for treason and revolt were the death penalty (and more specifically decapitation),

---

167   For example, after the repression of the great Ghent revolt in the middle of the fifteenth century: Fris 1901d, p. 104.
168   Fris 1911a; Dumolyn 1997.
169   Boone 1989a, pp. 74–5.
170   Doudelez 1974, pp. 188–292; Boone 1998.
171   Cuttler 1982, p. 7.
172   His 1964, vol. 1, p. 38.
173   Eggert 1975, p. 1153.

confiscation, and exile. Rebellious nobles saw their castles demolished.[174] In fourteenth-century Germany conspirators and rebels were often broken on the wheel or quartered.[175] In later medieval France, the typical penalties for treason were decapitation and quartering.[176]

In the punishment of crimes against the temporal majesty, Wielant distinguished a few different cases. Conspiring against and murdering the prince was such a horrendous and unspeakable crime, that no specific punishment was given. The guilty were publicly dragged to the scaffold, beheaded, and quartered as traitors, while all their property was confiscated. However, Wielant considered that when a judge dealt with a mutiny of the people against its governors, he should investigate what was the real cause of the troubles. If the governors bore some responsibility, as Wielant put it, the punishment was to be moderated. The Cockerulle-revolt in Ypres mentioned above, is a good example of this. When the people and their governors (practically meaning in most Flemish cases the city and its aldermen) stood up together against their natural prince, to kill his officers and usurp his rights, all were guilty, but in such cases grace should prevail over rigorous justice. A collective pardon was given and only the principal instigators punished in accordance with their participation. Some were to be punished corporally, others with exile and confiscation, others with pilgrimages. Seditious elements organising illicit assemblies and wars could be punished with the gallows or the sword or exiled, 'naer der qualiteyt van huerlieder vocatie' ('according to the quality of their status'). The body of a rebellious city in its entirety – or even the whole of the country – could be punished with poverty by imposing a great fine: an amende prouffitable.[177] The treaty of Athis-sur-Orge, imposed on Flanders by the king of France in 1305, aiming to avenge the defeat the French suffered in Kortrijk in 1302, stipulated that the land of Flanders had to pay 400,000 pounds to the king of France (and the fortifications of the big cities had to be demolished).[178] The two classic examples of these enormous fines are the sums Bruges and Ghent had to pay to Philip the Good after their failed large scale revolts (1438 and 1453), respectively 200,000 and 350,000 golden riders. Apart from the direct financial advantage for the duke, these fines also resulted in a tightening of his grip on urban fin-

---

174   Van Caenegem 1954, p. 83 quoting Galbert who mentions 'decollati, proscripti, banniti'.
175   His 1964, vol. 1, p. 41.
176   Cuttler 1982, pp. 116–17.
177   Wielant 1995; according to Jean de Terrevermeille a city on its whole could commit treason against the king, cfr. Cuttler 1982, p. 24.
178   De Smet, Jos 1931, p. 211.

ances, because they were indebted to him and had to sell rents to repay him.[179] But perhaps the fine of 50,000 *nobels* (240,000 *livre parisis*) to be paid by the Cassel district after its revolt, weighed relatively much more heavily on this small rural area.[180] Apart from fines paid to the duke, there were often compensations for nobles, officers or patricians who had sided with the duke and had suffered economic losses because of destruction of their property by rebels. A Ghent conflict in 1311 between weavers and fullers on the one hand and patricians on the other, not only led to the abolition of the *Vijftig Man* ('Fifty Men'), a revolutionary institution dominated by the popular classes,[181] but the city also had to pay a fine of 30,000 pounds *groten* to the count and 60,000 pounds *groten* as a compensation to the 'victims' (the *majores* who had actually provoked the revolt themselves trying to take over the city government). Also, after the Bruges revolt of 1436–8, important clients of the duke received large sums of money. This way, rebel's fines could also be used in the patronage system of the duke.[182]

The repression of a major revolt was made up of different ingredients out of which the fine was only one. A sentence given by the French king Charles VII, who tried to intervene in the conflict between Philip the Good and Ghent to extend his own power in the county of Flanders – although with formal respect for the duke's sovereignty – but never actually executed because Ghent did not want to accept it, directly inspired the following sentence given by the duke on the 28 July 1453, after the military repression of the revolt in the battle of Gavere. The way in which the contents of the punishment was concluded and the arguments used were very revealing. Ducal representatives had proposed some punishments to the royal ambassadors to be included in the king's sentence, which they knew, however, were inapplicable, but nevertheless gave them the opportunity to state what they judged to be a proper punishment in this case. The proposed complete demolition of the city was soon reduced to demolishing the two gates through which the urban militias had passed to leave their city to go to war against their prince, and in the end to just closing these two gates. Since the plan of a total confiscation of everything inside the city was not very realistic, confiscation of all weapons and banners seemed fit. Finally, it was concluded that the banners would be kept in a place where they could

---

179   For Bruges 1436–8, see Dumolyn 1997, pp. 289–92. The most important references for the 'Ghent Revolt' are: Fris 1901d; Fris 1914; Boone 1990a, 1990b and 1990c, pp. 60–7; Haemers 2004b.
180   Desplanque 1864–5, pp. 279–81.
181   Boone and Prevenier 1989a, p. 82.
182   Dumolyn 1997.

not be taken away without ducal permission. The same procedure of gradually toning down the measures to a realistic size was also used as far as privileges were concerned.[183]

When a revolt had started, the prince considered all privileges of the town or castellany involved as legally void, just as all property of rebels was automatically considered forfeited.[184] Almost every major revolt was repressed by the count or duke and already after the revolt of 1323–8 but especially after the Bruges revolt of 1436–8, legal repression was used by the prince as a political pretext to reform the institutions of the city (or sometimes rural castellany) in question, tightening his grip on the selection of the aldermen and the urban finances, and reducing the major city's grip on the surrounding countryside.[185] In Flemish historiography the new 'privileges' given to Bruges after the 1323–8 revolt have been seen as the classic example of the work of 'centralising legists' in the service of the count who used the repression of revolts as a welcome occasion to break part of the power of the cities.[186] The number of reserved cases was not extended by Louis of Nevers in the charters he issued during the years 1328–32, after the great revolt of maritime Flanders. The centralisation happened on the level of increased judicial, political and administrative control by the count over the cities and rural area.[187] The old and new privileges of all the pacified cities and localities were copied in a richly decorated chancery register for the count, to serve both as a commemoration of his victory and as an instrument for policies in similar cases in the future. A bit ironic in this context is the fact that the moderations the count had to add to his measures on five occasions in 1330, 1334 and 1338, to prevent a possible new revolt in Bruges, were also included at the time. When the count was again on the defensive in April 1338, fearing new revolts everywhere, he revoked his first repressive charter of 1329 and the register lost any direct value.[188]

The old customs of Cassel-Ambacht, which still held many old traditions of private settlement and feuds, were to be changed by the duke, the nobles and the Members of Flanders. Resistance against these 'novelties' had been

---

183　Boone 1990a, pp. 16–17; the text of the final sentence given by the duke is printed in Gachard 1833–4, vol. 2, pp. 143–56.

184　For example Espinas, Verlinden and Buntinx 1959–61, vol. 1, p. 21, 'pour lesquelles choses ilz estoient inhabiles de tous biens et de toutes graces, perdu et forfait tous leur biens, privileges, franchises, libertes et usaiges a eulx donnez et ottroies par nos predecesseurs, contes et contesses de Flandres'.

185　Blockmans, Willem 1988b; Blockmans, Willem 1985b, pp. 109–23.

186　Van Rompaey 1965; Boone 1996b.

187　Buntinx 1949, p. 213, n. 5; Van Rompaey 1965.

188　Prevenier 1998.

the reason for a revolt, but in fact, its repression in the end made this judicial centralisation much easier.[189] The foremost political and economic issues involved in revolutionary demands as well as in the prince's programme for centralisation – primarily the export industries, representation of craftsmen in urban government, urban particularism and the domination of the large cities over their rural hinterland – are not the issue in this article.[190] It may be clear, however, that the repressive measures of the counts and dukes on this level were on the long run the most disadvantageous for the cities (and sometimes rural districts) involved. In some authors' views, and with justification, the dukes of Burgundy provoked revolts themselves on some occasions, or did at least nothing to prevent them, hoping to be able to break the political power of the city later, and in the most effective way: with economic blockades and brutal armed force.[191]

Symbolic measures were an important feature in the punishment of rebellious communities. Peter Arnade wrote a fascinating study of the anthropological dimension of the phenomenon of *honorable amends* or *escondist honorable* imposed on rebellious Ghent,[192] so I will not go into great detail here. Suffice it is to say that these were usually processions of humiliation where bareheaded and barefooted townspeople, sometimes holding a burning candle, walked out to meet the prince, and knelt before him begging for his pardon, on the first occasion he entered a city after a revolt. Already in 1311 Robert of Béthune forced residents of Ghent to kneel down before him in this fashion. When the dukes of Burgundy became counts of Flanders, they put special emphasis on these ceremonies and refined them considerably. Another important symbolic element of repression consisted of oaths in which those submitting swore never again to rise against their natural prince and sovereign. After an abortive revolt by Ghent weavers, it was customary for the count to demand an oath of loyalty.[193] On 20 May 1380, the weavers of Bruges, supporting the revolt led by their Ghent brethren, were crushed by a reactionary coalition of Bruges's brokers, butchers and fishmongers, who enjoyed the support of most of the

---

189 Petit-Dutaillis 1908, pp. 112–16; Coussemaker 1873 and 1874.
190 See e.g. Blockmans, Willem 1996b and the literature mentioned there.
191 Boone 2005; Blockmans, Willem 1988b.
192 Arnade 1996a; though some of his social and political conclusions could be judged somewhat too one-sided, the value of this work is the fruitful use of an anthropological approach; for terminology see De Smet, Joseph Jean, ed. 1865, p. 338; Murray 1994, pp. 152; Soly 1984.
193 Fris 1913, p. 85; there is a clear connection with the 'oath of subjects', see Holenstein 1991; Heirbaut 1997, pp. 112–14.

smaller guilds within the city.[194] They were compelled to swear a solemn oath of submission on 18 December 1380.[195] The imposition of pilgrimages was another tried and true form of making honourable amends. In the peace treaty of Athissur-Orge, the king obliged 3,000 burghers of Bruges to make pilgrimages, 1,000 of whom had to go *'oultre mer'*. The logistical impossibility of realizing this stipulation compelled the city to buy out this clause for the handsome sum of 30,000 *livres tournois*. The pilgrimages imposed in the treaty of Arques (1326) were similarly redeemed by the residents of Bruges.[196] The practice rapidly turned such pilgrimages into little more than a thinly disguised fine.

Apart from the collective imposition of repressive mechanisms, the conditions for receiving a collective pardon for the entire community usually implied some individual punishments as well. In most cases, the repression of a collective action could not be secured without some harsh capital penalties, the taking of hostages, the imposition of exiles, or forfeiture of property.[197] The penalty for *burghstorm*, described in the thirteenth century *Boek van Tale ende Wedertale* was decapitation, the wheel, or exile for one hundred years.[198] According to the *Chronicon comitum Flandrensium*, the barons of the French army who defeated the rebels at Cassel in 1328 put pressure on the king to burn the whole region and slaughter everybody, women and children included. This never came to fruition, but the rebel captains, some of whom were bourgeois of Bruges, were beheaded, broken on the wheel, or drawn and quartered.[199] In addition, all the city privileges were confiscated and altered by the count, the city walls of Bruges and Ypres were ordered to be demolished and their moats filled in.[200] Furthermore, the goods of every one who had taken up arms against the king in Cassel would be confiscated and a commission of inquiry was installed to identify the guilty and determine compensation for the revolt's victims. The leader of the Cassel revolt Arnoud Kiekin and six of his principal accomplices were beheaded in 1430. Three hundred others who had played an important role were led to prisons in Saint-Omer and Aire-sur-la-Lys.[201] On different occasions – especially in the fourteenth century – hostages of rebellious cities or

---

194   De Smet, Jos 1947, p. 72.
195   Espinas and Pirenne, ed. 1906–66, vol. 1, p. 592.
196   Van Herwaarden 1978, pp. 56–7.
197   In a Mediterranean country like Sicily – apart from what is mentioned above – the reduction to slavery could be another punishment for rebellion, *cfr.* Romano 1995, p. 141.
198   Gilliodts-Van Severen 1890–3, vol. 1, pp. 288–90.
199   Stein 1899; Pirenne 1900, p. xxxi.
200   Gilliodts-Van Severen 1871–85, vol. 1, p. 401; Diegerick 1853–68, vol. 2, pp. 34–5.
201   Desplanque 1864–5, pp. 279–81 (Piéces justificatives C: partial edition of the duke's verdict).

areas were demanded by the count as a guarantee for the peace.[202] After the 1430 revolt in Geraardsbergen the principal rebels were put on the wheel and beheaded with the sword, while their heads were put on display at the city gates.[203] Others saw their property confiscated and were banished.[204] Death penalties for a little group of 'principal offenders' were a fixture in the repression of revolts.[205] Wielant clearly distinguishes between the principal offenders, the accomplices, and those who remained loyal. He mentions how some burghers of Bruges did not have to contribute to the fine that was imposed on the city in 1281 after the Moerlemaye revolt.[206] The inquiry organised by special commissioners of Maximilian of Austria for a revolt that took place in Ypres in 1477, revealed that a secret assembly had been organised, where the 'principaulx mouveurs' tried to 'seduce the people' into commotion against 'the government and welfare of the city' ('policie ende welvaert van der stede'). The instigators were those who spoke first at this meeting. They were banished together with those who had expressed insults or brutalised archducal officers. Some received pardon because of their old age or poverty.[207] Some French examples indicate the criteria used in distinguishing the principal offenders from the rest. In the later middle ages, generally the king of France punished a tumultuous collectivity by demanding exemplary victims, heavy collective fines, and by temporarily suspending the corps de ville.[208] After one French revolt (Saint-Lô in 1381–2), different levels of guilt were distinguished: some rebels incited others to 'sin', others wanted to sin but did not do it, still others just did so by error or temptation but were repentant.[209] After the revolts of Bourges (1474) and Rouen (1382), however, not only the rebels themselves and their active supporters were considered guilty, but everyone who had passively supported their cause, although in these cases this was clearly a pretext used by the king to reorganise the city administration.[210] Often a distinction was made along social lines: the new privileges granted to the city of Aalst in 1331 stated

---

202 Van den Auweele 1973; Limburg-Stirum 1879–89, vol. 1, pp. 405–7.

203 Gierts 1996, p. 170; some sources mention two victims, others 3, 4, 5 or 6!

204 Gierts 1996, pp. 175, 179.

205 De Smet, Joseph Jean, ed. 1865, p. 289: concerning the repression of the Bruges revolt of 1281, 'Mais le comte les mist tantot à la raison et a sa volenté de corps et de biens et feïst prendre les principaulx jusques à cinq et les exécuter'; for the degree of guilt, see Wielant 1995, p. 265; and the similarities in canon law in Kuttner 1935, pp. 22–30, 39–51.

206 De Smet, Joseph Jean, ed. 1865, p. 290.

207 Justice, Jean 1891, pp. 48, 67.

208 Chevalier 1982, p. 37.

209 Gauvard 1991, p. 837.

210 Cuttler 1982, p. 51.

that it was '*li communs*' who had perpetrated the '*horrible maleffachons*' against the count.[211] In Mechelen, a city and principality neighbouring Flanders, for which a thorough study of criminal law has been made, the leaders of revolts were usually beheaded. Their foremost accomplices were sent into exile and saw their property confiscated, but the common people who had been misled were pardoned.[212] Willem de Deken, one of the leaders of the 1323–8 revolt, was not drawn and quartered – as one author has presumed – though he was indeed punished in a rather crude manner, being hung, publicly exposed and put in the stocks. His hands were chopped off, he was dragged on a hurdle to the gallows and strung up.[213]

Exile, a typical penalty in medieval communal law, seemed to be a mitigation of the capital penalty.[214] It was a common punishment for collective action. We have already seen that it was used constantly in urban struggles for political power, certainly in Ghent, but also in Ypres and Bruges.[215] The Ghent aldermen and commune declared in 1358 that in the future only people who really had been against the count could be banned as rebels.[216] Apparently because the number of exiles had swelled after the Artevelde regime and people had been exiled under pretexts or false accusations, this practice had to be limited. According to Ghent's law, which we were unable to study thoroughly for this article, there are specific guidelines concerning the banishment of rebels. Ordinances of the aldermen of Ghent, proclaimed in the years 1485–6 made a distinction (as it was made in criminal law) between the use of wooden sticks and sharp (forbidden) weapons during a rebellion. The former was punished with only ten years of exile, while the latter normally carried fifty years of exile from the county of Flanders.[217] A Ghent weavers' revolt in 1354 was explicitly repressed only by means of capital punishment: as the count explicitly stated, exiled rebels could still create troubles and riots, as they had done in 1350.[218] The city repression normally seemed more lenient against collective action than comital justice. A statute issued by the Ghent aldermen in 1340–1 –

---

211   Limburg-Stirum 1878, p. 518.
212   Maes 1947, p. 321.
213   Van Caenegem 1953, pp. 140–1, correcting Stein 1899, p. 654.
214   Lenaerts 1972, p. 4.
215   See the description of the events in 1407–11 and 1429 above; '*Uutsecghen metter clocke*', the banishing of Bruges rebels without a trail and only by the sound of a bell, was abolished after the successful revolt of 1411, see Fris 1911a, p. 265; Gilliodts-Van Severen 1871–85, vol. 4, p. 208.
216   Van Duyse and de Busscher 1867, p. 148.
217   Lenaerts 1972, p. 6.
218   Ibid., p. 9.

under the Artevelde regime – decreed that *'tymult ofte wapeninghe'* ('collective action') would be punished by chastising the rebels so hard that they would never do it again.[219]

Finally, confiscations were a typical repressive measure used against collective action. A substantial number of lists of confiscated property, hostages, inquests for determining the compensation of victims, have been conserved in Flemish archives.[220] Though cities like Ghent and Bruges possessed privileges stating that the property of their citizens could not be confiscated, the prince did so anyway in times of revolt and legally he was entitled to do so, simply because in such a case a city legally had lost its privileges, and they could only be restored through princely grace.[221] John the Fearless granted the privilege of non-confiscation to the rural district of the Liberty of Bruges in 1410, except for crimes of *lèse-majesté* (the text says 'mutiny' but Wielant uses the term *lèse-majesté*, once more indicating how he was influenced by Roman Law much more than by the practical administration of justice) against the persons of the prince, his wife and legitimate children and the chancellor.[222] The confiscated property was sold by the sovereign bailiff and the receiver general of Flanders.[223] On several occasions the prince returned confiscated property to its owners in return for a lump sum payment for the damages of war.[224]

According to feudal law the fiefs of a rebellious vassal were obviously confiscated. The Flemish confiscation registers contain a number of fiefs that had belonged to rebels.[225] It is often hard to find out by which criteria they were confiscated. In other words: who was a rebel? When was somebody clearly considered a rebel? During the confiscations following the great revolt of 1379 only a limited number of those affected are explicitly identified as *muetenaers*

---

219   De Pauw 1885, p. 35.

220   See the list in Bautier, Sornay and Muret 1984, pp. 193–204. It is needless to say how valuable these registers are for social history. Not all have been thoroughly exploited, see a recent edition by Desreumaux 1999.

221   For a general evolution of confiscations in Flemish criminal law see Van Caenegem 1954, pp. 203–8. For Ghent: Lenaerts 1972, p. 95; Bruges: Fris 1911a.

222   De Smet, Joseph Jean, ed. 1865, p. 255, who wrongly dates the privilege to 1414 (though this could have been a confirmation of an earlier privilege): this seems to imply that he did not consider attacks on lower officers as *lèse-majesté*, see Gilliodts-Van Severen 1879–80, vol. 2, pp. 162–7 (See above n. 109); the question of freedom from confiscation in the case of conspiracy was itself a matter in dispute between Bruges and the duke in the fifteenth century, see Fris 1911a, p. 240; Gilliodts-Van Severen 1871–85, vol. 4, p. 115.

223   Van Rompaey 1967, pp. 101–4.

224   Lenaerts 1972, p. 96.

225   Opsommer 1995, pp. 778–9; Heirbaut 1997, pp. 272–6: a vassal who stood up against his prince *ipso facto* brought a *diffiducatio*.

('mutineers'). The general title of the registers of confiscation rather reflects the persecution of people who were of a somewhat anti-comital political persuasion.[226] And for the confiscation of the property of rebels in Bruges and some smaller Flemish cities during the same period, the criteria of the comital administration are not much clearer. Participation in armed struggle against the count was of course an obvious deed of rebellion. People who were executed while the confiscation registers do not mention the reason, or people next to whose names there was no comment at all, also figure in these sources.[227] Were they all guilty of some kind of 'rebellious behaviour'? Of course, arbitrary behaviour and plain greed on behalf of the receiving officers are never to be excluded. Using these documents as a reflection of the social composition of a revolt thus poses sometimes insoluble problems and reservations. The various series of confiscation documents of the final quarter of the fifteenth century have been thoroughly studied. Apparently a rebellious city like Ghent exactly copied the methods of repressive government and started imposing confiscation on her enemies of the pro-princely factions in the city, until the situation was again reversed by the next change of power. The motives for confiscation were clearly not always purely political and the confiscating party sometimes just took what they could get.[228]

10   Conclusion

In medieval Flanders, the legal repression of revolts and other political forms of collective action was an important element in the construction of a new public law and a repressive state apparatus, though most studies on medieval revolts have hitherto neglected these juridical aspects. Concepts of Roman law, Germanic, feudal and other customary law systems were applied in this process. During the last centuries of the Middle Ages, the great terminological diversity to describe collective action was gradually but slowly replaced by the concept of *lèse-majesté*. The counts of Flanders (later the dukes of Burgundy) thus tried to implicitly or explicitly define collective action in terms of this crime. Antagonistic forces within the county, the big cities with their particularistic attitude towards their customs and privileges, have both used collective action themselves to weaken the prince's position, and repressed it internally as an infringement of the urban peace and 'public interest'. As in other fields,

---

226   Van Oost 1975.
227   Van Oost 1978; De Smet, Jos 1947 and 1958.
228   Hancké 1995a.

competence problems in the repression of collective action were a typical feature of late medieval Flanders.

Collective action has been an ingredient of all developed social formations. Ruling classes and elites have always countered it with repressive action, militarily, legally and discursively. A typical element was the variability of the punishment according to the political balance of power. Cities preferred exiling rebels. Comital officers swiftly and brutally repressed small-scale collective action; the death penalty was the general rule. On top of this, the princes over the centuries developed a fixed punishment for the repression of rebellious communities. Cities were not tried before a court but the essential repressive method was the collective pardon with restrictive measures, determined by the prince and his enquiry commissions. It is hard to find criteria to distinguish between different punishments for different social groups because there are always so many complicating factors. In spite of general tendencies every revolt was a specific political situation, which led to specific legal reactions, ranging from 'pardon' and 'arbitration' to violent and bloody punishments. Usually, the 'principal offenders' did not receive a pardon and were executed (in most cases beheaded) and suffered confiscation. Sometimes rebels only suffered confiscation and were not executed. Furthermore, the body of the city was struck with important fines and the degradation of its privileges. This was another method used by the centralising prince to construct the new – repressive – modern state.

CHAPTER 13

The 'Terrible Wednesday' of Pentecost: Confronting Urban and Princely Discourses in the Bruges Rebellion of 1436–8

Jan Dumolyn

1 Introduction

On Wednesday 22 May 1437 an event of terrible violence occurred in the great Flemish city of Bruges which shocked medieval princes and nobility. The social order was violently disturbed.

During an armed intervention in a city that had been in a state of rebellion for almost a year, Philip the Good, duke of Burgundy and one of the most powerful princes of his day, only narrowly escaped from death, while one of his most loyal and valiant servants, Jean de Villiers, lord of L'Isle-Adam and knight of the Order of the Golden Fleece, did not survive the struggle. A few days before, the city had sent some of its officials to meet the advancing Burgundian army and ask the duke not to enter Bruges but to lead his troops through the adjacent village of Sint-Michiels to the hamlet of Male and from there to Middelburg in the neighbouring principality of Zeeland.[1] Instead, Philip attempted to enter the city with great force, a decision which led to an outright military confrontation. For the events of 22 May 1437, the Wednesday before the important Christian festival of Pentecost, thereafter called the 'Terrible Wednesday of Pentecost' (in Middle Dutch *de vreeslike sinxenwoensdag*), contradictory and competing accounts survive which reflect princely and urban discourses on the revolt of 1436–8. This chapter shows that purposes of political propaganda, princely honour and self-esteem and values of urban ideology, intermingled in the rhetorical strategies of the contemporaries. Careful analysis of the sources reveals that the social and political struggles between the centralising dukes of Burgundy and their powerful and autonomous Flemish cities were mirrored in a discursive struggle for the representation of political events.

---

1 Municipal Archives of Bruges, accounts of the city, 1436–8, fol. 120^r.

2   The Political and Socio-economic Context

The Bruges revolt of 1436–8 was not the first and certainly not the last of the widespread rebellions against the counts of Flanders and, after 1384, against the dukes of Burgundy.[2] Willem Blockmans has called this the 'Great Tradition' of revolts of Low Countries cities against their overlord, who was trying to centralise justice and administration while also taxing the towns heavily in order to wage his political and military campaigns.[3] Marc Boone and Maarten Prak have further refined this view by distinguishing a 'Little Tradition' of revolt: a struggle of power within the city, usually of the middle-class craft-guild workers against the urban patriciate, the former demanding financial control and participation in the urban government.[4] The 'Great' and 'Little' traditions constantly intermingled, especially after the accession of the Burgundian dukes, because the patricians, the urban political and economic elites who were mostly recruited among merchants and brokers, gradually started siding with the prince to win his favour and join his state bureaucracy. The Bruges revolt of 1436–8 and the Ghent revolt of 1449–53 were arguably the two most important obstacles faced by Duke Philip the Good in his pursuit to centralise finance and the administration of justice and to weaken the autonomous power position of the large towns.[5] The power of the large Flemish cities, which tried to control their rural hinterland and the economic infrastructure of the county, had to be broken by the Burgundian state and the repression of these revolts was an excellent opportunity for the duke to achieve this goal.[6]

The revolt of Bruges, however, was a political lesson that Philip would never forget, especially since it almost cost him his life. It took place against a backdrop of economic and military instability. At this time the Flemish drapery industry was to a great extent still dependent on supplies of English wool. The 1429 ordinances of the (English) wool staple of Calais had caused a considerable rise in prices which led to recession in the Flemish industry.[7] Meanwhile, Bruges organised armed raids against the rural drapery industry in the surrounding rural *kasselrij* ('district') of the 'Liberty of Bruges' to eliminate

---

2   See Below [Pattern of Urban Rebellion].
3   Blockmans, Willem 1988a.
4   Boone and Prak 1995.
5   On the Bruges revolt, Dumolyn 1997; on the Ghent revolt, Haemers 2004b. On the ducal administration, finance and centralisation, see the excellent biography of Vaughan 2002; on medieval Flanders see Nicholas, David 1992; Blockmans and Prevenier 1999; and Schnerb 1999.
6   Blockmans, Willem 1994b; Blockmans, Willem 1988d.
7   Munro 1973, p. 84.

this dangerous competition for the urban industry on account of its much cheaper labour. There were also ongoing conflicts with the Liberty about taxes.[8] Another source of discontent in Bruges was the deteriorating relations with its port city of Sluis which, though legally and economically subordinated to its capital city, was a stiff competitor and was trying to become more and more autonomous, thereby undermining Bruges's privileged staple position. Thus, town-countryside conflicts and inter-urban commercial rivalry were important factors in contributing to the outbreak of the Bruges revolt.

Moreover, the decade of the 1430s was a period of growing insecurity that was reflected in an increasing incidence of piracy in the North and Baltic Seas. There was a war between Denmark and the German Hanse, and Dutch, English and Castilian pirates hijacked many passing ships.[9] But the politico-military event which was to have the greatest negative influence on the Bruges economy was the 1435 Treaty of Arras.[10] This 'renversement des alliances' changed the position of the Burgundian dukes, who gave up their alliance with the English and now sided with the French in the Hundred Years War.[11] For the duke's subjects in the county of Flanders this alliance meant war with England, which dealt an enormous blow to the Flemish textile industry and its international commerce when conflict broke out in May 1436. One month later, the situation worsened, as several Hanse merchants were killed in Sluis.[12] The Hanse immediately called for a boycott of all Flemish ports. This was damaging for Bruges because crafts such as leather-working, building and the production of some luxuries depended on products, particularly furs, beeswax and amber, imported by Hanse merchants. Meanwhile, Philip the Good had planned an attack on Calais for which he had great trouble mobilising military support from the Flemings. In Bruges there was much protest against the fact that Sluis did not have to supply troops but could leave its men in the city for defence against English attacks from the sea.

On 4 July 1436 a Picard–Flemish army started besieging Calais, but the lack of a naval blockade resulted in the expedition quickly becoming a catastrophe. The urban militia of Ghent left the siege and their example was soon followed by the other Flemings. Humiliated by his subjects, Duke Philip was left behind as English troops started looting in Flanders. The Bruges militia returned to their city but refused to enter the gates and remained in the fields of the neigh-

---

8   Dumolyn 1997.
9   Blockmans, Willem, ed. 1990a, pp. 373, 394, 409, 433, 440, 509, 520, 556.
10   Dickinson 1955.
11   Thielemans 1966.
12   Paravicini 2006.

bouring village of Sint-Baafs, just as they had done in an earlier revolt in 1411.[13] The militia, which was mostly made up of the craftsmen, wanted the privileges of Bruges to be strictly observed and especially complained about the arrogance of Sluis. To neutralise this incipient popular uprising, Duchess Isabelle of Portugal, wife of Philip the Good, intervened, asking the Bruges militia to go to Sluis to man ships and attack the English at sea. However, the captain of that city, the Flemish nobleman Roland van Uutkerke,[14] and the Sluis elite refused to let them enter. Enraged and soaking wet – it had rained all night – the Bruges militia once again took up their position outside the walls of their city and demanded reprisals against Sluis and also against 'the inner rulers', their own political leaders who had permitted their subject port city to grow so strong and defiant. Although they did not enter Bruges, they killed the ducal *schout* ('sheriff') Stassaert Brisse, who was hated as an uncompromising representative of the central authority. The craft-guilds and the six district organisations of the city (*zestendelen*) ranged themselves in ritual fashion under their banners on the marketplace.[15] The duke, powerless on the side-lines, had to appoint new magistrates. But real power was now in the hands of the 'Great Council' of the fifty-four deans of the craft-guilds which assembled every month to oversee the observance of the Bruges privileges. The wealthy burghers who formed the political elite that had governed the city for the last thirty years were put in jail. Bruges requested all the small towns and villages within its sphere of influence to join the rebels in the marketplace with their banners, and many of them showed up. A short-lived revolt also broke out in Ghent, in support of the demands of the Bruges citizenry.

The duke and the city of Bruges concluded a negotiated peace on 17 October 1436. In a letter of pardon, Philip the Good forgave the inhabitants their rebellious acts and appointed a new sheriff. The balance of forces was not in his favour so long as the English military threat was still imminent, so he could do nothing more. However, a few days later the aldermen of Bruges exiled eighteen persons from Flanders, including Roland van Uutkerke and members of the Sluis elite. This represented a new declaration of war against the prince and against Sluis. In fact, a quasi-guerrilla war between the two cities would continue for over a year. The duke gave Sluis permission to block the River Zwin which connected the two cities and thus start an effective economic blockade.

---

13   Fris 1904 and 1911a.
14   See Boone 1995b.
15   This ritual gathering was called a *wapeninghe*. See [A Moody Community]; Arnade 1994, p. 497; Boone 2002a.

Inside Bruges, however, the middle classes eliminated the most radical rebels,[16] while collaborators and spies among the political elite assisted the duke. The situation remained a stalemate for several months. On 15 April 1437 the mayor of Bruges, Maurice van Varsenare, was lynched by a group of coopers who suspected (with reason) that he was an agent of the duke and would betray the city in any negotiations. The central authority's reaction was to strengthen the economic blockade and to try to subdue the rebellious city by starvation, a strategy that would eventually prove successful. But first the Bruges city government once more tried to ask the duke for mercy. In response to this plea, the duke came to Bruges with 3,000 heavily armed Picard soldiers, thus setting in motion the events of 22 May 1437.[17] In the ensuing events, the duke and his army were defeated inside the city walls and only narrowly escaped with their lives.

After this military confrontation, the radical faction in Bruges once more gained the upper hand and four military leaders (*upperhooftmannen*) were appointed to oversee the clandestine supply of food to the city. Most rich burghers fled the city. Armed confrontations multiplied in the countryside, and in July Bruges initiated a siege of Sluis, which was not successful. The rising spread further in the smaller towns and in the rural areas of western and coastal Flanders. The city of Ghent tried to intervene by organising a military campaign, but this was an utter failure due to a lack of clear objectives. Ultimately, it was the shortage of food which strengthened the moderate party in Bruges. The radicals were once again silenced and a transitional government of twenty-four notable burghers was installed to negotiate terms of surrender with the duke. By December 1437 the city had ceased its rebellion and on 4 March 1438 the duke promulgated his sentence. Forty rebels were executed in an exemplary manner, the city had to pay a heavy fine and many of its privileges, including much of its power over Sluis and the Liberty of Bruges, were revoked.[18] Philip the Good and his government had successfully stood the first test of a major rebellion in Flanders during what has been called 'the critical decade' (1430–40) of his reign.[19]

---

16   See Dumolyn 2005.

17   The duke claimed that he was not going to Bruges but to Holland and Zeeland. This is very possibly on account of an imminent English invasion, see Jansma 1932, p. 140 and Jansma 1950, pp. 16–17.

18   See [The Legal Repression].

19   Vaughan 2002, pp. 54–97.

3 A Variety of Accounts

A first series of accounts of the events of 22 May 1437 is part of a Flemish chronicle tradition mostly referred to as the *Flandria Generosa C* or the *Excellente Cronicke van Vlaenderen* ('Excellent Chronicle of Flanders'). This is a series of fifteenth- and sixteenth-century continuations of an original chronicle on the history of the land and the counts of Flanders between 621 and 1423.[20] The exact relationships between the different versions of this tradition have not yet been established but it is clear that there are Bruges and Ghent versions of the continuation. First of all, there is the so-called chronicle of the pseudo-Jan van Dixmude,[21] which belongs to the Bruges tradition together with manuscripts 436 and 437 of the Public Library of Bruges.[22] According to some authors, in the Bruges versions there were contributions from the famous poet-rhetorician (*rederijker*) Anthonis de Roovere and by the cleric Andries De Smet.[23] A sixteenth-century version of this tradition was compiled by Nicolas Despars and in some places contains details taken from other sources which have now been lost.[24] Finally, another fifteenth-century version, edited under the title *Kronyk van Vlaenderen* ('Chronicle of Flanders'), tells the story from a Ghent point of view.[25] However, the Bruges manuscript 437 gives the most interesting details and provides the most 'ideological' utterances on the 'Terrible Wednesday'.[26]

Another relevant Flemish chronicle is that of Olivier van Dixmude, a well-informed member of the Ypres city government who covered events in Flanders between 1377 and 1443.[27] Olivier fiercely defended the autonomy of the Flemish cities against the centralising dukes, but he was first of all an Ypres partisan and was often critical of the political actions of Ghent and Bruges, the other two big cities of the county.[28] There is also the 'Burgundian' chronicle of Enguerrand de

---

20   For the *Flandria Generosa* traditions see Lambert, Véronique 1993; Fris 1900b; Oosterman 2002.
21   Lambin, ed. 1839; De Smet, Joseph Jean, ed. 1856c. In fact, the attribution of this chronicle to Jan van Dixmuide was only a wild hypothesis of the editor.
22   See De Poorter, ed. 1934, pp. 491–3. A typed transcription is available in Dauwe 1987, vol. 2. A digitised version of Public Library of Bruges, ms. 437 can be found at Flandrica.be at www.flandrica.be/items/show/904/ (accessed 4 January 2021).
23   Fris 1900b; Oosterman 2002.
24   Despars 1837–40; on this chronicle see Fris 1901a, pp. 556–65.
25   Blommaert and Serrure, eds 1839–40. Other versions include Bibliothèque municipale, Douai, ms. 1110; and Royal Library of Belgium, Brussels, ms. 7384.
26   Public Library of Bruges, ms. 437, transcribed in Dauwe 1987, vol. 2.
27   Lambin, ed. 1835; Lambert, Véronique 1993, pp. 131–41.
28   Fris 1901c.

Monstrelet. The descendant of a noble family, he served as alderman of Cambrai and officer to the duke.[29] Clearly a ducal partisan, Monstrelet wanted to write a continuation of the famous chronicle of Froissart. He was, of course, an opponent of the Bruges revolt. The *Livre des trahisons de France envers la maison de Bourgogne* is another French-language chronicle,[30] an anonymous pro-Burgundian work written in the second half of the fifteenth century. In addition, there is a Latin chronicle, also composed in the second half of the fifteenth century by Adrian de Budt, monk and later prior of the important Flemish Ten Duinen abbey, though this source does not provide many important details on the events of 22 May 1437.[31] A final 'narrative source' is an anonymous Middle Dutch folk song on the events of 22 May 1437, called *Van mijn here van Lelidam* ('Of my lord of l'Isle-Adam').[32] Apparently, the bloodshed of that day had made a deep impression on the collective consciousness of the *Bruggelingen* (the inhabitants of Bruges), because it lived on in the form of a song, which was written down for the first time, as far as is known, in the *Het Antwerps Liedboek* ('Antwerp Songbook') of 1544. This folk song is one of the most interesting text traditions about the 'Terrible Wednesday'.

The two final sources used in this article are diplomatic texts issued by Duke Philip the Good. A first narrative is to be found in a propaganda letter written on 23 May 1437, in Middle Low German, one day after the events, to the German Hanse city of Lüneburg.[33] This letter is addressed to 'all venerable fathers in God, illustrious noble archbishops, bishops, dukes, counts, knights and squires, good cities and all others'[34] and had the clear intention of publicising the duke's point of view on the events. Apparently, the Lüneburg copy is the only one that was preserved, although it seems that this letter was written in reaction to similar circular letters issued by Bruges itself. According to the duke, Bruges had made efforts 'to harm our honour and good name [...] with letters and writings which they sent to different places'.[35] We are clearly dealing with a real medieval propaganda war, in which both parties tried to influence different European princes and cities, such as the town of Lüneburg with which Bruges had important commercial connections. Finally, the verdict the duke issued on 4 March 1438 includes a narrative of the events of the revolt to justify

---

29   Buchon, ed. 1826.
30   Kervyn de Lettenhove, ed. 1873.
31   Kervyn de Lettenhove, ed. 1870.
32   Van der Poel and Grijp, eds 2004, vol. 1, pp. 167–70; vol. 2, pp. 151–2.
33   Von der Ropp 1878, vol. 2, pp. 106–9.
34   Ibid., vol. 2, p. 106.
35   Gilliodts-Van Severen 1871–85, vol. 5, p. 141.

the repressive measures taken. The duke once more explained his own version of, among other details, the 'Terrible Wednesday of Pentecost'.[36]

4 Shocking and Violent Events

Wednesday 22 May was 'terrible' because on that day the existing social order was violently disturbed. Discrepancies between the different versions of the 'Terrible Wednesday' appeared even before it began. A few days earlier, the city had sent officials to meet the advancing army of the duke of Burgundy and ask him to send his troops directly to Middelburg and not to pass through Bruges. The city would provide food and drink for the soldiers at the nearby village of Male.[37] The 'official versions' found in the charters of the Burgundian duke about what happened on that day do not mention this fact but stress that the people of Bruges themselves had asked the duke 'in all humility' to come to Bruges when he was at the town of Roeselare, some thirty-five kilometres away.[38] The duke sent ahead a part of his following and his train to prepare accommodation for himself and his retainers. In Bruges, according to Monstrelet, some local inhabitants were spreading the word that he had come with his Picard soldiers to destroy and pillage the city. Frightened by this rumour, others may have started to take up arms.[39] The Flemish chronicles, however, do not mention arms in the hands of the people of Bruges at that time. On the contrary, manuscript 437 states that the order went out in Bruges that no one was to carry weapons or armour.[40]

Apparently the ducal army of nobles and Picard mercenary troops did not stop in Male but proceeded directly to the walls of Bruges. A procession of beguines, mendicant orders and other clergy went part of the way to meet the prince together with some aldermen and notable burghers, 'as it seemed, paying honour and reverence to him' and assured him of safe entrance to the city.[41]

---

36 Ibid., vol. 5, pp. 139–41.
37 Indeed, the city accounts mention the purchase of bread, eggs and wine: Municipal Archives of Bruges, accounts of the city, 1436–8, fol. 120^r. See also Dauwe 1987, vol. 2b, p. 360, which notes '*maer men zoude broodt ende bier te Malen zenden*' ('but they would send bread and beer to Male').
38 Gilliodts-Van Severen 1871–85, vol. 5, p. 139; Von der Ropp 1878, vol. 2, p. 107.
39 Buchon, ed. 1826, vol. 6, p. 336.
40 Dauwe 1987, vol. 2b, p. 360.
41 Von der Ropp 1878, vol. 2, p. 107; Gilliodts-Van Severen 1871–85, vol. 5, p. 139. It was part of the ritual of princely entries that the prince was received outside the city wall, see Lecuppre-Desjardin 2004a, pp. 135–44.

The prince, for his part, promised the *Bruggelingen* 'on his word as a prince' that his soldiers would not do them any harm whatsoever. However, when he approached the city he found on top of the Boeverie gate a great number of armed *Bruggelingen*. According to the Flemish chroniclers, he arrived there around three o'clock in the afternoon.[42] At issue was the fact that the county of Flanders did not normally permit 'foreign' (i.e. non-Flemish) troops to pass through its territory without explicit permission of the 'Four Members', the representative institution of Flanders consisting of Ghent, Bruges, Ypres, and the Liberty of Bruges (the rich rural district around the city).[43] At a time of revolt, however, Philip the Good did not concern himself with this custom. On the contrary, he needed foreign troops because Flemings were likely to be in sympathy with the revolt. His paid soldiers were originally from the regions of northern France ('Picards' was a term to denote all non-Flemish-speaking persons of the northern territories, including Picardy, Artois, Hainaut and Tournai) and must have felt little solidarity with the urban rebels of Bruges, whose language they could not speak and whose cause they probably did not understand. The Flemings referred to them as *Pyckaerts* or *Walen* ('Walloons', another general term for French-speaking peoples) and feared them as underpaid professional soldiers who in time of war looted their friends as well as their enemies. The presence of the Picards made this not only a military but also a cultural clash.

The duke and his army of 3,000 men had to wait for three to five hours outside the city gates.[44] Finally, he sent some nobles to the gate, and the aldermen came out to ask him to enter the city attended only by his councillors and nobles, because, as they said, 'in the whole city there was nobody armed against him'. But the duke replied that he would not enter Bruges before his people were able to take up their positions there to receive him. The Bruges aldermen and the deans of the craft-guilds, 'who were very ashamed', decided that they would let 300 or 400 men inside the city and then drop the gate so that the rest would have to stay outside. But the nobles sent in first by the duke held it open and, according to the Flemish chronicles, drove away the *Bruggelingen* thereby

---

42 Dauwe 1987, vol. 2b, p. 361; Lambin, ed. 1839, p. 77. The interesting question is whether this is a realistic detail or perhaps a biblical reference to the Passion to dramatise the setting?

43 Blockmans, Willem 1978, p. 459.

44 Dauwe 1987, vol. 2b, p. 361; according to one account it was even as many as 4,000 men. See Lambin, ed. 1839, p. 77. Numbers given by chronicles, however, tend to exaggerate and should always be treated with great circumspection. In Philip the Good's first version of the facts it was three to four hours, in his second version four to five. See Von der Ropp 1878, vol. 2, p. 108; Gilliodts-Van Severen 1871–85, vol. 5, p. 140. Lambin, ed. 1839, pp. 77–8, speaks of a two-hour period of waiting.

allowing some 1,100 troops to enter Bruges.[45] The duke claimed that he and his company 'peacefully' rode to the ducal palace in Bruges (the *Prinsenhof*) when he heard that the gate had been closed after him and the greater part of his troops were left outside it. He summoned the town government immediately to open the gate, but they refused to do so. Therefore, he said, he wanted to go back to the gate to leave the city peacefully. But suddenly he was attacked by the *Bruggelingen*, who, moreover, did so 'by design and treason' and tried to capture his noble person.[46]

On the subsequent events, the chronicles are, understandably, even more divergent. Olivier van Dixmude, the chronicler of Ypres, supports the duke's claim that the whole affair had been 'a treasonous plot to capture my esteemed lord'.[47] This is most unlikely. What occurred was the chaos associated with urban guerrilla warfare and street fighting. Neither the *Bruggelingen* nor the ducal army had any apparent scheme planned, and events most likely followed from the logic of military confrontation. Probably the duke had only planned to force the submission of the city by a 'show of strength', hoping it would have been already on its knees as a result of its isolation and economic blockade. But now the army was partly inside the city, the gate had closed behind it, and there was no going back. The ducal versions do not give many details about the confrontation, but the Flemish chronicles which can be linked to a Bruges origin speak apologetically about the reactions of the *Bruggelingen*. The Bruges manuscript 437 asserts that the Walloons had their bows bent and started shooting at the people who were looking out of their windows and taking off their hats to welcome the prince. According to the anonymous chronicler, Duke Philip wore black clothes and armour, rode a black horse and was waving a sword.[48] The symbolic meaning of this is very negative for the image of the duke because the chronicle was portraying him as a kind of 'knight of ven-

---

45 Dauwe 1987, vol. 2b, pp. 361–2; according to Lambin, ed. 1839, p. 77, by five o'clock already 1,400 Picards had entered the town; according to Lambin, ed. 1835, p. 154, the *Bruggelingen* had allowed the duke to enter with more than 1,000 soldiers; finally see the claim that only 400 or 500 Picardian soldiers had entered in Buchon, ed. 1826, vol. 6, p. 337.

46 Von der Ropp 1878, vol. 2, p. 108, notes 'that all the foresaid acts had been done by treason and had been planned long before' ('*dat alle saken voirscreven ghedaen waren bii opset ende verradereye van lang tevoren bedacht ende gesloten*'); Gilliodts-Van Severen 1871–85, vol. 5, p. 140 adds 'de propos advisé et machiné'.

47 Lambin, ed. 1835, p. 155.

48 Dauwe 1987, vol. 2b, p. 362. This detail does not appear in the other sources. This discourse is perhaps reminiscent of older chivalrous epic stories like the 'Karel ende Elegast' poem, in which the knight Elegast is described in a similar fashion, see Duinhoven, ed. 1982, p. 70, which notes: 'with arms as black as coals | Black was his helmet and his shield; | Which he wore around his neck; | His coat of mail was to be praised | Black was the tunic he wore |

geance'. The manuscript 437 and the chronicle of the pseudo-Jan van Dixmude also give another anecdote to show that the people of Bruges were innocent and had not planned an ambush for their lord. They tell the story of Raas Yweins, an old baker who stood unarmed before his duke, took off his cap and said, 'Be welcome, merciful prince', but the duke took his sword and slew him.[49]

The Flemish chronicles thus present the actions of the people of Bruges as an understandable reaction to the violent behaviour of the ducal army. The rebels had nothing to gain by a direct military confrontation with Philip the Good, though, as the facts would demonstrate, they stood a good chance of success inside their own walls against an army specifically trained for sieges and open-field battles rather than for fighting in the unfamiliar terrain of city streets. The rebels had always avoided blaming the prince, reserving their enmity for Sluis and the Liberty of Bruges. Conflicts were always the fault of 'the bad councillors', a strategy that kept open the possibility of negotiating with the prince.[50] Even Adrian de Budt, the religious chronicler of the Ten Duinen abbey, who cannot be thought of as an overt sympathiser with urban rebels, does not blame the *Bruggelingen* for the event. 'They saw themselves cruelly invaded, and they convened and manfully resisted', he wrote.[51] The Burgundian nobles and the Picards shouted, 'Kill them all, kill them all! The city is won!' (*Tuez tout, tuez tout! La ville gaignée!*). According to the Bruges manuscript 436, the duke specifically ordered the killing of the members of the textile guilds, who were – rightly – considered to be the hard core of the urban rebels.[52] The manuscript 437 reveals how the Bruges women were wringing their hands, pulling out their hair and crying, 'O dear men, by midnight the city will be won. And we, your wives and children, will be killed and all your property destroyed.'[53] This gave the *Bruggelingen* courage, as they grabbed their weapons and ran to the Friday Market and the Market, the two main squares of the city which had a military and ceremonial function. The commoners of Bruges even took their artillery (*'vueghelaers ende rybauden'*), as some of them assembled in the market and others near the gate. This scared the duke's soldiers who tried to flee the city

---

Black was the horse on which he sat' ('*Met wapenen swart als colen | Swart was helm ende scilt | Die hi aen den hals hilt; | Sinen halsberch mocht men loven; | Swart was den wapenroc daerboven, | Swart was dors daer hi op sat'*).

49 Dauwe 1987, vol. 2b, p. 362; Lambin, ed. 1839, p. 79. The same thing happened to a cooper by the name of Maerten van der Smisse.

50 See [Patterns].

51 Kervyn de Lettenhove, ed. 1870, p. 256.

52 Public Library of Bruges, ms. 436, fol. 198^r.

53 Dauwe 1987, vol. 2b, p. 363.

only to find the gates closed. Between Saint Julian's hospital and the Boeverie gate, according to pseudo-Jan van Dixmude, seventy-two Picards were killed.[54]

At some point the duke arrived at the Friday Market and sent Joos van Huele, lord of Lichtervelde, to see if they could take possession of the Market. Van Huele found the place empty and said to his companions: 'Let's go swiftly to our lord of Burgundy; he will have the market for him, for Bruges is won: we will kill those rebels of Bruges'. But a Bruges burgher heard him speak and allegedly said: 'O my lord! You do not know what is inside the city halls, it might be filled with men'. Frightened by this possibility, Joos van Huele returned to the duke who was on his way and advised him to return to the Friday Market.[55] This burgher, according to the manuscript 437, which gives the most expressive version of the events, came 'by the grace of God and as a miracle'. According to the *Livre des trahisons de France*, it was the *Bruggelingen* who were responsible for the aggression. They lined up along the streets with their guns and shouted, 'Kill them! Kill them' ('*Sela doit! Sela doit!*').[56] The people of Bruges assembled two battalions with heavy artillery in the *Steenstraat* and in the *Noordzandstraat*, two main streets connecting the Market to the Friday Market, and they soon gained the upper hand. The ducal troops inside the city tried to call for help by sounding their trumpets, but the rest of the army could not get into the town.[57] It was also near the gate that Jean de Villiers, lord of L'Isle-Adam, was killed by some *Bruggelingen*. He was, according to the Burgundian chronicles, one of the bravest and wealthiest knights in Burgundian service, who had twice helped the duke and his father, John the Fearless, capture Paris.[58] The duke said he was '*grandement renommé de vaillance en son vivant*' ('greatly renowned for valour during his life').[59] His killers tore the symbol of the golden fleece from around his neck. Monstrelet remarks that the duke 'had great sorrow in his heart' on account of de Villiers's death, but he could do nothing about it.[60]

Recognising that defeat was imminent, the duke and his forces inside the city, now clustered around the Boeverie gate, sought to fight their way out and escape as quickly as possible. They received help from a Bruges 'collaborator' (not all the *Bruggelingen* supported the rebellion), Jacob van Ardoye, chief of the *scarwetters*, the local police force, who fetched hammers, pliers and a chisel

---

54   Lambin, ed. 1839, p. 79. For the identification of these and other buildings in Bruges see Ryckaert 1991.
55   Lambin, ed. 1839, p. 78.
56   Kervyn de Lettenhove, ed. 1873, p. 214. This is a French transcription of the Dutch '*Sla doot!*'.
57   Dauwe 1987, vol. 2b, p. 364.
58   See Schnerb 2000 and 2001.
59   Gilliodts-Van Severen 1871–85, vol. 5, p. 140.
60   Buchon, ed. 1826, vol. 6, pp. 338–9.

to force the lock on the gate, effecting the duke's escape around seven o'clock in the evening.[61] Monstrelet claims that it was a smith who provided the duke with his tools. Philip the Good called the retreat and, 'as a good shepherd', he stayed at the back of his army until everybody had safely departed. His soldiers were so shocked and afraid that they could hardly march back in order.[62] However, not all managed to escape. The Flemish chronicles state that the ditches along the streets were full of dead Picards. Some had hidden in inns and houses, but the *Bruggelingen* spent the rest of the day and night chasing and killing them. The next day the dead were buried near Saint John's hospital. Eighty Walloons who belonged to the ducal court and had been captured, including the confessor of Duchess Isabelle of Portugal and some singers of the ducal chapel, were released. But the next Friday a scaffold was set up in the Market and twenty-two Picards were beheaded. There would have been even more victims if the foreign merchants residing in Bruges had not begged for mercy.[63] Jacob van Ardoye, too, was first beheaded and then quartered as a traitor.[64] The 'Terrible Wednesday' was over, the economic blockade against Bruges would be strengthened, and the revolt would enter its final phase before collapsing in failure.

5   The Song of Lelidam

One of the most fascinating sources on the events of 22 May 1437 is the historical folk song mentioned above.[65] It was preserved in the 'Antwerp Songbook' of 1544 and was still known in 1614 by the historian Emanuel van Meteren,

---

61   Lambin, ed. 1839, p. 80. This implies that the street-fighting took about two hours. According to one acount, however, this 'very cruel mortal storm' lasted about an hour and a half. See Buchon, ed. 1826, vol. 6, p. 339.

62   Buchon, ed. 1826, vol. 6, p. 340. Public Library of Bruges, ms. 437 says that Van Ardoye got the tools out of the house of a smith. See Dauwe 1987, vol. 2b, p. 365.

63   Dauwe 1987, vol. 2b, p. 366; Lambin, ed. 1839, p. 80.

64   Dauwe 1987, vol. 2b, p. 366. According to the – less-informed – Ghent version of the *Flandria Generosa C*, the blacksmith, who would supposedly have opened the gate, had fled the city with the duke but returned to see his wife and children and was then captured in Bruges. See Blommaert and Serrure, eds 1839–40, vol. 2, pp. 78–9.

65   The most recent edition is Van der Poel and Grijp, eds 2004, vol. 1, pp. 151–3; older editions are Hoffmann von Fallersleben, ed. 1855, pp. 97–9; Koepp 1929; Von Liliencron, ed. 1865–9, vol. 1, pp. 352–5; and Van de Graft, ed. 1904 pp. 80–4. On the Middle Dutch historical songs see Fredericq 1894; Kalff 1906–12, vol. 2, pp. 167–8; te Winkel 1922–7, vol. 2, p. 239; van Mierlo 1942, vol. 2, p. 205; Knuvelder 1957–61, vol. 1, p. 187; van Puffelen 1966. There are also indications of songs sung by the soldiers of the ducal army, see Boone 1997a, pp. 8–9; Thiry 1972, p. 118.

who said that a song was sung by the Flemish about these events.[66] Possibly this song was composed shortly after the events or perhaps during a later revolt against the Burgundian-Habsburg rulers, as in 1488, when earlier rebellious experiences were undoubtedly collectively remembered.[67] At any rate, the events of 1436–8 remained in the collective memory because, after the revolt, the duke had ordered that the Boeverie gate should be closed forever, and be transformed into a chapel where every day a mass was to be celebrated for the victims of the 'Terrible Wednesday'. The reason for this foundation was to be written down inside the chapel.[68] In 1453, however, the duke gave permission for the gate to be reopened because Bruges had stood by his side against the revolt of Ghent of 1449–53.[69] Moreover, the lord of L'Isle-Adam was buried in the collegiate church of Saint Donatian and his opulent sepulchre inside that church was visible for all.[70] The inscription on his grave said that, 'he was killed in Bruges by the common people when he thought of taking the city with his lord and master on the Wednesday of Pentecost in the year of Our Lord 1437'.[71]

The historical song 'Of my lord of Lelidam' ('L'Isle-Adam' was corrupted in the Dutch 'Lelidam' which literally means 'lilly-dam') gives a specific view on the events that caused the killing of its hero, Jean de Villiers. Indeed, the lord of L'Isle-Adam, leader of the Picard troops, is considered here a folk hero in a popular song that presumably has a Bruges origin or in any case a Flemish one. In the song, which curiously sets the events on a Tuesday and not a Wednesday, a conflict is constructed between de Villiers and Philip the Good.[72] De Villiers advises Philip not to attack Bruges, as he knows death awaits him in the city. The song starts with 'Count Philip of the land of Flanders' wanting to march on Holland. But that was not his real destination because it is against Bruges, 'the noble and pure city', that he leads his army. When the Burgundian troops are a mile from the city walls, the people of the city of Mechelen, a principality neighbouring the county of Flanders, leave the army because they do not want to fight against Bruges. This fact is mentioned in no other narrative source but symbolises inter-urban solidarity. The Picard troops arrive in the fields of Sint-

---

66   Van der Poel and Grijp, eds 2004, vol. 1, pp. 168–9.
67   Wellens 1965; See [Patterns].
68   Gilliodts-Van Severen 1871–85, vol. 5, p. 146.
69   Ibid., vol. 5, pp. 360–1; on the Ghent revolts see Haemers 2004b.
70   Gailliard, Victor 1861–7, vol. 1, pp. 93–5. He was first buried with the other Picardians in Saint John's hospital but after the ducal verdict on Bruges his body was transferred to Saint Donatian. On this church, which was demolished after the French Revolution, see Meulemeester 1988.
71   Gailliard, Victor 1861–7, vol. 1, p. 95.
72   Van der Poel and Grijp, eds 2004, vol. 1, p. 169.

Andries before Bruges when L'Isle-Adam says to the duke: 'Lord, what do you wish to do? You will find so many a fine nobleman on the streets of Bruges'. 'O noble lord of Lelidam', Philip answers: 'Why is it that you are so cowardly now? When you conquered Paris three times, you did not do it against your will!'[73] L'Isle-Adam replies that he had won Paris by a brave struggle, but that Philip wanted to take Bruges by *verraderije* ('treason'), a term with an extremely negative connotation within the discourse of the song which is also reminiscent of chivalrous epic.

When the army approaches the gates, the procession walks towards it, and as a divine sign, the cross they carried falls and breaks into four pieces before the prince's feet. 'O noble lord of Flanders, do not oppose God's will! God will not allow you to sack Bruges', L'Isle-Adam says, 'The *Bruggelingen* will kill me'. He asks for bread and wine for his 'last supper', he drinks and he entrusts himself to God. 'But before the day turned into the evening', the narrator remarks, 'he was in great peril'. The song goes on to describe the fighting between the *Bruggelingen* and the Picards (*die Pijckaerts*). In a knightly fashion, L'Isle-Adam shouts: 'Ransom! Ransom! Let me save my skin. I will have myself weighed on a scale and pay it all in fine gold.' The narrator answers 'Neither your silver nor your gold will be of use to you. Lelidam, however brave you are, you will loose your life here'. The narrator goes on to describe his death in the streets, and his burial in the church of Saint Donatian, 'may God have mercy on his soul.' The editors of the Antwerp songbook thought that the people of Bruges had begun to consider Jean de Villiers as one of them because he was buried in Bruges, and this is quite possible.[74] What is most striking in this historical song is the virulent anti-Burgundian tone in the guise of an almost chivalrous discourse with obvious religious elements, the story of a brave knight, a true Burgundian hero, who did not want to attack the 'noble' people of Bruges, and the bad prince ignoring the signs of God.

6   Ideology and Truth

The various accounts of the events of 22 May 1437 contain significant ideological elements that constitute ducal and urban registers of speech on social and political conflict in late medieval Flanders. The princely discourse is the most clear and unequivocal. In the Middle Low German propaganda letter

---

73   In fact, de Villiers had conquered Paris twice in 1418 and in 1436. On 'princely speech' see Lecuppre-Desjardin 2006.

74   Van der Poel and Grijp, eds 2004, vol. 1, p. 169.

that Philip the Good sent to the Hanse town of Lüneburg one day after the street-fighting in Bruges, he wishes to tell *warheit* ('the truth') about 'the strange manners' of the city of Bruges, 'the mutinies, murders and other great crimes' they have perpetrated 'to the great disadvantage of our lordship and to the great shame of law and justice'.[75] In this propaganda letter Philip the Good outlines his princely ideology, reminiscent of the general values to be found in the genre of 'mirrors of princes'.[76] He presents himself as a good prince who had always taken into account the opinions and the advice of the estates of his land. He had tried to bring peace between all conflicting parties and had always shown mercy and compassion. Most of all, he wanted to maintain the common good.[77] The people of Bruges, however, had been rebellious and unruly and had premeditated their acts of defiance. The duke had come to his city, so he says, to restore 'law, good government, unity and peace', political values that were shared by the urban political culture of medieval Flanders but are now appropriated by the ducal ideology.[78] Furthermore, in an ideological discourse reminiscent of the feudal contract between a lord and his retainers, Philip stresses 'the service and help [...] that good subjects should provide to their true lord and prince'.[79]

In the verdict of 3 March 1438 the same discursive elements can be found: the *'bonne justice et police'* and the *'bien de la chose publicque'*.[80] The honour and seigneury of his noble retainers is expressed: 'By the grace of our creator and the great courage and vigour of the nobles and valiant men' who were with the prince, they managed to escape from the city. Also emphasised is the fact that the captured Picards were executed 'without law or justice'. If he had wanted to, Philip states, with the worldly power God had granted him, he could have reduced Bruges to ashes.[81] Nevertheless, to avoid the shedding of Christian blood and all the other inconveniences and evils that arise from war, he had chosen to have mercy on the city, which had humbly subjected itself at the end of the revolt. The pro-Burgundian chronicler, Enguerrand de Monstrelet, for his part, adds an interesting ideological remark on the revolt. For him it was the work of 'people of little estate, who wished nothing else than to stir up

---

75   For what follows see Von der Ropp, 1878, vol. 2, pp. 106–9.
76   There is an extensive literature on different mirrors of princes but most of them show
      common characteristics. The classic reference remains Berges 1952.
77   On this 'ideological stereotype' see Kempshall 1999; Hibst 1991; Eberhard 1985.
78   See Dumolyn 2008b.
79   Von der Ropp 1878, vol. 2, pp. 106–9.
80   For what follows see Gilliodts-Van Severen 1871–85, vol. 5, pp. 134–58.
81   On the ducal idea of reducing cities to ashes, see Boone 1997a.

trouble to elevate themselves and have power over the richest'.[82] The writer of the *Livre des trahisons* calls the events a 'very great and very terrible rebellion of the people' but contains less of interest as far as ideological discourses are concerned.[83]

The urban ideology is less explicit in the sources. What is most clear is the accusation of treason that the writer of the song of the lord of L'Isle-Adam makes against Duke Philip, as opposed to the 'brave struggle' (*vroomen strije*) with which the lord of L'Isle-Adam had won Paris. This is a direct attack on the prince which was rare in Flemish urban discourse even during times of rebellion. Usually writers covered up the responsibility of the prince for the conflicts with his cities, and blamed stereotypical 'bad councillors and officials' for giving the prince bad advice.[84] Furthermore, the historical song presents the city of Bruges as 'noble' and 'pure', and it is said that many noblemen walked its streets. Rather than indicating a real noble presence in Bruges – which there certainly was, though during the revolt the urban nobles would have fled the city together with the rich patricians – this phrase is used because of the positive connotation that the word 'noble' carries.

It is, however, manuscript 437 that provides the most typical ideological passages from the urban point of view, and especially from the viewpoint of the middle classes since the voice of the patricians does not really emerge in the urban sources. When the officials of Bruges approached Philip and his advancing army, it is said that 'they saw no clemency in the prince'. Clemency was one of the typical aristocratic princely virtues (along with, among others, *spes, caritas, justitia, temperantia, prudentia, fortitudo* and *magnanimitas*).[85] This is therefore a heavy condemnation of the prince because he lacks a quality that a prince should hold in very high esteem. This can be contrasted with the clemency and mercy that the duke ascribed to himself in his own verdict. Another interesting allusion is to the shame felt by the Bruges aldermen and craft-guild deans when they initially tried to prevent the entrance of the duke, but after deliberation had to allow hundreds to enter the city anyway. Their honour was at stake because they suffered pressure from below, while at the same time they could not disobey their duke. Besides, in general, manuscript 437 is rich in 'emotional' contents.[86] It is an express-

---

82   Buchon, ed. 1826, vol. 6, p. 335.
83   Kervyn de Lettenhove, ed. 1873, p. 214.
84   See [Patterns].
85   Hibst 1991, pp. 154–6.
86   On the use of emotions in the discourses on revolts see Dumolyn and Lecuppre-Desjardin 2005.

ive source which evokes many very visual and dramatic scenes which have ideological connotations. Picture the duke all dressed in black on his black horse and with his brandished sword. Or the scene of the baker welcoming his prince and being killed by him or the mysterious burgher miraculously appearing and giving the wrong information to Joos van Heule that the city halls were filled with armed men. The most interesting passage, however, is a reproach made to the – unnamed – instigators of the whole 'Terrible Wednesday':

> O merciful God, what great mischief did those who were the instigators of this rebellion do! It seemed that they had little love for their prince when they brought this great peril down on his noble person, in which were so many thousands of people who only wanted virtue and honour for their prince and had to resist out of right necessity.[87]

The anonymous Bruges chronicler clearly does not mean his fellow citizens. He seems to point his finger at people in the vicinity of the prince who advised him to try to take the city by force.

7 Conclusion

In Georges Duby's famous study *Le dimanche de Bouvines*, a single event, the battle of Bouvines in 1214, revealed a good deal about thirteenth-century culture and ideology on war, peace and politics.[88] Following Duby this article also tries structurally to 'exploit the event' of the 'Terrible Wednesday' of 22 May 1437. In this major political incident and the written 'traces' it has left behind, contradictory political values and ideologies were crystallised. The logic of princely honour and propaganda violently opposed the values of the urban community of Bruges which was trying to preserve its autonomy and independent power and to justify its actions for future generations. In the 'propaganda war' these ideologies played off one another and deliberately intermingled. The prince was using the vocabulary of 'urban' discourse (namely, the emphasis on peace and good government) and appropriating it for his own use. The town similarly appropriated the vocabulary of princely and chivalric discourse and turned it against the prince. These contradictions were reflected in the differ-

---

87   Dauwe 1987, vol. 2b, p. 363.
88   Duby 1973 and its English translation Duby 1990. See Rüth 2001 and Stone, Lawrence 1979.

ent rhetorical strategies applied by the writers of princely charters, chronicles, and the historical folk song on the lord of L'Isle-Adam. In their turn, these ideological utterances reflected real social and political contradictions that deeply divided fifteenth-century Flanders.

CHAPTER 14

'The Good Causes of the People to Rise Up': Urban Freedoms and Power Struggles in the Southern Netherlands (1488)

Jan Dumolyn and Jelle Haemers (translated by Andrew Murray)

1 Introduction

The theory of the 'social contract', here in the sense of a 'political contract' (a term seldom used), as it was elaborated, well before Jean-Jacques Rousseau (*Du contrat social*, 1762) by Thomas Hobbes (*Leviathan*, 1651) and John Locke (his 'right of revolution' in his *Second Treatise of Government*, 1691), had known many precedents in the Middle Ages. Certainly, a written version of this political contract cannot be seen before the seventeenth century, and the expression 'political contract' is an anachronism, one posterior to medieval political thought. Nevertheless, it is certain that there existed a contractual political discourse in the Middle Ages, not written, but clearly present among the sovereign, the members of his court, the nobility, the clergy and the urban elites. This discourse was composed from a mixture of political ideas inspired by canon law, the bible, private law, feudal law and local customs. This 'juridical eclecticism' is formed in the Middle Ages under the pens of the clergy, jurists and the urban elite, and it will lead to the texts of Hobbes, Locke and Rousseau.

One could here multiply the references to the specialist literature, but we shall limit ourselves to a few obvious sources for a contractual conception of political relations between a prince and his subjects. In the Old Testament one finds, besides the 'contracts' between God and Noah or Abraham, the mutual obligations that King David concluded with the elders of Israel at Hebron,[1] which is translated as *foedus* in the Vulgate. One can also give the example of the Ark of the Covenant. Therefore, there are contracts between the prince and the people, but also between the prince and the Lord Almighty, and the two are intimately tied. In Roman law, one finds the notions – certainly, in private law and not public – of *contractus*, *pactum*, *stipulatio* and others. And one knows that the jurists used many of these kinds of concepts out of their

---

[1] 2 Chronicles 23.16.

original context in the *Digest*, as is also the case for the celebrated adage *quod omnes tangit* [...]. But, one could also read the famous *Lex Regia* (or more correctly the *Lex de imperio principis*) as containing the traces of a type of contractualism. However, it will be primarily the canonists rather than the Romanists who will insist on *pacta sunt observanda* as a sort of moral obligation. In the thirteenth century, canon law will consider more and more the notion of 'social contract' as being derived from natural law.[2] Furthermore, the influence of feudal law on all contractual thought of the modern era is of course obvious and there is no need here to explain it once more. But very early on this notion of a contract between lord and vassal was extended to the subjects in general. Thus, the whole ritual (or 'performance') by which the prince swore on the privileges of the cities of Flanders, studied by Élodie Lecuppre-Desjardin,[3] is nothing more than such a contract. One can even compare this princely oath to the *verborum obligatio* of Roman law. And what about 'organological' political thought, first with John of Salisbury and then retained by almost all medieval theorists? Perhaps we could also add the legal influence of the economic thinking of businessmen, an influence which also seems to have been important, although never seriously studied.

In analysing a historical example, dating from 1488, we would like to deconstruct the key elements of political contract in one of the most economically developed regions of Western Europe in the Middle Ages, the county of Flanders. We will analyse these elements in detail to find the sources on which the author of our documents, Willem Zoete, relied upon to write two texts. These texts were created during the Flemish revolt (1482–92) and as such they are completely steeped in the concrete facts of this revolt. Nevertheless, Willem was inspired by general ideas on the political relationship between the lord and his subjects. The analysis of these texts, and the comparison of their contents with the reality experienced by Willem, can help us reconstruct the 'political contract' in medieval Flanders. We will conclude that in the old county of Flanders at the end of the Middle Ages, the dominant political idea was, in the first instance, to seek harmony between the prince and subjects. Nevertheless, contractual ideas are sometimes very closely linked to the concept of *tyrannus* and to the justification of rebelling against an unjust prince.

---

2   Coleman, Janet, ed. 1996, pp. 11–15.
3   Lecuppre-Desjardin 2004a.

2 The Context: The Privileges of 1477 and the Flemish Revolt (1482–92)

The year 1477 offered the ideal opportunity for the urban elites of the county of Flanders to draft a 'political contract' between the sovereign and their subjects. In effect, the urban elites had profited from the unexpected death of the duke of Burgundy and count of Flanders, Charles the Bold, at the battle of Nancy on 5 January 1477, to oppose the autocratic politics of the deceased duke. The sudden political weakness of the Burgundian dynasty had obliged the new duchess, Mary of Burgundy, to make political concessions to the urban elites of the county of Flanders in exchange for military aid to combat the annexationist goals of the French king. In the spring of 1477, the principal towns of the county of Flanders (the 'Members of Flanders'. Ghent, Bruges and Ypres) had obtained many privileges that restored their ancient rights. For instance, with the 'Privilege for Flanders' (for the county in its entirety), the challengers of central power obtained the decentralisation of jurisdiction, financial management, administration, native judges, jurisdiction in the local language, a ban on leasing state functions, the cancelation of levies raised without the agreement of the towns, and other concessions. The duchess also promised to respect from now on the territorial integrity of the county and all the privileges, liberties and customs of her subjects. The privileges of 1477 have been described by Wim Blockmans as 'constitutional' texts, that is, they regulated in a fundamental manner the political relationship between the sovereign and their subjects.[4] Furthermore, in the privileges of 1477 one can discover some characteristics of a political contract between these two parties, since in the final sentences of the Great Privilege (the privilege for all the lands under the domination of the Burgundian dynasty from 11 February 1477) Mary of Burgundy was obliged to apply the text's instructions. By this clause the duchess exempted her subjects from all services to the dynasty in the event she violates the new privilege.[5]

The rupture of this contract between Mary of Burgundy and her subjects happened in the years followings, since Maximilian of Habsburg, Archduke of Austria and son of the Holy Roman Emperor Frederick III, who had mar-

---

4 Blockmans, Willem 1985b, pp. 97–125; Vaughan 1973, pp. 399–432.

5 'Ende waert dat wij, onse hoirs oft naercommers hierjeghen ghinghen [...], zo consenteren wij ende willekueren onsen vorseiden landen ende den ondersaten [...], dat zij ons ende onse naercommers nemmermeer gheenranden dienst doen en zullen noch onderhoorich zijn in gheenrande zaken die ons van noode zullen zijn [...], toter tijt toe dat wij hemlieden alsulc ghebrec als daerinne ghedaen ware, weder daden beteren ende uprechten', Blockmans, Arnould, and Strubbe 1985, p. 94. This passage is also found in all the Joyous Entries to Brabant granted at each accession from 1356 to 1794 (see Van Uytven 1985, p. 273).

ried Mary of Burgundy in August 1477, would repeatedly violate the privileges of 1477. For the Habsburg dynasty, the principal aim of the marriage between Mary and Maximilian was the reinforcement of the political position of the dynasty in the Empire.[6] The interests of the Habsburgs therefore directly conflicted with the privileges that the towns of the county of Flanders has received from Mary of Burgundy in the spring of 1477. The conflict between Maximilian and the Flemish towns, well-known for defending their privileges, was only a question of time. Already during the reign of Mary of Burgundy, but more intensely after her unexpected death in March 1482, the Members of Flanders had condemned Maximilian's politics. The grievances of the urban elite were numerous. The archduke had in fact waged war on France to regain the territories lost since 1477 without the Flemish towns having agreed to this military offensive. These wars resulted in a blockade of trade and a considerable increase in food prices. Maximilian's government was also characterised by an extremely autocratic monetary policy.[7] He devaluated the money on several occasions. Financial and material charges weighed heavily on the inhabitants and had degraded the economic position of the county of Flanders in general and of economic organisations and merchants in particular. 'O beautiful merchant town, it is pillage that you await, unless God saves us and grants us his grace!', as wrote a Bruges chronicler.[8] The Flemish towns, alongside the Flemish nobility, had revolted against this politics 'of theft' that had eroded their base of power.

During the revolt in question here, Maximilian's regency for Philip the Fair had constituted the stakes of the hostilities. Once started, the revolt would follow a typical pattern seen in prior examples.[9] After the death of Duchess Mary and until June 1485 a coalition that unifies the Flemish towns and nobility administrated the county by a council of regency in the name of the Philip the Fair. This council was composed of urban representatives and of 'nobles of the blood' (such as Adolph of Cleves and Louis of Gruuthuse),[10] but it had not been able to resist the military attack on the county by the archduke in 1485.

---

6   The incomes of the Habsburgs in their *Hausmacht* were not enough for their ambition to remain the dominant dynasty in the Empire. To enlarge his *Hausmacht* and improve his financial situation, Emperor Frederick III had subscribed to the marriage proposal of Charles the Bold. Debris 2005, pp. 8–12; Wiesflecker 1971–85, vol. 1.

7   Blockmans, Willem 1974a; Spufford 1970, pp. 141–6.

8   Despars 1837–40, vol. 4, p. 304: '*O schoone cooopstede* [sic], *gy wort een roofstede, tenzy dat Godt voorziet ende ons zijne gracie biet*'.

9   See [Patterns].

10   Haemers 2007a.

Maximilian's resumption of power that year was only short-lived. In November 1487, the Ghent rebels began, with the fall of Kortrijk, Hulst and Oudenaarde, to conquer the county. Maximilian, elected King of the Romans in 1486, wanted to prevent a pact of solidarity between the Bruges traders and their Ghent colleagues in January 1488, but the political ineptitude characteristic of this ruler who ignored local political sensibilities resulted in his own imprisonment in the town of Bruges from 1 February 1488 to 16 May of the same year.[11] Threatened by 'international' pressure supported by the elites of Brabant and Holland, by the pope and by the German Emperor Frederick III, who wanted to see his son, the King of Romans, released, the powers of the Flemish towns decided to free Maximilian on 16 May 1488. However, the Members of Flanders had forced the King of the Romans to sign on that day the 'Peace of Bruges', in which he renounced the regency of his son. The council of regency was re-established. We will come back to this. But contrary to what has been stipulated in the Peace of Bruges, once liberated, the King of the Romans attacked the county with an army and, in reaction, Philip of Cleves put himself at the head of the defence force of the county of Flanders. After a long war that exhausted the towns of the county, the leader of the political opposition to Maximilian had to capitulate on 12 October 1492 and sign the Peace of Sluis.[12] After ten year of revolt Maximilian of Austria's regency for Philip the Fair was no longer contested.

3   Willem Zoete and the Estates-General of March and April 1488

Certainly, the son of the emperor had finally won victory against the Flemish 'rebels'. But it is clear that the political resistance against his regency had fundamentally undermined the political authority of the prince of the House of Habsburg. The political climate of the revolt of Flanders was extremely favourable to the creation of texts that were to assess the political position of Maximilian as a regent for Philip the Fair as well as the general political relationship between a regent, sovereign and their subjects. On several occasions the Members of Flanders had written texts in which they explained their arguments against the regency of Maximilian. The Members tried to find political support for their cause not solely through a military conquest of the towns that remained loyal, led by Philip of Cleves, but also by using forceful propaganda.

---

11   Boone 2003b and 2007a.
12   Haemers 2007b and 2007c.

It is in the setting of this 'battle of paper' that the ideologue of the council of regency, the Ghentenaar Willem Zoete, had composed many speeches for the Estates-General, convening at Ghent during Maximilian's months of imprisonment, in March and April 1488, and in which the political arguments for the 'forfeiture' of the regent are defended. It is these texts of Willem Zoete to which we will now turn.

Before this analysis, it is necessary to give a brief biography of their author. Willem was the son of Jan Zoete and Johanna vander Capellen. He had married Elisabeth van Massemen, daughter of Barthelémy, a *maître des requêtes* for the Council of Flanders.[13] The father-in-law of Willem was therefore an important jurist, which can explain the marriage of his daughter to Willem. It is certain that Willem had also studied law, since he is titled *maître* ('master') in the sources, but we have not been able to discover the university at which he completed his studies. However, our analysis of the texts that he had written confirms that he was a man of great erudition and that he possessed an extensive knowledge of law. These qualities had also been remarked on by the magistrates of Bruges and Ghent, the two towns having employed Willem during the revolt of Flanders. The Ghentenaar therefore himself embodied the united opposition of the Flemish towns against Maximilian of Austria. Master Willem Zoete had been a 'pensionary' (*pensionaris*, a kind of city clerk responsible for juridical affairs) of the town of Bruges from September 1483 to June 1485. During these two years the jurist from Ghent often stayed in his native town to represent the town of Bruges to the council of regency and Philip the Fair, who resided at Ghent. According to the accounts of the town of Bruges, Willem was paid to 'occupy himself daily with the deputies of the other Members of Flanders in the affairs of the land and in the council of the regency of the lord'.[14] In the sources Willem thus appears to be a permanent representative of the town of Bruges in Ghent. It is therefore no coincidence that Bruges gave him his leave after the council of regency had been abolished by Maximilian in June 1485. Willem only reappears on the scene when his native town of Ghent recommenced the conflict against Maximilian in November 1487. When the latter's opponents took power in the town, Willem was named

---

13   Ghent City Archives, series 330, no. 41, fols. 62^r–62^v. Also see Van Hoecke 2005, pp. 111–2.
14   '*Omme aldaer daghelicx metten heeren van den bloede ende metten Grooten Rade ons gheduchts heeren ende princen* [Philip the Fair], *midsgaders den ghedeputeirden van den anderen tween Leden* [Ypres and Ghent], *besich te zine ende te besoingierne van zaken den lande int generale anegaende*', Municipal Archives of Bruges, accounts of the city, 1482–3, 127^r, and 1483–4, fol. 140^r.

'pensionary' of Ghent; he remained so until July 1491.[15] In the following months he became reattached to the council of regency and even to Philip of Cleves, the ideologue of the revolt against Maximilian. He accompanied Philip in Brabant, providing his captain with ideological ammunition in his efforts to unite political opposition in the Burgundian Netherlands.[16] After the town of Ghent had to capitulate by accepting the Peace of Cadzand in July 1492, it was logical that Willem disappeared from the political scene. It is probable that he died in November 1492, some weeks after the surrender of Philip of Cleves at Sluis.[17]

On the 13 March and the 28 April 1488 Willem presented two texts to the assembly of the Estates-General at Ghent with the aim of convincing the deputies of other towns and principalities of the Burgundian Low Countries to withdraw their confidence in the regent, Maximilian. On 13 March, Willem presented the first text in which he solemnly refutes the wardship of Philip the Fair by Maximilian. Only two deputies of the duchy of Brabant were present, but they drew up a report for the deputies of the other principalities of the Burgundian Netherlands who were assembled in Mechelen.[18] The deputies watched the evening of 13 March through the window of their Ghent hotel. They saw passing a noisy parade embodying the united military force of the Flemish cities.[19] That is to say, the city of Ghent, like the city of Bruges on the same day, organised a military parade of armed guildsmen (the *auweet*), thus wanting to show the military strength of the city: a word to the wise! In a less militarised atmosphere the deputies of nearly all the Estates of the northern Burgundian lands reassembled again at Ghent on 28 April 1488, where Willem presented the second text that we are going to analyse.[20] On this day, in the *hôtel Saint-Georges*, Ghent's intransigence spread out in the open. The Estates of Flanders, Brabant, Holland, Hainaut, Zeeland, Lille-Douai-Orchies, Luxembourg, Namur and Mechelen, as well as a delegation of the most important nobles of the Burgundian-Habsburg court, met for a great session of the Estates-General to discuss the liberation of the King of the Romans and his regency for Philip the Fair. After the session, which lasted two weeks, a treaty of alliance had been

---

15   Ghent City Archives, series 400, no. 30, fol. 332^r.
16   Ghent City Archives, series 20, no. 7, fols. 183^r–183^v; Gachard 1851, pp. 422–3.
17   He was buried in Ghent on 14 November 1492. Ghent City Archives, series 400, no. 31, fol. 80^r.
18   Wellens 1974, pp. 226–7. This report has been copied in a collection which is kept at the Bibliothèque nationale de France, Manuscrits Français 11590, fols. 252^r–255^v. It has been published and commented on in detail by Haemers 2010a, pp. 46–52.
19   Haemers and Lecuppre-Desjardin 2007.
20   Edited by Diegerick 1853–6, pp. xxxi–xlv (document G, beware the printing error on page numbers xliii, xliv and xlv).

signed between the principalities of the Low Countries on 12 May. The treaty re-established the council of regency in the county of Flanders, while stipulating that Maximilian would remain regent in the other principalities. On the 16 May, Maximilian confirmed this resolution with the 'Peace of Bruges', by which he renounced the regency in the county of Flanders. Willem and his political allies therefore had succeeded in installing a new council of regency in May 1488 in the county of Flanders, but they did not get this council to be recognised by the other principalities. The inability of the Members of Flanders to unite the political opposition against Maximilian of Austria, which will ultimately lead to the failure of the revolt, therefore already made itself felt at the beginning of the installation of the (second) council of regency in May 1488.[21]

4 The Two Speeches of Willem Zoete

Although Willem had not managed to persuade the deputies of the other Estates to reject Maximilian as the regent of his son, his two speeches are an excellent resource for reconstructing the 'political contract' in the county of Flanders.[22] His two texts, pearls of rhetoric, appear to be the result of a pre-established plan and were long-matured. The two speeches have characteristics typical for the legislation of customary law, which remained predominant in the Old Regime.[23] Leaving aside the numerous *ad hoc* passages, it is clear that Willem's texts are inspired not only by experience. The jurist had also used his great erudition to compose a veritable juridical accusation. In his *'J'accuse'* the pensionary summarises the reasons the Members of Flanders have for wanting to remove Maximilian from his regency. Juridical, historical, theoretical and even biblical arguments are enumerated in a dense style, but one clear for his audience. Because most of the deputies of the Estates-General were Dutch-speaking, the text was written in Middle Dutch. In its style, arguments and

---

21 Haemers and Sicking 2006.
22 A systematic analysis of the vocabulary and political ideas in these speeches was made using a large number of dictionaries and reference works for Middle Dutch, Middle French and Latin (legal, philosophical and Biblical). See Berger 1953; Keyt and Miller 1991; Berlioz 1994; Schrage 1987; Woolf 1913; Feenstra and Rossi 1961; Monier 1943; Ankum and Hartekamp 1973; Meinhart 1979; Reinsma, de Smidt, and de Schmidt 1969; Stallaert 1978. Also very useful are the Latin sources put online by Brepols in the Library of Latin Texts Online; and the *Monumenta Germaniae Historica*, see Boretius and Krause, eds 1883–97 and the on-line edition on www.mgh.de.
23 See, among others, Cauchies and De Schepper 1994.

purpose, the text often resembles the Act of Abjuration by which the Estates-General withdrew their confidence from the King of Spain, Philip II, in 1581. The speech of Willem Zoete is therefore one of the precedents of this Act of Abjuration, but because it had not achieved its aim it did not become as famous as that which was at the origin of the Dutch Revolt.[24]

Fundamentally, the two harangues pronounced by Willem translate the complaints and the claims of the great Flemish towns (the Members of Flanders) into a primarily juridical terminology which also concern questions of procedure as much as substantive argument. Some economic and political situations are then hidden in a stereotyped discourse of a legist specialised in the customary law enforced in the town, but are also clearly very much influenced by his studies in Roman and canon law, as we are going to demonstrate. The document of 28 April, for example, is a 'proposition' (*proposicie*),[25] that is, a juridical exposition elaborated by the lawyer from Ghent in response to the arguments of Pierre Rommerswalle, who expressed the point of view of the nobles of the blood, the Estates of Brabant, Hainaut, Zeeland and Namur. These Estates, who represent here the moderate wing of the revolt again Maximilian, sought in the first instance the liberation of the King of the Romans as the first step to reaching a compromise. In this session of the Estates-General of the Burgundian Low Countries held at Ghent on 28 April 1488, Willem's objective was to expound a series of juridical arguments to evade this strategy of moderation. As an experienced lawyer, he will first introduce a question of procedure. Willem argues that the liberation of Maximilian is neither the primary point, nor the preliminary question which the Estates must confront. On the contrary, one must in the first instance consider the questions evoked in the preceding sessions of the Estates, those concerning 'the unity of all the lands' ('*de eendrachtichede ende unye van allen den landen*'),[26] the peace treaty with France and the 'reduction of government ('*de reducxie van pollicie*'). Only after having discussed these preliminary questions could the freedom of the King of the Romans be placed on the agenda. To proceed otherwise would be an adjournment of the court, according to Willem, and even an 'perversion of order', an expression which must be understood here in its juridical sense of 'to pervert the course of justice', but which can also be associated with *perversio ordinis*, which one finds in Thomas Aquinas in the sense of tyranny as a perversion of the order wanted by God.

---

24   Blockmans, Willem 1983. The '*Placcaet van Verlatinghe*' has been edited by Mout 1979.
25   Diegerick 1853–6, p. xxxi; Haemers 2010a, p. 47.
26   Diegerick 1853–6, p. xxxii.

5   The 'Good Causes of the People'

According to Willem Zoete, the principle 'good cause' (the *bonae causae* or *justae causae* of Roman law) for which Maximilian should be deposed as regent of Philip the Fair was his mismanagement of his son's property. On the 28 June 1485 Maximilian had signed the Treaty of Bruges, in which the Members of Flanders recognised him as 'guardian [*mambour*] of My Lord the Duke Philip, his son, and in this capacity the government of the person of his said son and of the said lands is left to him'.[27] Therefore, Willem is accusing the King of the Romans of not having administered the wardship of Philip the Fair as he should.[28] Maximilian had borrowed large sums of money to finance his wars by offering jewels and precious items belonging to the Burgundian dynasty as collateral to his lenders. Willem was well informed, because, in fact, already during the reign of Mary of Burgundy, but also in 1486 for example, Maximilian had guaranteed his loans to foreign merchants with precious items from the treasury belonging to the counts of Flanders (conserved at the church of Saint Donatian in Bruges).[29] Due to the insolvency of Maximilian some of these pieces were not returned to the treasury, to the profit of Tommaso Portinari, among others.[30]

Philip the Fair's property was therefore managed 'poorly', said Willem, as in the expression *sobere regimente*, used in customary law of the towns of Flanders dealing with the management of the property of orphans. According to the private law of the southern Low Countries, guardianship could end by dismissal in the event of such management by the guardian of the property of his ward.[31] Willem includes the general management of the southern Low Countries in this 'mismanagement' of the count's personal property. The count should live 'from his own', and he therefore had the right to levy taxes in his domain.[32] But some taxes and customs imposed on the county by the officers of Maximilian of Austria were 'excessive'.[33] Furthermore, these taxes had served 'the appetite of some individual people'.[34] The King of the Romans had convened the Mem-

---

27   'mambour de monseigneur le duc Philippe, son filz, et en ceste qualité lui laisseront le gouvernement de la personne de son dit filz et du dit pays', Molinet 1935–7, vol. 1, p. 460.
28   Diegerick 1853–6, p. xxxvii.
29   Stabel and Haemers 2006.
30   Boone 1999.
31   Godding 1987, p. 137.
32   Scordia 2005.
33   Diegerick 1853–6, p. xxxvii.
34   Haemers 2010a, p. 51.

bers of Flanders only 'to have money'.[35] With these accusations Willem was therefore indicating to the 'relatives and friends' of Philip the Fair, that is, the 'nobles of blood' who were present at the convocation of the Estates-General,[36] that they could no longer accept the administration of the property of Count Philip by Maximilian of Austria.

The administration of the county of Flanders by the King of the Romans was an act of mismanagement, and worse, even of 'robbery, theft, slander, and misappropriation', according to Willem.[37] The Ghentenaar refers here to the taxes that Maximilian's officers had levied on the county, but also to the way in which the numerous subsidies that the Members of Flanders had granted to Maximilian had been spent. Willem Blockmans has calculated that during the regency of Maximilian (1485–8), the level of subsidies (aides) had reached the highest level in the century in Flanders if one excepts the year of 1475.[38] If it is not the volume of subsidies that is criticised by Willem, it is the expenditures of Maximilian that he condemns. The Members of Flanders had instructed Maximilian to defend the county of Flanders in exchange for the increase of these grants, and they had not asked him to begin an offensive war against France, a war which, furthermore, was detrimental to the commerce of the county of Flanders. Yet trade was the principal means of the county's prosperity, as already attested by the privileges of 1477.[39] The regent's wars had put a hypothec on the county and, consequently, it was preferable to withdraw guardianship from Maximilian's hands because he wasted his son's property.

The general thrust of Willem's case accuses the King of the Romans of having sought only his personal interest during the regency whereas the 'common good' of the lands should be the adage of princes (and regents). Willem proves that Maximilian is not concerned with this 'common good'. For example, he manipulated the exchange rate without the people's consent, despite the fact that money is 'the key to the people's coffers' and the basis of trade.[40] The regent had not acted in a just manner, but has imprisoned and punished arbit-

---

35   'Up de begheerten die de coninc dede omme ghelt thebbene', Ibid., p. 50.
36   On the 28 April, for example, Adolph of Cleves, Raphaël de Mercatel, and Philip of Burgundy, relatives of Philip the Fair, were present, Wellens 1974, pp. 462–3. Also see Haemers 2007e, cols 540–7; and Cauchies 1994, 275–6.
37   Diegerick 1853–6, p. xxxvii.
38   Blockmans, Willem 1974a, p. 293.
39   'Welvaert, orbore ende proffite van onsen vorseiden lande [...] alleenlic gefondeerd up de coopmanscepe ende neeringhe ende up de previlegen, vrijheden, costumen ende usagen', Blockmans, Willem 1985b, p. 129.
40   Haemers 2010a, p. 50.

rarily.[41] Maximilian had refused to defend the county effectively and he had even invaded the lands 'hostiliter' ('like an enemy'),[42] armed and surrounded by German troops (Willem here references the war led by Maximilian in the spring of 1485 to conquer the county). He had divided the county and he had sewn discord in order to reign.[43] The regent has not listened to the subjects of his son when they expressed their grievances to him.[44] He had lied to the Members so that they approve grants for him. While Maximilian had promised to use these grants for the maintenance of his son's court and the defence of the country, he 'wasted' them for other purposes.[45] In short, the regent did not behave as a good prince must.

Maximilian therefore broke his promise to be a good regent and, according to Willem, this oath was not the only commitment he had made. With the Treaty of Bruges, 28 June 1485, he had promised that he would 'confirm all the privileges, rights, customs and practices of the said lands'.[46] Even more, during his Joyous Entry into Bruges and into Ghent, Maximilian had solemnly sworn to maintain the privileges of the two cities and to keep the county 'in peace and in law'.[47] Despite this, the regent had imprisoned people without cause or reason. With some examples the pensionary proves that Maximilian had on many occasions violated the privileges of the county in general and those of 1477 in particular. The regent had not tolerated the Members of Flanders assembling without his consent, he had leased and sold comital offices, he had appointed foreigners to posts reserved for natives, etc.[48] Maximilian therefore had violated the privileges of 1477, whose final clauses mention that the subjects are not liable for services to a prince who perjures himself. In Willem's

---

41   Ibid., p. 49.
42   Diegerick 1853–6, p. xxxix.
43   Ibid., p. xxxiii.
44   Haemers 2010a, p. 52.
45   Ibid., p. 53.
46   'confirmerait tous les privilèges, droits, coutumes et usages du dit pays', Molinet 1935–7, vol. 1, p. 460.
47   His oath at Ghent: 'dat zwerdi wettelic voocht ende manbur te zijne van den hertooghe Phelips van Oostrijcke [...], tlandt van Vlaenderen in vreden ende in wette te houwene, de rechte, privilegen, oude ende nieuwe, van denzelven lande te houdene ende te doen onderhaudene', Ghent City Archives, series 93, no. 7, fol. 33ᵛ; at Bruges: 'dat wij den goeden lieden van der stede van Brugghe goed ende ghetrauwe heeren wesen zullen ende haerlieder previlegen, vriheden, goede costumen ende usaigen, alzo wel oude als nieuwe, houden ende doen houden, zullen ende al doen dat een goed ghetrauwe heere als vadere, vooght ende wettelic mamboir van zinen voorseiden zone schuldich es te doene zinen goeden lieden ende onderzaten', Municipal Archives of Bruges, cartulary 'Rodenboek', fol. 294ʳ.
48   Haemers 2010a, p. 51.

texts the privileges of 1477 are considered to be like contracts which the lord (or his regent) could not break. Maximilian is presented as a man without faith, who has not respected contracts not only with his subjects, but also with the king of France, of whom Philip the Fair was a vassal. Willem gives the example of the Peace of Arras that Maximilian had concluded with France in December 1482. Contrary to the stipulations of this treaty, Maximilian had waged war on France and therefore Willem claims that the King of the Romans breached the peace.[49] The regent therefore did not keep his promises, he made mistakes and he is the defaulting party.[50] Maximilian was 'the source of all the woe and disorder of the county' and consequently the Members of Flanders had good reasons to choose another regent.[51]

6 The Right to Resistance?

Did they have the right to choose another regent? It is clear that Willem played with a semantic association to convince the Estates-General of the Low Countries that Maximilian displays the characteristics of a tyrant.[52] His whole speech implies that the Roman king was the tyrant described by Thomas Aquinas. This latter, on this point followed by Bartolus de Saxoferrato, whom Willem had no doubt studied, distinguished the *tyrannus ex defectu tituli* and the *tyrannus ex pane exercitii*, respectively a tyrant who was not the 'natural prince' in the political language of the late Middle Ages, and a tyrant who abused his powers.[53] Willem suggests that Maximilian was both at the same time. Here, there was no question of legitimising a case of tyrannicide, as in the famous plea of Jean Petit and the *Policraticus* of John of Salisbury. However, the same semantic registers were used by Willem.[54] His principal argument was that the Flemish Revolt was not a true revolt but a lawful action of the subjects based in

---

49 Diegerick 1853–6, p. xxxviii. The Peace of Arras ended the war that Louis XI had led against the Burgundian dynasty after the death of Charles the Bold in 1477. It can be read in Molinet 1935–7, vol. 1, pp. 378–406.
50 Haemers 2010a, p. 47.
51 'Ten anderen es hy cause ende oorspronc van allen den quaden ende van alder desordene daerin men gherne remedieren soude', Diegerick 1853–6, p. xl.
52 'Car nul prince ne le peut autrement lever que par octroy, comme j'ay dit, si ce n'est par tyrannie et qu'il ne soit excommunié'. Commynes 1979, p. 435.
53 Deferrari 1960.
54 On the speech of Jean Petit, whose aim was to legitimatise the murder of the Duke of Orleans by John the Fearless, see Schnerb 2005, pp. 247–56. On John of Salisbury, see Rouse and Rouse 1967. Also see Rexroth 2004; and Valente 2003, pp. 18–32.

the principles of law. The members of Flanders, as argued Willem, have 'goede cause' (good/right causes) to proceed. According to this point of view, the revolt against a regent finds its legitimacy fundamentally in the notion of the common good. Anything that endangers the common welfare of the land, which God protects, can constitute a just motive for the replacement of a lord, who is thereby a tyrant.[55] In Willem's harangue, the incompetence of the lord is the motive most often invoked to prove that the politics of Maximilian of Habsburg resembles that of a tyrant.

Willem will therefore support his thesis, according to which the great towns of Flanders are within their rights, by putting forward a whole series of arguments found in the bible, history, natural law, Roman law, canon law and customary civil law. According to him, the Flemish were not in revolt, because medieval political theory, based on biblical and theological writings, does not accept the legitimisation of a revolt against the lord. However, as Philippe Depreux notes, political opposition to the prince – that is, to the unjust prince – is not completely unlawful.[56] To prove that Maximilian had governed 'unjustly', Willem claimed at the start of his speech that the Members of Flanders were simply using their right of appeal. The Members took themselves to be 'exempt' (*exemptus* as a form of juridical *immunitas*) of the guardianship of Maximilian over his son's lordship and also of the right of administration of his Flemish inheritance (*'hereditas administration, gestio, cura'*). Furthermore, they turned to the suzerain of the count of Flanders, the king of France. It was therefore not a rebellion and the Flemish were not 'mutineers' (*'meutmakers'*), it was simply an appeal, a defence procedure *'quae est de jure naturali'* (in Willem's words).[57]

The key words used by Willem reflect the central values in the political ideology of the urban elites of the county of Flanders. Some traces of this urban discourse can also be retrieved in many other sources that are not as scholarly as Willem's plea, some from Flanders but also from other European towns.[58] The harangues of Willem reflect central unsurprising notions: the common good, peace, unity, justice, commerce and industry, monetary stability and the political representation of subjects. For example, Maximilian is reproached for keeping the land and towns 'in division' (*'in divisien ende ghescille te houdene'*).[59] His soldiers engage in pillage and devastation. His officers, often foreigners to the lands of Flanders, are corrupt and ransom for-

---

55   Also see Cheynet 2008, p. 72.
56   See the introduction to Depreux, ed. 2008.
57   Diegerick 1853–6, p. xxxv.
58   Dumolyn 2008b.
59   Diegerick 1853–6, p. xxxv.

eign merchants. He is responsible for 'excess and violence' ('*overdaden ende violencie*')[60] and, according to Willem, Aristotle says in his *Politics* that because of such excesses governments and kingdoms were transferred '*de gente in gentem*' ('from one people to another'; in fact, this is more an allusion to Ecclesiastes).[61] Willem accuses the King of the Romans of very specific crimes in the language of criminal law found in the Code of Justinian: '*rapina*' (robbery), '*calomnia*' (slander), and the '*crime concussio*' (extortion, specifically, *extortio sub colore officii*: extortion under the colour of office).[62] He supports all this by evoking Gratian's Decretum.[63] Feudal law is also cited to argue that a vassal has no more obligations to his lord when the latter cannot assure his protection and security, without explicitly speaking of the *diffiducatio* or the *ius resistendi* (right to resist) because *strictu senso* these terms cannot be used to describe the relationships between a prince and his towns or other subjects. Elsewhere in his plea Willem emphasises that Maximilian had not kept the promises he made during his Joyous Entry into Flanders, a very grave accusation in the political universe of the Flemish citizens. Another charge: the breach of peace (*infractio pacis, 'denzelven paix imbreken*')[64] with France, to the detriment of his Flemish subjects. He refers to the book of Jeremiah to persuade his audience that if princes do not do their divine duty in protecting law and justice to avoid unreasonable burdens and the oppression of the poor,[65] they fall into the indignation of God 'and the people have good causes to rise up against them' ('*ende hevet tvolc goede cause jeghens hemlieden te rysene*').[66] One could thus multiply the examples in all the semantic registers that Willem uses, like the comparison between Maximilian and a series of supposedly bad kings formerly deposed by their subjects, such as Jeroboam, Nero, Childeric and others. The implicit bipolar opposition that Willem suggests with his argument is that between 'the natural prince' and the 'tyrant'. Even though this latter extremely grave

---

60   Haemers 2010a, p. 51: '*forchen, overdaden, crachten ende violencien*'.

61   '*Regnum a gente in gentem transfertur propter injustitias*'. Ecclesiastes 10.8.

62   Diegerick 1853–6, p. xxxvii.

63   *Pars* II, *causa* XXIII, *quaestio* 1, *capitula* 6.

64   Diegerick 1853–6, p. xxxvii.

65   Jeremiah 22.3–5. 'Thus saith the Lord; Execute ye judgment and righteousness, and deliver the spoiled out of the hand of the oppressor: and do no wrong, do no violence to the stranger, the fatherless, nor the widow, neither shed innocent blood in this place. For if ye do this thing indeed, then shall there enter in by the gates of this house kings sitting upon the throne of David, riding in chariots and on horses, he, and his servants, and his people. But if ye will not hear these words, I swear by myself, saith the Lord, that this house shall become a desolation'. King James Version.

66   Diegerick 1853–6, p. xxxvi.

accusation is not explicitly formulated, Willem plays on this dichotomy in the medieval political thought that we find, for example, this time word for word, in Christine de Pisan's *Livre de la Paix*.[67]

Willem's arguments, discourse and procedure together make the meeting of the Estates-General of March and April 1488 look like a tribunal. In effect, this assembly also had judicial powers, above all when it came to foreign policy, as was the case seen here since the peace treaty with the king of France had been broken. The legal procedure implicitly refers to the feudal contract where each of the parties could consider itself released from its obligations if the other party perjured themselves. But it also brings to mind historical precedents in Flanders. Already in 1128 the new count of Flanders, William Clito, after a grave succession crisis in the county, had to justify himself before a comparable tribunal.[68] In 1452 the duke of Burgundy, Philip the Good, also had to appear before an exceptional royal tribunal which had to consider whether he had violated the rights of the Flemish towns in general and those of the town of Ghent in particular.[69] In the years of 1483–5 the Members of Flanders had brought a lawsuit against Maximilian before the Parliament of Paris due to the bad management of the property of Philip the Fair, a vassal of the king of France.[70] The juridical procedure had aimed to depose the King of the Romans as guardian of his son and thus withdraw from him the management of his inheritance in the Low Countries. But this process never resulted in a sentence.

The outcome of such a trial, like the granting of a privilege from the lord to his subjects, always depends on concrete political circumstances and, more specifically, on the lord's political resilience. Once his power was restored, he could challenge the sentence of the trial or the existence of any particular privilege.[71] In 1488, the sentence of the 'trial against Maximilian' would also reflect a certain balance of power. The document that would end the assembly of the Estates-General of April 1488, the 'Treaty of Union' of 12 May 1488, would judge that Maximilian should be deposed of his regency in the county. The imprisoned King of the Romans did not have the means to oppose this 'sentence' which have given the Members of Flanders the right to remove Maximilian from his regency and to choose another regent, that is to say, the council of regency. During a humiliating ceremony, Maximilian himself signed this

---

67 See Pisan 1958 (143/9).
68 Blockmans, Willem 1983, p. 146; Boone 2007a, pp. 195–6; Van Caenegem 1990, p. 105; Demyttenaere 2003; Boone, 2007b.
69 Boone 1990a; and Haemers 2004b, pp. 341–51.
70 Dauchy 1995, pp. 199–206.
71 Van Uytven and Blockmans 1969, p. 423.

treaty on 16 May 1488 (the 'Peace of Bruges'), through which the political claim of the Members of Flanders to choose another regent became a written law. But, as we have already explained in detail, the son of the German Emperor never accepted his dismissal. As soon as he was released he contested the Peace of Bruges with the same means that Willem had himself used: a legal struggle, one accompanied with intensive propaganda. But, as was often the case in the Middle Ages, the sword decided the outcome of this dispute.

7 Conclusion: The Political Contract in Flanders

Just as Willem Blockmans has argued for the 1581 Act of Abjuration, we also conclude that in 1488 Willem wanted the Estates-General to consider themselves the ultimate guarantors of the rights of the prince's subjects.[72] The observation that the Flemish 'rebels' had failed to unite the political opposition of the Burgundian lands against Maximilian of Habsburg does not change the fact that the set of rights, customs and privileges that the Flemish urban elites fervently defended can be considered as the key element of the political contract between the subjects and their lord. Willem insisted that the regent Maximilian guarantee this contract; if he violated it, he overstepped the law and should be replaced by a better guarantor. The prince's power was therefore reduced, not even to a bilateral contract between equal parties, but to an assignment revocable by its mandator. According to the documents that we have analysed here, the subjects, and more specifically their representatives in the assemblies of the Estates, have therefore the right to no longer recognise Maximilian as their prince. They have such recourse especially if the prince has neglected their entreaties and requests for the redress of grievances justified by their rights. With a juridical eclecticism, that is to say arguments based on natural law, biblical citations, Roman law, customary law and precedent, Willem justifies such a procedure. In addition, the oath Maximilian had taken in 1485, and the resulting contractual relationship, legitimised the removal from his regency in 1488. The King of the Romans had frequently violated the laws of the land and the contract with his subjects, that is to say that he had never respected the privileges of his subjects. As a guardian, he had badly managed the property and the lands of his son because he had governed them only for his own profit. The regent was recalcitrant and even incapable of demonstrating sensitivity to the

---

72 Blockmans, Willem 1983, pp. 139 and 141. See also Ganshof 1950; Kossmann 1980; and Königsberger 2001.

remonstrations and grievances of his subjects. Consequently, the Members of Flanders had 'good causes' and even the right to choose another regent.

Well before John Locke, the Ghent jurist Willem Zoete had thus composed in 1488 a 'hypothesis for rebellion'. Willem's harangue was a juridical plea and used arguments derived from different juridical sources: Roman, canon, customary, feudal and even natural law. Substantive arguments were found to support legal reasoning, and it is this intertextuality – one using biblical, juridical, historical and philosophical registers – which strikingly reflects a typically medieval way of reasoning. Although Willem had been the prisoner of his juridical logic and of very specific legal categories, all the fundamental values of the urban ideology of the great Flemish towns were present in his discourse: self-governance in dialogue with the prince, monetary stability, the burden of taxation, a stable environment for investment, juridical and military security, etc. In addition, each legal allegation and each ideological expression in turn reflects very concrete political, economic and social problems. There is therefore a real dialectic between words and things in the texts that we have analysed.

By way of a conclusion: what is the difference between the work of Locke and the rhetoric of Willem? Locke wrote that the people revolt against an unjust prince. Willem cannot legitimate a revolt because this would be unthinkable in the framework of medieval political thought and above all in juridical arguments before an assembly of the Estates-General that in the majority consisted of representatives more moderate than the three great Flemish towns with their revolutionary tradition. He therefore concluded that the people had 'good reasons to rise up against the prince'. For him, a rising was not necessarily a revolt; it was self-defence 'according to natural law'. A pearl of rhetoric then, and also an example of juridical hypocrisy at a moment when the prince was in prison in Bruges and there was already an open armed revolt in his lands. But behind all this phraseology one perceives the true motivations of the people of the Flemish towns, and certainly a vision, early but highly developed, of social or political contract.

Bibliography

Primary Sources

Archives départementales du Nord, Lille
Series B (Chambre des Comptes) 2121
B 2140
B 3495, Nr. 123686
B 4121
B 5346
B 17732

Municipal Archives of Bruges (Stadsarchief Brugge)
Accounts of the city, 1436–8, 1467–77, 1476–7, 1477–8, 1478–9, 1479–80, 1481–2, 1482–3, 1483–4, 1485–6, 1487–8, 1488–9, 1491–2
Accounts of the war, no. 5 (1488–89)
Cartulary Rodenboek
Charters ambachten, nos. 236; 546
Fonds Adornes, nos. 361, 363, 368
Klerk van de Vierschare, no. 828bis
Memoriael van de Camere, 1478
Political charters, first series, nos. 163; 165
Procuraties, 1485; 1492
Register of the city council, 1468–1501
Register van de Vierschaar

State Archives of Belgium, Bruges (Algemeen Rijksarchief Brugge)
Burg van Brugge, no. 64
Chambers of accounts, nos. 13788; 14118; 17404; 17412
Oud archief stad Nieuwpoort, charter 124

Public Library of Bruges (Openbare bibliotheek Brugge)
Ms. 436
Ms. 437

Royal Library of Belgium, Brussels (KBR)
Ms. 7384

Ghent City Archives (Stadsarchief Gent)
Charter 582
Series 20, no. 7
Series 93, no. 7
Series 330, nos. 41; 44; 45
Series 400, nos. 30; 31

Bibliothèque municipale, Douai
Ms. 1110

Bibliothèque nationale de France
Manuscrits Français 11590

Veurne Municipal Archives (Stadsarchief Veurne)
Charter 206

Haus-, Hof-, und Staatsarchiv, Vienna
Belgica PC, Liasse 1, Konvolut 2 (Ghent, 1476–92).

Online Resources

De Digitale Bibliotheek voor de Nederlandse Letteren (DBNL), www.dbnl.org.
Flandrica.be, www.flandrica.be.
Library of Latin Texts Online, http://www.brepols.net/Pages/BrowseBySeries.aspx?Tree
   Series=LLT-O, Brepols.
Thesaurus Diplomaticus, www.diplomata-belgica.be.
Monumenta Germaniae Historica, www.mgh.de.
Woordenboek der Nederlandsche Taal, http://gtb.inl.nl/.

Secondary Sources

Abu-Lughod, Lila, and Catherine Lutz 1990. 'Introduction: Emotion, Discourse and the
   Politics of Everyday Life'. In *Language and the Politics of Emotion*, edited by Cather-
   ine Lutz and Lila Abu-Lughod, 1–23. Cambridge: Cambridge University Press.
Acke, Renaat 1986. 'De schepenbank van Ieper (1280–1330)'. *De Leiegouw* 28: 165–70.
Alberts, Wybe Jappe, ed. 1957. *Dit sijn die wonderlijcke oorloghen van den doorluchtighen
   hoochgheboren prince, keyser Maximiliaen*. Groningen: Wolters.
Allison, James, and Joseph Cloud 1962. 'The Lex Julia Maiestatis'. *Latomus* 21 (4): 711–31.

Althoff, Gerd 1996. 'Empörung, Tränen, Zerknirschung: Emotionen in der öffentlichen Kommunikation des Mittelalters'. *Frühmittelalerliche Studien* 16: 60–79.

Althoff, Gerd 1998. 'Ira Regis: Prolegomena to a History of Royal Anger'. In *Anger's Past. The Social Uses of an Emotion in the Middle Ages*, edited by Barbara Rosenwein, 59–74. Ithaca, NY: Cornell University Press.

Althoff, Gerd 2002a. 'Die Kultur der Zeichen und Symbole'. *Frühmittelalerliche Studien* 36: 1–17.

Althoff, Gerd 2002b. 'The Variability of Rituals in the Middle Ages'. In *Medieval Concepts of the Past. Ritual, Memory, Historiography*, edited by Gerd Althoff, Johannes Fried, and Patrick Geary, 71–87. Cambridge: Cambridge University Press.

Ankum, Johan, and Arthur Hartkamp 1973. *Romeinsrechtelijk handwoordenboek*. Zwolle: Tjeenk Willink.

Ardant, Gabriel 1965. *Théorie sociologique de l'impôt*. 2 vols. Paris: S.E.V.P.E.N.

Arens, Werner 1989. 'Late Middle English Political Poetry as "Public Poetry"'. In *The Living Middle Ages: Studies in Mediaeval English Literature and its Tradition*, edited by Uwe Böker, Manfred Markus, and Rainer Schöwerling, 166–82. Stuttgart: Belser.

Arnade, Peter 1991. 'Secular Charisma, Sacred Power: Rites of Rebellion in the Ghent Entry of 1467'. *Handelingen der Maatschappij voor Geschiedenis en Oudheidkunde te Gent* 45: 69–94.

Arnade, Peter 1994. 'Crowds, Banners and the Market Place: Symbols of Defiance and Defeat during the Ghent War of 1452–1453'. *Journal of Medieval and Renaissance Studies* 24 (3): 471–97.

Arnade, Peter 1996a. *Realms of Ritual. Burgundian Ceremony and Civic Life in Medieval Ghent*. Ithaca, NY: Cornell University Press.

Arnade, Peter 1996b. 'Writing and Social Experience: Narratives of Urban Life in the Burgundian Netherlands'. In *Verhalende bronnen. Repertoriëring, editie en commercialisering*, edited by Ludo Milis, Véronique Lambert, and Ann Kelders, 95–118. Ghent: Studia Historica Gandensia.

Arnade, Peter 1997. 'City, Court and Public Ritual in the Late-Medieval Burgundian Netherlands'. *Comparative Studies in Society and History* 29: 296–314.

Arnade, Peter 2000. 'The Emperor and the City: The Cultural Politics of the Joyous Entry in Early Sixteenth-Century Ghent and Flanders'. *Handelingen der Maatschappij voor Geschiedenis en Oudheidkunde te Gent* 54: 65–92.

Arnade, Peter 2003. 'Privileges and the Political Imagination in the Ghent Revolt of 1539'. In *Charles V in Context: The Making of a European Identity*, edited by Marc Boone and Marysa Demoor, 103–24. Brussels: Ghent University-VUB University Press.

Arnade, Peter 2005. 'The Rage of the "Canaille": The Logic of Fury in the Iconoclasm Riots of 1566'. In Lecuppre-Desjardin and Van Bruaene, eds 2005, 93–111.

Arnade, Peter 2008. *Beggars, Iconoclasts, and Civic Patriots: The Political Culture of the Dutch Revolt*. Ithaca, NY: Cornell University Press.

Arnade, Peter, Martha Howell, and Walter Simons 2002. 'Fertile Spaces: The Productivity of Urban Space in Northern Europe'. *The Journal of Interdisciplinary History* 32 (4): 515–48.

Arnold, John 2001. *Inquisition and Power: Catharism and the Confessing Subject in Medieval Languedoc*. Philadelphia, PA: University of Pennsylvania Press.

Arnold, John 2009. 'Religion and Popular Rebellion, from the Capuciati to Niklashausen'. *Cultural and Social History* 6 (2): 149–70.

Arnould, Maurice-Aurélien 1985. 'Les lendemains de Nancy dans les "Pays de par deça" (Janvier-Avril 1477)'. In Blockmans, Willem, ed. 1985a, 1–83.

Assmann, Jan 1992. *Das kulturelle Gedächtnis: Schrift, Erinnerung und politische Identität in frühen Hochkulturen*. Munich: Beck.

Assmann, Jan 2008. 'Communicative and Cultural Memory'. In *Cultural Memory Studies. An International and Interdisciplinary Handbook*, edited by Astrid Erll and Ansgar, 109–18. Nünning. Berlin.

Austin, John 1971. *How to Do Things with Words*. London: Oxford University Press.

Avonds, Piet 1994. '"Ghemeyn oirbaer". Volkssoevereiniteit en politieke ethiek in Brabant in de veertiende eeuw'. In Reynaert, ed. 1994, 164–80.

Axters, Stephanus 1943. *Jan van Leeuwen. Een bloemlezing uit zijn werken*. Antwerp: De Sikkel.

Bailly, Marie-Charlotte 1998. 'Un cas particulier de lèse-majesté. Les injures verbales contre le conseil de Hollande en tant que collège (1428–1491)'. *Tijdschrift voor Rechtsgeschiedenis* 66: 97–113.

Bakhtin, Mikhail 1981. 'Discourse in the Novel'. In *The Dialogic Imagination: Four Essays*, edited by Michael Holquist, translated by Caryl Emerson and Michael Holquist, 259–422. Austin, TX: University of Texas Press.

Bakhtin, Mikhail. 1984. *Rabelais and His World*, translated by Hélène Iswolsky. Bloomington and Indianapolis: Indiana University Press.

Barbey, Jean 1983. *La fonction royale: essence et légitimité*. Paris: Nouvelles éditions latines.

Bardoel, Agatha 1994. 'The Urban Uprising at Bruges, 1280–81. Some New Findings about the Rebels and the Partisans'. *Revue Belge de Philologie et d'Histoire* 72: 761–91.

Barr, Helen 2001. *Socioliterary Practice in Late Medieval England*. Oxford: Oxford University Press.

Barron, Caroline 2004. 'The Political Culture of Medieval London'. In *The Fifteenth Century IV: Political Culture in Late Medieval Britain*, edited by Linda Clark and Christine Carpenter, 111–34. Woodbridge: The Boydell Press.

Barry, Jonathan 1994. 'Bourgeois Collectivism? Urban Association and the Middling Sort'. In *The Middling Sort of People: Culture, Society and Politics in England, 1550–1800*, edited by Jonathan Barry and Christhopher Brooks, 84–112. London: Palgrave Macmillan.

Barth, Reinhard 1974. *Argumentation und Selbstverständnis der Bürgeropposition in städtischen Auseinandersetzungen des Spätmittelalters: Lübeck 1403–1408, Braunschweig 1374–1376, Mainz 1444–1446, Köln 1396–1400*. Cologne: Böhlau.

Barton, Richard 1998. ' "Zealous Anger" and the Renegotiation of Aristocratic Relationships in Eleventh- and Twelfth-Century France'. In *Anger's Past. The Social Uses of an Emotion in the Middle Ages*, edited by Barbara Rosenwein, 153–70. Ithaca, NY: Cornell University Press.

Battard, Marius, and Jean Lestocquoy 1948. *Beffrois, halles, hôtels de ville dans le nord de la France et la Belgique*. Arras: Brunet.

Bauman, Richard 1967. *The Crimen Maiestatis in the Roman Republic and Augustan Principate*. Johannesburg: Witwatersrand University Press.

Bauman, Richard 1974. *Impietas in Principem. A Study of Treason against the Roman Emperor with Special Reference to the First Century A. D.* Munich: Beck.

Bautier, Robert-Henri, Janine Sornay, and Françoise Muret 1984. *Les sources de l'histoire économique et sociale du Moyen Âge. Les états de la maison de Bourgogne, 1: Archives des principautés territoriales, Part 2: Les principautés du Nord*. Paris: CNRS Éditions.

Beik, William 1987. 'Urban Factions and the Social Order during the Minority of Louis XIV'. *French Historical Studies* 15: 36–67.

Beik, William 1997. *Urban Protest in Seventeenth-Century France. The Culture of Retribution*. Cambridge: Cambridge University Press.

Beik, William 2007. 'The Violence of the French Crowd from Charivari to Revolution'. *Past & Present* 197: 75–110.

Bellingradt, Daniel 2011. *Flugpublizistik und Öffentlichkeit um 1700. Dynamiken, Akteure und Strukturen im urbanen Raum des Alten Reiches*. Stuttgart: Franz Steiner Verlag.

Bellingradt, Daniel 2012. 'The Early Modern City as a Resonating Box: Media, Public Opinion, and the Urban Space of the Holy Roman Empire, Cologne and Hamburg ca. 1700'. *Journal of Early Modern History* 16 (3): 201–40.

Benad, Matthias 1990. *Domus und Religion in Montaillou. Katholische Kirche und Katharismus im Überlebenskampf der Familie des Pfarrers Petrus Clerici am Anfang des 14. Jahrhunderts*. Tübingen: Mohr.

Bercé, Yves-Marie 1976. *Fête et révolte: des mentalités populaires du XVI e au XVIIIe siècle*. Paris: Hachette.

Bercé, Yves-Marie 1980. *Révoltes et révolutions dans l'Europe moderne: XVIe–XVIIIe siècles*. Paris: Presses Universitaires de France.

Berger, Adolf 1953. *Encyclopedic Dictionary of Roman Law*. Philadelphia, PA: The American Philosophical Society.

Berges, Wilhelm 1952. *Die Fürstenspiegel des hohen und späten Mittelalters*. Stuttgard: Hiersemann.

Berlioz, Jacques 1994. *Identifier sources et citations*. Turnhout: Brepols.

Berten, Dirk 1913. 'Un ancien manuscrit flamand de la bibliothèque de Vienne'. *Bulletin de la Commission Royale des Anciennes Lois et Ordonnances de Belgique* 9: 436–92.

Bertin, Paul 1947. *Une commune flamande-artésienne, Aire-sur-la-Lys, des origines au xvie siècle.* Arras: Brunet.

Billen, Claire 2010. 'Dire le Bien Commun dans l'espace public. Matérialité épigraphique et monumentale du bien commun dans les villes des Pays-Bas, à la fin du Moyen Âge'. In *De Bono Communi. The Discourse and Practice of the Common Good in the European City*, edited by Élodie Lecuppre-Desjardin and Anne-Laure Van Bruaene, 71–88. Turnhout: Brepols.

Bisschop, Willem, and Eelco Verwijs, eds 1870. *Gedichten van Willem van Hildegaersberch.* The Hague: Nijhof.

Black, Anthony 2002. *Political Thought in Europe, 1250–1450.* Cambridge: Cambridge University Press.

Black, Anthony 2003. *Guild and State: European Political thought from the Twelfth Century to the Present.* New Brunswick: Transaction Publishers.

Blickle, Peter 1988. *Unruhen in der ständischen Gesellschaft 1300–1800.* Munich: Walter de Gruyter GmbH.

Blickle, Peter 2000. *Kommunalismus: Skizzen einer gesellschaftlichen Organisationsform.* 2 vols. Munich: Oldenbourg.

Bloch, Marc 1925. 'Mémoire collective, tradition et coutume. A propos d'un livre récent'. *Revue de Synthèse Historique* 40: 73–84.

Block, Joseph 1993. *Factional Politics and the English Reformation.* Woodbridge: Boydell & Brewer.

Blockmans, Frans 1938a. 'De oudste privileges der groote Vlaamsche steden'. *Nederlandsche Historiebladen* 1: 421–46.

Blockmans, Frans 1938b. *Het Gentsche stadspatriciaat tot omstreeks 1302.* Antwerp: De Sikkel.

Blockmans, Frans 1940. 'De bestraffing van den opstand van Brugge en van westelijk Vlaanderen in 1328'. In *Beknopte handelingen van het 15de Vlaams philologencongres*, 38–45. Louvain: Peeters.

Blockmans, Willem 1971. 'Nieuwe gegevens over de gegoede burgerij in Brugge in de 13e en vooral 15e Eeuw'. In *Studiën betreffende de sociale strukturen te Brugge, Kortrijk en Gent in de 14e en 15e Eeuw. Deel I: tekst*, edited by Willem Blockmans, 133–54. Kortrijk: UGA.

Blockmans, Willem 1973. 'De belastingbetalers te Brugge (1488–1490) en te Gent (1492–1494). Register van persoonsnamen'. In *Studiën betreffende de sociale strukturen te Brugge, Kortrijk en Gent in de 14e en 15e Eeuw. Deel III: Tabellen en register van persoonsnamen*, edited by Willem Blockmans, Cécile Pauwelyn, and Liliane Wynant, 211–86. Kortrijk: UGA.

Blockmans, Willem 1974a. 'Autocratie ou polyarchie? La lutte pour le pouvoir politique en Flandre de 1482 à 1492 d'après des documents inédits'. *Bulletin de la Commission Royale d'Histoire* 140: 257–368.

Blockmans, Willem 1974b. 'Revolutionaire mechanismen in Vlaanderen van de 13ᵉ tot de 16ᵉ eeuw'. *Tijdschrift voor Sociale Wetenschappen* 19: 123–40.

Blockmans, Willem 1978. *De volksvertegenwoordiging in Vlaanderen in de overgang van middeleeuwen naar nieuwe tijden (1384–1506)*. Brussels: Koninklijke Academie voor Wetenschappen.

Blockmans, Willem 1983. 'Du contrat féodal à la souveraineté du peuple. Les précédents de la déchéance de Philippe II dans les Pays-Bas (1581)'. In *Assemblee di stati e istituzioni rappresentative nella storia del pensiero politico moderno, secoli XV–XX. Atti del convegno internazionale tenuto a Perugia dal 16 al 18 settembre, 1982*, 135–50. Rimini: Universita di Perugia.

Blockmans, Willem, ed. 1985a. *1477. Le Privilège Général et les privilèges régionaux de Marie de Bourgogne pour les Pays-Bas (1477. Het Algemene en de gewestelijke privilegien van Maria van Bourgondië voor de Nederlanden)*. Kortrijk: UGA.

Blockmans, Willem 1985b. 'Breuk of continuïteit? De Vlaamse Privilegiën van 1477 in het licht van het staatsvormingsproces'. In Blockmans, Willem, ed. 1985a, 97–144.

Blockmans, Willem 1985c. 'La position du comté de Flandre dans le royaume à la fin du XVe siècle'. In *La France de la fin du XVe siècle. Renouveau et apogée: économie, pouvoirs, arts, culture et conscience nationales. Colloque international du Centre national de la recherche scientifique: Tours, Centre d'études supérieures de la Renaissance, 3–6 octobre 1983: actes*, edited by Bernard Chevalier and Philippe Contamine, 71–89. Paris: CNRS Éditions.

Blockmans, Willem 1988a. 'Alternatives to Monarchical Centralisation: The Great Tradition of Revolt in Flanders and Brabant'. In *Republiken und Republikanismus im Europa der frühen Neuzeit*, edited by Helmut Königsberger, 145–54. Munich: Oldenbourg.

Blockmans, Willem 1988b. 'La répression des révoltes urbaines comme méthode de centralisation dans les Pays-Bas bourguignons'. In *Milan et les états bourguignons. Deux ensembles politiques princiers entre Moyen Âge et Renaissance (XIVe–XVIe s.)*, edited by Jean-Marie Cauchies and Giorgio Chittolini, 5–9. Publications du Centre Européen d'Études Bourguignonnes (XIVe–XVIe siècles) 28. Basel: Centre Européen d'Études Bourguignonnes (XIVe–XVIe siècles).

Blockmans, Willem 1988c. 'Patronage, Brokerage and Corruption as Symptoms of Incipient State Formation in the Burgundian-Habsburg Netherlands'. In *Klientelsysteme im Europa der Frühen Neuzeit*, edited by Antoni Maçzak and Elisabeth von Müller-Luckner, 117–26. Munich: Oldenbourg.

Blockmans, Willem 1988d. 'Princes conquérants et bourgeois calculateurs. Le poids des réseaux urbains dans la formation des états'. In *La ville, la bourgeoisie et la genèse de l'état moderne (XIIe–XVIIIes.)*, edited by Neithard Bulst and Jean-Philippe Genet, 167–80. Paris: CNRS Éditions.

Blockmans, Willem 1989. 'Voracious States and Obstructing Cities: An Aspect of State Formation in Preindustrial Europe'. *Theory and Society* 18: 733–55.

Blockmans, Willem, ed. 1990a. *Handelingen van de Leden en van de Staten van Vlaanderen. Regering van Filips de Goede (10 September 1419–15 Juni 1467): excerpten uit de rekeningen van de vlaamse steden en kasselrijen en van de vorstelijke ambtenaren, dl. 1: tot de onderwerping van Brugge (4 maart 1438)*. Brussels: Paleis der Academiën.

Blockmans, Willem 1990b. 'Vete, partijstrijd en staatsmacht, een vergelijking (met de nadruk op Vlaanderen)'. In *Bloedwraak, partijstrijd en pacificatie in laat-middeleeuws Holland*, edited by Jannis Marsilje, 9–33. Hilversum: Verloren.

Blockmans, Willem 1994a. 'Urban Space in the Low Countries, 13th–16th Centuries'. In *Spazio urbano e organizzazione economica nell'Europa medievale*, edited by Alberto Grohmann, 163–75. Napels: Edizioni Scientifiche Italiane.

Blockmans, Willem 1994b. 'Voracious States and Obstructing Cities'. In *Cities and the Rise of States in Europe, AD 1000–1800*, in Tilly and Blockmans, eds 1994, 218–50. Boulder, CO: Westview.

Blockmans, Willem 1996a. '"Crisme de leze majesté", Les idées politiques de Charles le Téméraire'. In *Les Pays-Bas bourguignons, histoire et institutions. Mélanges André Uyttebrouck*, edited by Jean-Marie Duvosquel and André Uyttebrouck, 71–81. Brussels: Archives et Bibliothèques de Belgique.

Blockmans, Willem 1996b. 'La manipulation du consensus, systèmes de pouvoir à la fin du Moyen Âge'. In *Principe e città alla fine del medioevo*, edited by S. Gensini, 433–47. Pisa: Firenze University Press.

Blockmans, Willem 1997a. 'The Impact of Cities on State Formation: Three Contrasting Territories in the Low Countries, 1300–1500'. In *Resistance, Representation, and Community*, edited by Peter Blickle, 256–71. Oxford: Oxford University Press.

Blockmans, Willem 1997b. *A History of Power in Europe. Peoples, Markets and States*. Antwerp: Mercatorfonds.

Blockmans, Willem 1999a. 'Regionale Vielfalt in Zunftwesen in den Niederlanden vom 13. bis 16. Jahrhundert'. In *Handwerk in Europa vom Spätmitteralter bis zur Frühen Neuzeit*, edited by Knut Schulz, 51–63. Munich: Oldenbourg.

Blockmans, Willem 1999b. 'Städtenetzwerke in den Niederlanden'. In *Mitteleuropäisches Städtewesen in Mittelalter und Frühneuzeit. Edith Ennen Gewidnet*, edited by Wilhelm Janssen and Margaret Wensky, 91–104. Cologne: Böhlau.

Blockmans, Willem 2000. *Keizer Karel V, 1500–1558: de utopie van het keizerschap*. Louvain: Halewyck.

Blockmans, Willem 2002. *Emperor Charles V, 1500–1558*. London: Arnold.

Blockmans, Willem 2010. 'Inclusiveness and Exclusion: Trust Networks at the Origins of European Cities'. *Theory and Society* 39: 315–26.

Blockmans, Willem, and Esther Donckers 1999. 'Self-Representation of Court and City in Flanders and Brabant in the Fifteenth and Early Sixteenth Centuries'. In *Showing Status: Representation of Social Positions in the Late Middle Age*, edited by Willem Blockmans and Antheun Janse, 81–113. Turnhout: Brepols.

Blockmans, Willem, and Walter Prevenier 1999. *The Promised Lands. The Low Countries under Burgundian Rule, 1369–1530*. Philadelphia, PA: University of Pennsylvania Press.

Blockmans, Willem, Maurice-Aurélien Arnould, and Egied Strubbe 1985. 'Privilegie voor alle landen van herwaarts over, verleend door Maria, hertogin van Bourgondië ter bekrachting van de klachten die de Staten-Generaal haar hadden voorgelegd, 11 februari 1477'. In Blockmans, Willem, ed. 1985a, 85–95.

Blockmans, Willem, and Paul van Peteghem 1976. 'De Pacificatie van Gent als uiting van kontinuïteit in de politieke opvattingen van de standenvertegenwoordiging'. *Tijdschrift voor Geschiedenis* 89: 322–34.

Bloemendal, Jan, ed. 2009. *Een Spel van zinnen van den Zieke Stad van Jacob Jacobsz. Jonck (UBU 5 M 19 ms 1336): politieke en religieuze satire in zestiende-eeuws Amsterdam*. Amersfoort: Florivallis.

Blommaert, Philip, ed. 1847. *Politieke balladen, refereinen, liederen en spotdichten der XVIe eeuw, naar een gelyktydig handschrift*. Ghent: Annoot-Braeckman.

Blommaert, Philip, and Constant Serrure, eds 1839–40. *Kronyk van Vlaenderen van 580–1467*. 2 vols. Ghent: Vanderhaeghen-Hulin.

Blommaert, Willem 1915. *Les châtelains de Flandre: étude d'histoire constitutionnelle*. Ghent: Van Goethem.

Boas, George 1969. *Vox Populi: Essays in the History of an Idea*. Baltimore, MD: The Johns Hopkins University Press.

Boffa, Serge 2001. 'Réflexions sur la révolte des métiers bruxellois (22 Juillet 1360)'. In *Bruxelles et la vie urbaine. Archives–Art–Histoire*, edited by Frank Daelemans and André Vanrie, vol. 1, 163–85. Brussels: Archives et bibliothèque de Belgique.

Bois, Guy 2000. *La grande dépression médiévale, XIVe–XVe siècles. Le précédent d'une crise systémique*. Paris: Presses Universitaires de France.

Boissevain, Jeremy 1974. *Friends of Friends: Networks, Manipulators and Coalitions*. Oxford: Blackwell.

Bonicel, Mathieu, and Katell Lavéant 2010. 'Le théâtre dans la ville. Pour une histoire sociale des représentations dramatiques'. *Médiévales* 59: 91–105.

Bonney, Richard, ed. 1999. *The Rise of the Fiscal State in Europe, c. 1200–1815*. Oxford: Oxford University Press.

Boogaart, Thomas 2001a. 'Our Saviour's Blood: Procession and Community in Late Medieval Bruges'. In *Moving Subjects: Processional Performance in the Middle Ages and the Renaissance*, edited by Kathleen Ashley and Wim Hüsken, 69–116. Amsterdam: Rodopi.

Boogaart, Thomas 2001b. 'Reflections on the Moerlemaye: Revolt and Reform in Late Medieval Bruges'. *Revue Belge de Philologie et d'histoire* 79 (4): 1133–57.

Boogaart, Thomas 2004. *An Ethnogeography of Late Medieval Bruges: Evolution of the Corporate Milieu 1280–1349*. Lewiston, NY: Edwin Mellen Press.

Boone, Marc 1989a. 'De souverein-baljuw van Vlaanderen: breekijzer in het conflict tussen stedelijk particularisme en bourgondische centralisatie'. *Handelingen van het Genootschap voor Geschiedenis te Brugge* 126: 57–78.

Boone, Marc 1989b. ' "Want remitteren is princelijck." Vorstelijk genaderecht en sociale realiteiten in de bourgondische periode'. In *Liber amicorum Achiel de Vos*, 53–9. Evergem: Oost-Vlaams Verbond van de Kringen voor Geschiedenis.

Boone, Marc 1990a. 'Diplomatie et violence d'état. La sentence rendue par les ambassadeurs et conseillers du roi de France, Charles VII, concernant le conflit entre Philippe le Bon, duc de Bourgogne, et Gand en 1452'. *Bulletin de La Comission Royale d'Histoire* 156: 1–54.

Boone, Marc 1990b. *Gent en de Bourgondische hertogen, ca. 1384–ca. 1453, een sociaalpolitieke studie van een staatsvormingsproces*. Brussels: Koninklijke Academie voor Wetenschappen.

Boone, Marc 1990c. *Geld en macht. De Gentse stadsfinanciën en de bourgondische staatsvorming (1384–1453)*. Ghent: Maatschappij voor Geschiedenis en Oudheidkunde.

Boone, Marc 1990d. 'Lanchals (Pieter)'. In *Nationaal Biografisch Woordenboek*, vol. 13: 471–80. Brussels: Paleis der Academiën.

Boone, Marc 1991. ' "Plus dueil que joie." Renteverkopen door de stad Gent in de Bourgondische Periode: tussen private belangen en publieke financiën'. *Gemeentekrediet van België, driemaandelijks tijdschrift* 45: 3–26.

Boone, Marc 1993. 'L'industrie textile à Gand au bas Moyen Âge ou les résurrections successives d'une activité réputée moribonde'. In *La draperie ancienne des Pays-Bas: débouchés et stratégies de survie (14e–16e siècles)*, edited by Marc Boone and Walter Prevenier, 15–61. Louvain: Garant.

Boone, Marc 1994. 'Les métiers dans les villes flamandes au bas Moyen Âge (XIVe– XVIe siècles): images normatives, réalités sociopolitiques et économiques'. In *Les métiers au Moyen Âge. Aspects économiques et sociaux*, edited by Pascale Lambrechts and Jean-Pierre Sosson, 1–21. Louvain-la-Neuve: Institut d'Études Médiévales.

Boone, Marc 1995a. 'Schöffe, Schöffengericht, Schöffenbank, II: Stadtsgeschichte'. *Lexicon des Mittelalters*, vol. 7: 1514–17. Turnhout: Brepols.

Boone, Marc 1995b. 'Une famille au service de l'état bourguignon naissant. Roland et Jean d'Uutkerke, nobles flamands dans l'entourage de Philippe Le Bon'. *Revue du Nord* 72: 233–56.

Boone, Marc 1995c. 'Brugge und Gent um 1250: die Entstehung der Flämischen Städtelandschaft'. In *Europas Städte zwischen Zwang und Freiheit: die Europäische Stadt um die Mitte des 13. Jahrhunderts*, edited by Wilfried Hartmann, 97–107. Regensburg: Universiteitsverlag.

Boone, Marc 1996a. 'Les gens de métiers à l'époque corporative à Gand et les litiges professionels (1350–1450)'. In *Statuts individuels, statuts corporatifs et judiciaires dans les villes européennes (Moyen Âge et Temps Modernes)*, edited by Marc Boone and Maarten Prak, 23–47. Louvain: Garant.

Boone, Marc 1996b. 'Les juristes et la construction de l'état bourguignon aux Pays-Bas, état de la question, pistes de recherches'. In *Les Pays-Bas bourguignons, histoire et institutions. Mélanges André Uyttebrouck*, edited by Jean-Marie Duvosquel, Jacques Nazet, and André Vanrie, 105–20. Brussels: Archives et bibliothèques de Belgique.

Boone, Marc 1997a. 'Destroying and Reconstructing the City: the Inculcation and Arrogation of Princely Power in the Burgundian-Habsburg Netherlands (14th–16th Centuries)'. In *The Propagation of Power in the Medieval West: Selected Proceedings of the International Conference, Groningen 20–23 November, 1996*, edited by Martin Gosman, Arie Vanderjagt, and Jan Veenstra, 1–33. Groningen: Egbert Forsten.

Boone, Marc 1997b. 'La construction d'un républicanisme urbain. Enjeux de la politique municipale dans les villes flamandes au bas Moyen Âge'. In *Enjeux et expressions de la politique municipale (XIIe–XXe siècles)*, edited by Denis Menjot and Jean-Luc Pinol, 41–60. Paris: L'Harmattan.

Boone, Marc 1997c. 'Städtische Selbstverwaltungsorgane vom 14. bis 16. Jahrhundert. Verfassungsnorm und Verwaltwirklichkeit im Spätmittelalterlichen Flämischen Raum am Beispeil Gent'. In *Verwaltung und Politik in Städten Mitteleuropas. Beitrage zu Verfassungsnorm und Verfassungswirklichkeit in Altständischer Zeit*, edited by Wilfried Ehrbrecht, 21–46. Cologne: Böhlau.

Boone, Marc 1998. 'Social Conflicts in the Cloth Industry of Ypres (Late 13th–Early 14th Centuries): The Cockerulle Reconsidered'. In *Ypres and the Medieval Cloth Industry in Flanders. Archaeological and Historical Contributions*, edited by Marc Dewilde, Anton Ervynck, and Alexis Wielemans, 147–55. Zellik: Instituut voor het Archeologisch Patrimonium.

Boone, Marc 1999. 'Apologie d'un banquier médiéval: Tommaso Portinari et l'état bourguignon'. *Le Moyen Âge* 105: 31–54.

Boone, Marc 2000. '"Le dict mal s'est espandu comme peste fatale". Karel V en Gent, stedelijke identiteit en staatsgeweld'. *Handelingen der Maatschappij voor Geschiedenis en Oudheidkunde te Gent* 54: 31–63.

Boone, Marc 2001a. 'Élites urbaines, noblesse d'état. Bourgeois et nobles dans la société des Pays-Bas bourguignons (principalement en Flandre et en Brabant)'. In *Liber Amicorum Raphaël De Smedt. 3. Historia*, edited by Jacques Paviot, 61–85. Louvain: Peeters.

Boone, Marc 2001b. 'Législation communale et ingérence princière: la "restriction" de Charles le Téméraire pour la ville de Gand (13 juillet 1468)'. In *Faire bans, edictz et statuz'. Légiférer dans la ville médiévale. Sources, objets, acteurs de l'activité législative communale en occident, ca. 1200–1500*, edited by Jean-Marie Cauchies and Eric Bousmar, 139–51. Brussels: Publications des Facultés Universitaires Saint-Louis.

Boone, Marc 2002a. 'Urban Space and Political Conflict in Late Medieval Flanders'. *The Journal of Interdisciplinary History* 32 (4): 621–40.

Boone, Marc 2002b. 'Une sociètè urbanisèe sous tension. Le comté de Flandre vers 1302'. In Van Caenegem, ed. 2002, 27–77.

Boone, Marc 2003a. 'Het "Charter van Senlis" (november 1301) voor de stad Gent. Een stedelijke constitutie in het spanningsveld tussen vorst en stad'. *Handelingen van de Maatschappij voor Geschiedenis en Oudheidkunde te Gent* 57: 1–45.

Boone, Marc 2003b. 'La justice en spectacle. La justice urbaine en Flandre et la crise du pouvoir "bourguignon" (1477–1488)'. *Revue Historique* 125: 43–65.

Boone, Marc 2005. 'Armes, coursses, assemblees et commocion. Les gens de métiers et l'usage de la violence dans la société urbaine Flamande à la fin du Moyen Âge'. *Revue du Nord* 87 (359): 7–33.

Boone, Marc 2007a. 'La justice politique dans les grandes villes flamandes. Étude d'un cas: la crise de l'état bourguignon et la guerre contre Maximilien d'Autriche (1477–1492)'. In *Les procès politiques (XIVe–XVIIe siècle)*, edited by Yves-Marie Bercé, 183–218. Rome: École Française de Rome.

Boone, Marc 2007b. 'The Dutch Revolt and the Medieval Tradition of Urban Dissent'. *Journal of Early Modern History* 11: 351–75.

Boone, Marc. 2008a. "'L'automne du Moyen Âge': Johan Huizinga et Henri Pirenne ou 'plusieurs vérités pour la même chose'". In *Autour du XVe siècle. Journées d'étude en l'honneur d'Alberto Vàrvaro. Communications présentées au Symposium de clôture de la Chaire Francqui au titre étranger (Liège, 10–11 mai 2004)*, edited by Paola Moreno and Giovanni Palumbo, 27–51. Geneva: Librairie Droz.

Boone, Marc 2008b. 'Le comté de Flandre dans le long XIVe siècle: une société urbanisée face aux crises du Bas Moyen Âge'. In *Rivolte urbane e rivolte contadine nell'Europa del Trecento: un confronto*, edited by Giovanni Cherubini, Giuliano Pinto, and Monique Bourin, 17–48. Florence: Firenze University Press.

Boone, Marc 2010. *Á la recherche d'une modernité civique: la société urbaine des anciens Pays-Bas au bas Moyen Âge*. Brussels: Éditions de l'Université de Bruxelles.

Boone, Marc 2013. 'From Cuckoo's Egg to "Sedem Tyranni": the Princely Citadels in the Cities of the Low Countries, or the City's Spatial Integrity Hijacked (15th–early 16th Centuries)'. In *The Power of Space in Late Medieval and Early Modern Europe: The Cities of Italy, Northern France and the Low Countries*, edited by Marc Boone and Martha Howell, 77–95. Turnhout: Brepols.

Boone, Marc. 2019. 'Yet another failed state? The Huizinga-Pirenne controversy on the Burgundian state reconsidered'. In *Rereading Huizinga: Autumn of the Middle Ages, a century later*, edited by Peter Arnade, Martha Howell and Anton van der Lem, 105–120. Amsterdam: Amsterdam University Press.

Boone, Marc, and Hanno Brand 1993. 'Vollersoproeren en collectieve actie in Gent en Leiden in de 14e en 15e Eeuw'. *Tijdschrift voor Sociale Geschiedenis* 19: 168–93.

Boone, Marc, and Heleni Porfyriou 2007. 'Markets, Squares, Streets: Urban Space, a Tool for Cultural Exchange'. In *Cultural Exchange in Early Modern Europe. Volume II: Cities and Cultural Exchange in Europe, 1400–1700*, edited by Donatella Calabi and Stephen Turk Christensen, 227–53. Cambridge: Cambridge University Press.

Boone, Marc, and Maarten Prak 1995. 'Rulers, Patricians and Burghers: the Great and Little Traditions of Urban Revolt in the Low Countries'. In *A Miracle Mirrored. The Dutch Republic in European Perspective*, edited by Karel Davids and Jan Lucassen, 99–134. Cambridge: Cambridge University Press.

Boone, Marc, and Martha Howell 2013. 'Introduction'. In *The Power of Space in Late Medieval and Early Modern Europe: The Cities of Italy, Northern France and the Low Countries*, edited by Marc Boone and Martha Howell, 1–10. Turnhout: Brepols.

Boone, Marc, and Thérèse de Hemptinne 1997. 'Espace urbain et ambitions princières. Les présences matérielles de l'autorité princière dans le Gand médiéval (12e siècle–1540)'. In *Zeremoniell und Raum*, edited by Werner Paravicini, 279–304. Sigmaringen: Thorbecke.

Boone, Marc, and Walter Prevenier 1989a. 'De "stadsstaat"-droom'. In *Gent: Apologie van een rebelse stad*, edited by Johan Decavele and Herman Balthazar, 80–105. Antwerp: Mercatorfonds.

Boone, Marc, and Walter Prevenier 1989b. 'The City-State Dream (1300–1500)'. In *Ghent. In Defence of a Rebellious City: History, Art, Culture*, edited by Johan Decavele and Herman Balthazar, 81–105. Antwerp: Mercatorfonds.

Boone, Marc, and Peter Stabel, eds 2000. *Shaping Urban Identity in Late Medieval Europe*. Louvain: Garant.

Borchert, Till-Holger, ed. 2005. *De portretten van Memling*. Ghent: Ludion.

Boretius, Alfredus, and Victor Krause, eds 1883–97. *Capitularia Regum Francorum*. 2 vols. Hannover: Impensis Bibliopolii Hahniani.

Bouhier, Jean 1742. *Les coutumes du Duché de Bourgogne: avec les anciennes coutumes, tant générales, que locales, de la même province, non encore imprimées et les observations de M. Bouhier*. 2 vols. Dijon: Arnauld Jean-Baptiste Augé.

Bourdieu, Pierre 1972. 'Les stratégies matrimoniales dans le système de reproduction'. *Annales. Economies, sociétés, civilisations* 27: 1105–27.

Bourdieu, Pierre 1991. *Language and Symbolic Power*, edited by John Thompson, translated by Gino Raymond and Matthew Adamson. Oxford: Oxford University Press.

Bourdieu, Pierre 1994. 'Rethinking the State: Genesis and Structure of the Bureaucratic Field'. *Sociological Theory* 12: 1–18.

Bourdieu, Pierre, and Loïc Wacquant 1992. *An Invitation to Reflexive Sociology*. Chicago, IL: University of Chicago Press.

Bourin, Monique 2008. 'Les révoltes dans la France du XIVe siècle: traditions histori-ographiques et nouvelles recherches'. In *Rivolte urbane e rivolte contadine nell'Europa del Trecento: un confronto*, edited by Giovanni Cherubini, Giuliano Pinto, and Monique Bourin, 49–72. Florence: Firenze University Press.

Boutillier, Jean 1603. *Somme rural, ou le grand coustumier general de practique civil et canon*, edited by Loys Charondas le Caron. Paris: Barthelemy Macé.

Bouza, Fernando 1999. *Communication, Knowledge, and Memory in Early Modern Spain*. Philadelphia: University of Pennsylvania Press.

Bowsky, William 1981. *A Medieval Italian Commune: Siena under the Nine, 1287–1355*. Berkeley, CA: University of California Press.

Braekevelt, Johan, Frederik Buylaert, Jan Dumolyn, and Jelle Haemers 2012. 'The Politics of Factional Conflict in Late Medieval Flanders'. *Historical Research* 85: 13–31.

Brand, Hanno, Pierre Monnet, and Martial Staub, eds 2003. *Memoria, communitas, civitas: mémoire et conscience urbaines en occident à la fin du Moyen Âge*. Ostfildern: Thorbecke.

Brassart, Félix 1883a. 'Émeute contre les marchands de blé, du 28 octobre 1322'. *Souvenirs de la Flandre Wallonne, 2e Série* 3: 133–41.

Brassart, Félix 1883b. 'Émeute des tisserands, 1280 (vers le mois d'octobre)'. *Souvenirs de la Flandre Wallonne, 2e Série* 3: 123–29.

Brewer, Ebenezer 1898. *Dictionary of Phrase and Fable: Giving the Derivation, Source, or Origin of Common Phrases, Allusions, and Words that have a Tale to Tell*. Philadelphia, PA: Henry Altemus Company.

Brinkman, Herman 1991. 'De stedelijke context van het werk van Jan de Weert (veertiende eeuw)'. In *Op belofte van profijt. Stadsliteratuur en burgermoraal in de nederlandse letterkunde van de middeleeuwen*, edited by Herman Pleij, 101–20. Amsterdam: Prometheus.

Brinkman, Herman 1997. *Dichten uit liefde. Literatuur in Leiden aan het einde van de middeleeuwen*. Hilversum: Verloren.

Brinkman, Herman 2002. 'Het Kerelslied: van historielied tot lyriek van het beschavingsoffensief'. *Queeste* 9: 98–116.

Brinkman, Herman 2004. 'Een lied van hoon en weerwraak. "Ruters" contra "kerels" in het Gruuthuse-handschrift'. *Queeste* 11: 1–43.

Brinkman, Herman 2011. 'De Gentse dichter Everaert Taybaert en het stadsdichterschap in de Late Middeleeuwen'. *Spiegel der Letteren* 53: 419–42.

Brinkman, Herman, and Janny Schenkel, eds 1997. *Het Comburgse handschrift: Hs. Stuttgart, Württembergische Landesbibliothek, Cod. poet. et phil. 2° 22*. 2 vols. Hilversum: Verloren.

Brinkman, Herman, and Janny Schenkel, eds 1999. *Het Handschrift-van Hulthem*. Hilversum: Verloren.

Brown, Andrew 2011. *Civic Ceremony and Religion in Medieval Bruges c. 1300–1520.* Cambridge: Cambridge University Press.

Bruch, Hettel 1971. *Slaat op den trommele. Het Wilhelmus en de geuzenliederen.* Leiden: Sijthof.

Brucker, Gene 1972. 'The Florentine Popolo Minuto and its Political Role, 1340–1450'. In *Violence and Civil Disorder in Italian Cities, 1200–1500,* edited by Lauro Martines, 155–83. Berkeley, CA: University of California Press.

Brucker, Gene 1983. *Renaissance Florence.* Berkeley, CA: University of California Press.

Bruhns, Hinnerk 1988. 'Ville et état chez Max Weber'. *Les Annales du Recherche Urbaine* 38: 3–12.

Bruins, Luitje 1977. 'De herkomst van de termen gilde en ambacht'. In *Ondernemende Geschiedenis. 22 Opstellen geschreven bij het afscheid van Mr. H. van Riel als voorzitter van de Vereniging Het Nederlands Economisch-Historisch Archief, 's Gravenhage,* 15–33. 's Gravenhage: Nijhoff.

Brunner, Heinrich 1890. 'Abspaltungen der Friedlosigkeit'. *Zeitschrift der Savigny-Stiftung für Rechtsgeschichte, Germanistische Abteilung* 2: 62–100.

Brunner, Heinrich 1892. *Deutsche Rechtsgeschichte.* vol. 2. Berlin: Duncker & Humblot.

Brunner, Karl 1979. *Oppositionelle Gruppen im Karolingerreich.* Vienna: Böhlau.

Brustein, William, and Margaret Levi 1987. 'The Geography of Rebellion: Rulers, Rebels, and Regions, 1500 to 1700'. *Theory and Society* 16 (4): 467–95.

Buchon, Jean, ed. 1826. *Chroniques d'Enguerrand de Monstrelet.* 8 vols. Paris: Carez.

Buitendijk, Willem 1977. *Nederlandse strijdzangen (1525–1648).* Culemborg: Tjeenk Willink.

Buntinx, Jan 1949. *De audiëntie van de graven van Vlaanderen: studie over het centraal grafelijk gerecht (c. 1330–c. 1409).* Brussels: Standaard-Boekhandel.

Buntinx, Jan 1972. 'Wielant (Filips)'. In *Nationaal Biografisch Woordenboek,* vol. 5: 1009–19. Brussels: Paleis der Academiën.

Burke, Peter 1987. 'Introduction'. In *The Social History of Language,* edited by Peter Burke and Roy Porter, 1–20. Cambridge: Cambridge University Press.

Burke, Peter 1989. 'History as Social Memory'. In *Memory, History, Culture and the Mind,* edited by Thomas Butler, 97–113. Oxford: Oxford University Press.

Burns, James Henderson, ed. 1988. *The Cambridge History of Medieval Political Thought c. 350–c. 1450.* Cambridge: Cambridge University Press.

Burns, James MacGregor 1978. *Leadership.* New York, NY: Harper & Row.

Buylaert, Frederik 2005. 'Sociale mobiliteit bij stedelijke elites in laatmiddeleeuws Vlaanderen. Een gevalstudie over de Vlaamse familie De Baenst'. *Jaarboek voor Middeleeuwse Geschiedenis* 8: 201–51.

Buylaert, Frederik 2007. 'Familiekwesties. De beheersing van vetes en private conflicten in de elite van het laatmiddeleeuwse Gent'. *Stadsgeschiedenis* 2: 1–19.

Buylaert, Frederik and Jan Dumolyn 2020. 'Van Eyck's World. Court Culture, Luxury

Production, Elite Patronage and Social Distinction within an Urban Network'. In *Van Eyck. An Optical Revolution*, edited by Till-Holger Borchert, Jan Dumolyn, and Maximiliaan Martens, 84–125. New York: Thames & Hudson Inc.

Buylaert, Frederik, Jelle De Rock, Jan Dumolyn, and Ingrid Geelen 2015. 'De Poortersloge van Brugge: een sociale en culturele geschiedenis van een uniek laatmiddeleeuws gebouw'. *Handelingen van het Genootschap voor Geschiedenis te Brugge* 152 (2): 225–84.

Callewier, Hendrik 2011. *De papen van Brugge: de seculiere clerus in een middeleeuwse wereldstad (1411–1477)*. Louvain: Universitaire Pers Leuven.

Canning, Joseph 1996. *A History of Medieval Political Thought, 300–1450*. London/New York, NY: Routledge.

Carlyle, Robert, and Alexander Carlyle 1903–36. *A History of Medieval Political Theory in the West*. 6 vols. Edinburgh/London: William Blackwood and Sons.

Carrington, Peter, John Scott, and Stanley Wasserman, eds 2005. *Models and Methods in Social Network Analysis*. Cambridge: Cambridge University Press.

Carruthers, Mary 2008. *The Book of Memory. A Study of Memory in Medieval Culture*. Cambridge: Cambridge University Press.

Carson, Patricia 1980. *James van Artevelde, the Man from Ghent*. Ghent: Story-Scientia.

Carton, Charles, ed. 1859. *'t Boeck van al 't gene datter gheschiedt is binnen Brugghe sichten jaer 1477 tot 1491*. Ghent: Annoot-Braeckman.

Casagrande, Carla, and Silvana Vecchio 1991. *Les péchés de la langue: discipline et éthique de la parole dans la culture médiévale*. Paris: Cerf.

Cauchies, Jean-Marie 1994. 'Bourgogne (Philippe de)'. In *Nouvelle Biographie Nationale*, vol. 3: 275–6.

Cauchies, Jean-Marie 2003. *Philippe le Beau. Le dernier duc de Bourgogne*. Turnhout: Brepols.

Cauchies, Jean-Marie, and Hugo De Schepper 1994. *Justice, grâce et législation*. Brussels: Facultés Universitaires Saint-Louis.

Certeau, Michel de 1994. *La prise de parole. et autres écrits politiques*, edited by Luce Giard. Paris: Éditions du Seuil.

Challet, Vincent 1998. 'La révolte des tuchins: banditisme social ou sociabilité villageoise?' *Médiévales* 34: 101–12.

Challet, Vincent 2005a. 'Les tuchins ou la grande révolte du Languedoc'. *L'Histoire* 298: 62–67.

Challet, Vincent 2005b. '"Moyran, los traidors, moyran". Cris de haine et sentiment d'abandon dans les villes languedociennes à la fin du XIVe siècle'. In Lecuppre-Desjardin and Van Bruaene, eds 2005, 83–92.

Challet, Vincent 2008. 'Peuple et élites. Stratégies sociales et manipulations politiques dans les révoltes paysannes (France, $XIVe$–XVe siècle)'. In Depreux, ed. 2008, 213–28.

Cheesman, Tom 1994. *The Shocking Ballad Picture Show: German Popular Literature and Cultural History*. Oxford: Berg.

Cherubini, Giovanni 2008. 'Les pouvoirs dans la ville en Flandre et en Italie'. In Crouzet-Pavan and Lecuppre-Desjardin, eds 2008, 235–44.

Chevalier, Bernard 1982. 'Corporations, conflits politiques et paix sociale en France (à l'exclusion de la Flandre) aux XIVe et XVe siècles'. *Revue Historique* 268: 17–44.

Cheynet, Jean-Claude 2008. '"Se révolter légitimement contre le Basileus"?' In Depreux, ed. 2008, 57–73.

Chorley, Patrick 1987. 'The Cloth Exports of Flanders and Northern France during the Thirteenth-Century: a Luxury Trade?' *Economic History Review* 40: 349–79.

Ciapelli, Giovanni, and Patricia Rubin, eds 2000. *Art, Memory, and Family in Renaissance Florence*. Cambridge: Cambridge University Press.

Clanchy, Michael 1979. *From Memory to the Written Record. England, 1066–1307*. London: Harvard University Press.

Clark, Peter 1983. *The English Alehouse, 1200–1830*. London: Longman.

Clark, Robert 1999. 'Community versus Subject in Late Medieval French Confraternity Drama and Ritual'. In *Drama and Community: People and Plays in Medieval Europe*, edited by Alan Hindley, 34–56. Turnhout: Brepols.

Classen, Albrecht 2009. 'Urban Space in the Middle Ages and the Early Modern Age: Historical, Mental, Cultural, and Social-Economic Investigations'. In *Urban Space in the Middle Ages and the Early Modern Age*, 1–146. Berlin: De Gruyter.

Clay, Steven 1997. 'La guerre des plumes. La presse provinciale et la politique de factions sous le premier Directoire à Marseille, 1796–1797'. *Annales Historiques de la Révolution Française* 308: 221–47.

Climo, Jacob, and Maria Cattel 2002. 'Meaning in Social Memory and History: Anthropological Perspectives'. In *Social Memory and History. Anthropological Perspectives*, edited by Jacob Climo and Marie Cattel, 1–36. Walnut Creek: Altamira.

Clopper, Lawrence 1989. 'Lay and Clerical Impact on Civic Religious Drama and Ceremony'. In *Contexts for Early English Drama*, edited by Marianne Briscoe and John Coldewey, 102–36. Bloomington, IN: Indiana University Press.

Cohn, Samuel 1999. *Creating the Florentine State: Peasants and Rebellion, 1348–1434*. Cambridge: Cambridge University Press.

Cohn, Samuel 2006. *Lust for Liberty: The Politics of Social Revolt in Medieval Europe, 1200–1425. Italy, France, and Flanders*. Cambridge, MA: Harvard University Press.

Cohn, Samuel 2012a. 'Enigmas of Communication: Jacques, Ciompi, and the English'. In Oliva Herrer, Challet, Dumolyn et al., eds 2012, 227–50.

Cohn, Samuel 2012b. 'The Modernity of Medieval Popular Revolt'. *History Compass* 10: 731–41.

Cohn, Samuel 2013. *Popular Protest in Late Medieval English Towns*. Cambridge: Cambridge University Press.

Coleman, Janet 1981. *English Literature in History, 1350–1400: Medieval Readers and Writers.* London: Columbia University Press.

Coleman, Janet, ed. 1996. *The Individual in Political Theory and Practice.* Oxford: Clarendon Press.

Coleman, Joyce 1996. *Public Reading and the Reading Public in Late Medieval England and France.* Cambridge: Cambridge University Press.

Commynes, Philippe de 1979. *Philippe de Commynes, sieur d'Argenton. Mémoires sur Louis XI: 1464–1483*, edited by Jean Dufournet. Paris: Gallimard.

Confino, Alon 1997. 'Collective Memory and Cultural History: Problems of Method'. *American Historical Review* 102 (5): 1386–1403.

Coornaert, Emile 1941. *Les corporations en France avant 1789.* Paris: Gallimard.

Coornaert, Emile 1948. 'Les ghildes médiévales (ve–ixe siècles)'. *Revue Historique* 199: 22–55; 208–43.

Coppens, Greta 1969. 'Revolte en repressie in Vlaanderen in de xvde eeuw'. Unpublished dissertation, Ghent: Ghent University.

Coussemaker, Edmond de 1873. 'Sources du droit public et coutumier de la Flandre maritime'. *Annales du Comité Flamand de France* 11: 183–290.

Coussemaker, Edmond de 1874. 'Sources du droit public et coutumier de la Flandre maritime'. *Annales du Comité Flamand de France* 12: 157–332.

Crombie, Laura 2011. 'Honour, Community and Hierarchy in the Feasts of the Archery and Crossbow Guilds of Bruges, 1445–81'. *Journal of Medieval History* 37 (1): 102–13.

Crouzet-Pavan, Élisabeth 1992. *'Sopra le acqua salse'. Espaces, pouvoir et société à Venise à la fin du Moyen Âge.* Rome: École française de Rome.

Crouzet-Pavan, Élisabeth 1994. 'Les mots de Venise: sur le contrôle du langage dans une cité-état italienne'. In *La circulation des nouvelles au Moyen Âge. Actes des congrès de la Société des historiens médiévistes de l'enseignement supérieur public, 24ᵉ Congrès, Avignon, 1993*, 205–18. Paris: Publications de la Sorbonne.

Crouzet-Pavan, Élisabeth 2000. 'Cultures et contre-cultures: à propos des logiques spatiales de l'espace public Vénétien'. In Boone and Stabel, eds 2000, 89–107.

Crouzet-Pavan, Élisabeth 2001. *Enfers et paradis. L'Italie de Dante et de Giotto.* Paris: Albin Michel.

Crouzet-Pavan, Élisabeth and Élodie Lecuppre-Desjardin, eds 2008. *Villes de Flandre et d'Italie, XIIIe–XVIe siècle: les enseignements d'une comparasion.* Turnhout: Brepols.

Cubitt, Geoffrey 2007. *History and Memory.* Manchester: Manchester University Press.

Cuttler, Simon 1982. *The Laws of Treason and Treason Trials in Later Medieval France.* Cambridge: Cambridge University Press.

Czok, Karl 1958–9. 'Zunftkämpfe, Zunftrevolutionen oder Bürgerkämpfe'. *Wissenschaftliche Zeitschrift der Karl Marx-Universität Leipzig, Gesellschafts- und Sprachwissenschaftliche Reihe* 8: 129–43.

Czok, Karl 1960. 'Zur Volksbewegung in den deutschen Städten des 14. Jahrhunderts. Bürgerkämpfe and antikuriale Opposition'. In *Städtische Volksbewegungen im 14. Jahrhundert*, edited by Erika Engelmann, 157–69. Berlin: Akademie.

Dambruyne, Johan 1990. 'Keizer Karel: meester of knecht?'. In *Keizer tussen stropdragers. Karel v, 1500–1558*, edited by Johan Decavele, 156–73. Louvain: Davidsfonds.

Dambruyne, Johan 1998. 'Guilds, Social Mobility and Status in Sixteenth-Century Ghent'. *International Review of Social History* 43: 31–78.

Dambruyne, Johan 2001. *Mensen en centen. Het 16de-eeuwse Gent in demografisch en economisch perspectief*. Ghent: Maatschappij voor Geschiedenis en Oudheidkunde.

Dambruyne, Johan 2002. *Corporatieve middengroepen: aspiraties, relaties en transformaties in de 16de-eeuwse Gentse ambachtswereld*. Ghent: Academia Press.

Dambruyne, Johan 2003. 'De middenstand in opstand. Corporatieve aspiraties en transformaties in het zestiende-eeuwse Gent'. *Handelingen der Maatschappij voor Geschiedenis en Oudheidkunde te Gent* 57: 71–122.

Dambruyne, Johan 2006. 'Corporative Capital and Social Representation in the Southern and Northern Netherlands, 1500–1800'. In Prak, Lis, Lucassen et al., eds 2006, 194–223.

Darnton, Robert 1996. *The Forbidden Best-Sellers of Pre-Revolutionary France*. London: W.W. Norton.

Darnton, Robert 2010. *Poetry and the Police: Communication Networks in Eighteenth-Century France*. Cambridge, MA: Harvard University Press.

Dauchy, Serge 1995. *De processen in beroep uit Vlaanderen bij het Parlement van Parijs (1320–1521): een rechtshistorisch onderzoek naar de wording van staat en souvereiniteit in de Bourgondisch-Habsburgse periode*. Brussels: Paleis der Academiën.

Dauwe, Marie-Rose 1987. 'De Cronicke van Vlaenderen, historiografische studie en transcriptie van f° 137vo tot f° 420vo'. 2 vols. Unpublished dissertation, Ghent: Ghent University.

Davies, Rees 2003. 'The Medieval State: the Tyranny of a Concept?' *Journal of Historical Sociology* 16 (2): 280–300.

Davies, Rees. 1995. *The Revolt of Owain Glyndwr*. Oxford: Oxford University Press.

De Baecker, Louis 1855. *Chants historiques de la Flandre*. Lille: Ernest Van Ackere.

De Beer, Joseph 1931. 'Sceaux des corporations et communautés religieuses d'Audenaerde'. In *Jaarboeken van Oudheid- en Geschiedkundige Verbond van België. XXVIIIe zitting. Congres van Antwerpen 1930. Aflevering 2: verhandelingen*, 395–414. Antwerp: V. Resseler.

de Bock, Eugène 1969–70. 'Waardering van de Rederijkers'. *Spiegel der Letteren*, 12: 241–67.

de Bruin, Martine 2001. 'Luik 1578. De driejarige Fransje Vanden Cruycen zingt een lang lied over de martelaren van Gorkum: geuzen- en anti-geuzenliederen'. In *Een muziekgeschiedenis der Nederlanden*, edited by Louis Grijp, 174–81. Amsterdam: Amsterdam University Press.

de Bruin, Martine, Johan Oosterman, and Clara Strijbosch, eds 2001. *Repertorium van het Nederlandse lied tot 1600*. Ghent: KANTL.

De Clercq, Charles 1936. *La législation religieuse franque: étude sur les actes de conciles et les capitulaires, les statuts diocésains et les règles monastiques*. 2 vols. Louvain: Bibliothèque universitaire.

De Clercq, Wim, Jan Dumolyn, and Jelle Haemers 2007. ' "Vivre Noblement": Material Culture and Elite Identity in Late Medieval Flanders'. *The Journal of Interdisciplinary History* 38 (1): 1–31.

De Coninck, Christiane, and Willem Blockmans 1967. 'Geschiedenis van de Gentse leprozerie "Het Rijke Gasthuis": vanaf de stichting (ca. 1146) tot omstreeks 1370'. *Annales de la Société Belge d'Histoire des Hôpitaux* 5: 3–43.

de Hemptinne, Thérèse, Adriaan Verhulst, and Lieve De Mey 1988–2009. *De oorkonden der graven van Vlaanderen (juli 1128-september 1191)*. 3 vols. Brussels: Paleis der Academiën.

Dean, Trevor, ed. 2000. *The Towns of Italy in the Later Middle Ages*. Manchester: Manchester University Press.

Debris, Cyrille 2005. *'Tu felix Austria, nube': la dynastie de Habsbourg et sa politique matrimoniale à la fin du Moyen Âge (XIIIe–XVIe siècles)*. Turnhout: Brepols.

Decavele, Johan, and Paul Van Peteghem 1989. 'Ghent, "Absolutely" Broken'. In *Ghent. In Defence of a Rebellious City: History, Art, Culture*, edited by Johan Decavele and Herman Balthazar, 107–33. Antwerp: Mercatorfonds.

Deferrari, Roy 1960. *A Latin-English Dictionary of St. Thomas Aquinas: Based on the Summa Theologica and Selected Passages of his other Works*. Boston, MA: St. Paul Editions.

De Fouw, Arie, 1937. *Philips van Kleef: een bijdrage tot de kennis van zijn leven en karakter*. Groningen: Wolters.

De Gryse, Louis 1969. 'The Reform of Flemish Judicial and Fiscal Administration in the Reign of Philip of Alsace (1157/63–1191)'. Unpublished dissertation, Minneapolis, MN: University of Minnesota.

Dekker, Rudolf, and van de Pol, Lotte 1982. ' "Wat hoort men niet al vreemde dingen ..." ' *Spiegel Historiael* 17: 486–94.

Dekker, Therese 1987. 'Medieval Theatre in the Lowlands: Secular Drama'. *Dutch Crossing* 11 (32): 37–55.

De Keyser, Raphael, and Amber Verrycken 1983. 'De pseudo-profetie van Amisins: een Vlaamse visie op de veertiende eeuw'. In *Pascua mediaevalia: studies voor Prof. Dr. J.M. De Smet*, edited by Robrecht Lievens, Erik Van Mingroot, and Werner Verbeke, 398–451. Louvain: Universitaire Pers Leuven.

Delcourt, André 1930. *La vengeance de la commune: l'arsin et l'abattis de maison en Flandre et en Hainaut*. Lille: É. Raoust.

Deligne, Chloé 2013. 'Powers over Space, Spaces over Power. The Constitution of Town

Squares in the Cities of the Low Countries (12th–14th Century)'. In *The Power of Space in Late Medieval and Early Modern Europe: The Cities of Italy, Northern France and the Low Countries*, edited by Marc Boone and Martha Howell, 21–8. Turnhout: Brepols.

Deligne, Chloé, and Claire Billen 2007. 'Introduction'. In *Voisinages, coexistences, appropriations: groupes sociaux et territoires urbains (Moyen Âge–16e siècle)*, edited by Chloé Deligne and Claire Billen, 3–15. Turnhout: Brepols.

De Meester, Toon, Jan Dumolyn, and Susan Frances Jones 2020. 'Meester Jans Huus van Eicke. Jan van Eyck's House, Workshop and Milieu in Bruges: New Archival Data'. In *Van Eyck: An Optical Revolution*, edited by Till-Holger Borchert, Jan Dumolyn, and Maximiliaan Martens, 126–37. New York: Thames & Hudson Inc.

Demets Lisa, 2021. 'Spies, instigators and troublemakers. Gendered perceptions on rebellious women in late medieval Flemish chronicles'. *Journal of Women's History* 33: forthcoming.

Demonty, Philippe 2000. 'Le Thesaurus Diplomaticus, un instrument de travail pour une nouvelle approche en diplomatique médiévale'. In *La diplomatique urbaine en Europe au Moyen Âge*, edited by Walter Prevenier and Thérèse de Hemptinne, 122–32. Louvain: Garant.

De Munck, Bert, Steven Kaplan, and Hugo Soly, eds 2007. *Learning on the Shop Floor: Historical Perspectives on Apprenticeship*. New York, NY: Berghan Books.

De Munck, Bert, Peter Lourens, and Jan Lucassen 2006. 'The Establishment and Distribution of Craft Guilds in the Low Countries, 1000–1800'. In Prak, Lis, Lucassen et al., eds 2006, 32–73.

Demuynck, Roger 1951. 'De Gentse oorlog (1379–1385). Oorzaken en karakter'. *Handelingen der Maatschappij voor Geschiedenis en Oudheidkunde te Gent* 5: 305–18.

Demyttenaere, Albert 2003. 'Galbert of Bruges on Political Meeting Culture: Palavers and Fights in Flanders during the Years 1127 and 1128'. In *Political Assemblies in the Earlier Middle Ages*, edited by Paul Barnwell and Marco Mostert, 151–92. Turnhout: Brepols Publishers.

Deneckere, Gita 1993. 'The Transforming Impact of Collective Action: Belgium, 1886'. *International Review of Social History* 38 (3): 345–67.

Pas, Justin de 1930. *Le bourgeois de Saint-Omer: sa condition juridique dans les institutions communales*. Lille: É. Raoust.

de Pauw, Napoléon 1878. *Conspiration d'Audenarde sous Jacques van Artevelde (1342): critique historique*. Ghent: Rogghé.

de Pauw, Napoléon 1885. *De voorgeboden der stad Gent in de XIVe Eeuw (1337–1382)*. Ghent: Annoot-Braeckman.

de Pauw, Napoléon 1890. *Dit es tbesouch van dien dat Pieter Bou ende Leusz sijn broeder ontcracht waren den here vor Sinte Verrilden Kerke te Ghent*. Ghent: Annoot-Braeckman.

de Pauw, Napoléon 1893–1914. *Middelnederlandsche gedichten en fragmenten*. 2 vols. Ghent: Siffer.

de Pauw, Napoléon 1899a. 'L'enquête de Bruges après la bataille de Cassel, documents inédits publiés'. *Bulletin de la Commission Royale d'Histoire* 68: 665–704.

de Pauw, Napoléon 1899b. *Ypre jeghen Poperinghe angaende den verbonden: gedingstukken der XIVe eeuw nopens het laken*. Ghent: Siffer.

de Pauw, Napoléon 1910. 'L'enquête sur les capitaines de Courtrai sous Artevelde'. *Bulletin de la Commission Royale d'Histoire* 79: 219–91.

de Pauw, Napoléon 1920. *Cartulaire historique et généalogique des Artevelde*. Brussels: Hayez.

De Pelsmaeker, Prosper 1914. *Coutumes des pays et comté de Flandre: Quartier d'Ypres, registres aux sentences des echevins d'Ypres*. Brussels: Goemaere.

Pisan, Christine de 1958. *The Livre de la paix of Christine de Pisan*, edited by Charity Cannon Willard. 's-Gravenhage: Mouton.

Deploige, Jeroen 2008. 'Revolt and the Manipulation of Sacral and Private Space in 12th-Century Laon and Bruges'. In *Power and Culture: New Perspectives on Spatiality in European History*, edited by Pieter François, Taina Syrjaama and Henri Terho, 89–107. Pisa: Pisa University Press.

De Poerck, Guy 1931. 'Note critique sur le grand privilège brugeois de 1304 et le réglement d'élection du magistrat'. *Annales de la Société d'Emulation de Bruges* 74: 139–57.

De Poorter, Alphonse, ed. 1934. *Catalogue des manuscrits de la bibliothèque publique de la ville de Bruges*. Gembloux and Paris: Les Belles Lettres.

De Potter, Frans 1882–1933. *Gent van den oudsten tijd tot heden. Geschiedkundige beschrijving der stad*. 15 vols. Ghent: Annoot-Braeckman.

De Potter, Frans, ed. 1885. *Chronijcke van Ghendt door Jan van den Vivere en eenige andere aanteekenaars der XVIe en XVIIe Eeuw*. Ghent: Siffer.

De Potter, Frans, and Jan Broeckaert 1873–6. *Geschiedenis der stad Aalst voorgegaan van eene historische schets van 't voormalige land van Aalst*. 5 vols. Ghent: Annoot-Braeckman.

Depreux, Philippe, ed. 2008. *Revolte und Sozialstatus von der Spätantike bis zur Frühen Neuzeit / Révolte et statut social de l'Antiquité Tardive aux Temps Modernes*. Munich: Oldenbourg Wissenschaftverlag.

De Ridder-Symoens, Hilde. 1993. 'Prosopographical Research in the Low Countries Concerning the Middle Ages and the Sixteenth Century'. *Medieval Prosopography* 14: 27–120.

De Roos, Marjoke 1994. 'Le monde a l'envers. Fêtes de carnaval dans les Pays-Bas Bourguignons (XIV–XVIe Siecles)'. In *Fêtes et cérémonies aux XIVe–XIVe siècles*, edited by Jean-Marie Cauchies, 221–32. Publications du Centre Européen d'Etudes Bourguignonnes (XIVe–XVIe siècles) 34. Turnhout: Brepols.

De Roover, Raymond 1999. *Money, Banking and Credit in Mediaeval Bruges*. London/ New York, NY: Routledge.

Derville, Alain 1993. 'Les métiers de Saint-Omer'. In *Les métiers au Moyen Âge. Aspects économiques et sociaux*, edited by Pascale Lambrechts and Jean-Pierre Sosson, 99–108. Louvain-la-Neuve: Institut d'Études Médiévales.

Derville, Alain 1995. *Saint-Omer: des origines ou débuts du 14e siècle*. Lille: Presses Universitaires du Septentrion.

Derycke, Laurence 2003. 'The Public Annuity Market in Bruges at the End of the 15th Century'. In *Urban Public Debts. Urban Government and the Market for Annuities in Western Europe, 14th–18th Centuries*, edited by Marc Boone, Karel Davids, and Paul Janssens, 165–81. Turnhout: Brepols.

De Sagher, Henri 1922. 'Schutrecht, diefstal, compositie en pijniging in het vijftiende-eeuwsche Vlaamsche strafrecht'. *Handelingen van het Genootschap voor Geschiedenis te Brugge* 72: 94–163.

De Schrevel, Arthur 1922. *Le traité d'alliance conclue en 1339 entre la Flandre et le Brabant, renouvelé en 1578*. Bruges: De Plancke.

Des Marez, Guillaume 1900. *Les luttes sociales en Flandre au Moyen Âge*. Brussels: Lefevre.

Des Marez, Guillaume 1905–6. 'Les luttes sociales à Bruxelles au Moyen Âge'. *Revue de l'Université de Bruxelles* 11: 287–323.

De Smet, Anton 1950. 'De klacht van de "Ghemeente" van Damme in 1280, enkele gegevens over politieke en sociale toestanden in een kleine Vlaamse stad gedurende de tweede helft der XIIIde eeuw'. *Handelingen van de Koninlijke Commissie voor Geschiedenis* 115: 1–15.

De Smet, Joseph Jean, ed. 1837a. 'Chronicon comitum Flandrensium'. In *Corpus chronicorum Flandriae* 1: 37–257. Brussels: Hayez.

De Smet, Joseph Jean, ed. 1837b. 'Chronicon Flandriae scriptum ab Adriano de Budt'. In *Corpus chronicorum Flandriae* 1: 261–367. Brussels: Hayez.

De Smet, Joseph Jean, ed. 1841. 'Chronicon majus de Li Muisis'. In *Corpus chronicorum Flandriae* 2: 93–294. Brussels: Hayez.

De Smet, Joseph Jean, ed. 1856a. 'Histoire des Païs-Bas depuis 1477 jusqu'en 1492. Écrite en forme de journal par un auteur contemporain'. In *Corpus chronicorum Flandriae* 3: 689–742. Brussels: Hayez.

De Smet, Joseph Jean, ed. 1856b. 'Chronique des Pays-Bas, de France, d'Angleterre et de Tournai'. In *Corpus chronicorum Flandriae* 3: 111–569. Brussels: Hayez.

De Smet, Joseph Jean, ed. 1856c. 'Laetste deel der kronyk van Jan van Dixmude'. In *Corpus chronicorum Flandriae* 3: 31–109. Brussels: Hayez.

De Smet, Joseph Jean, ed. 1865. 'Philippe Wielant. Receuil des antiquités de Flandre'. In *Corpus chronicorum Flandriae* 4: 1–442. Brussels: Hayez.

De Smet, Jos 1929. 'Les effectifs brugeois à la bataille de Courtrai en 1302'. *Revue Belge de Philologie et d'Histoire* 8: 863–70.

De Smet, Jos 1931. 'Les comptes des confiscations de biens opérées par ordre du comte de Flandre à Courtrai et dans la châtellenie (1304–1305)'. *Handelingen van de Geschied- en Oudheidkundige Kring van Kortrijk, nieuwe reeks* 10: 210–28.

De Smet, Jos 1933. 'L'effectif des milices brugeoises et la population de la ville en 1340'. *Revue Belge de Philologie et d'Histoire* 12: 631–36.

De Smet, Jos 1947. 'De repressie te Brugge na de Slag bij Westrozebeke, 1 december 1382–31 augustus 1384'. *Handelingen van het Genootschap voor Geschiedenis* 84 (1): 71–118.

De Smet, Jos 1958. 'De verbeurdverklaringen in het Brugse Vrije en in de smalle steden aldaar na de Slag bij Westrozebeke (1382–1384)'. *Handelingen van het Genootschap voor Geschiedenis* 95: 115–36.

Despars, Nicolas 1837–40. *Cronijcke van den lande ende graefscepe van Vlaenderen, gemaect door jo.r Nicolaes Despars, van de jaeren 405 tot 1492*, edited by Jean De Jonghe, 4 vols. Bruges: s.n.

Desplanque, Alexandre 1864–5. 'Troubles de la châtellenie de Cassel sous Philippe le Bon (1427–1431)'. *Annales du Comité Flamand de France* 8: 218–81.

Desreumaux, John 1999. *Sociaal-economische achtergrond van de Kortrijkse rebellen uit het confiscatieregister van 1383*. 3 vols. Geluwe: Davidsfonds.

De Vigne, Felix 1857. *Moeurs et usages des corporation de métiers de la Belgique et du nord de la France*. Ghent: De Busscher.

De Vries, Sj. 1942. 'Rederijkersspelen als historische documenten'. *Tijdschrift voor Geschiedenis* 57: 185–98.

Dewilde, Marc, and Stephan van Bellingen 1998. 'Excavating a Suburb of Medieval Ypres (Belgium): Evidence for the Cloth Industry?' In *Ypres and the Medieval Cloth Industry in Flanders: Archaeological and Historical Contributions*, edited by Marc Dewilde, Anton Ervynck, and Alexis Wielemans, 57–72. Zellik: Instituut voor het archeologisch patrimonium.

Dewitte, Alfons 1982. 'Chronologie van de reformatie te Brugge en in het Brugse Vrije (1485–1593)'. In *Brugge in de geuzentijd: bijdragen tot de geschiedenis van de hervorming te Brugge en in het Brugse Vrije tijdens de 16de Eeuw*, edited by Dirk Van der Bauwhede and Marc Goetinck, 34–41. Bruges: Werkgroep herdenkingsbundel en uitgaven Westvlaamse gidsenkring.

Dhondt, Jan 1948. 'Développement urbain et initiative comtale en Flandre au 11e siècle'. *Revue du Nord* 30: 133–56.

Dhondt, Jan 1950a. 'Les origines des états de Flandre'. *Anciens Pays et Assemblées d'États* 1: 5–52.

Dhondt, Jan 1950b. 'Ordres ou puissances: l'exemple des états de Flandre'. *Annales. Économies, sociétés, civilisations* 5: 289–305.

Dhondt, Jan 1957. 'Les solidarités médiévales. Une société en transition: la Flandre en 1127–1128'. *Annales. Économies, sociétés, civilisations* 12: 529–60.

Dickinson, Jocelyn 1955. *The Congress of Arras 1435: A Study in Medieval Diplomacy.* Oxford: Clarendon Press.

Diegerick, Isidore 1848. 'Épisode de l'histoire d'Ypres sous le règne de Marie de Bourgogne, 1477'. *Annales de la Société d'Émulation de Bruges* 10: 423–76.

Diegerick, Isidore 1853–68. *Inventaire analytique et chronologique des chartes et documents appartenant aux archives de la ville d'Ypres.* 4 vols. Bruges: Vandecasteele-Werbrouck.

Diegerick, Isidore 1853–6. *Correspondance des magistrats d'Ypres députés à Gand et à Bruges pendant les troubles de Flandre sous Maximilien, deuxième partie.* Bruges: Vandecasteele-Werbrouck.

Diegerick, Isidore 1855–6. 'Les drapiers Yprois et la conspiration manquée. Épisode de l'histoire d'Ypres (1428–1429)'. *Annales de La Société d'Emulation de Bruges* 14: 285–310.

Diegerick, Isidore 1856. *Les drapiers yprois et la conspiration manquée. Épisode de l'histoire d'Ypres (1428–1429).* Bruges: Vandecasteele-Werbrouck.

Dilcher, Gerhard 1967. *Die Entstehung der lombardischen Stadtkommune. Eine rechtsgeschichtliche Untersuchung.* Aalen: Scientia.

Dilcher, Gerhard 1988. 'I comuni italiani come movimento sociale e forma giuridica'. In *L'evoluzione delle città italiane nell'XI secolo,* edited by Renato Bordone and Jörg Jarnut, 71–98. Bologna: Il Mulino.

Doehard, Renée 1963. *Études Anversoises. Documents sur le commerce international à Anvers.* 3 vols. Paris: S.E.V.P.E.N.

Dollinger, Philippe 1977. *Pages d'histoire. France et Allemagne Médiévale.* Paris: Ophrys.

Doudelez, Gustave 1974. 'La révolution communale de 1280 à Ypres'. In *Prisma van de geschiedenis van Ieper: een bundel historische opstellen,* edited by Octaaf Mus, 188–294. Tielt: Lannoo.

Doudet, Estelle 2008–9. 'Contraintes, concurrences et écriture personnelle chez les rhétoriqueurs francophones'. *Jaarboek De Fonteine* 58: 69–86.

Douglas, Mary, and Aaron Wildavsky 1982. *Risk and Culture.* Berkeley, CA: University of California Press.

Duby, Georges 1973. *Le dimanche de Bouvines.* Paris: Gallimard.

Duby, Georges 1990. *The Legend of Bouvines: War, Religion and Culture in the Middle Ages,* translated by Catherine Tihany. Berkeley, CA: University of California Press.

Duffin, Anne 1996. *Faction and Faith. Politics and Religion of the Cornish Gentry before the Civil War.* Exeter: University of Exeter Press.

Duinhoven, Antonius, ed. 1982. *Karel ende Elegast.* The Hague: Nijhoff.

Dümmler, Ernst, ed. 1895. *Monumenta Germaniae Historica. Epistolae (in Quart) vol. 4. Epistolae Karolini Aevi 2.* Berlin: Weidmann.

Dumolyn, Jan 1995. 'De Brugse opstand van 1436–1438'. Unpublished dissertation, Ghent: Ghent University.

Dumolyn, Jan 1997. *De Brugse opstand van 1436–1438.* Kortrijk: UGA.

Dumolyn, Jan 1999. 'Population et structures professionnelles à Bruges au XIVe et XVe siècles'. *Revue du Nord* 81: 43–64.

Dumolyn, Jan 2002. 'Investeren in sociaal kapitaal. Netwerken en sociale transacties van Bourgondische ambtenaren'. *Tijdschrift voor Sociale Geschiedenis* 28: 417–38.

Dumolyn, Jan 2003. *Staatsvorming en vorstelijke ambtenaren in het graafschap Vlaanderen (1419–1477).* Louvain: Garant.

Dumolyn, Jan 2005. 'Marginalen of radicalen? Het vertoog over de "roepers en krijsers" tijdens stedelijke opstanden, voornamelijk in het laatmiddeleeuwse Vlaanderen'. *Tijdschrift voor Sociale en Economische Geschiedenis* 2 (2): 29–53.

Dumolyn, Jan 2006a. 'Justice, Equity and the Common Good. The State Ideology of the Councillors of the Burgundian Dukes'. In *The Ideology of Burgundy: the Promotion of National Consciousness, 1364–1565,* edited by Jonathan Boulton and Jan Veenstra, 1–20. Leiden: Brill.

Dumolyn, Jan 2006b. 'Nobles, Patricians and Officers: the Making of a Regional Political Elite in Late Medieval Flanders'. *Journal of Social History* 40 (2): 431–52.

Dumolyn, Jan 2007. 'The Political and Symbolic Economy of State Feudalism. The Case of Late-Medieval Flanders'. *Historical Materialism* 15: 105–31.

Dumolyn, Jan 2008a. '"Criers and Shouters": The Discourse on Radical Urban Rebels in Late Medieval Flanders'. *Journal of Social History* 42: 111–37.

Dumolyn, Jan 2008b. 'Privileges and Novelties: The Political Discourse of the Flemish Cities and Rural Districts in their Negotiations with the Dukes of Burgundy (1384–1506)'. *Urban History* 35: 5–23.

Dumolyn, Jan 2009. 'Le peuple seroit moult opprimé. The Discourse on the People in the Chronicles of Jean Molinet'. *French History* 23: 171–92.

Dumolyn, Jan 2010a. 'Une idéologie urbaine "bricolée" en Flandre médiévale: les sept portes de Bruges dans le manuscrit Gruuthuse (début du XVe siècle)'. *Revue Belge de Philologie et d'Histoire.* 88: 1039–84.

Dumolyn, Jan 2010b. '"Our Land is only Founded on Trade and Industry": Economic Discourses in Fifteenth-Century Bruges'. *Journal of Medieval History* 36: 374–89.

Dumolyn, Jan 2012a. 'Economic Development, Social Space and Political Power in Bruges, c. 1127–1302'. In *Contact and Exchange in Later Medieval Europe: Essays in Honour of Malcolm Vale,* edited by Hannah Skoda, Patrick Lantschner, and Robert Shaw, 33–58. Woodbridge: The Boydell Press.

Dumolyn, Jan 2012b. 'Urban Ideologies in Later Medieval Flanders: Towards an Analytical Framework'. In *The Languages of Political Society,* edited by Jean-Philippe Genet and Andrea Gamberini, 69–96. Milan: Viella.

Dumolyn, Jan 2015. 'Les "plaintes" des villes flamandes à la fin du treizième siècle et les discours et pratiques politiques de la commune'. *Le Moyen Âge* 121 (2): 383–407.

Dumolyn, Jan, and Jelle Haemers 2015a. '"A Blabbermouth Can Barely Control His Tongue"': Political Poems, Songs and Prophecies in the Low Countries (Fifteenth–Sixteenth Centuries)'. In *Spoken Word and Social Practice: Orality in Europe (1400–1700)*, edited by Thomas Cohen and Lesley Twomey, 280–299. Leiden: Brill.

Dumolyn, Jan, and Jelle Haemers 2015b. 'Reclaiming the Common Sphere of the City: the Revival of the Bruges Commune in the Late Thirteenth Century'. In *La légitimité implicite au Moyen Âge. Le pouvoir symbolique en occident (1300–1640)*, edited by Jean-Philippe Genet, vol. 2, 161–88. Paris: Publications de la Sorbonne.

Dumolyn, Jan, and Jelle Haemers 2016, 'Takehan, Cokerulle, and Mutemaque: Naming Collective Action in the Later Medieval Low Countries'. In *The Routledge History Handbook of Medieval Revolt*, edited by Justine Firnhaber-Baker, and Dirk Schoenaers, 39–54. London: Routledge.

Dumolyn, Jan, and Jelle Haemers 2017. 'Je dis à cheus où fu rebellion. Chansons politiques en moyen néerlandais autour de 1500'. In: *Pour la singuliere affection qu'avons à luy. Etudes bourguignonnes offertes à Jean-Marie Cauchies*, edited by Pierre Delsalle, Gilles Docquier, Alain Marchandisse, and Bertrand Schnerb, 207–19. Turnhout: Brepols.

Dumolyn, Jan, and Jelle Haemers 2018a. 'Political Songs and Memories of Rebellion in the Later Medieval Low Countries'. In *Rhythms of Revolt: European Traditions and Memories of Social Conflict in Oral Culture*, edited by Eva Guillorel, David Hopkin, and William Pooley, 43–63. New York, NY: Routledge.

Dumolyn, Jan, and Jelle Haemers 2018b. '"We Will Ask for a New Artevelde." Names, Sites and the Memory of Revolt in the Late Medieval Low Countries'. In *La mémoire des révoltes en Europe à l'époque moderne*, edited by Alexandra Merle, Stéphane Jettot and Manuel Herrero Sanchez, 231–49. Paris: Classiques Garnier.

Dumolyn, Jan, Luc De Grauwe, and Jelle Haemers 2019. 'Moerlemaye: een taalkundige en historische verklaring. Over de naamgeving van politieke conflicten in de middeleeuwse Nederlanden'. *Tijdschrift voor Nederlandse Taal- en Letterkunde*, 135 (1): 1–22.

Dumolyn, Jan, and Jelle Haemers 2020, 'Mauvais mercredi et vendredi saint. Conflits politiques urbains et temps liturgique dans les Pays-Bas du Moyen Âge tardif'. *Annales. Histoire, Sciences Sociales* 75 (2): 249–82.

Dumolyn, Jan, Jelle Haemers, Hipólito Rafael Oliva Herrer, and Vincent Challet, eds 2014. *The Voices of the People in Late Medieval Europe. Communication and Popular Politics*. Turnhout: Brepols.

Dumolyn, Jan, and Élodie Lecuppre-Desjardin 2005. 'Propagande et sensibilité: la fibre émotionnelle au cœur des luttes politiques et sociales dans les villes des anciens Pays-Bas Bourguignons. L'exemple de la révolte Brugeoise de 1436–1438'. In Lecuppre-Desjardin and Van Bruaene, eds, 2005, 41–62.

Dumolyn, Jan, and Kristof Papin 2012. 'Y avait-il des "révoltes fiscales" dans les villes médiévales des Pays-Bas méridionaux? L'exemple de Saint-Omer en 1467'. *Revue du Nord* 94 (4): 827–70.

Dumolyn, Jan, and Peter Stabel 2002. 'Aan de zijlijnen van een conflict? Gent en het Gentse in 1302'. In *Omtrent 1302*, edited by Paul Trio, Dirk Heirbaut, and Dirk Van den Auweele, 37–63. Louvain: Louvain University Press.

Duplessis, Robert, and Martha Howell 1982. 'Reconsidering the Early Modern Urban Economy: the Cases of Leiden and Lille'. *Past & Present* 94: 49–84.

Dupont, Guy 1996. *Maagdenverleidsters, hoeren en speculanten: prostitutie in Brugge tijdens de Bourgondische periode (1385–1515)*. Bruges: Marc Van de Wiele.

Dupont, Sophie 1999. 'Onderzoek naar het democratisch gehalte van het Kortrijkse stadsbestuur tijdens de 13e en 14e Eeuw'. *De Leiegouw* 41: 275–304.

Dupuy, Roger 2002. *La politique du peuple: XVIIIe–XXe siècle. Racines, permanences et ambiguïtés du populisme*. Paris: Albin Michel.

Eberhard, Winfried 1985. '"Gemeiner Nutzen" als oppositionelle Leitvorstellung im Spätmittelalter'. In *Renovatio et Reformatio: Wider das Bild von 'Finsteren' Mittelalter: Festschrift für Ludwig Hödl zum 60. Geburtstag*, edited by Manfred Gerwing and Godehard Ruppert, 195–214. Münster: Aschendorff.

Eersels, Ben, and Jelle Haemers, eds 2020. *Words and Deeds. Shaping Urban Politics from Below in Late Medieval Europe*. Turnhout: Brepols.

Eggert, Wolfgang 1971. 'Formen der sozialen Auseinandersetzung im frühmittelalterlichen Frankenreich'. *Jahrbuch für Wirtschaftgeschichte* 4: 273–85.

Eggert, Wolfgang 1975. 'Rebelliones servorum. Bewaffnete Klassenkämpfe im früh- und frühen Hochmittelalter und ihre Darstellung in Zeitgenössischen erzählenden Quellen'. *Zeitschrift für Geschichtswissenschaft* 23: 1147–64.

Ehbrecht, Wilfried 1976. 'Hanse und spätmiddelalterliche Bürgerkämpfe in Niedersachsen und Westfalen'. *Niedersächsisches Jahrbuch für Landesgeschichte* 48: 77–105.

Elias, Norbert 1939. *Über den Prozess der Zivilisation. Soziogenetische und psychogenetische Untersuchungen*. 2 vols. Basel: Haus zum Falken.

Elliott, J.H. 1969. 'Revolution and Continuity in Early Modern Europe'. *Past & Present* 42: 35–56.

Emirbayer, Mustafa, and Jeff Goodwin 1994. 'Network Analysis, Culture, and the Problem of Agency'. *American Journal of Sociology* 99: 1411–54.

Ennen, Edith 1972. *Die europäische Stadt des Mittelalters*. Göttingen: Vandenhoeck & Ruprecht.

Epperlein, Siegfried 1969. *Herrschaft und Volk im karolingischen Imperium. Studien über soziale Konflikte und dogmatisch-politische Kontroversen im fränkischen Reich*. Berlin: Akademie-Verlag.

Epperlein, Siegfried 1975. 'Volksbewegungen im Frühmittelalterlichen Europa – Eine Skizze'. In *Die Rolle der Volksmassen in der Geschichte der Vorkapitalistischen Gesell-*

schaftformationen, edited by Joachim Herrmann and Irmgard Sellnow, 211–28. Berlin: Akademie-Verlag.

Epperlein, Siegfried 1989. 'Bauerlicher Widerstand im Frühen und Hohen Mittelalter, Resultate, Probleme und Aufgaben der Forschung'. *Zeitschrift für Geschichtswissenschaft* 37: 314–28.

Epstein, Stephen 1998. 'Craft Guilds, Apprenticeship and Technological Change in Pre-Industrial Europe'. *Journal of Economic History* 58: 684–713.

Epstein, Stephen and Maarten Prak, eds 2008. *Guilds, Innovation, and the European Economy, 1400–1800.* Cambridge: Cambridge University Press.

Erickson, Bonnie 1997. 'Social Networks and History'. *Historical Methods* 30: 149–57.

Erll, Astrid 2005. *Kollektives Gedächtnis und Erinnerungskulturen. Eine Einführung.* Weimar: Metzler.

Erné, Benjamin 1934. *Twee zestiende-eeuwse Spelen van de Hel.* Groningen: Wolters.

Ertman, Thomas 2005. 'State Formation and State Building in Europe'. In *The Handbook of Political Sociology. States, Civil Societies, and Globalization,* edited by Thomas Janoskin, Robert Alford, and Alexander Hicks, 367–83. Cambridge: Cambridge University Press.

Espinas, Georges 1913. *La vie urbaine de Douai au Moyen Âge.* 4 vols. Paris: Picard.

Espinas, Georges 1933. *Les origines du capitalisme. 1: Sire Jehan Boinebroke: patricien et drapier Douaisien (?–1286 environ).* Lille: É. Raoust.

Espinas, Georges 1941–2. *Les origines du droit d'association dans les villes de l'Artois et de la Flandre française jusqu'au début du xvie siècle.* 2 vols. Lille: É. Raoust.

Espinas, Georges 1947. 'Le Privilège de Saint-Omer de 1127'. *Revue du Nord* 29: 43–8.

Espinas, Georges, Charles Verlinden, and Jan Buntinx 1959–61. *Privilèges et chartes de franchise de la Flandre.* 2 vols. Brussels: SCT.

Espinas, Georges, and Henri Pirenne, eds 1906–66. *Recueil de documents relatifs à l'histoire de l'industrie drapière en Flandre.* 4 vols. Brussels: Kiessling et Imbreghts.

Everaert, John 1993. 'Les Lem, alias Leme. Une dynastie marchande d'origine flamande au service de l'expansion Portugaise'. In *Actas. III Colóquio Internacional de História da Madeira,* 817–38. Madeira: Secretaria Regional do Turismo e Cultura, Centro de Estudos de História do Atlântico.

Faems, An 2009. 'Sporen van het utopische in de Middelnederlandse literatuur. Een lezing van Jan van Boendales "Boec vander Wraken"'. In *Paradijzen van papier. Utopie in de Nederlandse literatuur,* edited by Anne Decelle, An Faems, and Tom Sintobin. 17–41. Louvain: Peeters.

Fargeix, Caroline 2007. *Les élites lyonnaises du xve siècle au miroir de leur langage: pratiques et représentations culturelles des conseillers de Lyon d'après les registres de délibérations consulaires.* Paris: De Boccard.

Farr, James 1988. *Hands of Honor. Artisans and their World in Dijon, 1550–1650.* Ithaca, NY: Cornell University Press.

Farr, James 2000. *Artisans in Europe 1300–1914*. Cambridge: Cambridge University Press.

Favresse, Félicien 1961. *Études sur les métiers bruxellois au Moyen Âge*. Brussels: Institut de Sociologie Solvay.

Fayen, Arnold 1912. *Lettres de Jean XXII (1316–1334): textes et analyses*. 3 vols. Rome: Bretschneider.

Feenstra, Robert 1970. *Philip of Leyden and his Treatise De Cura Reipublicae et Sorte Principantis*. Glasgow: University of Glasgow.

Feenstra, Robert, and Guido Rossi 1961. *Ius romanum medii Aevi. Index adbreviationum et de modo citandi fontes*. Milan: Giuffré.

Fentress, James, and Chris Wickham 1992. *Social Memory*. Oxford: Oxford University Press.

Fieuws, Jacques 1977. 'Een Engels volkslied over de Slag der Gulden Sporen'. *Brugs Ommeland* 2: 186–95.

Finnegan, Ruth 1988. *Literacy and Orality. Studies in the Technology of Communication*. Oxford: Blackwell.

Fletcher, Christopher 2008. 'Morality and Office in Late Medieval England and France'. In *Fourteenth-Century England V*, edited by Nigel Saul, 178–90. Woodbridge: Boydell & Brewer.

Fletcher, Christopher, and Rosamund Oates 2009. 'Religious Thought, Political Practice, 1200–1600'. *Cultural and Social History* 6 (3): 297–304.

Fögen, Marie, ed. 1995. *Ordnung und Aufruhr im Mittelalter: historische und juristische Studien zur Rebellion*. Frankfurt am Main: V. Klostermann.

Foncke, Robert 1928. 'Verboden liedjes en paskwillen'. *Mechlinia. Maandschrift voor Oudheidkunde-Geschiedenis* 7: 81–86.

Foot, Sarah 1999. 'Remembering, Forgetting and Inventing: Attitudes to the Past in England at the End of the First Viking Age'. *Transactions of the Royal Historical Society* 9: 185–200.

Foronda, François, ed. 2011. *Avant le contrat social: le contrat politique dans l'occident médiéval, XIIIe–XVIe siècle*. Paris: Éditions de la Sorbonne.

Forster, Robert, and Jack Greene 1970. 'Introduction'. In *Preconditions of Revolution in Early Modern Europe*, edited by Robert Forster and Jack Greene, 1–18. Baltimore: John Hopkins University Press.

Fossier, Robert 1973. 'Remarques sur l'étude des "commotions" sociales aux XIe et XIIe siècles'. *Cahiers de Civilisation Médiévale, Xe–XIIe Siècles* 16: 45–50.

Foucault, Michel 1971. 'Nietzsche, la généalogie, l'histoire'. In *Hommage à Jean Hyppolite*, 145–72. Paris: Presses Universitaires de France.

Foucault, Michel 1977. *Language, Counter-Memory, Practices. Selected Essays and Interviews*, edited by Donald Bouchard. Ithaca, NY: Cornell University Press.

Foucault, Michel 1991. *The Foucault Reader*. London: Penguin.

Foucault, Michel 1994. 'Nietzsche, la généalogie, l'histoire'. In *Dits et Ecrits, 1954–1988*, edited by Daniel Defert, François Ewald, and Jacques Lagrange, vol. 2, 136–56. Paris: Gallimard.

Fourquin, Guy 1972. *Les soulèvements populaires au Moyen Âge*. Paris: Presses Universitaires de France.

Fox, Adam 1997. 'Rumour, News and Popular Political Opinion in Elizabethan and Early Stuart England'. *Historical Journal* 40: 597–620.

Fox, Adam 1999. 'Remembering the Past in Early Modern England: Oral and Written Tradition'. *Transactions of the Royal Historical Society* 9: 233–56.

François, Etienne, and Hagen Schulze, eds 2003. *Deutsche Erinnerungsorte*. Munich: Beck.

Fredericq, Paul 1894. *Onze historische volksliederen van vóór de godsdienstige beroerten der 16de Eeuw*. Ghent: Vuylsteke.

Frijda, Nico 1998. 'De structuur van emoties'. In *Emoties in de Middeleeuwen*, edited by René Stuip and Cees Vellekoop, 9–28. Hilversum: Verloren.

Fris, Victor 1900a. 'De onlusten te Gent in 1432–1435'. *Bulletin de la Société d'Histoire et d'Archéologie de Gand* 8: 163–78.

Fris, Victor 1900b. 'Ontleding van drie Vlaamsche kronijken'. *Handelingen der Maatschappij voor Geschied- en Oudheidkunde van Gent* 3: 135–71.

Fris, Victor 1901a. 'La Cronycke van den lande ende graefscepe van Vlaenderen de Nicolas Despars'. *Bulletin de la Commission Royale d'Histoire* 70: 545–65.

Fris, Victor 1901b. 'Les antiquités de Flandre par Philippe Wielant'. *Bulletin de la Commission Royale d'Histoire* 70: 393–407.

Fris, Victor 1901c. 'Les idées politiques d'Olivier van Dixmude'. *Bulletin de l'Academie Royale Belge* 3: 295–326.

Fris, Victor 1901d. 'Oorkonden betreffende den opstand van Gent tegen Philips den Goede (1450–53)'. *Handelingen der Maatschappij voor Geschied- en Oudheidkunde te Gent* 4: 55–146.

Fris, Victor 1901e. 'Pehaert (Mathieu)'. In *Biographie Nationale*, vol. 16: 867–9. Brussels: Paleis der Academiën.

Fris, Victor, ed. 1901–4. *Dagboek van Gent van 1447 tot 1470, met een vervolg van 1477 tot 1515*. 2 vols. Ghent: Annoot-Braeckman.

Fris, Victor 1903. 'Het oproer te Gent in 1479'. *Tijdschrift van het Willemsfonds* 8: 98–111.

Fris, Victor 1904. 'Documents Gantois concernant la levée du siège de Calais en 1436'. In *Mélanges Paul Frédéricq*, 22–35. Brussels: Lamertin.

Fris, Victor 1906a. 'Blavotins et Ingherkins. Une guerre privée dans la Flandre maritime au XIIme siècle'. *Bulletin de la Société d'Histoire et d'Archéologie de Gand* 14: 133–85.

Fris, Victor 1906b. 'Jan van Coppenhole, een Gentsch politicus in de 15e eeuw'. *Bulletin de la Société d'Histoire et d'Archéologie de Gand* 14: 93–114.

Fris, Victor 1907. 'Les origines de la réforme constitutionnelle de Gand de 1360–1369'. *Fédération archéologique et historique de Belgique. Annales du XXe congrès*, edited by Paul Bergmans, vol. 3, 427–59. Ghent: Siffer.

Fris, Victor 1909. 'L'émeute de Gand en février 1479'. *Bulletijn van de Maatschappij voor Geschied- en Oudheidkunde te Gent* 17: 179–97.

Fris, Victor 1911a. 'Het Brugsche Calfvel van 1407–1411'. *Bulletin de l'Académie royale d'Archéologie de Belgique* 4: 183–274.

Fris, Victor 1911b. *Geschiedenis van Geraardsbergen*. Ghent: Vanderpoorten.

Fris, Victor 1912. 'Twee episoden uit de geschiedenis van Geerardsbergen in het midden der 15de eeuw'. *Handelingen der Maatschappij voor Geschied- en Oudheidkunde te Gent* 12: 3–79.

Fris, Victor 1913. *Histoire de Gand*. Brussels: Van Oest.

Fris, Victor 1914. 'Bewijsstukken betreffende den opstand van Gent tegen Philips den Goede 1451–1454'. *Bulletijn der Maatschappij voor Geschied- en Oudheidkunde te Gent* 22: 3–123.

Fris, Victor 1923. 'La Restriction de Gand, 13 Juillet 1468'. *Bulletijn der Maatschappij voor Geschied- en Oudheidkunde te Gent* 31: 57–142.

Funck-Brentano, Frantz, ed. 1896. *Annales Gandenses*. Paris: Picard.

Gachard, Louis 1833–4. *Collection de documents inédits concernant l'histoire de la Belgique*. 2 vols. Brussels.

Gachard, Louis 1851. 'Lettres inédites de Maximilien, duc d'Autriche, Roi des romains et Empereur, sur les affaires des Pays-Bas, de 1478 à 1508. Première partie, 1478–1488'. *Compte rendu des séances de la Commission Royale d'Histoire ou Recueil de ses bulletins. 2e Série* 2: 263–452.

Gaggio, Dario 2004. 'Do Social Historians Need Social Capital?'. *Social History* 29: 499–513.

Gailliard, Jean-Jacques 1854. *De ambachten en neringen van Brugge, of beschryving hunner opkomst, bloei, werkzaemheden, gebruiken en voorregten*. Bruges: Gailliard.

Gailliard, Jean-Jacques 1857–64. *Bruges et le Franc ou leur magistrature et leur noblesse, avec des données historique et généalogiques sur chaque famille*. 6 vols. Bruges: Gailliard.

Gailliard, Victor 1861–7. *Inscriptions funéraires et monumentales de la Flandre Occidentale avec des données historiques et généalogiques: arrondissements de Bruges*. 5 vols. Bruges.

Gallacher, Stuart 1945. 'Vox Populi, Vox Dei'. *Philological Quarterly* 24: 12–19.

Ganshof, François 1932. *Recherches sur les tribunaux de châtellenie en Flandre avant le milieu du XIIIe siècle*. Antwerp: De Sikkel.

Ganshof, François 1935. 'Étude sur le faussement de jugement dans le droit Flamand des XIIe et XIIIe siècles'. *Bulletin de la Commission Royale des Anciennes Lois et Ordonnances de Belgique* 14: 115–40.

Ganshof, François 1938. 'Die Rechtsprechung des Gräflichen Hofgerichtes in Flandern'. *Zeitschrift der Savigny-Stiftung für Rechtsgeschichte, Germanistische Abteilung* 58: 163–77.

Ganshof, François 1950. 'Les origines du concept de souveraineté nationale en Flandre'. *Revue d'Histoire du Droit* 18 (2): 135–58.

Ganshof, François 1951. 'Le droit urbain en Flandre au début de la première phase de son histoire'. *Revue d'Histoire du Droit* 19 (4): 387–416.

Ganshof, François 1955. *Wat waren de capitularia?* Brussels: Paleis der Academiën.

Ganshof, François 1957. *Qu'est-ce que la féodalité?* Brussels: Office de publicité.

Garrioch, David 2003. 'Sounds of the City. The Soundscape of Early Modern European Towns'. *Urban History* 30: 5–25.

Gauvard, Claude 1989. 'Les révoltes du règne de Charles VI : tentative pour expliquer un échec'. In Gambrelle and Trébitsch, eds 1989, vol. 1, 53–61.

Gauvard, Claude 1991. *"De grâce especial": crime, état et société en France à la fin du Moyen Âge*. Paris: Publications de la Sorbonne.

Gauvard, Claude 1994. 'Rumeurs et stéréotypes à la fin du Moyen Âge'. In *La circulation des nouvelles au Moyen Âge – XXIVe Congrès de la SHMES (Avignon, juin 1993)*, 157–77. Paris: Éditions de la Sorbonne.

Geary, Patrick 1994. *Phantoms of Remembrance: Memory and Oblivion at the End of the First Millennium*. Princeton, NJ: Princeton University Press.

Geary, Patrick 2000. 'The Historical Material of Memory'. In Ciapelli and Rubin, eds 2000, 17–25.

Geary, Patrick 2005. 'Medieval Archivists as Authors. Social Memory and Archival Memory'. In *Archives, Documentation, and Institutions of Social Memory*, edited by Francis Blouin and William Rosenberg, 106–13. Ann Arbor: University of Michigan Press.

Geeraedts, Loek 1986. *Het volksboek van Ulenspieghel. naar de oudste, bewaard gebleven druk van Michiel Hillen van Hoochstraten te Antwerpen uit de eerste helft van de 16de eeuw*. Amsterdam: DNB/Uitgeverij Pelckmans.

Geirnaert, Noël and Ludo Vandamme 1996. *Bruges: Two Thousand Years of History*. Bruges: Stichting Kunstboek.

Geirnaert, Noël, and André Vandewalle, eds 1983. *Adornes en Jeruzalem: internationaal leven in het 15de- en 16de-eeuwse Brugge*. Bruges: Stad Brugge.

Genet, Jean-Philippe 1992. 'Which State Rises?' *Historical Research* 65: 119–33.

Giancarlo, Matthew 2007. *Parliament and Literature in Late Medieval England*. Cambridge: Cambridge University Press.

Gierts, Stephane 1996. 'De opstand te Geraardsbergen in 1430'. Unpublished dissertation, Ghent: Ghent University.

Gilli, Patrick 2011. 'Aux sources de l'espace politique: techniques électorales et pratiques délibératives dans les cités italiennes (XIIe–XIVe siècles)'. In *L'espace public au*

Moyen Âge: Débats autour de Jürgen Habermas, edited by Patrick Boucheron and Nicolas Offenstadt, 229–247. Paris: Presses Universitaires de France.

Gilliodts-van Severen, Louis 1871–85. *Inventaire des archives de la ville de Bruges. Section 1: inventaire des chartes*. 9 vols. Bruges: Gailliard.

Gilliodts-van Severen, Louis 1874. *Coutumes des pays et comté de Flandre. Quartier de Bruges. Coutume de la ville de Bruges*. 2 vols. Brussels: Gobbaerts.

Gilliodts-van Severen, Louis 1879–80. *Coutumes des pays et comté de Flandre. Quartier de Bruges. Coutumes du Franc de Bruges*. 3 vols. Brussels: Gobbaerts.

Gilliodts-van Severen, Louis 1890–3. *Coutumes des pays et comté de Flandre. Quartier de Bruges. Coutumes des petites villes et seigneuries enclavées*. 6 vols. Brussels: Gobbaerts.

Gilliodts-van Severen, Louis 1897–1902. *Coutumes des pays et comté de Flandre. Quartier de Furnes*. 6 vols. Brussels: Goemaere.

Gilliodts-van Severen, Louis 1908. *Coutumes de pays et comté de Flandre. Quartier d'Ypres*. 2 vols. Brussels: Hayez.

Ginzburg, Carlo 1976. *The Cheese and the Worms: The Cosmos of a Sixteenth-Century Miller*, translated by John and Anne C. Tedeshi.

Giry, Arthur 1877. *Histoire de la ville de Saint-Omer et des institutions jusqu'aux XIVe siècle*. Paris: F. Vieweg.

Gambrelle, Fabienne, and Michel Trebitsch, eds 1989. *Révolte et société. Actes du IVe Colloque d'Histoire au present 4e mai 1988 Paris*. 2 vols. Paris: Histoire au present/Publications de la Sorbonne.

Gleba, Gudrun, 1989. *Die Gemeinde als alternatives Ordnungsmodell. Zur sozialen und politischen Differenzierung des Gemeindebegriffes in den innerstädtischen Auseinandersetzungen des 14. und 15. Jahrhunderts. Mainz, Magdeburg, München, Lübeck.* Cologne and Vienna: Böhlau.

Godding, Philippe 1987. *Le droit privé dans les Pays-Bas méridionaux du 12e au 18e siècle*. Brussels: Académie Royale de Belgique.

Grijp, Louis 1977. 'Zingende de dood in'. In *Veelderhande liedekens: studies over het Nederlandse lied tot 1600*, edited by Frank Willaert, 118–48. Louvain: Peeters.

Grijp, Louis 2000. 'Zangcultuur'. In *Volkscultuur: een inleiding in de Nederlandse etnologie*, edited by Ton Dekker, Herman Roodenburg, and Gerard Rooijakkers, 337–80. Nijmegen: SUN.

Grijp, Louis 2004. 'Gruwelijk geblèr of indringende voordracht? De performance van het straatlied'. *Literatuur* 20: 20–5.

Grijp, Louis, and Martine de Bruin, eds 2006. *De kist van Pierlala: straatliederen uit het geheugen van Nederland*. Amsterdam: Bakker.

Gruijs, Albert, and Thom Mertens 1975. 'A New Fragment of Jacob van Maerlant's Eerste and Tweede Martijn (in cod. Bodmer 101, Bibliotheca Bodmeriana, Geneva)'. *Quaerendo* 5: 346–52.

Guenée, Bernard 2002. *L'opinion publique à la fin du Moyen Âge: d'après la chronique de Charles VI du religieux de Saint-Denis*. Paris: Perrin.

Guilcher, Jean-Michel 1989. *La chanson folklorique de la langue française. La notion et son histoire*. Paris: ADP.

Guillorel, Eva 2010. *La complainte et la plainte. Chanson, justice, cultures en Bretagne (XVIe–XVIIIe siècles)*. Rennes: Presses Universitaires de Rennes.

Guldi, Jo 2011. 'What Is the Spatial Turn?', URL: https://spatial.scholarslab.org/spatial-turn/ (accessed 14 November 2020).

Haegeman, Marc 1988. *De anglofilie in het graafschap Vlaanderen tussen 1379 en 1435: politieke en economische aspecten*. Kortrijk: UGA.

Haemers, Jelle 2002. '"Diverssche wonderlic zaken". De Gentse opstand (1449–1453)'. Unpublished dissertation, Ghent: Ghent University.

Haemers, Jelle 2004a. 'De dominante staat. De Gentse opstand (1449–1453) in de negentiende- en twintigste-eeuwse historiografie'. *Bijdragen en Mededelingen betreffende de Geschiedenis der Nederlanden* 119 (1): 39–61.

Haemers, Jelle 2004b. *De Gentse opstand (1449–1453). De strijd tussen rivaliserende netwerken om het stedelijke kapitaal*. Kortrijk: UGA.

Haemers, Jelle 2005a. 'Boone (Lieven)'. In *Nationaal Biografisch Woordenboek*, vol. 17: 120–4. Brussels: Paleis der Academiën.

Haemers, Jelle 2005b. 'Middelburg na Pieter Bladelin. De juridische en militaire strijd tussen vorst, stad en adel om sociale erkenning en politieke macht (1472–1492)'. *Handelingen van het Genootschap voor Geschiedenis* 142 (3): 215–65.

Haemers, Jelle 2007a. 'Adellijke onvrede. Adolf van Kleef en Lodewijk van Gruuthuse als beschermheren en uitdagers van het Bourgondisch-Habsburgse hof (1477–1492)'. *Jaarboek voor Middeleeuwse Geschiedenis* 10: 178–215.

Haemers, Jelle 2007b. 'Kleef (Filips Van)'. In *Nationaal Biografisch Woordenboek*, vol. 18: 547–57. Brussels: Paleis der Academiën.

Haemers, Jelle 2007c. 'Philippe de Clèves et la Flandre. La position d'un aristocrate au cœur d'une révolte urbaine (1477–1492)'. In Haemers, Van Hoorebeeck, and Wijsman, eds 2007, 21–99.

Haemers, Jelle 2007d. 'Moreel (Willem)'. In *Nationaal Biografisch Woordenboek*, vol. 18: 681–9. Brussels: Paleis der Academiën.

Haemers, Jelle 2007e. 'Kleef (Adolf Van)'. In *Nationaal Biografisch Woordenboek*, vol. 18: 540–7. Brussels: Paleis der Academiën.

Haemers, Jelle 2007f. 'Zegels, eden, taal en liturgie. Ideologie, propaganda en het symbolische gebruik van ruimte in Gent (1483)'. *Handelingen van Maatschappij voor Geschiedenis en Oudheidkunde te Gent* 61: 183–212.

Haemers, Jelle 2008. 'Opstand adelt? De rechtvaardiging van het politieke verzet van de Bourgondisch-Habsburgse adel in de Vlaamse opstand (1482–1492)'. *Bijdragen en Mededelingen betreffende de Geschiedenis der Nederlanden* 123: 586–608.

Haemers, Jelle 2009. *For the Common Good? State Power and Urban Revolts in the Reign of Mary of Burgundy, 1477–1482.* Turnhout: Brepols.

Haemers, Jelle 2010a. 'Geletterd verzet. Diplomatiek, politiek en herinneringscultuur van opstandelingen in de laatmiddeleeuwse en vroegmoderne stad (Casus: Brugge en Gent)'. *Bulletin de la Commission Royale d'Histoire de Belgique* 176: 5–54.

Haemers, Jelle 2010b. 'Un miroir à double face: les chroniques de Jean Molinet et de Nicolas Despars. La lutte discursive entre centralisme et constitutionalisme dans le cadre de la révolte brugeoise de 1488'. *Le Moyen Âge* 116: 269–301.

Haemers, Jelle 2011. 'Social Memory and Rebellion in Fifteenth-Century Ghent'. *Social History* 36 (4): 443–63.

Haemers, Jelle 2012. 'Bloed en inkt. Een nieuwe blik op opstand en geweld te Leuven'. *Stadsgeschiedenis* 7: 141–64.

Haemers, Jelle 2016a. 'Révolte et requête. Les gens de métiers et les conflits sociaux dans les villes de Flandre (XIIIe–XVe siècle)'. *Revue Historique* 677: 27–56.

Haemers, Jelle 2016b. 'The Identity of the Urban 'Commoners' in Thirteenth-Century Flanders'. *Imago Temporis. Medium Aevum* 10: 191–213.

Haemers, Jelle 2018. 'Diffuser des lettres pour contracter des alliances. La communication des rebelles en Flandre et en Brabant au bas Moyen Âge'. *Revue francaise d'histoire du livre* 138: 131–50.

Haemers, Jelle, Andrea Bardyn, and Chanelle Delameillieure 2019. *Wijvenwereld: Vrouwen in de middeleeuwse stad.* Antwerpen: Uitgeverij Vrijdag.

Haemers, Jelle, and Anke Demeyer 2019. 'Le cri du rebelle, le cri du criminel. Slogans, insultes et langage des "malfaiteurs" dans les villes des Pays-Bas méridionaux, XIVe–XVIe siècles'. *Histoire, Économie & Société* 37 (1): 15–31.

Haemers, Jelle, Céline Van Hoorebeeck, and Hanno Wijsman, eds 2007. *Entre la ville, la noblesse et l'état: Philippe de Clèves (1456–1528), homme politique et bibliophile.* Turnhout, Belgium: Brepols.

Haemers, Jelle, and Chanelle Delameillieure 2017. 'Women and Contentious Speech in Fifteenth-Century Brabant', *Continuity & Change* 32 (3): 323–47.

Haemers, Jelle, and Élodie Lecuppre-Desjardin 2007. 'Conquérir et reconquérir l'espace urbain. Le triomphe de la collectivité sur l'individu dans le cadre de la révolte brugeoise de 1488'. In *Voisinages, coexistences, appropriations: groupes sociaux et territoires urbains (Moyen Âge–16e siècle)*, edited by Chloé Deligne and Claire Billen, 119–42. Turnhout: Brepols.

Haemers, Jelle, and Élodie Lecuppre-Desjardin 2020. 'La voix des "sans-voix". Réflexion sur les prises de parole des leaders des révoltes populaires à la fin du Moyen Âge'. In *La voix au Moyen Âge. Le Congrès de la SHMESP*, pp. 233–47. Paris: Éditions de la Sorbonne.

Haemers, Jelle, and Louis Sicking 2006. 'De Vlaamse opstand van Filips van Kleef en de Nederlandse opstand van Willem van Oranje: een vergelijking'. *Tijdschrift voor Geschiedenis* 119 (3): 328–47.

Haemers, Jelle, and Tim Soens 2007. 'Lauwerein (Yeronimus Van)'. In *Nationaal Biografisch Woordenboek*, vol. 18: 584–92. Brussels: Paleis der Academiën.

Haemers, J., and Valeria Van Camp 2018. '« Li ville est mal gouvernee ». Les registres du conseil de la ville de Mons, la crise politique de 1424–1428, son impact sur l'audition des comptes communaux'. *Histoire urbaine* 52 (2): 137–66.

Haemers, Jelle, and Valerie Vrancken 2017. 'Libels in the City. Bill Casting in Fifteenth-Century Flanders and Brabant'. *The Medieval Low Countries* 4: 165–87.

Haines, Margaret 2000. 'Artisan Family Strategies: Proposals for Research on the Families of Florentine Artists'. In Ciapelli and Rubin, eds 2000, 163–75.

Halbwachs, Maurice 1923. *Les cadres sociaux de la mémoire*. Paris: Librairie Félix Alcan.

Halbwachs, Maurice 1950. *La mémoire collective*. Paris: Presses Universitaires de France.

Halbwachs, Maurice 1992. *On Collective Memory*, translated by Lewis Coser. Chicago, IL: University of Chicago Press.

Halpern, David 2005. *Social Capital*. Cambridge: Cambridge Polity Press.

Hanagan, Michael, Leslie Moch, and Wayne Te Brake, eds 1998. *Challenging Authority: the Historical Study of Contentious Politics*. Minneapolis, MN: University of Minnesota Press.

Hancké, Katia 1995a. 'Confiscaties als politiek wapen in intern stedelijke conflicten, casus: Gent 1477–1492'. *Handelingen der Maatschappij voor Geschiedenis en Oudheidkunde te Gent* 49: 197–220.

Hancké, Katia 1995b, 'Conflict en confiscatie, Een bijdrage tot de kennis van de sociale structuren te Gent op het einde van de xve eeuw' Unpublished dissertation, Ghent: Ghent University.

Häpke, Rudolf 1908. *Brügges Entwicklung zum mittelalterlichen Weltmarkt*. Bruges: K. Curtius.

Harvey, Isabel 1991. *Jack Cade's Rebellion of 1450*. Oxford: Oxford University Press.

Harvey, Isabel 1995. 'Was there Popular Politics in Fifteenth-Century England?' In *The McFarlane Legacy: Studies in Late Medieval Politics and Society*, edited by Richard Britnell and Anthony Pollard, 155–74. Stroud: Alan Sutton Publishing.

Haverkamp, Alfred 1991. 'Innerstädtische Auseinandersetzungen und überlokale Zusammenhänge in deutschen Städten während der ersten Hälfe des 14. Jahrhunderts'. In *Stadtadel und Bürgertum in den italienischen und deutschen Städten des Spätmittelalters*, edited by Reinhard Elze and Gina Fasoli, 89–126. Berlin: Duncker & Humblot.

Haverkamp, Alfred 1996. '… An die große Glocke hängen. Über Öffentlichkeit im Mittelalter'. *Jahrbuch des Historischen Kollegs 1995*, 71–112.

Haverkamp, Anselm, and Renate Lachmann, eds 1993. *Memoria: Vergessen und Erinneren*. Munich: Wilhelm Fink.

Heers, Jacques 1977. *Factions and Political Life in the Medieval West*. Amsterdam/New York, NY: North-Holland.

Heirbaut, Dirk 1997. *Over heren, vazallen en graven: het persoonlijk leenrecht in Vlaanderen ca. 1000–1305*. Brussels: Algemeen Rijksarchief.

Hennequin, Gilles 1955. 'La révolte des bourgeois de Saint-Omer de 1306, et ses conséquences'. *Bulletin Trimestriel de la Société Académique des Antiquaires de la Morinie* 18: 417–44.

Herlihy, David 1976. 'Società e spazio nella città italiana del medioeve'. In *La storiografia urbanistica*, edited by Ricardo Martinelli, 174–94. Lucca: Ciska-Marsilio Editori.

Hermersdorf, Bernard 1980. *Rechtsspiegel. Een rechtshistorische terugblik in de Lage Landen van het herfsttij*, edited by Pieter Verdam. Nijmegen: Dekker & Van de Vegt.

Hibst, Peter 1991. *Utilitas publica, gemeiner Nutz, Gemeinwohl: Untersuchungen zur Idee eines politischen Leitbegriffes von der Antike bis zum späten Mittelalter*. Frankfurt am Main: Peter Lang.

Hicks, Michael 1995. *Bastard Feudalism*. Harlow: Longman.

Highley, Christopher 1998. 'The Royal Image in Elizabethan Ireland'. In *Dissing Elizabeth: Negative Representations of Gloriana*, edited by Julia Walker, 60–76. Durham/London: Duke University Press.

Higounet, Arlette, and Claudine Billot 1984. 'Bannissement et repeuplement dirigé à Arras (1479–1484)'. In *La faute, la répression et le pardon. Actes du 107e Congrès National des Sociétés Savantes (Brest 1982)*, 107–24. Paris: Comité des Travaux Historiques et Scientifiques.

Hilton, Rodney 1973. *Bond Men Made Free: Medieval Peasant Movements and the English Rising of 1381*, edited by Christopher Dyer. New York, NY: Viking Press.

Hilton, Rodney 1974. 'Peasant Society, Peasant Movements and Feudalism in Medieval Europe'. In *Rural Protest: Peasant Movements and Social Change*, edited by Henry Landsberger, 67–94. London: Palgrave Macmillan.

Hilton, Rodney 1989. 'Révoltes rurales et révoltes urbaines au Moyen Âge'. In Gambrelle and Trebitsch, eds 1989, vol. 2, 25–33.

Hilton, Rodney 1999. 'The Origins of Robin Hood'. In *Robin Hood. An Anthology of Scholarship and Criticism*, edited by Stephen Knight, 197–210. Woodbridge: Boydell & Brewer.

Hilton, Rodney, and Trevor Aston, eds 1984. *The English Rising of 1381*. Cambridge, Cambridge University Press.

His, Rudolf 1964. *Das Strafrecht des deutschen Mittelalters*. 2 vols. Aalen: Scientia.

Hoare, Quintin, and Geoffrey Nowell Smith, trans and eds 1971. *Selections from the Prison Notebooks of Antonio Gramsci*. London: Lawrence & Wishart.

Hoffmann, Hartmut 1964. *Gottesfriede und Treuga Dei*. Stuttgart: Hiersemann.

Hoffmann von Fallersleben, August, ed. 1830–62. *Horae Belgicae*. 12 vols. Vratislaviae: Grass, Barth et Soc.

Hoffmann von Fallersleben, August, ed. 1855. *Antwerpener Liederbuch von Jahre 1544*. Hanover: Carl Rümpler.

Hogenelst, Bernardina 1997. *Sproken en sprekers. Inleiding op en repertorium van de middelnederlandse sproke.* 2 vols. Amsterdam: Prometheus.

Holbach, Rudolf 1993. 'Some Remarks on the Role of "Putting-out" in Flemish and Northwestern European Cloth Production'. In *La draperie ancienne des Pays-Bas: débouchés et strategies de survie (14e–16e siècles)*, edited by Marc Boone and Walter Prevenier, 207–50. Louvain: Garant.

Holden, Anthony, ed. 1970. Le roman de Rou de Wace. 3 vols. Paris: Picard.

Holenstein, André 1991. *Die Huldigung der Untertanen: Rechtskultur und Herrschaftsordnung (800–1800).* Stuttgard: De Gruyter Oldenbourg.

Holquist, Michael 2002. *Dialogism: Bakhtin and his World.* 2nd ed. London: Psychology Press.

Honemann, Volker 1997. 'Politische Lieder und Sprüche im Späten Mittelalter und der Frühen Neuzeit'. *Die Musikforschung* 50 (4): 399–421.

Honemann, Volker 2008. '"Herzog Casimir von Pommern" und "Busse von Erxleben": Zwei politische Lieder des deutschen Spätmittelalters im Vergleich'. In *Literaturlandschaften. Schriften zur Deutschsprachigen Literatur im Osten des Reiches*, edited by Rudolf Suntrup and Volker Honemann, 227–46. Frankfurt am Main: Peter Lang.

Hopkin, David 2012. *Voices of the People in Nineteenth-Century France.* Cambridge: Cambridge University Press.

Howell, Martha 1986. *Women, Production, and Patriarchy in Late Medieval Cities.* Chicago, IL: University of Chicago Press.

Howell, Martha 1993. 'Achieving the Guild Effect without Guilds: Crafts and Craftsmen in Late Medieval Douai'. In *Les métiers au Moyen Âge. Aspects économiques et sociaux*, edited by Pascale Lambrechts and Jean-Pierre Sosson, 109–28. Louvain-la-Neuve: Institut d'Études Médiévales.

Howell, Martha 2001. 'The Social Logic of the Marital Household in Cities of the Late Medieval Low Countries'. In *The Household in Late Medieval Cities, Italy and Northwestern Europe Compared*, edited by Myriam Carlier and Tim Soens, 185–202. Louvain: Garant.

Howell, Martha 2007. 'From Land to Love. Commerce and Marriage in Northern Europe during the Late Middle Ages'. *Jaarboek voor Middeleeuwse Geschiedenis* 10: 216–53.

Howell, Martha, and Marc Boone 1996. 'Becoming Early Modern in the Late Medieval Low Countries: Ghent and Douai from the Fourteenth to the Sixteenth Century'. *Urban History* 23: 300–24.

Hugenholtz, Frederik 1949. *Drie boerenopstanden uit de veertiende eeuw: Vlaanderen, 1323–1328; Frankrijk, 1358; Engeland, 1381. Onderzoek naar het opstandig bewustzijn.* Haarlem: Tjeenk Willink.

Hugenholtz, Frederik 1964. 'The 1477 Crisis in the Burgundian Duke's Dominions'. In *Britain and the Netherlands* 2, edited by John Bromley and Ernst Kossmann, 33–46. Groningen: J.-B. Wolters.

Hummelen, Willem 1968. *Repertorium van het rederijkersdrama, 1500–ca. 1620*. Assen: Van Gorcum.

Hummelen, Willem, and Geert. Dibbets, eds 1985. *Een Spel van sinnen beroerende het cooren (1565) van Lauris Jansz.* Zutphen: Thieme.

Hüsken, Wim 1992. 'Kroniek van het toneel in Brugge (1468–1556)'. *Verslagen en Mededelingen van de Koninklijke Academie voor Nederlandse Taal en Letterkunde* 103: 219–52.

Hüsken, Wim 1996. 'The Fool as Social Critic: the Case of Dutch Rhetoricians' Drama'. In *Fools and Folly*, edited by Clifford Davidson, 112–45. Kalamazoo, MI: Medieval Institute Publications.

Hüsken, Wim 1997. 'Politics and Drama: the City of Bruges as Organizer of Drama Festivals'. In *The Stage as a Mirror: Civic Theatre in Late Medieval Europe*, edited by Alan Knight, 165–87. Cambridge: Brewer.

Hüsken, Wim 1999. 'Cornelis Everaert on Power and Authority'. In *The Growth of Authority in the Medieval West*, edited by Martin Gosman, Arie Vanderjagt, and Jan Veenstra, 241–56. Groningen: Forsten.

Hüsken, Wim, ed. 2005. *De spelen van Cornelis Everaert: opnieuw uitgegeven, van inleiding, annotaties en woordverklaringen voorzien.* 2 vols. Hilversum: Verloren.

Hüsken, Wim, Bart Ramakers, and Frans Schaars, eds 1992. *Trou moet blijcken. Bronnenuitgave van de boeken der Haarlemse rederijkamer 'de Pellicanisten'.* Asse: Quarto.

Hutton, Shennan 2011. *Women and Economic Activities in Late Medieval Ghent.* New York, NY: Palgrave Macmillan.

Hyde, John 1973. *Society and Politics in Medieval Italy: the Evolution of the Civil Life, 1000–1350.* New York, NY: St. Martin's Press.

Hymes, Dell 1977. *Foundations in Sociolinguistics: an Ethnographic Approach.* London: Tavistock Publications.

Innes, Matthew 1998. 'Memory, Orality, and Literacy in an Early Medieval Society'. *Past & Present* 158: 3–36.

Innes, Matthew 2000. 'Introduction: Using the Past, Interpreting the Present, Influencing the Future'. In *The Uses of the Past in the Early Middle Ages*, edited by Yitzhak Hen and Matthew Innes, 1–8. Cambridge: Cambridge University Press.

Isenmann, Eberhard 2012. *Die deutsche Stadt im Mittelalter, 1150–1550.* Cologne: Böhlau.

Ives, Eric 1979. *Faction in Tudor England.* London: Historical Association.

Jackman, Robert, and Ross Miller 1998. 'Social Capital and Politics'. *Annual Review of Political Science* 1: 47–73.

Jameson, Fredric 1988 'Cognitive Mapping'. In *Marxism and the Interpretation of Culture*, edited by Cary Nelson and Lawrence Grossberg, 347–57. Urbana and Chicago: University of Illinois.

Jansma, Taeke 1932. *Raad en Rekenkamer in Holland en Zeeland tijdens hertog Philips van Bourgondië.* Utrecht: Instituut voor Middeleeuwsche Geschiedenis.

Jansma, Taeke 1950. *Het vraagstuk van Hollands welvaren tijdens hertog Philips van Bourgondië*. Groningen: Wolters.

Janssens, Albert 1983. 'Het Brugse bevolkingsaantal in 1477'. In *Van middeleeuwen tot heden. Bladeren door Brugse kunst en geschiedenis*, 29–35. Bruges: Jong Kristen Onthaal voor Toerisme.

Janssens, Albert 1996. 'Macht en onmacht van de Brugse schepenbank in de periode 1477–1490'. *Handelingen van het Genootschap voor Geschiedenis te Brugge* 133 (1–3): 5–45.

Janssens, Albert 2003. 'Willem Moreel en Hans Memling. Bijdrage tot het onderzoek naar de schilderijen van Memling in opdracht van de familie Moreel'. *Handelingen van het Genootschap voor Geschiedenis* 140: 66–110.

Janssens, Albert 2006. 'Daar komen de Brugse kruisboogschutters van de "oude" Gilde van Sint-Joris (tweede helft vijftiende eeuw)'. *Brugs Ommeland* 46: 52–75; 83–113.

Jente, Richard, ed. 1947. *Proverbia Communia: a Fifteenth Century Collection of Dutch Proverbs together with the Low German Version*. Bloomington, IN: Indiana University Press.

Johanek, Peter 2002. 'Geschichtsüberlieferung und ihre Medien in der Gesellschaft des späten Mittelalters'. In *Pragmatische Dimensionen mittelalterlicher Schriftkultur*, edited by Christel Meier, Volker Honemann, Hagen Keller, and Rudolf Suntrup, 339–57. Munich: Fink.

Johnson, Chalmers 1982. *Revolutionary Change*. Palo Alto, CA: Stanford University Press.

Johnstone, Hilda, ed. 1951. *Annals of Ghent*. London: Nelson.

Jones, Amanda 2009. *'Commotion Time': the English Risings of 1549*. London: Taylor & Francis.

Jones, Michael 1984. 'Trahison et l'idée de lèse-majesté dans la Bretagne du xve siècle'. In *La faute, la répression et le pardon. Actes du 107e Congrès National des Sociétés Savantes (Brest 1982)*, 91–106. Paris: Comité des Travaux Historiques et Scientifiques.

Jones, Philip 1997. *The Italian City-State: from Commune to Signoria*. Oxford: Clarendon Press.

Jouhaud, Christine 2009. ' "Camisard! We were Camisard!" Remembrance and the Ruining of Remembrance through the Production of Historical Absences'. *History and Memory* 21 (1): 5–24.

Joutard, Philippe 1977. *La légende des Camisard*. Paris: Gallimard.

Joutard, Philippe 1983. *Ces voix qui nous viennent du passé*. Paris: Hachette.

Justice, Jean 1891. 'La répression à Ypres après la révolte de 1477. Documents faisant suite à l'épisode de l'histoire d'Ypres sous le règne de Marie de Bourgogne'. *Annales de la Société d'Émulation de Bruges* 41: 1–285.

Justice, Steven 1994. *Writing and Rebellion: England in 1381*. Berkeley, CA: University of California Press.

Kalff, Gerrit 1884. *Het lied in de Middeleeuwen*. Leiden: Brill.

Kalff, Gerrit 1906–12. *Geschiedenis der Nederlandsche letterkunde*. 7 vols. Groningen: Brill.

Kansteiner, Wulf 2002. 'Finding Meaning in Memory: a Methodological Critique of Collective Memory Studies'. *History and Theory* 41: 179–97.

Keene, Derek 1990. 'Suburban Growth'. In *The English Medieval Town: a Reader in English Urban History, 1200–1540*, edited by Richard Holt and Gervase Rosser, 97–119. London: Longman.

Keene, Derek 2004. 'Towns and the Growth of Trade'. In *The New Cambridge Medieval History. 4: c. 1024–c. 1198*, edited by David Luscombe and Jonathan Riley-Smith, Part 1: 47–85. Cambridge: Cambridge University Press.

Keller, Hagen 1988. 'Gli inizi de comune in Lombardia: limiti della documentazione e metodi di ricerca'. In *L'evoluzione delle città italiane nell'xi secolo*, edited by Renato Bordone and Jörg Jarnut, 45–70. Bologna: Il Mulino.

Kellermann, Karina 2000. *Abschied vom 'Historischen Volkslied'. Studien zu Funktion, Ästhetik und Publizität der Gattung Historisch-Politische Ereignisdichtung*. Berlin: De Gruyter.

Kempshall, Matthew 1999. *The Common Good in Late Medieval Political Thought*. Oxford: Clarendon Press.

Kent, Dale 1978. *The Rise of the Medici: Faction in Florence, 1426–1434*. Oxford: Oxford University Press.

Kern, Fritz 1954. *Gottesgnadentum und Widerstandsrecht im früheren Mittelalter zur Entwicklungsgeschichte der Monarchie*. Münster: Böhlau.

Kertzer, David 1988. *Ritual, Politics and Power*. New Haven, CT: Yale University Press.

Kervyn de Lettenhove, Joseph, ed. 1850. *Mémoires de Jean de Dadizeele, souverain bailli de Flandre*. Bruges: Vandecasteele-Werbrouck.

Kervyn de Lettenhove, Joseph, ed. 1863–6. *Œuvres de Georges Chastellain*. 8 vols. Brussels: Heussner.

Kervyn de Lettenhove, Joseph, ed. 1867–77. *Œuvres de Froissart: Chroniques*. 25 vols. Brussels: Devaux.

Kervyn de Lettenhove, Joseph, ed. 1870. 'Adriaen de But: Chronicon Flandriae'. In *Chroniques relatives à l'histoire de Belgique sous la domination des ducs de Bourgogne 1: Chroniques des religieux des Dunes, Jean Brandon, Gilles de Roye, Adrien de But [1384–1488] (textes latins)*, 211–710. Brussels: Hayez

Kervyn de Lettenhove, Joseph, ed. 1873. 'Le livre des trahisons de France'. In *Chroniques relatives à l'histoire de Belgique sous la domination des ducs de Bourgogne 2: Le livre des trahisons de France. La geste des ducs de Bourgogne. Le pastoralet (textes fraçais)*, 1–258. Brussels: Hayez.

Kesselring, Krista 2007. *The Northern Rebellion of 1569: Faith, Politics, and Protest in Elizabethan England*. New York, NY: Palgrave Macmillan.

Keyt, David, and Fred Miller 1991. *A Companion to Aristotle's Politics*. Oxford: Blackwell.

Kinable, Dirk 1998. *Facetten van Boendale. Literair-historische verkenningen van Jans Teesteye en de Lekenspiegel*. Leiden: Internationaal Forum voor Afrikaanse en Nederlandse Taal en Letteren.

Klapisch-Zuber, Christiane 1991. 'Comptes et mémoires: l'écriture des livres de famille florentine'. In *L'écrit dans la société médiévale. Divers aspects de sa pratique du XIe au XVe siècle. Textes en hommage à Lucie Fossier*, edited by Caroline Bourlet and Annie Dufour, 251–58. Paris: Centre National de la Recherche Scientifique.

Knoke, David, and Song Yang 2008. *Social Network Analysis*. Los Angeles: Sage Publications.

Knuvelder, Gerard 1957–61. *Handboek tot de geschiedenis der Nederlandse letterkunde*. 4 vols. Den Bosch: Malmberg.

Koepp, Johannes 1929. *Untersuchungen über das Antwerpener Liederbuch vom Jahre 1544*. Antwerp: De Sikkel.

Köhn, Rolf 1991. 'Freiheit als Forderung und Ziel bauerlichen Widerstandes (Mittel- und Westeuropa, 11.–13. Jahrhundert)'. In *Die abendländische Freiheit vom 10. zum 14. Jahrhundert. Der Wirkungszusammenhang von Idee und Wirklichkeit im europäischen Vergleich*, edited by Johannes Fried, 325–87. Sigmaringen: Thorbecke.

Königsberger, Helmut 1986. 'Fürst und Generalstaaten: Maximilian I. in den Niederlanden (1477–1493)'. *Historischer Zeitschrift* 242: 557–79.

Königsberger, Helmut 2001. *Monarchies, States Generals and Parliaments. The Netherlands in the Fifteenth and Sixteenth Centuries*. Cambridge: Cambridge University Press.

Koopmans, Jelle 2001. 'Toneelgeschiedenis rond de grens. Drama in de Noord-Franse Steden'. In *Spel en spektakel. Middeleeuws toneel in de Lage Landen*, edited by Bart Ramakers and Hans van Dijk, 83–97. Amsterdam: Prometheus.

Kossmann, Ernst 1980. 'Volkssouvereiniteit aan het begin van het Nederlandse Ancien Régime'. *Bijdragen en Mededelingen van de Geschiedenis der Nederlanden* 95: 1–34.

Krynen, Jacques 1993. *L'empire du roi: idées et croyances politiques en France, XIIIe–XVe siècle*. Paris: Gallimard.

Kuhn, Christian 2007. 'Urban Laughter as a "Counter-Public" Sphere in Augsburg: the Case of the City Mayor, Jakob Herbrot (1490/95–1564)'. *International Review of Social History* 52: 77–93.

Kuijpers, Erika, and Judith Pollmann 2013. 'Why Remember Terror? Memories of Violence in the Dutch Revolt'. In *Ireland 1641. Contexts and Reactions*, edited by Jane Ohlmeyer and Michaél O'siochrú, 176–96. Manchester: Manchester University Press.

Kuttner, Stephan 1935. *Kanonistische Schuldlehre von Gratian bis auf die Dekretalen Gregors IX*. Vatican City: Biblioteca Apostólica Vaticana.

La Roncière, Charles-Marie de 1991. 'Corporations et mouvements sociaux en Italie du Nord et du Centre au XIVe siècle'. In *Forme ed evoluzione del lavoro in Europa: XII–XVIII secc.*, edited by Annalisa Guarducci, 397–416. Florence: Le Monnier.

Laenen, Joseph 1924. *Les archives de l'état à Vienne au point de vue de l'histoire de Belgique*. Brussels: Kiessling.

Lalou, Élisabeth 1990. 'Les révoltes contre le pouvoir à la fin du XIIIe et au début de XIVe siècle'. In *Violence et contestation au Moyen Âge*, edited by François-Olivier Touati, 159–84. Paris: Éditions du Comité des Travaux Historiques et Scientifiques.

Lambert, Bart 2006. *The City, the Duke and their Banker: the Rapondi Family and the Formation of the Burgundian State (1384–1430)*. Turnhout: Brepols.

Lambert, Véronique 1993. *Chronicles of Flanders, 1200–1500. Chronicles Written Independently from Flandria Generosa*. Ghent: Maatschappij voor Geschiedenis en Oudheidkunde te Gent.

Lambert, Véronique 1999. 'Réalité et fiction: les flamands et la Bataille des Éperons d'Or'. In *Actes du Colloque, 1ère journée de Coordination universitaire pour l'étude du flamand (CEUF), 16 octobre 1998*, edited by Jean Heuclin, 19–25. Lille: Université Catholique de Lille.

Lambert, Véronique 2002. 'Over carrière, promotie, degradatie en rehabilitatie. 700 jaar Jan Breydel en Pieter de Coninck'. In *Omtrent 1302*, edited by Paul Trio, Dirk Heirbaut, and Dirk Van den Auweele, 207–28. Louvain: Louvain University Press.

Lambert, Véronique, and Jan Dumolyn 2002. 'De cruciale decennia in de geschiedenis van een Europese Stad. Brugge tussen 1280 en 1302'. In *Omtrent 1302*, edited by Paul Trio, Dirk Heirbaut, and Dirk Van den Auweele, 65–79. Louvain: Louvain University Press.

Lambin, Jean-Jacques, ed. 1831. *Verhael van den moord van eenige schepenen, raeden en andere inwooners der stad Ypre, gebeurd den 29n en 30n november 1303*. Ypres: Lambin et fils.

Lambin, Jean-Jacques, ed. 1835. *Olivier Van Dixmuide: merkwaerdige gebeurtenissen, vooral in Vlaenderen en Brabant, en ook in de aengrenzende landstreken: van 1377 tot 1443*. Ypres: Lambin et fils.

Lambin, Jean-Jacques, ed. 1839. *Dits de cronike ende genealogie van den prinsen ende graven van den foreeste van Buc, dat heet Vlaenderlant, van 863 tot 1436, gevolgd naar het oorspronkelijk handschrift van Jan van Dixmude*. Ypres: Lambin et fils.

Langley, Frederick 1999. 'Community Drama and Community Politics in Thirteenth-Century Arras: Adam de la Halle's "Jeu de la Feuillée"'. In *Drama and Community: People and Plays in Medieval Europe*, edited by Alan Hindley, 57–77. Turnhout: Brepols.

Lansing, Carol 1991. *The Florentine Magnates: Lineage and Faction in a Medieval Commune*. Princeton, NJ: Princeton University Press.

Lantschner, Patrick 2009. 'The Ciompi Revolution Constructed: Modern Historians and the Nineteenth-Century Paradigm of Revolution'. *Annali di Storia di Firenze* 4: 277–97.

Larrington, Carolyne 2001. 'The Psychology of Emotion and Study of the Medieval Period'. *Early Medieval Europe* 10: 251–6.

Lavéant, Katell 2007. *Théâtre et culture dramatique d'expression française dans les villes des Pays-Bas méridionaux, xve–xvie siècles*. Amsterdam: University of Amsterdam.

Le Roy Ladurie, Emmanuel 1975. *Montaillou, village occitan de 1294 à 1324*. Paris: Gallimard.

Lear, Floyd 1965. *Treason and Related Offences in Roman and Germanic Law*. Austin, TX: University of Texas Press.

Lecuppre-Desjardin, Élodie 1999. 'Les lumières de la ville: recherche sur l'utilisation de la lumière dans les cérémonies bourguignonnes'. *Revue Historique* 123: 23–43.

Lecuppre-Desjardin, Élodie 2002. 'Grote schoonmaak in de stad. De sanering, beveiliging en ruimtelijke inrichting van de stad naar aanleiding van vorstelijke plechtigheden in de Bourgondische Nederlanden (14e–15e eeuw)'. *Jaarboek voor Ecologische Geschiedenis*, 19–35.

Lecuppre-Desjardin, Élodie 2003. 'Des pouvoirs inscrits dans la pierre? Essai sur l'édilité urbaine dans les anciens Pays-Bas bourguignons'. *Memini. Travaux et documents publiés par la société des études médiévales de Québec* 7: 7–35.

Lecuppre-Desjardin, Élodie 2004a. *La ville des cérémonies: essai sur la communication politique dans les anciens Pays-Bas Bourguignons*. Turnhout: Brepols.

Lecuppre-Desjardin, Élodie 2004b. 'Parcours festifs et enjeux de pouvoirs dans les villes des anciens Pays-Bas Bourguignons au xve siècle'. *Histoire Urbaine* 9: 29–45.

Lecuppre-Desjardin, Élodie 2006. '"Et le prince respondit de par sa bouche". Monarchal Speech Habits in Late Medieval Europe'. In *Mystifying the Monarch: Studies on Discourse, Power, and History*, edited by Gita Deneckere and Jeroen Deploige, 55–64. Amsterdam: Amsterdam University Press.

Lecuppre-Desjardin, Élodie 2007. 'Multipolarité et multifonctionalité des places publiques dans les villes des anciens Pays-Bas Bourguignons'. In *La place publique urbaine du Moyen Âge à nos jours*, edited by Laurence Baudoux-Rousseau, 45–52. Arras: Artois Presses Université.

Lecuppre-Desjardin, Élodie 2010. 'Des portes qui parlent: placards, feuilles volantes et communication politique dans les villes des Pays-Bas à la fin du Moyen Âge'. *Bibliothèque de l'École des Chartes* 168: 151–72.

Lecuppre-Desjardin, Élodie 2011. 'La Grande Procession de Lille à la fin du Moyen Âge: entre dévotion populaire et enjeux de pouvoir'. In *Sentiments religieux et piété populaire de l'an mil à nos jours*, edited by Jean Heuclin, 43–56. Villeneuve d'Ascq: Revue du Nord.

Lecuppre-Desjardin, Élodie, and Anne-Laure Van Bruaene, eds 2005. *Emotions in the Heart of the City (14th–16th Century)*. Turnhout: Brepols.

Lecuppre-Desjardin, Élodie, and Anne-Laure Van Bruaene 2013. 'Déambuler sous le regard de Dieu et parmi les siens: les habitudes processionnelles dans les villes des anciens Pays-Bas (XIIIe–XVIe siècles)'. In *Ommegang!*, edited by Jean-Paul Heerbrant, 49–58. Brussels: Centre Albert Marinus.

Leendertz, Pieter 1924–5. *Het Geuzenliedboek naar de oude drukken*. 2 vols. Zutphen: Thieme.

Lefebvre, Henri 1974. *La production de l'espace*. Paris: Anthropos.

Leguai, André 1967. 'Émeutes et troubles d'origine fiscale pendant le règne de Louis XI'. *Le Moyen Âge* 73: 447–87.

Leguai, André 1976. 'Les troubles urbains dans le Nord de la France à la fin du XIIIe et au début du XIVe siècle'. *Revue d'histoire Économique et Sociale* 54 (3): 281–303.

Leguay, Jean-Pierre 1984. *La rue au Moyen Âge*. Rennes: Éditions Ouest-France Université.

Lenaerts, Robert 1972. 'Het strafrecht en het strafprocesrecht in de XIVe en XVe eeuw te Gent'. Unpublished dissertation, Ghent: Ghent University.

Lentz, Matthias 2002. 'Rechtsstreit, Kommunikation und Öffentlichkeit im späten Mittelalter. Das Beispiel der Schmähbriefe und Schandbilder'. In *Propaganda, Kommunikation und Öffentlichkeit, 11.–16. Jahrhundert*, edited by Karel Hruza, 189–208. Vienna: Verlaf der Österreichischen Akademie der Wissenschaften.

Lett, Didier, and Nicolas Offenstadt, eds 2003. *Haro! Noël! Oyé! Pratique du cri au Moyen Âge*. Paris: Publications de la Sorbonne.

Leupen, Piet 1981. *Philip of Leyden, a Fourteenth Century Jurist. A Study of His Life and Treatise 'De Cura Reipublicae et Sorte Principantis'*. The Hague: Tjeenk Willink.

Lévi-Strauss, Claude 1949. *Les structures élémentaires de la parenté*. Paris: Presses Universitaires de France.

Lévy, René, and Xavier Rousseau 1992. 'États, justice pénale et histoire: bilan et perspectives'. *Droit et Société* 20/21: 249–79.

Leyte, Guillaume 1996. *Domaine et domanialité publique dans la France médiévale (XIIe–XVe siècles)*. Strasbourg: Presses Universitaires de Strasbourg.

Liddy, Christian 2011. 'Bill Casting and Political Communication: a Public Sphere in Late Medieval English Towns?' In *La gobernanza de la ciudad europea en la Edad Media*, edited by Jesus Solorzano Telechea and Beatriz Arizaga Bolumburu, 447–61. Logrono: Instituto de Estudios Riojanos.

Liddy, Christian, and Jelle Haemers 2013. 'Popular Politics in the Late Medieval Town: York and Bruges'. *English Historical Review* 128 (533): 771–805.

Limburg-Stirum, Thierry de 1878. *Coutumes des pays et comté de Flandre. Quartier de Gand. Coutumes des deux villes et pays d'Alost (Alost et Grammont)*. Brussels: Gobbaerts.

Limburg-Stirum, Thierry de 1879–89. *Codex diplomaticus Flandriae inde ab anno 1296 ad usque 1325 ou recueil de documents relatifs aux guerres et dissensions suscitées par Philippe-le-Bel, roi de France, contre Gui de Dampierre, comte de Flandre*. 2 vols. Bruges: De Zuttere.

Limburg-Stirum, Thierry de 1882–6. *Coutumes des pays et comté de Flandre. Quartier de Gand. Coutumes de la ville d'Audenaerde*. 2 vols. Brussels: Gobbaerts.

Limburg-Stirum, Thierry de 1898–1901. *Cartulaire de Louis de Male, comte de Flandre. Decreten van den grave Lodewyck van Vlaenderen, 1348 à 1358*. 2 vols. Bruges: De Plancke.

Limburg-Stirum, Thierry de 1905. *Coutumes des pays et comté de Flandre. Quartier de Gand. Coutumes de la ville et de la châtellenie de Courtrai*. Brussels: Goemaere.

Lilley, Keith 2002. *Urban Life in the Middle Ages 1000–1450*. Basingstoke: Palgrave.

Lilley, Keith 2014. 'Conceptualising the City: Historical Mapping, Spatial Theory, and the Production of Urban Spaces'. In *Cities and their Spaces: Concepts and their Use in Europe*, edited by Michel Pauly and Martin Scheutz, 114–22. Weimar: Böhlau.

Lindorfer, Bettina 2003. 'Peccatum Linguae and the Punishment of Speech Violations in the Middle Ages and Early Modern Times'. In *Speaking in the Medieval World*, edited by Jean Godsall-Myers. Leiden: Brill.

Lipsitz, George 1989. *Time Passages. Collective Memory and American Popular Culture*. Minneapolis, MN: University of Minnesota Press.

Lis, Catharina, and Hugo Soly 1994a. 'An Irresistible Phalanx. Journeymen Associations in Western Europe, 1300–1800'. In *Before the Unions. Wage Earners and Collective Action in Europe, 1300–1850*, edited by Catharina Lis, Jan Lucassen, and Hugo Soly, 11–52. Cambridge: Cambridge University Press.

Lis, Catharina, and Hugo Soly, eds 1994b. *Werken volgens de regels: ambachten in Brabant en Vlaanderen, 1500–1800*. Brussels: Vrije Universiteit Brussel Press.

Lis, Catharina, and Hugo Soly, eds 1997. *Werelden van verschil: ambachtsgilden in de Lage Landen*. Brussels: Vrije Universiteit Brussel Press.

Lis, Catharina, and Hugo Soly 2006a. 'Craft Guilds in Comparative Perspective: the Northern and Southern Netherlands. A Survey'. In Prak, Lis, Lucassen et al., eds 2006, 1–31.

Lis, Catharina, and Hugo Soly 2006b. 'Export Industries, Craft Guilds and Capitalist Trajectories, 13th to 18th Centuries'. In Prak, Lis, Lucassen et al., eds 2006, 107–32.

Lis, Catharina, and Hugo Soly 2008. 'Subcontracting in Guild-Based Exports Trades, 13th–18th Centuries'. In Epstein and Prak, eds 2008, 81–113.

Loman, Abraham. 1872. *Twaalf Geuzenliedjes*. Amsterdam: Nederlandse Muziekgeschiedenis.

Loncke, Eline 2007. 'De kronieken van Vlaanderen: uitgave en studie van het Handschrift 436 van de Stadsbibliotheek te Brugge'. Unpublished dissertation, Ghent: Ghent University.

Lucas, Stephen 1929. *The Low Countries and the Hundred Years' War, 1326–1347*. Ann Arbor, MI: University of Michigan Press.

Luebke, David 1997. *His Majesty's Rebels. Communities, Factions & Rural Revolt in the Black Forest, 1725–1745*. Ithaca, N.Y./London: Cornell University Press.

Lutz, Catherine 1987. 'Goals, Events and Understanding in Ifaluk Emotion Theory'. In *Cultural Models in Language and Thought*, edited by Dorothy Holland and Naomi Quinn, 290–312. Cambridge: Cambridge University Press.

Lutz, Catherine, and Geoffrey White 1986. 'The Anthropology of Emotions'. *Annual Review of Anthropology* 15: 405–36.

Lyna, Frederik, and Willem van Eeghem, eds 1929–30. *Jan van Stijevoorts refereinenbundel Anno MDXXIV*. 2 vols. Antwerp: De Sikkel.

Maddicot, John 1986. 'Poems of Social Protest in Early Fourteenth-Century England'. In *England in the Fourteenth Century*, edited by William Omrod, 130–44. Woodbridge: The Boydell Press.

Maertens, Alfons 1940. *Gids der Brugsche godshuizen*. Bruges: Walleyndruk.

Maes, Louis-Theo 1947. *Vijf eeuwen stedelijk strafrecht. Bijdrage tot de rechtsen cultuurgeschiedenis der Nederlanden*. Antwerp: De Sikkel.

Maire-Vigueur, Jean-Claude 1995. 'Éspace urbain et système de relations'. *Le Moyen Âge* 105: 297–309.

Maire-Vigueur, Jean-Claude 2003. *Cavaliers et citoyens. Guerre et société dans l'Italie communale, XIIe–XIIIe siècles*. Paris: École des Hautes Études en Sciences Sociales.

Mairey, Aude 2007a. *Une Angleterre entre rêve et réalité. Littérature et société dans l'Angleterre du XIVe siècle*. Paris: Éditions de la Sorbonne.

Mairey, Aude 2007b. 'Poésie et politique dans l'Angleterre de la fin du Moyen Âge: le cas du parlement'. *Revue Française d'Histoire des Idées Politiques* 26 (2): 231–50.

Mak, Jacobus 1944. *De rederijkers*. Amsterdam: P.N. van Kampen.

Mak, Jacobus, ed. 1955. *De gedichten van Anthonis De Roovere, naar alle tot dusver bekende handschriften en oude drukken*. Zwolle: Tjeenk Willink.

Marchandisse, Alain, and Bernard Schnerb 2016. 'Chansons, ballades et complaintes de guerre au XVe siècle: entre exaltation de l'esprit belliqueux et mémoire des événements'. In *Les 'paysages sonores' au Moyen-Âge et à la Renaissance*, edited by Laurent Hablot and Laurent Vissière, 113–24. Rennes: Presses Universitaires de Rennes.

Maréchal, Griet 1978. *De sociale en politieke gebondenheid van het Brugse hospitaalwezen in de middeleeuwen*. Kortrijk: UGA.

Mareel, Samuel 2008. 'Entre ciel et terre. Le théâtre socio-politique de Cornelis Everaert'. *European Medieval Drama* 12: 93–108.

Mareel, Samuel 2010a. 'Theatre and Politics in Brussels from Charles the Bold to Philip the Fair: the Leemans' Collection'. In *Books in Transition: Manuscripts and Printed Books at the Time of Philip the Fair*, edited by Hanno Wijsman, Ann Kelders, and Susie Speakman Sutch, 213–30. Turnhout: Brepols.

Mareel, Samuel 2010b. *Voor vorst en stad: rederijkersliteratuur en vorstenfeest in Vlaanderen en Brabant 1432–1561*. Amsterdam: Amsterdam University Press.

Mareel, Samuel 2011. 'You Serve Me Well. Representations of Gossip, Newsmongering and Public Opinion in the Plays of Cornelis Everaert'. In *Literary Cultures and Public Opinion in the Low Countries, 1450–1650*, edited by Jan Bloemendal and Arjan van Dixhoorn, 37–53. Leiden: Brill.

Martin, Fred 1984. 'De liedjeszanger als massamedium: straatzangers in de achttiende en negentiende eeuw'. *Tijdschrift voor Geschiedenis* 97: 422–46.

Martines, Lauro 1972. 'Political Violence in the Thirteenth Century'. In *Violence and Civil Disorder in Italian Cities, 1200–1500*, edited by Lauro Martines, 331–53. Berkeley, CA: University of California Press.

Martines, Lauro 2000. 'Poetry as Politics and Memory in Renaissance Florence and Italy'. In Ciapelli and Rubin, eds 2000, 48–63.

Martines, Lauro 2001. *Strong Words: Writing and Social Strain in the Italian Renaissance*. Baltimore, MD: John Hopkins University Press.

Martines, Lauro 2003. *April Blood. Florence and the Plot against the Medici*. Oxford: Oxford University Press.

Martines, Lauro 2005. 'The Authority of Violence: Notes on Renaissance Florence'. In Lecuppre-Desjardin and Van Bruaene, eds 2005, 31–41.

Märtins, Renate 1976. *Wertorientierungen und wirtschaftliches Erfolgsstreben mittelalterlicher Großkaufleute: das Beispiel Gent im 13. Jahrhundert*. Cologne-Vienna: Böhlau.

Maschke, Erich 1959. 'Verfassung und soziale Kräfte in der deutschen Stadt des späten Mittelalters, vornehmlich in Oberdeutschland'. *Vierteljahrschrift für Sozial- und Wirtschaftsgeschichte* 46: 289–349; 433–76.

Mayer, Thomas 1985. 'Faction and Ideology: Thomas Starkey's Dialogue'. *The Historical Journal* 28: 1–25.

McAdam, Doug, Sidney Tarrow and Charles Tilly 2003. *The Dynamics of Contention*. New York, N.Y./London: Cambridge University Press.

McRee, Benjamin 1994. 'Unity or Division? The Social Meaning of Guild Ceremony in Urban Communities'. In *Cities and Spectacle in Medieval Europe*, edited by Barbara Hanawalt and Kathryn Reyerson, 189–207. Minneapolis, MN: University of Minnesota Press.

Meder, Theo 1991. *Sprookspreker in Holland: leven en werk van Willem van Hildegaersberch (circa 1400)*. Amsterdam: Prometheus.

Meinhart, Marianne 1979. *Vocabularium iurisprudentiae romanae*. Berlin: Reimer.

Mérindol, Christian de 1990. 'Mouvements sociaux et troubles politiques à la fin du moyen âge. Essai sur la symbolique des villes'. In *Violence et contestation au Moyen Âge, actes du 114e Congrès national des sociétés savantes (Paris, 1989). Section d'histoire médiévale et de philologie*, 267–303. Paris: Comité des Travaux Historiques et Scientifiques.

Mertens, Jacques 1961. 'De verdeling van de Brugse schepenzetels op sociaal gebied (14de eeuw)'. *Wetenschappelijke Tijdingen* 21: 451–66.

Mertens, Jacques 1973. 'Twee weversopstanden te Brugge (1387–1391)'. *Handelingen van het Genootschap voor Geschiedenis* 110: 5–20.

Mertens, Jacques 1978. 'De boerenopstand onder Zannekin'. In *Nikolaas Zannekin en de Slag bij Kassel, 1328–1978. Bijdrage tot de Studie van de 14de eeuw en de Landelijke Geschiedenis van de Westhoek*, 96–103. Diksmuide: Kulturele raad Diksmuide Werkgroep Zannekin.

Mertens, Jacques 1981. 'De Brugse ambachtsbesturen (1361–1374, n.st.): een oligarchie'. In *Recht en instellingen in de oude Nederlanden tijdens de Middeleeuwen en de Nieuwe Tijd. Liber Amicorum Jan Buntinx*, edited by Gustaaf Asaert, 185–98. Louvain: Leuven Universitaire Pers.

Mertens, Jacques 1987. 'Woelingen te Brugge tussen 1359 en 1361'. In *Album Carlos Wyffels: aangeboden door zijn wetenschappelijke medewerkers*, edited by Georges Hansotte, Herman Coppejans, and Carlos Wyffels, 325–32. Brussels: Algemeen Rijksarchief.

Mertens, Jacques 1996. 'Brugge en Gent. De vertegenwoordiging van de Leden in de stadsmagistraat'. In *Qui valet ingenio. Liber Amicorum aangeboden aan dr. Johan Decavele*, edited by Joris de Zutter, Leen Charles, and André Capiteyn, 385–91. Ghent: Stichting Mens en Kultuur.

Meulemeester, Jean-Luc 1988. *Sint-Donaas en de voormalige Brugse kathedraal*. Bruges: Jong Kristen Onthaal voor Toerisme.

Middleton, Anne 1978. 'The Idea of Public Poetry in the Reign of Richard II'. *Speculum* 53: 94–114.

Milani, Giuliano 2005. *I comuni Italiani: secoli XII–XIV*. Rome: Gius. Laterza & Figli Spa.

Millet, Hélène, ed. 2003. *Suppliques et requêtes: le gouvernement par la grâce en occident, XIIe–XVe siècle*. Rome: École Française de Rome.

Molinet, Jean 1935–7. *Chroniques*, edited by Georges Doutrepont and Omer Jodogne. 3 vols. Brussels: Palais des Académies.

Mollat, Michel 1978. *Les pauvres au Moyen Âge*. Paris: Hachette.

Mollat, Michel, and Philippe Wolff 1970. *Ongles bleus, Jacques et Ciompi, les révolutions populaires en Europe aux XIVe et XVe siécles*. Paris: Calmann-Lévy.

Mollat, Michel, and Philippe Wolff 1973. *The Popular Revolutions of the Late Middle Ages*, translated by Arthur Lytton-Sells. London: Allen & Unwin.

Monier, Raymond 1928. 'Le recours au chef de sens au Moyen Âge dans les villes flamandes'. *Revue du Nord* 14: 5–19.

Monier, Raymond 1943. *Petit vocabulaire du droit romain*. Paris: Domat-Montchrestien.

Monnet, Pierre 2001. 'Ville réelle et ville idéale à la fin du Moyen Âge. Une géographie au prisme des témoignages autobiographiques allemands'. *Annales. Histoire, Sciences Sociales* 56 (3): 591–621.

Morris, William 1910. *The Revolt of Ghent*, Huddersfield: The Worker Office.

Moscovici, Serge 1981. *L'âge des foules. Un traité historique de psychologie de masses.* Paris: Fayard.

Moser, Dietz-Rüdiger 2006. 'Sozialkritische Volkslieder vom Mittelalter bis zur Gegenwart'. *Jahrbuch des Österreichischen Volkliedwerkes* 55: 12–32.

Mout, Marianne 1979. *Plakkaat van verlatinge 1581.* 's-Gravenhage: Staatsuitgeverij.

Müller, Jacob 1907. 'Cornelis Everaerts Spelen als spiegel van den maatschappelijke toestanden zijns tijds'. *Verslagen en Mededeelingen der Koninklijke Vlaamsche Academie voor Taal- en Letterkunde*, 442–8.

Munro, John 1973. *Wool, Cloth and Gold: the Struggle for Bullion in Anglo-Burgundian Trade 1340–1478.* Brussels/Toronto: Éditions de l'Université de Bruxelles.

Munro, John 1991. 'Industrial Transformation in the North-West European Textile Trades, c. 1250–c. 1340: Economic Progress and Economic Crisis?' In *Before the Black Death. Studies in the 'Crisis' of the Early Fourteenth Century*, edited by Bruce Campbell, 110–48. Manchester: Manchester University Press.

Murray, James 1994. 'The Liturgy of the Count's Advent in Bruges, from Galbert to Van Eyck'. In *Cities and Spectacle in Medieval Europe*, edited by Barbara Hanawalt, 137–52. Minneapolis, MN: University of Minnesota Press.

Murray, James 2005. *Bruges. Cradle of Capitalism.* Cambridge: Cambridge University Press.

Mus, Octaaf 1964. 'De Brugse compagnie Despars op het einde van de 15e eeuw'. *Handelingen van het Genootschap voor Geschiedenis* 101: 5–118.

Najemy, John 1979. 'Guild Republicanism in Trecento Florence. The Successes and Ultimate Failure of Corporate Politics'. *The American Historical Review* 84: 53–71.

Najemy, John 1982. *Corporatism and Consensus in Florentine Electoral Politics, 1280–1400.* Chapel Hill, NC: The University of North Carolina Press.

Najemy, John 1991. 'The Dialogue of Power in Florentine Politics'. In *City States in Classical Antiquity and Medieval Italy: Athens and Rome, Florence and Venice*, edited by Antonio Molho, 269–88. Stuttgard: Steiner.

Najemy, John 2006. 'Florentine Politics and Urban Spaces'. In *Renaissance Florence: a Social History*, edited by Roger Crum and John Paoletti, 19–54. Cambridge: Cambridge University Press.

Newton, Kenneth 2006. 'Political Support: Social Capital, Civil Society, and Political and Economical Performance'. *Political Studies* 54: 846–64.

Nicholas, David 1971. *Town and Countryside: Social, Economic, and Political Tensions in Fourteenth-Century Flanders.* Bruges: De Tempel.

Nicholas, David 1987. *The Metamorphosis of a Medieval City: Ghent in the Age of the Arteveldes, 1302–1390.* Lincoln, NE: University of Nebraska Press.

Nicholas, David 1988. *The van Arteveldes of Ghent: the Varieties of Vendetta and the Hero in History.* Ithaca, NY: Cornell University Press.

Nicholas, David 1992. *Medieval Flanders*. London: Longman.

Nicholas, Ralph 1977. 'Factions: a Comparative Analysis'. In *Friends, Followers, and Factions: a Reader in Political Clientelism*, edited by Steffen Schmidt, 55–73. Berkeley, CA: University of California Press.

Niermeyer, Jan 1935. *Onderzoekingen over Luikse en Maastrichtse oorkonden en over de Vita Baldrici Episcopi Leodiensis: een bijdrage tot de geschiedenis van burgerij en geestelijkheid in het Maasgebied tot het begin van de dertiende eeuw*. Groningen: Wolters.

Niermeyer, Jan 1976. *Mediae latinitatis lexicon minus*. Leiden: Brill.

Nora, Pierre 1984–92. *Les lieux de mémoire*. Paris: Gallimard.

Nowé, Henri 1928. *Les baillis comtaux de Flandre, des origines à la fin du XIVe siècle*. Brussels: Lamartin.

Oexle, Otto 1982a. 'Der mitteralterliche Zunft als Forschungsproblem'. *Blätter für Deutsche Landesgeschichte* 118: 1–44.

Oexle, Otto 1982b. 'Liturgische Memoria und historische Erinnerung. Zur Frage nach dem Gruppenbewusstsein und dem Wissenschaft der eigenen Geschichte in den mittelalterlichen Gilden'. In *Tradition als historische Kraft. Interdisziplinäre Forschungen zur Geschichte des früheren Mittelalters*, edited by Norbert Kamp and Joachim Wollasch, 323–40. Berlin: De Gruyter.

Oexle, Otto 1985. 'Conjuratio und Gilde im frühen Mittelalter. Ein Beitrag zum Problem der sozialgeschichtlichen Kontinuität zwischen Antike und Mittelalter'. In *Gilden und Zünfte. kaufmännische und gewerbliche Genossenschaften im frühen und hohen Mittelalter*, edited by Berent Schwineköper, 151–214. Sigmaringen: Thorbecke.

Oexle, Otto 1995 'Die Kultur der Rebellion, Schwureinigung und Verschwörung im früh- und hochmittelalterlichen Okzident'. In Fögen, ed. 1995, 119–37.

Oexle, Otto 1996a. 'Friede durch Verschwörung'. In *Träger und Instrumentarien des Friedens im hohen und späten Mittelalter*, edited by Johannes Fried, 115–50. Sigmaringen: Jan Thorbecke Verlag.

Oexle, Otto 1996b. 'Gilde und Kommune: über die Entstehung von "Einung" und "Gemeinde" als Grundformen des Zusammenlebens in Europa'. In *Theorien kommunaler Ordnung in Europa*, edited by Peter Blickle and Elisabeth Müller-Luckner, 75–97. Munich: Oldenbourg.

Offenstadt, Nicolas 2007. *Faire la paix au Moyen Âge: discours et gestes de paix pendant la Guerre de Cent Ans*. Paris: Jacob.

Olick, Jeffrey 1999. 'Collective Memory: the Two Cultures'. *Sociological Theory* 17 (3): 338–48.

Olick, Jeffrey, and Joyce Robbins 1998. 'Social Memory Studies: from "Collective Memory" to the Historical Sociology of Mnemonic Practices'. *Annual Review of Sociology* 24: 105–40.

Oliva Herrer, Hipólito Rafael 2007. 'La circulation des idées politiques parmi les élites rurales'. In *Les élites rurales dans l'Europe médiévale et moderne*, edited by François Menant and Jean-Pierre Jessenne. 179–94. Toulouse: Presses Universitaires du Midi.

Oliva Herrer, Hipólito Rafael 2012. '¡Viva el rey y la comunidad! Arqueología del discurso político de las comunidades'. In Oliva Herrer, Challet, Dumolyn et al., eds 2012, 315–56.

Oliva Herrer, Hipólito Rafael, Vincent Challet, Jan Dumolyn and María Antonia Carmona Ruiz, eds 2012. *La comunidad medieval como esfera pública*. Seville: Prensa de la Universidad de Sevilla.

Oosterman, Johan 1995–6. 'Anthonis de Roovere. Het werk: overlevering, toeschrijving en plaatsbepaling'. *Jaarboek De Fonteine* 45–6: 29–140.

Oosterman, Johan 1999. 'Oh Flanders, Weep! Anthonis de Roovere and Charles the Bold'. In *The Growth of Authority in the Medieval West*, edited by Martin Gosman, Arjo Vanderjagt, and Jan Veenstra, 257–67. Groningen: Forsten.

Oosterman, Johan 2001. 'Spelen, goede moraliteiten en eerbare esbattementen. Anthonis de Roovere en het toneel in Brugge'. In *Spel en Spektakel. Middeleeuws Toneel in de Lage Landen*, edited by Bart Ramakers and Hans van Dijk, 154–77. Amsterdam: Prometheus.

Oosterman, Johan 2002. 'De "Excellente cronike van Vlaenderen" en Anthonis de Roovere'. *Tijdschrift voor Nederlandse Taal- en Letterkunde* 118: 22–37.

Oosterman, Johan 2003. 'Brugge, bid God om vrede. Vroomheidsoffensief van vijftiende-eeuwse rederijkers'. In *Conformisten en rebellen. Rederijkerscultuur in de Nederlanden (1400–1650)*, edited by Bart Ramakers, 149–61. Amsterdam: Amsterdam University Press.

Oosterman, Johan 2005. 'O Fortuna. Tragiek, troost en vastberadenheid'. *Nederlandse Letterkunde* 10: 98–105.

Opsommer, Rik 1995. *'Omme dat leengoed es thoochste dinc van der weerelt': het leenrecht in Vlaanderen in de 14de en 15de Eeuw*. Brussels: Algemeen Rijksarchief.

Ormrod, Mark 2009. 'Murmur, Clamour and Noise: Voicing Complaint and Remedy in Petitions to the English Crown, c. 1300–c. 1460'. In *Medieval Petitions: Grace and Grievance*, edited by Mark Ormrod, Gwilym Dodd, and Anthony Musson, 135–55. York: York Medieval Press/Woodbridge: Boydell & Brewer.

Oschema, Klaus 2006. *Freundschaft und Nähe im spätmittelalterlichen Burgund. Studien zum Spannungsfeld von Emotion und Institution*. Cologne: Böhlau.

Padgett, John, and Christopher Ansell 1993. 'Robust Action and the Rise of the Medici, 1400–1434'. *American Journal of Sociology* 98: 1259–1319.

Paravicini, Werner 2006. 'Schuld und Sühne. Der Hansenmord zu Sluis in Flandern anno 1436'. In *Wirtschaft, Gesellschaft, Mentalitäten im Mittelalter. Festschrift Rolf Sprandel*, edited by Hans-Peter Baum, Rainer Leng, and Joachim Schneider, 401–51. Stuttgart: Steiner.

Paris, Gaston, ed. 1935. *Chansons du XVe siècle publiées d'après le manuscrit de la Bibliothèque nationale de Paris*. Paris: Société des Anciens Textes Français.

Paviot, Jacques 2002. *Bruges 1300–1500*. Paris: Autrement.

Paviot, Jacques 2006. 'Les flamands au Portugal au XVe siècle (Lisbonne, Madère, Açores)'. *Anais de Historia de Alem-Mar* 7: 7–40.

Perrot, Ernest 1910. *Les cas royaux. Origines et développement de la théorie aux XIIIe et XIVe siècles*. Paris: Rousseau.

Petti Balbi, Giovanna 2008. 'La mémoire dans les cités italiennes à la fin du Moyen Âge: quelques exemples'. In Crouzet-Pavan and Lecuppre-Desjardin, eds 2008, 131–47.

Petit-Dutaillis, Charles 1908. *Documents nouveaux sur les mœurs populaires et le droit de vengeance dans les Pays-Bas au XVe siècle: lettres de rémission de Philippe le Bon*. Paris: Honoré Champion.

Petit-Dutaillis, Charles 1947. *Les communes françaises. Caractères et évolutions des origines au XVIIIe siècle*. Paris: Albin Michel.

Pirenne, Henri 1900. *Le soulèvement de la Flandre maritime de 1323–1328*. Brussels: Kiessling.

Pirenne, Henri, ed. 1902. *Chronique rimée des troubles de Flandre 1379–1380*. Ghent: Siffer et Vuylsteke.

Pirenne, Henri 1910. *Les anciennes démocraties des Pays-Bas*. Paris: Flammation.

Pirenne, Henri 1933. 'Le mouvement économique et social'. In *Histoire du Moyen Âge. vol. VIII: La civilisation occidentale au moyen âge du XIe au milieu du XVe siècle*, edited by Gustave Glotz, 1–189. Paris: Presses Universitaires de France.

Pirenne, Henri 1939. *Les villes et les institutions urbaines*. 2 vols. Paris/Bruxelles: Alcan/N.S.E.

Pirenne, Henri 1963. *Early Democracies in the Low Countries: Urban Society and Political Conflict in the Middle Ages and the Renaissance*. New York, NY: Norton.

Planitz, Hans 1954. *Die deutsche Stadt im Mittelalter*. Graz/Cologne: Böhlau.

Platelle, Henri 1971. 'La violence et ses remèdes en Flandre au XIe siècle'. *Sacris Erudiri* 20: 101–73.

Pleij, Herman 1973. 'Een onbekend historielied over het Beleg van Poederooijen in 1507'. In *Weerwerk. Opstellen aangeboden aan Garmt Stuiveling*, edited by G. Huygens, 19–31. Assen: Van Gorcum.

Pleij, Herman 1983. *Het Gilde van de Blauwe Schuit. Volksfeest en burgermoraal in de Late Middeleeuwen*. Amsterdam: Meulenhoff.

Pleij, Herman 1990. 'Urban Elites in Search of a Culture: The Brussels Snow Festival of 1511'. *New Literary History* 21 (3): 629–47.

Pleij, Herman 1994. 'The Rise of Urban Literature in the Low Countries'. In *Medieval Dutch Literature in its European Context*, edited by Erik Kooper, 62–77. Cambridge: Cambridge University Press.

Pleij, Herman 2000. 'Anna Bijns als pamflettiste? Het refrein over de beide Maartens'. *Spiegel der Letteren* 42: 187–225.

Pleij, Herman 2007. *Het gevleugelde woord. Geschiedenis van de Nederlandse literatuur, 1400–1650.* Amsterdam: Bert Bakker.

Pleij, Herman 2011. *Anna Bijns, van Antwerpen.* Amsterdam: Bert Bakker.

Pocock, John 1987. 'The Concept of a Language and the Métier d'historien'. In *The Languages of Political Theory in Early-Modern Europe,* edited by Anthony Pagden, 19–38. New York, NY: Cambridge University Press.

Postless, David 2006. 'Identity and Identification: Some Recent Research into the English Medieval Forename'. In *Studies on the Personal Name in Later Medieval England and Wales,* edited by David Postless and Joel Rosenthal, 29–62. Kalamazoo, MI: Medieval Institute Publications.

Postlewate, Laurie, and Wim Hüsken, eds 2007. *Acts and Texts: Performance and Ritual in the Middle Ages and the Renaissance.* Amsterdam: Brill.

Potter, David 2007. 'Politics and Faction at the Court of Francis I: the Duchesse d'Étampes, Montmorency and the Dauphin Henri'. *French History* 21 (2): 127–46.

Prak, Maarten 1991. 'Citizen Radicalism and Democracy in the Dutch Republic: the Patriot Movement of the 1780s'. *Theory and Society* 20 (1): 73–102.

Prak, Maarten 2000. 'Politik, Kultur und politische Kultur: die Zünfte in den nördlichen Niederlanden'. In *Zunftlandschaften in Deutschland und den Niederlanden im Vergleich: Kolloquium der Historischen Kommission für Westfalen am 6. und 7. November 1997 auf Haus Welbergen,* edited by Wilfried Reininghaus, 71–83. Münster: Aschendorff.

Prak, Maarten 2006. 'Corporate Politics in the Low Countries: Guilds as Institutions, 14th to 18th Centuries'. In Prak, Lis, Lucassen et al., eds 2006, 74–106.

Prak, Maarten, Catharina Lis, Jan Lucassen, and Hugo Soly, eds 2006. *Craft Guilds in the Early Modern Low Countries: Work Power, and Representation.* Aldershot: Ashgate.

Prevenier, Walter 1961. 'Réalité et histoire. Le quatrième membre de Flandre'. *Revue du Nord* 43: 5–14.

Prevenier, Walter 1964–71. *De oorkonden der graven van Vlaanderen: 1191-aanvang 1206.* 3 vols. Brussels: Palais des Académies.

Prevenier, Walter 1975. 'Bevolkingscijfers en professionele strukturen der bevolking van Gent en Brugge in de 14de Eeuw'. In *Album aangeboden aan Charles Verlinden ter gelegenheid van zijn dertig jaar professoraat,* 270–303. Wetteren: Universa.

Prevenier, Walter 1978. 'La bourgeoisie en Flandre au XIIIe siècle'. *Revue de l'Université de Bruxelles* 4: 407–28.

Prevenier, Walter 1983. 'La démographie des villes du comté de Flandre aux XIVe et XVe siècles. État de la question. Essai d'interprétation'. *Revue du Nord* 65: 255–75.

Prevenier, Walter 1985. 'De charmes van de diplomatie: centraliserende hertogen van Bourgondië in de (machts-)balans met een autonomistisch Gents stadspatriciaat, 1379–1438'. *Naamkunde* 17: 293–300.

Prevenier, Walter 1998. 'La conservation de la mémoire par l'enregistrement dans les chancelleries princières et dans les villes des Anciens Pays-Bas du Moyen Âge'. In *Forschungen zur Reichs-, Papst- und Landesgeschichte. Peter Herde zum 65. Geburtstag von Freunden, Schülern und Kollegen dargebracht*, edited by Karl Borchard and Enno Bünz, 551–64. Stuttgart: Hiersemann.

Prevenier, Walter 2002. 'Conscience et perception de la condition sociale chez les gens du commun dans les anciens Pays-Bas des XIIIe et XIVe siècles'. In *Le petit peuple dans l'occident médiéval: terminologies, perceptions, réalités*, edited by Pierre Boglioni, Robert Delort, and Claude Gauvard, 175–89. Paris: Publications de la Sorbonne.

Prevenier, Walter 2010. 'Utilitas Communis in the Low Countries (13th–15th Centuries): from Social Mobilisation to Legitimation of Power'. In *De Bono Communi. The Discourse and Practice of the Common Good in the European City (13th–16th c.)*, edited by Élodie Lecuppre-Desjardin and Anne-Laure Van Bruaene, 205–16. Turnhout: Brepols.

Propp, Vladimir 1984. *Theory and History of Folklore*, edited by Anatoly Liberman. Manchester: Manchester University Press.

Racine, Pierre 1985. 'Associations de marchands et associations de métiers en Italie de 600 à 1200'. In *Gilden und Zünfte: kaufmännische und gewerbliche Genossenschaften im Frühen und Hohen Mittelalter*, edited by Berent Schwineköper, 127–49. Sigmaringen: Thorbecke.

Ramakers, Bart 2003. 'Ter inleiding'. In *Conformisten en rebellen. Rederijkerscultuur in de Nederlanden (1400–1650)*, edited by Bart Ramakers, 11–20. Amsterdam: Amsterdam University Press.

Ramakers, Bart 2006. 'Dutch Allegorical Theatre: Tradition and Conceptual Approach'. In *Urban Theatre in the Low Countries, 1400–1625*, edited by Elsa Strietman and Peter Happé, 127–48. Turnhout: Brepols.

Randall, Adrian 2006. *Riotous Assemblies: Popular Protest in Hanoverian England*. Oxford: Oxford University Press.

Raveschot, Patrick, and Marie Christine Laleman 1986. *Wat 'n leven binnen die muren! Gent 1100–1350: een stadsarcheologische benadering van de Gentse binnenstad*. Ghent: Dienst Monumentenzorg en Stadsarcheologie.

Reddy, William 1997. 'Against Constructionism: the Historical Ethnography of Emotions'. *Current Anthropology* 38 (3): 327–51.

Reiffenberg, Frédéric de, ed. 1835–6. *Mémoires sur le régne de Philippe le Bon, Duc de Bourgogne*. 4 vols. Brussels: Lacrosse.

Reinsma, Riemer, Jan de Smidt, and Jacobus de Schmidt 1969. *Glossarium van Nederlandse en Franse oude rechtstermen*. Amsterdam: Werkgroep Grote Raad van Mechelen.

Rexroth, Frank 2004. 'Tyrannen und Taugenichtse. Beobachtungen zur Ritualität europäischer Königsabsetzungen im späten Mittelalter'. *Historische Zeitschrift* 278 (1): 27–53.

Reynaert, Joris, ed. 1994. *Wat is wijsheid? Lekenethiek in de Middelnederlandse letterkunde*. Amsterdam: Prometheus.

Reynaert, Joris 1999. *Laet ons voort vroylijc maken zanc. Opstellen over lyriek in het Gruuthuse-handschrift*. Ghent: Rijksuniversiteit.

Reynolds, Susan 1982. 'Medieval Urban History and the History of Political Thought'. *Urban History* 9: 14–23.

Reynolds, Susan 1984. *Kingdoms and Communities in Western Europe, 900–1300*. Oxford: Clarendon press.

Reynolds, Susan 2003. 'There were States in Medieval Europe: a Response to Rees Davies'. *Journal of Historical Sociology* 16 (4): 550–5.

Richard, Olivier 2009. *Mémoires bourgeoise. Memoria et identité urbaine à Ratisbonne à la fin du Moyen Âge*. Rennes: Presses Universitaires de Rennes.

Ricour, Alain 1857–9. 'Complaintes et chansons inédites en langue flamande'. *Bulletin du Comité Flamand de France* 1: 174–92.

Rider, Jeff, ed. 1994. *Galbertus notarius Brugensis. De multro, traditione et occisione gloriosi Karoli comitis Flandriarum*. Turnhout: Brepols.

Robbins, Kevin 1995. 'The Social Mechanisms of Urban Rebellion: a Case Study of Leadership in the 1614 Revolt at La Rochelle'. *French Historical Studies* 19 (2): 559–90.

Robbins, Rossell, ed. 1959. *Historical Poems of the XIVth and XVth Centuries*. New York, NY: Columbia University Press.

Rogghé, Paul 1942. *Vlaanderen en het zevenjarig beleid van Jacob van Artevelde, 1338–1345. Een critisch-historische studie*. 2 vols. Brussels: Manteau.

Rogghé, Paul 1944. 'Het Gentsche stadsbestuur van 1302 tot 1345 en een en ander betreffende het Gentsche stadspatriciaat'. *Handelingen der Maatschappij voor Geschiedenis en Oudheidkunde te Gent* 1: 135–63.

Rogghé, Paul 1949–50. 'De samenstelling der Gentse schepenbanken in de 2de helft der 14de eeuw'. *Handelingen der Maatschappij van Geschiedenis en Oudheidkunde te Gent* 4: 22–31.

Rogghé, Paul 1952. 'Gemeente ende vrient. Nationale omwentelingen in de XIVe Eeuw'. *Annales de la Société d'Émulation de Bruges* 89: 101–35.

Rogghé, Paul 1961. 'Het eerste bewind der Gentse hoofdmannen (1319–1329)'. *Appeltjes van het Meetjesland* 12: 181–227.

Rolland, Paul 1931. *Les origines de la commune de Tournai: histoire interne de la seigneurie épiscopale tournaisienne*. Tournai: M. Lamertin.

Rollison, David 1992. *The Local Origins of Modern Society: Gloucestershire 1500–1800*. London: Taylor & Francis.

Romano, Andrea 1995. 'I ribelli nella legislazione e nella dottrina giuridica del Regnum Siciliae'. In Fögen, ed. 1995, 139–61.

Rosenwein, Barbara 1998a. 'Introduction'. In *Anger's Past. The Social Uses of an Emotion in the Middle Ages*, edited by Barbara Rosenwein, 1–6. Ithaca, NY: Cornell University Press.

Rosenwein, Barbara, 1998b 'Controlling Paradigms'. In *Anger's Past. The Social Uses of an Emotion in the Middle Ages*, edited by Barbara Rosenwein, 233–47. Ithaca, NY: Cornell University Press.

Rosenwein, Barbara, 2001. 'Writing without Fear about Early Medieval Emotions'. *Early Medieval Europe* 10 (2): 229–34.

Rosenwein, Barbara, 2002. 'Worrying about Emotions in History'. *American Historical Review* 107: 821–45.

Ross, James 1959. 'Rise and Fall of a Twelfth-century Clan: the Erembalds and the Murder of Count Charles of Flanders, 1127–1128'. *Speculum* 34: 367–90.

Ross, James, ed. 1991. *Galbert of Bruges, The Murder of Charles the Good.* Toronto: University of Toronto Press.

Rosser, Gervase 1993. 'Workers' Associations in English Medieval Towns'. In *Les métiers au Moyen Âge. Aspects économiques et sociaux*, edited by Pascale Lambrechts and Jean-Pierre Sosson, 283–305. Louvain-la-Neuve: Institut d'Études Médiévales.

Rosser, Gervase 1997. 'Craft, Guilds and the Negotation of Work in Medieval Town'. *Past & Present* 154: 3–31.

Rosser, Gervase 2006a. 'Big Brotherhood: Guilds in Urban Politics in Late Medieval England'. In *Guilds and Associations in Europe, 900–1900*, edited by Ian Gadd and Patrick Wallis, 27–42. London: Institute of Historical Research.

Rosser, Gervase 2006b. 'Roles in Life: The Drama of the Medieval Guilds'. In *REED in Review: Essays in Celebration of the First Twenty-Five Years*, edited by Audrey Douglas and Sally-Beth Maclean, 140–56. Toronto: University of Toronto.

Roth, Gunhild 1996. 'Leonard Assenheimer und Heinz Dompnig. Zwei "Historische Volkslieder" aus Breslau im Vergleich'. In *Lied im Deutschen Mittelalter: Überlieferung, Typen, Gebrauch*, edited by Cyril Edwards, Ernst Hellgardt, and Ott Norbert, 257–80. Tübingen: Niemeyer.

Rotz, Rhiman 1973. 'Urban Uprisings in Germany? Revolutionary or Reformist? The Case of Brunswick, 1374'. *Viator. Medieval and Renaissance Studies* 4: 207–23.

Rotz, Rhiman 1976. 'Investigating Urban Uprisings with Examples from Hanseatic Towns, 1374–1416'. In *Order and Innovation in the Middle Ages: Essays in Honor of Joseph R. Strayer*, edited by Joseph R. Strayer, William C. Jordan, Teofilo F. Ruiz, and Bruce McNab, 215–33. Princeton, NJ: Princeton University Press.

Rotz, Rhiman 1985. ' "Social Struggles" or the Price of Power? German Urban Uprisings in the Late Middle Ages'. *Archiv für Reformationsgeschichte* 76: 64–95.

Rouse, Richard, and Mary Rouse 1967. 'John of Salisbury and the Doctrine of Tyranni-cide'. *Speculum* 42 (4): 693–709.

Rozin, Paul, Laura Lowery, Sumio Imada, and Jonathan Haidt 1999. 'The CAD Triad Hypothesis: A Mapping between Three Moral Emotions (Contempt, Anger, Disgust) and Three Moral Codes (Community, Autonomy, Divinity)'. *Journal of Personality and Social Psychology* 76 (4): 574–86.

Rudé, George 1981. *The Crowd in History; a Study of Popular Disturbances in France and England 1730–1848*. London: Lawrence & Wishart

Rüth, Axel 2001. 'The Battle of Bouvines: Event History vs. Problem History'. *Modern Language Notes* 116 (4): 816–43.

Ryckaert, Marc 1991. *Historische Stedenatlas van België 2: Brugge*. Brussels: Gemeen-tekrediet van België.

Ryckaert, Marc, Maurice Vandermaesen, and Maurits Coornaert 1979. *De Witte Kaproe-nen: de Gentse opstand (1379–1385) en de geschiedenis van de Brugse Leie*. Ghent: Provinciebestuur Oost-Vlaanderen.

Sabbe, Jacques 1970. 'De opstand van Brugge tegen graaf Robrecht van Bethune en zijn zoon Robrecht van Kassel in 1321–1322. Het laatste politieke optreden van de volk-sleiders Pieter de Coninc en Jan Breidel'. *Annales de la Société d'Émulation de Bruges* 107: 217–49.

Sabbe, Jacques 1992. *Vlaanderen in opstand, 1323–1328: Nikolaas Zannekin, Zeger Jans-zone en Willem de Deken*. Bruges: Van de Wiele.

Sabbe, Maurits 1928. *De muziek in Vlaanderen*. Antwerp: L. Opdebeek.

Saint Genois, Jules de 1843–6. *Inventaire analytique des chartes des comtes de Flandre, avant l'avènement des princes de la Maison de Bourgogne, [...] précédé d'une notice historique sur l'ancienne trésorerie des chartes de Rupelmonde*. Ghent: Vanryckegem-Hovaere.

Saint-Denis, Alain 1994. *Apogée d'une cité: Laon et le Laonnois aux XIIe et XIIIe siècles*. Nancy: Presses Universitaires de Nancy.

Salzberg, Rosa 2010. 'In the Mouths of Charlatans: Street Performers and the Dissem-ination of Pamphlets in Renaissance Italy'. *Renaissance Studies* 24: 638–53.

Salzberg, Rosa, and Massimo Rospocher 2012. 'Street Singers in Italian Renaissance Urban Culture and Communication'. *Cultural and Social History* 9: 9–26.

Sauermann, Dietmar 1975. 'Das Historisch-Politischen Lied'. In *Handbuch des Volk-sliedes*, edited by Rolf Brednich and Lutz Röhrich, vol. 1: 293–322. Münich: Fink.

Sbriccoli, Mario 1974. *Crimen laesae maiestatis: il problema del reato politico alle soglie della scienza penalistica moderna*. 2 vols. Milano: Giuffre.

Scase, Wendy 1998. 'Strange and Wonderful Bills: Bill-Casting and Political Discourse in Late Medieval England'. In *New Medieval Literatures* 2, edited by Rita Copeland, David Lawton, and Wendy Scase, 225–47. Oxford: Clarendon Press.

Scase, Wendy 2007. *Literature and Complaint in England, 1272–1553*. Oxford: Oxford Uni-versity Press.

Scattergood, John 1971. *Politics and Poetry in the Fifteenth Century*. New York, NY: Barnes & Noble.

Scattergood, John 2000. 'Remembering Richard II: John Gower's Cronica Tripartita, Richard the Redeles, and Mum and the Sothsegger'. In *The Lost Tradition. Essays on Middle English Alliterative Poetry*, edited by John Scattergood, 200–25. Dublin: Four Courts Press.

Schilling, Heinz 1988. 'Gab es im späten Mittelalter und zu Beginn der Neuzeit in Deutschland einen städtsichen "Republikanismus"? Zur politischen Kultur des alt-europäischen Stadtbürgertums'. In *Republiken und Republikanismus im Europa des Frühen Neuzeit*, edited by Helmut Königsberger, 101–44. Munich: Oldenbourg.

Schilling, Heinz 1992. 'Civic Republicanism in Late Medieval and Early Modern Cities'. In *Religion, Political Culture, and the Emergence of Early Modern Society: Essays in German and Dutch History*, edited by Heinz Schilling, 3–60. Leiden/New York: E.J. Brill.

Schmoller, Gustav 1875. *Strassburg zur Zeit der Zünftkämpfe und die Reform seiner Verfassung und Verwaltung im 15. Jahrhundert*. Strasbourg: K.J. Trübner.

Schnerb, Bertrand 1999. *L'État bourguignon (1363–1477)*. Paris: Perrin.

Schnerb, Bertrand 2000. 'Jean de Villiers, seigneur de l'Isle-Adam'. In *Les chevaliers de la Toison d'Or au xve siècle*, edited by Raphaël De Smedt, 47–9. Frankfurt am Main: Peter Lang.

Schnerb, Bertrand 2001. 'Jean de Villiers, seigneur de l'Isle-Adam, vu par les chroniqueurs bourguignons'. In *Le héros bourguignon: histoire et épopée (41e rencontres du Centre Européen d'Études Bourguignonnes)*, edited by Jean-Marie Cauchies, 105–122. Publications du Centre Européen d'Etudes Bourguignonnes (xive–xvie siècles) 41. Turnhout: Brepols.

Schnerb, Bertrand 2005. *Jean sans peur: le prince meurtrier*. Paris: Payot.

Schofield, John, and Alan Vince 1994. *Medieval Towns*. London: Leicester University Press.

Scholliers, Etienne 1965. 'Lonen te Brugge en in het Brugse Vrije (xve–xviie eeuw)'. In *Dokumenten voor de geschiedenis van prijzen en lonen in Vlaanderen en Brabant*, edited by Charles Verlinden and Jan Craeybeckx, vol. 2, 87–160. Bruges: De Tempel.

Schott, Clausdieter, and Ruth Schmidt-Wiegand, eds 1984. *Der Sachsenspiegel / Eike von Repgow*. Zurich: Manesse.

Schouteet, Albert 1962. 'Jurisdictie over ambachtslieden te Brugge in de 16de eeuw'. *Bulletin de la Commission Royale pour la Publication des Anciennes Lois et Ordonnances de la Belgique* 20 (2): 403–50.

Schrage, Eltjo 1987. *Das römische Recht im Mittelalter*. Darmstadt: Wissenschaftliche Buchgesellschaft.

Schubert, Ernst 1975. ' "Bauerngeschrey": zum Problem der öffentlichen Meinung im spätmittelalterlichen Franken'. *Jahrbuch für Fränkische Landesforschung* 34 (5): 883–907.

Schudson, Michael 1995. 'Dynamics of Distortion in Collective Memory'. In *Memory Distortion. How Minds, Brains, and Societies Reconstruct the Past*, edited by Daniel Schacter, 346–64. Cambridge, MA: Harvard University Press.

Schulte, Aloys 1904. *Die Fugger in Rom, 1495–1523: mit Studien zur Geschichte des kirlichen Finanswesens jener Zeit*. 2 vols. Leipzig: Duncker & Humblot.

Schulz, Knut 1992. *'Denn sie lieben die Freiheit so sehr ...': kommunale Aufstände und Entstehung des europäischen Bürgertums im Hochmittelalter*. Darmstadt: Wissenschaftliche Buchgesellschaft.

Schulz, Knut 1994. 'Die Politische Zunft. Eine die spätmittelalterliche Stadt prägende Institution?' In *Verwaltung und Politik in Städten Mitteleuropas. Beitrage zu Verfassungsnorm und Verfassungswirklichkeit in altständischer Zeit*, edited by Wilfried Ehbrecht, 1–20. Cologne: Böhlau.

Schwerhoff, Gerd 1998. 'Zivilisationsprozeß und Geschichtswissenschaft'. *Historische Zeitschrift* 266 (1): 561–605.

Scordia, Lydwine 2005. *Le roi doit vivre du sien: la théorie de l'impôt en France (XIII–XVe siècles)*. Paris: Institut d'Études Augustiniennes.

Scott, James 1990. *Domination and the Arts of Resistance: Hidden Transcripts*. London: Yale University Press.

Scott, James 2009. 'Preface'. In *Political Space in Pre-Industrial Europe*, edited by Beat Kümin, 1–4. Aldershot: Ashgate.

Scott, John 2000. *Social Network Analysis*. London: Sage Publications.

Serrarens, Eduard 1928. 'Kommunisme in de Middelnederlandse Letterkunde'. *Tijdschrift voor Taal en Letterkunde* 16: 1–32; 77–127.

Serrure, Constant-Philippe 1855. 'Kleine gedichten uit de dertiende en veertiende eeuw'. In *Vaderlandsch museum voor nederduitsche letterkunde, oudheid en geschiedenis* 1: 296–401. Ghent: Annoot-Braeckman.

Shagan, Ethan 2001. 'Rumours and Popular Politics in the Reign of Henry VIII'. In *The Politics of the Excluded, c. 1500–1850*, edited by Tim Harris, 30–66. London: Macmillan Education UK.

Shephard, Robert 1992. 'Court Factions in Early Modern England'. *Journal of Modern History* 64 (4): 721–45.

Sieg'l, Christian 1993. *Arbeitskämpfe seit dem Spätmittelalter*. Cologne: Böhlau.

Simon-Muscheid, Katherina 1992. 'Konfliktkonstellationen im Handwerk des 14. bis 16. Jahrhunderts'. *Aevum Quotidianum* 27: 87–108.

Skocpol, Theda 1979. *States and Social Revolutions: a Comparative Analysis of France, Russia, and China*. Cambridge: Cambridge University Press.

Small, Greame 2005. 'When "Indiciaires" meet "Rederijkers": a Contribution to the History of the Burgundian "Theatre State"'. In *Stad van koopmanschap en vrede. Literatuur in Brugge tussen Middeleeuwen en Rederijkerstijd*, edited by Johan Oosterman, 133–61. Louvain: Peeters.

Snellaert, Ferdinand, ed. 1869. *Nederlandsche gedichten uit de veertiende eeuw van Jan Boendale, Hein van Aken en anderen.* Brussels: Hayez.

Soens, Ernest 1900–2. 'Onuitgegeven gedichten van Anna Bijns'. *Leuvense Bijdragen* 4 (3): 199–368.

Soly, Hugo 1983. 'Kroeglopen in Brabant en Vlaanderen, 16de–18de eeuw'. *Spiegel Historiael* 18: 569–77.

Soly, Hugo 1984. 'Plechtige Intochten in de steden van de Zuidelijke Nederlanden tijdens de overgang van de Middeleeuwen naar Nieuwe Tijd: communicatie, propaganda, spektakel'. *Tijdschrift voor Geschiedenis* 97: 341–61.

Soly, Hugo 2008. 'The Political Economy of European Craft Guilds. Power Relations and Economic Strategies of Merchants and Master Artisans in the Medieval and Early Modern Textile Industries'. *International Review of Social History* 53: 45–71.

Sommers, Shula 1988. 'Understanding Emotions: Some Interdisciplinary Considerations'. In Stearns and Stearns, eds 1988, 23–38.

Sosson, Jean-Pierre 1966. 'La structure sociale de la corporation médiévale. L'example des tonneliers de Bruges de 1350 à 1500'. *Belgisch Tijdschrift voor Filologie en Geschiedenis* 44: 457–78.

Sosson, Jean-Pierre 1977. *Les travaux publics de la ville de Bruges (XIVe–XVe siècles). Les travaux. Les hommes.* Brussels: Crédit communal de Belgique.

Sosson, Jean-Pierre 1984. 'Die Körperschaften in den Niederlanden und Nordfrankreich: neue Forschungsperspectiven'. In *Gilden und Korporationen in den Nordeuropäischen Städten des späten Mittelalters*, edited by Klaus Friedland, 79–90. Cologne: Böhlau.

Sosson, Jean-Pierre 1986. 'Structures associatives et réalités socio-économiques dans l'artisanat d'art et du bâtiment aux Pays-Bas (XIVe–XVe siècles). Perspectives de recherches'. In *Artistes, artisans et production artistique au Moyen Âge. Colloque international du Centre National de la Recherche Sientifique, Université de Rennes II – Haute-Bretagne, 2–6 mai 1983*, edited by Xavier Barral i Altet, vol. 1, 111–21. Paris: Picard.

Sosson, Jean-Pierre 1990. 'Les métiers: norme et réalité. L'exemple des anciens Pays-Bas Méridionaux aux XIVe et XVe siècles'. In *Le travail au Moyen Âge: une approche interdisciplinaire*, edited by Jacqueline Hamesse and Colette Muraille-Samaran, 339–48. Louvain-la-Neuve: Institut d'Études Médiévales.

Spufford, Peter 1970. *Monetary Problems and Policies in the Burgundian Netherlands 1433–1496.* Leiden: Brill.

Staab, Franz 1975. *Untersuchungen zur Gesellschaft am Mittelrhein in der Karolingerzeit.* Wiesbaden: Steiner.

Stabel, Peter 1990. 'De Bourgondische periode. Lokale instellingen'. In *750 Jaar Eeklo*, 35–51. Eeklo: Taptoe.

Stabel, Peter 1992. 'Van schepenen en ontvangers: politieke elite en stadsfinanciën in Axel en Hulst'. *Tijdschrift voor Sociale Geschiedenis* 18: 1–21.

Stabel, Peter 1993. 'L'encadrement corporatif et la conjoncture économique dans les petites villes de la Flandre orientale: contrainte et possibilités'. In *Les métiers au Moyen Âge. Aspects économiques et sociaux*, edited by Pascale Lambrechts and Jean-Pierre Sosson, 335–48. Louvain-la-Neuve: Institut d'Études Médiévales.

Stabel, Peter 1995. *De kleine stad in Vlaanderen: bevolkingsdynamiek en economische functies van de kleine en secundaire stedelijke centra in het Gentse kwartier (14de–16de Eeuw)*. Brussels: Paleis der Academiën.

Stabel, Peter 1996. 'Entre commerce international et économie locale. Le monde financier de Wouter Ameyde (Bruges fin xve-début xvie siècle)'. In *Finances publiques et finances privés au bas Moyen Âge*, edited by Marc Boone and Walter Prevenier, 75–99. Louvain: Garant.

Stabel, Peter 1997. *Dwarfs among Giants. The Flemish Urban Network in the Late Middle Ages*. Louvain: Garant.

Stabel, Peter 2000 'Marketing Cloth in the Low Countries: Manufacturers, Brokers and Merchants (14th–16th Centuries)'. In *International Trade in the Low Countries (14th–16th Centuries): Merchants, Organisation, Infrastructure*, edited by Peter Stabel, Bruno Blondé, and Anke Greve. 15–36. Louvain: Garant.

Stabel, Peter 2001. 'Markets and Retail in the Cities of the Late Medieval Low Countries. Economic Networks and Socio-cultural Display'. In *Fiere e mercati nella integrazione delle economie europee, secc. XIII–XVII*, edited by Simonetta Cavaciocchi, 797–817. Florence: Le Monnier.

Stabel, Peter 2002. 'Urbanization and its Consequences: Spatial Developments in Late Medieval Flanders'. In *Raumerfassung und Raumbewusstsein im Späteren Mittelalter*, edited by Peter Moraw, 179–202. Stuttgart: Thorbecke.

Stabel, Peter 2004. 'Guilds in Late Medieval Flanders: Myths and Realities of Guild Life in an Export-Oriented Environment'. *Journal of Medieval History* 30 (2): 187–212.

Stabel, Peter 2008a. 'Composition et recomposition des réseaux urbains des Pays-Bas au bas Moyen Âge'. In Crouzet-Pavan and Lecuppre-Desjardin, eds 2008, 29–64.

Stabel, Peter 2008b. 'From the Market to the Shop. Retail and Urban Space in Late Medieval Bruges'. In *Buyers & Sellers: Retail Circuits and Practices in Mediaeval and Early Modern Europe*, edited by Peter Stabel, Jon Stobart, Ilja Van Damme, and Bruno Blondé, 79–108. Turnhout: Brepols.

Stabel, Peter 2008c. 'Public or Private, Collective or Individual? The Space of Late Medieval Trade in the Low Countries'. In *Il mercante patrizio: palazzi e botteghe nell'Europa del Rinascimento*, edited by Donatelle Calabi and Silvia Beltramo, 37–54. Milan: Mondadori.

Stabel, Peter 2011. 'Militaire organisatie, bewapening en wapenbezit in het laatmiddeleeuwse Brugge'. *Revue Belge de Philologie et Histoire* 89: 1049–73.

Stabel, Peter, and Jelle Haemers 2006. 'From Bruges to Antwerp. International Commercial Firms and Governement's Credit in the Late 15th and Early 16th Century'. In

Banca, crédito y capital. La monarquía Hispánica y los antiguos Países Bajos, 1505–1700, edited by Carmen Sanz Ayán and Bernardo García García, 21–37. Madrid: Fundación Carlos de Amberes.

Stallaert, Karel 1978. *Glossarium van verouderde rechtstermen, kunstwoorden en andere uitdrukkingen uit Vlaamsche, Brabantsche en Limburgsche oorkonden.* 2 vols. Handzame: Familia et Patria.

Stalpaert, Hervé 1959. *Oudvlaamse volksliederen op vliegende bladen: historie en folklore.* Kortrijk: UGA.

Stearns, Carol, and Peter Stearns, eds 1988. *Emotion and Social Change. Toward a New Psychohistory.* London/New York: Holmes & Meier.

Stein, Henri 1899. 'Les conséquences de la bataille de Cassel pour la ville de Bruges et la mort de Guillaume de Deken, son ancien bourgmestre'. *Bulletin de La Commission Royale d'Histoire* 68: 647–64.

Stein, Robert, Anita Boele and Willem Blockmans 2010. 'Whose Community? The Origin and Development of the Concept of Bonum Commune in Flanders, Brabant and Holland (twelfth–fifteenth century)'. In *De Bono Communi. The Discourse and Practice of the Common Good in the European City (13th–16th c.)*, edited by Élodie Lecuppre-Desjardin and Anne-Laure Van Bruaene, 149–69. Turnhout: Brepols.

Steiner, Emily 2003. 'Commonalty and Literary Form in the 1370s and 80s'. In *New Medieval Literatures* 6, edited by David Lawton, Wendy Scase, and Rita Copeland, 199–221. Oxford: Oxford University Press.

Stella, Alessandro 1993. *La révolte des Ciompi: les hommes, les lieux, le travail.* Paris: École des Hautes Études en Sciences Sociales.

Stiennon, Jacques 1951. *Étude sur la chartrier et le domaine de l'abbaye de Saint-Jacques de Liège (1015–1209).* Paris: Les Belles Lettres.

Stock, Brian 1990. *Listening for the Text. On the Uses of the Past.* Philadelphia, PA: University of Pennsylvania.

Stockton, Eric, ed. 1962. *The Major Latin Works of John Gower: The Voice of One Crying, and the Tripartite Chronicle*, translated by Eric Stockton. Seattle, WA: University of Washington Press.

Stone, Clarence 1995. 'Political Leadership in Urban Politics'. In *Theories of Urban Politics*, edited by David Judge, Gerry Stoker, and Harold Wolman, 96–117. London/Thousand Oaks, CA: Sage Publications.

Stone, Lawrence 1979. 'The Revival of the Narrative: Reflections on a New Old History'. *Past & Present* 85: 3–24.

Stoop, Patricia 2001. '"Dboec vanden Tien Gheboden" van Jan van Leeuwen. Een kritische tekstuitgave'. *Ons Geestelijk Erf* 75 (2): 182–235.

Strassner, Erich 1970. 'Politische Relevanz "Historischer Volkslieder"'. In *Formen Mittelalterlicher Literatur*, edited by Otmar Werner and Bemd Nauman, 229–46. Göpingen: Verlag Alfred Kümmerle.

Strietman, Elsa 1991. 'The Low Countries'. In *The Theatre of Medieval Europe: New Research in Early Drama*, edited by Eckhard Simon, 225–52. Cambridge: Cambridge University Press.

Strietman, Elsa 1997. 'The Rhetoricians and the Reformation'. *European Medieval Drama* 1: 119–31.

Strietman, Elsa 1998. 'Pawns or Prime Movers? The Rhetoricians in the Struggle for Power in the Low Countries'. *European Medieval Drama* 2: 111–21.

Strietman, Elsa 1999. 'A Tale of Two Cities: Drama and the Community in the Low Countries'. In *Drama and Community: People and Plays in Medieval Europe*, edited by Alan Hindley, 126–47. Turnhout: Brepols.

Strohm, Paul 1992. *Hochon's Arrow: the Social Imagination of Fourteenth-Century Texts*. Princeton, NJ: Princeton University Press.

Strohm, Paul 2005. *Politique. Languages of Statecraft between Chaucer and Shakespeare*. Notre Dame: Notre Dame University Press.

Strohm, Reinhard 1985. *Music in Late Medieval Bruges*. Oxford: Clarendon Press.

Strubbe, Egied 1950. 'Het "motyf nopende der costumen ende husagen van den sterfhuze van Ghend" door Martin van den Bundere'. *Handelingen van de Koninklijke Commissie voor de Uitgave van Oude Wetten en Verordeningen van België* 17: 1–32.

Strubbe, Egied 1963. 'Van de eerste naar de tweede omwalling van Brugge'. *Handelingen van het Genootschap voor Geschiedenis* 100 (1–3): 271–300.

Strubbe, Egied 1984. 'La paix de Dieu dans le Nord de la France'. *Recueils de la Société Jean Bodin* 14: 489–501.

Struve, Tilman 1984. 'The Importance of the Organism in the Political Theory of John of Salisbury'. In *The World of John of Salisbury*, edited by Michael Wilks. Oxford: Blackwell.

Studt, Birgit, ed. 2007. *Haus- und Familienbücher in der städtischen Gesellschaft des Spätmittelalters und der Frühen Neuzeit*. Cologne: Böhlau.

Sutch, Susie 2003. 'Jan Pertcheval and the Brussels Leliebroeders (1490–1500): the Model of a Conformist Rhetorician's Chamber?' In *Conformisten en Rebellen. Rederijkerscultuur in de Nederlanden (1400–1650)*, edited by Bart Ramakers, 95–106. Amsterdam: Amsterdam University Press.

Symes, Carol 2007. *A Common Stage: Theater and Public Life in Medieval Arras*. London: Cornell University Press.

Szreter, Simon 2002. 'The State of Social Capital: bringing back in Power, Politics, and History'. *Theory and Society* 31 (5): 573–621.

Te Brake, Wayne 2003. 'Charles v and his Contentious Subjects'. In *Charles v in Context: the Making of a European Identity*, edited by Marc Boone and Marysa Demoor, 125–46. Ghent: Ghent University, Faculty of Arts and Philosophy.

TeBrake, William 1993. *A Plague of Insurrection: Popular Politics and Peasant Revolt in Flanders, 1323–1328*. Philadelphia, PA: University of Pennsylvania Press.

Ter Braake, Serge 2007. *Met recht en rekenschap. De ambtenaren bij het Hof van Holland en de Haagse Rekenkamer in de Habsburgse Tijd (1483–1558)*. Hilversum: Verloren.

Te Winkel, Jan 1877. *Maerlants werken beschouwd als spiegel van de dertiende eeuw.* Leiden: Brill.

Te Winkel, Jan 1884. *Het middeleeuwsch lierdicht.* Bruges: Barbiaux.

Te Winkel, Jan 1887. *Geschiedenis der Nederlandsche letterkunde.* Haarlem: De Erven Bohn.

Te Winkel, Jan 1922–7. *De ontwikkelingsgang der Nederlandsche letterkunde.* 7 vols. Haarlem: Bohn.

Thielemans, Marie-Rose 1966. *Bourgogne et Angleterre. Relations politiques et économiques entre les Pays-Bas Bourguignons et l'Angleterre (1435–1467)*. Brussels: Presses Universitaires de Bruxelles.

Thiry, Claude 1972. 'Les poèmes de langue française relatifs aux sacs de Dinant et de Liège'. In *Liège et Bourgogne. Actes du colloque tenu à Liège les 28, 29 et 30 octobre 1968*, 101–27. Paris: Les Belles Lettres.

Thoen, Erik 1988. 'Rechten en plichten van plattelanders als instrumenten van machtspolitieke strijd tussen adel, stedelijke burgerij en grafelijk gezag in het laat-middeleeuwse Vlaanderen'. In *Les structures du pouvoir dans les communautés rurales en Belgique et dans les pays limitrophes (XIIe–XIXe siècle)*, 469–90. Brussels: Crédit communal de Belgique.

Thoen, Erik 2001. 'A "Commercial Survival Economy" in Evolution. The Flemish Countryside and the Transition to Capitalism (Middle Ages–19th Century)'. In *Peasants into Farmers? The Transformation of Rural Economy and Society in the Low Countries (Middle Ages–19th Century) in Light of the Brenner Debate*, edited by Peter Hoppenbrouwers and Jan Luiten van Zanden, 102–57. Turnhout: Brepols.

Thoen, Erik, and Adriaan Verhulst 1986. 'Le réseau urbain et les campagnes dans l'ancien comté de Flandre (ca. 1350–1800)'. *Storia della città: rivista internazionale di storia urbana e territoriale* 36: 53–66.

Thompson, E.P. 1993. *Customs in Common.* London: Penguin.

Tilly, Charles 1969. 'Collective Violence in European Perspective'. In *Violence in America: Historical and Comparative Perspectives*, edited by Hugh Davis Graham and Tedd Gurr, 2 vols., vol. 1., 5–34. Washington, D.C.: U.S. Government Printing Office Government Printing Office.

Tilly, Charles 1978. *From Mobilization to Revolution.* Reading, MA: Addison-Wesley Pub. Co.

Tilly, Charles 1985. 'Warmaking and Statemaking as Organized Crime'. In *Bringing the State Back In*, edited by Dietrich Rueschemeyer, Theda Skocpol, and Peter Evans, 169–91. Cambridge: Cambridge University Press.

Tilly, Charles 1986. *The Contentious French.* Cambridge, MA: Belknap Press.

Tilly, Charles 1989. 'History, Sociology and Dutch Collective Action'. *Tijdschrift voor Sociale Geschiedenis* 5: 142–57.

Tilly, Charles 1990. *Coercion, Capital, and European States, AD 990–1990*. Cambridge: B. Blackwell.

Tilly, Charles 2003. *The Politics of Collective Violence*. Cambridge: Cambridge University Press.

Tilly, Charles 2005. *Trust and Rule*. Cambridge: Cambridge University Press.

Tilly, Charles 2008. *Contentious Performances*. Cambridge: Cambridge University Press.

Tilly, Charles, and Willem Blockmans, eds 1994. *Cities and the Rise of States in Europe, A.D. 1000 to 1800*. Boulder, CO: Westview Press.

Tollebeek, Johan 1998. 'Historical Representation and the Nation-State in Romantic Belgium (1830–1850)'. *Journal of the History of Ideas* 59 (2): 329–53.

Tollebeek, Johan, Geert Buelens, Gita Deneckere, Chantal Kesteloot, and Sophie de Schaepdrijver, eds 2008. *België, een parcours van herinnering*. 2 vols. Amsterdam: Bert Bakker.

Touati, François-Olivier 1990. 'Révolte et Société: l'exemple du Moyen Âge'. In *Violence et contestation au Moyen Âge. Actes du 114e Congrès national des sociétés savantes (Paris, 1989)*, 7–17. Paris: Éditions du Comité des Travaux Historiques et Scientifiques.

Trexler, Richard 1980. *Public Life in Renaissance Florence*. New York, NY: Academic Press.

Trexler, Richard 1984a. 'Correre la terra. Collective Insults in the Late Middle Ages'. *Mélanges de l'École française de Rome. Moyen Âge, Temps Modernes* 96: 872–91.

Trexler, Richard 1984b. 'Follow the Flag: The Ciompi Revolt seen from the Streets'. *Bibliothèque d'Humanisme et Renaissance* 46: 357–92.

Trio, Paul 1990. *De Gentse broederschappen (1182–1580): ontstaan, naamgeving, materiële uitrusting, structuur, opheffing en bronnen*. Ghent: Maatschappij voor Geschiedenis en Oudheidkunde te Gent.

Trio, Paul 1997. 'Bestuursinstellingen van de stad Ieper'. In *De gewestelijke en lokale overheidsinstellingen in Vlaanderen tot 1795*, edited by Walter Prevenier and Beatrijs Augustyn, 333–60. Brussels: Algemeen Rijksarchief.

Trio, Paul 2008. 'The Chronicle Attributed to "Olivier van Diksmuide": a Misunderstood Town Chronicle of Ypres from Late Medieval Flanders'. In *The Medieval Chronicle V*, edited by Erik Simon Kooper, 211–25. Leiden: Brill.

Trio, Paul 2009. 'The Social Positioning of Late Medieval Confraternities in Urbanized Flanders'. In *Medieval Confraternities in European Towns*, edited by Monika Escher-Apsner, 99–110. Frankfurt am Main: Peter Lang.

Tuan, Yi-Fu 1977. *Space and Place: The Perspective of Experience*. London: Arnold.

Vaes, Maurice 1919. 'Les fondations hospitalières flamandes à Rome du XVe au XVIIIe siècle'. *Bulletin de l'Institut historique belge de Rome* 1: 161–371.

Valente, Claire 2003. *The Theory and Practice of Revolt in Medieval England*. Aldershot: Ashgate.

Van Anrooij, Wim 1985. 'Dichter, kroniekschrijver en wapenkundige. Heraut Gelre en zijn werk'. *Literatuur* 2: 244–51.

Van Anrooij, Wim 1994. 'Recht en rechtvaardigheid binnen de Antwerpse School'. In Reynaert, ed. 1994, 149–63.

Van Anrooij, Wim 2002a. 'Het korte lied over de moord op graaf Floris v. Een nieuwe versie in het handschrift-Jochems'. *Spiegel der Letteren* 44: 299–321.

Van Anrooij, Wim 2002b. '"Poenten" in de Middelnederlandse letterkunde. Een geledingssysteem in het zakelijke en discursieve vertoog'. In *Al t'Antwerpen in die stad: Jan van Boendale en de literaire cultuur van zijn tijd*, edited by Wim van Anrooij, 65–80. Amsterdam: Prometheus.

Van Bavel, Bas 2010a. *Manors and Markets: Economy and Society in the Low Countries, 500–1600*. Oxford: Oxford University Press.

Van Bavel, Bas 2010b. 'Rural Revolts and Structural Change in the Low Countries, Thirteenth–Early Fourteenth Centuries'. *In Survival and Discord in Medieval Society: Essays in Honour of Christopher Dyer*, edited by Richard Goddard, John Langdon, and Miriam Müller, 249–68. Turnhout: Brepols.

Van Bork, Gé, Dirk Delabastita, Hendrik Van Gorp et al., eds 2012a. 'Geuzenlied'. In *Algemeen Letterkundig Lexicon*. Leiden: Stichting Digitale Bibliotheek voor de Nederlandse Letteren.

Van Bork, Gé, Dirk Delabastita, Hendrik Van Gorp et al., eds 2012b. 'Historielied'. In *Algemeen Letterkundig Lexicon*. Leiden: Stichting Digitale Bibliotheek voor de Nederlandse Letteren.

Van Bruaene, Anne-Laure 1998. *De Gentse memorieboeken als spiegel van stedelijk historisch bewustzijn, 14de tot 16de eeuw*. Ghent: Maatschappij voor Geschiedenis en Oudheidkunde te Gent.

Van Bruaene, Anne-Laure 2002. 'Harmonie et honneur en jeu: les compétitions dramatiques et symboliques entre les villes flamandes et brabançonnes aux quinzième et seizième siècles'. In *Le verbe, l'image et les représentations de la société urbaine au Moyen Âge*, edited by Marc Boone, Élodie Lecuppre-Desjardin, and Jean-Pierre Sosson, 227–38. Louvain: Garant.

Van Bruaene, Anne-Laure 2006. '"A Wonderfull Tryumfe, for the Wynnyng of a Pryse". Guilds, Ritual, Theater, and the Urban Network in the Southern Low Countries, ca. 1450–1650'. *Renaissance Quarterly* 59 (2): 374–405.

Van Bruaene, Anne-Laure 2008. *Om beters wille. Rederijkerskamers en de stedelijke cultuur in de Zuidelijke Nederlanden (1400–1650)*. Amsterdam: Amsterdam University Press.

Van Bruaene, Anne-Laure 2010. 'Princes, Emperors, Kings and Investiture in the Festive Culture of Flanders (Fifteenth–Sixteenth Century)'. In *Les 'autres' rois. Études sur la royauté comme notion hiérarchique dans la société au bas Moyen Âge et au début de l'époque moderne*, edited by Torsten Hiltmann, 131–44. Munich: De Gruyter.

Van Buuren, Alphonsus, ed. 1998. *Den Duytschen Catoen*. Hilversum: Verloren.

Van Caenegem, Raoul 1953. 'Nota over de terechtstelling van Willem de Deken te Parijs in 1328'. *Handelingen van Het Genootschap voor Geschiedenis te Brugge* 90: 140–2.

Van Caenegem, Raoul 1954. *Geschiedenis van het strafrecht in Vlaanderen van de XIe tot de XIVe eeuw*. Brussels: Koninklijke Vlaamse Academie voor Wetenschappen.

Van Caenegem, Raoul 1956. *Geschiedenis van het strafprocesrecht in Vlaanderen van de XIe tot de XIVe eeuw*. Brussels: Koninklijke Vlaamse Academie voor Wetenschappen.

Van Caenegem, Raoul 1968. 'Coutumes et législation en Flandre aux XIe et XIIe siècles'. In *Les libertés urbaines et rurales du XIe au XIVe siècles*, 245–79. Brussels: Crédit Communal de Belgique.

Van Caenegem, Raoul 1971. 'Considérations critiques sur l'ordonnance comtale flamande connue sous le nom d'Ordonnance sur les baillis'. In *Actes du congrès international de la Société italienne de l'histoire du droit*, 133–52. Ghent: Rijksuniversiteit.

Van Caenegem, Raoul 1978. 'Galbert van Brugge en het recht', *Mededelingen van de Koninklijke Academie voor Wetenschappen, Letteren en Schone Kunsten van België* 40 (1): 3–35.

Van Caenegem, Raoul 1982. 'De keure van Sint-Omaars van 1127'. *The Legal History Review* 50 (3): 253–62.

Van Caenegem, Raoul 1990. 'Galbert of Bruges on Serfdom, Prosecution of Crime and Constitutionalism (1127–28)'. In *Law, Custom, and the Social Fabric in Medieval Europe: Essays in Honor of Bryce Lyon*, edited by Bernard Bachrach and David Nicholas, 89–112. Kalamazoo, MI: Medieval Institute Publications.

Van Caenegem, Raoul 1991. *Legal History: A European Perspective*. London: Hambledon Press.

Van Caenegem, Raoul 1994a. 'Considerations on the Customary Law of Twelfth-Century Flanders'. In *Law, History, the Low Countries and Europe*, edited by Ludo Milis, 97–106. London: Hambledon Press.

Van Caenegem, Raoul 1994b. 'The Ghent Revolt of 1128'. In *Law, History, the Low Countries and Europe*, edited by Ludo Milis, 107–12. London: Hambledon Press.

Van Caenegem, Raoul 2000. 'L'état de droit dans la Flandre médiévale'. In *Excerptiones iuris. Studies in honor of André Gouron*, edited by Bernard Durand and Laurent Mayali, 759–72. Berkeley, CA: Robbins Collection.

Van Caenegem, Raoul, ed. 2002. *1302. Le désastre de Courtrai. Mythes et réalités de la Bataille des éperons d'or*. Antwerp: Mercatorfonds.

Van Caenegem, Raoul 2009. 'De keure van Sint-Omaars van 1127: een politiek document'. *Bulletin de la Commission Royale d'Histoire* 175 (1): 185–202.

Vandecandelaere, Hans 2008. 'Een opstand in de zeven "actes", 1303–1306'. *Cahiers Bruxellois* 40: 3–67.

Vandenbroeck, Paul 1990. 'Stadscultuur in de Nederlanden, ca. 1400–ca. 1600. Ideologische zwaartepunten, evenwichtsmechanismen, dubbelbinding'. *Driemaandelijks Tijdschrift van het Gemeentekrediet* 44: 17–41.

Van de Graft, Cornelia, ed. 1904. *Middelnederlandsche historieliederen.* Epe: Hooiberg.

Van de Graft, Cornelia, ed. 1968. *Middelnederlandsche historieliederen.* Arnhem: Gysbers & Van Loon.

Van den Auweele, Dirk 1973. 'De Brugse gijzelaarslijsten van 1301, 1305 en 1328, een comparatieve analyse'. *Handelingen van het Genootschap voor Geschiedenis* 110: 105–67.

Van den Auweele, Dirk 1974. 'Schepenbank en schepenen te Brugge (1127–1384). Bijdrage tot de studie van een gewone stedelijke rechts- en bestuursinstelling'. Unpublished dissertation, Louvain: Catholic University of Louvain.

Van den Auweele, Dirk, and Michel Oosterbosch 1995. 'Vergeten handschriften. Het cartularium van het Hendrik Kempegasthuis in Diest (1313–1676)'. In *Serta devota in memoriam Guillelmi Lourdaux*, edited by Werner Verbeke, vol. 2, 255–84. Louvain: Leuven University Press.

van den Berg, Arie 2004. 'Lopend nieuws. De marktzangers als wandelend journaal'. *Literatuur* 20: 43–9.

Vandenpeereboom, Alphonse, ed. 1878–83. *Ypriana: notices, études, notes et documents sur Ypres.* 7 vols. Bruges: De Zuttere.

Van der Bom, Jacques 1985. 'Maarten van Rossum en de publiciteit'. *Literatuur* 2: 11–17.

van der Hallen, Erik 1977. 'Het Gentse meerseniersambacht (1305–1540)'. *Handelingen van de Maatschappij voor Geschiedenis en Oudheidkunde te Gent* 31: 77–149.

Vanderjagt, Arie 1981. *Qui sa vertu anoblist. The Concepts of Noblesse and Chose Publique in Burgundian Political Thought.* Meppel: Krips Repro.

Vanderkindere, Léon 1909a. 'La première phase de l'évolution constitutionnelle des communes flamandes' *Choix d'études historiques*, 251–304. Brussels: G. Des Marez.

Vanderkindere, Léon 1909b. 'La politique communale de Philippe d'Alsace et ses conséquences'. *Choix d'études historiques*, 305–41. Brussels: G. Des Marez.

Vandermassen, Maurice 1993. 'Brugse en Ieperse gijzelaars voor koning en graaf, 1329–1329. Een administratief dossier'. *Handelingen van het Genootschap voor Geschiedenis* 130: 119–44.

Van der Meersch, Polydore-Charles 1852–61. *Memorieboek der stad Ghendt van 't jaer 1301 tot 1737.* 4 vols. Ghent: Annoot-Braeckman.

Van der Poel, Dieuwke, and Louis Grijp, eds 2004. *Het Antwerps liedboek.* 2 vols. Tielt: Lannoo.

Vanderputten, Steven 2004. '"Literate Memory" and Social Reassessment in Tenth-Century Monasticism'. *Mediaevistik* 17: 65–94.

Van der Wee, Herman 1988. 'Industrial Dynamics and the Process of Urbanization and Deurbanization from the Late Middle Ages to the Eighteenth Century. A Synthesis'. In *The Rise and Decline of Urban Industries in Italy and in the Low Countries (Late*

Middle Ages–Early Modern Times), edited by Herman Van der Wee, 307–82. Louvain: Louvain University Press.

Vandewalle, André 1999. 'De Brugse stadsmagistraat en de deelname van de ambachten aan het bestuur, 14de–15de Eeuw'. In *De Vlaamse instellingen tijdens het Ancien Régime: Recent onderzoek in nieuw perspectief*, edited by Walter Prevenier and Beatrijs Augustyn, 27–40. Brussels: Algemeen Rijksarchief.

Van Dievoet, Guido 1951. *Jehan Boutillier en de Somme rural*. Louvain: Leuvense Universitaire Uitgaven.

Van Dijck, Maarten 2006. 'De stad als onafhankelijke variabele en centrum van moderniteit. Langetermijntrends in stedelijke en rurale criminaliteitsprocessen in de Nederlanden (1300–1800)'. *Stadsgeschiedenis* 1: 7–26.

Maximilianus, Pater (Van Dun, Petrus), ed. 1954. *Sinte Franciscus leven van Jacob van Maerlant*. Zwolle: Tjeenk Willink.

Van der Linden, Marcel 2009. 'Charles Tilly's Historical Sociology'. *International Review of Social History* 54: 237–74.

Van Duyse, Prudens, and Edmond de Busscher 1867. *Inventaire analytique des chartes et documents appartenant aux archives de la ville de Gand*. Ghent: Annoot-Braeckman.

Van Eeckhoudt-De Jaeger, Marceline 1983. 'Bijdrage tot de studie van het Oudenaardse ambachtswezen in de 14e en 15e Eeuw'. *Handelingen van de Geschied- en Oudheidkundige Kring van Oudenaarde* 20: 71–93.

Van Elslander, Antonin 1953. *Het refrein in de Nederlanden tot 1600*. Ghent: Erasmus.

Van Gelder, Hendrik Enno 1911. 'Satiren der XVIe-eeuwsche kleine burgerij'. *Oud Holland* 29 (4): 201–32.

Van Gent, Michiel 1990. 'De Hoekse factie in Leiden circa 1445–1490: het verhaal van verliezers'. In *Bloedwraak, partijstrijd en pacificatie in laat-middeleeuws Holland*, edited by Jannis Marsilje, 122–40. Hilversum: Verloren.

Van Gent, Michiel 1994. *'Pertijelike saken': Hoeken en Kabeljauwen in het Bourgondisch-Oostenrijkse tijdperk*. Den Haag: Stichting Hollandse Historische Reeks.

Van Gerven, Jan 1976. 'Nationaal gevoel en stedelijke politieke visies in het 14de-eeuwse Brabant. Het voorbeeld van Jan van Boendale'. *Bijdrage tot de Geschiedenis* 59: 145–64.

Van Gerven, Jan 1978. 'Sociale werkelijkheid en mentale konstructie in het werk van Jan van Boendale (eerste helft 14de eeuw)'. *Tijdschrift voor Sociale Geschiedenis* 13: 47–70.

Vanhaverbeke, Katrien 1998. 'De reële machtsstrukturen binnen het stadsbestuur van Brugge in de periode 1375–1407. Verslag van een prosopografische studie'. *Handelingen van het Genootschap voor Geschiedenis* 135: 3–54.

Van Herwaarden, Jan 1978. *Opgelegde bedevaarten. Een studie over de praktijk van opleggen van bedevaarten (met name in de stedelijke rechtspraak) in de Nederlanden gedurende de Late Middeleeuwen (ca. 1300–ca. 1550)*. Amsterdam: Van Gorcum.

Van Hoecke, Karel 2005. 'Het ontstaan van Oudenaarde in het licht van laatmiddeleeuwse bronnen'. *Handelingen van de Geschied- en Oudheidkundige Kring van Oudenaarde* 42 (2): 31–154.

Van Honacker, Karin 1994. *Lokaal verzet en oproer in de 17de en 18de eeuw: collectieve acties tegen het centraal gezag in Brussel, Antwerpen en Leuven.* Kortrijk: UGA.

van Houtte, Jan 1950. 'Makelaars en waarden te Brugge van de 13e tot de 16e Eeuw'. *Bijdragen voor de Geschiedenis der Nederlanden* 5: 1–30.

van Houtte, Jan 1982. *De geschiedenis van Brugge.* Tielt: Lannoo.

Van Krieken, Robert 1989. 'Violence, Self-Discipline and Modernity: Beyond the "Civilizing Process"'. *The Sociological Review* 37 (2): 193–218.

Van Leeuwen, Jacoba 2004. 'Over slapscheten en levereters: pamfletten en strooibriefjes in de laatmiddeleeuwse Vlaamse stad'. *Madoc: Tijdschrift over de Middeleeuwen* 18: 77–85.

Van Leeuwen, Jacoba 2005. 'Municipal Oaths, Political Virtues and the Centralised State: The Adaptation of Oaths of Office in Fifteenth-Century Flanders'. *Journal of Medieval History* 31 (2): 185–210.

Van Leeuwen, Jacoba, 2006a. 'Balancing Tradition and Rites of Rebellion: The Ritual Transfer of Power in Bruges on 12 February 1488'. In Van Leeuwen, ed. 2006b, 65–82.

Van Leeuwen, Jacoba, ed. 2006b. *Symbolic Communication in Late Medieval Towns.* Louvain: Louvain University Press.

Van Leeuwen, Jacoba 2008. 'Rebels, Texts and Triumph: The Use of Written Documents during the Revolt of 1477 in Bruges'. In *Strategies of Writing: Studies on Text and Trust in the Middle Ages: Papers from 'Trust in Writing in the Middle Ages' (Utrecht, 28–29 November 2002)*, edited by Petra Schulte, Marco Mostert, and Irene van Renswoude, 301–22. Turnhout: Brepols.

Van Mierlo, Jozef 1942. *Geschiedenis van de letterkunde der Nederlanden.* 4 vols. Den Bosch/Brussels: Standaard-Boekhandel.

Van Mierlo, Jozef 1946. *Jacob van Maerlant. Zijn leven, zijn werken, zijn beteekenis.* Turnhout: Van Mierlo-Proost.

Van Moerkerken, Pieter 1904. *De satire der nederlandsche kunst der middeleeuwen.* Amsterdam: Van Looy.

Van Nierop, Henk 1997. 'Popular Participation in Politics in the Dutch Republic'. In *Resistance, Representation and Community*, edited by Peter Blickle, 272–90. New York, NY: Clarendon Press.

Van Oost, Angeline 1975. 'Sociale stratifikatie van de Gentse opstandelingen van 1379–1386, een kritische benadering van konfiskatiedokumenten'. *Handelingen der Maatschappij voor Geschiedenis en Oudheidkunde te Gent* 29: 59–92.

Van Oost, Angeline 1978. 'Sociale stratifikatie van de Brugse opstandigen en van de opstandige ingezetenen van de kleinere kasselrijsteden en van de kasselrijdorpen in Vlaanderen van 1379–85, kritische benadering van konfiskatiedokumenten'. *Belgisch Tijdschrift voor Filologie en Geschiedenis* 61: 830–77.

Van Oostrom, Frits 1996. *Maerlants wereld.* Amsterdam: Prometheus.

Van Oostrom, Frits 2006. *Stemmen op schrift. De nederlandse literatuur vanaf het begin tot 1300.* Amsterdam: Bakker.

Van Oostrom, Frits 2013. *Wereld in woorden. Geschiedenis van de nederlandse literatuur.* Amsterdam: Bert Bakker.

Van Puffelen, S.A.E. 1966. 'Het historielied als dichtsoort'. *Wetenschappelijke Tijdingen* 25: 31–8.

Van Rompaey, Jan 1961. 'Het compositierecht in Vlaanderen van de veertiende tot de achttiende eeuw'. *Tijdschrift voor Rechtsgeschiedenis* 29 (1): 43–79.

Van Rompaey, Jan 1965. 'De Brugse Keure van 1329 en de aanvullende privileges'. *Handelingen van de Koninklijke Commissie voor de Uitgave der Oude Wetten en Verordeningen van België* 21: 35–105.

Van Rompaey, Jan 1967. *Het grafelijk baljuwsambt in Vlaanderen tijdens de boergondische periode.* Brussels: Paleis der Academiën.

Van Rompaey, Jan 1973. *De Grote Raad van de Hertogen van Boergondië en het Parlement van Mechelen.* Brussels: Paleis der Academiën.

Van Rompaey, Jan 1978. 'De opstand in het Vlaamse kustland van 1323 tot 1328 en de figuur van Nikolaas Zannekin'. In *Nikolaas Zannekin en de slag bij Kassel 1328–1978: bijdrage tot de studie van de 14de eeuw en de landelijke geschiedenis van de Westhoek,* 104–28. Diksmuide: Werkgroep Zannekin.

Vansina, Jan 1973. *Oral Tradition: A Study in Historical Methodology,* translated by H.M. Wright. Harmondsworth: Penguin Books.

Vansina, Jan 1985. *Oral Tradition as History.* Madison, WI: University of Wisconsin Press.

Van 't Hooft, Bart 1948. *Honderd jaar Geldersche geschiedenis in historieliederen.* Arnhem: Gouda Quint.

Van Uytven, Raymond 1962. 'Plutokratie in de "oude demokratieën der Nederlanden". Cijfers en beschouwingen omtrent de korporatieve organisatie en de sociale struktuur der gemeenten in de Late Middeleeuwen'. *Handelingen van de Koninklijke Zuidnederlandse Maatschappij voor Taal- en Letterkunde en Geschiedenis* 17: 373–409.

Van Uytven, Raymond 1963. 'Pieter Couthereel en de troebelen te Leuven van 1350 tot 1363. kritische nota over de persoon van een hertogelijk ambtenaar en zijn rol in de politieke geschiedenis van Brabant en Leuven'. *Mededelingen van de Geschied- en Oudheidkundige Kring voor Leuven en Omgeving* 3 (2): 63–97.

Van Uytven, Raymond 1982. 'Stadsgeschiedenis in het Noorden en Zuiden'. In *Algemene geschiedenis der Nederlanden. Band 2: Middeleeuwen. Het sociaal-economische leven ca. 1000–1500. Het stedelijk leven ca. 1000–1400. Politieke ontwikkeling ca. 1100–1400,* 188–253. Haarlem: Fibula-Van Dishoeck.

Van Uytven, Raymond 1983. 'Scènes de la vie sociale dans les villes des Pays-Bas du XIVe au XVIe siècles'. In *Actes du Colloque 'La sociabilité urbaine en Europe du Nord-Ouest du XIVe au XVIIIe siècle'*, 11–31. Douai: Lefebvre-Leveque.

Van Uytven, Raymond 1985. '1477 in Brabant'. In Blockmans, Willem, ed. 1985a, 253–85.

Van Uytven, Raymond 1995. 'Stages of Economic Decline: Late Medieval Bruges'. In *Peasants and Townsmen in Medieval Europe. Studia in Honorem Adriaan Verhulst*, edited by Jean-Marie Duvosquel and Erik Thoen, 259–69. Ghent: Snoeck-Ducaju & Zoon.

Van Uytven, Raymond 1998. 'Flämische Belfriede und südniederländische städtische Bauwerke im Mittelalter: Symbol und Mythos'. In *Information, Kommunikation und Selbstdarstellung*, edited by Alfred Haverkamp and Elisabeth Müller-Luckner, 125–59. Munich: Oldenbourg.

Van Uytven, Raymond 2001. *Production and Consumption in the Low Countries, 13th–16th Centuries*. Aldershot: Ashgate Publishing.

Van Uytven, Raymond 2002. 'Het Antwerpen van Jan van Boendale'. In *Al t'Antwerpen in die stad. Jan van Boendale en de literaire cultuur van zijn tijd*, edited by Wim Van Anrooij, 17–29. Amsterdam: Prometheus.

Van Uytven, Raymond, and Willem Blockmans 1969. 'Constitutions and Their Application in the Netherlands during the Middle Ages'. *Revue Belge de Philologie et d'Histoire* 47: 399–424.

Van Vloten, Johannes 1864. *Nederlandsche Geschiedzangen*. 2 vols. Amsterdam: Muller.

Van Werveke, Hans 1943a. 'De medezeggenschap van de knapen (gezellen) in de middeleeuwse ambachten', *Mededelingen van de Koninklijke Vlaamsche Academie voor Wetenschappen, Letteren en Schoone Kunsten van België. Klasse der Letteren* 5: 5–24.

Van Werveke, Hans 1943b. *Jacques van Artevelde*. Brussels: La Renaissance du Livre.

Van Werveke, Hans 1946a. 'De koopman-ondernemer en de ondernemer in de Vlaamsche lakennijverheid van de Middeleeuwen'. *Mededeelingen van de Koninklijke Vlaamsche Academie voor Wetenschappen, Letteren en Schoone Kunsten van België. Klasse der Letteren* 8 (4): 5–26.

Van Werveke, Hans 1946b. *Gand. Esquisse d'histoire sociale*. Brussels: La Renaissance du Livre.

Van Werveke, Hans 1959. 'La famine de l'an 1316 en Flandre et dans les régions voisines'. *Revue du Nord* 41: 5–14.

van Wissing, Pieter 1993. '"Kinders, ic weet secreet goed en rijkdom". Maarten van Rossem voor Leuven. Anti-Gelderse historieliederen uit het Antwerps Liedboek (1544)'. In *Verdrag en tractaat van Venlo. Herdenkingsbundel, 1543–1993*, edited by Frank Keverling Buisman, 235–46. Hilversum: Verloren.

Vaughan, Richard 1970. *Philip the Good: The Apogee of Burgundy*. London: Longman.

Vaughan, Richard 1973. *Charles the Bold: The Last Valois Duke of Burgundy*. London: Longman.

Vaughan, Richard 2002. *Philip the Good: The Apogee of the Burgundian State.* Woodbridge: Boydell Press.

Vellekoop, Cornelis 1985. 'Hoe oud is "oudt" in het Antwerps Liedboek?' In *Tussentijds. Bundel studies aangeboden aan W.P. Gerritsen ter gelegenheid van zijn vijftigste verjaardag,* edited by Alphonseus van Buuren, 272–9. Utrecht: HES.

Verboven, Koenraad, Myriam Carlier and Jan Dumolyn 2007. 'A short manual to the art of prosopography'. In *Prosopography: Approaches and Application. A Handbook,* edited by Katharine S.B. Keats-Rohan, 35–70. Oxford: Prosopographica and Genealogica.

Verbruggen, Christophe 2007. 'Literary Strategy during Flanders' Golden Decades: Combining Social Network Analysis and Prosopography'. In *Prosopography Approaches and Applications: A Handbook,* edited by Katharine S.B. Keats-Rohan, 579–601. Oxford: Prosopographica et Genealogica.

Verbruggen, Jan 1948. 'De Brugse effectieven van de slag bij Kortrijk'. *Bijdragen voor de Geschiedenis der Nederlanden* 2: 241–7.

Verbruggen, Jan 1954. *De krijgskunst in West-Europa in de middeleeuwen.* Brussels: Paleis der Academiën.

Verbruggen, Jan 1956. 'Beschouwingen over 1302'. *Annales de la Société d'Émulation de Bruges* 93: 38–83.

Verbruggen, Jan 1960. *Het leger en de vloot van de graven van Vlaanderen vanaf het ontstaan tot in 1305.* Brussels: Paleis der Academiën.

Verbruggen, Jan 1962. *Het gemeenteleger van Brugge van 1338 tot 1340 en de namen van de weerbare mannen.* Brussels: Paleis der Academiën.

Verbruggen, Jan 1977. *The Art of Warfare in Western Europe during the Middle Ages.* Amsterdam: North-Holland.

Verbruggen, Jan 1991. *Vlaanderen na de Guldensporenslag.* Bruges: Westvlaamse Gidsenkring.

Verbruggen, Jan 1993. *De Slag bij Guinegate, 7 Augustus 1479. De verdediging van het graafschap Vlaanderen tegen de Koning van Frankrijk, 1477–1480.* Brussels: Koninklijk Legermuseum.

Verbruggen, Raf 2002. '"Wapenninghe, meute ende beroete". Het collectief geweld van de 14de-eeuwse ambachten in de grote Vlaamse steden'. Unpublished dissertation, Ghent: Ghent University.

Verbruggen, Raf 2005. *Geweld in Vlaanderen: macht en onderdrukking in de Vlaamse steden tijdens de veertiende eeuw.* Bruges: Van de Wiele.

Vercauteren, Fernand 1943. *Luttes sociales à Liège (XIIIe et XIVe siècles).* Brussels: Renaissance du Livre.

Verhulst, Adriaan 1967. 'Un exemple de la politique économique de Philippe d'Alsace: la fondation de Gravelines (1163)'. *Cahiers de Civilisation Médiévale* 10: 15–28.

Verhulst, Adriaan 1999. *The Rise of Cities in North-West Europe.* Cambridge: Cambridge University Press.

Verlinden, Charles 1935. *Robert Ier le Frison, comte de Flandre: étude d'histoire politique.* Antwerp: De Sikkel.

Vermeesch, Albert 1966. *Essai sur les origines et la signification de la commune dans le Nord de la France (XIe et XIIe siècles).* Heule: UGA.

Verriest, Léo 1913. *Les luttes sociales et le contrat d'apprentissage à Tournai jusqu'en 1424.* Brussels: Hayez.

Verwijs, Eelco, and Jacob Verdam 1907. *Middelnederlandsch woordenboek.* 11 vols. The Hague: Nijhof.

Verwijs, Eelco, ed. 1879. *Jacob van Maerlant's strophische gedichten.* Groningen: Wolters.

Viaene, Dieter 2004. 'De drang naar macht. De Ieperse stadsmagistraat in de veertiende eeuw (1328–1383)'. *Handelingen van het Genootschap voor Geschiedenis* 141: 3–42.

Vink, Ester 2001. 'Hieronymous Bosch's life in 's-Hertogenbosch'. In *Hieronymous Bosch: New Insights into His Life and Work*, edited by Jos Koldeweij, Bernard Vermet, and Barbera van Kooij, 19–24. Rotterdam, Ghent and Amsterdam: Boymans van Beuningen Museum.

Vlietinck, Edward 1910. *Cartulaire d'Ostende: texte original avec notes et additions précédé d'une introduction historique.* Antwerp: De Vlijt.

Vogüé, Adalbert de, and Jean Neufville, eds 1972–3. *La règle de saint Benoît.* 7 vols. Paris: Cerf.

Volpe, Gioacchino 1970. *Studi sulle istituzioni comunali a Pisa.* Florence: G.C. Sansoni.

Von der Ropp, Goswin 1878. *Hanserecesse von 1431–1476.* 7 vols. Leipzig: Duncker & Humblot.

Von Gierke, Otto 1868–1881. *Das deutsche Genossenschaftsrecht.* 4 vols. Berlin: Weidmannsche Buchhandlung.

Von Liliencron, Rochus, ed. 1865–9. *Die historischen Volkslieder der Deutschen vom 13. bis 16. Jahrhundert.* 5 vols. Leipzig: Vogel.

Vorsterman van Oyen, George 1892. *Rechtsbronnen der stad Aardenburg.* 's-Gravenhage: Nijhoff.

Vorsterman, Willem, ed. 1531. *Dits die excellente cronike van Vlaenderen.* Antwerp: Willem Vorsterman.

Vrancken, Valerie 2017. 'United in Revolt, Common Discourse: Urban and Noble Perceptions of 'Bad Government' in Fifteenth-Century Brabant, 1420–1421.' *Journal of Medieval History* 43: 579–99.

Vuylsteke, Julius 1895. ' "De Goede Disendach", 13 Januari 1349'. *Handelingen der Maatschappij voor Geschiedenis en Oudheidkunde te Gent* 1: 9–47.

Vuylsteke, Julius 1906. *Uitleggingen tot de Gentsche stads- en baljuwrekeningen 1280–1315.* Ghent: Vuylsteke.

Waite, Gary 2006. 'Rhetoricians and Religious Compromise during the Early Reformation (c. 1520–1555)'. In *Urban Theatre in the Low Countries, 1400–1625*, edited by Elsa Strietman and Peter Happé, 79–102. Turnhout: Brepols.

Walker, Simon 2000. 'Rumour, Sedition and Popular Protest in the Reign of Henry IV'. *Past & Present* 166: 31–65.

Walter, John 2006. *Crowds and Popular Politics in Early Modern England*. Manchester: Manchester University Press.

Walter, John 2007. 'Politicising the Popular? The "Tradition of Riot" and Popular Political Culture in the English Revolution'. In *The English Revolution, c. 1590–1720: Politics, Religion and Communities*, edited by Nicholas Tyacke, 95–110. Manchester: Manchester University Press.

Walter, John 2009. '"The Pooremans Joy and the Gentlemans Plague": A Lincolnshire Libel and the Politics of Sedition in Early Modern England'. *Past & Present* 203: 29–67.

Walther, Hans, ed. 1967. *Proverbia sententiaeque latinitatis Medii Aevi. Vol. 5*. Göttingen: Vandenhoeck & Ruprecht.

Wandhoff, Haiko 2004. 'Une moult belle conjointure. Die Schrift, der Roman und das kulturelle Gedächtnis des mittelalterlichen Adels'. In *Medium und Gedächtnis. von der Überbietung der Grenze(n)*, edited by Franziska Sick and Beate Ochsner, 111–24. Frankfurt am Main: Lang.

Warlop, Ernest 1975–6. *The Flemish Nobility before 1300*. 2 vols. Kortrijk: G. Desmet-Huysman.

Warnkönig, Leopold 1835. *Flandrische Staats- und Rechtsgeschichte bis zum Jahr 1305*. 3 vols. Tübingen: Fues.

Warnkönig, Leopold, and Albert Gheldolf 1835–64. *Histoire de la Flandre et de ses institutions civiles et politiques, jusqu'à l'année 1305*. 5 vols. Brussels: Verbeyst.

Wasserman, Stanley, and Katherina Faust 1994. *Social Network Analysis. Methods and Applications*. Cambridge: Cambridge University Press.

Waterschoot, Werner, and Dirk Coigneau, eds 1979. *Eduard de Dene. Testament rhetoricael*. 2 vols. Ghent: Rijksuniversiteit.

Watts, John 2004. 'The Pressure of the Public on Later Medieval Politics'. In *The Fifteenth Century IV: Political Culture in Late Medieval Britain*, edited by Linda Clark and Christine Carpenter, 159–80. Woodbridge: Boydell & Brewer.

Watts, John 2007. 'Public or Plebs: The Changing Meaning of "the Commons", 1381–1549'. In *Power and Identity in the Middle Ages: Essays in Memory of Rees Davies*, edited by Huw Pryce and John Watts, 242–60. Oxford: Oxford University Press.

Watts, John 2009. *The Making of Polities: Europe, 1300–1500*. Cambridge: Cambridge University Press.

Weber, Max 1968. *Economy and Society. An Outline of Interpretive Sociology*, edited by Guenther Roth and Claus Wittich. New York, NY: Bedminister Press.

Wellens, Robert 1965. 'La révolte brugeoise de 1488'. *Annales de la Société d'Émulation de Bruges* 102: 5–52.

Wellens, Robert 1974. *Les États Généraux des Pays-Bas des origines à la fin du règne de Philippe le Beau (1464–1506)*. Kortrijk: UGA.

White, Geoffrey 1990. 'Moral Discourse and the Rhetoric of Emotions'. In *Language and the Politics of Emotion*, edited by Catherine Lutz and Lila Abu-Lughod, 46–68. Cambridge: Cambridge University Press.

White, Stephen 1998. 'The Politics of Anger'. In *Anger's Past. The Social Uses of an Emotion in the Middle Ages*, edited by Barbara Rosenwein, 127–53. Ithaca, NY: Cornell University Press.

Whittle, Jane, and Stephen Rigby 2003. 'England: Popular Politics and Social Conflict'. In *A Companion to Britain in the Later Middle Ages*, edited by Stephen Rigby, 65–86. Oxford: Blackwell.

Whyte, Nicola 2007. 'Landscape, Memory and Custom: Parish Identities, c. 1550–1700'. *Social History* 32 (2): 166–86.

Wickham, Chris 1998. 'Gossip and Resistance among the Medieval Peasantry'. *Past & Present* 160: 3–24.

Wielant, Filips 1872. *Practijcke criminele van Philips Wielant*, edited by Auguste Orts. Ghent: Annoot-Braeckman.

Wielant, Filips 1995. *Filips Wielant, verzameld werk I: Corte instructie in materie criminele*, edited by Jos Monballyu. Brussels: Paleis der Academiën.

Wiesflecker, Hermann 1971–85. *Kaiser Maximilian I.: das Reich, Österreich und Europa an der Wende zur Neuzeit.* 5 vols. Munich: R. Oldenburg.

Willaert, Frank, ed. 1992. *Een zoet akkoord: middeleeuwse lyriek in de Lage Landen*. Amsterdam: Prometheus.

Willaert, Frank, ed. 1997. *Veelderhande liedekens: studies over het nederlandse lied tot 1600*. Louvain: Peeters.

Willaert, Frank 2008. *De fiere nachtegaal. Het nederlandse lied in de middeleeuwen.* Amsterdam: Amsterdam University Press.

Willems, Jan, Constant Serrure, and Ferdinand Snellaert 1848. *Oude Vlaemsche liederen ten deele met de melodiën*. Ghent: Gyselynck.

Wood, Andy 2001. ' "Poore Men Woll Speke One Daye": Plebeian Languages of Deference and Defiance in England, c. 1520–1640'. In *The Politics of the Excluded, c. 1500–1850*, edited by Tim Harris, 67–98. New York, NY: Palgrave.

Wood, Andy 2007. *The 1549 Rebellions and the Making of Early Modern England.* Cambridge: Cambridge University Press.

Wood, Andy 2013. *The Memory of the People. Custom and Popular Senses of the Past in Early Modern England.* Cambridge: Cambridge University Press.

Woolf, Cecil 1913. *Bartolus of Sassoferrato*. London: University Press.

Wuttke, Ulrike 2010. 'Apocalyptische angstdromen van een Antwerpse stadsklerk? De eindtijd in het "Boec van der Wraken"'. *Madoc* 24: 33–42.

Wyffels, Carlos 1949–50. 'De oudste rekening der stad Aardenburg (1309–1310) en de opstand van 1311'. *Archief. Uitgegeven door het Zeeuwsch Genootschap der Weten-schappen*, 10–52.

Wyffels, Carlos 1950a. 'Les corporations flamandes et l'origine des communautés de métiers'. *Revue du Nord* 128: 193–205.

Wyffels, Carlos 1950b. 'Twee oude Vlaamse ambachtskeuren: de vleeshouwers van Brugge (2 December 1302) en de smeden van Damme (eerste helft 1303)'. *Annales de la Société d'Emulation de Bruges* 87: 93–109.

Wyffels, Carlos 1951. *De oorsprong der ambachten in Vlaanderen en Brabant*. Brussels: Paleis der Academiën.

Wyffels, Carlos 1966. 'Nieuwe gegevens betreffende de XIIIde eeuwse "demokratische" stedelijke opstand: de Brugse "Moerlemaye" (1280–1281)'. *Handelingen van de Konin-lijke Commissie voor Geschiedenis* 132: 37–142.

Wyffels, Carlos 1968. 'Is de Brugse keure betreffende het "Poortersgeding", gedagtekend van 1229, in werkelijkheid zestig jaar jonger?'. *Tijdschrift voor Rechtsgeschiedenis* 36: 525–533.

Wyffels, Carlos 1973. 'Kanttekeningen bij de Brugse "Moerlemaye", 1280–1281'. In *Album Albert Schouteet*, 253–58. Bruges: Westvlaams Verbond van Kringen voor Heem-kunde.

Xhayet, Geneviève 1993. 'Le rôle politique des métiers liégeois à la fin du Moyen Âge'. In *Les métiers au Moyen Âge. Aspects économiques et sociaux*, edited by Pascale Lam-brechts and Jean-Pierre Sosson, 361–78. Louvain-la-Neuve: Institut d'Études Médi-évales.

Xhayet, Geneviève 1997. *Réseaux de pouvoir et solidarités de parti à Liège au Moyen Âge (1250–1468)*. Geneva: Droz.

Zagorin, Perez 1982. *Rebels and Rulers, 1500–1660*. 2 vols. Cambridge: Cambridge Uni-versity Press.

Zerubavel, Eviatar 1997. *Social Mindscapes. An Invitation to Cognitive Sociology*. Cam-bridge, MA: Harvard University Press.

Zerubavel, Eviatar 2003. *Time Maps. Collective Memory and the Social Shape of the Past*. Chicago: University of Chicago Press.

Zerubavel, Yael 1995. *Recovered Roots. Collective Memory and the Making of Israeli National Tradition*. Chicago: University of Chicago Press.

Zotz, Thomas 2000. 'Der Stadtadel im spätmittelalterlichen Deutschland und seine Erinnerungskultur'. In *Adelige und bürgerliche Erinnerungskulturen des Spätmit-telalters und der Frühen Neuzeit*, edited by Werner Rösener, 145–61. Göttingen: Vand-enhoeck & Ruprecht.

Zumthor, Paul 1983. *Introduction à la poésie orale*. Paris: Éditions du Seuil.

Index

Great Council (ducal), See *Raad van Vlaanderen*
'Great Council of Bruges', See *'Ghemeene buucke'*
'Great Council of Ghent', See *Collacie*
'Great Council of Ypres', of Twenty-Seven 70, 218, 266, 313
    of Holland 302
    of Leiden 215
    of Paris (614) 292
    of State 302
    of the Liberty of Bruges 106
    Privy 302
    regency- 28, 81, 88, 89–93, 95, 104, 357–61, 369
councillors 23, 36, 63, 73, 77, 89, 94, 100, 107, 167, 182, 292, 300, 315–16, 321, 300, 345
Count of Clermont 300
Count of Flanders 1, 11–12, 14–15, 17, 20–27, 29–30, 33–34, 37–38, 40, 50–52, 61–63, 65–68, 71–74, 79, 81, 87, 92, 105, 117, 124–25, 141–43, 145, 147–60, 156, 161–62, 167, 169, 176, 180–82, 202, 204–05, 208, 215, 219, 230, 244–45, 247–48, 250, 253, 266, 270–71, 290, 294, 296–99, 304–11, 316–18, 321–24, 328–31, 333, 348, 356, 363–64, 367, 369
Count of Holland 216, 299, 323
Count of Namur 149
counter-memory/-ies 172, 179, 189, 192–93
courpse 100
Coutumes 365
anciennes 300, 303
creesers, clamantibus, roepers ('criers', 'shouters') 168, 248, 277–79
crossbowmen 94, 164
Cubitt, Geoffrey 171
cueillote 156, 273
cultural hegemony, See hegemony, cultural
custom(s), costumary, xi 5–7, 63, 121, 124, 137, 143, 154, 16–66, 176, 182, 184, 192, 198–99, 238, 242, 268, 271, 276, 293, 298, 309, 311, 327–28, 333, 343, 354, 356, 363, 365, 370–71
customary law, costumary justice, xii 29, 137, 140, 142–44, 158, 163, 169, 175, 333, 361–63, 367, 370
Cuul, Willem Van 276
Czok, Karl 12, 26, 52, 55

d'Heere, Lucas 225
Dadizeele, John of 122, 414
Dagboek van Gent ('Dairy of Ghent') 315
Daghelicxschen Snaetere, See plays
Damme 15–17, 50, 64, 146, 149, 244, 270, 273, 304
Dampierre, Guy de 50–51, 63, 324
David, See King David
Dboec van den Tien Gheboden ('Book of the Ten Commandments') 243
De Cura rei Publicae et Sorte Principantis ('On the Care of the State and the Role of the Ruler') (Philip of Leyden) 299
De hel vant brouwergilde, See plays
De Munt (tavern 'The Mint') 217
De natura rerum 244
death penalty 292, 310, 324, 330, 334
decapitation, decapitated 28, 89, 91, 107, 116, 133, 158, 324–25, 329
Degrassalius 300
Deinze 74, 279, 308
deken(s) 48, 50, 64, 66
Deken, Willem de 61, 318, 331
Delcourt, André 137
Delft, Nicolas van 105
demagogue(s), demagogic 249, 256, 258, 269, 278
Den Beer (tavern) 250
Den Bosch 53
Den droom van Roovere op die doot van Kaerle van Borgonnyen saleger gedachten ('Roovere's Dream on the death of the Charles of Burgundy of Blessed Memory') 215
Dendermonde 204, 219, 308
Dene, Eduard de 236
Denis, Foriaen 279
Denmark 337
Depreux, Philippe 367
Der leken spieghel ('Layman's Mirror') 245
Der nature bloeme (Dutch adaptation of *De natura rerum*) 244
Despars, Nicolas 340
Dhamere, Jan 100–102
Dheere
    Jacob 105, 107
    Michiel 105
Dhondt 15, 32, 141, 396
    Jan (academic) xi